SUMMA VIRTUTUM DE REMEDIIS ANIME

MS. Einsiedeln, Stiftsbibliothek 275, f. 137v

Actual size. Reproduced with permission of the Stiftsbibliothek.

SUMMA VIRTUTUM DE REMEDIIS ANIME

EDITED BY

SIEGFRIED WENZEL

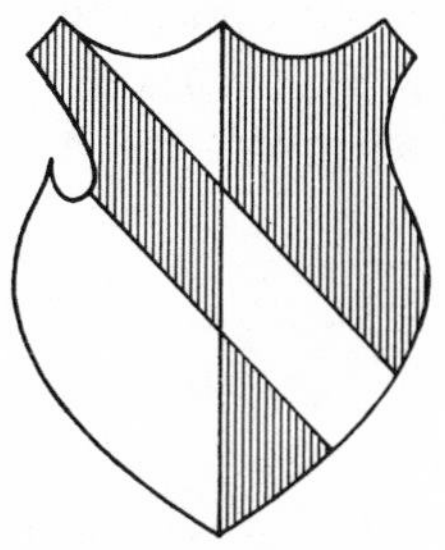

THE CHAUCER LIBRARY

THE UNIVERSITY OF GEORGIA PRESS
ATHENS

Designed by Martyn Hitchcock
Set in Mergenthaler Bembo type
Printed in the United States of America

The paper in this book meets the guidelines for permanence and durability of the Committee on Production Guidelines for Book Longevity of the Council on Library Resources.

Library of Congress Cataloging in Publication Data

Summa virtutum de remediis anime. English & Latin.
Summa virtutum de remediis anime.

(The Chaucer library)
English and Latin.
Includes bibliographical references.

1. Chaucer, Geoffrey, d. 1400—Sources. 2. Virtues—Early works to 1800. 3. Theology—Middle Ages, 600–1500. I. Wenzel, Siegfried. II. Series.

PR1912.S913 1984 241′.4 82-13430
ISBN 0-8203-0638-X

Portions of the introduction are based on an article by Siegfried Wenzel, "The Source for the *Remedia* of the Parson's Tale," *Traditio* 27 (1971): 433–53. Used by permission of Fordham University Press.

Quotations from the Parson's Tale are from F. N. Robinson, ed., *The Works of Geoffrey Chaucer*, 2d ed. Copyright © 1957 by the President and Fellows of Harvard College. Used by permission of Houghton Mifflin Company.

CONTENTS

FOREWORD

The purpose of the Chaucer Library is to present the classical and medieval works that the English poet Geoffrey Chaucer (ca. 1343–1400) knew, translated, or made use of in his writings in versions that are as close as possible to those that were in existence, circulating, and being read by him and his contemporaries. These versions were, of course, not critical editions—they were filled with readings that the original authors did not write, with additions and omissions, and sometimes with glosses and commentaries—and the Chaucer Library was created in 1946 in the belief that only by reproducing such nonoriginal material could one have a true understanding of the ways in which classical and medieval texts were read and understood by medieval readers. The Chaucer Library has followed this traditional policy, as in the first volume published by the University of Georgia Press, Pope Innocent III's *De Miseria Condicionis Humane*, and will continue to do so, while at the same time striving to present readable texts, with punctuation and capitalization modernized, abbreviations expanded, some letters regularized, and accompanied by English translations.

At the same time, however, it is clear that some works known to and used by Chaucer do not warrant this kind of presentation, and the Chaucer Library Committee has widened the range of editorial possibilities to include critical editions. Nicholas of Lynn's *Kalendarium*, the second volume, was a critical edition, and the *Summa virtutum de remediis anime*, the present volume, is one as well. As Professor Wenzel demonstrates in his introduction, the *Summa* was the ultimate source for the *remedia* sections of Chaucer's Parson's Tale, but the verbal evidence is both too limited and too evenly balanced to permit him to choose a single manuscript to be printed in its entirety; moreover, the *Summa* has never been printed before. In this case, and in cases like it, it is more useful to print a critical edition, prepared according to whatever editorial method is most appropriate, than to follow the traditional policy of the Chaucer Library. The present volume, as Wenzel describes it, is "a fully critical edition" that attempts "to present a text which approaches the form of the archetype for all extant manuscripts in as much as the careful selection of a base text and analysis of all variant readings will allow." One can feel confident, therefore, that the text printed here is very close to the author's original, and because all readings closer to Chaucer's translation have been asterisked in the corpus of variants, one can see at a glance how Chaucer's manuscript would have differed from the edited text. It is with great pleasure that the

Chaucer Library Committee now adds the *Summa virtutum de remediis anime*, a work of importance for students both of Chaucer and of medieval theology, to the list of books in Chaucer's library.

Robert E. Lewis, General Editor

For the Chaucer Library Committee:
Ruth J. Dean
John H. Fisher
Albert C. Friend
Traugott Lawler
Robert A. Pratt
A. G. Rigg
Siegfried Wenzel
Edward Wilson

ACKNOWLEDGMENTS

In preparing this edition I have received various kinds of help, which it is a great pleasure to acknowledge. Above all, I wish to thank the former librarian of the Stiftsbibliothek Einsiedeln, Fr. Kuno Bugmann, O.S.B., and his successor, Fr. Dr. Odo Lang, O.S.B., for providing me with a microfilm and giving me access to the manuscript, for hospitably sharing their knowledge of the library and its holdings, and for their permission to use MS 275 as the base of my edition. I am equally grateful to the owners of the other manuscripts used in this edition and to the respective librarians and their staff for their courtesy and help in allowing me to examine the manuscripts and acquiring microfilms. To Morton W. Bloomfield, Leonard E. Boyle, Susan Cavanaugh, A. Ian Doyle, Julian G. Plante, and Richard H. Rouse I am indebted for various kinds of information and suggestions concerning the manuscripts and textual questions. Robert E. Lewis has been a friendly critic and a catalyst in establishing my editorial principles, and George Rigg has saved me from a number of embarrassing slips. Grants from the American Philosophical Society (1972) and the National Endowment for the Humanities (1975–76) allowed me to examine and to collate the manuscripts. To all these go my heartfelt thanks.

INTRODUCTION

THE *SUMMA VIRTUTUM DE REMEDIIS ANIME*

The sections in the Parson's Tale in which Chaucer describes the virtues that are opposed to the seven deadly sins as their remedies derive from a Latin treatise which bears the title *Summa virtutum de remediis anime*[1] and begins with the words "Postquam dictum est de morbis ipsius anime, idest peccatis, addendum est de remediis, scilicet de uirtutibus." For the sake of clarity I shall refer to this *Summa* by its opening word.

Postquam is clearly divided into chapters, even though these are not numbered in the manuscripts and though the extant manuscripts are not consistent in marking possible chapter divisions by such devices as enlarged capitals and rubrics. My division of the work into nine chapters is based on its internal structure. This division appears most clearly in manuscript L (where these nine sections, and only these, are marked by enlarged capitals) and is not contradicted by any external marking devices which appear in the other manuscripts.

The treatise begins with a chapter on virtues in general. After an initial division (lines 6–7) into *virtutes naturales* (the natural faculties of our body and soul), *politicae*, and *gratuitae*, it develops each kind at increasing length. *Virtutes politicae* (22–155) are what later Schoolmen would call the natural or moral virtues and include the traditional cardinal virtues. Three reasons are given why there are four cardinal virtues (44–86), and then each virtue is defined and described with respect to its function in man's moral life (87–155). *Virtutes gratuitae* (156–430) comprise both natural and political virtues when these are infused with grace, but more specifically they are the traditional theological virtues (164–208). After a developed definition of *virtus gratuita* according to St. Augustine (209–51), the author discusses grace: its nature (255–314), how it is given (315–86: by Christ, through the Virgin, and through the seven sacraments), how it is lost (through the seven deadly sins, 387–404), and how it is restored (405–14). A short section on external graces, such as beauty, strength, health, and wealth, closes the chapter (415–30).

Chapter II turns to particular virtues and begins with humility, not because this virtue is first in greatness and importance (which would be charity) or in the order of psychological progression or acquisition (which would be faith), but because it is opposed to the first deadly sin which it combats, pride (2–15). Humility is divided into true and false (16–20). True humility in turn is divided into three kinds—of heart, mouth, and deed—and each of these has several subdivisions (20–97). Next we learn how true humility can be acquired: by considering Christ's

own humility and the miseries of our human condition (98–173). Eight points follow that list the good effects of this virtue (174–96), and then the author presents a series of examples which can teach us true humility, such as the peacock and the bear, little children, Saracen merchants, or the moon, whose eleven properties are moralized at some length (197–356). Somewhat less space is devoted to false humility or hypocrisy (357–401), and the chapter ends with a mere reference to the twelve degrees of true humility according to St. Bernard (402–3) and a short listing of punishments that may befall pride (404–9). One manuscript adds a section on the four signs of humility, which is directly borrowed from Peraldus.

The following, long chapter (III) on charity returns to the earlier comparison of humility to the moon and now likens charity to the sun. The reason why charity is treated only after humility is that the vice it opposes, envy, is born of pride, which was opposed by humility. The chapter falls into four large sections. After an introductory part (2–97) it discusses at great length the love of God (98–815), then turns to love of one's neighbor, including one's enemy (816–943), and concludes with a paragraph on the punishment of envy (944–59). The introduction, after placing charity in the order of virtues and vices, distinguishes between uncreated love (that is, God) and created love (that is, a human virtue) and takes some pain to show that, while "charity" can have various meanings (27–38), it is indeed "a good quality of the mind," that is, natural to man (8ff.), and can be defined in various ways (45–66). The precise relation between the two loves which form the bulk of the chapter—love of God and of one's neighbor—also receives some analytical attention (67–97). Love of God, then, is shown to be very commendable (98–120) and to have a number of good effects (121–50); it can also be compared to a variety of natural objects (151–575), on some of which (for example, the sun, fire, light, and heart) the author dwells at length, extracting a series of moral lessons from their properties. After this he turns to "that charity which is at once created and uncreated, which is the love of Christ," and discusses Christ's love for man and conversely man's love for him (576–815). Christ's love appeared in ten things, and he loved man in seven ways (sweetly, wisely, and so forth). In return, man should love him in the same seven ways. The last of them, loving him "from our whole mind, . . . that is to say, in our whole memory," leads the author to discuss *memoria passionis Christi*, that is, meditation on Christ's passion (765–815).

Chapter IV is equally extensive. It actually offers two virtues as remedies to the sin of wrath: meekness and patience. The two are initially distinguished from each other, and meekness (*mansuetudo*, praised in Psalm 31:11) is shown to be essentially the same as mildness (*mititudo*,

listed among the beatitudes of Matthew 5:4). Starting with its etymology, our author develops several similitudes for *mansuetudo*, gives reasons why it is praiseworthy, and lists its good effects and degrees (27–136). Turning to a much longer discussion of patience (137–1013), he follows a similar process of definition, commendation, and illustration by comparing the virtue to various natural objects. He then reaches the heart of the matter: based on four "external vexations" whose endurance requires patience, he can now speak of four forms of patience to which we are exhorted by the word and example of Christ; and to these four another three (patience in temptation, sickness, and contempt of the world) are easily added (285–948). The section continues with briefer mention of three types of suffering men (Christ and the two thieves, 949–85), of three forms of long-suffering (985–1006), and of the reward for long-suffering, which is expressed in the beatitude "Blessed are the peacemakers" (1007–13), which leads to a digression on "peace" (1014–1174). The chapter finally ends with a few lines on the punishment of the sin that is counteracted by patience (1175–82).

The next chapter (v) appears to be a further digression in that its subject matter, obedience, is not opposed directly to one of the seven deadly sins; yet the author clearly conceives of it as a discrete section which follows "after the chapter on humility and patience," and the reason for its inclusion lies in the fact that obedience is the daughter of humility and nursling of patience (3-6). Following his habitual procedures, the author defines and commends this virtue, discusses its conditions (62ff.), distinguishes three forms (92ff.), and lists its good effects (160ff.). Then he employs a literary form which he had used in part before and which we will encounter again in later chapters: the scholastic *quaestio*, in which a question ("queritur an") or objection ("videtur quod") is introduced, a series of authorities are quoted (sometimes in mutual contradiction), and a *solutio* or determination is given. Here, the author thus discusses whether obedience is meritorious (183–200), whether it is virtue in general or a specific virtue (201–16), whether an obedient person may retain any part of his own will (217–44), and whether one should obey an evil superior (245–66).

Chapter vi returns to the strictly remedial virtues by opposing fortitude to sloth. It defines the virtue (3–15) and then lists and develops its traditional five species (16–147). Finally, it adds a number of "special remedies" against sloth, such as considering God's creating the world, the movement of heavenly bodies and the constant change in all things, the behavior of ants and bees, as well as engaging in prayer, holy reading, and saintly conversation (148–213).

Chapter vii discusses the remedy for the vice of greed: *misericordia* and *pietas*, which are defined and distinguished from each other as being

merely two aspects of the same virtue (3–12). After indicating the scriptural basis for mercy (13–21), the author shows how praiseworthy this virtue is, whether in God or in man (22–128), and then indicates reasons that invite us (129–93) and causes that compel us (194–247) to practice it. After distinguishing mercy from such similar virtues as *pietas, indulgencia,* and *compassio* (248–56), he compares it to several natural objects, such as a tree, the fountain of paradise, Jacob's ladder, and oil, whose properties are moralized at some length (257–338). A final paragraph (339–52) lists the five species or rather acts of the virtue.

The next chapter (VIII), the shortest of the treatise, deals with abstinence. After distinguishing between abstaining from evil inclinations in general and from food in particular (3–11), the author shows that the latter is indeed a virtue (12–29) and lists five sinful aspects of eating which one must avoid (30–44). This virtue is taught even by irrational animals (45–66). It has seven companions, which, together with abstinence itself, form the conventional species of moderation (67–106). Christ taught abstinence by his example and teaching (107–14), and his words "Blessed are they that hunger and thirst after justice, for they shall have their fill" lead to two extensions: first, the question whether saints enjoy "their fill" spiritually already in this life (115–34), and next a brief *distinctio* on the word "hunger" (135–41). Nine reasons are then given why abstinence is praiseworthy (142–64). In contrast, indiscreet or exaggerated abstinence is to be reproached (165–88). A short paragraph on the evil consequences of gluttony (189–94) closes this chapter.

Last, in Chapter IX continence is offered as the remedy for lechery. After distinguishing between a general and a specialized meaning of the term, the author divides continence into three parts according to the state of those who have this virtue (that is, marriage, widowhood, and virginity; 3–15), and this division furnishes the structure for the entire chapter. Modesty in spouses (16–163) is safeguarded by the sacrament of matrimony, which is defined (16–25) and shown to be praiseworthy with the help of a conventional memory verse (26–47). Marriage, however, does not allow for sex at all times (48–75); and several reasons for monogamy are adduced (76–89). Two paragraphs explain what attitude husbands should have towards their wives and vice versa (90–115), and the question is raised and scholastically determined whether the sex act is always sinful (116–63). Next, continence in widows (164–404) is similarly defined, praised, and illustrated with several biblical images. The quotation of "Blessed are the clean of heart, for they shall see God" leads to a listing of the good effects which cleanness of heart has (253–89). Then ten ascetic practices which help in preserving chastity are discussed (290–334), and finally the notion that "a person who makes a vow of continence dedicates a temple to God" leads to a long moraliza-

tion of the rite of dedicating a church (335–404). Finally, virginity (405–871) also is first defined, and its good effects are listed and praised (405–66). The question is raised whether virginity is a virtue (467–90), and the implication in distinguishing between physical and mental or spiritual virginity results in two additional paragraphs (491–511). Then the author turns to "foolish virginity" (512–56), whose great archetype, Eve, leads him to her even greater opposite, Mary. An extended eulogy of the Blessed Virgin follows (556–871), in which more than two dozen traditional images, mostly from the Old Testament (especially Ecclesiasticus 24:17–23), are moralized in praise of this virtue.

As this summary already indicates, in its tone and style *Postquam* is thoroughly "scholastic." Its discussion of abstract concepts proceeds by definition and divisions. A number of topics are treated in the format of scholastic disputations. In addition, the author is eager to find logical foundations for such traditional units and topics as the four cardinal or the three theological virtues or the two kinds of love. It is interesting to note in this respect that occasionally the author presents several such rationales (as in the case of the cardinal virtues) or definitions, which he juxtaposes without singling any one out as the best—a method which seems to have been characteristic of the Franciscan masters writing in the first half of the thirteenth century, before the appearance of the more unified theological *summae.*[2] At the same time, the search for logical foundations leads further to the construction of a system in which each part has its rational place. Thus, we hear not only why the remedial virtues are taken up in the order adopted for the work, but are also shown several connecting links between them.

The desire to give reasons and to prove extends to the smallest details of this work: if at all possible, every assertion is backed up by authoritative quotations which are taken either from the Bible or from a number of theological and secular writers, including the Church Fathers, Anselm, Bernard of Clairvaux, Aristotle, Boethius, and several pagan and Christian poets. While this urge to prove by "authorities" shows the strong influence of scholastic dialectic, it betrays even more the impact of rhetoric. *Postquam* clearly belongs to that practical literature which, around the middle of the thirteenth century, came to be written for preachers, literature which combines a firm logical and systematic structure with a rich collection of pertinent subject matter for use in persuasive oratory. The latter characteristic is very evident in that all the chapters on individual virtues in *Postquam* contain long sections that give a *commendatio* of the respective virtue, in which the writer explains point by point such matters as how the particular virtue is taught by Christ and by Scripture, what its good effects in us are, and how it may be compared to many visible objects in creation. This, of course, is the

stuff of which sermons were made after the impact of the universities and the mendicant orders. Its rhetorical orientation is further manifest in its use of many small devices that are equally ubiquitous in later medieval preaching, such as "etymology," verbal concordance, *distinctiones,* and the use of *exempla* and memory verses.

BACKGROUND AND LITERARY GENRE OF THE *SUMMA VIRTUTUM*

The extended, systematic treatment of the virtues itself is likewise a product of the scholastic period. In earlier centuries, one finds nothing on "the virtues" which would parallel the detailed and seminal analyses of the chief vices given by Cassian and Gregory the Great and their successors.[3] This relative neglect is not as astonishing as it may appear if one considers that Christian ethical literature until the twelfth century (and in fact far beyond) had an eminently practical, ascetic orientation. Its attention focused on man in the here and now, as a being created good but having become flawed through the Fall, with reformation made possible through Christ's redemptive work and necessary for his progression to future happiness. The primary object of moral theology, thus, was sinful man who must struggle against his innate evil inclinations. Attention to these inclinations or "vices," therefore, must and did come first.[4] "First we must uproot the vices, and afterwards plant the virtues," said Othlo of St. Emmeran in the twelfth century,[5] reflecting the commonplace practical thought of Gregory and Cassian.[6] Similarly, the literary genre of the *summa* on the virtues came into being only as a companion and sequel to the *summa* on the vices.

If in literary treatments the virtues took second place to the vices in the order and degree of attention they received, their historical development was also considerably less straightforward than that of the vices. Were one to ask Bishop Bradwardine or Geoffrey Chaucer or a real-life Haukyn the Active Man to name the chief vices, their answers would be immediate and identical: a series of seven beginning with pride and ending with lechery. But a similar request to name the chief virtues would probably have occasioned a puzzled "Which ones?" For throughout the Middle Ages, systematic theology as well as popular catechetical instruction recognized two different series of chief virtues, depending on whether "virtue" was considered as a principle of morally right action, or as a counterpart to or replacement for a specific vice. In the first case, one would think of the four cardinal virtues (prudence, justice, fortitude, and moderation), which theologians from the early Fathers on had accepted from pagan philosophers,[7] enriched with

"branches" to cover a wide spectrum of behavior,[8] and combined with the three "catholic" or "theological" virtues (faith, hope, and charity) of I Corinthians 13:13.[9] In the second case, one would think of such virtues as humility, patience, chastity, and so on. Because the chief vices, or deadly sins, were considered to be wounds or diseases in human nature after the Fall which Christ had come to heal,[10] these opposite virtues were called *remedia*.[11] Though attempts to develop a list of "remedial virtues" began in the patristic period, complete lists seem to have appeared only later,[12] and they never became as definitely fixed as did the corresponding list of deadly sins.[13] The competition between cardinal-plus-theological and remedial virtues can still be seen very clearly in *Postquam*, whose first chapter deals with the former while chapters II–IX, forming the true subject of the work, deal with the latter.

In analyzing the notion of "remedial virtue" and developing a complete list, theologians also had to consider at least two other concepts and series, both endowed with biblical authority, whose members could be related to the chief vices: the beatitudes of Matthew 5:3–9 (or 11), which promise bliss to specified spiritual attitudes,[14] and the gifts of the Holy Spirit, mentioned in Isaiah 11:2–3, which create or support positive spiritual attitudes in their recipient.[15] Needless to say, the members of these various lists are by no means synonymous, and while twelfth-century theologians delighted in correlating these and several other septenaries,[16] they were faced with a conglomerate of confusing traditions in which the precise relationships between virtues, gifts, and beatitudes, between cardinal-plus-theological and remedial virtues, between natural and infused virtue, and ultimately between human effort and divine grace, all constituted so many problems which sooner or later had to be solved.

The solution was given by the early scholastic masters of the twelfth and beginning thirteenth centuries.[17] The collection, questioning, and analysis of theological traditions undertaken by such writers as Peter Lombard, Alanus of Lille, William of Auxerre, Jean de la Rochelle, and many others led to the establishment of a rational system in which these various series and their members found their logical, interrelated place. This systematic analysis was to provide the framework for the full-fledged, monographic treatment of the virtues as we find it in *Postquam*, especially in its opening chapter, which distinguishes between different kinds of "virtue," offers rationales for both series of virtues, and places them in the larger contexts of psychology (by considering *virtutes* as *vires animae*) and of theology (by considering them in relation to nature and grace). Although *Postquam* is not an original treatise of systematic theology but rather a product of *haute vulgarisation*, it neatly reflects the results of theological thought current in the period ca. 1230–50.

The second major aspect of the work and its genre—its homiletic orientation—similarly marks an intensification of earlier efforts to collect material or "authorities" which could be used for exhortation either in private reading or in preaching. The *florilegium* by Peter the Chanter entitled *Verbum abbreviatum* (1191–92),[18] for example, collects biblical quotations and examples to show how the virtues were taught by Christ's words and deeds; its chapter on humility also contains a story from *Vitas Patrum* which recurs in *Postquam* (II.191–93).[19] A similar distant predecessor is the *Summa de arte praedicatoria* by Alanus of Lille (1199?).[20] Its chapter on patience, for example, foreshadows *Postquam* not only by giving biblical examples and a variety of authoritative quotations for the virtue but also by proposing the scheme of the four kinds of injury which patience can overcome (IV.286–90).[21] But the immediate progenitor of *Postquam* and its genre is the work on the vices and virtues by the French Dominican William Peraldus, in which the efforts of Peter the Chanter, Alanus, and other flower gatherers, as well as the work of biblical commentators culminated in a rich and firmly structured bouquet. Like this illustrious predecessor, *Postquam* was evidently composed in response to the demand for handbooks on the vices and virtues which had been created by the new stimulus the mendicant orders had given to preaching and the concomitant emphasis on the sacrament of penance.[22]

The strong, even if indirect, influence of Peraldus on *Postquam* is evident from the following. In three of its nine manuscripts *Postquam* is preceded by a copy of Peraldus's *Summa vitiorum*.[23] But more importantly, in five other manuscripts[24] *Postquam* is preceded by a different treatise on the vices, which begins with the words "Primo uidendum est quid sit peccatum" (henceforth referred to as *Primo*), which is clearly an abbreviation and reworking of Peraldus's *Summa vitiorum* (see below). That *Postquam* was written as a sequel to *Primo*, and most likely by the same author, is established by the following facts:

(*a*) DIRECT REFERENCES IN *POSTQUAM* TO *PRIMO*. *Postquam* contains six references to chapters that are not part of it (at I.390–91; IV.253–54; VIII.55–56; VIII.105–6; IX.74–75; IX.114–15). Although all six references could be to *Primo*, two are very general in nature and two others could also be to Peraldus's *Summa vitiorum*. But the two remaining references can only be to *Primo*:[25] "Consider the properties of the pig treated in the chapter on gluttony above" (VIII.55–56) points to a number of properties of the pig which are mentioned and moralized in *Primo* in the chapter on gluttony (ff. 67^{v}–68 in E); and the reference to Christ the physician (IV.253–54) is to a chapter at the beginning of *Primo* (f. 4^{v} in E). Neither passage occurs in Peraldus.

(*b*) USE OF THE SAME INITIAL IMAGE. *Postquam* begins with the words:

"After having spoken of the soul's diseases, that is, the sins, we must now add the discussion of their remedies, that is, the virtues." While the comparison of the vices to different kinds of sickness, and of the virtues to healing remedies, had some currency in the late Middle Ages,[26] it does not occur prominently in Peraldus. In contrast, *Primo* (and *Quoniam*) calls the seven deadly sins *vulnera anime*, compares them to seven *morbi corporales* (ff. 3^{v}–4^{v}), and then extends the simile further: "Against these seven wounds of our nature the heavenly physician has brought healing medicine" ("Contra hec septem uulnera nature celestis medicus tulit salubrem medicinam," f. 4^{v}a). Various steps in the healing process are indicated, including a healing potion, which is grace; *medicina conservativa*, which consists in "the virtues inserted in the habit of grace"; *medicina restaurativa*, the seven gifts of the Holy Spirit; and the "vessels of grace," which are the seven sacraments. Next follow specific remedies for the specific vices/diseases, as for instance: "Against the blindness of envy he brought the eye-salve of his charity, which is made from burnt calamine extinguished in vinegar" ("Contra cecitatem inuidie tulit collirium caritatis sue, quod fit ex lapide calamine combuste et in aceto extincte," f. 4^{v}b).

(*c*) REPEATED MATERIAL. Like the initial image that has just been discussed, a fairly large number of images and quotations found throughout *Primo* are used again in *Postquam*, such as: the bear that is blinded by looking at a shining basin (II.204–5; cf. *Primo*, f. 13); the bat that walks on its wings because it has no forefeet (V.111–12; cf. f. 40^{v}); "virtutes gregatim volant," attributed to Gregory (II.11 and IX.468–69; cf. f. 4^{v}); the name Herod or Herodias said to signify "gloria pellis" (I.388; cf. f. 7^{v}); the reasons for monogamy (IX.76–89; cf. f. 79^{v}); and many others. It should be noted that these examples are not part of the commonplaces which can be found in just any medieval treatise on the vices and virtues.

It is therefore evident that *Primo* and *Postquam* form a unit. Although this is not the place for a detailed analysis of *Primo*,[27] it should be pointed out that this work on the seven chief vices represents an abbreviation and reworking of Peraldus's *Summa vitiorum*. Though its author has added a good deal of homiletic matter, among which a greater interest in moralized properties of natural objects (such as the pig, mentioned above) is especially noteworthy, and though he has rearranged the Peraldian series of chief vices (which had included a "sin of the tongue" with many branches) to bring it in line with the traditional "seven deadly sins," a large amount of *Primo*'s material is directly taken over from Peraldus.

While *Primo*, thus, is a reworking of Peraldus's work on the vices, its sequel on the virtues, *Postquam*, is substantively independent of

Peraldus's *Summa virtutum*. In composing a monograph on the virtues, Peraldus had adopted the traditional series of cardinal-plus-theological virtues, to which he added, by simple juxtaposition, the gifts of the Holy Spirit and the beatitudes. Quite differently, the author of *Primo-Postquam* chose to focus on the series of remedial virtues, each directly opposed to one of the seven deadly sins. The result is not only one of the earliest monographs on the virtues, but the first extensive treatment of the remedial virtues. *Postquam* thus holds an importance in medieval theological and pastoral literature that is quite independent of its significance as a source of Chaucer's Parson's Tale.

AUTHORSHIP AND DATE

Primo and *Postquam* give no direct indication of the identity of their author. The fact that the virtue of obedience receives a separate chapter may suggest that *Postquam* was written by a member of a religious order, and the citation of St. Francis at IV.371 may cause one to think of a Franciscan author, but neither of these features carries sufficient proof. The treatise on the vices contains a story which mentions persons and a place that have some relation to the work's author. It is an *exemplum* of the bad ending lawyers can come to: "My companion Stephen, rector of the church of Caldecote, when he had studied law for many years and was about to die, said to his brother, the knight Robert de Bloy: 'Do you know the cleric Stephen of Caldecote?' His brother replied: 'You are the one. Make the sign of the cross on your forehead!' And Stephen said: 'I do not know that cleric. But whoever he was, there are two black monks in the corner who have brought a judgment against him which can never be revoked.' And after saying this he at once died."[28] Unfortunately, the passage holds more problems than answers, because no Robert de Bloy seems to be known, nor have I found any incumbent of Caldecote named Stephen de Bloy, nor is it clear which of the many villages by that name is referred to, nor is the relation between Stephen ("my companion," *socius meus*) and the writer at all patent. If one admits the possibility that the family name may have become corrupted very early in the scribal transmission, one may think of Robert de Brus (or Bruce) V (died 1245) or his son by the same name (died 1295).[29] Robert V's wife, Isabel, had inherited lands in Huntingdonshire, including Caldecote, and her son acted as patron of the church of Caldecote in 1268; the patronage of the Bruce family continued at least into the fourteenth century.[30] At an unspecified date, Hugh of Welles, bishop of Lincoln (1209–35), conferred the church of Caldecote[31] on a Stephanus de Holewella, who at this point was to go

to school so that he "in officio cantandi se faciat edoceri."[32] Again, the identity of this Stephen with the protagonist of our story is by no means assured, and even if it were it would not throw any light on his "companion," our author.

The quoted story provides a little more help for the dating of *Postquam*, because it is repeated in the *Liber exemplorum*, which was written by an unnamed English Franciscan between 1275 and 1279. This collection of stories that illustrate a variety of moral topics in alphabetical order begins its section on *advocati* as follows: "Terrible to say and awful to hear is the *exemplum* that one finds about Stephen, the rector of the church of Caldecote. In England, though, there are very many villages by the name of Caldecote, but as we have found, a certain Stephen, who was rector of some Caldecote, after he had studied law for many years . . ."[33] Since the story continues from that point on verbatim as it is found in *Primo*, the author of *Liber exemplorum* clearly copied it from a written source. This would place the date of composition for *Primo* before 1275/79.

It is possible to narrow the probable period of composition still further, for in connection with the Caldecote story the author of *Primo* makes the following remark about the papal prohibition against the study of civil law: "Excluded from practicing civil law are not only *plebani*, that is, higher members of the clergy, as is stated in the decretal *Super specula*, but also all who have the cure of souls, as stated in the rescript which the Lord Pope sent to the bishop of Orleans."[34] The first part of this reference is to the famous constitution of Honorius III, of 1219, which was incorporated in the Decretals of Gregory in 1234. The second part refers to a rescript of Gregory to the bishop of Orleans of 17 January 1235.[35] If the wording allows us to interpret *dominus papa*, "the Lord Pope," as referring to the ruling pope, *Primo* would have been written between 1235 and 1241, and it is reasonable to assume that its sequel, *Postquam*, was produced not many years later.[36]

POSTQUAM AND CHAUCER'S *REMEDIA*

Earlier investigations into the sources of the Parson's Tale have shown that while Chaucer's treatment of the sins and their remedies is ultimately indebted to the great work on the vices and virtues by William Peraldus, the latter contains hardly any specific parallels to Chaucer's discussions of the remedial virtues which follow each of the seven deadly sins. Kate O. Petersen's basic study, which first brought Peraldus to the attention of Chaucerians, offered no parallels for the sections that discuss the *remedia* except for parts of lines 918–22, 939, and 951–55, for

which she referred to the section on temperance in Peraldus's *Summa virtutum*, and to the end of the section on lechery in his *Summa vitiorum*. (Peraldus provides, in fact, other parallels not noticed by Petersen, as will be shown later.) Petersen also emphasized that Peraldus is at best the *ultimate* source for the respective parts of the Parson's Tale, whose material underwent considerable change before it reached Chaucer.[37] In the two generations after Petersen's work, several scholars studied the relevant literature on the vices and virtues that originated in the century between Peraldus and Chaucer,[38] but no treatise came to light which could be claimed as a closer analogue or source, so that Germaine Dempster, in her contribution to *Sources and Analogues of Chaucer's "Canterbury Tales,"* could only restate Petersen's findings. In her own reproduction of source texts she included a section from Peraldus's treatment of lechery as a possible though remote source for the Parson's Tale, lines 951–55, and added the note that "for the remedies against the other six sins Chaucer does not seem to owe anything to either the *Summa virtutum* or the *Summa vitiorum*."[39] Richard Hazelton suggested several years later that "in translating the *remedia*, and probably the entire sins tractate (if not the treatise as a whole), Chaucer relied on both a Latin text and a French translation" of the *Moralium dogma philosophorum*, a highly influential treatment of the virtues composed in the twelfth century.[40] Hazelton does not make a convincing case for this work, because *Moralium dogma philosophorum* contains parallels for only a small percentage of lines in Chaucer's *remedia* sections; its material does not appear in the same sequence as in the Parson's Tale; and, most important, the work offers only definitions of the cardinal virtues and their species, definitions which by Chaucer's time had become commonplaces in theological literature.[41]

In contrast to these proposed sources in Latin, French, and English, the work here edited, which had been unknown until the late 1960s, contains passages whose similarity to Chaucer's discussion of the *remedia* is extensive and striking. *Postquam* offers the following parallels:[42]

Parson's Tale	*Postquam*
SUPERBIA	cap. II
[475] Now sith that so is that ye han understonde what is Pride, and whiche been the speces of it, and whennes Pride sourdeth and spryngeth,	
[476] now shul ye understonde which is the remedie agayns the synne of Pride; and that is humylitee, or mekenesse.	[3] Et primo de humilitate quia ipsa est remedium superbie . . .
[477] That is a vertu thurgh which a man hath verray knoweleche of hymself, and	[16] "Humilitas est uirtus quia quis uerissima sui cognicione sibi ipsi uilescit."

Parson's Tale	*Postquam*
holdeth of hymself no pris ne deyntee, as in regard of his desertes, considerynge evere his freletee.	[19] ". . . intuitu conditoris uel proprie fragilitatis." . . .
[478] Now been ther three maneres of humylitee: as humylitee in herte; another humylitee is in his mouth; the thridde in his werkes.	[20] Vera humilitas sic diuiditur: alia est cordis, alia oris, alia operis.
[479] The humilitee in herte is in foure maneres. That oon is whan a man holdeth hymself as noght worth biforn God of hevene. Another is whan he ne despiseth noon other man.	[21] Illa que est cordis consistit in quatuor, quorum primum est semetipsum abnegare . . . [24] "ante Dei oculos." . . . [25] Secundum est ut neminem . . . contempnat. . . .
[480] The thridde is whan he rekketh nat, though men holde hym noght worth. The ferthe is whan he nys nat sory of his humiliacioun.	[32] Tercium est ut contempnat se contempni. . . . [45] Quartum est ut non contristetur in sua deiectione. . . .
[481] Also the humilitee of mouth is in foure thynges: in attempree speche, and in humblesse of speche, and whan he biknoweth with his owene mouth that he is swich a hym thynketh that he is in his herte.	[53] Humilitas oris consistit in quatuor, quorum primum est taciturnitas. . . . [57] "sermo tuus discretum sumat inicium et cum moderamine finem." . . . [63] Secundum est propria facta humili uerbo [*var.* uoce] referre. . . . [68] Tercium est seipsum uilem et contaminatum proclamare. . . .
Another is whan he preiseth the bountee of another man, and nothyng therof amenuseth.	[69] Quartum est aliena bona sine diminucione commendare. . . .
[482] Humilitee eek in werkes is in foure maneres. The firste is whan he putteth othere men biforn hym. The seconde is to chese the loweste place over al. The thridde is gladly to assente to good conseil.	[73] Humilitas operis consistit in quinque, quorum primum est alios sibi preponere. . . . [75] Secundum est inferiorem locum eligere. . . . [76] Tercium est aliorum . . . consilio facile assentire. . . .
[483] The ferthe is to stonde gladly to the award of his sovereyns, or of hym that is in hyer degree. Certein, this is a greet werk of humylitee.	[79] Quartum est libenter subici maioribus et obedire. . . . [81] Triplex humilitas: vna minor . . . , alia maior.

INVIDIA — cap. III

[515] Now wol I speke of remedie agayns this foule synne of Envye. First is the love of God principal, and lovyng of his neighebor as hymself; for soothly, that oon ne may nat been withoute that oother.	[3] Dicendum est quid sit . . . [4] curacio [*var.* remedium] inuidie. . . . [67] Est autem caritas que dilectio Dei est et proximi una uirtus. . . .
[516] And truste wel that in the name of thy neighebor thou shalt understonde the name of thy brother; for certes alle we have o fader flesshly, and o mooder, that is to seyn, Adam and Eve; and eek o fader espiritueel, and that is God of hevene.	[*See below, 837 and 839*]

Parson's Tale	*Postquam*
[517] Thy neighebor artow holden for to love,	[816] Sequitur de dilectione proximi. . . . "Diliges proximum tuum sicut teipsum." . . .
[*See below, at 519*]	[818] "Prout uultis ut faciant uobis homines, et uos facite illis." . . .
and wilne hym alle goodnesse; and therfore seith God, "Love thy neighebor as thyselve," that is to seyn, to salvacioun bothe of lyf and of soule.	[823] quo teneor ei desiderare bonum, et hoc notat Dominus cum dicit, "sicut teipsum," idest . . . ad uitam eternam. . . .
[518] And mooreover thou shalt love hym in word, and in benigne amonestynge and chastisynge, and conforten hym in his anoyes, and prey for hym with al thyn herte.	[829] Item diligendus est uerbo ut instruas, corripias, consoleris, et ores pro eo. . . .
[519] And in dede thou shalt love hym in swich wise that thou shalt doon to hym in charitee as thou woldest that it were doon to thyn owene persone.	[831] Item diligendus est beneficio. . . . [*See above, 818*]
[*See above, at 516*]	[837] "Nomine proximi omnis homo intelligitur." . . . [839] Et nomine fratris intelligitur omnis homo, quia omnes eundem patrem habent carnalem, scilicet Adam, et spiritualem, Deum. . . .
[520] And therfore thou ne shalt doon hym no damage in wikked word, ne harm in his body, ne in his catel, ne in his soule, by entissyng of wikked ensample.	[845] Si igitur fratrem leseris . . . [847] aut uerbo, scilicet obiurgando uel detrahendo . . . [848] aut dampno pecunie . . .[850] aut lesione corporis . . . [851] aut lesione anime prouocando ad peccatum . . . [853] aut prauo exemplo. . . .
[521] Thou shalt nat desiren his wyf, ne none of his thynges. Understoond eek that in the name of neighebor is comprehended his enemy.	[*No parallel*]
[522] Certes, man shal loven his enemy, by the comandement of God; and soothly thy freend shaltow love in God. [523] I seye, thyn enemy shaltow love for Goddes sake, by his comandement. For if it were reson that man sholde haten his enemy, for sothe God nolde nat receyven us to his love that been his enemys.	[860] Sub nomine proximi cadunt eciam inimici. Quod expressius ostendit Dominus . . . "diligite inimicos uestros." . . . [862] Amicos debemus diligere in Deo . . . , et inimicos propter Deum . . . , [865] idest propter eius preceptum. . . . [*See below, 939*]
[524] Agayns three manere of wronges that his enemy dooth to hym, he shal doon three thynges, as thus. [525] Agayns hate and rancour of herte, he shal love hym in herte. Agayns chidyng and wikkede wordes, he shal preye for his enemy.	[880] Et tria precepit Dominus circa dilectionem inimici contra triplicem iniuriam, quarum prima est cordis, ut odium uel rancor, contra quam dicit "diligite." Secunda est oris, ut contumelia uel rixa, contra quam dicit "orate pro persequentibus et calumpniantibus uos."

Parson's Tale	*Postquam*
Agayns the wikked dede of his enemy, he shal doon hym bountee.	Tercia est operis, contra quam dicit "benefacite hiis qui uos oderunt." . . .
[526] For Crist seith: "Loveth youre enemys, and preyeth for hem that speke yow harm, and eek for hem that yow chacen and pursewen, and dooth bountee to hem that yow haten." Loo, thus comaundeth us oure Lord Jhesu Crist to do to oure enemys.	[*In the preceding sentences*] [906] Multum placet Deo, qui tam sollicite ammonet de inimico diligendo. . . .
[527] For soothly, nature dryveth us to loven oure freendes,	[909] De dilectione amici . . . naturaliter hoc facimus. . . .
and parfey, oure enemys han moore nede to love than oure freendes; and they that moore nede have, certes to hem shal men doon goodnesse;	[910] Secundo, quia inimici magis indigent, et indigentibus conferendum est beneficium. . . .
[528] and certes, in thilke dede have we remembraunce of the love of Jhesu Crist that deyde for his enemys.	[913] Tercio, quia in dilectione inimici memores sumus dilectionis Dei, qui pro inimicis . . . orauit. . . .
[529] And in as muche as thilke love is the moore grevous to perfourne, so muche is the moore gret the merite;	[919] Quarto, quia magnum beneficium meriti nobis accumulamus propter difficultatem huiusmodi dilectionis. . . .
and therfore the lovynge of oure enemy hath confounded the venym of the devel.	[933] Octauo, quia per dilectionem inimici maxime confunditur inuidia diaboli. . . .
[530] For right as the devel is disconfited by humylitee, right so is he wounded to the deeth by love of oure enemy.	[935] Vnde sicut humilitate prosternitur, ita dilectione uulneratur. . . .
[*See above, at 523*]	[939] "Si iustum fuisset inimicos odire, Deus te ex gentibus inimicum nunquam in suam suscepisset dilectionem." . . .
[531] Certes, thanne is love the medicine that casteth out the venym of Envye fro mannes herte.	[*No parallels*]
[532] The speces of this paas shullen be moore largely declared in hir chapitres folwynge.	

IRA — cap. IV

[654] The remedie agains Ire is a vertu that men clepen Mansuetude, that is Debonairetee; and eek another vertu, that men callen Pacience or Suffrance.	[2] Sequitur de mansuetudine et paciencia, que sunt remedia ire. . . .
[655] Debonairetee withdraweth and refreyneth the stirynges and the moevynges of mannes corage in his herte, in swich manere that they ne skippe nat out by angre ne by ire.	[4] Mansuetudo est in reprimendo motus interiores ne iram prouocent,
[656] Suffrance suffreth swetely alle the anoyaunces and the wronges that men doon to man outward.	paciencia est in sustinendo molestias exteriores. . . .
[657] Seint Jerome seith thus of debonairetee, that "it dooth noon harm to no	[7] Ieronimus: "Mansuetus neminem ledit." . . . [23] "Tranquillitas mentis

Parson's Tale	*Postquam*
wight ne seith; ne for noon harm that men doon or seyn, he ne eschawfeth nat agayns his resoun."	que nec illatis malis exasperari . . . potest." . . .
[658] This vertu somtyme comth of nature; for, as seith the philosophre, "A man is a quyk thyng, by nature debonaire and tretable to goodnesse;	[27] Dicitur autem mansuetus . . . tractabilis. Philosophus: "Homo est animal mansuetum natura." . . .
but whan debonairetee is enformed of grace, thanne is it the moore worth."	[*No parallel*]
[659] Pacience, that is another remedie agayns Ire, is a vertu that suffreth swetely every mannes goodnesse, and is nat wrooth for noon harm that is doon to hym.	[140] "Paciencia est aliena mala [*var.* bona] equanimiter perpeti et aduersus eum qui mala ingerit nullo dolore morderi."
[660] The philosophre seith that pacience is thilke vertu that suffreth debonairely alle the outrages of adversitee and every wikked word.	[141] Philosophus: "Paciencia est uirtus contumeliarum et omnis aduersitatis inpetus equanimiter portans."
[661] This vertu maketh a man lyk to God, and maketh hym Goddes owene deere child, as seith Crist.	[143] Paciencia . . . assimilat nos Deo et filios eius constituit . . . ; Matthei v: "Beati pacifici, quoniam filii Dei uocabuntur." . . .
This vertu disconfiteth thyn enemy. And therfore seith the wise man, "If thow wolt venquysse thyn enemy, lerne to suffre."	[164] Item paciencia uincit hostem, secundum quod solet dici [*var.* dicit Philosophus]: ". . . si uis uincere, disce pati." . . .
[662] And thou shalt understonde that man suffreth foure manere of grevances in outward thynges, agayns the whiche foure he moot have foure manere of paciences.	[286] Ideo sciendum quod quadruplex est exterior molestia, et necessaria quadruplex paciencia.
[663] The firste grevance is of wikkede wordes. Thilke suffrede Jhesu Crist withouten grucchyng, ful paciently, whan the Jewes despised and repreved hym ful ofte.	[287] Molestia exterior est in contumelia uerborum. . . . [290] Pacienciam ad uerba docuit qui tot contumelias, tot contradictiones, tot conuicia, tot obprobria sine murmure sustinuit. . . .
[664] Suffre thou therfore paciently; for the wise man seith, "If thou stryve with a fool, though the fool be wrooth or though he laughe, algate thou shalt have no reste."	[306] Sciuit enim esse scriptum: "Vir sapiens si cum stulto contenderit, siue irascatur siue rideat, non inueniet requiem." . . .
[665] That oother grevance outward is to have damage of thy catel. Theragains suffred Crist ful paciently, whan he was despoyled of al that he hadde in this lyf, and that nas but his clothes.	[391] Pacienciam ad dampna rerum exhibuit Christus cum se propriis denudari permisit uestimentis. . . .
[666] The thridde grevance is a man to have harm in his body. That suffred Crist ful paciently in al his passioun.	[549] Sequitur de paciencia in lesione proprii corporis. . . . Hanc exhibuit Christus precipue in sua passione. . . .
[667] The fourthe grevance is in outrageous labour in werkes. Wherfore I seye that folk that maken hir servantz to tra-	[656] Sequitur de paciencia ad angarias [*var.* in angariis] operum. Et est angaria operum coactio seruicii corporalis inde-

vaillen to grevously, or out of tyme, as on haly dayes, soothly they do greet synne.

biti in propria alicuius persona. . . . [667] Vnde grauiter peccant qui sabbatum soluunt precipiendo uel exequendo pro temporali precio uel commodo. Et per sabbatum intellige omne festum sollempne. . . .

[668] Heer-agayns suffred Crist ful paciently and taughte us pacience, whan he baar upon his blissed shulder the croys upon which he sholde suffren despitous deeth.

[694] Ad angariam operum exemplo nos inuitat qui proprio humero tulit patibulum. . . .

[669] Heere may men lerne to be pacient; for certes noght oonly Cristen men been pacient, for love of Jhesu Crist, and for gerdoun of the blisful lyf that is perdurable, but certes, the olde payens that nevere were Cristene, commendeden and useden the vertu of pacience.
[670] A philosophre upon a tyme, that wolde have beten his disciple for his grete trespas, for which he was greetly amoeved, broghte a yerde to scoure with the child;
[671] and whan this child saugh the yerde, he seyde to his maister, "What thenke ye do?" "I wol bete thee," quod the maister, "for thy correccioun."
[672] "For sothe," quod the child, "ye oghten first correcte youreself, that han lost al youre pacience for the gilt of a child."
[673] "For sothe," quod the maister al wepynge, "thow seyst sooth. Have thow the yerde, my deere sone, and correcte me for myn impacience."

[*No parallel*]

[674] Of pacience comth obedience,

cap. v

[2] Post capitulum de humilitate et paciencia sequitur de obediencia. . . .

thurgh which a man is obedient to Crist and to alle hem to whiche he oghte to been obedient in Crist.
[675] And understond wel that obedience is perfit, whan that a man dooth gladly and hastily, with good herte entierly, al that he sholde do.
[676] Obedience generally is to perfourne the doctrine of God and of his sovereyns, to whiche hym oghte to ben obeisaunt in alle rightwisnesse.

[28] Quibus autem exhibenda sit obediencia . . . : [29] "Obedite prepositis uestris. . . ."
[62] Tria exiguntur ad perfectam obedienciam. Primo ut sit uoluntaria. . . . [65] Item debet esse cita . . . , [69] integra, ut fiant omnia que precipiuntur. . . . [80] Item bene debet homo obedire suo superiori. . . . [206] Obediencia generalis . . . [207] est adinplecio mandati, et ipsa est idem quod iusticia generalis. . . . [265] Et de ordine nature omnia inferiora obedienciam debent superioribus.

ACCIDIA — cap. VI

Parson's Tale	*Postquam*
[728] Agayns this horrible synne of Accidie, and the branches of the same, ther is a vertu that is called *fortitudo* or strengthe,	[2] Sequitur de remedio accidie, idest de uirtute fortitudinis. . . .
[*Cf. below, at 730*]	[4] "Fortitudo est periculorum considerata suscepcio et laborum diuturna perpessio." . . .
that is an affeccioun thurgh which a man despiseth anoyouse thinges.	[7] "Fortitudo est affectio qua omnia incommoda contempnimus."
[729] This vertu is so myghty and so vigerous that it dar withstonde myghtily and wisely kepen hymself fro perils that been wikked, and wrastle agayn the assautes of the devel.	Huius uirtutis est aggredi forcia. . . .
[730] For it enhaunceth and enforceth the soule, right as Accidie abateth it and maketh it fieble. For this *fortitudo* may endure by long suffraunce the travailles that been covenable.	[8] Ipsa enim eleuat animam et roborat, accidia econtra deprimit eam et debilitat. . . . [*Cf. above, 4*]
[731] This vertu hath manye speces; and the firste is cleped magnanimitee, that is to seyn,	[16] Huius uirtutis quinque sunt species. . . . [17] Magnanimitas est difficilium spontanea et racionalis aggressio.
greet corage. For certes, ther bihoveth greet corage agains Accidie, lest that it ne swolwe the soule by the synne of sorwe, or destroye it by wanhope.	[18] Et oportet magnum animum habere contra accidiam, ne ipsa absorbeat hominem per tristiciam uel frangat per desperacionem. . . .
[732] This vertu maketh folk to undertake harde thynges and grevouse thynges, by hir owene wil, wisely and resonably.	[*See above, 17*]
[733] And for as muchel as the devel fighteth agayns a man moore by queyntise and by sleighte than by strengthe, therfore men shal withstonden hym by wit and by resoun and by discrecioun.	[*No parallel*]
[734] Thanne arn ther the vertues of feith and hope in God and in his seintes, to acheve and acomplice the goode werkes in the whiche he purposeth fermely to continue.	[45] Fiducia est certa spes perducendi ad finem rem inchoatam. . . . [63] Item in sanctis habenda est fiducia suffragii, quia in solo Deo fiducia est premii. . . .
[735] Thanne comth seuretee or sikernesse; and that is whan a man ne douteth no travaille in tyme comynge of the goode werkes that a man hath bigonne.	[75] Securitas est incommoditates imminentes et rei inchoate affines non formidare. . . .
[736] Thanne comth magnificence, that is to seyn, whan a man dooth and perfourneth grete werkes of goodnesse; and that is the ende why that men sholde do goode werkes, for in the acomplissynge of grete goode werkes lith the grete gerdoun.	[89] Magnificencia est difficilium et preclarorum consumacio. . . . [91] Nostra uero magnificencia finem respicit in opere, que est potissima causarum, propter quam mouentur cetere. . . .

Parson's Tale	*Postquam*
[737] Thanne is ther constaunce, that is, stablenesse of corage; and this sholde been in herte by stedefast feith, and in mouth, and in berynge, and in chiere, and in dede.	[121] Constancia est stabilitas animi firma. . . . [122] Alia est cordis, ut sit homo "nichil in fide hesitans." . . . [124] Alia est oris. . . . [126] Alia est constancia uultus . . . [136] gestum. . . . [138] Quarta est constancia operis. . . .
[738] Eke ther been mo speciale remedies against Accidie in diverse werkes, and in consideracioun of the peynes of helle and of the joyes of hevene, and in the trust of the grace of the Holy Goost, that wole yeve hym myght to perfourne his goode entente.	[148] Specialia remedia contra accidiam sunt hec. . . . [*No further parallels*]

AVARICIA — cap. VII

[804] Now shul ye understonde that the releevynge of Avarice is misericorde, and pitee largely taken.	[2] Sequitur de remedio auaricie, idest de misericordia siue [*var.* et] pietate. . . .
And men myghten axe why that misericorde and pitee is releevynge of Avarice. [805] Certes, the av[a]ricious man sheweth no pitee ne misericorde to the nedeful man, for he deliteth hym in the kepynge of his tresor, and nat in the rescowynge ne releevynge of his evene-Cristen. And therfore speke I first of misericorde.	[*No parallel*]
[806] Thanne is misericorde, as seith the philosophre, a vertu by which the corage of a man is stired by the mysese of hym that is mysesed.	[4] Misericordia sic diffinitur a Philosopho: "Misericordia est uirtus per quam mouetur animus super calamitate afflictorum."
[807] Upon which misericorde folweth pitee in parfournynge of charitable werkes of misericorde.	[6] Pietas . . . sumitur pro operibus misericordie. . . .
[808] And certes, thise thynges moeven a man to the misericorde of Jhesu Crist, that he yaf hymself for oure gilt, and suffred deeth for misericorde, and forgaf us oure originale synnes,	[13] Misericordiam docuit Dominus . . . : [18] "Dedit semetipsum pro peccatis nostris, ut nos eriperet a seculo nequam." . . .
[809] and thereby relessed us fro the peynes of helle, and amenused the peynes of purgatorie by penitence, and yeveth grace wel to do, and atte laste the blisse of hevene.	[48] Item sicut misericordia redemit, sic ipsa miseros custodit et a peccato et a supplicio. . . .
[810] The speces of misericorde been, as for to lene and for to yeve, and to foryeven and relesse, and for to han pitee in herte and compassioun of the meschief of his evene-Cristene, and eek to chastise, there as nede is.	[339] Species misericordie . . . : dare . . . ; commodare . . . ; condonare . . . ; "Dimittite . . ."; conpati . . . ; [347] correpcio. . . .
[811] Another manere of remedie agayns avarice is resonable largesse; but soothly, heere bihoveth the consideracioun of the	[*No parallels*]

grace of Jhesu Crist, and of his temporeel goodes, and eek of the goodes perdurables, that Crist yaf to us;

[812] and to han remembrance of the deeth that he shal receyve, he noot whanne, where, ne how; and eek that he shal forgon al that he hath, save oonly that he hath despended in goode werkes.

[813] But for as muche as som folk been unmesurable, men oghten eschue fool-largesse, that men clepen wast.

[814] Certes, he that is fool-large ne yeveth nat his catel, but he leseth his catel. Soothly, what thyng that he yeveth for veyne glorie, as to mynstrals and to folk, for to beren his renoun in the world, he hath synne therof, and noon almesse.

[815] Certes, he leseth foule his good, that ne seketh with the yifte of his good nothyng but synne.

[816] He is lyk to an hors that seketh rather to drynken drovy or trouble water than for a drynken water of the clere welle.

[817] And for as muchel as they yeven ther as they sholde nat yeven, to hem aperteneth thilke malisoun that Crist shal yeven at the day of doom to hem that shullen been dampned.

GULA cap. VIII

[831] Agayns Glotonye is the remedie abstinence, as seith Galien; but that holde I nat meritorie, if he do it oonly for the heele of his body. Seint Augustyn wole that abstinence be doon for vertu and with pacience.

[832] "Abstinence," he seith, "is litel worth, but if a man have good wil thereto, and but it be enforced by pacience and by charitee, and that men doon it for Godes sake, and in hope to have the blisse of hevene."

[833] The felawes of abstinence been attemperaunce, that holdeth the meene in alle thynges; eek shame, that eschueth all deshonestee;

[2] Sequitur de remedio gule, idest de abstinencia . . . [4] sicut dicit Galienus quod abstinencia est medicina omnium morborum. . . . [19] Augustinus . . . : "Passionibus non meremur nisi paciencia informentur."

[21] Vnde ipsa priuacio alimentorum non est meritoria nisi assit uoluntas caritate informata, ut cum quis abstinet spe refectionis que erit in gloria. . . .

[67] Comites autem abstinencie sunt . . . [70] modestia cultum et motum et omnem nostram occupacionem ultra defectum et citra excessum faciens sistere . . . , docet medium. . . . [77] Verecundia . . . quandoque enim pauet honestatem. . . .

suffisance, that seketh no riche metes ne drynkes, ne dooth no fors of to outrageous apparaillynge of mete;

[87] Honestas est nec lauciores cibos querere nec in nimio apparatu operam dare. . . .

[834] mesure also, that restreyneth by resoun the deslavee appetit of etynge;

[93] Moderancia est nimium appetitum ciborum racionis inperio reuocare [*var.* refrenare] . . . in edendo. . . .
[97] Parcitas est mensuram refectionis non excedere. . . .

sobrenesse also, that restreyneth the outrage of drynke;

[100] Sobrietas est excessuum inpetum cohibere. . . . [101] libidinem potus temperat. . . .

[835] sparynge also, that restreyneth the delicaat ese to sitte longe at his mete and softely, wherfore some folk stonden of hir owene wyl to eten at the lasse leyser.

[Parcitas, *at 97?*]

LUXURIA — cap. IX

[915] Now comth the remedie agayns Leccherie, and that is generally chastitee and continence, that restreyneth alle the desordeynee moevynges that comen of flesshly talentes.
[916] And evere the gretter merite shal he han, that most restreyneth the wikkede eschawfynges of the ardour of this synne.

[2] Sequitur de continencia, que est remedium luxurie . . . [4] generalis . . . specialis: "Continencia est uirtus reprimens motus illicitos ad carnalem concupiscenciam. . . .
[6] Castitas . . . [8] specialis uero est uirtus motus restringens illicitos, que tanto meretur amplius, quanto ualidius carnalis fomitis reprimit incentiuum [*var.* incendium].

And this is in two maneres, that is to seyn, chastitee in mariage, and chastitee of widwehod.

[*See below, at 948*]

[10] Continencie siue castitatis tres sunt partes [*var.* species]: Pudicicia coniugalis, continencia uidualis,
integritas uirginalis [*cf. varr.*]. . . .

[917] Now shaltow understonde that matrimoyne is leefful assemblynge of man and of womman that receyven by vertu of the sacrement the boond thurgh which they may nat be departed in al hir lyf, that is to seyn, whil that they lyven bothe.

[21] Est autem matrimonium "legittima uiri et mulieris coniunctio." . . .

[918] This, as seith the book, is a ful greet sacrement.

[*See below, 78*]

God maked it, as I have seyd, in paradys, and wolde hymself be born in mariage.
[919] And for to halwen mariage he was at a weddynge, where as he turned water into wyn; which was the firste miracle that he wroghte in erthe biforn his disciples.

[27] Deus illud instituit . . . de illo nasci uoluit . . . nubciis sanctificandis interfuit. . . .

[920] Trewe effect of mariage clenseth fornicacioun and replenysseth hooly chirche of good lynage; for that is the ende of mariage; and it chaungeth deedly

[28] Bonos effectus . . . [32] mundat a fornicacione . . . [35] fecundat ecclesiam prole, quia hec est causa finalis matrimonii. . . . [38] Mutat mortale peccatum

Parson's Tale	Postquam
synne into venial synne bitwixe hem that been ywedded, and maketh the hertes al oon of hem that been ywedded, as wel as the bodies.	in ueniale. . . . [42] Vnit et mentes et corpora . . .
[*See below, at 940*]	[44] quia neuter habet potestatem sui ipsius. . . .
[921] This is verray mariage, that was establissed by God, er that synne bigan, whan natureel lawe was in his right poynt in paradys;	[45] Commendatur ab auctore, Deo . . . ante peccatum institutum . . . sub lege naturali . . . in paradyso.
and it was ordeyned that o man sholde have but o womman, and o womman but o man, as seith Seint Augustyn, by manye resouns.	[76] Item una uni coniungitur pluribus de causis, ut docet [*var.* dicit] Augustinus. . . .
[922] First, for mariage is figured bitwixe Crist and holy chirche.	[77] Prima est figura unionis Christi et Ecclesie. . . .
[*See above, at 918*]	[78] "Sacramentum hoc magnum est." . . .
And that oother is for a man is heved of a womman; algate, by ordinaunce it sholde be so.	[79] Secunda, quia "uir est capud mulieris." . . .
[923] For if a womman hadde mo men than oon, thanne sholde she have moo hevedes than oon, and that were an horrible thyng biforn God;	[80] Et si una haberet plures uiros, quasi plura haberet capita et esset matrimonium monstruosum.
and eek a woman ne myghte nat plese to many folk at oones.	[81] Item non posset una simul et semel pluribus obedire [*var.* satisfacere]. . . .
And also ther ne sholde nevere be pees ne reste amonges hem; for everich wolde axen his owene thyng.	[84] Item inter plures uix staret pax et concordia, cum quilibet uendicaret equale ius dominandi. . . .
[924] And forther over, no man ne sholde knowe his owene engendrure, ne who sholde have his heritage;	[87] Item non posset agnosci cuius esset suscepta proles, nec ad quem pertineret hereditas.
and the womman sholde been the lasse biloved fro the tyme that she were conjoynt to many men.	[88] Item minus diligeretur uxor a singulis, eo quod esset communis pluribus.
[925] Now comth how that a man sholde bere hym with his wif, and namely in two thynges, that is to seyn, in suffraunce and reverence, as shewed Crist whan he made first womman.	[90] Qualiter se habeant uiri ad uxores in paciencia et reuerencia docuit Dominus in opere creacionis,
[926] For he ne made hire nat of the heved of Adam, for she sholde nat clayme to greet lordshipe.	[91] cum de costa formaret mulierem et non de parte alia—non de capite, non de pede, ut [93] doceret esse uiri sociam, non dominam, non ancillam.
[927] For ther as the womman hath the maistrie, she maketh to muche desray. Ther neden none ensamples of this; the experience of day by day oghte suffise.	[*No parallel*]
[928] Also, certes, God ne made nat womman of the foot of Adam, for she ne sholde nat been holden to lowe;	[*See above, 93*]
for she kan nat paciently suffre.	[*No parallel*]

Parson's Tale	*Postquam*
But God made womman of the ryb of Adam, for womman sholde be felawe unto man.	[*See above, 91 and 93*]
[929] Man sholde bere hym to his wyf in feith, in trouthe, and in love, as seith Seint Paul, that a man sholde loven his wyf as Crist loved hooly chirche, that loved it so wel that he deyde for it. So sholde a man for his wyf, if it were nede.	[96] Item qualiter se habeant uiri ad uxores docet Apostolus . . . : "Viri, diligite uxores uestras . . . sicut Christus dilexit Ecclesiam." . . . mortuus est pro illa, ita et uos pro uxoribus uestris, si opus sit. . . .
[930] Now how that a womman sholde be subget to hire housbonde, that telleth Seint Peter. First in obedience.	[105] Item qualiter se habeant mulieres ad uiros suos docet Petrus . . . : In obediencia,
[931] And eek, as seith the decree, a womman that is wyf, as longe as she is a wyf, she hath noon auctoritee to swere ne to bere witnesse withoute leve of hir housbonde, that is hire lord; algate, he sholde be so by resoun.	[*No parallel*]
[932] She sholde eek serven hym in alle honestee, and been attempree of hire array.	[106] in officio, ut sint modeste in spiritu, irreprehensibiles in habitu. . . .
I woot wel that they sholde setten hire entente to plesen hir housbondes, but nat by hire queyntise of array.	[109] Item studere debet uxor qualiter "uiro suo placeat," . . . [110] non qualiter . . . [111] in risu, in uisu, in gestu, in habitu . . . [113] per pellem fucatam. . . .
[933] Seint Jerome seith that "wyves that been apparailled in silk and in precious purpre ne mowe nat clothen hem in Jhesu Crist." Loke what seith Seint John eek in thys matere?	[*No parallels*]
[934] Seint Gregorie eek seith that "no wight seketh precious array but oonly for veyne glorie, to been honoured the moore biforn the peple."	
[935] It is a greet folye, a womman to have a fair array outward and in hirself be foul inward.	
[936] A wyf sholde eek be mesurable in lookynge and in berynge and in lawghynge, and discreet in alle hire wordes and hire dedes.	[*See above, 111*]
[937] And aboven alle worldly thyng she sholde loven hire housbonde with al hire herte, and to hym be trewe of hir body.	[*No parallels*]
[938] So sholde an housbonde eek be to his wyf. For sith that al the body is the housbondes, so sholde hire herte been, or elles ther is bitwixe hem two, as in that, no parfit mariage.	
[939] Thanne shal men understonde that for thre thynges a man and his wyf flesshly mowen assemble. The firste is	[138] Ad hoc sciendum quod quatuor de causis cognoscitur uxor: aut causa prolis procreande,

Parson's Tale	*Postquam*
in entente of engendrure of children to the service of God; for certes that is the cause final of matrimoyne.	[*See above, 35*]
[940] Another cause is to yelden everich of hem to oother the dette of hire bodies;	[139] aut debiti reddendi,
for neither of hem hath power of his owene body.	[*Cf. above, 44*]
The thridde is for to eschewe leccherye and vileynye. The ferthe is for sothe deedly synne.	aut incontinencie uitande, aut libidinis explende.
[941] As to the firste, it is meritorie; the seconde also,	[140] In primo casu potest esse meritorium; in secundo
for, as seith the decree, that she has merite of chastitee that yeldeth to hire housbonde the dette of hir body, ye, though it be agayn hir likynge and the lust of hire herte.	[*No parallel*]
[942] The thridde manere is venyal synne; and, trewely, scarsly may ther any of thise be withoute venial synne, for the corrupcion and for the delit.	[141] et tercio similiter, licet comitetur ueniale.
[943] The fourthe manere is for to understonde, as if they assemble oonly for amorous love and for noon of the foreseyde causes, but for to accomplice thilke brennynge delit, they rekke nevere how ofte. Soothly, it is deedly synne; and yet, with sorwe, somme folk wol peynen hem moore to doon than to hire appetit suffiseth.	[142] In quarto. . . . Si uero tanta sit libido . . . mortale est. . . .
[944] The seconde manere of chastitee is for to been a clene wydewe, and eschue the embracynges of man, and desiren the embracynge of Jhesu Crist.	[164] Continencia uidualis est uirtus humanos declinans et in diuinos se colligens amplexus. . . .
[945] Thise been tho that han been wyves and han forgoon hire housbondes, and eek wommen that han doon leccherie and been releeved by penitence.	[*See below, 213*]
[946] And certes, if that a wyf koude kepen hire al chaast by licence of hir housbonde, so that she yeve nevere noon occasion that he agilte, it were to hire a greet merite.	[*No parallel*]
[947] Thise manere wommen that observen chastitee moste be clene in herte as wel as in body and in thought, and mesurable in clothynge and in contenaunce; and been abstinent in etynge and drynkynge, in spekynge, and in dede. They been the vessel or the boyste of the blissed Magdelene, that fulfilleth hooly chirche of good odour.	[193] Item continencia siue castitas est quoddam preciosum uas in quo sunt species aromatice, ut puritas mentis, mundicia cordis, modestia in gestu, honestas in habitu, abstinencia in cibo et potu, verecundia in uultu, discrecio in uerbo et facto. Hoc uas figuratur in alabastro Magdalene, cuius odor inplet latitudinem Ecclesie. . . .

Parson's Tale	*Postquam*
[*See above, at 945*]	[213] Continencia . . . uidualis . . . large conplectitur conuersionem cuiuslibet penitentis post lapsum. . . .
[*See below, at 951*]	[290] Plura sunt que faciunt ad conseruacionem continencie. . . . [304] Tercium est modestia cibi et potus. . . .
[*See below, at 953*]	[314] Quartum est uitacio mulierum . . . [318] temptamenta. . . .
	[*Cf. above, 10*]
[948] The thridde manere of chastitee is virginitee, and it bihoveth that she be hooly in herte and clene of body.	[405] Uirginitas est carnis integritas, que nullum habet meritum nisi mens fuerit incorrupta. . . .
Thanne is she spouse to Jhesu Crist,	[411] Ipsa est sponsa Christi. . . .
[*See below, at 950*]	[415] Item ipsa genuit Christum. . . .
and she is the lyf of angeles.	[429] Item . . . [430] "uiuere angelicum est." . . .
[949] She is the preisynge of this world, and she is as thise martirs in egalitee; she hath in hire that tonge may nat telle ne herte thynke.	[456] Item pro martirio reputatur. . . .
[950] Virginitee baar our Lord Jhesu Crist, and virgine was hymselve.	[*See above, 415*]
[951] Another remedie agayns Leccherie is specially to withdrawen swiche thynges as yeve occasion to thilke vileynye, as ese, etynge, and drynkynge. For certes, whan the pot boyleth strongly, the beste remedie is to withdrawe the fyr.	[*See above, 290 and 304*]
[952] Slepynge longe in greet quiete is eek a greet norice to Leccherie.	[*No parallel*]
[953] Another remedie agayns Leccherie is that a man or a womman eschue the compaignye of hem by whiche he douteth to be tempted; for al be it so that the dede be withstonden, yet is ther greet temptacioun.	[*See above, 314*]
[954] Soothly, a whit wal, although it ne brenne noght fully by stikynge of a candele, yet is the wal blak of the leyt.	[*No parallels*]
[955] Ful ofte tyme I rede that no man truste in his owene perfeccioun, but he be stronger than Sampson, and hoolier than David, and wiser than Salomon.	

These extracts from *Postquam* furnish close verbal parallels for the majority of Chaucer's lines on the *remedia*. The parallels cover all seven remedial virtues; they are precisely the same remedies, to the point that *Postquam* mentions two virtues against wrath and two against avarice, as does the Parson's Tale; and the sequence of the virtues is exactly the same in both treatises. The material which the Parson's Tale shares with

Postquam occurs in the same sequence as in the earlier Latin work, with only a handful of minor exceptions where two phrases appear in reversed order (for example, at 658 or at 731–32), a point is anticipated by several sentences (516, 523, and so on), or a remark is picked up a few sentences later (for example, at 920 and 947). In no instance does material which *Postquam* uses in the treatment of one virtue turn up, in Chaucer, under a different virtue. The agreement between the two works extends beyond commonplace definitions of the virtues and their species to many smaller schemes, such as the "three maneres of humylitee" (478–83), the "foure manere of grevances in outward thynges" (662–68), and others, which seem to be peculiar to *Postquam*. It is true that Chaucer's lines contain a number of sentences which are commonplaces and which can be separately found in various theological works. For example, the remarks on Eve's having been created not from Adam's head or foot but from his rib (lines 925–28), or the four reasons for intercourse (lines 939–43) also appear in Raymund of Pennafort's *Summa de poenitentia et matrimonio*.[43] But the combination of such material and its peculiar wording, sequence, organization in smaller schemes, and place within the larger frame of remedial virtues occur only in one other known treatise, *Postquam*, which may therefore confidently be considered the source of Chaucer's *remedia*.

The material utilized in the Parson's Tale, however, represents only a minimal portion of *Postquam*. The translator-redactor—whether he was Chaucer himself or an intermediary[44]—evidently went through the Latin work with care and selected what served his purpose. He concentrated on schemes and divisions but disregarded almost completely the sections which praise the virtues and the wealth of similes which form a major part of *Postquam*. Similarly, the various *quaestiones* and the entire first chapter were left untouched. This process of selecting material over long stretches of prose may explain the occasional logical and stylistic flaws one finds in the Parson's Tale.

Postquam accounts for approximately 70–75 percent of Chaucer's sections on the *remedia*. With regard to the derivation of the remaining portions for which *Postquam* furnishes no parallels, the following comments can be made:

521a. Quotation of the ninth and tenth commandments, "Non concupisces domum proximi tui, nec desiderabis uxorem eius, non servum, non ancillam, non bovem, non asinum, nec omnia quae illius sunt" (Exodus 20:17), which follows the subject matter of 520 logically. *Postquam* here similarly cites biblical authorities for the various misdeeds listed, but not Exodus 20:17. It is possible that Chaucer found that authority in a copy of *Postquam* which is currently unknown; but it is not unreasonable to think that he might have added the line on his own.

531–32. This notoriously difficult conclusion and transition seems to be of Chaucer's devising, based on several key ideas running through *Postquam* and *Primo*, which I have analyzed at some length in *The Chaucer Review* 16 (1982): 245–48.

658b. The addition "but whan debonairetee is enformed of grace, thanne is it the moore worth" may be Chaucer's. It expresses the common scholastic teaching that virtues are natural habits which become meritorious when infused by or with grace. Cf. *Postquam* I. 32–33, 160–63, and 270–72.

669–73. No source for this *exemplum* against impatience is known. But Peraldus, *Summa virtutum* III.v.11.4, "de modo faciendi correptionem," says one must discipline others "in mansuetudine" and quotes a saying by Diogenes "cum esset iratus servo suo" (p. 353).[45]

729 and 733. The inclusion of the assaults of the devil, and the need for discretion rather than fortitude in withstanding them, is peculiar, though not illogical. Cf. Peraldus, *Summa virtutum* III.iv.6.5, under patience, which is a branch of fortitude: "Item notandum quod ad repugnandum diabolo multum valet sapientia, cum ipse astutia maxime impugnat. . . . Sap. 5: 'Melior est sapientia quam vires' " (p. 287). Other scriptural passages follow, and then Peraldus speaks of faith (*fides* and *fiducia*) as another help in fighting the devil (cf. Parson's Tale, line 734).

738. Although *Postquam* contains a paragraph on *specialia remedia*, the particular ones here summarized come from Peraldus, *Summa vitiorum* V.iii: "Sequitur de remediis contra acediam: . . . diuersitas occupationum. . . . Secundum est consideratio poenae futurae. . . . Tertium est consideratio aeterni praemii. . . . / Octauum et summum est gratia Dei" (pp. 207–8).

804b–5. The reason why mercy and pity are opposed to avarice seems to be Chaucer's own addition, suggested by 804a.

811–17. These lines first list several remedies against avarice, though very confusingly (811–12), and then distinguish foolish from reasonable *largesse* (813–17; cf. 811). Both parts are at least remotely suggested by Peraldus, *Summa vitiorum* IV.iv. In the next-to-the-last part on avarice, Peraldus deals with remedies against the sin and mentions among others, in this order: "mortis consideratio . . . , labor quaerentium diuitias v[a]nus ostenditur, quum homo nudus in terram reuertitur. . . . / Consideratio aeternarum diuitiarum" (pp. 158–59). The following part (IV.v) continues: "Post remedia auaritiae, dicendum est de prodigalitate. . . . Possumus in hoc prodigum a largo distinguere: quia prodigus sua non tribuit, sed perdit . . . quando dat ea histrionibus, vel aliis inhonestis personis. . . . Prodigus etiam pro nihilo rem suam dat, quando dat eam pro vana gloria, quae nihil est in valore" (p. 160).

"Ipse similis est canali, ex aqua retinenti faeces et limositatem" (p. 162). "Consideratio districti iudicii. Si enim . . . illaturus est Dominus in iudicio, 'Ite ergo maledicti in ignem aeternum,' quid dicturus est prodigis dispensatoribus?" (p. 164).

927 and 928b. Evidently Chaucer's expansions of his source, though by no means uncommon sentiments.

931. Reference to *Decretum*, pars II, causa 33, quaestio 5, canon 17; ed. E. Friedberg (Leipzig, 1879; reprint ed., Graz, 1959), 1:1255. The canon ("Mulierem constat") is cited in Raymund of Pennafort, *Summa* II.viii.9 (p. 251).

933–34. The three authorities are: Cyprian, *De habitu virginum* 13 (PL 4:464); Revelation 18:16–17; and Gregory, *Homiliae in Evangelia* II.xl.3 (PL 76:1305). All three occur in Peraldus, *Summa vitiorum* VI.iii.10 and 14 (pp. 254 and 261), the section on pride of clothing, and similarly in *Quoniam*. The first two quotations derive from a gloss on 1 Peter 3:3 (cf. Parson's Tale, line 930).

935. May be likewise derived from Peraldus, *Summa vitiorum* VI.iii.12, a passage between the second and third quotation just mentioned: "Tertio, valet contra superbiam ornatus, si ostendantur multiplices stultitiae ornantium se. Prima est, quod exteriora sua vilia interioribus, quae pretiosa sunt, praeponunt" (p. 256); also in *Quoniam*.

937–38. Possibly Chaucer's expansion.

941. Cf. *Decretum*, pars II, causa 33, quaestio 5, canon 1 (ed. Friedberg, 1:1250), which, however, states the matter from the husband's point of view. Cited in Raymund, *Summa* IV.ii.13 (p. 519).

946. The notion of complete abstinence in marriage derives from scholastic discussions of the marriage between Joseph and Mary. See *Decretum*, pars II, causa 33, quaestio 5, canon 4 (pp. 1251–52), cited by Raymund, *Summa* IV.ii.15 (p. 522).

951–55. Though *Postquam* mentions several ascetic practices as remedies for lechery, Peraldus has closer parallels. 951a and 952 appear to be based on *Summa vitiorum* II.iii.1: "De his quae praestant occasionem huic peccato . . . ocium, indiscreta sumptio cibi et potus" (p. 28). The boiling-pot image of 951 and the material of lines 953–55 come from *Summa vitiorum* III.iv.1–2: "De remediis contra hoc peccatum . . . per . . . lignorum subtractionem. . . . Si olla, quae iuxta ignem est, adeo ebulliat . . . de lignis subtrahitur. . . . Secundum remedium est, vt homo subtrahat sibi de cibo et potu. . . . Tertium remedium est, vt homo elonget se ab igne luxuriae . . . exemplo Joseph, de quo legitur Gen. 39" (p. 34). "Mulieres nobis fugiendae sunt. . . . Nec Dauide sanctior, nec Samsone fortior, nec Salomone potes esse sapient[i]or. . . . Etsi murus a candela iuxta se posita non comburatur, tamen denigratur"

(p. 35). The material of lines 953–55 also appears in *Quoniam* and *Primo*, where it follows (against Peraldus) the same order as in Chaucer, including the sequence Samson–David–Salomon.

The lines in Chaucer's *remedia* sections which have no direct counterpart in *Postquam* may therefore either be free additions, created by Chaucer in response to a suggestion that he found in *Postquam*, such as lines 521, 531–32, 738, 804b–5, and others; or else they may derive from other source texts which Chaucer remembered or perhaps even consulted for the purpose. Interestingly enough, nearly all the latter passages can be found in the two major sources which Chaucer is known to have utilized elsewhere in the Parson's Tale: the *summae* by Raymund of Pennafort and Peraldus (or *Quoniam*). But whether Chaucer added sentences of his own making or drew on other texts, the mold for the entire sections on the *remedia* undoubtedly came from *Postquam*. His adapting this material and incorporating it into the larger structure of the Parson's Tale shows that, far from being a slavish translator, Chaucer made deliberate selections, combined material from different sources, and transformed the somewhat terse and dry Latin of *Postquam* into his much more fluid and relaxed English prose.

THE MANUSCRIPTS AND THEIR RELATIONS

Postquam has been preserved in the following nine copies:

A London, British Library, MS Additional 5667, ff. 40–62^{v}.[46] Vellum, iii + 147, s. xiii^{2}. Modern binding, rebound in 1982.

Contents: (1) *Compilacio de viciis*, "Primo videndum est," ff. 3–38^{v} (incomplete). List of the final chapters of *Primo* and of the chapters of *Postquam*, f. 39. (2) *Compilacio de virtutibus*, "Postquam dictum est," ff. 40–62^{v}, ends incomplete. (3) Sermon notes, ff. 63–64. (4) Treatise on the seven deadly sins, "Superbia est elacio viciosa," ff. 65–78^{v}. (5) Sermon outlines and sermons, in a variety of hands, and a list of epistles and gospels; ff. 79–145. (6) Several inscriptions and notes, ff. 146–147^{v} (flyleaves).

Primo and *Postquam* are written in the same textura of the second half of the thirteenth century, in one column. Folio size: ca. 125 × 90; written space, ca. 87 × 60.

The volume comes from the Cistercian Hailes Abbey, Gloucestershire. The end flyleaves (ff. 146–47) bear the names of several fifteenth-century monks of the abbey: Thomas Harwood and John Brystow (professed in 1451 under Abbot Richard Landreke), in fifteenth-century hands.[47]

E Einsiedeln, Stiftsbibliothek, MS 275, ff. 91^{v}–147^{v}.[48] Vellum, i + xiv + 166 + i, s. xiii^{2}. Bound in stamped white leather over wooden boards, fifteenth or sixteenth century. Metal clasps. Folio size: 153 × 113; written space, 127 × 87/90. Collation: paper flyleaf; fourteen vellum leaves (i–xiv), of which ii–xiv form a quire of fourteen, with one leaf between iv and v cut out; main: vellum, quires i-xiii^{12}, xiiii^{8} (f. 164 stub), 165–66; end flyleaf, paper.

The main part (ff. 1–166) contains the following: (1) *Summa viciorum*, "Primo videndum est," ff. 1–91^{v}. (2) *Summa virtutum de remediis anime*, "Postquam dictum est," ff. 91^{v}–147^{v}. (3) *Summa de confessione*, "Quoniam circa confessiones animarum," ff. 147^{v}–163, by Paul of Hungary; see Morton W. Bloomfield et al., *Incipits of Latin Works on the Virtues and Vices, 1100–1500 A.D.* (Cambridge, Mass.: Medieval Academy of America, 1979), no. 4919. (4) *Interrogaciones Anshelmi ad fratrem agonizantem*, "Anshelmus Cantuariensis episcopus docuit," f. 163.[49] (5) *Absolucio domini Alexandri quarti*, "Dominus noster Iesus Christus per piissimam suam misericordiam," f. 163. 164 stub. 165–66 blank.

All texts except 5, which is in a different and later script, are in the same textura of the second half of the thirteenth century, with many German features. Written in two columns, thirty-three lines per column, below top line. Ruled in ink, prickmarks occasionally visible at top and bottom. Written in black ink; initials and paragraph marks in red; capital letters touched in red. Red ink is also used for brackets in the margins and for cancellations. Quires numbered with Roman numerals on first and last pages of quire; catchwords.

Ff. i–xiv contain the following: (*a*) *Tractatus de redempcionibus*, "Queritur utrum condicio reuendicionis viciet empcionis contractum," ff. i–viii. Written in cursive script, one column, with red initial. (*b*) Alphabetical subject index to the treatises contained in the main part, Abstinencia–Ypocrisis, with references to folio and column (a–d), ff. viii^{v}–x^{v}. (*c*) *Questio*, "Hugo cardinalis magister in theologia ordinis predicatorum queritur vtrum aliquis cum salute anime possit habere plura beneficia . . . et tunc vterque peccat," f. x^{v}b. (*d*) *De vngelt*. Two letters, the first: "Predilecto in Christo fratri Ber. de Ratispona ordinis fratrum minorum frater Albertus episcopus Ratisponensis salutem. De questione mihi a dilectione vestra proposita . . . liberos pone onus disrumpe. Vale," f. xi^{r}a. (*e*) The second letter: "In Christo sibi karissimo fratri Iohanni lectori Wormacensi frater G. [Gi?] magister in theologia salutem et pacem in domino. Super hiis questionibus quas mihi determinandas misistis. . . . Set hec possunt eciam in simplicibus testimoniis communiri ex sacra scriptura. Vale," f. xi^{r}a–b.

Items *c, d*, and *e* are written in the same hand, a very small notula that may still belong to xiii ex. All three pieces, in the same order, occur

also in Osnabrück, Rathsgymnasium, MS C.I. (s. xiii^2), f. 118.[50] Item *c*, which in addition appears in Basel, Universitätsbibliothek B.II.20, ff. 66–67 (xiv in.), was printed from the latter MS by Friedrich Stegmüller in *Historisches Jahrbuch* 72 (1953): 176–207. Item *d*, which in addition appears in Donaueschingen, Hofsbibliothek, MS 267, f. 94 (s. xiv ex.), was printed from the Osnabrück MS by Karl Rieder, *Das Leben Bertholds von Regensburg* (Freiburg i.B.: Charitas-Druckerei, 1901), pp. 46–47. The author of *e*, who in the Osnabrück MS is further described as master at Paris and "lector fratrum Coloniensium," has been identified as Gilbert van Eyen, O.P., who lectured in Cologne after 1269.[51] The Osnabrück MS belonged to Magister Heinrich de Capella, canon at the Chorherrenstift St. Johann in Constance; his name appears in diocesan records of Constance between 1267 and 1277.[52]

F Cambridge, University Library, MS Ff.1.17, part II, ff. 77–104^v.[53] Vellum, 292 folios, s. xiii^2. Originally the volume had eight more leaves, ff. 1–4 and 297–300, which are now bound separately as MS Ff.1.17, part I.

Contents: (1) *Summa de viciis abbreuiata,* "Primo uidendum est," ff. 1–74^v, in 296 numbered columns; followed by a paragraph on confession. 75–76 blank. (2) *Summa de virtutibus abbreuiata*, "Postquam dictum est," ff. 77–104^v. 105 apparently pencil notes, now illegible. (3) A series of theological distinctions and commonplaces, including a *Modus predicandi* ("Octo sunt modi ampliandi," ff. 199^v–201), in several different hands, ff. 106–292^v.

Postquam is written in two columns, in three different hands of the second half of s. xiii: (*a*) 77–86^v, an anglicana; (*b*) 87–104, a small textura; (*c*) 104 (mid column)–104^v, cursive anglicana (which could be by the same scribe as *a*, but in very deteriorated form). Folio size: 196 × 155; written space: (*a*) 139 × 112; (*b*) 143 × 111; (*c*) 145 × 121. Text ends imperfectly: "in siccos" and catchword "homines" (IX. 723).

Provenance: "Fratris Rogeri de shepeheued," f. 239, lower margin; "Summa de viciis et virtutibus abbreuiata ex dono Fratris Rogeri de Schepiswed," f. 4^v of part I, lower margin.[54]

G London, Gray's Inn, MS 12, ff. 261–86^v.[55] Vellum, 286 folios, s. xiii ex. Original binding: leather on wooden boards, metal clasps.

For contents, see Ker, *Medieval Manuscripts,* 1:59–60. The first part of the volume contains various theological works, including the *Contes moralisés* by Nicholas Bozon, all written in the fourteenth century. The second part contains *Postquam* preceded by a copy of Peraldus, *Summa vitiorum*, ff. 79–260^v. Both works are written in the same small textura of the end of the thirteenth century and bear a continuous foliation

1–204 (that is, excluding the introductory list of chapters of Peraldus), which seems to be later than the text. Folio size: 280 × 200; written space, c. 195 × 130; two columns. *Postquam* ends incomplete.

The volume bears the inscriptions: "Summa de viciis et virtutibus. A. De communitate Minorum cestrie de dono Conewey Ministri," f. i^{v}. Roger de Conway, provincial minister of the Franciscans, died in 1360. The book apparently came to Gray's Inn in the early seventeenth century; see Ker, *Medieval Manuscripts*, 1:50–51.

H London, British Library, MS Harley 406, ff. 68^{v}–93.[56] Vellum, 167 folios, s. xv. Nineteenth-century binding.

Contents: (1) "Primo dicendum est," ff. 1–68^{v}, beginning missing. (2) *De virtutibus,* "Postquam dictum est," ff. 68^{v}–93, end incomplete and at least one gathering of text missing between ff. 69 and 70. (3) *Evangelium de infantia Salvatoris,* preceded by a paragraph on Anna and Esmeria, the mothers of Mary and Elizabeth, and the epistle of Bishops Chromatius and Heliodorus to Jerome "de transferendo libro de nativitate beate Marie," ff. 94–102. (4) *Gesta Romanorum,* ff. 102^{v}–43^{v}, end incomplete. (5) *Liber scintillarum,* attributed to Bede, end incomplete, ff. 144–67.

Primo and *Postquam* are written in the same hand, a bastard anglicana of the fifteenth century, in one column. Folio size: 250 × 160; written space, 190 × 130.

I Cambridge, University Library, MS Ii.4.8, ff. 147–71^{v}.[57] Vellum, 171 folios, s. xiv in. Modern binding.

Postquam is preceded by *Tractatus de virtutibus criminalibus,* that is, Peraldus, *Summa vitiorum,* ff. 1–147, both written in the same fourteenth-century textura.

Provenance: perhaps from the Benedictine Cathedral Priory of the Holy Trinity, Norwich.[58]

J Cambridge, Jesus College, MS 20, ff. 87^{v}–142.[59] Vellum, ii + 142 + ii, s. xiii ex. The flyleaves front and back, one bifolium each, contain parts of an alphabetical index to *distinctiones.* Bound in a leaf from a twelfth-century liturgical manuscript.

Postquam is preceded by the *Summa de viciis,* "Primo uidendum est," ff. 1–87. Both works are written in the same hand, a curious, large, thirteenth-century set anglicana in two columns. Folio size: 280 × c.183; written space, 220/224 × 134/140. The text is heavily corrected; see below, pp. 35 and 39.

The volume comes from the cathedral library of Durham, where it is mentioned in a list of books kept in the Spendement of 1391.[60]

L Oxford, Bodleian Library, MS Laud Misc. 171, ff. 7–49.[61] Vellum, 175 folios, s. xiii ex. Bound in calf, seventeenth century.

The volume contains a variety of theological works, written in various hands, but no treatise on the vices.

Postquam is written in two columns, in anglicana formata. Folio size: 160 × 120; written space, c. 140 × 92.

W Worcester, Cathedral Library, MS F.38, ff. 132^{v}–55.[62] Vellum, 370 folios, s. xiv in. Modern binding.

Contents: (1) Peraldus, *Summa vitiorum*, ff. 4–129^{v}. Table of chapters, ff. 130–32. (2) *Summa de vii virtutibus oppositis vii criminalibus peccatis*, "Postquam dictum est," ff. 132^{v}–55. (3) *Parva summula*, attributed to "a certain John" in the list of contents; beginning illegible; ff. 155^{v}–216^{v}. (4) *Speculum iuniorum*, ff. 216–70; Bloomfield, *Incipits*, no. 5103. Table of chapters, ff. 271–72. (5) *Summa de dispensacionibus episcoporum*, "Attendens ego Bonaguida de Arecia," ff. 272^{v}–74^{v}. (6) *Liber provincialis*, a list of dioceses, ff. 274^{v}–78, and kingdoms, 278^{v}. (7) *Concordancie auctoritatum bibliotece,* biblical authorities on specified theological and moral topics, ff. 280–301. (8) *Proverbia Senece secundum alphabetum*, ff. 301^{v}–3. (9) *Casus legum super dec. que suffragia monachorum dic[untur?]*, "Gregorius episcopus etc. Quia sicut per seruum," ff. 304–69^{v}.

The entire volume is written in an early-fourteenth-century textura, in two columns. Folio size: 333 × 210, written space, c. 259 × 135; sixty lines per column. Medieval foliation and quire numbering. Throughout the volume, the handwriting in the upper part of the folios has frequently become illegible due to water damage.

In addition to these extant manuscripts, *Postquam* also appeared in a manuscript of Dover Priory which is now lost.[63]

The work, thus, enjoyed a certain popularity. It was copied not only in England but also on the Continent, and in medieval times it was certainly in the hands of the Benedictines (I,J), Cistercians (A), and Franciscans (G). Composed about the middle of the thirteenth century, it continued to be copied into the fifteenth (H). Moreover, parts of it were used as a source for two separate English translations. The earlier one is Chaucer's Parson's Tale, where extracts from *Postquam* appear in English as the *remedia* which Chaucer appends to the individual seven deadly sins. Exactly the same process of placing material from *Postquam* directly after each corresponding vice was followed in the anonymous English *Memoriale credencium*, a handbook of popular religious instruction apparently written in the first half of the fifteenth century.[64] The two translations do not use the same material, nor do they show similarities in the shared passages; in addition, *Memoriale* reverses the order

of fortitude (Chapter VI in *Postquam*) and mildness/patience (Chapter VII) and combines obedience (Chapter V) with humility (Chapter II).[65]

Each of the extant manuscript copies presents numerous unique readings. On the basis of common variants, shared errors, and shared omissions, it is possible to group the texts as follows:

1. F and L are closely related; they share many omissions (for example, III. 473–74, 488–90, and 573), peculiar readings (for example, I.53; II. 158, 188, 364, and 376; VII.287; and VIII.99–100), and the tendency to abbreviate scriptural quotations drastically. Neither text seems to be a copy of the other.

2. G, I, and W share a large number of peculiar variants (for example, II. 64, 94–95, 100, 126, and 188) and omissions (for example, II. 184 and 216–19). In all three manuscripts, and only in these, *Postquam* is not preceded by *Primo* but instead by the *Summa vitiorum* of Peraldus. Within this group, I seems closer to the archetype because of its smaller number of peculiar readings. In contrast, W is characterized not only by a larger number of unique readings but also by the greater painfulness of its mistakes (for example, IX.536). G, on the other hand, very frequently goes its own way in shortening the received text by omitting transitional phrases and by other stylistic shortenings.

3. E and J share a number of significant readings against groups 1 and 2 (see examples below). J is unique among all manuscripts in that it has undergone an extensive process of scribal correction and emendation. A fairly large part of its material is written over erasures, and in addition it contains a large number of interlinear and—more often—marginal corrections to the text, in the form of "vel X." These corrections are written in a slightly more cursive hand, though the difference could be due to the same scribe's writing on a rougher surface and/or with a softer quill. These marginal "*vel*-readings" often present a better or the correct reading (as at III.416; IV. 69–70 and 439), but they also frequently offer a variant which does not improve the text and which is not supported by any of the other witnesses (as at VI.207). Evidently, the corrector of J collated his text against a second manuscript; but he also seems to have introduced emendations of his own devising.

4. H and A cannot be as easily grouped. H patterns strikingly with F, especially in Chapter IV. But it also shares important readings with E or J or both against the other groups (see examples below). Its scribal errors, however, place it later in the line of descent than E and J. A shares some important variants with H (I. 12, 129, and 142–43; III. 289–90, 635, 704, and so on), but elsewhere it also follows GIW (II. 188, 209, 315, for instance) or the other groups (as at I.103).

On occasion, the first three groups are neatly separated by their readings, as in the following examples:

II.188 (ad demonis) deuictionem (EJ) : deuitacionem (FL) : deuicti/diuiti confusionem (GIW) : confusionem (A) (H out).

II.315 recolit (EJ) : recolligit (FL) : reputat (AGIW) (H out).

More often, any two groups combine against the third, as in the examples given above for the three groups. But there are a good many cases in which individual manuscripts do not follow their stipulated group but join another. Thus, the groupings FGIW and GILW occur frequently, with peculiar variants or shared omissions; and a wide variety of other combinations appear as well, as the corpus of variants demonstrates. While the classification suggested above, thus, can be observed as a general tendency, it does not obtain in each and every instance of variation.

In order to determine the relation of Chaucer's Parson's Tale to the extant manuscripts of *Postquam*, the following substantive variants in the latter are of significance:

Parson's Tale 481 **humblesse of speche** humili uerbo EJFL; humili uoce GIW; humili uerbo uel uoce A (II.64).

482 **to assente** assentire EJAFIL; consentire GW (II.77).

515 **remedie** curacio EJAFLW; remedium G; remedium siue curacio I (III.4).

659 **every mannes goodnesse** aliena mala EJGL; aliena bona FHW; aliena bona mala I (IV.140).

661 **seith the wise man** solet dici/dicere EJFGHIW; dicit philosophus L (IV.165).

664 **though the fool . . . reste** *full quotation* EJGHILW; etc. F (IV.307–8).

675 **entierly al** omnia EJFGH; *om* ILW (V.70).

730 **accidie abateth it** accidia econtra deprimit eam EJGHW; accendit/accidia contrahit FL; accidia deprimit eam I (VI.9).

734–37 **thanne . . . thanne . . . thanne . . . thanne** *no introductory words* EJG; secunda . . . tercia . . . quarta . . . quinta FILW (VI.45, 75, 89, 121).

738 **speciale** spiritualia EFG; specialia JHILW (VI.148).

833 **apparailynge** apparatu EJIW; appetitui/appetitu FGL (VIII.88).

834 **restreyneth** reuocare EJGILW; refrenare F (VIII.94).

915 **ardour** incendium E; incentiuum JFGILW (IX.10).

923 **plese** satisfacere E; obedire JFGILW (IX.82).

926–27 **heved . . . foot** capite . . . pede EJILW; pede . . . capite F; *om* G (IX.92).

947 **in clothynge** in habitu EJGILW; in ritu F (IX.196).

Of these variants, Parson's Tale 659 seems to be the most significant. Chaucer's definition of patience as "a vertu that suffreth swetely every mannes goodnesse" is patently wrong: to be patient does not mean

to willingly endure other people's *goodnesse*, but rather their evil and wickedness. Indeed the latter reading ("aliena mala") appears in several manuscripts, is textually superior, and has the support of the source quoted here; but Chaucer's translation does have a firm base ("aliena bona") in three manuscripts (FHW), with a fourth (I) giving both readings. Did Chaucer, therefore, work from F, H, W, or a manuscript textually related to these? Further examinations reveals that none of these three witnesses is so *consistently* close to the Parson's Tale that one may claim for it a greater degree of kinship than for any other Latin manuscript. Against W are the variants for lines 482, 515, 661, 675; against H is the reading at 661, as well as the fact that H lacks most of the material Chaucer borrowed and that it shows minor differences as at 528 and 737; against F, finally, are the variants for lines 515, 661, 730, 738, 833, 926–27, and 947, as well as its characteristic tendency to abbreviate biblical quotations (for example, at 664). Conversely, other manuscripts have as good a claim for paternity to the Parson's Tale as do these three. J, for instance, quite often preserves the better reading for Chaucer's translation; and E, though it is unique in these cases, comes closer to Chaucer's lines 915 and 923 than any other witness. The available evidence, therefore, does not show any of the Latin manuscripts, or any group of them, to be more closely related to the Parson's Tale than the others.

EDITORIAL PRINCIPLES

Since the respective passages of the Parson's Tale cannot be unequivocally related to any of the manuscript groups, let alone to a single manuscript of *Postquam* as their immediate base; and since the Parson's Tale contains, in translation, only a very small part of the verbal material of *Postquam* (roughly 2.5 per cent); and finally, since *Postquam* has never been edited or even printed before, it was decided, with the consent of the Chaucer Library Committee and the general editor, to prepare a fully critical edition of the treatise. The following text is therefore an attempt to present a text which approaches the form of the archetype for all extant manuscripts as far as the careful selection of a base text and analysis of all variant readings will allow.

In selecting the base text, consideration was given to the following factors: the number of omissions, clear scribal errors, and unique readings; the quality of individual or group readings in the light of the entire textual transmission; completeness of the text; presence in the codex of the related *Summa* on the vices, *Primo*; and the date of the manuscript.

Following these criteria, A and H can be eliminated at once because they lack substantial parts of the text. The incidence of scribal errors and omissions varies somewhat in different sections of *Postquam*, but overall W, L, and G have the largest number of errors and omissions, in descending order, with W consistently showing about twice as many as the manuscript with the lowest number of errors. The remaining manuscripts—E, J, F, and I—all show a considerably lower number of errors and omissions. None of them, however, occupies the lowest place consistently throughout the entire text. In selecting my base manuscript from this group, then, I have applied the following line of reasoning:

(1) Manuscript I, though in itself a good text, does not have *Postquam* preceded by *Primo* but rather by Peraldus's *Summa vitiorum*. In addition, it tends to abbreviate single words more frequently than other manuscripts, which would force the editor very often to interpret its text in the light of the other codices.

(2) Manuscript F has approximately the same number of (unique) errors and omissions as I, E, and J; but if one adds to these the errors and omissions it shares with L (and which are unique to FL), it decidedly becomes inferior to I, E, and J. In addition, it lacks the equivalent of one column of text in chapter III and approximately one leaf of text at the end.

(3) E and J can be shown to have superior readings at crucial points, as the following cases will exemplify:

IV.1048 Ephesios EJH : Philippenses FGILW.
The text immediately afterwards quoted is Ephesians 2:14.

VI.137–38 epistula Ieremie EJH : epistulǎ Iude IW : Iude FGL.
The text quoted is indeed from the "Letter of Jeremiah," preserved in an appendix to the Book of Baruch, chapter 6, a somewhat unusual citation.

IV.642 curare EJH : quandoque curare FGILW.
In the sentence "Item carnem infirmam, quam non potuerit curare fomentum siue emplastrum, quandoque curat cauterium," the cited *quandoque* makes no sense; it is apparently a case of anticipation which occurred in the immediate ancestor of FGILW.

IV.1099–1100 disceptacio EJ : deceptacio FHI : deceptio GLW.
The required word is *disceptacio*, "dispute"; the other readings are lexically in opposition to the context. It is possible that the author's copy had *decertacio*, "dispute," written with a long *r* which was subsequently misread as *p*. But the extant witnesses do not provide direct evidence for this possibility.

IV.98 mansionis EJ : mansuetudinis GILW : beatitudinis FH.
In interpreting the Psalm verse "mansueti hereditabunt terram," the author moralizes *terra* variously, including: "terra uiuencium, in qua est porcio iustorum, que terra dicitur racione stabilitatis et eterne mansionis." *Mansuetudinis* is nonsensical, a slip due to inattention and association with the general topic of the context (the virtue of *mansuetudo*). *Beatitudinis* would appear to be the result of scribal emendation.

(4) J has several points in its favor. It seems to have undergone a process of careful revision and correction, apparently by collation with at least one manuscript other than its exemplar. Besides, it is early and of English provenance. After prolonged deliberation, however, I decided against using it as the base because the process and the result of recording the actual state of its text, which would be required in order to give the reader of this edition a faithful account of the base manuscript, would be enormously cumbersome. Not only are its interlinear and marginal additions (including its *vel*-readings) very frequent, but its corrections over erasure are most numerous, and it is not always clear exactly where they begin and end. J is an interesting specimen for the study of scribal habits and textual transmission, but as a base for a critical edition it is thoroughly impractical. Fortunately, a different, equally good witness is available. My choice for base text, therefore, is E.

The main argument against using E for an edition in the Chaucer Library is that it was written on the Continent, in the territory of High German. This fact is manifest from such paleographical details as its letter formation, the numbering of its quires, and some characteristic spellings, especially of names: *Anshelmus* (passim, consistently), *Růberto* for *Roberto* (f. 47^{r}b), *Odmundus* and *Otmundus* for *Eadmundus* (f. 54^{r}b). Except for these few idiosyncrasies, however, its spelling is remarkably like that found in its English counterparts, and in general it is the work of a careful, intelligent, and consistent scribe. It does have its share of scribal errors and omissions by eyeskip, as well as unique readings. It also shows some definite scribal tendencies that result in recurring errors or unique readings. For example, its scribe evidently did not understand the abbreviation *f.* for *fine* ("at the end" of a biblical book) or mistook it for a paragraph mark (which in his own writing is very similar to *f*). Similarly, several times he misunderstood abbreviated references to Osee and either interpreted them in various idiosyncratic ways (I.295; IV.873; VII.210) or omitted them (II.156; III.315; VII.149). He also had some difficulty with the abbreviation sign for *con-* in his exemplar, which he consequently reproduced as *o-* (I. 212–13; II.318), and with initial

m- (for example, at IX.723). On the other hand, he liked to write "in libro" instead of "libro" (for example, I. 130 and 141) and to supply the preposition *a* (as at I.32). But these peculiarities are minor in nature and easy to spot and to correct.

This edition, then, is based on E with emendations to reflect the archetype as it can be inferred from all extant manuscripts. The text of E has been faithfully reproduced, with the following exceptions: (*a*) abbreviations are silently expanded; (*b*) though its punctuation has guided me, I have not reproduced it but instead introduced modern punctuation and paragraph divisions; (*c*) likewise, I have followed the modern (English) usage of capitalization as closely as seemed reasonable; (*d*) chapter numbers (I–IX) have been added, for easier reference; (*e*) I have normalized the use of numbers by consistently reproducing numbers referring to books and chapters with numerals as they appear in E, and other numbers with number words regardless of E's practice. Unless the context establishes otherwise, I have interpreted E's references to biblical books and chapters as the chapter number standing in the ablative and the title of the book in the genitive case; thus, "Isaie v" should be interpreted as "quinto [capitulo] Isaie."

The emendations have been arrived at by complete analysis of all variant readings throughout the work. All emendations have the authority of at least one manuscript. When I have selected a reading from a witness other than E, my selection has been guided by recension of the respective variants, the nature of the probable error, the meaning and context of the passage in question, and in case of quotations the source that is quoted. The relative weight given to the witnesses normally follows the manuscript groups EJH–GIW–FL, in descending order. The following cases may illustrate the process of recension that has been followed:

IV.784. In enumerating the moral benefits that may come from patiently enduring bodily sickness, the author writes: "Quintum est depuracio (EILW) : sobrietas (J) : depurgacio (F) : deputacio (H) anime; Ecclesiastici xxxi: 'Infirmitas grauis sobriam facit animam.'" (G has a longer omission; A is out.) The archetype must have had *depuracio*, a rare (but not unattested) word, which is changed to *depurgacio* in F as the *lectio facilior*, and replaced by *sobrietas* in J (over erasure), evidently a scribal guess under the influence of the following quotation. The form *deputacio* in H gives witness to both the reading *depuracio* in the archetype and the unfamiliar nature of the word.

IV.288. Patience is necessary in four kinds of "external vexation." The fourth kind is "in angaria (EGH) : angustia (JFILW) operum." As the following development shows (IV.656 ff.), the required word is *angaria*. Evidently the archetype contained the word with the normal

abbreviation sign for *-ar-*, which was misinterpreted as *-us(t)-* by JFILW.

VI.129. Composure in facial expression is attributed to Socrates: "quod de Socrate philosopho (EIL) : falso (JGH) : *om* F (W *illegible*) gloriantur philosophi." According to the source here quoted, the correct reading is *falso*. The variant can probably be explained as a wrong interpretation of the normal suspension *fº* in anticipation of the following *philosophi*.

III.550. Charity is like a garment which protects its wearer "contra cupiditatem male incedentem (EF) : incendentem (JH) : accendentem (AG) / ascendentem (I) / attendentem (W) : *om* (L)." *Incendentem* has been preferred because (a) the root *-cend-* has the authority of JAHGIW over *-ced-* (EF); (b) the prefix *in-* has the authority of the better manuscripts (EJFH) over *ac-*, *as-*, *at-*; (c) the context seems to demand a verb referring to the heat of desire; it is possible that the author's copy had *ascendentem*, and the meaning of "climbing" would to some degree fit the sentence even better than "heating up"; but the unique testimony of I was not deemed sufficient to reject the combined weight of the other texts. The correctness of this emendation is further supported by the use of "vel ex timore male humiliante, vel ex amore male incendente" by Bonaventura (see the source note to III.550–51).

IV.420. By sloughing off its skin the snake "reiunescit (E) : iuuenescit (J) : reuiuiscit (FI) : reiuuenescit (GHL) : reiunscit (?W)." The archetype must have had a word with *re-*, which was wrongly interpreted as *reiuuenescit* as the *lectio facilior* and replaced (in J) with *iuuenescit*, the normal, classical verb.

Unique readings of E have been rejected in favor of the best variant, weighed in the order of J(H)—GIW—FL. In four or five cases all manuscripts appear to be in substantive error, which would mean that either the archetype made or the author's copy contained a mistake. Two instances involve erroneous references to biblical books: II.101 and III.718–19. All manuscripts apparently have a sentence out of its expected logical sequence, at IX.650–54. And at I.365, "per ipsa sacramenta" (*ista* in J) very probably is a mistake for "per vii sacramenta," shared by all manuscripts. In none of these cases have I emended the base text.

Where the base text has been emended, this fact is signaled in the text by square brackets around material not in E, and the mark ° for material in E that has been omitted from my text. The apparatus will record the reading of E in these places as well as the readings of all other manuscripts. Consequently, a variant note such as "I.23 **agere** genere E" means that E reads *genere* whereas all other manuscripts (JAFGHILW) have *agere*.

In addition to listing all rejected readings of E, the apparatus also records group readings (that is, variants shared by two or more manuscripts) and omissions of two or more words in any manuscript. Further, it presents a number of unique variants that make some syntactic or lexical sense and could be of importance in the textual history of the work (for example, I. 5, 21, 39, 46; II.172). For every lemma in the corpus of variants the readings of all manuscripts are recorded, directly (to the right of the lemma) or indirectly (implied in the lemma). These principles for recording variants do not, however, apply to biblical quotations. Very probably the author's copy or the archetype or both gave biblical quotations in abbreviated form, not only by shortening the sentence with *etc.* but also by abbreviating individual words. As a result, the surviving manuscripts show very much variation in this, whose recording here would serve no useful purpose. Shared variant readings and longer omissions in biblical quotations are therefore not consistently recorded in the apparatus. Again, in its handling of the biblical quotations E is a more sensible text than, for instance, FL, which often terminate a biblical quotation before reaching the key word that is commented on in the following sentence. Finally, minor variations in the use of such words as *uel / siue, enim / autem, autem / uero, uero / enim, idest / uel, item / ipsa, quia / quasi,* or *nec / non* have been mostly disregarded. Likewise, variations in spelling and in the word order within a sentence are ordinarily disregarded. The variants are given without punctuation, except in one or two cases where scribal punctuation elucidates the nature of an error (for example, VII.285) and in longer additions where my punctuation will help the reader to understand the added text, which is usually an authoritative quotation (for example, II. 159–60, 207; III.370).

In the corpus of variants, the witnesses are quoted in the order E–J–A–F–G–H–I–L–W. In determining which manuscripts support the reading of the edited text, the reader will have to keep in mind that the following omissions (longer *lacunae* through loss of leaves) are not recorded in each single lemma:

A lacks III.876 to the end;
F lacks III.599–634 and IX.723 to the end;
G lacks IX.759 to the end;
H lacks I.166–III.241 and VII.323 to the end;
L lacks III.889–959.

Thus, the interpretation of the variant notes will be as follows:

I.8 **uires** uirtutes GLW; uirtutes ⟨vel vires⟩ J.
The reading *uires* of the text is found in EAFHI and marginally, as a *vel*-reading, in J; whereas GLW and the body of J read *uirtutes.*

vii.328 **misericordiam** penitenciam E; penam FL; fidem et misericordiam G *and source.*
The reading of the base text (E), *penitenciam*, has been rejected in favor of *misericordiam*, found in JIW (and supported by G and the quoted source); A and H are out at this point.

ix.772 **fine** *om* EL.
The supplied *fine* is attested by JW and omitted in EL; I has a longer omission at this point (as noted in variant to ix.771–72), and AFGH are out.

ix.787 Bernardus *marg* E.
The word *Bernardus* appears in E in the margin next to the quotation attributed to Bernardus which begins at line 787.

In the apparatus the following abbreviations and diacritic signs are used:

add	added
canc	canceled, either crossed out or expunged
corr	corrected
interl	interlinear, written between the lines above the text
marg	marginal, written in the margin
om	omitted
rubr	rubric
⟨ ⟩	added in the margin
*	reading closer to Chaucer's English

Parenthetical numbers ***(1st)***, ***(2nd)***, and so on, after a single-word lemma are used to identify the first, second, and so forth, occurrence of the word in lines where the same word appears more than once.

Finally, the apparatus also records all scribal cancellations and marginalia (mostly names of the authorities quoted in the text) which appear in E in the text hand. The text of the base manuscript can therefore be fully recovered from the edited text and the apparatus, except for its abbreviations, punctuation marks, and capitalization.

The translation which accompanies the edition is intended primarily as a help to the understanding of the Latin text, and I have consequently tried to follow the original as closely as possible but without—I hope—sacrificing intelligibility. The punctuation in the translation consistently follows that of the Latin text with the exception of commas. For biblical quotations I have drawn on the Douay version, although I have modernized pronouns and verb forms and have always followed the quotations as given by *Postquam.* In citing biblical books I have used the standard modern titles, but I have kept the chapter numbers as they appear in *Postquam.*

NOTES

1. The title varies in the manuscripts; see variants to I.1. I have adopted the title as given by the base manuscript, E.

2. A good example is Jean de la Rochelle, *Tractatus de divisione multiplici potentiarum animae*, ed. Pierre Michaud-Quantin (Paris: J. Vrin, 1964); the virtues are treated in part III, iv–xvii (pp. 149–78). For such multiplication of definitions and rationales, see Odo Lottin, *Psychologie et morale*, vol. 3 (Louvain: Abbaye du Mont César; Gembloux: J. Ducolot, 1949), pp. 154–94.

3. See Morton W. Bloomfield, *The Seven Deadly Sins* (East Lansing: Michigan State College Press, 1952). Notice that Cassian's *De institutis coenobiorum* (published ca. 425; ed. Michael Petschenig, CSEL 17, Vienna: F. Tempsky, 1888) proposes to give "remedies [*remedia*] for the eight principal vices," in books 5–12. But primary attention focuses on "battles" (*certamina*) against the vices, most of which are described in detail, while the "virtues" receive considerably less attention. Some of the *remedia* are ascetic practices like fasting or manual work; others are such virtuous attitudes as humility or continence. The treatise does not offer a consistent series of abstract moral qualities, as does *Postquam*. Book V of the *Collationes Patrum* (426–28; ed. M. Petschenig, CSEL 13, Vienna: F. Tempsky, 1886), which is devoted to the eight principal vices, declares that the virtues occupy the places in our soul left vacant after the vices have been driven out. He specifies only four virtues (*Coll.* V.23). Similarly, Gregory speaks of the virtues as "singulis quibusque vitiis obviantia . . . medicamenta" but mentions only four; *Homiliae in Evangelia* XXXII.1 (PL 76:1232–33); his important discussion of the seven principal vices, in *Moralia in Job* XXXI.xlv.87–91 (PL 76:620ff.) says nothing about the virtues. The same "neglect" of the virtues existed on the level of popular catechesis. In the published synodal statutes of the English Church in the thirteenth century, the virtues are listed once (A.D. 1281) and not separately mentioned, whereas the chief vices are listed four and mentioned an additional ten times; F. M. Powicke and C. R. Cheney, *Councils and Synods with Other Documents Relating to the English Church*, vol. 2, *A.D. 1205–1313* (Oxford: Clarendon Press, 1964).

4. There are, of course, exceptions. Grosseteste's *Templum Domini*, for example, gives priority to the (three) cardinal plus three theological virtues in the process of building God's temple, which is man. Here the seven chief vices are treated as forces which battle against charity. For a synopsis of the work, see Siegfried Wenzel, "Robert Grosseteste's Treatise on Confession, 'Deus est,'" *Franciscan Studies* 30 (1970): 234–35.

5. "Vitia prius exstirpanda sunt in homine, deinde virtutes inserendae"; *Libellus proverbiorum* V.49; ed. W. C. Korfmacher (Chicago: Loyola University Press, 1936), p. 88.

6. "Nisi prius perversa destrueret, aedificare utiliter recta non posset" (Gregory, *Regula pastoralis* III.34 [PL 77:117]); "Mortificatione uoluntatum extirpantur atque marcescunt uniuersa uitia. Expulsione uitiorum uirtutes fruticant atque succrescunt" (Cassian, *Instituta* IV.43, ed. M. Petschenig, p. 78). First we must know the nature of the vices; to drive them out takes twice as much sweat as to acquire the virtues (*Collationes* XIV.3).

7. For the biblical (Wisdom 8:7), classical (Cicero, Macrobius), and patristic background of, as well as the scholastic concern with, the four cardinal virtues, see Lottin, *Psychologie*, 3:154–94.

8. The development of the cardinal virtues with large schemata of branches, on the basis of Cicero and Macrobius, can be seen in such twelfth-century works as *Moralium dogma philosophorum*, ed. J. Holmberg (Uppsala: Almqvist & Wiksells, 1929), and Alanus of Lille, *De virtutibus et de vitiis et de donis Spiritus Sancti*, ed. Lottin, in *Psychologie*, vol. 6 (1960), pp. 27–92.

9. The combination occurs already in a fragment attributed to Augustine: *Epistulae*, 171.A, ed. A. Goldbacher, CSEL 44 (Vienna: F. Tempsky, 1904), pp. 635–36.

10. The image of Christ the physician derives from Mark 2:17 (Luke 5:31).

11. For Cassian ("*remedia*") and Gregory ("*medicamenta*"), see above, note 3. A rival metaphor for the opposition between vices and virtues was that of spiritual battle, as in Prudentius, Rabanus, and many other writers. But notice that both metaphors appear almost side by side as early as Cassian and Gregory.

12. Isidore, in his *Differentiae* II.40 (PL 83:97–98), still mixes abstractions ("patience") with practices ("almsgiving"), as noted above, note 3; in his *Sententiae* II.37 he pits abstract virtues (patience, generosity) against the vices, though the latter come in a much larger number than the Gregorian seven. Aelfric, however, presents a series of eight (abstract) virtues which "overcome" the chief vices: *Sermo XVI de memoria sanctorum*, ll. 312–68, in *Aelfric's Lives of Saints*, ed. W. W. Skeat, vol. 2 (EETS 82; London: N. Trübner, 1885), pp. 359–63; and his "Second Old English Letter to Archbishop Wulfstan," ll. 151–74, in *Die Hirtenbriefe Aelfrics in altenglischer und lateinischer Fassung*, ed. Bernhard Fehr, Bibliothek der angelsächsischen Prosa, 9 (Hamburg: H. Grand, 1914). A similar opposition occurs in a lengthy twelfth-century poem in Latin; see Heinz-Willi Klein, "Johannis abbatis Liber de VII viciis et VII virtutibus," *Mittellateinisches Jahrbuch 9* (1973): 173–247.

13. Avarice, thus, may be opposed by generosity (*largitas*), voluntary poverty, contempt of the world, mercy, or compassion.

14. An early attempt to set the beatitudes systematically against the eight capital vices appears in Smaragdus, *Collectiones* (PL 102:546–47), a commentary on Matthew by Frigulus or Figulus (who wrote "between Isidore and Bede"); see Bernhard Bischoff, *Mittelalterliche Studien*, vol. 1 (Stuttgart: A Hiersemann, 1966), pp. 251–52.

15. Gregory, *Moralia* II.xlix.77 (PL 75:592–93), sets the seven gifts against seven temptations; his successors relate them to the seven unclean spirits of Matthew 12:45 (*Glossa ordinaria*, PL 114:129) or seven vices (Bernard of Clairvaux, *Sermo 14 de diversis*; PL 183:574–77). They are opposed to the seven deadly sins by Hugh of St. Victor (see next note) and William of Auxerre, *Summa aurea* (Paris: Nicolaus Vaultier & Durandus Gerlier, 1500; reprint ed., Frankfurt/Main: Minerva G.m.b.H., 1964), f. 181d.

16. Especially Hugh of St. Victor in his influential *De quinque septenis* (PL 175:405–14). The "virtues" here are those of the beatitudes. Cf. Lottin, *Psychologie*, 3:434–35. Notice that *Postquam* sets the seven gifts against the seven deadly sins in its comparison of charity to fire: III.328–55.

17. The development has been traced by Lottin, especially in *Psychologie* 3:97–456.

18. See John W. Baldwin, *Masters, Princes, and Merchants: The Social Views of Peter the Chanter and His Circle*, 2 vols. (Princeton, N.J.: Princeton University Press, 1970).

19. *Verbum abbreviatum* 13 (PL 205:59).

20. James J. Murphy, *Rhetoric in the Middle Ages* (Berkeley: University of California Press, 1974), pp. 303–9.

21. *Summa de arte praedicatoria* 15 (PL 210:140).

22. For the vices and virtues as a topic that was highly recommended for preaching after 1200, see Siegfried Wenzel, "Vices, Virtues, and Popular Preaching," in *Medieval and Renaissance Studies: Proceedings of the Southeastern Institute of Medieval and Renaissance Studies, Summer, 1974*, ed. Dale B. J. Randall (Durham, N.C.: Duke University Press, 1976), pp. 28–32. Peraldus's *Summa vitiorum* was published in 1236, his *Summa virtutum* before 1248/49; see Antoine Dondaine, "Guillaume Peyraut, vie et oeuvres," *Archivum Fratrum Praedicatorum* 18 (1948), esp. pp. 184–97.

23. Manuscripts G, I, and W.

24. Manuscripts E, J, A, F, and H.

25. Notice that there exists a longer redaction of *Primo* which begins with the words "Quoniam ut ait sapiens, 'peccantem virum involvet laqueus,'" which I have briefly discussed in "The Source of Chaucer's Seven Deadly Sins," *Traditio* 30 (1974): 351ff. To the two manuscripts listed there must be added Dublin, Trinity College, MS 306, ff. 1–121ᵛ (beginning missing). The relation between Peraldus, *Quoniam*, and *Primo*, and the apparent process of redaction await further study. *Quoniam* also contains the two passages referred to.

26. A close parallel to the medical image of *Primo* and *Postquam* appears in Hugh of St. Victor, *De sacramentis* II.xiii.2 (PL 176:527).

27. See my earlier discussion in *Traditio* 30 (1974): 351–78.

28. "Socius meus Stephanus rector ecclesie de Caldecote, cum per plures annos audisset leges, tandem moriturus dixit fratri suo militi Roberto de Bloy: 'Nosti clericum Stephanum de Caldecote?' Cui frater respondit: 'Tu es ille. Signa frontem tuam cruce!' Et ait Stephanus: 'Non noui illum clericum. Set quicumque ille fuerit, duo nigri monachi in angulo tulerunt sentenciam contra ipsum, / que nunquam poterit reuocari.' Et hoc dicto statim expirauit." Reproduced from J, ff. 42ᵛ–43. For manuscripts of *Primo*, see note 29. The tale does not appear in A, H, and O (which are incomplete at this point), and M; I have not been able to examine D. The story in the same form also appears in *Quoniam*, for whose manuscripts see note 27. The name of the knight is also spelled Rŭberto Lebrei (E) and Roberto le Bloy (R1, Du) or Roberto de Bloye (F). Variants of the name of the village are: Caldescore (E), Caldecoche (?F), Caldechote (R2, once), and Saldecote (Ha, once; TCD, both times).

29. *Dictionary of National Biography*, s.v. "Bruce, Robert de, V."

30. F. N. Davis, ed., *Rotuli Ricardi Gravesend*, Lincoln Record Society, no. 20 (Lincoln, 1925), p. 173. Willelmus de Brus is "advocatus ecclesie" of Caldecote, and holds the manor and village from Robert de Brus, in 7 Edward I, *Rotuli Hundredorum*, vol. 2 (London: Record Commission, 1818), pp. 636; and

for 32 Edward I see John Caley and John Bayley, eds., *Calendarium inquisitionum post mortem sive escaetarum*, vol. 1 (London: Record Commission, 1806), pp. 188.

31. There were, however, two churches of Caldecote in the diocese of Lincoln, archdeanery Huntingdon: one in Huntingdonshire, the other in Hertfordshire.

32. W. P. W. Phillimore, ed., *Rotuli Hugonis de Welles*, Canterbury and York Society, no. 1 (London, 1909), pp. 49–50.

33. "Terribile est dictu et auditu horribile exemplum quod de Stephano rectore ecclesie de Caldecote reperitur. In Anglia siquidem sunt plures ville quarum nomen Caldecote appellatur, set sicut invenimus, quidam Stephanus nomine, qui / rector erat unius Caldecote, cum per plures annos audisset leges . . ." A. G. Little, ed., *Liber exemplorum*, British Society of Franciscan Studies, no. 1 (Aberdeen: University Press, 1908; reprint ed., Farnsborough, Hants.: Gregg Press, 1966), pp. 40–41; my translation.

34. "Non solum excluduntur ab exercicio legum plebani, idest maiores persone ecclesie, ut in illa decretali *Super specula*, et eciam omnes curam animarum habentes, vt in rescripto quod mandauit dominus papa episcopo Aurelianensi." *Primo*, MS E, f. 44^{r}b.

35. The terms of the decretal and the rescript, as well as the entire subject, are discussed by Stephan Kuttner, "Papst Honorius III. und das Studium des Zivilrechts," in *Festschrift für Martin Wolff*, ed. Ernst von Caemmerer et al. (Tübingen: Mohr, 1952), pp. 79–101.

36. The prohibition was repeated in simplified form by Bishop Grosseteste, in his Statutes of Lincoln of 1239(?); see *Councils and Synods* 2:274 and note 2. Notice that in 1279 Archbishop Pecham regrets that curates cannot study *iura civilia* for lack of benefices; ibid., pp. 844 and 863.

37. Kate O. Petersen, *The Sources of the Parson's Tale*, Radcliffe College Monographs, no. 12 (Boston: Ginn & Company, 1901), esp. pp. 79–80.

38. Notably Homer G. Pfander, "Some Medieval Manuals of Religious Instruction in England and Observations on Chaucer's Parson's Tale," *JEGP* 35 (1936): 243–58. A more recent comparison of the Parson's Tale with medieval English and French manuals for penitents has been made by Lee W. Patterson, "The 'Parson's Tale' and the Quitting of the 'Canterbury Tales,'" *Traditio* 34 (1978): 331–80.

39. Germaine Dempster, in *Sources and Analogues of Chaucer's "Canterbury Tales,"* ed. W. F. Bryan and G. Dempster (Chicago: University of Chicago Press, 1941), pp. 723–60, esp. p. 744 n. 1.

40. Richard Hazelton, "Chaucer's Parson's Tale and the *Moralium Dogma Philosophorum,*" *Traditio* 16 (1960): 255–64, esp. p. 255.

41. For a more detailed critique, see p. 434 of my article referred to in the following note.

42. The following parallel text and its discussion represents a revision of my article "The Source for the 'Remedia' of the Parson's Tale," *Traditio* 27 (1971): 433–53. Besides expanding the discussion of Chaucer's relation to *Postquam*, I here give the Latin parallels according to the edited text (instead of MS F). I have reduced the parallels to verbal material that corresponds to Chaucer's text, since the larger context in *Postquam* can be found in the edition below.

Where manuscripts offer a reading which is closer to Chaucer's wording than the edited text, this fact is here indicated parenthetically with "*var.*"; the complete information can be found in the corpus of variants which accompanies the edition. The text of the Parson's Tale is taken from F. N. Robinson, ed., *The Works of Geoffrey Chaucer*, 2d ed. (Boston: Houghton Mifflin, 1957).

43. Raymund of Pennafort, *Summa de poenitentia et matrimonio* (Rome: Ioannes Tallinus, 1603; reprint ed., Farnborough, Hants.: Gregg Press, 1967). The cited passages occur at IV.ii.3 (p. 512) and 13 (p. 519).

44. That Chaucer may have worked from an intermediate source in Latin or French which placed the *remedia* directly after each corresponding vice (as does the Parson's Tale) is a possibility, but no such work is known.

45. References to Peraldus are to *Gvillelmi Peraldi . . . Svmmae virtvtvm ac vitiorvm*, 2 vols. (Lyon: Pierre Compagnon & Robert Taillandier, 1668), without indication of volume number. *Summa vitiorum* can be found in vol. 2, *Summa virtutum* in vol. 1 of this edition. Notice that a story about Plato who, as he is about to chastize his servant, checks himself because he is angry appears in Walter Burley, *De vita et moribus philosophorum*, chap. 52 (ed. Hermann Knust, Bibliothek des Litterarischen Vereins in Stuttgart, no. 177 [Tübingen, 1886], pp. 220–22). Knust points out that the anecdote conflates passages from Valerius and Seneca. A similar story is told of Plutarch, who, however, is only accused of anger by a servant who is being flogged: John of Salisbury, *Policraticus* IV.8 (ed. C. C. J. Webb [Oxford: Clarendon Press, 1909], 1:265–66). See also ibid., V.7 (Webb 1:308).

46. [F. Madden et al.], *Index to the Additional Manuscripts . . . Acquired in the Years 1783–1835* (London: Trustees of the British Museum, 1849), p. 448 ("Theology").

47. Neil R. Ker, *Medieval Libraries of Great Britain*, 2d ed. (London: Royal Historical Society, 1964), p. 266.

48. Gabriel Meier, *Catalogus codicum manu scriptorum qui in bibliotheca Monasterii Einsidlensis OSB. servantur*, vol. 1 (Einsiedeln: Sumptibus Monasterii; Leipzig: O. Harrassowitz, 1899), p. 245.

49. For this short work, see R. W. Southern and F. S. Schmitt, eds., *Memorials of St. Anselm* (London: Oxford University Press, 1969), pp. 252–54.

50. See Heinrich Finke, *Konzilstudien zur Geschichte des 13. Jahrhunderts* (Münster: Regensberg, 1891), pp. 1–2, n. 1.

51. Palémon Glorieux, *Répertoire des maîtres en théologie à Paris au XIIIe siècle*, vol. 1 (Paris: J. Vrin, 1933), p. 118; and Stephanus G. Axters, *Bibliotheca Dominicana Neerlandica manuscripta 1224–1500* (Louvain: Publications Universitaires, 1970), pp. 51–52.

52. Cf. P. Ladewig and T. Müller, eds., *Regesta episcoporum Constantiensium*, vol. 1 (Innsbruck: Wagner, 1895), nos. 2168–377 passim.

53. *A Catalogue of the Manuscripts Preserved in the Library of the University of Cambridge*, vol. 2 (Cambridge: University Press, 1857), pp. 305–7.

54. A Roger Shepesheued was rector of the church of St. Denis, Evington, at some time between 1312 and 1330; A. Hamilton Thompson, *The Abbey of St. Mary of the Meadows Leicester* (Leicester: E. Backus, 1949), p. 137.

55. Neil R. Ker, *Medieval Manuscripts in British Libraries,* vol. 1, *London* (Oxford: Clarendon Press, 1969), pp. 59–60.

56. [R. Nares et al.], *A Catalogue of the Harleian Manuscripts in the British Museum,* vol. 1 (London: British Museum, 1808), p. 235; and J. A. Herbert, *Catalogue of Romances in the Department of Manuscripts in the British Museum,* vol. 3 (London: Trustees of the British Museum, 1910), p. 221.

57. *A Catalogue . . . Cambridge,* vol. 3 (Cambridge: University Press, 1858), pp. 447–48.

58. Cf. Ker, *Medieval Libraries,* p. 137.

59. M. R. James, *A Descriptive Catalogue of the Manuscripts in the Library of Jesus College, Cambridge* (London and Cambridge: C. J. Clay and Sons, 1895), p. 21.

60. J. Raine, *Catalogi veteres librorum Ecclesiae Cathedralis Dunelmensis,* Surtees Society, no. 7 (London: J. B. Nichols and Son, 1838), pp. 24 and 100; and Ker, *Medieval Libraries,* p. 61.

61. H. O. Coxe, *Catalogi codicum manuscriptorum Bibliothecae Bodleianae. Pars secunda Codices Latinos et Miscellaneos Laudianos complectens* (Oxford: Oxford University Press, 1858–85; reprint ed. with corrections and additions by R. W. Hunt, Oxford: Bodleian Library, 1973), cols. 155–57 and p. 550.

62. J. K. Floyer, *Catalogue of Manuscripts Preserved in the Chapter Library of Worcester Cathedral,* ed. and rev. S. G. Hamilton (Oxford: James Parker and Co., 1906), p. 18, does not identify *Postquam.* It was, however, noticed by Patrick Young in his *Catalogus librorum manuscriptorum bibliothecae Wigorniensis Made in 1622–23,* ed. I. Atkins and N. R. Ker (Cambridge: Cambridge University Press, 1944), p. 49.

63. Given as 140 in the catalogue of 1389; preceded by a *Summa de septem viciis capitalibus,* which on account of its length and of its *secundo folio* (*demonibus iocun-*[*dius*], not *iocum* as printed), must be *Primo.* See M. R. James, *The Ancient Libraries of Canterbury and Dover* (Cambridge: Cambridge University Press, 1903), pp. 420 and 456.

64. *"Memoriale Credencium." A Late Middle English Manual of Theology for Lay People Edited from Bodley MS Tanner 201,* ed. J. H. L. Kengen (Nijmegen: [privately printed], 1979).

65. I have briefly discussed the relation of *Memoriale* to *Postquam* in my review of the edition, in *Anglia* 99 (1981): 511–13.

SUMMA VIRTUTUM
DE REMEDIIS ANIME

Here begins the Summa of the Virtues on the Remedies of the Soul.

I

After having spoken of the soul's diseases, that is, the sins, we must now add the discussion of their remedies, that is, the virtues—not, however, the individual virtues in their own order, but the seven virtues that are opposed to the seven deadly sins. But before we define virtue, we must present a division of the virtues, for division is the way toward definition. Virtues are divided into natural virtues, political virtues, and virtues of grace. Natural virtues are the powers of the soul and the body, according to Rabanus in his book *On the Nature of Things,* where he says: "Some powers belong to the body, others to the heart." Of the natural and spiritual powers, some are located in the rational spirit, such as intelligence, memory, and will; others belong to the animal spirit, such as imagination, memory, appetite or desire; and others belong to the vegetative spirit, such as the augmentative, nutritive, and generative powers. The sensitive powers of the body are also called "bodily powers" by many philosophers, because they are located in the instruments of the body, according to what is said in the *Timaeus,* that bodies are the base of the senses. For what the mind perceives, it obtains by the activity of the body. Among the spiritual as well as the bodily powers, some are motive and others are apprehensive, because of the affects of the soul and the concepts that are to be generated.

A political virtue is a virtue acquired through the exercise of deeds that are good by their nature. And since such a virtue derives from repeated action, it is named from *"polus,"* that is, plurality, for just as through often playing the harp well one becomes a good harpist, so through acting well in many ways one becomes good, as is said in the *Ethics.* Or else it is named after *"polis,"* that is, city, because in ancient times, when the laws of nations had not yet been handed on, cities were ruled through such virtues, by the teaching of philosophers. This is manifestly true since Socrates himself was stoned to death for his moral teaching long before the age of faith.

The political virtues also include the cardinal virtues as long as these are un-

1 **Incipit . . . anime** *rubr* E, *with punctus between* uirtutum *and* de; Incipit tractatus de virtutibus J; Incipit quedam compilacio de virtutibus A; Incipit summa de virtutibus abbreviata F; de virtutibus assit principio sancta Maria meo G; de virtutibus H; Incipit de virtutibus I; *om* L; Incipit summa de septem uirtutibus oppositis septem criminalibus peccatis W. **I** *om all MSS.* 2 **idest** *add* de FILW. 2–3 **peccatis . . . uirtutibus** viciis hic de uirtutibus dicendum est I. 5 **peccatis** viciis I. 6 **diffinicionem** diffinicione FHL. 7 **alia est naturalis** *om* W. **politica** pollicita AGHI *here and in the following instances.* 8 Philosophus *marg* E. **uires** uirtutes GLW; uirtutes ⟨vel vires⟩ J. **Rabanum** philosophum E. 10 **Virtutes . . . spirituales** Virtutum autem naturalium et spiritualium E. 11 **racionali** racionabili JAFGHI. 11–12 **uoluntas . . . memoria** *om* L. 12 **animali** sensuali AH; sensibili FGIW. 13 **in** cum AH. 14 **eciam** autem JGIW. 15 **philosophis** *om* G. 16 **insint** insunt FGLW; instar I; insunt ⟨vel insint⟩ J. 17 **Thimeo** Thimotheo HL. **corpora** copora E. 18 **sentit** sentit, *corr to* seruit *marg* J; senti H; sensus I. **percipit . . . uigore** et percipit racio est in corporis uigore E. **racio et** ponitur J; ponitur tamen G; ponitur eciam ILW. **Virium** Virtutum JGW. 19 **tam . . . spiritualium** spiritualium tam corporalium E. 21 **insinuandos** instruandos I. 23 **agere** genere E. 25 **bene** *om* E; boni G. 26 **agere** genere *exp* agere E. **ut dicitur** Aristoteles G. 28 **antiquitus**

Incipit Summa uirtutum de remediis anime f. 91va

[I]

Postquam dictum est de morbis ipsius anime, idest peccatis, addendum est de remediis, scilicet de uirtutibus—non tamen de singulis per ordinem, set de septem oppositis septem criminalibus peccatis. Set priusquam dicatur quid sit uirtus, facienda est diuisio uirtutum, quia diuisio est uia in diffinicionem. Virtutum alia est naturalis, alia politica, alia gratuita. Virtutes naturales dicunter uires anime / et corporis secundum [Rabanum] in libro *De* f. 91vb *naturis rerum* sic dicentem: “Quedam sunt uirtutes corporum, quedam cordium.” [Virtutes] autem [naturales] et [spirituales] quedam sunt in spiritu racionali, ut intelligencia, memoria, uoluntas; quedam sunt in spiritu animali, ut ymaginacio, memoria, appetitus siue desiderium; quedam sunt in spiritu uegetabili, ut augmentatiua, nutritiua, generatiua. Vires eciam sensitiue ipsius corporis “uirtutes corporee” a multis philosophis appellantur, eo quod insint instrumentis corporeis, secundum quod dicitur in *Thimeo,* quod fundamenta sensuum sunt [corpora]. Illud tamen quod sentit, ° percipit racio [et] in [corporeo] uigore. Virium autem [tam corporalium quam spiritualium] quedam sunt motiue, quedam apprehensiue, propter affectus anime et conceptus insinuandos.

Uirtus politica est uirtus aquisita per exercicium operum que sunt de genere bonorum. Et quia ipsa est ex multiplici [agere], ideo dicitur a “polis,” quod est pluralitas, quia sicut ex multociens bene cytharizare fit bonus cytarista, sic ex multiplici [bene] agere fit bonus, ut dicitur in *Ethicis*. Vel dicitur a “polis,” quod est ciuitas, eo quod ciuitates per tales uirtutes ex doctrina philosophorum [antiquitus] regerentur, cum nondum essent tradita iura gencium. Patet hoc esse uerum cum ipse Socrates pro doctrina morum longe ante fidem lapidatus fuerit.

Virtus autem polytica conprehendit eciam uirtutes cardinales

formed, because once they have been formed with grace, they belong to the virtues of grace. There are four cardinal virtues: prudence, justice, fortitude, and moderation. They are called "cardinal" as if of the heart, because according to Isidore *"cardias"* in Greek means heart. Whence a passion is also called *cardiaca*. For as the heart is the principle of life in an animate being, giving it motion and sensitivity through which the soul goes outside itself into external actions, so these virtues rule actions and direct them toward a proper end and teach the means by which one comes to the good. Or else they are named after *cardo,* "hinge," because just as a hinge supports a door, so these virtues support the mind in its workings, whether it receives from the outside or proceeds to an action from within, just as a door opens the way for entrance and exit.

There are four for several reasons. Three will suffice for now. The first derives from the nature of action and its proper circumstances. As natural powers are related to doing, so are the political virtues related to doing well; as are likewise the virtues of grace. Hence the Ten Commandments and the virtues are concerned with the same subject, but the Commandments are concerned with what is to be done, the virtues with how it is to be done; hence the virtues aim at removing difficulties about the good, because many evils surround one good. In book III of the *Ethics* we can find the image of center and circumference, for the good exists indivisible, but evil manifold. Therefore, since the good is difficult to find, counsel must come first of all, as Sallust says: "Before you begin, take counsel, and after you have taken counsel, promptly do the work!" And Proverbs 4: "Let your eyelids walk before your steps." To this function prudence is well suited, because it considers the beginning and the end of a thing, as it is said in the *Consolation*: "Prudence measures the outcome of things." It likewise regulates the mean. Therefore, it is said in the *Ethics*: "Prudence examines the mean." After counsel has been taken and a choice has been made, that virtue is called for which puts an action into effect; and that is justice, which rules all the others and teaches them to act with reason and measure, so that no one in his action should pursue his own dishonorably or assume himself what belongs to others. But since two fortunes work against justice and the execution of good deeds, namely prosperity and adversity, justice must be assisted by two companions, that is, fortitude in adversity, so that troubles may

om EW. **nondum** non AGW. 31 **eciam** *om* JL. 32 **cum** *add* a E. 33 de uirtutibus cardinalibus *marg* E; de cardinalibus *rubr* I. 35 **quasi cordiales** *om* F. **cordiales** cardiales AH. **cardias** *corr from* cordias E; cordias IW; cordas G. **cor** *add* latine JGIW. 36 Ysidorus *marg* E. **Unde et** et inde E. 37 **dans** creans L; *add* ei F. 38 **exit ad** excitat W. 39 **debitum** bonum F. 41 **subuehunt** *om* E. 42 **cum** eum E. **recipiat** recipiant H. **siue** ***(2nd)*** *add* cum GW. **prodeat** prodeant H. 44 **racionibus** *add* quarum E. 44–45 **Sufficiant . . . presens** scilicet tribus I; *om* L. 46 **potencie** acciones F. 47 **sic . . . agere** *om* E. **ut** et E; *om* J. 50 **ammouendas** *sic* EI; admovendas A; amovendas FHLW; movendas J. 52 **III** 2 GL. 53 **indiuisibiliter** GW(?); indiuisibili E; in indiuisibili JFHL; indivisibile AI. **omnifariam** omnipharium JA; multipharium FL. 55 Salustius *marg* E. 55–56 **consulto . . . consuleris** et postquam inceperis consulto G. 56 **consuleris** inceperis IW. 57 **tuos** *add* et E. 58 **ut** unde JFHI; *add* Boecius JG. 58–59 **Prudencia** Prudencie E, *not preceded by punctuation, but followed by punctus and capital letter.* 60–61 **consiliatum** consultum JAG; saliatum H. 61 **illa** *om* E; et J. 62 **monet** mouet(?) JFGHIW. 64–65 **due . . . execucionem** duo inpediunt boni execucionem G. 66 **comitibus** modis comitis bonis J; bonis comitibus G. 67 **superent** *marg for* surriperent J; caperent G.

dum sunt informes, quia cum / ° gracia informantur, sub uirtute gratuita continentur. Sunt autem uirtutes cardinales quatuor: prudencia, iusticia, fortitudo, temperancia. Et dicuntur "cardinales" quasi cordiales. "Cardias" enim Grece idem est quod cor, secundum Ysidorum. [Unde et] cardiaca passio dicitur. Sicut enim cor est principium uite in animali dans motum et sensum per quos anima exit ad operaciones exteriores, sic iste uirtutes regunt actiones et dirigunt in debitum finem et docent medium quo uenitur ad bonum. Vel dicuntur a cardine, quia sicut cardo subuehit hostium, sic iste uirtutes [subuehunt] animum in suis operacionibus, siue [cum] recipiat ab exterioribus siue prodeat in opus ab interioribus, sicut per hostium patet ingressus et exitus. f. 92ra

Sunt autem quatuor pluribus racionibus. ° Sufficiant tres ad presens. Prima sumitur ex natura ipsius actionis et circumstanciis debitis. Quia sicut potencie naturales sunt ad ipsum agere, [sic uirtutes politice sunt ad bene agere]; similiter [ut] gratuite. Vnde Decem Preceptorum et uirtutum eadem est materia, set Precepta respiciunt id quod agendum est, virtutes uero qualiter sit agendum; vnde uirtutes sunt ad ammouendas difficultates circa bonum, quia unum bonum multa mala circumstant. Vnde ponitur exemplum III *Ethicorum* de centro et circumferencia, quia bonum est [indiuisibiliter], malum autem omnifariam. Quia igitur difficile est inuenire bonum, necesse est precedere consilium, ut dicit / Salustius: "Priusquam incipias, consulto, et postquam consuleris, mature opus facito!" Et Prouerbiorum iiii: "Palpebre tue precedant gressus tuos." ° Ad hoc opus apta est prudencia, que inicium rei considerat et finem, ut in *Consolacionibus*: "[Prudencia] rerum exitus metitur." Ipsa eciam ordinat de medio. Vnde in *Ethicis*: "Prudencia est inspectrix medii." Postquam consiliatum est et electum, necessaria est [illa] uirtus que iubet producere in opus; et hec est iusticia, que ceteris inperat et monet eas ad actum cum racione et moderamine, ne quis in agendo quod suum est turpiter ingerat nec alienum usurpet. Set quia due fortune iusticiam inpediunt et boni execucionem, que sunt prosperitas et aduersitas, necesse fuit iusticiam duobus comitibus fulciri, fortitudine scilicet in aduersis, ne molestie mentem superent [uel] f. 92rb

not overcome or break one's mind, and moderation in prosperity, so that pleasures may not charm and seduce it.

The second reason stems from the necessary elements of virtue which constitute it as a virtue. The first of these is to know what is to be chosen and what to be done, which is the proper function of prudence, whose "inner plumbline of the heart measures out a deed in advance." The second element is the ability to do it, which since it is weak in us requires fortitude. The third element is will, which since it is idle and roving in us needs to be bridled by reason, and this is the function of moderation. The fourth element is action itself, which belongs to justice, whose function it is to rule the other virtues and carry out a deed.

The third reason derives from our needs after human nature has become corrupted, because as Bede says: "When man sinned he fell into four: into malice, weakness, ignorance, and concupiscence." Against malice, justice was needed in order to curb it and to draw a line between what is allowed and what is not; against weakness, fortitude was needed, which would strengthen our injured nature; against ignorance, prudence; against concupiscence, moderation.

Now we turn to the definitions and the actions of the four cardinal virtues, the first of which is prudence. According to Augustine in his book *Whence Evil Comes,* prudence is "the knowledge of what things are to be desired and which must be shunned." According to Tullius, prudence is "the knowledge of good and evil things and the ability to distinguish between the two." The acts of prudence in this life are: "to guard against snares," *Sentences,* book III; "to avoid evil," Augustine, *On Genesis*; "to put incorruptible things before corruptible ones," Augustine, *On the Freedom of the Will*; "to distinguish good from evil," *The City of God,* book XIX; "to put eternal goods before temporal ones," Augustine, *On Music,* book VI. Its acts in heaven are: "to prefer no other good to God," *Sentences* III; "to contemplate pure Truth," Augustine, *On Music* VI. But its principal act is "to choose the better over the worse," as Augustine says in his book of *Eighty-three Questions.* Its preceding acts are "to distinguish good from evil" and "to contemplate pure Truth," as was said above. Its subsequent acts are "to guard against snares and avoid evil," according to Augustine, *On*

uel et E. 68 **blanda** blande AH; *add* animum GIW. 71 **et quid** quidve E. 72 **sit** est JAW; *om* FGHIL. 72–73 **quia . . . opus** *marg for* unde in poetria intrinseca linea cordis prevenitus est J. 72 **eius** *om* E. 75 **uanum** uarium FGL. 76 **opus** *om* E. 79 **nostra** mea W. 80 **Beda** *marg* E. **ut** *om* E; vbi H. 81 **quatuor** *add* incommoda A. **inpotenciam** inopiam W. 82 **fuit** est E. 83 **cohiberet** *corr from* chohiberet E. 84 **inpotenciam** inopiam W. 85 **ignoranciam** *add* necessaria fuit IW. 86 **temperancia** *add* de diffinicione cardinalium uirtutum *rubr* J; *add* de quatuor virtutibus cardinalibus *rubr* A; *add* de diffinicionibus cardinalium *rubr* I; *add* de diffinicionibus quatuor virtutum cardinalium *rubr* W. 88 **actibus** accionibus FW. **quarum prima** quorum primum E. 89 Augustinus *marg* E. 90 Tullius *marg* E. **uitandarum** fugiendarum G. 93 Augustinus *marg* E. 94 Augustinus *marg* E. **corrupcioni** corporum EHL; corrupcionem AW; quorumpcioni G. 95 Augustinus *marg* E. 96–104 **eterna . . . temporalibus** *om* H. 97 **in** *om* FGILW; *marg* J. 98 Augustinus *marg* E. 100 Augustinus *marg* E. **libro** *om* EILW. 103 Augustinus

frangant, temperancia in prosperis, ne blanda demulceant et seducant.

Secunda racio sumitur ex hiis que necessario postulat uirtus ut uirtus sit. Quorum primum est scire quid eligendum [et quid] agendum sit, quod est officium prudencie, quia [eius] “intrinseca linea cordis premetitur opus.” Secundum est posse, quod quia in nobis infirmum est indiget fortitudine. Tercium est uelle, quod quia in nobis uanum et uagum est necesse est racione ipsum refrenari, quod est [opus] temperancie. Quartum est ipsum operari, quod est iusticie, cuius / est inperare ceteris uirtutibus et in opus f. 92ᵛa producere.

Tercia racio sumitur ex nostra indigencia postquam fuit corrupta humana natura, quia [ut] dicit Beda: “Homo cum peccauit incidit in quatuor: in maliciam, in inpotenciam, in ignoranciam, in concupiscenciam.” Contra maliciam necessaria [fuit] iusticia, ut cohiberet eam et inter licitum et illicitum limites poneret; contra inpotenciam necessaria fuit fortitudo que naturam lesam roboraret; contra ignoranciam, prudencia; contra concupiscenciam, temperancia.

Sequitur de diffinicionibus quatuor cardinalium uirtutum et earum actibus, [quarum prima] est prudencia. Et est prudencia secundum Augustinum in libro *Vnde malum*: “Rerum appetendarum et uitandarum sciencia.” Secundum Tullium prudencia est “bonarum rerum atque malarum utrarumque discrecio.” Actus uero prudencie sunt quoad uiam: “precauere insidias,” ut in III *Sentenciarum*; “mala deuitare,” vt Augustinus *Super Genesim*; “incorrupcionem [corrupcioni] preponere,” vt Augustinus *De libero arbitrio*; “discernere bona a malis,” vt XIX *De ciuitate Dei*; “preponere temporalibus eterna,” Augustinus libro VI *Musice*. Actus eius in patria sunt: “nullum bonum Deo preponere,” vt in III *Sentenciarum*; “conspicere puram Ueritatem,” vt Augustinus VI *Musice*. Principalis uero actus eius est “meliora peioribus preeligere,” vt Augustinus [libro] *LXXXIII questionum*. / Actus uero f. 92ᵛb eius precedentes sunt “discernere bona a malis,” “Ueritatem puram conspicere,” ut supra dictum est. Consequentes uero actus eius sunt “insidias [precauere] et malum deuitare,” ut Augustinus

Genesis, and "to place God before all else, and eternal things before temporal ones," as was said earlier.

Justice is the virtue "by which each is given his own," according to Augustine in his book *Whence Evil Comes.* Or according to Tullius, justice is "the virtue which gives everyone his right." Its acts are to subordinate the lower to the higher, to serve only God spiritually, to worship and to fear him. Deuteronomy 6: "You shall adore the Lord your God, and shall serve him only." Moreover, this virtue teaches us to give reverence and obedience to men of higher rank; Hebrews, at the end: "Obey your prelates," etc. It also teaches to give counsel and aid to one's equals, to unite oneself with one's equals, not to desire to be like others, and to do unto others as we would have them do to us, Luke 6. It also teaches us to show compassion and sympathy to our inferiors, so that we may judge of the disposition of our neighbors by ourselves, Ecclesiasticus 31. And it teaches us to help the suffering and to punish evil habits; Exodus 22: "Wizards you shall not suffer to live." In heaven the act of justice is to subject all things to God and to prefer him surpassingly to all things. We should know that justice is twofold: one is general and embraces all virtues and has as its subject what is owed and what is worthy; the other is a special virtue, on the same level with the other three cardinal virtues, and has as its subject what pertains to each individual.

Fortitude, according to Augustine in his book *Whence Evil Comes,* is "the disposition by which we disdain all inconveniences." According to Tullius, "fortitude is the well-advised undertaking of perilous actions and the prolonged endurance of hardships." Its chief act is to adhere most firmly to what has been chosen with prudence. Its antecedent act is to strengthen one's mind against temporal inconveniences, according to Augustine in his book of *Eighty-three Questions.* Another act is not to be fearful in the face of any adversity or sickness or even death, according to Augustine, *On Music* VI. Hence Gregory says well that fortitude teaches how to undertake troublesome things. Its following acts in this life are, not to let any fear or pain turn us away from what we have wisely chosen, as Augustine says in *On Free Will.* After this follows still another act, that is, willingly to suffer inconveniences in order to obtain what has been chosen, as is stated in *Sentences* III; and "to endure misfortunes," as Augustine says in his *On Genesis.* In heaven its act will be to cling to God most firmly, *Sentences* III. Upon which follows, not to suffer any inconveniences there.

marg E. **precauere** GIW *and line* 92; uitare EJAFL. 106 Augustinus *marg* E. 107 **ius** *add* suum AF. 109 **spiritualiter** specialiter JAFHILW. 110 **adorabis** timebis JAGH; adhereas I; etc W. 111 **hominibus superioribus** superiori E; superioribus GL; omnibus superioribus I. 112 **fine** servi E, *as part of following quotation*; xii A; 13 F; ultimo G; 3 I; xiii f W. 113 **etc.** vestris E; *om* FGILW. **ipsa docet** *written twice, the repetition canc* E. **paribus** *om* AL; subditis F; perhibet W. **et auxilium** *om* I. 114 **coequari** preesse FH; preesse vel coequari A. **et** *om* E. 115 **sic** hoc E; ut JF; ita A; nec ita H. **faciamus** *add* nos GIW. 119 **Exodi . . . uiuere** *om* W. 121 **sciendum** *add* est FGIW. 123 **que** *om* E. **specialis** spiritualis E. 125 Augustinus *marg* E. 126 **contempnimus** contemnuntur G. 127 Tullius *marg* E. **Fortitudo** *om* E. 128–29 **actus . . . adherere** *marg* E, *the words* actus . . . for- *cut off by binder.* 129 **electo** eligere AH. 130 Augustinus *marg* E. **Augustinus** *add* in E. 131 **est** *om* E. **ad** *om* AF. **aduersitatem uel** *om* G. 132 Augustinus *marg* E. 133 Gregorius *marg* E. 134 **electo** eligere AH. 135 Augustinus *marg* E. 136 **perferre** proferre GI. 137 Augustinus *marg* E. 138 **firmissime** fortissime E. 141 Augusti-

Super Genesim, et "Deum omnibus preponere et eterna temporalibus," ut supra dictum est.

Iusticia est "qua cuique sua tribuuntur," ut Augustinus in libro *Vnde malum*. Vel secundum Tullium iusticia est "uirtus ius unicuique conferens." Huius actus sunt inferiora pocioribus subdere, soli Deo spiritualiter seruire, reuereri ipsum et timere. Deuteronomi vi: "Dominum Deum tuum adorabis et illi soli seruies." Preterea ipsa docet [hominibus superioribus] reuerenciam exhibere et obedienciam; vnde Hebreorum [fine]: "Obedite prepositis uestris," [etc.]. Item ipsa docet paribus exhibere consilium et auxilium, pares sibi copulare, nulli uelle coequari, [et] prout uolumus quod fiat nobis [sic] faciamus proximis, Luce vi. Item ipsa docet inferioribus exhibere conpassionem et condescensum, ut intelligamus que sunt proximi ex nobismetipsis, Ecclesiastici xxxi. Item ipsa docet miseris subuenire et prauos mores punire; Exodi xxii: "Maleficos non pacieris uiuere." Actus iusticie in patria est omnia Deo subdere et illum excellenter omnibus preferre. Et sciendum quod est iusticia duplex: vna que est generalis et omnes uirtutes continet et habet pro subiecto debitum vel dignum; alia [que] est [specialis] / f. 93[r]a condiuidens cum tribus cardinalibus, et habet pro subiecto proprium siue suum.

Fortitudo secundum Augustinum in libro *Vnde malum* est "affectio qua omnia incommoda contempnimus." Secundum Tullium: "[Fortitudo] est periculorum considerata suscepcio et laborum diuturna perpessio." Huius [actus principalis est prudenter electo for]tissime adherere. Actus antecedens est firmare animum contra temporales molestias, ut Augustinus ° libro *LXXXIII questionum*. Alius [est] ad nullam aduersitatem uel infirmitatem uel eciam mortem formidare, vt Augustinus VI *Musice*. Ideo bene dicit Gregorius quod fortitudo docet agredi ardua. Actus eius consequentes sunt quidam in via, ut sapienter electo nullis terroribus penisque depelli, ut Augustinus *De libero arbitrio*. Adhuc consequitur alius, scilicet pro electo habendo libenter perferre molestias, ut III *Sentenciarum*; "tolerare aduersa," vt Augustinus *Super Genesim*. In patria erit eius actus [firmissime] Deo adherere, vt III *Sentenciarum*. Ad quem consequitur nichil molestie ibidem pati.

Moderation, as Augustine states in *Whence Evil Comes,* is "the disposition that restrains our desire from those objects which it craves for dishonorably." According to Tullius, moderation is "the virtue which curbs those desires which attack us by the allurement of prosperity." Its chief act is to keep measure in things that belong to the flesh, that "we may not live according to the flesh," Romans 8. Its preceding act withdraws the mind from the love of an inferior beauty, Augustine, *On Music* VI. Another act is to curb impulses, and this in various ways, namely: "to repress improper delights," *Sentences* III; "to restrain lust," Augustine, *On Genesis*; to restrain our desire from those things which give temporal pleasure, Augustine in his book of *Eighty-three Questions.* Its following act in heaven is "not to take pleasure in any harmful weakness," *Sentences* III. From it arises another act: always "to remain pure," according to Augustine, *On Music* VI.

Now we turn to the virtue of grace, which can be considered in two ways: either as *gratis data,* "gratuitously given," or as *gratum faciens,* "rendering acceptable." The first comprises not only the virtues of grace proper but also the political and natural virtues, as well as all spiritual and temporal gifts, for "every best gift and every perfect gift is from above," James 1, gratuitously given. The second kind of virtue of grace, which "renders acceptable," comprises the theological virtues and the cardinal virtues inasmuch as they are formed with grace, because before the coming of grace they are numbered among the political virtues.

The theological virtues are three: faith, hope, and charity, and they are called theological from *"theos,"* which is God, and *"logos,"* word or reason, because they prompt us to know and to love God according to reason. Whereas the cardinal virtues with their species dispose us to good external deeds and diminish the difficulties and remove obstacles which we meet in obtaining the good, the three theological virtues dispose us to know and to desire God. Thus, faith is concerned with knowing God in this life; it is "the illumination of the mind to see God," as Augustine says in his book *On Seeing God.* Or else it is "the substance of things to be hoped for," Hebrews 11, that is, faith is the foundation on which the eternal goods for which we hope exist in us; that is to

nus *marg* E. **Augustinus** *add* in E. 142 **cohercens** cohibens E. 142–43 **ab . . . appetuntur** *om* AH. 143 Tullius *marg* E. **temperancia** *om* E. **cohibens** cohercens IL; artans G. 144 **suasu** suos E; *om* G. **prosperitatis** *add* eciam GI; proprietatis eciam W. 146 **Romanorum viii** II Ro xiii E. 147 Augustinus *marg* E. 149 **multiplex** multipliciter AFGIW; multipliciter ⟨vel multiplex⟩ J; videtur L. 150 Augustinus *marg* E. 151 Augustinus *marg* E. 151–52 **Augustinus** *add* in E. 153 **noxio** noxie E. 154 Augustinus *marg* E. 155 **Musice** *add* de uirtute gratuita *rubr* JA; *add* virtus gratuita *marg* G; *illeg* W. 156 **duplex** dupliciter FHIW. 158–59 **data temporalia** *om* L; temporalia J. 159 **omne *(2nd)*** *om* E. 162 **quod** *add* a E. **informantur** conformantur G; reformantur W. 164 de uirtutibus theoloycis *marg* E. *In the text* E *consistently contracts to* theo^{ce} *or* theolo^{ce}. J *gives* theologicas *at* 161 *and contracts as* E *elsewhere.* **theologice** theorice F. 165 **theologice** theorice F. 165–66 **sermo uel** quod est EFLW; quod est sermo vel A; quod est sermo (*om* vel racio) H. 166 **de** *text of* H *ends here; lacuna to ch. III, line 241.* 168 **exteriora** *marg, to re-*

Temperancia est, ut ait Augustinus ° libro *Vnde malum*, "affectio [cohercens] appetitum ab hiis rebus que turpiter appetuntur." Secundum Tullium [temperancia] est "uirtus cohibens motus [suasu] prosperitatis in nos inpetum facientes." Principalis actus temperancie est in hiis que carnis sunt modum tenere, ut "non secundum carnem uiuamus," [Romanorum viii]. Actus eius precedens est subtrahere ab amore inferior- / is pulcritudinis, Augustinus 93^{r}b VI *Musice*. Alius est refrenare inpellencia, et huiusmodi multiplex: "cohercere scilicet prauas delectaciones," ut III *Sentenciarum*; "libidinem refrenare," Augustinus *Super Genesim*; refrenare cupiditatem ab hiis que temporaliter delectant, ut Augustinus ° libro *LXXXIII questionum*. Actus consequens in patria est "nullo defectu [noxio] delectari," ut III *Sentenciarum*. Ex quo alius sequitur: semper "immaculatum permanere," vt Augustinus VI *Musice*.

Sequitur de uirtute gratuita, que duplex dicitur: aut gratis data aut gratum faciens. Gratis data conprehendit non solum gratuitas set eciam politicas et naturales et omnia dona spiritualia et data temporalia, quia "omne datum optimum et [omne] donum perfectum desursum est," gratis datum, Iacobi i. Virtus uero gratuita, idest gratum faciens, conprehendit theologicas et cardinales secundum quod ° gracia informantur, quia ante graciam inter politicas numerantur.

Virtutes autem theologice sunt tres: fides, spes, caritas, et dicuntur theologice a "theos," quod est Deus, et "logos," [sermo uel] racio, quia de Deo cognoscendo et diligendo racionabiliter persuadent. Et sicut cardinales cum suis speciebus ordinant nos ad opera bona exteriora et difficultates circa bonum alleuiant et inpedimenta remouent, ita tres theologice ordinant nos ad Deum / cognoscendum et appetendum. f. 93^{v}a Vnde de eius cognicione in uia est fides; que est "mentis illuminacio ad uidendum Deum," ut dicit Augustinus in libro *De uidendo [Deo]*. [Vel] ipsa est "substancia rerum sperandarum," Hebreorum xi, [idest] fides est fundamentum per quod eterna bona sperata subsistunt in nobis;

place cum suis speciebus, *canc*, E. **bonum** *marg, to replace* hominem, *canc*, E. 169 **theologice** theorice F. 170 **et appetendum** *om* L; *add* et diligendum F. 172 Augustinus *marg* E. **Deo** deum E. **Vel** item E; et F. 173 **idest** item E; *om*

say, faith is the first habit through which the other virtues exist in our soul. But hope is the desire to obtain the highest good, so that what is known by faith in this life may through manifest hope be obtained in heaven. Augustine: "Hope is a firm expectation of the future good, based on grace and one's merits." Charity is love or the embracing of the highest good, by which our soul clings to the highest good in so far as it is known and hoped for in this life, because "as much as you believe, you hope for, and as much as you hope for, you love," as Ambrose says. Thus, charity is love "by which God is loved for himself and our neighbor for God's sake," as Augustine states. And according to Bernard, charity is the well-ordered desire for the good. Although every virtue is love or belongs to the order of love, as Augustine says in *The City of God,* yet the individual virtues are not differentiated on the basis of the love in which they agree, because in that case there would be only one virtue, charity, which is love of the good; rather, they are differentiated on the basis of the difficulties which they solve concerning the good. Therefore, each virtue has its own end and its own love with regard to the good. Hence, as the three theological virtues are directed toward the highest good—which is not merely simple but the simplest of all—, they yet find their individual delights in it according to the different aspects that are found in this good as well as according to the different effects that come from it. That means: faith is directed toward the highest good as toward the first truth; hope, as toward the greatest bounty; and charity, as toward the greatest goodness. Though these three qualities are absolutely one in God's simple essence, they yet have different effects and are different aspects. That such a thing should be possible can be shown by an example from everyday experience: though milk is one thing in its substance, it yet contains aspects that appeal to different senses, for sight perceives in it whiteness, taste sweetness, and touch wetness. In the same fashion, if we may speak like stammering children, the soul's sight directed to the first principle is faith, its taste is hope, its touch is charity, because it unites us with him, just as touching means to have the furthest points in common. And the faithful soul barely has its furthest point united with God because, while by nature it is most different from God in its substance, yet in its will and the conformity which comes by grace it can be said to be like him because of his image which is impressed on reason.

Virtue of grace is defined by Augustine as follows: "Virtue is a good quality of the mind by which we live rightly, which no one misuses, and which God

FGL. 175 **idest** item E; vel FL. 178 Augustinus *marg* E. **Spes** fides JLW. 181 **et . . . speras** *om* AG. 181–82 **et . . . diligis** *om* W. 182 Ambrosius *marg* E. 183 **ipsum** *om* E. 184 Bernardus *marg* E. **Bernardum** hoc F. 185 Augustinus *marg* E. 185–86 **Augustinus** *add* in libro E. 188 **caritas** caritatis E. 189 **circa bonum** *om* I. 189–90 **Vnde . . . bonum** *om* EFIW. 190 **delectacionem** dileccionem JL. 191 **theologice** theorice F. 192 **solum** *om* E. 193 **delectaciones** dilecciones F; delectaciones ⟨vel dilecciones⟩ J. **connotata** conuocata AGW (*also at line* 198). 194 **effectus** affectus E; *corr from* affectus A. **Verbi gracia** ut dicit Gregorius AILW. 195 **ueritatem** uirtutem JAF; caritatem W. 200 **subiecto** substancia G. 205 **cum *(1st)*** *add* est E. **unita** in vita L; unita ⟨vel in vita⟩ J. 206 **uoluntate** nobilitate J. 207 **propter** preter AGIW. **ymaginem** ymaginacionem J. 209 Augustinus *marg* E. **Virtus autem** ipsa autem virtus JFL; ipsa virtus

[idest,] fides est primus habitus per quem cetere uirtutes anime
insunt. Spes uero est appetitus summi boni habendi, ut quod per
fidem cognoscitur in via per manifestam spem habeatur in patria.
Augustinus: "Spes est certa expectacio futuri boni ex gracia et
meritis proueniens." Caritas est amor siue amplexus summi boni,
quo inheret ei anima in quantum cognoscitur in uia et speratur,
quia "quantum credis, tantum speras, et quantum speras, tantum
diligis," ut dicit Ambrosius. Caritas igitur amor est quo diligitur
Deus propter se [ipsum] et proximus propter Deum, ut dicit Augustinus. Et secundum Bernardum caritas est uoluntas ordinata
boni. Et licet omnis uirtus sit amor uel ordo amoris, ut dicit Augustinus ° *De ciuitate Dei,* tamen non distinguntur uirtutes penes amorem in quo conueniunt, quia sic esset solum una uirtus,
[caritas] scilicet, que est amor boni; set distinguntur penes difficultates quas explicant circa bonum. [Vnde quelibet uirtus habet
proprium finem et propriam delectacionem circa bonum.] Vnde
cum tres theologice uirtutes sint in summum bonum—quod non
[solum] est sim- / plex immo simplicissimum—, inueniunt ta- f. 93vb
men in ipso proprias delectaciones penes diuersa connotata in
ipso et penes diuersos [effectus] qui sunt ab ipso. Verbi gracia:
fides est in ipsum tanquam in primam ueritatem; spes tanquam in
summam largitatem; caritas tanquam in summam bonitatem.
Hec tria licet unum sint omnino in simplici Dei essencia, diuersos
tamen habent effectus et diuersa connotata. Et quod hoc possibile
sit sensibili monstratur exemplo: quia quamuis lac sit unum in
subiecto, tamen diuersorum sensuum continet obiecta, vnde uisus in eo percipit albedinem, gustus dulcedinem, tactus humidita-
tem. Ita, ut balbuciendo loquamur, visus anime in ipsum primum est fides, gustus quidem est spes, caritas tactus, quia unit
cum ipso, sicut tangere est habere ultima simul. Et anima fidelis
uix ultima habet cum ° Deo unita, quia cum in natura ualde
dissimilis sit substancia, in uoluntate tamen et conformitate que
per graciam est dicitur ei assimilata propter ymaginem que racioni est inpressa.

Virtus autem gratuita sic diffinitur ab Augustino: "Virtus est bona qualitas mentis qua recte uiuitur, qua nullus male utitur, quam operatur Deus in nobis sine nobis." Et nota quod sicut ani-

alone works in us without us." Notice that just as the soul stands in three relationships to the body, so virtue has three relationships to the soul and a fourth to God, who is its giver. In one way, the soul is related to the body as its form, to fulfil it; in the same way is virtue related to the soul, when it is said to be "a good quality of the mind." In another way, the soul is the act of the physical, organic body, that is, the principle of life within it, giving it motion and sensitivity. The same is spiritually the case with the soul, as is indicated in the words "by which we live rightly," etc. In a third way the soul is said to be the body's act or form in so far as it moves its organs in their functions, just as a natural form is the principle of action in a natural substance. And this is expressed in the words "which no one misuses," for the use of anything lies in its actual function. This part of the definition excludes the evil habit of vice, which no one uses well. What is said in the last place, "which God works in us," indicates that virtue comes from the bounty of its giver and not from man. And this excludes the heresy of Sabellius, who claimed that man is sufficient for his own justice through his own free will, which is false and heretical, because as man could not create himself, so he cannot restore himself, since nothing has ever engendered itself or brought itself into being, according to the Philosopher. Moreover, if grace came from man, and consequently his justification, then the merit as well as the reward should be attributed to man and not to God; which is a most impious claim, for in that case God would have created man for nothing, for he should receive no service from man, nor would he be man's reward. Likewise, every cause is better than what it causes or equally good. Then, if man were the cause of grace and, consequently, of his justification, he would be equally good before and after the coming of grace, and equally good in the state of wickedness as in that of justice; which is not only heretical but also absurd. Notice also that virtue and grace are the same in substance, but we speak of grace in reference to its giver; Augustine: "Grace is God's gift without merit." Virtue is the same habit of grace, because all virtues are united in one habit of grace, but "virtue" refers to external actions, as Tullius says: "Virtue lies in action." Notice also that just as the natural powers relate to doing, so the virtues relate to doing well, but the gifts of the Holy Spirit relate to the vigor of the same virtues. The last words of the definition, "without us," and so forth, should be understood as without our operation—because we are not able to create grace or infuse it—but not as without our cooperation, because "we are

AGIW. 210 **utitur** uiuitur F. 212 **conparaciones** operaciones EJI. 213 **conparaciones** operaciones EJI. 217 **motum** nomen E. 221 **Huic** hoc FGL; hoc ⟨vel huic⟩ J. 223 **eciam hoc** in E. 224 **quo . . . utitur** *om* G. 230 Philosophus *marg* E. **gracia** *add* dei AFL. 233 **tunc** *om* E. 235 **suo** *om* E. 237 **ut** et JGW. 237–38 **et . . . insanum** *om* L. 239 **sunt** sit E. 240 Augustinus *marg* E. 242 **operaciones** conparaciones E. 243 Tullius *marg* E. 244 **uires** virtutes IL. 245 **bene agere** ipsum bene E. 247–49 **graciam . . . cooperantibus** *om* E; *marg* J. 247 **graciam enim** quia graciam AFGL. 249 **iii** ii E; xv J. 250 **reci-**

ma habet tres [conparaciones] ad corpus, sic uirtus tres habet [conparaciones] ad animam, quartam ad Deum qui dator est eius. Anima uero uno modo se habet ad / corpus sicut forma eius f. 94ra ad conplementum; sic uirtus ad animam, cum dicitur "bona qualitas mentis." Alio modo est anima actus corporis organici phisici, idest principium uite in ipso dans ei [motum] et sensum. Hoc idem est uirtus anime spiritualiter, quod in illa parte notatur "qua recte uiuitur," etc. Tercio modo dicitur anima actus uel forma in quantum mouet organa corporis ad operaciones, sicut forma naturalis principium est actionis in naturali subiecto. Huic respondet quod dicitur "qua nullus male utitur," quia usus rei est in actuali exercicio. Excluditur [eciam hoc] membro malus habitus uicii quo nullus bene utitur. Quod dicitur ultimo "quam operatur Deus in nobis," ostenditur quod a datoris largitate sit uirtus et non ab homine. Et excluditur heresis Sabellii qui dixit hominem sibi sufficere ad iusticiam per liberum arbitrium, cum hoc sit falsum et hereticum, quia sicut homo non potuit seipsum creare, ita nec recreare, quia nichil seipsum genuit neque ad esse conduxit, ut dicit Philosophus. Preterea, si gracia esset ab homine et per consequens iustificacio, tam meritum quam premium esset homini ascribendum et non Deo; quod est inpiissimum dicere, quia [tunc] creasset hominem pro nichilo, a quo nec haberet famulatum, nec teneretur ei ad premium. Item omnis causa est melior [suo] causato uel eque bona. Vnde, si homo esset causa gracie et per consequens iustificacionis sue, eque bonus esset ante graciam ut post, et inpius sicut iustificatus; quod / non solum est f. 94rb hereticum set eciam insanum. Et nota quod idem in subiecto [sunt] gracia et uirtus, set gracia in conparacione ad datorem dicitur; Augustinus: "Gracia est donum Dei sine meritis." Virtus est idem habitus gracie, quia omnes uirtutes in uno habitu gracie conueniunt, set "uirtus" respicit [operaciones] exteriores, secundum quod dicit Tullius: "Virtus in operacione consistit." Et nota quod sicut uires naturales sunt ad ipsum agere, ita uirtutes ad [bene agere], dona uero Spiritus Sancti sunt ad robur ipsarum uirtutum. Quod autem dicitur in ultima parte diffinicionis, "sine nobis," etc., intellige sine nobis operantibus [—graciam enim creare non possumus nec infundere—, non tamen sine nobis cooperan-

God's coadjutors," Corinthians 3, since it lies in us either to accept grace that is offered or to reject it. And thus Augustine says: "He who has created you without you, will not justify you without you."

Since it has been said earlier that grace and virtue are the same in substance, though different in their relations, we must now consider what grace is, what its effect is, how it is received, how lost, and how regained. Grace is defined in various ways. Sometimes with respect to its giver, and thus Augustine calls it God's gift without merit, as above. Sometimes with respect to the subject in which it is, and in this case it shares the definition of virtue, because both are a good habit of the mind. Sometimes it is defined with respect to its effects; Romans 1: "Grace to you and peace"; Gloss: "Grace, that is, the remission of sin," because, you should add, that is an effect of grace. For grace remits sin as a joint cause, while God is a separate cause, just as a physician heals and medicine heals.

Grace is divided into many kinds. Corinthians 12: "Now there are diversities of graces," and so forth, for some graces are spiritual, others bodily, some are external, others internal. But internal graces are twofold, for some are natural graces, such as reason, memory, talent, and the like. When these are abused, grace is turned into guilt; Ecclesiasticus 20: "The grace of the fools shall be poured out." Other graces are internal, namely the virtues of grace, that is, faith, hope, charity, meekness, humility, etc., which Peter commands us to minister willingly to one another, I Peter 4: "As every man has received grace, ministering the same one to another; so that, if any man speak, let him speak as if it were the words of God," etc.

Grace has various effects. Its first effect is to wipe out the stain of sin and to reform God's image in the soul and to prepare the soul to receive God. This grace is like that disposition in matter which prepares it to receive a form, which is glory itself. For glory is grace confirmed, as Augustine says in *On the Psalms*. The same is expressed in John 1: "Grace for grace," that is to say, glory freely given through the merits of grace itself. Likewise in Zacharias 4, that the Lord "shall give equal grace to the grace"; this you should understand as a general comparison, because a greater grace deserves a greater glory, but not in an equal proportion, for God rewards all above their desert. Grace is like the ray of

pere accipere E. **graciam oblatam** *om* G; graciam IW. 251 Augustinus *marg* E. **te *(4th)*** *add* dicendum est quid sit gracia *rubr* A. 254 **quis** quid EW. 255 **Diffinitur . . . gracia** gracia diffinitur E. **pluribus** multis JI. 256 Augustinus *marg* E. 257–60 **in . . . Quandoque** *om* A. 257 **Quandoque** deinde J; denique W. 258 **eandem** *om* E. 259 **est** *om* E. 261 **Glossa gracia** *om* E; gracia JI. 262 **ipsa** ipse E. 262–63 **peccatum** peccata E. 264 **sanat *(2nd)*** *add* de gracia *rubr* J. 270 **effundentur** effunduntur EW; effundetur J (*with* gracia). 271 **gracia** *om* EL. 272–73 **libenter in alterutrum** *om* L. 273 **iiii** iii E. 273–75 **Vnusquisque . . . etc.** *om* G. 274–75 **quasi . . . Dei** siquis ministrat JAFL; *om* GIW. 277 **peccati** *om* G. 280 Augustinus *marg* E. **confirmata** conformata IW; conformata ⟨vel confirmata⟩ J. 280–81 **Psalmos** *add* graciam et gloriam dabit dominus *marg* J. 282–83 **Idem . . . gracie** *om* A. 284 **gracia** *om* F. **debetur** tenetur F; detur L.

tibus], quia "coadiutores Dei sumus," Corinthiorum [iii], quia in nobis est aut [recipere] graciam oblatam aut repellere. Ideo dicit Augustinus: "Qui creauit te sine te, non iustificabit te sine te."

Quia predictum est quod gracia et uirtus sunt in subiecto idem, racione tamen differentes, dicendum est quid sit gracia, [quis] eius effectus, qualiter detur, et qualiter amittatur, et quomodo recuperetur. [Diffinitur autem gracia] pluribus modis. Quandoque in conparacione ad datorem, et sic dicit Augustinus quod est donum Dei sine meritis, ut supra. Quandoque in conparacione ad subiectum in quo est, et sic habet [eandem] diffinicionem cum uirtute, quia utraque bonus habitus mentis [est]. Quandoque diffinitur in conparacione ad suos effectus; Romanorum i: "Gracia uobis et pax"; [Glossa: "gracia,] idest remissio peccati," quia suple [ipsa] est effectus gracie. / Gracia enim remittit [peccatum] ut causa coniuncta, Deus uero ut causa separata, uel sicut medicus sanat et pocio sanat. f. 94va

Diuiditur autem gracia multipliciter. Corinthiorum xii: "Diuisiones graciarum sunt," etc., quia quedam sunt spirituales, quedam corporales, quedam exteriores, quedam interiores. Interiores uero dupliciter, quia quedam naturales, ut racio, memoria, ingenium, etc. Quibus cum quis abutitur, gracia in culpam mutatur; Ecclesiastici xx: "Gracie stultorum [effundentur]." Alie sunt [gracie] interiores, idest gratuite uirtutes, idest fides, spes, caritas, mansuetudo, humilitas, etc., quas precipit Petrus libenter in alterutrum ministrari, I Petri [iiii]: "Vnusquisque sicut accepit graciam in alterutrum amministrantes, vt siquis loquitur, quasi sermones Dei," etc.

Effectus gracie plures sunt. Primus est quod delet maculam peccati et reformat Dei similitudinem in anima et preparat eam ad suscepcionem Dei. Ipsa enim est sicut disposicio in materia que preparat eam ad suscepcionem forme, que est ipsa gloria. Gloria enim est gracia confirmata, ut dicit Augustinus *Super Psalmos*. Hoc est quod dicitur Iohannis i: "Graciam pro gracia," idest gloria gratis data meritis ipsius gracie. Idem dicitur Zacharie iiii, quod Dominus "exequabit graciam gracie"; et intellige conparacionem generalem, quia maiori gracie debetur maior gloria, non ex equa [proporcione], quia Deus remunerat omnes supra meri-

the sun which dissolves the raincloud. The cloud, which hides the sun, is sin; Lamentations 3: "You have set a cloud before you," etc. This cloud the Lord dissolves through the warming ray of the sun, that is, through grace which makes the soul grow warm through contrition and devotion; Isaias 44: "I have blotted out your iniquities as a cloud, and your sins as a mist." A cloud also stands for sin because of its origin. For a cloud rises out of vapors, sin out of delights; Job 36: "The air on a sudden will be thickened into clouds and the wind will pass," etc. A cloud is dissolved by wind and heat; similarly, sin by contrition and confession; Osee 13: "They will be as a morning cloud and as the dew that passes away," add: sins at the coming of grace. A second effect of grace is to give life to the soul; Habacuc 2: "The just shall live in his faith." Faith is the first grace, according to Augustine, and it is the first life of the soul, just as the vegetative soul is the first life of nature. And as the soul is the life of the body, so grace is the life of the spirit. Thus, when grace is lost, the soul dies spiritually; Wisdom 16: "A man kills his soul through mischief." Another effect of grace is to enlighten our rational and to kindle our concupiscible power. John 5: "John was a burning and a shining light." "John" signifies the grace which enlightens the intellect and kindles our affect, according to Bernard. It also appeases the irascible power; Colossians 1: "Grace be to you and peace"; the Gloss explains: the remission of sin and tranquillity of the mind, and both come from grace. It further brings spiritual joy; Colossians 3: "Singing in grace in your hearts to the Lord." It also strengthens us against our spiritual foes; Timothy 1: "Grace, that is, the strength to resist." And it is the nurse of all good; Wisdom 16: "I was obedient to your grace that nourishes all."

Next we must consider how grace has been given, for it has flowed to us in two manners: through Christ as through its full well-spring, "of whose fullness we all have received," John 1, and through the Blessed Virgin as through a channel, through whom the water of grace has flowed to the garden of the Church. Christ himself is its well-spring for several reasons. First, because having sprung from the land of the virginal womb he waters all the land of paradise, that is, all the Church. He is that same river "which is divided into four heads," Genesis 2; and Ecclesiasticus 24: "He fills up wisdom as the Phison."

285 **proporcione** conparacione E. 289 **calefactionem radii** calefacientem radium JF. 292–93 **uaporibus** *add* aeris *marg* A. 293 **delectacionibus** *add* carnis A. 294 **et uentus . . . etc.** *om* IW. 295–96 **sic . . . nubes** *om* F. 295 **Osee** eodem E. 296 **preteriens** mane pertransiens G; matutinus pertransiens I. 297 **gracie** *add* item E. **uiuificat** iustificat E. 299 Augustinus *marg* E. 303 **suam** *add* item E. **effectus** *add* eius E. **quod** quia E. 304 **racionabilem** racionalem JFI. 306 **gracia** anima I. 307 Bernardus *marg* E. **Item** *om* JIW. 307–9 **Item . . . est** *after* Domino *line 311* L. 308 Glossa *marg* E. **Glossa** *add* ibi GIW. 309 **et utraque** *om* E. 313 **gracie** gracia E. 318 **canalem** cananalem E; carnalem JA. 321 **Ipse**

tum. Item gracia est sicut radius solis qui / dissoluit nubem aquosam. Nubes que solem abscondit peccatum est; Trenorum iii: "Opposita est nubes," etc. Hanc nubem dissoluit Dominus per calefactionem radii solis, idest per graciam que feruescere facit animam per contricionem et deuocionem; Ysaie xliiii: "Deleui ut nubem iniquitates tuas, et quasi nebulam peccata tua." Item peccatum est nubes racione sui ortus. Oritur enim nubes ex uaporibus; sic peccatum ex delectacionibus; Iob xxxvi: "Subito aer cogetur in nubes et uentus transiens," etc. Vento et calore soluitur nubes; sic peccatum contricione et confessione; [Osee] xiii: "Erunt quasi nubes matutina et sicut ros preteriens," peccata suple in aduentu gracie. ° Alius effectus eius est quod [uiuificat] animam; Abacuc ii: "Iustus ex fide uiuit." Fides est prima gracia, secundum Augustinum, et ipsa est prima uita anime, sicut uegetatiua anima est prima uita nature. Et sicut anima est uita corporis, sic gracia est uita spiritus. Ideo cum gracia perditur, anima spiritualiter moritur; Sapiencie xvi: "Homo per maliciam occidit animam suam." ° Alius effectus ° est [quod] ipsa illuminat uim racionabilem et accendit concupiscibilem. Iohannis v: "Iohannes erat lucerna lucens et ardens." "Iohannes" interpretatur gracia que illuminat intellectum et accendit affectum, secundum Bernardum. Item ipsa sedat irascibilem; Ad Colossenses i: "Gracia uobis et pax"; Glossa: peccati remis- / sio et mentis tranquillitas, [et utraque] ex gracia est. Item ipsa inducit leticiam spiritualem; Colossensium iii: "Cantantes in gracia in cordibus uestris Domino." Item ipsa roborat contra spirituales hostes; Ad Thymotheum i: "Gracia, idest robur resistendi." Item ipsa est nutrix omnium bonorum; Sapiencie xvi: "Omnium nutrici [gracie] deseruiebam."

f. 94vb

f. 95ra

Uidendum est qualiter data sit gracia, quia duobus modis emanauit ad nos: per Christum tanquam per fontalem plenitudinem, "de cuius plenitudine nos omnes accepimus," Iohannis i, et per Beatam Uirginem tanquam per canalem, per quam aqua gracie fluxit ad ortum Ecclesie. Ipse Christus est fons pluribus de causis. Primo quia ortus de terra uirginalis uteri irrigat terram tocius paradysi, idest tocius Ecclesie. [Ipse idem] est fluuius "qui diuiditur in quatuor capita," Genesis ii; et Ecclesiastici xxiiii:

"Phison" means change of the mouth. Christ was the Phison in his preaching, when he spoke to all in a way they could understand, Matthew 4. He was the Tigris in the days of new things, when he "created a new thing on earth," that is, in his incarnation; Jeremias 31: "The Lord will create a new thing upon the earth." Indeed he was the Tigris then, because like a tiger he was striped in his nature, that is, God and man. He was Gyon in his passion and in the opening of his wounds, for "Gyon" means a cleft of the earth; Isaias 2: "Hide in the pit." And he was Euphrates in the sending of the Holy Spirit, when the apostles spoke in the tongues of all men, Acts 2. "Euphrates" means fruitful or producing fruit, which indicates his abundant knowledge and teaching. Likewise, spring water comes from the sea, but in the veins of the earth it is filtered and made sweet; thus the nature of sinful man, in being taken on by Christ, has been made sweet through his bitter passion. For he "cast wood into the waters of Marath, which were turned into sweetness," Exodus 15, that is, through the suffering of his cross he has taken away the salty taste of our former bitterness. Also, a well-spring that wells up from the deep carries small pebbles with it. Thus, Christ carries the small and humble with him; Job 21: "He has been sweet to the gravel of Cocytus, and he has drawn every man behind him, and there are innumerable before him." Although this is interpreted with reference to the wicked one, it can be meaningfully interpreted *in bono,* for Christ has become sweet for the humble and the little ones whom he has carried with him, who formerly tumbled around in sensual pleasure and tended to come to grief, as Gregory says. "Gravel" are small pebbles, "Cocytus" is the river which means grief; he himself "has drawn every man behind him," that is, some from every nation, after he came in the flesh; and "there are innumerable before him," that is, the patriarchs, prophets, and other faithful. Likewise, this well-spring gave warmth in the cold. There was cold in his passion, when water and blood flowed from him. This well-spring also grows cold in the heat, because it cools his faithful in their temptation and tribulation; Jeremias 6: "You will find refreshment for your souls." This is "the little fountain" which "grew into a great river," Esther 6, because in his faith the Church of believers grows. This is the "fountain open to the house of David, for the washing of the unclean woman," Zacharias 13. It cleanses from original sin by baptism and from actual sin by penance. Further, if anyone drinks from its water, it quenches in him the thirst of worldly desires; John 4: "He who will drink," and so forth. From this

idem item ipse E; ipse L. 323 **inplet . . . Physon** qui L. 324 **fuit** semper E. 326–27 **in incarnacione** incarnacionem JGW; *om* L. 326 **nouum . . . terram** *om* J, *but it and the other manuscripts continue the quotation*: femina circumdabit uirum, *in various forms.* 329 **in (2nd)** *om* E. **uulnerum** misteriorum F; infernorum L. 331–32 **fuit . . . Eufrates** *om* L. 331 **missione** emissione AGIW; J *with* e *canc.* 338–40 **deposuit . . . secum** *om* W. 339 **antique** *add* con *canc* E. 340 **attollit** attulit E. 341 **trahit** *om* E; detrahit W. **Cochiti** Conchiti E. 343 **inpio** *add* antichristo *marg* J. 345 **ad luctum** *om* E. 346 Gregorius *marg* E. **Gregorius** Origenes G; Glossa W. 353 **Ieremie** Iohannis E. **refrigerium** requiem E. 356 **Iacob** *om* E. 360 **etc.** *add* item E. 362 Bernardus *marg* E. **quem** quam AGIW; *om* J.

"Ipse quasi Physon inplet sapienciam." "Physon" interpretatur oris mutacio. Physon [fuit] Christus in predicacione, loquens singulis prout poterant intelligere, Matthei iiii. Tigris fuit in diebus nouorum, quando "nouum fecit super terram," scilicet in incarnacione; Ieremie xxxi: "Nouum faciet Dominus super terram." Et bene tunc fuit Tigris, quia in natura uarius, idest Deus et homo. Geon fuit in passione et [in] uulnerum apercione, quia Geon interpretatur hyatus terre; Ysaie ii: "Abscondere in fossa humo." Eufrates fuit in Spiritus Sancti missione, quando omnium linguis locuti sunt apostoli, / f. 95rb Actuum ii. "Eufrates" interpretatur frugifer uel fructificans, in quo notatur habundancia sciencie eius et doctrine. Item aqua fontis a mari ducit originem, set per uenas terre colatur et dulcoratur; sic natura hominis peccatoris a Christo assumpta facta est dulcis per amaritudinem passionis. Ipse enim "misit lignum in aquas Marath, que in dulcedinem uerse sunt," Exodi xv, idest per penam sue crucis deposuit salsedinem antique amaritudinis. Item fons profunde scaturiginis paruos lapillos secum [attollit]. Ita Christus paruos et humiles secum [trahit]; Iob xxi: "Dulcis fuit glareis [Cochiti], et post se omnem hominem traxit, et ante se innumerabiles." Licet istud exponatur de inpio, signanter tamen exponitur in bono, quia Christus dulcis factus est humilibus et paruulis quos secum traxit, qui prius uoluebantur cum uoluptate et tendebant [ad luctum], sicut dicit Gregorius. "Glaree" enim sunt parui lapilli, "Cochitus" fluuius, qui interpretatur luctus; ipse "post se omnem hominem traxit," idest ueniens per carnem de omni gente aliquem; et "ante se innumerabiles," idest patriarchas, prophetas, et alios fideles. Item iste fons calefiebat in frigore. Erat enim frigus in passione, quando ex illo emanauit unda cum sanguine. Item iste fons frigescit in calore, quia suos refrigerat in temptacione et tribulacione; [Ieremie] / f. 95va vi: "Inuenietis [refrigerium] animabus uestris." Item iste est "fons paruus" qui "creuit in fluuium maximum," Hester vi, quia in sua fide multiplicatur Ecclesia credencium. Item est "fons patens domui [Iacob] in ablucionem sordium menstruate," Zacharie xiii. Lauat enim per baptismum ab originali et per penitenciam ab actuali. Item siquis de eius aqua biberit, sitim secularium cupiditatum in eo extinguit; Iohannis iiii: "Siquis bi-

well-spring which never runs dry flows the water of all spiritual grace. The Blessed Virgin is, as it were, a channel or aqueduct through whom the stream of mercy has watered this parched world. Bernard: "So long the world lacked the streams of grace, because the aqueduct had not yet interceded."

Grace is given in another way daily through the sacraments. Through the Eucharist, as is shown in John 6: "He that eats me lives through me." Therefore "Eucharist" means good grace. Grace is also given through baptism, when faith is infused together with the other virtues. Augustine says in his book *On the Presence of God*: A child has all the virtues as a gift, that is, as a habit, in whom "the spark of reason lies dormant, waiting to be kindled at the coming of the proper age." In addition, Bede says that as the fish is nourished by water, so faith by baptism. Grace is also given in confirmation. Timothy 4: "Neglect not the grace that was given you through imposition of hands of the bishop," that is, in confirmation. Grace is, further, given in extreme unction; James, last chapter: "We are anointed with oil," etc., "and sins are forgiven," etc. Also in holy orders is grace given. Thus, the priest is a minister of grace, so that he may obtain grace for those whom he prays for. Ecclesiasticus 35: "He shall render grace that offers fine flour," that is, a likeness of flour, in which Christ is hidden under the form of bread. Grace is further given in matrimony, where sometimes a nonbelieving husband is sanctified by his wife who is a believer, that is, he is converted to the faith; sometimes vice-versa the wife is converted through her husband, Corinthians 7. And grace is finally given in penance, because in penance is "the shame which brings grace," Ecclesiasticus 4. These seven sacraments give grace, augment it, and preserve it, and ward off what is opposed to it.

What takes grace away are the seven deadly sins. Gluttony takes it away. Thus, "Herodias," that is, the glory of the skin, killed "John," that is, grace, at the banquet, Matthew 14; for whose murder she used her daughter, that is, lust, which is born of gluttony, as is shown in the chapters on these vices. Similarly, covetousness takes grace away, as is clear from Ananias, Acts 5, whose name means the gifts of God and who earned death for his covetousness. Also wrath takes grace away. Ecclesiasticus 20: "A fool will have no grace"; for a fool is he who "immediately shows his anger," Proverbs 12. Envy also takes grace away, as is symbolized in 2 Kings 10: Ammon shaved off the beards of David's ser-

363 **mundo** *om* E. **quia** quamdiu E. 365 **gracia** *add* scilicet E. **ipsa** ista J. 365–66 **Eucharistiam** *add* quod E. 369 Augustinus *marg* E. **Augustinus** *add* in EA. **presencia** presciencia JIL. 371 Beda *marg* E. 373 **gracia** *om* FGILW. 375 **gracia** *om* AFGLW. 376 **in** *om* E. 377 **confertur** datur J. 380 **gracia** *marg* E; *om* AGILW. 381 **uir** *om* E. **sanctificatur** sanctifatur E. 383 **Corinthiorum vii** *om* E; th 6 G. 383–84 **Item . . . septem** *om* I. 383 **gracia** *om* FGLW. **quia in ipsa** ibi enim GW. 385 **graciam** gloriam GW. **conseruant** confirmant J; servant G. 387 **Gula** vana gloria E. 388 **eam** graciam E. **Vnde . . . interfecit** *om* L. 390–91 **ut . . . viciis** *om* GW. 390 **patet** *om* EI. 391 **ut** quod E; *om* JFL. 392 **Ananya** *add* et Saphira E. 392–93 **qui . . . meruit** *om* L. 394 **uero** *om* EAW; enim FL. **indicat** vindicat AI. 395–96 **figuratum est** figuratur GIW. 396 **II** *om*

berit," etc. ° Ex isto fonte indeficiente fluit omnis aqua spiritualis gracie. Beata Virgo quasi canalis est siue aqueductus per quem mundum aridum irrigauit misericordie fluctus. Bernardus: "Tamdiu defuerunt [mundo] fluenta gracie, [quia] aqueductus nondum intercesserat."

Alio modo datur cottidie gracia ° per ipsa sacramenta. Per Eucharistiam, ° patet Iohannis vi: "Qui manducat me uiuit propter me." Vnde "Eucharistia" interpretatur bona gracia. Item per baptismum datur gracia, vbi fides infunditur cum ceteris uirtutibus. Augustinus libro *De presencia Dei*: Paruulus habet omnes uirtutes in munere, idest in habitu, in quo "sopita est scintilla racionis excitanda etatis accessu." Preterea dicit Beda quod sicut piscis aqua, sic fides baptismo nutritur. Item in confirmacione datur gracia. Thymothei iiii: "Noli negligere graciam que data est tibi per inposicionem manuum episcopi," idest in confirmacione. Item in extrema unc- / cione datur gracia. Iacobi ultimo: "Vn- f. 95vb gentes oleo," etc., "et dimittuntur peccata," etc. Item [in] ordine confertur gracia. Ideo sacerdos minister est gracie, ut pro quibus oret graciam inpetret. Ecclesiastici xxxv: "Retribuet graciam qui offert similaginem," idest similitudinem simile, vbi latet Christus sub panis specie. Item in coniugio datur gracia, vnde infidelis [uir] per fidelem mulierem quandoque [sanctificatur], idest, conuertitur ad fidem; quandoque e conuerso mulier per uirum, [Corinthiorum vii]. Item in penitencia datur gracia, quia in ipsa est "confusio adducens graciam," Ecclesiastici iiii. Hec septem sacramenta dant graciam, augmentant, et conseruant, et prohibent eius contraria.

Que auferunt graciam sunt septem mortalia. [Gula] aufert [eam]. Vnde "Herodias," idest gloria pellis, interfecit "Iohannem," idest graciam, in conuiuio, Matthei xiiii; ad cuius necem fecit eius filia, idest luxuria, que de gula nascitur, ut [patet] in capitulis de istis viciis. Item cupiditas aufert graciam, [ut] patet in Ananya °, Actuum v, qui interpretatur donum Dei et pro cupiditate mortem meruit. Item ira aufert graciam. Ecclesiastici xx: "Fatuo non erit gracia"; fatuus [uero] est qui "statim indicat iram suam," Prouerbiorum 12. Item inuidia aufert graciam, quod figuratum est II Regum x: Amon rasit barbas seruorum Dauid et

vants and tore their garments. "Ammon" means murmuring against kindness and signifies the envious person who disparages grace. Pride, too, takes grace away; James 4: "God resists the proud and gives grace to the humble." Likewise, sloth takes grace away; Ecclesiasticus 20: "The grace of fools shall be poured out." Bernard: "When grace has smiled on someone, he should fear lest he lose it. When it has gone from him, he should fear lest he fall into ruin. When he has received it back after his fall, he should fear lest he do not use it to bear fruit."

The following things restore grace: shame, that is, in penance; Ecclesiasticus 4: "There is a shame which brings grace." Further, the tears of compunction. Whence Moses found favor before the Lord, Exodus 33. "Moses" means watery or taken from the waters, and signifies him who weeps for his sins. Further, the bitterness of contrition; whence Mary "found grace before the Lord," Luke 1. "Mary" means bitter sea, that is, contrition, or in the Syriac language "Mary" is the same as lady. Also alms preserve grace; Ecclesiasticus 29: "The alms of a man is as a sack," etc.; and further: "and it will preserve his grace," etc.

Yet there are external graces which either hinder internal grace or take it completely away. The first of them is bodily beauty; Proverbs at the end: "Favor is deceitful and beauty is vain"; and Augustine says: "Beauty is a gift of God, but suspect." Another is strength; the Psalm: "The giant will not be saved by his own great strength." Another is health of body; Corinthians 12: "To another, the grace of health." Another is temporal riches; Proverbs 25: "Grace and friendship deliver a man; keep these for yourself, lest you fall under reproach." The rich man in the Gospel had such a grace, that is, worldly affluence, but he lacked the friendship of a single saint; thus he is not known in heaven but is called "a certain man," and he fell under reproach when he was told, "Son, remember," and so forth. These graces kill that grace which makes a man acceptable, so that one may say of them what Boethius in book I of his *Consolation* says of worldly knowledge: "They kill the fruitful harvest of reason with the sterile thorns of the passions; they do not liberate the minds of men from disease but infect them."

JAFGLW. 397 **gratificacionem** gratificacioni JFIL. 400 **xx** *om* E. 401 Bernardus *marg* E. **effundentur** effunduntur E. 402 **arriserit** promissa fuerit F; commissa est G; commissa fuerit W; accesserit I. 402 **est** *om* E. 403 **interitum** peccatum E; meritum L. **reddita sit** redierit E. 404 **non** bene E; *om* GLW. 405–6 **penitencialis** spiritualis AW; spiritualis *(canc)* penitencialis E. 406 **confusio** *add* uerecundie scilicet E. 408 **xxxiii** xxiii E. 410 **Maria** *in capital letters* E. 414 **et sequitur** *om* EAFL; et legitur W. **et sequitur . . . etc.** *om* F. 417 **Prouerbiorum** *add* in E; *add* 31 F. 418 Augustinus *marg* E. **et** *om* E. 419–21 **Alia . . . sanitatum** *after* etc *line 426* L. 421 **rerum** *om* F. 424 **in celo** *written twice* E. 425 **notus** *add* uel nominatus E. 426 **dicatur** dictum est GIW. 427 **necant** negant vel necant J; negant L; uocant W. 428 Boecius *marg* E. **sunt** *add* gracie E. 429 **racione** racionis F *and source.*

precidit uestes. “Amon” interpretatur remurmurans gratificacionem et signat inuidum qui gracie detrahit. Item superbia aufert graciam; Iacobi iiii: “Superbis Deus resi- / stit, humilibus autem f. 96ra dat graciam.” Item accidia aufert graciam; Ecclesiastici [xx]: “Gracie fatuorum [effundentur].” Bernardus: “Timendum est cum arriserit alicui gracia, ne eam perdat. Timendum [est] cum recesserit, ne in [interitum] cadat. Timendum est cum [reddita sit] post lapsum, ne ipsa [non] utatur ad fructum.”

Hec sunt que restituunt graciam: verecundia, scilicet penitencialis; Ecclesiastici iiii: “Est confusio ° adducens graciam.” Item lacrime conpunctionis. Vnde Moyses inuenit graciam coram Domino, Exodi [xxxiii]. “Moyses” aquosus uel assumptus ex aquis interpretatur, et lacrimantem pro peccatis signat. Item amaritudo contricionis; vnde Maria “inuenit graciam coram Domino,” Luce i. “Maria” interpretatur mare amarum, hoc est contricio, vel Syra lingua idem est quod domina. Item graciam conseruat elemosina; Ecclesiastici xxix: “Elemosina uiri quasi sacculus,” etc.; [et sequitur:] “et graciam eius conseruabit,” etc.

Sunt autem gracie exteriores que graciam interiorem uel inpediunt uel omnino auferunt. Quarum prima est pulcritudo corporis; Prouerbiorum ° fine: “Fallax gracia et uana est pulcritudo”; [et] Augustinus: “Pulcritudo donum Dei est, set suspectum.” Alia est fortitudo; Psalmus: “Non salvabitur gygas in multitudine virtutis sue.” Alia est sanitas corporis; Corinthiorum xii: “Alii gracia sanitatum.” Alia facultas rerum temporalium; Prouerbiorum xxv: “Gracia et amicicia liberant; quas tibi serua, / ne exprobrabilis fias.” Diues epulo habuit istam graciam, f. 96rb idest rerum affluenciam, set nullius sancti amiciciam; ideo in celo ° non est notus ° set dicitur “homo quidam,” et factus est exprobrabilis cum dicatur ei: “Fili, recordare,” etc. Iste gracie graciam gratum facientem necant, ut possit de eis dici quod de scienciis secularibus dicit Boecius I *Consolacionum*: “Hee sunt ° que infructuosis affectuum spinis uberem fructibus racione segetem necant, hominumque mentes afficiunt, morbo non liberant.”

II

ON HUMILITY

After having spoken of the virtues in general, we will now discuss them individually and begin with humility, for it is the remedy for pride—not because it is the first in the order of the virtues but in their preservation. Charity is the first as their mistress and form, for it gives to all others the power to gain merit. Faith is the first in terms of their origin, because it is the first habit of grace by which the other virtues exist in man. Therefore is faith called "substance," Hebrews 11; the Gloss: "that is, one foundation of believers." Even though faith is the first virtue in origin, nevertheless all virtues are simultaneous in time; Gregory: "The virtues fly in one flock." Humility is the first in the safekeeping of the virtues; Gregory: "Whoever gathers all the other virtues without humility, carries as it were dust into the wind." Bernard: "The religious life is built on poverty and is kept safe by humility."

Humility is either true or false. True humility is defined by Bernard as follows: "Humility is the virtue by which through perfect self-knowledge one becomes of small value to oneself." Another definition says: "Humility is the voluntary bending down of the mind when it considers its Creator or its own weakness." And this definition touches on the causes of becoming humble. True humility is divided into: humility of heart, of mouth, and of deed. Humility of heart has four aspects, the first of which is self-abasement. Matthew 8: "He who will come after me, let him deny," etc. Gregory: "He abases himself who, after trampling upon the swelling of pride, shows himself in God's eyes to be a stranger to himself." The second aspect is to despise no man in one's mind; Jerome: "The humble man despises no one, the meek man hurts no one." Moreover, Michol despised David for his humility and was punished with perpetual sterility, 2 Kings 6. This means: those who despise others become less able to receive grace and more prone to commit sins; Proverbs 28: "He that is easily stirred up to wrath, shall be more prone to sin." The third is to despise being despised, and this will arise from one's own deficiency when one notices that one is in no way self-sufficient but has all things from God's generosity.

II *om all MSS.* 1 **De humilitate** *rubr* JI; de uirtutibus in specie *rubr* EG; de humilitate uera *rubr* A; de [*erasure*] F; *om* L; de virtute humilitatis *rubr* W. 4 **prima** *add* in ordine JGW. 7 **ipse** *corr to* ipsa E. 9 Glossa *marg* E. 11 De humilitate *marg* E. **Gregorius** cuius E. 12 Gregorius *marg* E. 13–14 **congregat . . . portat** *om* L. 13 **quasi** *add* qui E. 13–14 **quasi . . . portat** etc FG. 14 Bernardus *marg* E. 17 Bernardus *marg* E. 18 **cognicione** congregacione I. **sibi ipsi** ipse sibi JFIW; *om* GL. **Alia . . . Humilitas** item E; humilitas alia W. 19–20 **uel . . . fragilitatis** *om* G. 20 **humiliacionis** diffinicionis F. 21 **operis** corporis JAI. 23 Gregorius *marg* E. **Matthei . . . etc.** *om* E. 23–24 **Gregorius** *om* GW. 26 Ieronimus *marg* E. 27 **Preterea** propterea GIW. 29 **est** *add* quod JAGILW. **alios** ceteros GIW. 30 **proniores** prompciores F. 31 **xxviii** xxix AW; 24 G. **peccata** peccandum AIL. 31–32 **procliuior** pronior I. 35 **suffragium** suffragia E. **proximorum** amicorum

[II]

[DE HUMILITATE]

Postquam dictum est de uirtutibus in genere, dicendum est de eis in specie, et primo de humilitate, quia ipsa est remedium superbie—non quod ipsa sit prima in ordine uirtutum set in earum conseruacione. Caritas est prima tanquam magistra uirtutum et forma, quia omnibus aliis dat efficaciam merendi. Fides est prima origine, quia ipsa est primus habitus gratuitus quo mediante cetere uirtutes insunt. Ideo dicitur fides "substancia," Hebreorum xi; Glossa: "idest unum credencium fundamentum." Et licet fides sit prima origine, omnes tamen uirtutes sunt simul tempore; [Gregorius]: "Uirtutes gregatim uolant." Humilitas est prima in conseruacione uirtutum; Gregorius: "Qui ceteras uirtutes sine humilitate congregat, quasi ° in uentum puluerem portat." Bernardus: "Religio in paupertate fun- / datur, in hu- f. 96va
militate custoditur."

Alia est humilitas uera, alia ficta. Humilitas uera sic diffinitur secundum Bernardum: "Humilitas est uirtus qua quis uerissima sui cognicione sibi ipsi uilescit." [Alia est huiusmodi: "Humilitas] est uoluntaria mentis inclinacio intuitu Conditoris uel proprie fragilitatis." Et hec tangit causas humiliacionis. Vera humilitas sic diuiditur: Alia est cordis, alia oris, alia operis. Illa que est cordis consistit in quatuor, quorum primum est semetipsum abnegare. [Matthei viii: "Qui uult post me uenire, abneget," etc.] Gregorius: "Semetipsum abnegat, qui calcato typo superbie ante Dei oculos sese a se alienum demonstrat." Secundum est ut neminem in animo contempnat; Ieronimus: "Humilis neminem contempnit, mansuetus neminem ledit." Preterea Michol contempsit Dauid propter suam humilitatem et recepit in penam perpetuam sterilitatem, II Regum vi. Hoc est: qui alios contempnunt, minus habiles ad graciam fiunt et proniores ad peccandum; Prouerbiorum xxviii: "Qui ad indignandum facilis est, erit ad peccata procliuior." Tercium est ut contempnat se contempni, et hoc erit ex defectu sui si se conspiciat in nullo sibi sufficere et omnia ex lar-

Thus one will always flee to God's help, the support of the saints, and the advice of one's neighbors. Such are the "poor in spirit," Matthew 5; the Greek text has "God's beggars or needy," that is, the humble who recognize that they need God in all things; and to them is promised the kingdom of heaven. The humble person trusts in God, the proud in himself. Therefore, he is like the bull who in his pride bellows against the thunder and is struck by lightning in the field; to whom it is said, Ecclesiasticus 6: "Do not extol yourself in the thoughts of your soul like a bull." Such a man is not poor in spirit but very rich and puffed up; to him Job 15 says: "Why does your spirit swell against God?" The proud of heart is like a bladder which swells up with the wind of vanity; that is, he becomes "puffed up by the sense of his flesh," Colossians 2. The fourth aspect is not to grieve when one is put down, but rather to "lay down one's greatness without tribulation," Job 36. One cannot do this as long as one is puffed up with the wind of pride, for one will yet burst in the furnace, that is, in tribulation, as Gregory says. Impure gold, which is alloyed with some other metal, bursts in the furnace; thus pride in tribulation. Ecclesiasticus 2: "Gold and silver are tried in the fire, but acceptable men in the furnace of humiliation."

Humility of mouth has four aspects, the first of which is to keep silence "until one is asked," according to Bernard. And Ecclesiasticus 32: "If you are asked twice, let your answer have an end"; that is, in addition bow your head out of humility, or let your speech begin discreetly and end with due measure, so as not to be superfluous. But many people are like the jackdaw or the parrot, which are very garrulous birds that learn human words and talk to themselves, ask and answer and greet passers-by without being themselves addressed. Of these it is said in Proverbs 18: "He that answers before he hears shows himself to be a fool and worthy of confusion." The second is to report one's deeds with humble words and not to praise them; and even when we have done all things well, let us say that "we are unprofitable servants," Luke 18, for the Lord threatens those who enlarge their own fringes. Sophonias 3: "I will take away your proud boasters." The third is to confess oneself low and impure. Such was the law for the leper, who signifies the sinner, Leviticus 13. The fourth is to praise other people's good without belittling it; Gregory: "True humility thinks little of itself and praises another man's good without malice."

I. **consilium** consilia E. 37 **recognoscunt** cognoscunt JFL. 39 **pre** *written twice* E. 43 **dicit** dicitur FL. **xv** xvi AGIW; 3 FL. 44 **que** qui JAF. **uanitatis** *add* sue J. 44–45 **uanitatis . . . inflatus** sic iste uento uanitatis sue inflatur E. 49 Gregorius *marg* E. **adultero** adulterino AI; ultimo F; altero GLW. 52 **receptibiles** acceptabiles F. **humiliacionis** humilitatis J; tribulacionis A. 53 **quorum** *om* EW. 54 Bernardus *marg* E. **usque** AF *and source*; ut EJ; *om* GILW. **interrogacionem** *add* loquatur solum E. 55 **xxxii** xxii E; xxii ⟨vel 32⟩ J; 3 I. 57 **vel** ut J. 59 **siccato** sicorico A; fiscato F; phitaco L. 62 **se** *om* E. 63 **et . . . dignum** *om* EL. 64 **uerbo** voce GIW; uerbo uel uoce A. **referre** proferre JFGIW. 65 **sumus** simus E. 66 **magnificantibus** *add* auferre E. 70 Gregorius *marg* E. 75 **preuenientes**

gitate Dei possidere. Ita semper confugiet ad Dei adiutorium et sanctorum [suffragium] et proximorum [consilium]. Tales sunt "pauperes spiritu," Matthei v; Grecus habet "Dei mendici uel egeni," idest humi- / les qui in omnibus se recognoscunt Deo indigere; f. 96vb
et istis promittitur regnum celorum. Humilis confidit in Deo, superbus in seipso. Vnde similis est thauro qui pre superbia contra tonitruum mugiens fulminatur in agro; cui dicitur Ecclesiastici vi: "Non te extollas in cogitacione tua ut thaurus." Talis non habet pauperem spiritum set ualde diuitem et inflatum; cui dicit Iob xv: "Quid tumet contra Deum spiritus tuus?" Superbus corde similis est vesice que tumet uento [uanitatis; scilicet "inflatus] sensu carnis sue," Colossensium ii. Quartum est ut non contristetur in sua deiectione, set ut "deponat magnitudinem suam sine tribulacione," Iob xxxvi. Hoc non posset quamdiu tumet uento superbie, quia adhuc crepabit in fornace, idest in tribulacione, ut dicit Gregorius. Aurum enim non purum de adultero metallo habens interceptum crepat in fornace; sic superbia in tribulacione. Ecclesiastici ii: "Aurum et argentum in igne probatur, homines uero receptibiles in camino humiliacionis."

Humilitas oris consistit in quatuor, [quorum] primum est taciturnitas "[usque] ad interrogacionem °," secundum Bernardum. Et Ecclesiastici [xxxii]: "Et si bis interrogatus fueris, habeat capud responsum tuum"; idest, adhuc inclina capud propter humilitatem, vel sermo tuus discretum sumat inicium et cum moderamine finem, ne / sit superfluus. Set multi sunt similes f. 97ra
graculo et siccato, que sunt aues multe garrulitatis et humana addiscunt uerba et cum seipsis locuntur, querunt, et respondent, et salutant transeuntes non salutati. De talibus dicitur Prouerbiorum xviii: "Qui prius respondit quam audiat, stultum [se] esse demonstrat [et confusione dignum]." Secundum est propria facta humili uerbo referre, non extollere; et eciam cum omnia bene fecerimus, dicamus quod "serui inutiles [sumus]," Luce xviii, quia Dominus comminatur proprias fimbrias magnificantibus °. Sophonie iii: "Auferam magniloquos superbie tue." Tercium est seipsum uilem et contaminatum proclamare. Hec enim fuit lex leprosi, qui peccatorem signat, Leuitici xiii. Quartum est aliena bona sine diminucione commendare; Gregorius: "Vera humilitas est que parua de se estimat et alterius bona sine liuore commendat."

Humility in deed has five aspects, the first of which is to place others above oneself or to give them greater honor; Romans 12: "With honor anticipating one another." The second is to choose the lower place; Luke 14: "Sit down in the lowest place." The third is to agree easily with the view or counsel of other people. For this teaches us "the wisdom that is from above"; for it is "easy to be persuaded and consenting to the good," James 3. The fourth is to submit oneself willingly to one's superiors and obey them; Jerome glosses Matthew 4 as follows: "Humility is true when obedience does not abandon it as its companion." And notice that humility is threefold: one is lesser, to submit oneself to people of higher standing; the second is greater, to submit oneself to one's equals; the third is the greatest and most perfect, namely, to submit oneself to one's inferiors. Of the last kind is said in Matthew 3: "So it becomes us to fulfill all justice"; Gloss: that is, perfect humility. And humility is fittingly called justice, because it is just that man, who in his sin refused to submit to his Creator, should humble himself so that he be subject. This is the saying of Gregory. The fifth is to do humble deeds, such as the works of penance in ashes and sackcloth, in waking and fasting. These are the works of husbandmen, that is, of simple people who do true penance, not of proud noblemen. Ecclesiasticus 7: "Hate not laborious works, nor husbandry ordained by the most High." "Husbandry" is the work of a husbandman, that is, humble penance, which the nobility that is worthy of damnation considers detestable; Ecclesiasticus 13: "Humility is an abomination to the proud." And since proud noblemen do not humble themselves in penance, they are to be humbled in pain; Proverbs 29: "Humiliation will follow the proud."

There are many ways to acquire and to protect humility. The first is to think of Christ's humility, which was the beginning of our salvation, just as the pride of the devil and of man was the beginning of our ruin. Ecclesiasticus 10: "All perdition," etc. Gregory: "We have an admirable example of humility, an admirable remedy against pride. Why, then, are you puffed up, man? O carrion skin, why do you inflate yourself? O ugly mass of blood, why do you swell up?" You are proud, and your prince is humble? Far be it! Behold how much Christ humbled himself, that he not only became like a man in the likeness of sinful flesh, but even that he could be compared to a worm, as in the Psalm: "But I am a worm and no man," etc. He can be compared to the woodworm, which is a worm that bores in wood. For when Christ was fastened on the wood of sal-

add etc JAFL. 77 **sensui** consensui E. **assentire** consentire GW. 80 Ieronimus *marg* E. 82 **humilitas** obediencia AW. **alia** altera FL. 84 **Sic** *add* enim E. 85 Glossa *marg* E. 85–87 **Et . . . humiliari** *om* E. 87 **subdatur** *add* homini A; *add* omnibus F; *add* creature L. 88 Gregorius *marg* E. **Sentencia . . . est *(1st)*** *om* L. **exercicium** *add* bonorum FL. 89 **penitencie** misericordie L. **cilicio** *add* et E. 89–90 **uigiliis** uigilia AGIW. 90 **et** *add* in E. **Hec . . . rusticorum** *om* L. **idest** et EJ; scilicet W. 92 **ab** in E. 94 **dampnabilis** *om* E. **nobilitas** uoluptas L. 94–95 **Abhominacio** abhominabilis GIW. 95 **non** *marg* E. 99–100 **que . . . salutis** *om* W. 100 **et hominis** est omnis J. **perdicionis** dampnacionis GIW. 101 Gregorius *marg* E. **x** *add* ab ipsa sumpsit inicium GIW. 101–2 **Habemus mirum** hoc est mirum J; habemus AG; huiusmodi F; habeamus uirum I. 103–4 **extenderis** *add* o E. 104 **feda** fetida GW. **Tu** *om* E. **es** *om* JFL; et inflatus AGIW. 109 **ligno** *add*

Humilitas operis consistit in quinque, quorum primum est alios sibi preponere siue honore preuenire; Romanorum xii: "Honore inuicem preuenientes." Secundum est inferiorem locum eligere; Luce xiiii: "Recumbe in nouissimo loco." Tercium est aliorum [sensui] uel consilio facile assentire. Hoc enim docet "sapiencia que desursum est"; est enim "suadibilis et bonis consenciens," Iacobi iii. Quartum est libenter subici maioribus et obedire; Glossa Ieronimi super Matthei iiii: "Vera humili- / tas est quam non deserit obediencia comes." Et nota quod est triplex humilitas: vna minor, subdere se maioribus; alia maior, subdere se equalibus; tercia maxima et perfectissima, scilicet subdere se minoribus. De qua Matthei iii: "Sic ° decet nos inplere omnem iusticiam"; Glossa: idest, perfectam humilitatem. [Et bene uocatur humilitas iusticia, quia iustum est hominem in tantum humiliari] ut subdatur, qui renuit peccando subesse Conditori. Sentencia Gregorii est. Quintum est exercicium humilium operum, ut sunt opera penitencie in cinere et cilicio, ° in uigiliis et ° ieiunio. Hec sunt opera rusticorum, [idest] simplicium uere penitencium, non nobilium superborum. Ecclesiastici vii: "Ne oderis laboriosa opera et rusticacionem [ab] Altissimo creatam." "Rusticacio" est opus rustici, scilicet humilis penitencia, quam [dampnabilis] nobilitas execratur; Ecclesiastici xiii: "Abhominacio est superbo humilitas." Et quia nobiles superbi non humiliantur in penitencia, ideo humiliandi sunt in pena; Prouerbiorum xxix: "Superbum sequetur humilitas."

f. 97rb

Sunt autem plura per que acquiritur humilitas et custoditur. Primum est consideracio humilitatis Christi, que fuit inicium salutis, sicut superbia dyaboli et hominis inicium perdicionis. Ecclesiastici x: "Omnis perdicio," etc. Gregorius: "Habemus mirum humilitatis exemplum, mirum superbie medicamentum. Quid ergo intumescis, o homo? O pellis morticina, quid extenderis? ° Sanies feda, quid inflaris?" [Tu] superbus es, et prin- / ceps tuus humilis? Absit! Et uide quantum humiliatus est Christus, ut non solum assimilaretur homini in similitudinem carnis peccati, set ut eciam conpararetur uermi, ut in Psalmo: "Ego autem sum uermis et non homo," etc. Potest autem conparari teredoni, idest vermi qui lignum terebrat. Ipse enim affixus ligno

f. 97va

vation, he bored, as it were, and devoured the wood of damnation. He is, therefore, prefigured by David, who is called "the most tender little worm of the wood." And Christ is called a worm because of his origin and lowness. Because of his origin: he was born of a virgin without fleshly sin, just as a worm is bred without intercourse either from some vapor or from putrefaction. Some other worm is bred from the earth which is called earthworm, and it lives in low and moist places, is long and soft, pulls itself along by its mouth, and does not stretch out until it has contracted itself. In these properties Christ is a worm. He was born of earth, that is, he took flesh from a virgin; the Psalm: "Truth is sprung out of earth." Therefore, in his incarnation he was truly humble, that is, "bent to humus," according to Isidore, when he assumed the nature of an earthly creature. He was further *intestinum terre,* "an earthworm," full of men's abuse and mockery, just as *intestina,* "entrails," contain ugly things. For he took upon himself punishment, he endured disgrace, he bore the pain "of our sins in his body upon the wood," 1 Peter 2. Further, *intestinum,* "entrails," refers to God's internal mercy, because he patiently endures our filth until he casts it out through penance or through punishment; Luke 2: "Through the bowels of the mercy of God," etc. Further, Christ pulled himself along on the earth by his mouth when he converted many by his preaching; Luke 4: "They wondered at the words of grace that proceeded from his mouth." Further, he first contracted himself when he was enclosed in the Virgin's womb before he stretched himself out in his teaching and working of miracles; but after he was taken from the manger and exalted on the gibbet, he became visible to the whole world by his teaching and miracles, and he has become "the light of the Gentiles and their salvation even to the farthest part of the earth," Isaias 49.

Another thing which induces humility is to consider our miserable status. For man is formed "from the slime of the earth," Genesis 2, and he dissolves into clay; Job 13: "Your necks will be brought to clay." The third is to consider our own baseness, for man is nothing else than a sackful of dung and food for worms; Micheas 7: "Your humiliation is in your midst," that is, the cause for your humiliation, for in our stomach lies a lump of phlegm, which looks extremely disgusting when it is thrown up in drunkenness; in our bowels are excrements, and in our loins the most vile matter of the human body. The fourth is the fragility of our flesh; Job 30: "I am compared to dirt, embers, and ashes." The human body is a very fragile vessel, and once it is broken, it cannot be repaired by man, just as pottery once it has been broken "with a mighty break-

crucis idest ligno E. 112–13 **et . . . originis** *om* FGILW. 113 **culpa** copula FGIW; concupiscencia L. 118–19 **idest . . . incarnatus** *om* AI. 120 Ysidorus *marg* E. 122 **plenus** plenum L; plenus ⟨vel plenum⟩ J. **irrisionibus** illusionibus E. 125–26 **interna** *om* F. 126 **pacienter** per pacienciam GIW. 127 **emittat** emittit E; exuat AGW; dimittat F. **ii** *om* EW. 128 **traxit** trahit EIL. 129 **multitudinem** *add* gencium AFIW. 130 **Mirabantur** *add* omnes E. **in** de E. **gracie** *om* E. **que** *marg* E. 131 **eius** dei E. **clausus** *om* F. 132 **assumptus** *add* est E. 134 **factus** *add* est E. **salutem** salute E. 136 **Aliud** secundum E. 137 **formatus** formatur FL. 139 **proprie** perpetue E. 140 **homo** *add* scilicet E. 141 **tua** *om* E. 142 **tissanaria** fimaria J; tussanaria F; fisanaria G. 143 **cum reicitur** cum reuertitur F; *om* I. 144 **materia** membra IW. 146 **uas** *om* EW. 149 **dicit** *marg* E.

° salutis quasi terebrauit et consumpsit lignum dampnacionis. Vnde ipse figuratur per Dauid, qui dicitur "tenerrimus ligni uermiculus." Et dicitur Christus uermis racione originis et uilitatis. Racione originis: natus de uirgine sine culpa carnis, sicut sine coitu nascitur uermis aut exalacione aut ex putrefactione. Item quidam uermis de terra oritur qui intestinum terre dicitur, in locis humidis et humilibus manens, longus et mollis, ore se trahens, nec extenditur prius quam in se contrahatur. Hiis proprietatibus est Christus uermis. De terra natus, idest de uirgine incarnatus; Psalmus: "Veritas de terra orta est." Vnde in incarnacione uere fuit humilis, idest "humo acclinis," secundum Ysidorum, cum scilicet assumpsit naturam terreni generis. Item ipse fuit terre intestinum plenus obprobriis et [irrisionibus] hominum, sicut intestina continent feda. Ipse enim penalitates assumpsit, feda sustinuit, penam eciam "peccatorum nostrorum tulit in corpore suo super lignum," I Petri ii. Preterea intestinum dicitur interna Dei misericordia, quia fe- / da nostra pacienter tolerat do- f. 97vb
nec ea per penitenciam uel per penam [emittat]; Luce [ii]: "Per uiscera misericordie Dei," etc. Item Christus ore se [traxit] super terram quando predicacione sua multitudinem conuertit; Luce iiii: "Mirabantur ° [in] uerbis [gracie] que procedebant de ore [eius]." Item prius se contraxit clausus utero Uirginis quam extenderetur in doctrina et miraculis; set postea assumptus ° de presepio et exaltatus in patibulo, doctrina et miraculis claruit toti mundo, factus ° "in lucem Gencium et [salutem] usque ad extremum terre," Ysaie xlix.

[Aliud] quod humilitatem inducit est consideracio nostre abiecte condicionis. Homo enim formatus "de limo terre," Genesis ii, in lutum resoluitur; Iob xiii: "Redigentur in lutum ceruices uestre." Tercium est consideracio [proprie] uilitatis, quod nichil aliud sit homo ° quam saccus stercorum et cibus uermium; Michee vii: "Humiliacio [tua] in medio tui," idest, causa humiliacionis, quia in stomacho est massa tissanaria, que ualde uilis apparet cum reicitur in crapula; in uisceribus sunt stercora, in renibus uilissima humani corporis materia. Quartum est carnis fragilitas; Iob xxx: "Conparatus sum luto, fauille, et cineri." Valde fragile [uas] est corpus humanum, et cum frangitur, ab ho-

ing," Isaias 30. The fifth is the instability of our heart, for as Gregory says: "Nothing is flightier than our heart." Job 20: "Various thoughts succeed one another, and my mind is hurried away to different things." The sixth is our inclination to sin. Genesis 9: "The senses and thought of man are prone to evil from his youth." Galatians, near the end: "Considering yourself, lest you also be tempted." Bernard: "Considering how prone to sin, how easy to be tempted." The seventh is how we sin continuously; Proverbs 24: "A just man falls seven times a day." The eighth is the difficulty of rising again; Osee 13: "Destruction is your own, O Israel, says the Lord; from me is your help"; that is, man is the cause of his own damnation but not of his salvation, nor does he rise without the help of the Savior. This is what is meant by the Psalm: "A breath that goes and does not return." The ninth is to consider what is greater and better than we are. Bernard: "Just as examining what is worse fosters pride, so looking at what is better cautions us to be humble." Job 33 says of the humble penitent: "He shall look upon men and shall say, 'I have sinned and indeed I have offended, and I have not received what I have deserved.'" The tenth is the uncertainty of our merits, for "man does not know whether he is worthy of hatred or love," Ecclesiastes 9. It is very hard if one knows beyond doubt that one has sinned a hundred times and not once truly repented. The eleventh is the shortness of life; Job 16, at the end: "Short years pass away, and I am walking in a path by which I shall not return." The twelfth is the inevitability of death. Ecclesiastes 2: "The learned dies in like manner as the unlearned." Boethius in his *Consolation*: "Death shrouds the lowly together with the lofty head." And Seneca says: "Death tramples under the same foot the rich man's castle and the poor man's hovel."

Humility is good for many things. First, for receiving grace. An example is the Blessed Virgin: "He has regarded the humility of his handmaid," Luke 1. Humility is the proper receptacle for grace, as a hollow vessel holds more liquid and soft wool more dye. Also, a river spreads out from its bed to fill low-lying lands. The Holy Spirit is like a full river, whose waters are the gifts of grace which flow to the humble. The Psalm: "The stream of the river makes the city of God joyful." Second, humility is good for the increase of grace; the Psalm: "The vales shall abound with wheat," that is, the humble with grace. Third, for the preservation of grace; Gregory: "Everything we do perishes unless it is

149 Gregorius *marg* E. **fugacius** *add* Basilius: "Talis est vita nostra ut neque ea que prospera sunt nec ea que tristia perseverent" F. 151 **cogitacio** cogitaciones GI. **hominis** humani cordis AILW; humani corporis vel cordis FG. 152 **fine** *om* EG; 6 f F. 153 Bernardus *marg* E. 155 **xxiiii** xiiii JAI; 29 G. 156 **resurgendi** *om* I. **Osee** *om with blank* E. 157 **dicit . . . ex** tantummodo in F. 158 **dampnacionis** perdicionis dampnacionis FL. **resurgit** resurget FL; redire potest GIW. 159 **rediens** *add* Bernardus: "Si me inspicio, tolerare meipsum non possum, tanta in me que digna sunt reprehensione et confusione inuenio; et quanto sepius me et subtilius discucio, tanto plures abhominaciones in angulis cordis mee inuenio" F. 160–61 **maiorum . . . consideracio** *om* A. 161 Bernardus *marg* E. **peioris** prioris E. 164 **non** *om* E. 166 **Ecclesiaste** Ecclesiastici E. 167 **peccasse** peccare EAFL. **uere . . . penituisse** se semel uere uelit penituisse J. 168 **fine** *om* EL. **transeunt** transierunt E. 169 **reuertar** reuertor E. 170 **Ecclesiaste** Ecclesiastici E. **Moritur** morientur E. **et** ut AFILW; et *interl for canc* ut J; similiter et G. 171 Boecius *marg* E. 172 Seneca *marg* E. **turres** edes L. 177 **recipit** continet I. 179 **est** *om* E. **Spiritus Sanctus** *om* G. 180–81 **Fluminis . . . Psalmus** *om* L. 182 **humiles** *om* F. **gra-**

mine non reparatur, sicut nec testa cum frangitur "contricione perualida," Ysaie xxx. Quintum est cordis mutabilitas, quia ut dicit Gregorius: "Nichil / corde fugacius." Iob xx: "Cogitaciones f. 98ra uarie succedunt sibi et mens in diuersa rapitur." Sextum est peccandi pronitas. Genesis ix: "Sensus et cogitacio hominis prona sunt in malum ab adolescencia sua." Galatarum [fine]: "Considerans teipsum, ne et tu tempteris." Bernardus: "Considerans quam pronus ad peccandum, quam facilis ad temptandum." Septimum est peccandi assiduitas; Prouerbiorum xxiiii: "Sepcies in die cadit iustus." Octauum est resurgendi difficultas; [Osee] xiii: "Perdicio tua, Israel, dicit Dominus; ex me auxilium tuum"; idest, homo est sibi causa dampnacionis set non salutis, nec resurgit sine adiutorio Saluatoris. Hoc est in Psalmo: "Spiritus uadens et non rediens." Nonum est consideracio maiorum et meliorum. Bernardus: "Sicut incentiuum est elacionis [peioris] consideracio, ita cautela humilitatis est respectus melioris." Iob xxxiii de humili penitente dicit: "Respiciet homines et dicet, 'Peccaui et uere deliqui, et ut dignus eram [non] recepi.'" Decimum est incertitudo meritorum, quia "nescit homo utrum odio an amore dignus sit," [Ecclesiaste] ix. Satis durum est homini quod absque dubio nouit se cencies [peccasse] nec tamen uere semel penituisse. Undecimum est uite breuitas; Iob xvi [fine]: "Breues anni [transeunt], et semitam per quam non [reuertar] ambulo." Duodecimum est moriendi necessitas. [Ecclesiaste] / ii: "[Moritur] doctus et indoc- f. 98rb tus." Boecius in *Consolacionibus*: "Mors inuoluit simul humile et excelsum capud." Seneca: "Mors pulsat equo pede diuitum turres et pauperum tuguria."

Humilitas ualet ad plura. Primo ad gracie suscepcionem. Exemplum de Beata Uirgine: "Respexit humilitatem ancille sue," Luce i. Humilitas est proprium receptaculum gracie, sicut uas concauum plus recipit de liquore et lana mollis de colore. Fluuius eciam facit diuerticula a canali suo, ut inpleat loca humilia. Quasi fluuius [est] habundans Spiritus Sanctus, cuius aque sunt dona gracie que ad humiles fluunt. Psalmus: "Fluminis inpetus letificat ciuitatem Dei." Secundo, ualet ad gracie augmentum; Psalmus: "Valles habundabunt frumento," idest humiles [gracia]. Tercio, ad gracie conseruacionem; Gregorius: "Perit omne quod agitur

carefully protected by humility." Fourth, humility is good for the resting of the Holy Spirit; Isaias at the end: "On whom shall my spirit rest but the humble?" Fifth, humility is good for God's remembrance, namely that God may remember the humble; the Psalm: "The Lord was mindful of us in our humility." Sixth, for victory over the devil, because as we read in the *Lives of the Fathers*, the devil is not overcome in fasting, because he does not eat; nor in waking, because he does not sleep; but he is defeated by humility and charity. In the seventh place, humility is good for avoiding the snares of the devil. Blessed Antony saw the whole world full of the snares of demons and said: "Who will avoid these?" And he was told: "Humility." In the eighth place, it is good for being raised to heaven; Luke 14: "He that humbles himself shall be exalted." Daniel 4: "The Lord will appoint the most humble man over the kingdom."

Humility can be learned from examples, so that if someone becomes exalted on account of the grace he has received, he may become humble because of the sin he has committed. For the peacock, when it looks at its shining feathers, has reason for pride; but when it looks at its black feet and listens to its awful voice, it has reason to blush. So the Apostle says meaningfully at the end of Galatians: "Considering yourself, lest you also be tempted," as if he were saying: see what you have of your self, and not only of your self but from the gift of grace. Likewise, if we look constantly into the light, our eye grows either dim or blind. The bear, for example, when it looks at a shining basin, loses its eyesight. Thus, when man pays too much attention to the gifts of grace in himself and forgets his own abject state, he falls into the blindness of vainglory, and then "he stumbles at noonday as in darkness," Isaias 59. Further, if one wanted to climb a steep mountain, it would be necessary for him to bend forward; but if he were to descend, he could walk erect. Thus, with humility man climbs to heaven, with pride he goes down to hell, for "easy is the descent to Avernus; and to pass out to the upper air, this is the toil. Few are those whom their virtue has lifted up to heaven." This is what is reported in Kings 14, that Jonathan climbed the slope of a mountain, "creeping on his hands and feet, and his armorbearer after him." In this way Christ ascended to heaven, with his hands and feet nailed down and his head bent low. His armorbearer

cia *om* E. 183 Gregorius *marg* E. 184 **caute** *blank* J; *om* GIW. 185 **requiem** suscepcionem E; replecionem A; repleciones I. **fine** *om* E; ultimo G; 7 FL. 186–87 **ut . . . humilium** iam nos erit memor nostri I. 188 **deuictionem** confusionem A; deuitacionem FL; deuicti confusionem GI; diuiti confusionem W. 189–90 **non . . . quia** ieiuno non comedit, uigilo E; ieiunio non *(apparently to be replaced by:)* ⟨quod ieiunio non uincitur diabolus⟩ quia non commedit vigiliis non quia J; non uincitur ieiunio quia non comedit uigilia non quia A; de diabolo quod non uincitur ieiunio quia non comedit uigiliis quia F; ieiunio non quia diabolus non comedit uigilia non quia G; quod diabolus non ieiunio quia non comedit non vigilia quia I; ieiunio non quia non comedit vigiliis non quia L; quod diabolus non ieiunat quia non comedit nec vigilat quia W. 191 **Septimo** *add* ualet JAFL; est W. 194 **exaltacionem** *add* quia J; *add* unde A. 194–95 **humiliat exaltabitur** exaltat humiliabitur et qui se humiliat exaltabitur E; exaltat humiliabitur J. 199 **si** *add* uero GIW. 200–201 **signanter dicit** *om* GIW. 201 **Galatarum** *om* E. **fine** *om* EG; v J; 8 F. 202–3 **ex te set quid** *om* EAGIW. 203 **quid** *om* FL. **assidue** continue GI; *om* W. 205 **nimis** *om* FL; nimium GW. 206 **incurrit** *add* propriam E. 207 **lix** *add*

nisi in humilitate caute custodiatur." Quarto, ad Spiritus Sancti [requiem]; Ysaie [fine]: "Super quem requiescet spiritus meus nisi super humilem?" Quinto, ad Dei memoriam, ut Deus scilicet memoretur humilium; Psalmus: "Dominus in humilitate nostra memor fuit nostri." Sexto, ad demonis deuictionem, quia ut legitur in *Uitas Patrum* [non uincitur diabolus ieiunio, quia non comedit; uigiliis non, quia] non dormit; set humilitate uincitur et caritate. Septimo, ad laqueorum demonis euasionem. Vnde beatus Antonius uidit totum mundum plenum laqueis demonum et dixit: "Quis euadet / istos?" Et responsum est ei: "Humilitas." f. 98^{v}a
Octauo ualet ad celestem exaltacionem; Luce xiiii: "Qui se [humiliat, exaltabitur]." Danielis iiii: "Humillimum Dominus constituet hominem super regnum."

Per exempla potest humilitas edoceri, ut siquis eleuetur de gracia sibi collata, humilietur de culpa perpetrata. Pavo enim si lucentes pennas respiciat, habet unde superbiat; si nigros pedes et horribilem uocem attendat, habet unde erubescat. Ideo signanter dicit Apostolus, [Galatarum fine]: "Considerans teipsum ne et tu tempteris," quasi: vide quid sit ex te, et non solum quid [ex te set quid] ex dono gracie. Item, si oculus assidue respiciat lucem, uel tenebrescit uel excecatur. Exemplum de urso qui respiciens peluim candentem perdit uisum. Sic cum quis nimis attendit in se dona gracie oblitus proprie miserie, incurrit ° cecitatem uane glorie, et tunc inpingit "meridie quasi in tenebris," Ysaie lix. Item siquis uellet ascendere montem prominentem, necesse esset ipsum inclinari; si uero descenderet, posset erectus incedere. Ita cum humilitate ad celum ascenditur, cum superbia ad inferos descenditur, quia "facilis descensus Auerni; [superasque] euadere ad auras, [hic labor est. Pauci quos vexit ad ethera uirtus]." Hoc est quod dicitur ° Regum xiiii, quod [Ionathas] ascendit cliuum montis "reptans manibus et pedibus, et armiger eius post eum."
Ita Christus ascendit [in] celum manibus et / pedibus affixis et f. 98^{v}b

Gregorius: "Cum bona, fratres, agitis, semper ad memoriam mala acta revocate, ut cum caute culpa aspicitur, nunquam de bono opere animus incaute letetur" I. 209 **inclinari** inclinare JFL; incuruare se GIW; incuruare se siue inclinare A. 211 **superasque** superasset E; superas et J. 212 **hic . . . uirtus** *om* EGW. **vexit** vexat J; vehit I; *om* L. 212–13 **Hoc . . . dicitur** unde GIW. 213 **dicitur** *add* II E; *add* I I. **Ionathas** *om* E. 215 **in** *om* EA; ad GW. **affixis** *add* in ligno crucis A. 216 **qui se-**

who follows him is any faithful who imitates the humility of his passion and who with the newt "supports himself with his hands," Proverbs, near the end, that is, who follows Christ by creeping on his affections and deeds. Further, if one wants to see the stars by day, one must go down into a deep well. Thus he who wants to know the life of saints and follow their teaching must go down into deep humility, and thus he will know the truth which the Lord reveals to little ones, that is, the humble, and hides from the wise, Matthew 11. In the well of humility lies hidden the knowledge of truth. Hence the Academy said that truth hides in a deep well. The same is said in Luke 10: "Mary was sitting at the Lord's feet so that she might hear God's word"; the Gloss: "The lower she sits, the more abundantly she receives." On the other hand, Gregory states: "A puffed-up mind is a hindrance to truth." Likewise, the deeper the roots of the tree penetrate into the ground, the higher its branches rise. Thus, the deeper humility's root lies in our heart, the loftier will be the fruit of our virtues, that is, our reward itself. Isaias 37: "That which is saved of Juda shall take root downward and shall bear fruit upward." In contrast, of the wicked who has neither virtues nor reward Job 18 says: "Let his roots dry up beneath; let his harvest be destroyed above." Also, the deeper the foundations of a castle are, the more firmly will its tower withstand the blows from the siege engines. The castle is the company of virtues; Canticles 7: "What will you see in the Shulamite but the companies of camps?" The Shulamite stands for the faithful soul that is fortified with companies of camps, that is, with virtuous habits and deeds and with guardian angels. The foundation of this castle is humility, the siege engines are demonic temptations. Nebuchadnezzar, the king of Babylon, "sets battering rams," that is engines, "against our gates," that is, against the five bodily senses, Ezechiel 21. To build this tower is to ground our virtues in humility, Luke 14. Further, if someone brought the king or the prince a tiny gift in a large container, such as an apple in a hamper or a cupful of wine in a barrel, it would be a ludicrous present; but if the container were proportionate to its content, the present would be acceptable. Thus, since our deeds are small and imperfect, if we offer them with a puffed-up heart, we do not appease God; only if we do so with a contrite and humble heart, Daniel 3. And Ecclesiasticus 3: "The greater you are, humble yourself all the more in all things, and you shall find grace before God."

quitur *om* GIW. 217–19 **et . . . sequitur** *om* GIW. 218 **fine** *om* EL. 220 **est** *om* E. **profundum** *om* E. 222 **ueritatem** uirtutem F. 224 **xi** *add* f AFGIW. **latet** iacet J. **agnicio** cognicio AGI. 225 **Achademici** *corr from* achedemici E; achademia F. 225–26 **hoc . . . dicitur** unde GIW. 227 Glossa *marg* E. 227–28 **Glossa . . . Econtra** *om* L. 228 Gregorius *marg* E. **Tumor** timor JIW. 232 **xxxvii** xxxiii E; vii W. 233–34 **de inpio** *om* E. 234 **xviii** xxviii E. 235 **atteratur** atteritur E. 238 **uidebis** uidebitis E. 242 **enim** *om* EL. 244 **Turrem** turrim AFLW. 245 **Item** *om* EFLW. 246 **offerret** offert EW; offert ⟨vel offerret⟩ J; afferret FL; conferret G. 247 **ut** *add* unum GIW. **ciphatum** ciphum E. 248 **mensurabile** commensurabile AIW. 249 **parua . . . inperfecta** sint opera nostra inperfecta vel eciam perfecta GIW. **inperfecta** *add* uel eciam perfecta A. 251–52 **magnus** maior

capite inclinato. Armiger eius qui sequitur est quilibet fidelis qui humilitatem passionis eius imitatur et cum stellione "manibus nititur," Prouerbiorum [fine], idest affectibus et operibus reptans Christum sequitur. Item siquis uult stellas de die uidere, necesse [est] ipsum in puteum [profundum] descendere. Ita qui uult cognoscere sanctorum uitam et sequi doctrinam, descendat in profundam humilitatem, et sic cognoscet ueritatem quam Dominus reuelat paruulis, idest humilibus, et abscondit a sapientibus, Matthei xi. In puteo humilitatis latet agnicio ueritatis. Vnde Achademici dixerunt ueritatem latere in puteo profundo. Hoc est quod dicitur Luce x: "Maria sedebat secus pedes Domini ut audiat uerbum Dei"; Glossa: "Quanto humilius sedet, tanto amplius capit." Econtra Gregorius: "Tumor mentis obstaculum ueritatis." Item quanto radices arboris penetrant terram profundius, tanto rami surgunt sublimius. Sic quanto radix humilitatis fuerit in corde profundior, tanto uirtutum fructus erit sublimior, idest ipsa remuneracio. Ysaie [xxxvii]: "Quod saluatum est de Iuda mittet radices deorsum et faciet fructum sursum." Econtra [de inpio] qui nec habet uirtutes nec meritum, Iob [xviii]: "Deorsum radices eius siccentur; sursum autem [atteratur] messis eius." Item quanto fundamentum castri est profundius, / tanto turris eius f. 99ra
contra machinarum ictus resistit forcius. Castrum est uirtutum congeries; Canticorum vii: "Quid [uidebis] in Sunamite nisi choros castrorum?" Sunamitis est anima fidelis que munitur castrorum choris, idest uirtutum habitibus et operibus et angelicis custodiis. Fundamentum castri humilitas est, machine inpugnantes sunt demonum temptaciones. Nabuchodonosor [enim] rex Babylonis "ponit arietes," idest machinas, "contra portas nostras," idest contra quinque corporis sensus, Ezechielis xxi. Turrem istam edificare est uirtutes in humilitate fundare, Luce xiiii. [Item] siquis [offerret] regi uel principi exiguum munus in magno uase, ut pomum in sporta uel [ciphatum] uini in dolio, ridiculosum esset exenium; set si uas esset contento mensurabile, fieret exenium acceptabile. Ita cum parua sunt opera nostra et inperfecta, si cum tumido corde offerimus, Deum non placamus; set cum corde contrito et humili, Danielis iii. Et Ecclesiastici iii: "Quanto magnus es, humilia te in omnibus, et coram Deo inuenies graciam."

This is what the Lord said to his apostles, Matthew 18: "Unless you are converted and become as little children, you shall not enter into the kingdom of heaven." "Converted," add: from the state of sin to that of innocence, from the state of pride to that of humility; "and you shall become as little children," that is, you shall have through grace what they have by nature, humility and cleanness. That is what the Lord commanded in Exodus 13: "The firstborn of an ass you shall change for a sheep." To do so "means to transform the beginning of an unclean life into sincere innocence," as Gregory says. Moreover, a child is content with little; thus also the humble. Timothy, at the end: "Having food and wherewith to be covered, with these let us be content." And Ecclesiasticus 29: "Be contented with little instead of much, and you will not hear the reproach." A little child also is pure and innocent. Such cling to the Lord; the Psalm: "The innocent and the upright have adhered to me." A child does not remember its hurt. Leviticus 19: "You shall not be mindful of the injury of your citizens." Seneca: "It is hurtful to remember one's hurt." Also, when a little child has fallen down, he runs to his mother and shows her his hands. Thus, the humble of heart shows his fall to the Church; Ecclesiasticus 18: "Humble yourself before you are sick, and in the time of sickness show your way of life." Further, we must not think it below our dignity to become like little children, since Christ became a child, he who is boundless in power and wisdom. This child gave his bread for an apple, that is to say, he gave himself as living bread, John 6, in place of that forbidden fruit which the woman had plucked from the tree. And Christ hung this bread on the tree so that, in contrast, salvation might spring from it. Jeremias 11: "Let us put wood on his bread," that is, on him who is bread. These are the words of those who put him on the cross. The Hebrew text reads *"lechen,"* which means back or bread.

Another example of humility comes from the Saracen merchants who, as they travel through various countries and fear thieves or robbers, pulverize their gold with quicksilver, which is a powerful solvent; and when they arrive at their destination, they melt their gold down and have it again pure. Our gold is the substance of our virtues; Proverbs 12: "The substance of a man is precious gold," that is virtues and merits. To pulverize this gold means to think little or nothing of our virtues and merits, as Abraham did, Genesis 18: "Whereas I am dust and ashes." Quicksilver is the humility of an active nature, which is ready

JAI. 256 **a . . . humilitatis** *om* L. **statum** *add* humiliacionis uel E. 258 **Hoc est quod** unde GIW. 261 Gregorius *marg* E. **conuertere** auertere GL; aduertere I; adultere W. 262 **fine** *om* E; 6 FG. 266 **meminit** *add* iniuriarum A; *add* lesum FL. 267–68 **ciuium . . . iniurie** *om* I. 267 Seneca *marg* E. 268 **meminisse** *add* suple ad uindictam non ad correpcionem J. 269 **humilis** humiles E. 270 **manifestat** manifestant E; *add* matri L. 272 **fieri** esse GILW. 273 **Christus** *om* A; *add* pro nobis L. **immensus** *om* L. 275 **Et** *om* E. 275–76 **Et . . . ligno** *om* W. 276 **oriretur** *add* mundo J. 277 **in *(2nd)*** *om* E. 278 **Verbum . . . est** verba crucifixorum sunt GIW. 278–79 **Verbum . . . panem** *om* E. 279 **dorsum** deorsum FGLW. 280 **Aliud . . . est** item exemplum GIW. 281 **regna** loca GIW; regiones L. **transeuntes** transfretantes J. 281–82 **pertimentes** pertimescentes J; timentes FGILW. 285 **nostrum** *om* GW. 286–87 **idest . . . est** que est puluerizanda idest I. **istud . . . merita** *om* GLW. 287 **reputare** *add* debemus GIW. 288 **xviii** *add* dicens AFGILW. **puluis et** *om* E. **cinis** *add* etc E. 289 **nature** uite FL. 289–90 **bona parata** parata bona E; bona productiua I; bona perdita W. 290 **examinatum** probatum J. 292 **argentariis** argentarii

Hoc est quod Dominus dixit apostolis, Matthei xviii: "Nisi conuersi fueritis et efficiamini sicut paruuli, non intrabitis in regnum celorum." "Conuersi," suple: a statu culpe ad statum innocencie, a statu elacionis ad statum ° humilitatis; "et efficiamini sicut paruuli," idest habentes per graciam quod illi per naturam, / [f. 99rb] humilitatem scilicet et mundiciam. Hoc est quod Dominus precepit Exodi xiii: "Primogenitum asini commutabis oue." Hoc enim facere "est inmunde uite primordia in innocencie simplicitatem conuertere," ut dicit Gregorius. Item paruulus contentus est modicis; ita et humilis. Thymothei [fine]: "Habentes alimenta et quibus tegamur, hiis contenti simus." Et Ecclesiastici xxix: "Minimum pro magno placeat tibi, et inproperium non audies." Item mundus et innocens est. Tales adherent Domino; Psalmus: "Innocentes et recti adheserunt michi." Item lesus non meminit. Leuitici xix: "Non eris memor iniurie ciuium tuorum." Seneca: "Iniuria est iniurie meminisse." Item paruulus post casum ad matrem currit et manus ostendit. Sic [humilis] corde lapsum suum [manifestat] Ecclesie; Ecclesiastici xviii: "Ante languorem humilia te, et in tempore infirmitatis ostende conuersacionem tuam." Item non debemus dedignari fieri paruuli, ex quo paruulus factus est Christus potencia et sapiencia immensus. Iste paruulus dedit panem suum pro pomo, idest seipsum panem uiuum, Iohannis vi, pro fructu uetito quem mulier sumpsit de ligno. [Et] Christus affixit panem ligno ut salus oriretur a contrario. Ieremie xi: "Mittamus lignum in panem eius," idest [in] ipsum qui est panis. [Verbum crucifixorum est. Hebreus habet "lechen," quod sonat dorsum uel panem.]

Aliud exemplum humilitatis est de mercatoribus Sarracenis qui per diuersa regna transeuntes et latrones / [f. 99va] uel predones pertimentes puluerizant aurum suum cum argento uiuo, quod est ualde penetratiue nature; et cum uenerint ad locum propositum, conflant aurum suum et habent illud purgatissimum. Aurum nostrum est substancia uirtutum; Prouerbiorum xii: "Substancia hominis auri precium," idest uirtutes et merita. Istud aurum puluerizare est uirtutes et merita parua uel nulla reputare, sicut fecit Abraham, Genesis xviii: "Cum sim [puluis et] cinis" °. Argentum uiuum est humilitas actiue nature, quia ad omnia [bona

for all good things. Humility is "silver tried in fire" because it is purified by tribulation. And just as quicksilver is found in places of small value, such as the furnaces of silversmiths, or the mire in wells, or very old waste in sewers, according to Isidore, thus humility is quite easily found when we think of our own small value. Micheas 6: "Your humiliation is in your midst." And our gold must be pulverized because of thieves, that is, demons who stealthily lie in wait for us. Job 19: "His thieves have come by me." And Gregory says in his *Homilies on the Gospels*: "Demons, like thieves, are on the lookout on our journey." Therefore, he who carries his treasure openly on his way invites being plundered. But when we arrive at our destination, that is, our heavenly home, all the dust will be melted down, because then all the humiliation of this life and all the disdain of other people will end, and then "the trial of our faith," that is, its reward, "will be much more precious than gold that is tried by the fire," 1 Peter 1.

In the beginning the Lord created two lights: "a greater light," Genesis 1, which prefigures charity; "and a lesser light," which prefigures humility. Humility is like the moon for several reasons. First, in Greek the moon is called *"mene,"* which means defect, from which *mensis,* "the month," has its name; thus, humility always judges itself deficient in itself and from itself. The Psalm says: "Their soul," that is, of the humble, "fainted in them"; and in another Psalm: "When my spirit failed me," that is, when I judged my own spirit deficient, "you knew," that is, you approved of, "my paths," that is, my deeds and intentions. Secondly, the moon borrows all its light from the sun. Thus humility takes everything as received from Christ and credits nothing to itself; Corinthians 4: "What do you have that you have not received?" The third is that the more light the moon receives from the sun, the more clearly appears the spot in it which comes from the earth's shadow or from its own composition. Thus, the more humility grows, the more clearly does it recognize its defects, just as specks of dust in the sunbeam. Gregory, towards the end of his *Morals*: "The more light of grace one receives, the more reprehensible he finds himself to be." The fourth is that the moon is a wandering star; and true humility is always afraid of wandering astray. Gregory: "It is a sign of a good conscience to acknowledge fault in itself even where there is none." The fifth is that the moon is closer to the earth than any other planet; thus, humility holds itself to be lower than anyone else. For this reason, *humilis,* "humble," is derived

E. 293 Ysidorus *marg* E. 294 **inuenitur** reperitur EF. 295 **vi** v EA. **Et aurum** item argentum E. 297 Gregorius *marg* E. 297–98 **in . . . Euangeliorum** *om* E. **Omeliis** omelia AF. 298 **Euangeliorum** *om* A; euangeliis W. **iter nostrum** terram nostram I. 299 **thesaurum** *add* suum E. 301 **patriam** Ierusalem L. 301–4 **quia . . . probatur** *om* J. 302 **despectio** despectacio E. 304 **et argento** *om* EAF. **i** ii EW. 305 **Fecit . . . inicio** dominus ab inicio creauit JAFL; item dominus ab inicio instituit GIW. 307 **plura** multa GIW; plurima L. 308 **Grecum** *add* a AGIW. 310 **in ipsis** *om* E. 311 **et in alio** idem E; et alibi GIW; *add* Psalmo FL. 312 **ex *(1st)*** in FGILW. 313 **idest** *add* tu E. 314 **mutuatur** mutuat EI; mutatur A. 315 **recolit** reputat AGIW; recolligit FL. 316 **est *(1st)*** habes AFIW. 317 **luna** *om* E. 318 **conposicione** opposicione E. 319 **limpidius** uerius A. 320 Gregorius *marg* E. **radio** lumine GIW. 323 Gregorius *marg* E. **timet** *add* se AFGILW. 324 **culpas**

parata] est. Ipsa est "argentum igne examinatum" quod purgatur per tribulacionem. Et sicut argentum uiuum inuenitur in locis uilibus, ut in fornacibus [argentariis] uel luto puteorum uel in uetustissimo stercore cloacarum, secundum Ysidorum, ita humilitas in consideracione proprie uilitatis cicius [inuenitur]. Michee [vi]: "Humiliacio tua in medio tui." [Et aurum] nostrum puluerizandum est propter latrones, idest demones latenter insidiantes. Iob xix: "Venerunt latrones eius per me." Et Gregorius [in *Omeliis Euangeliorum*]: "Isti demones quasi latrunculi iter nostrum obsident." Vnde depredari desiderat qui thesaurum ° in uia publice portat. Cum autem uenerimus ad regionem nostram, idest celestem patriam, totus puluis exsufflabitur, quia omnis humiliacio presentis uite et hominum [despectio] terminabitur, et tunc "probacio fi- / dei" nostre, idest merces fidei, "multo preciosior f. 99vb
erit auro [et argento] quod per ignem probatur," I Petri [i].

Fecit Dominus ab inicio duo luminaria: "luminare maius," Genesis i, quo figuratur caritas; et "luminare minus," quo figuratur humilitas. Ipsa enim conparatur lune propter plura. Primo, quia luna secundum Grecum "mene" dicitur, idest defectus, vnde mensis nomen habet; et humilitas ex se et in se semper deficit sui reputacione. Psalmus: "Anima eorum, idest humilium, [in ipsis] defecit"; [et in alio]: "In deficiendo ex me spiritum meum," idest, ex eo quod reputaui ex me defectum spiritus, "tu cognouisti," idest ° approbasti, "semitas meas," idest opera et intenciones. Secundo, quia luna totum lumen [mutuatur] a sole. Sic humilitas totum recolit acceptum a Christo et nichil sibi ascribit; Corinthiorum iiii: "Quid est quod non accepisti?" Tercium est quod quanto [luna] magis a sole illustratur, tanto magis in ea apparet macula que ex umbra terre est uel ex [conposicione] propria. Ita quanto magis humilitas proficit, tanto defectus suos limpidius cognoscit, uelut attomos in radio solis. Gregorius in fine *Moralium*: "Quanto quis maioris gracie lumen percipit, tanto magis se esse reprehensibilem cognoscit." Quartum est quod luna est planeta erraticus; et uera humilitas semper timet errare. Gregorius: "Bonarum mencium est ibi [culpas] agnoscere ubi culpa non est." Quintum est quod luna omnibus plane- / tis terre propinquior f. 100ra
est; sic humilitas ceteris omnibus inferiorem se reputat. Vnde hu-

from *humo acclinis,* "lying close to the ground," as Isidore says. Moreover, true humility is compassionate and bends down to its neighbor, as is shown in him who said, Corinthians 2: "Who is weak," etc. The sixth is that the full moon, as it were, shows the image of a man suspended in it. And true humility remembers Christ's passion and, looking at him, "crucifies its flesh with its vices and lusts," Galatians, at the end; that is, by taming the flesh it suppresses its lusts. The seventh is that the waxing moon points its horns to the east, and humility, when it grows, links its beginning and end to the orient, that is, to Christ—Zacharias 6: "A man, the orient is his name"—, knowing that "of him and by him are all things," Romans 12. The eighth is that as the physical dew comes from the moon, so abundant spiritual dew comes from humility. Isaias 26: "Your dew is the dew of light"; that is, grace itself is the main cause for the knowledge of God in our soul. This is "the dew that meets the heat and overpowers it," Ecclesiasticus 43; that is, the dew of grace quenches the heat of lust. The ninth is that the moon appears to be smaller the closer it is to the sun; thus, humility appears to itself smaller, the closer it is to Christ. We find an example in the Blessed Virgin, and in Job 42: "Now my eye sees you; therefore I reprehend myself and do penance," and so forth. The tenth is that the moon waxes and wanes. Thus humility, the more it wanes in self-esteem, the more it grows in God's approval; Kings 15: "When you were a little one in your own eyes, were you not made the head of the tribes of Israel?" The eleventh is that as soon as the moon is full, it begins to wane. Thus, in the fullness of the virtues we must always begin anew to practice good deeds; Ecclesiasticus 18: "When a man has done, then shall he begin." Paul understood this when he said: "I do not count myself to have apprehended; I shall run, if I may by any means apprehend," Philippians 3.

Now we turn to false humility, which is the same as pretense or hypocrisy, which is so named from *"hypos,"* which means false, and *"crisis,"* judgment, because it causes a false judgment of itself when it does one thing and shows forth another. Of the humility of such a person is said in Ecclesiasticus 19: "There is one that humbles himself wickedly, and his interior is full of deceit." It is a grave deceit to display saintliness and live after one's pleasure. The Gloss re-

culpam E. 327 Ysidorus *marg* E. **quasi . . . acclinis** *om* G. **acclinis** acclinus JL. 327–28 **preterea uera** prima G. 328 **uera** *om* EIW. **et condescensum** *om* E; et descensum FG. 329 **patet in illo** illo patet E. 332 **crucifigit** crucifixit E. 333 **fine** *om* EJ; 4 f F. 334 **concupiscencias** concupiscenciam EFGL. **habet** sint E; immittit GIW. 335 **orientem** ***(1st)*** arietem E. **proficiens** proficit GIW. 335–36 **idest . . . eius** Zacharie vi vir oriens nomen eius Christus EW; Iacobi iii et Zacharie vi oriens nomen eius idest ad Christum J. *The passage is very garbled; I have reconstructed it on the basis of* A: Christum Zacharie vi vir oriens nomen eius refert . . . (*similarly* IW), *and of* FL: idest Christum refert suum principium et finem Zacharie vi vir oriens nomen eius. 337 **sciens** *om* EL. 338 **ros** res JGW. 339 **materialis** matutinalis F. **roris** rei GW. 341 **ardori** *add* superbie A. 345 **proximior** propinquior JFL; uicinior I. 346 **te** me E. 351 **decrementum** detrimentum J. 352 **cumulo** curriculo F. 354 **Hoc . . . dixit** unde GIW. 355 **curram si** sed G; non I; *om* W. **curram . . . conprehendam** *om* E. 356 **iii** *add* de humilitate ypocriti *rubr* J; *add* de falsa humilitate *rubr* AI; *add* de humilitate falsa *rubr* F. 358 **crisis** *add* quod est E. 362 **ostentare** ostendere FL. 363 Glossa *marg* E. 364 Bernardus *marg* E. **ueri-**

milis dicitur quasi humo acclinis, ut dicit Ysidorus. Et preterea [uera] humilitas habet conpassionem proximi [et condescensum], ut patet [in] illo qui dicebat, Corinthiorum ii: "Quis infirmatur," etc. Sextum est quod luna plena representat ymaginem quasi hominis in ea pendentis. Et uera humilitas memoriam habet passionis Christi, cuius intuitu "carnem [crucifigit] cum uiciis et concupiscenciis," Galatarum [fine]; idest domando carnem reprimit [concupiscencias]. Septimum est quod crescens [habet] cornua ad [orientem], et humilitas proficiens ad orientem, [idest Christum—Zacharie vi, "uir oriens nomen eius"—,] refert suum principium et finem, [sciens] "quoniam ab ipso et per ipsum sunt omnia," Romanorum xii. Octauum est quod sicut a luna est ros materialis, ita ab humilitate habundancia roris spiritualis. Ysaie xxvi: "Ros lucis ros tuus"; idest, ipsa gracia precipua est causa cognicionis Dei in anima. Hic est "ros qui obuiat ardori et humilem efficit eum," Ecclesiastici xliii; idest, ros gracie extinguit ardorem concupiscencie. Nonum est quod luna tanto apparet minor quanto soli est uicinior; sic humilitas quanto Christo est proximior, tanto sibi uidetur minor. Exemplum de Beata Virgine, et Iob xlii: "Nunc oculus meus uidet [te]; idcirco me reprehendo et ago penitenciam," etc. Decimum est quod luna / crescit f. 100rb et decrescit. Sic humilitas quanto decrescit in estimacione sua, tanto crescit in estimacione diuina; Regum xv: "Nonne cum esses paruulus in oculis tuis, capud in tribubus Israel factus es?" Undecimum est quod post plenilunium statim incipit decrementum. Sic in cumulo uirtutum semper reincipiendum est exercicium bonorum operum; Ecclesiastici xviii: "Cum consumauerit homo, tunc incipiet." Hoc intellexit Paulus cum dixit: "Nondum arbitror me conprehendisse; [curram si quomodo conprehendam,]" Philippensium iii.

Sequitur de falsa humilitate, que idem est quod simulacio uel ypocrisis, que dicitur ab "ypos," quod est falsum, et "crisis," ° iudicium, quia falsum iudicium de se relinquit cum aliud agat et aliud ostendat. De cuius humilitate Ecclesiastici xix dicitur: "Est qui se nequiter humiliat, et interiora eius plena sunt dolo." Magnus dolus est ostentare sanctitatem et uiuere secundum uoluptatem. Vnde Glossa hic dicit: "Ypocrite et heretici os-

marks on this passage: "Hypocrites and heretics make a show of virtues but do not possess them in truth." Bernard: "Many pursue the shadow of this virtue, few its reality." The same: "It is the appearance of virtue, not its reality; a quality, not the substance itself." The word hypocrisy is otherwise derived from *"hypos,"* which means under, and *"crisis,"* gold, as if it were *sub-auratus,* "gilded over," for the hypocrite is thought to be within what he makes himself out to be outside. Gregory: "The life of a hypocrite is like the sight of a phantom, one sees in the vision what does not exist in reality." Hence the hypocrite is well typified by Beel, who was silver on the outside and clay within, Daniel 13. He is further the whited sepulcher, which on the outside is beautiful to the eyes, "but within full of all filthiness," Matthew 23. He is also a wolf in sheep's clothing, Matthew 7. And there is an ancient proverb:

Under the wool of a lamb often hides the heart of a wolf.

Likewise, the hypocrite is a rush which looks green but bears no fruit. Job 8: "Can the rush be green without moisture?" Gregory on this verse: "The hypocrite is green in the color of saintliness without bringing forth good deeds." He is also the angel of Satan who "transforms himself into an angel of light," 2 Corinthians 11. Moreover, he is the dungheap covered with snow in which salt is useless, Luke 14, because its external show suggests holiness, but its inner falseness has the stench of decay. Hence the hypocrite is that Diotrephes, who seeks to have the preeminence and does not receive the brethren but prates against them, 3 John. "Diotrephes" means splendidly tasteless or insinuating elegance. This is the dungheap covered with snow which without salt, that is, without the spice of virtues, rots away in the stench of his life. The hypocrite is also an idol or image, which seems to have something numinous about it while in reality it leads to error; Jeremias 2: "My people have changed their glory into an idol." An idol is so called as if it were *in dolo factum,* "made in deceit," that is to say, so that it may cause people to go astray. And an image, *simulacrum,* is so called as if it were *simulatum sacrum,* "fake-holy." These things apply to the falsely humble. In addition, the hypocrite is the devil's *symia,* "ape," who bears the *similitudo,* "likeness," of man, but a ludicrous one; Jeremias 10: "It is a ridiculous work." He is, further, a firefly, which gives light in the dark and is dark in the light; that is, he is beautiful in the eyes of men, ugly in the sight of the angels. Hence his proud show will become the height of his damnation. And thus it is said in Job 20 that he "glitters in his bitterness." Finally, the hypocrite

tatem sanctitatem FL. 365 Idem *marg* E. 366 **uirtutis** uirtutum E. 367 **crisis** *add* quod est EL. 368 **uidetur** non est JG; non videtur I; putatur L. 369 Gregorius *marg* E. 371 **ipse** *om* AGIW. **intus** intra E. 373 **pulcrum** *add* et E. **intus** *add* uero GIW. 374 **xxiii** xiiii E; xxiiii J; 13 GI. 374–75 **Item . . . vii** *om* A. 375 **Et est** *om* GIW. **prouerbium** *add* versus E. 376 Versus *marg* E. **agnina** ovina FL. 377 **cyrpus** pinus E; surculus I, *corr.* 378 Gregorius *marg* E. **cyrpus** surculus I, *corr.* **Gregorius** Glossa GIW. 379 **colore** calore E. 380 **ipse** *om* GIW. 382 **sapit** capit GILW. 385 **non** *add* benigne E. 386 **speciose** sponse GW; sponsus I. **insulsus** infulsus EA. **uel** et E. 387 **insinuans** insaniens FIL. **idest** *add* sine AFGIW. 388 **in . . . conputrescens** *om* L. 389 **numinis** ueritatis E. 391 **Et . . . ydolum** *om* A. 392 **simulatum** simulacrum E; simul J; *om* I. 395 **risu** risui E. **noctiluca** nocticula E; noctuluca AG. 397 **ostentacionis** sustentacionis GW. 398 **fulgurat** ful-

tendunt uirtutum speciem set non habent ueritatem." Bernardus: "Multi umbram huius uirtutis, pauci ueritatem secuntur." Idem: "Species [uirtutis] et non ueritas; qualitas est et non substancia." V.el ypocrisis dicitur ab "ypos," quod est sub, et "crisis," ° aurum, quasi sub-auratus, quia talis uidetur intra qualem se simulat extra. Gregorius: "Vita ypocrite est quasi quedam uisio fantasmatis, que hoc habet in ymagine quod non habet in ueritate." Vnde ipse bene fi- / guratur per Bel, qui extra fuit argenteus et [intus] f. 100va luteus, Danielis xiii. Item ipse est sepulcrum dealbatum, quod extra oculis est pulcrum, ° "intus omni spurcicia plenum," Matthei [xxiii]. Item ipse est lupus in uestimentis ouium, Matthei vii. Et est antiquum prouerbium: °

Pelle sub agnina latitat mens sepe lupina.

Item ipse est [cyrpus] uirens et non fructificans. Iob viii: "Nunquid uirescere potest cyrpus absque humore?" Gregorius ibidem: "Ypocrita uirescit [colore] sanctitatis sine fructu operis." Item ipse est angelus Sathane "transfigurans se in angelum lucis," II Corinthiorum xi. Item ipse est sterquilinium niue tectum in quo sal inutile est, Luce xiiii, quia simulacio exterior sapit discrecionem sanctitatis, set falsitas interior fetorem habet corrupcionis. Vnde ypocrita est ille Dyotrephes, qui querit principatum gerere et non ° recipit fratres set maligne garrit in eos, Canonica Iohannis iii. "Dyotrephes" interpretatur speciose [insulsus] [uel] decor insinuans. Hic est sterquilinium niue tectum sine sale, idest condimento uirtutum, in fetore uite conputrescens. Item ipse est ydolum siue simulacrum, quod uidetur habere aliquid [numinis] cum sit uia erroris; Ieremie ii: "Populus meus mutauit gloriam suam in ydolum." Et dicitur ydolum quasi in dolo factum, scilicet ut errare faciat. Et dicitur simulacrum quasi / [simulatum] sa- f. 100vb crum. Hec ficto humili conueniunt. Item ipse est symia dyaboli habens similitudinem hominis, set ridiculosam; Ieremie x: "Opus est [risu] dignum." Item ipse est [noctiluca] in tenebris lucens et in luce tenebrescens; idest pulcher in conspectu hominum, fedus in conspectu angelorum. Vnde gloria ostentacionis cedit ei ad cumulum dampnacionis. Ideo dicitur Iob xx quod "[fulgurat] in amaritudinem suam." Item ipse est anus aureus iuxta archam,

is the gold ring on the ark, Kings 6, that is, under the show of holiness he hides his baseness within Holy Church.

True humility has twelve steps, for which see the book *On the Steps of Humility* by blessed Bernard.

After the remedy against pride follows its punishment, which is being cast down with a heavy crash. Isaias 14: "How are you fallen, o Lucifer," and so forth. And Luke 10: "I saw Satan like lightning from," and so forth. Likewise, the proud will be trampled down by demons; Job 20: "The terrible ones shall go and come upon them." Also, they will become black and deformed; Isaias 13: "Their countenances shall be as faces burnt."

gatur E; figurat W. 400 **celans** operatur E. 402 **uere** *om* EG. **require** quere E. 403 Bernardus *marg* E. 407 **conculcandi** calcandi E. 408 **eos** eo E. 409 **xiii** xiiii E. **eorum** *add two columns on* signa humilitatis E, *reproduced in Appendix*.

Regum vi, idest, sub specie sanctitatis turpitudinem [celans] intra Sanctam Ecclesiam.

Gradus autem [uere] humilitatis sunt duodecim; [require] in libro beati Bernardi *De gradibus humilitatis.*

Post remedium superbie sequitur de pena eiusdem, que est deiectio cum graui allisione. Ysaie xiiii: "Quomodo cecidisti, Lucifer," etc. Et Luce x: "Vidi Sathanam quasi fulgur de," etc. Item superbi [conculcandi] sunt a demonibus; Iob xx: "Vadent et uenient super [eos] horribiles." Item erunt nigri et deformes; Ysaie [xiii]: "Facies combuste uultus eorum." °

III

ON CHARITY

We have said what is the lesser light, that is, humility, which is the remedy for pride. Now we shall speak of the greater light, that is, charity, which is the remedy for envy; for envy is born first of pride. Here we do not deal with the virtues according to their order, but according to the origin of the vices to which the virtues are opposed. Charity is twofold: uncreated, which is God himself, and created, which is "a good quality of the mind," according to Augustine, even though it was the opinion of some that man's charity is the Holy Spirit alone, which is contradicted by the authority of the saints who say that it is a created habit. The reasons for this are evident in the following way: just as faith, which is the perfection of our rational power, is a created habit, and hope, which is the perfection of our irascible part, so is charity, the perfection of our concupiscible part, a created habit. Also, all merit is dependent on charity, according to Augustine, which means that the ability to gain merit comes from it, even if the other virtues assist in meriting. Therefore, if charity in men were only the Holy Spirit, as they say, merit and reward are due only to him and not to men, and consequently man is rewarded for nothing; in that case the Apostle is wrong in saying, in Timothy 4: "There is laid up for me a crown of justice"; which it is a blasphemy to assert. Further, man's charity receives more and less, which could not be true of the Holy Spirit since he is fully God in himself. Further, according to Corinthians 13, charity is never made void, which could not be said of the Holy Spirit to any purpose, since he always remains untouched and unstained, whether man has charity or not; Augustine in Book I of the *Confessions*: "Even if the vessels are broken, you will not run out."

Now we must know that charity can mean different things: sometimes God himself, John 4: "God is charity"; sometimes the created virtue, Augustine *On the Psalms*: "Charity is the name of God and of virtue"; sometimes the movement of virtue, Augustine: "Charity I call a movement of the mind"; sometimes the whole Trinity, Augustine in his book *On the Trinity,* and on the verse of John quoted above. Sometimes the Holy Spirit is properly called charity; 1 John

III *om all MSS.* 1 **De caritate** *rubr* EJIW; *om* AFGL. 3–4 **superbie . . . que est** siue W. 4 **curacio** *remedium G; remedium siue curacio I. 8 Augustinus *marg* E. 9 **hominis** hominum AFGIW. 12 **modo** *add* dicens E. **perfectio** operacio FL. 13 **que est** *om* AFGLW. 15 Augustinus *marg* E. 16 **licet** et FL. **efficacia** efficiencia J. 17 **debetur** deberetur JFLW; debentur G. 18 **remuneratur** remuneraretur JL; remunerabitur GIW. 18–19 **remuneratur . . . nichilo** non remuneratur A; non remunerabitur GIW. 19 **ergo . . . quod** quod falsum est quia JFL; quod falsum est cum AGIW. **dicit** dicat AGW. 20 **quod . . . dicere** *om* GIW. **est** *om* E; esset FL. 21 **magis** maius JAFLW. 25 Augustinus *marg* E. 27 **est** *om* E. 29 Augustinus *marg* E. 30 Augustinus *marg* E. **quandoque . . . uirtutis** *om* IW. 31 Au-

[III]

DE CARITATE

Dictum est quid sit luminare minus, idest humilitas, que est remedium superbie. Dicendum est quid sit luminare maius, idest caritas, que est curacio inuidie; inuidia enim primo nascitur de superbia. Non enim agitur hic de uirtutibus secundum suum ordinem, set secundum uiciorum originem quibus opponuntur uirtutes. Est autem duplex caritas: increata, que est ipse Deus, et creata, que est "bona qualitas mentis" secundum Augustinum, licet fuerit opinio quorundam hominis caritatem solum esse Spiritum / Sanctum, cui satis obuiant auctoritates sanctorum qui (f. 101^{v}a) dicunt ipsam esse habitum creatum. Et est euidens ostensio racionum hoc modo °: sicut fides, que est perfectio racionalis, est habitus creatus, et spes, que est perfectio irascibilis, ita caritas perfectio concupiscibilis est habitus creatus. Item penes caritatem est omne meritum, secundum Augustinum, idest, efficacia merendi ex ipsa est, licet alie uirtutes commereantur. Si ergo caritas hominum tantum esset Spiritus Sanctus, ut illi dicunt, illi debetur meritum et premium et non hominibus, et sic remuneratur homo pro nichilo; ergo falsum est quod dicit Apostolus, Thymothei iiii: "Reposita est michi corona iusticie"; quod nephas [est] dicere. Item caritas hominis recipit magis et minus, quod Spiritui Sancto est inpossibile cum sit plenus Deus in se. Item, Corinthiorum xiii, caritas non euacuatur, quod de Spiritu Sancto frustra diceretur, qui semper manet incontactus et incontaminatus, siue homo habeat caritatem siue non; Augustinus in primo *Confessionum*: "Etsi uasa frangantur, tu tamen non effunderis."

Ideo sciendum [est] quod caritas dicitur pluribus modis: quandoque ipse Deus, Iohannis iiii: "Deus caritas est"; quandoque ipsa uirtus creata, Augustinus *Super Psalmos*: "Caritas est nomen Dei et uirtutis"; quandoque motus uirtutis, Augustinus: "Caritatem uoco motum animi"; quandoque tota Trinitas, Augustinus in libro *De Trinitate,* et in predicta auctoritate Iohannis. / Quandoque (f. 101^{v}b) appropriate Spiritus Sanctus dicitur caritas; I Iohannis iii: "Videte

3: "Behold what manner of charity the Father has bestowed upon us"; he bestowed charity when he sent the Holy Spirit to the faithful, through which he adopted them to himself. Sometimes it is called the sign of charity, that is, its deed; John 15: "No man has greater love," that is, a greater sign of love, "than that he lay down his life."

Further, that man's charity is a created habit can be clearly seen in Romans 5: "The charity of God is poured forth in your hearts." Just as the Holy Spirit is not poured out when man sins, as Augustine says, so is it not poured forth in his heart when he repents except by the gifts of grace when it is extended in a deed. Bernard, *On Canticles*: "Charity is poured forth when it is extended to one's neighbor."

Charity is defined in various ways. Sometimes it is defined according to the origin from which it comes, and thus charity is to love with God and to hate with God. Sometimes it is defined according to its habit, and thus charity is said to be the order of love, as Augustine declares in *The City of God*. In a different way he defines it according to its being a habit: "Love is the well-spring which the stranger does not share." In another way it is defined according to the subject in which it is; Augustine: "Love is the sign by which the sons of God can be distinguished from the sons of the devil"; and this the Lord intimates in John 13: "By this shall all men know that you are my disciples, if you have love one for another." In another way it is defined according to its chief end to which it is directed, which is the good; therefore, since it finds the highest good in God, it loves him the most. And thus Bernard defines: "Charity is the well-ordered love of the good." Sometimes it is defined according to its objects; Augustine: "Charity is love of God and of one's neighbor." Sometimes it is defined according to its acts; Bernard: "While any virtue is a vehicle for the tired wanderer, provision on the way for the traveler, and light for him who walks in darkness, only charity brings rest to the tired, a home to the wayfarer, and eternal light to the pure mind." With regard to the same aspect Gregory defines it as follows: "Charity is the mistress of all the virtues, which has in it nothing that is harsh, strange, or confused; her office is to nourish concord, to keep what has been bound together, to bind together what is disjointed, to straighten what is crooked, and to strengthen all the other virtues with the gift of her protection."

Charity, the love of God and one's neighbor, is one and the same virtue in its kind. Gregory: "Charity has one root, though different acts"; add: its movements are divers in number. Thus, there can be a greater movement toward

gustinus *marg* E. 34 **cum** quando E. 35 **fidelibus** *om* E. 37 **habet** *add* etc EL. 38 **suam** *om* EGW. 39 **hominis** *om* GIW. **habitus creatus** creata FL. 40 **est** *om* E. 41–42 **ut dicit** *om* E. 42 Augustinus *marg* E. 43 Bernardus *marg* E. **nisi** nec EA; penitet enim GI; insuper L; *om* W. **cum** *om* E. 44 **dilatatur** dilatetur GIW. 45 **pluribus** multis JGIW. 47–50 **dicitur . . . cui non** *om* G. 48 Augustinus *marg* E. 50 **cui** quo FILW; quo uel cui J. 51 Augustinus *marg* E. **Augustinus** *om* F. 52–53 **et . . . In** *om* G. 52 **hoc** *om* E. **Dominus** *repeated and canc* E. 55 **qui** quod GIW. 58 Augustinus *marg* E. **obiecta** subiecta AFLW; substanciam G. 59 Bernardus *marg* E. **Bernardus** *om* W. 60 **autem** omnis F; *om* GW. 62 Gregorius *marg* E. 66 **protectionis** perfectionis vel directionis A; directionis GW; discrecionis I. 68 Gregorius *marg* E. **est** *om* E. 69 **est** *om* EW. 72 Augustinus *marg* E. **ut di-**

qualem caritatem dedit nobis Pater"; caritatem dedit [cum] Spiritum Sanctum [fidelibus] misit, per quem sibi illos adoptauit. Quandoque dicitur signum caritatis, scilicet ipsum opus; Iohannis xv: "Maiorem caritatem nemo habet," ° idest, maius signum, "quam ut animam [suam] ponat."

Item quod caritas hominis sit habitus creatus manifeste patet Romanorum v: "Caritas Dei diffusa [est] in cordibus vestris." Sicut enim Spiritus Sanctus non effunditur cum quis peccat, [ut dicit] Augustinus, sic nec diffunditur in corde eius cum penitet [nisi] per dona gracie [cum] extenditur in opere. Bernardus, *Super Cantica*: "Caritas diffunditur cum ad proximum dilatatur."

Diffinitur autem caritas pluribus modis. Quandoque penes principium a quo est, et sic est caritas amare cum Deo et odire cum Deo. Quandoque diffinitur penes suum habitum, et sic dicitur caritas ordo amoris, quod habetur ab Augustino *De ciuitate Dei*. Alio modo ab eodem diffinitur prout est habitus: "Dilectio est fons cui non communicat alienus." Aliter diffinitur penes subiectum in quo est; Augustinus: "Dilectio est signum quo discernuntur filii Dei a filiis dyaboli"; et [hoc] innuit Dominus in Iohannis xiii: "In hoc cognoscent omnes quia discipuli mei estis, si dilectionem habueritis ad inuicem." Aliter diffinitur penes principalem finem ad quem est, qui est bonum; vnde quia in Deo inuenit summum bonum, sum- / me diligit ipsum. Sic diffinit Ber- f. 102ra
nardus: "Caritas est ordinata uoluntas boni." Quandoque penes sua obiecta diffinitur; Augustinus: "Caritas est dilectio Dei et proximi." Quandoque diffinitur penes suos actus; Bernardus: "Cum autem uirtus sit fesso uehiculum, uiatori uiaticum, lux caligantibus, sola caritas fatigato est requies, uiatori mansio, lux perpetua pure menti." Eodem respectu diffinit Gregorius: "Magistra omnium uirtutum est caritas, que nichil sapit asperum, nichil extraneum, nichil confusum; cuius proprium est nutrire concordiam, sociata seruare, dissociata coniungere, praua dirigere, atque protectionis sue munere ceteras uirtutes solidare."

Est autem caritas que dilectio Dei est et proximi una uirtus secundum speciem. Gregorius: "Vna [est] radix caritatis, set diuersitas [est] operis"; suple: motus eius sunt diuersi secundum numerum. Ideo potest esse maior motus in Deum et minor in

God and a lesser one toward one's neighbor, even though the one toward one's neighbor is at the same time directed toward God, for Augustine says that he who truly loves his neighbor, loves nothing in him but God. And although the movement which is toward one's neighbor is ultimately directed toward God, yet there is another movement toward God which is not directed toward one's neighbor, such as the movement of devotion, contemplation, and loving God more than all things. Since there are principally two acts of charity, namely, to love God and to love one's neighbor, there are consequently two commandments of love concerning them. And charity appears in a commandment because of its deeds, in which human free will is involved; in so far as charity is a habit, it could not appear in a commandment, because as such it exists by God's gift alone. Further, whereas *latria* and *dulia,* which are concerned with the honor due to the Creator and to his creation, are different virtues in kind, the love of God and the love of his creatures do not differ in kind, because they have one and the same end, as they have one and the same root. For *latria,* which is the service owed to and shown to God, is directed toward God as the highest being; whereas *dulia,* which is the honor given to creation, concerns creation alone; and thus these two virtues have different objects and different ends. The same must be said of wisdom, which is cognition of the Creator, and knowledge, which is cognition of creatures. That the movement of charity toward one's neighbor can at the same time be directed toward God may be seen in an example, because according to Augustine in one and the same act of vision we see the image, the mirror, the window, and the passers-by. Likewise, in the same act of taste we taste something sweet as well as sweetness, and in the same act of love we love what is good and goodness itself. Master Praepositinus gives an example about fire, that two men get warm by the same fire, one more, the other less, because of the difference in their complexions; in the same way, one and the same movement is greater toward God and less so toward one's neighbor because of the enormous distance between the two goodnesses.

Charity is to be recommended for many reasons. First, for its dignity, because charity loves the good so much that it bears the name of the highest good; hence, "God is charity." Second, for its forming power, because charity is the form of all virtues, and as the form in natural things is the principle of their action, so charity in the virtues; because while every virtue of grace has its merit, nevertheless without charity none of them would be sufficient to earn reward. Thus, an authority states that charity alone is crowned; add: as to its supremacy and ability to gain merit. Third, for its joy, because charity always serves the

cit dicit EFL; *om* GIW. 74 **finaliter** similiter E. 76 **precipue** precipua E. 77 **istis** *add* scilicet E. 80 **qui** quia AGL. 87 **Idem** secundo E; ideo FGW; item L. **est** *om* EGIW. 88 **sciencia** *add* est *canc* E. 90 **in Deum** *marg* E. 91 Augustinus *marg* E. **fenestra et transeuntes** per fenestram transeuntes FL; per fenestras transeuntes G. 91–92 **secundum Augustinum** *om* L. 93 **ipsa** *om* EL. 94 **Prepositini** propositum JAL; prepositi FIW. **ad . . . ignem** de eodem igne E. 98 **Caritas . . . plura** item caritas est commendabilis propter plura J; commendabilis est caritas propter plura GIW; *om* A. 99 **amat** habet E. **habet** sit FL; *om* W. 106 **efficaciam** efficienciam J; sufficienciam A. 106 **tercio** iiii° *corr by erasure to* iii° E. 106–8 **quia . . . facilitatis** *om* E. 107 **xiii** xiiii J; 12 FL. 108 **facilitatis** facul-

proximum, licet ille qui est in proximum sit eciam in Deum, quia [ut] dicit Augustinus, qui uere diligit proximum nichil diligit in eo preter Deum. Et licet ille motus qui est in proximum [finaliter] sit in Deum, est tamen alius motus in Deum qui non est in proximum, ut motus deuocionis, contemplacionis, et Deum diligere super omnia. Item quia duo sunt [precipue] opera caritatis, scilicet diligere Deum et proximum, ideo de istis ° du- / obus sunt duo precepta dilectionis. Et est caritas in precepto f. 102rb racione operum, quibus se admiscet liberum arbitrium; racione habitus non potuit esse in precepto, qui solum est ex Dei dono. Et licet latria et dulia sint diuerse uirtutes secundum speciem, in quibus est honor Creatoris et creature, tamen dilectio Dei et creature non differunt secundum speciem, quia ponunt unum finem, sicut unam habent radicem. Latria uero, que est seruitus Deo exhibita et debita, soli Deo intendit tanquam summo; dulia uero, que est honor creature, solum circa creaturam consistit; et ita habent diuersa subiecta et diuersos fines. [Idem] dicendum [est] de sapiencia, que est cognicio Creatoris, et sciencia, que est cognicio creature. Et quod idem motus caritatis qui est in proximum possit esse in Deum patet per exemplum, quia eadem uisione uidetur ymago et speculum et fenestra et transeuntes, secundum Augustinum. Item eodem gustu gustatur dulce et dulcedo, et eadem dilectione diligitur bonum et [ipsa] bonitas. Exemplum Magistri Prepositini est de igne, quia duo [ad eundem ignem] calefiunt magis et minus propter diuersitatem conplexionum; ita unus motus in Deum maior est et in proximum minor propter uehementem distanciam bonitatum.

Caritas est commendabilis propter plura. Primo racione dignitatis, quia tantum [amat] caritas bonum quod ipsa habet nomen summe bonitatis; vnde "Deus caritas est." Secundo racione / informacionis, quia ipsa forma est uirtutum, et sicut forma in f. 102va naturalibus est principium actionis, ita caritas in uirtutibus; quia licet unaqueque uirtus gratuita habeat suum meritum, sine caritate tamen non sufficerent omnes ad premium. Ideo dicit auctoritas quod sola caritas coronatur; suple: quoad auctoritatem et efficaciam merendi. Tercio racione iocunditatis, [quia caritas semper seruit Domino in leticia; unde Ad Corinthios [xiii]: ipsa

Lord in joyfulness; Corinthians 13: charity "rejoices with the truth." Fourth, for its ease; Bede's comment on Luke: "Love makes all things light." And Matthew 22: "On these two hangs the whole Law and the prophets"; that is, in the two commandments of love all things become easy, for a weight which hangs can be moved easily; or else, the Law and prophets come to this, the love of God and one's neighbor. Fifth, for its breadth, because charity extends itself to friends and enemies. Augustine: "Charity is wider than the ocean"; and in the Psalm: "Your commandment is exceeding broad." Sixth, for its fullness, because charity fulfills the law; Romans 13: "Charity is the fulfilling of the Law." Seventh, for its activity, because it never stands idle, for it either gains ground or loses it, as Augustine says. Eighth, for its permanence, because it is not made void but remains increased in heaven; Corinthians 13: "Charity never falls away."

Charity can achieve many things. It can bring God's presence, because "he that abides in charity, abides in God and God in him," 1 John 4. Further, it brings unity of minds; Ephesians 4: "Careful to keep the unity of the Spirit in the bond of peace." For charity is the bond of perfection, according to the Apostle and to Augustine. It further helps in supporting one's neighbor; Ephesians 4: "Supporting one another in charity." Also, in overcoming our enemy, for charity is "terrible" to our enemies "as an army set in array," Canticles 6. And Jerome: "Every battle that is entered in one accord leads to victory"; on the contrary, a "kingdom divided against itself shall be made desolate," Matthew 12, and Judith 15: "Because the Assyrians were not united together they went without order in their flight." There is the example of the four bulls which, as long as they were united, the lion could not attack or harm, but he finally fell upon one after it had been separated. Charity also helps to obtain things more easily; Bernard: "Pray together with many, for a crowd is hardly ever repelled." It also aids in distinguishing the good from the bad, for charity is a special sign of God, so that the good may say: "The light of your countenance is signed upon us, O Lord." A sheep marked with the proper sign of its shepherd is admitted into the sheepfold; one marked with a stranger's sign remains outside. Charity further helps to enlighten the mind, for as Bernard says it is the light of our mind, but envy is the mind's darkness, for it does not allow us to see our neighbor's good. 1 John 1: "He that hates his brother walks in darkness and knows not where he goes." Also, in charity rests the salvation of our soul, for the least amount of it is sufficient for salvation; this is shown by the fact that

tatis GW. Beda *marg* E. 110–12 **idest . . . prophete** *om* E. 110 **in** *om* J. 112 **Quinto** quarto E. 114 Augustinus *marg* E. 115 **Sexto** quinto E. 116 **dilectio** caritas FL. 117 **Septimo** sexto E. 118 Augustinus *marg* E. **ut . . . Augustinus** Augustinus AGI; *om* E. **Octauo** septimo E. 120 **excidit** excidet E. 121 **Caritas . . . multa** *om* A. 123 **animorum** animarum E. 125 Augustinus *marg* E. 129 Ieronimus *marg* E. **Ieronimus** ideo F; Gr L. 133 **leo** *add* deo *canc* E. **inuadere uel** *om* EFL. **uel** nec AGIW. **potuit** poterat E. 134 Bernardus *marg* E. 136 **speciale** spirituale FL; spirituale ⟨uel speciale⟩ J. 140 Bernardus *marg* E. 142–43 **nescit quo eat** non uidet quo uadat E; *om* FGILW. 143 **minima** nimia E. 144 **excidit**

"congaudet ueritati." Quarto racione facilitatis;] Beda super Lucam: "Amor omnia facit leuia." Et Matthei xxii: "In hiis tota Lex pendet et prophete"; [idest, in duobus preceptis caritatis omnia fiunt facilia, onus enim pendens facilius mouetur; uel ad hoc sunt Lex et prophete,] ut diligatur Deus et proximus. [Quinto] racione amplitudinis, quia caritas extenditur ad amicos et inimicos. Augustinus: "Caritas lacior est occeano"; et in Psalmo: "Latum mandatum tuum nimis." [Sexto] racione inplecionis, quia caritas Legem inplet; Romanorum xiii: "Plenitudo Legis est dilectio." [Septimo] racione operacionis, quia nunquam est ociosa, quia semper aut proficit aut deficit, ut dicit Augustinus. [Octauo] racione duracionis, quia non euacuatur set manet aucta in patria; Corinthiorum xiii: "Caritas nunquam [excidit]."

Caritas ualet ad multa. Valet enim ad Dei presenciam, quia "qui manet in caritate, in Deo manet et Deus in eo," I Iohannis iiii. Item ad [animorum] unitatem; Ephesiorum iiii: "Solliciti seruare unitatem Spiritus in uinculo pacis." Caritas enim est uinculum perfectionis, secundum Apostolum et secundum Augustinum. Item ualet ad proximorum subportacionem; Ephesiorum iiii: "Subportantes inuicem in caritate." / Item ad hostis inpugnacionem, quia caritas est "terribilis" hostibus "ut castrorum acies ordinata," Canticorum vi. Et Ieronimus: "Omnis pugna unanimiter aggressa uictoriam parit;" econtra "regnum in se diuisum desolabitur," Matthei xii, et Iudith xv: "Assyrii non adunati in fugam ibant precipites." Exemplum de quatuor thauris, quos adunatos leo [inuadere uel] ledere non [potuit], set tandem unum separatum inuasit. Item, ad faciliorem inpetracionem; Bernardus: "Ora cum multis, quia multitudo uix patitur repulsam." Item, ad distinctionem bonorum a malis, quia caritas est speciale signaculum Dei, vt dicere ualeant boni: "Signatum est super nos lumen uultus tui, Domine." Ouis signata proprio signo pastoris in ouile colligitur; alieno uero excluditur. Item, ad mentis illuminacionem, quia caritas lux mentis est, dicit Bernardus, inuidia uero mentis tenebra, que bonum proximi uidere non patitur. I Iohannis i: "Qui odit fratrem suum, in tenebris ambulat et [nescit quo eat]." Item in ipsa salus anime posita est, quia [minima] caritas sufficit ad salutem; quod probatur ex eo quod nunquam [excidit]

f. 102vb

charity never falls away but remains with him who possesses it. Further, on it depend our merit and reward. Thus, charity is "the shekel of the sanctuary" according to which "all estimation shall be made," end of Leviticus, for without it no deed is meritorious. Job 28: "Silver shall not be weighed in exchange for it, nor shall the finest gold purchase it."

Charity is the greater light in the firmament of heaven, that is, in God's Church. The "greater light" is the sun, and to it charity can be compared for many reasons. The sun is the fountain of all light. Though the stars are bright bodies, yet they do not shine for us without the light of the sun; Ecclesiasticus 43: "The Lord enlightens the world on high," that is, by the light of the sun he gives the stars their brightness. In the same way does charity give light to the other virtues, that is, their power to merit reward; and so Gregory rightly calls charity the "mistress of the virtues." Moreover, the sun is the fountain of heat, since it consists of a fiery substance; and charity, too, is of a fiery nature, as it makes the spirit burn toward God, as the Psalmist testifies: "My heart grew hot within me," and so forth, that is to say, from the charity it has acquired. And this heat sets our neighbors on fire when by its example it incites other people to follow good ways. In addition, the sun is shared by all. So is charity, which does not seek out the corners; that is, it does not pay attention to people's individual characteristics, whether someone is blue-blooded, or wise, or powerful, or rich, but simply considers what is good in a man, so that it may avoid the "respect of persons"; for as Gregory says: "When a man looks, not at what someone is, but at what he can do, he is being led to the respect of persons." The fact that charity belongs to all was in the Apostle's mind when he said: "I became all things to all men, that I might gain all for Christ," Corinthians 9. "All things to all men," and so forth—Gregory explains: "Not by becoming an apostate but through compassion." Furthermore, the sun brings life to things that grow on earth; in the same way, charity gives our works spiritual life; as a result, what is done without it, is dead. Therefore, the Apostle calls himself "born out of due time" before grace came to him, Corinthians 15. Also, the sun is very large, eight times larger than the earth according to Augustine, *On Genesis*; and according to Ptolemy 166 times larger, which, however, is a lie and the former statement is true. Similarly, charity appears very small in its merit, but it will be very large in its reward, when "the least shall become a thousand and a little one a most strong nation," Isaias 60. For charity will raise the de-

excidet E; excedit I. 147 **fine** *om* E. 148 **Non** nec E. 152 **luminare . . . conparatur** sol scilicet G. 153 **plura** multa GIW. 154 **splendent** splenderent E. 157 Gregorius *marg* E. **lucem** lucere E. 161 **ex concepta** excepta E. **hic** *om* E. 165 **quod potens** *om* E. 167 Gregorius *marg* E. 168 **persone** personarum GIW. **ducitur** dicimus E; ducimur A; inducimur L; ductum W. 169 **qui dicebat** *om* I. 171 Gregorius *marg* E. **set conpaciendo** *om* W. 172 **sic** *add* et E. 174 **aduentum** tempus G. 176 Augustinum *marg* E. **Genesim** *add* i JAGILW. 177 Ptolomeus *marg* E. **tamen** *om* FL. 178 **ita** item EJ. **ualde parua** parua I; *om* W. 182 **et** *om* GIW.

set manet cum eo cuius est. Item penes ipsam est premium et meritum. Vnde ipsa est "syclus sanctuarii" ad cuius quantitatem "omnis estimacio ponderabitur," Leuitici [fine], quia extra ipsam nullum opus est meritorium. Iob xxviii: "[Non] appendetur argentum in commutacione, nec dabitur aurum ob- / f. 103ra risum pro ea."

Caritas est luminare maius in firmamento celi, idest in Ecclesia Dei. "Luminare maius" est sol, et ipsa soli conparatur propter plura. Sol enim fons est tocius luminis. Licet enim stelle sint corpora perspicua, tamen non [splendent] nobis sine luce solis; Ecclesiastici xliii: "Mundum illuminans in excelsis Dominus," idest, per lucem solis dans claritatem stellis. Ita caritas ceteris uirtutibus dat [lucem], idest merendi efficaciam; ideo bene uocat eam Gregorius "magistram uirtutum." Item sol est fons caloris, cum sit ignee substancie; et caritas ignee nature est, vnde spiritum feruere facit in Deum, teste Psalmista: "Concaluit cor meum intra me," etc., hoc est, [ex concepta] caritate. Et [hic] ardor accendit proximos dum per exemplum animat ceteros ad bonos mores. Item sol est communis omnibus. Sic et caritas, que non querit angulos; idest, non respicit condiciones persone, scilicet quod sit generosus, quod sapiens, [quod potens,] quod opulentus, set pure bonum respicit in homine, ut uitet "accepcionem persone"; quia ut dicit Gregorius: "Cum homo intuetur non in eo quod sit, set in eo quod possit, in accepcionem persone [ducitur]." Comunitatem caritatis attendebat qui dicebat: "Omnia omnibus factus sum, ut omnes Christo lucrifacerem," Corinthiorum ix. "Omnia omnibus," etc.—Gregorius: "Non apostatando set conpaciendo." Item sol confert uegetacionem terre nascentibus; sic ° caritas uiuificacionem spiritualem confert operibus; vnde que extra ipsam / f. 103rb fiunt, mortua sunt. Vnde Apostolus ante aduentum gracie uocat se "abortiuum," Corinthiorum xv. Item sol est ualde magnus, quia octies maior terra secundum Augustinum *Super Genesim*; secundum Ptolomeum cencies sexagesies sexies, quod tamen mendacium est et primum uerum. [Ita] caritas ualde parua uidetur in merito, set ualde magna erit in premio, quando "minimus erit in mille et paruulus in gentem robustissimam," Ysaie lx. Caritas enim contemptos et abiectibiles suscitabit in reges et principes.

spised and contemptible to kings and princes. In addition, the sun is by nature incapable of suffering pain; so is true charity incapable of being overcome. Corinthians 13: "It bears all things," add: the world's afflictions; "it endures all things," by patiently waiting for the promises of heaven. Hence, "many waters cannot quench it," end of Canticles, that is, many tribulations. Also, the sun moves easily, and charity is ready to do all good. Hence, the bridegroom is said to have "his hands turned," Canticles 5, as if ready and prepared to every good. Further, the sun has fine rays. Thus charity with its ray of compassion and affection at once perceives the needs of one's neighbor and helps him if it can, or commiserates with him if it cannot help. For it understands its neighbor's condition from its own need, as in Ecclesiasticus 31. And this is why charity is called *"benigna,"* "kind," Corinthians 13, as if *bene ignita,* "well kindled"; for it has a penetrating quality like fire when it suffers with the needy, for otherwise he who has no charity "shuts up his bowels in his brother's need," 1 John 3. The sun, further, shines forth in its light, and charity shines on its neighbors through good deeds; end of Canticles: "The lamps of its fire and flames." Moreover, the sun runs its course in eighteen years, according to Isidore, and charity distributes its commandments through the Old and New Testament, which lead us to merit and reward. In the Old Testament are ten commandments, in the New are eight parts, by which together charity educates us towards the eternal life; Ecclesiasticus 24: "All these things are the book of life, the covenant of the Most High, and the knowledge of truth." And this is the definition of theology. The sun also runs its plenary course through all its degrees in thirty-two and a half years, as Alcabitius says in his treatise *On Astrology.* Thus the sun of justice, Christ, ran the course of his appointed task during thirty-two and a half years in our mortal life, if we count the time by the solar year, which has 365 days and a quarter, that is, six hours. In terms of the lunar year, however, which has 354 days, Christ was on earth for thirty-three full years. After that the sun returned to his place, that is, heaven, where he lives in his visible shape which he drew from the Virgin, for in his divinity he is everywhere; Jeremias 23: "I fill heaven and earth, says the Lord." This sun has returned to his own place after rising in his nativity and setting in his passion, and in both he appeared red because of earthly vapors, that is, because of the human frailties which he had taken on himself on earth. He appeared red in his circumcision and in his passion; therefore the lover of the bride is called "ruddy," Canticles 5.

inuincibilis inuisibilis E; inmutabilis F. 183 **Omnia** cum E. 185 **eam** *written twice* E. **fine** *om* EF. 187 **sponsus** sponsa E. 188 **omne** *add* opus E. 193–94 **quasi . . . ignita** quia benignitas FGIL; quasi benignitas W. 194 **est** *om* JAIW. 196 **fratris** *om* E; patris G. **splendidus** splendidius ELW. 197 **proximis** pro tuis E; propriis I. **fine** *om* EF; viii d A. 199 Ysidorus *marg* E. 199–200 **Ysidorum . . . per** *om* W. 200 **sua per** sua et per E; secundum I. 202 **nos** non E. 206 **Alcabiz** Alcalueri(?) E. 212 **quatuor** iii E. 215 **diuinitate** deitate JAILW. 215–16 **inpleo** inplebo E. 218 **idest** et FL. 224 Crisostomus *marg* E.

Item sol est natura inpassibilis; ita et caritas uera [inuincibilis] est. Corinthiorum xiii: "[Omnia] suffert," mundi aduersa suple; "omnia sustinet," celi promissa pacienter exspectans. Vnde "multe aque non possunt eam extinguere," Canticorum [fine], idest multe tribulaciones. Item sol est agilis in motu, et caritas ad omne bonum est parata. Vnde [sponsus] dicitur habere "manus tornatiles," Canticorum v, quasi ad omne ° bonum promptas et paratas. Item sol est radio subtilis. Ita caritas radio conpassionis et affectionis statim percipit necessitates proximi et succurrit si potest, uel conpatitur si non potest. Intelligit enim que sunt proximi ex defectu proprii subiecti, vt Ecclesiastici xxxi. Et hoc est quod caritas dicitur "benigna," Corinthiorum xiii, quasi bene ignita; penetratiue nature est sicut ignis dum conpatitur egenis, quoniam e contrario / qui caritatem non habet, "claudit uiscera in f. 103va necessitate [fratris]," I Iohannis iii. Item sol est luce [splendidus], et caritas lucet [proximis] bonis operibus; Canticorum [fine]: "Lampades eius ignis atque flammarum." Item sol per octodecim annos conplet cursum suum, secundum Ysidorum, et caritas distribuit precepta sua ° per Uetus et Nouum Testamentum, que nobis sunt ad meritum et premium. In Ueteri decem precepta sunt, in Nouo sunt octo partes, quibus omnibus caritas [nos] erudit ad uitam eternam; Ecclesiastici xxiiii: "Hec omnia liber uite, testamentum Altissimi, et agnicio ueritatis." Et hec diffinicio theologie. Item plenarium cursum perficit sol secundum omnes gradus per triginta et duo annos et dimidium, ut dicit [Alcabiz] *De iudiciis astrorum*. Sic sol iusticie, Christus, per triginta et duo annos et dimidium in nostra mortalitate prefiniti laboris conpleuit cursum, ut conputemus tempus secundum annum solarem, qui continet trecentos et sexaginta quinque dies et quadrantem, idest sex horas. Secundum annum uero lunarem, qui continet trecentos et quinquaginta [quatuor] dies, fuit in terris Christus triginta tribus annis integris. Et postea reuersus est sol ad locum suum, idest celum, vbi est in uisibili specie quam traxit de Uirgine, quia diuinitate est ubique; Ieremie xxiii: "Celum et terram ego [inpleo], dicit Dominus." Reuersus est autem sol iste ad locum suum post ortum natiuitatis et occasum passionis, et utrobique rubeus / apparuit propter uapores terrestres, idest, propter huma- f. 103vb nas infirmitates quas in terra suscepit. Rubuit in circumcisione et in passione; vnde dilectus sponse "rubicundus" dicitur, Canticorum v. Item cum sol fertur per obliquum circulum, proximior

Further, as the sun runs through its oblique orbit, it is the proximate cause that generates things. Charity runs through an oblique orbit when it is extended to one's enemy and so becomes more meritorious to the one who has it. Chrysostom: "When we pray for our enemies, we commend not so much them as ourselves to God, and we are heard more when we pray for our enemies than when we pray for ourselves. He who prays for himself performs not an act of grace but of nature; but he who prays for his enemy performs an act of grace." Also, through the cloud of sin or the moon of worldliness, the light of grace in us is eclipsed; Jeremias 5: "Our iniquities and our sins have withholden and turned away good things from us."

Charity is the fire which the Lord came to light on earth, that is, in the hearts of the faithful. It is lighted in various ways. First through motion, as in a piece of wood or iron when it is given strong movement. This fire the Lord lighted through the motion of the Apostles, who "went about" through towns and "cities preaching" the kingdom of God, Matthew 10. Second, it is lighted in the blowing of preaching and prayer, which the Lord prefigured by blowing on the Apostles and giving them the Holy Spirit, John 20. They were like "a firebrand amongst wood or amongst hay," Zacharias 12. Hence, if a preacher burns with the fire of love, he changes his listeners more easily into a flame of devotion; Gregory: "What does not first burn in itself, does not light anything else." And Abdias, near the end: "The house of Jacob shall be a fire, and the house of Joseph a flame, and the house of Esau stubble." "Jacob," whose name means wrestler or overthrower, is the preacher, whose job it is to wrestle with demons and overthrow vices. The preacher is likewise "Joseph," whose name means growing, for he must always grow in virtues and in good works. If such a preacher is "fire" in spiritual fervor with regard to God and "flame" with regard to his zeal for other souls, he will convert the house of Esau to grace, just as fire changes stubble into its own nature. "Esau" means shaggy or hairy and stands for sinners. Fire is lighted in a third manner by the collision of solid bodies, such as of stone against iron. Stones were the martyrs struck by the world's tribulations, through whose example charity should be kindled in us. These are the "holy stones lifted up over the land" of the living, Zacharias 9. They are struck by the afflictions of the world, which the Lord rebukes on account of his martyrs under the figure of Babylon, Jeremias 51: "You dash together for me the weapons of war." The "weapons of war" were the martyrs killed for Christ's sake, dashed so cruelly that they were given over to death. In a fourth way is fire lighted by two concave mirrors placed against the sunbeam at a cer-

228 **peccati** peccatorum E. **per lunam** pluuiam F. 231 **accendere in terra** accendere JG; mittere in terram F. 233 **Hunc** homo(?) E. 234 **motum** predicacionem W. 235 **ewangelizantes** ewangelizare E; *add* uerbum dei et FL. 239 **feno** ferro E; sono F. **caritate** igne caritatis FL. 240 **deuocionis** conuersionis uel deuocionis F. 241 Gregorius *marg* E. **Gregorius** *om* G. **arserit** ardet E. **aliud** alios GW. **non** ***(2nd)*** H *resumes*. 242 **Et** *om* E. **fine** *om* E; x H. 248 **zelum** salutem A. 248–49 **domum . . . graciam** *om* L. 249 **conuertet** conuertit E; conuertent F. 250 **uel pilosus** *om* G. **Tercio modo** item FL. 258 **Quarto** tercio L. 260

causa est generacioni rerum. Caritas per obliquum circulum fertur cum ad inimicum extenditur et habenti eam magis meritoria efficitur. Crisostomus: “Orantes pro inimicis non tantum illos quantum nos commendamus Deo, et magis orantes pro inimicis exaudimur quam pro nobis. Qui enim pro se orat, non opus gracie exequitur set nature; qui uero pro inimico, opus gracie.” Item per nubem [peccati] uel per lunam temporalitatis eclypsatur in nobis lumen caritatis; Ieremie v: “Iniquitates nostre et peccata nostra prohibent et declinant bonum a nobis.”

Caritas est ignis quem Dominus uenit accendere in terra, idest cordibus fidelium. Accenditur autem pluribus modis. Primo per motum, ut patet in ligno fortiter moto uel in ferro. [Hunc] ignem accendit Dominus per motum apostolorum qui “circuibant” ciuitates et “castella [ewangelizantes]” regnum Dei, Matthei x. Secundo accenditur per flatum predicacionis et oracionis, in cuius signum insufflauit Dominus et dedit apostolis Spiritum Sanctum, Iohannis xx. Ipsi enim fuerunt tanquam “fax ignis in lignis uel in [feno],” Zacharie xii. Vnde si predicator caritate exarserit, facilius auditores in flammam deuocionis conuertit; Gregorius: “Quod in se prius non [arserit], aliud non accendit.” / [Et] Abdyas [fine]: “Erit domus Iacob ignis, et domus Ioseph f. 104[r]a flamma, et domus Esau stipula.” “Iacob,” qui interpretatur luctator uel subplantator, est predicator, cuius est luctari contra demonia et subplantare uicia. Idem est “Ioseph,” qui interpretatur accrescens, ut semper sit crescens in uirtutibus et bonis operibus. Hic uero, si sit “ignis” in feruore spiritus quoad Deum et “flamma” quoad zelum animarum, domum Esau [conuertet] in graciam, sicut ignis conuertit stipulam in sui naturam. “Esau” interpretatur yspidus uel pilosus et signat peccatores. Tercio modo accenditur ignis per collisionem solidorum corporum, ut lapidis ad ferrum. Lapides fuerunt martires, collisi per mundi tribulaciones, quorum exemplis debet accendi caritas in nobis. Hii sunt “lapides sancti eleuati super terram” uiuencium, Zacharie ix. Hii sunt collisi per afflictiones mundi, quem increpat Dominus pro martiribus suis sub typo Babylonis, Ieremie li: “Collidis tu michi uasa belli.” “Vasa belli” fuerunt martires pro Christo interfecti, tam crudeliter collisi ut darentur morti. Quarto modo accenditur

tain angle, because the rays of the sun will converge behind the mirrors in a cone and their intersection will kindle fire. The two mirrors are the two testaments, which kindle a fire in us, that is, they preach to us of the love of God and of our neighbor. Of these mirrors was the laver made, that is, a washing-bowl for the souls; Exodus 38: "You shall make a laver of the mirrors of the women who lie watching at the door of the tabernacle." The mirrors, thus, are the two testaments. Gregory: "Holy Scripture is held up to the eyes of the mind like a mirror, so that the inner face of the soul may be seen. For there we see what is ugly and disgraceful in us, how much we have progressed and how far we still are from the goal." Women look into these mirrors, that is, the holy souls who, anxious about their salvation, detect their blemishes in the mirrors and wash them away. These women "lie watching at the door of the tabernacle," because with their whole desire they sigh for the entrance to the kingdom. Holy Scripture is rightly called a mirror, because when a mirror is broken there appear many images, just as Holy Scripture has many explanations, for "many shall pass over, and knowledge shall be manifold," Daniel 12. Likewise, in this mirror appears the likeness of God, true charity and true humility, what is right and what is wrong, what God wants and what he does not want. Thus Scripture is called God's face, Exodus 33. Moreover, when a woman in her period looks into a mirror, she produces a stain on it. So does the sinful soul when it looks into Holy Scripture, "for wisdom will not enter into a malicious soul," Wisdom 1. It should be noted that there are three kinds of mirrors. The first is plane, in which things appear as they are. Such is Holy Scripture; James 1: In this mirror we see "our own countenance," etc. The second kind is concave, which is worldly knowledge, in which all things appear upside-down, because it "perverts the paths of judgment," Proverbs 17. The third is convex, in which the images appear raised, by which philosophical enterprise is indicated, such as mathematics and metaphysics, which raise above and puff up; Corinthians 8: "Knowledge puffs up." The fifth way in which fire is lighted is by means of a glass vessel with water placed against the sunbeams. The glass vessel is the Blessed Virgin filled with the water of graces, through whom the fire of divine charity is lighted in the churches of the faithful. Apocalypse 3: "A sea of glass round about the throne like to a crystal." The "sea of glass" is the Virgin Mary, a sea for her abundance of graces; wherefore she is also called Mother of Grace,

specula *om* E. **cono** *add* non *canc* E. 261 **intersectio** interfectio EGH; interiectio A; intercisio F. 263 **labrum** F; labium EJAGHILW. 264 **labrum** *source and* F; labium EJAGHILW. 265–66 **que . . . testamenta** *om* IW. 266 Gregorius *marg* E. 268 **et . . . conspicimus** conspicimus et probra E. **probra** obprobria J; pulchra A *and source.* 268 **nostra** *om* EL. 269 **profectu** perfectione E. 271 **et abluunt** *om* G. 274 **sicut** *add* sacre JF. 276 **apparet** est E. 277 **humilitas** *add* et J; *add* etc AFGHL. 278 **Exodi xxxiii fine** Exodi xiii E; *om* L. 282 **Et** *om* E; set A. 284 **consideramus** conspicimus FL; considerat W. 285 **qua** quo E. 286 **peruertit** peruertet E. 288 **philosophia** prophecia EHIW; plura G. **mathematica** mare vincial E. 289 **et inflant** *om* A; *add* corda ILW. 289–90 **Corinthiorum . . . inflat** *om* AH. 290 **Quintum** quartum AHW; quarto L. 291 **oppositum** appositum FHL. 292 **aqua** *om* E; aquis G. 293 **fidelium** fidelibus E. 294 **in . . . sedis** *om* FL. **circuitu** conspectu I; *om* W. 296–97 **nec *(1st)* . . . estatis** *om*

ignis per duo specula concaua debita proporcione ad radium solis opposita, quia radii solares retro [specula] in cono concurrent, quorum [intersectio] generabit ignem. Duo specula sunt duo testamenta, que ignem in nobis generant, idest, dilectionem Dei et proximi nobis predicant. Ex istis speculis / (f. 104rb) fit [labrum], idest animarum lauatorium; Exodi xxxviii: "Facies [labrum] de speculis mulierum que cubant in hostio tabernaculi." Specula igitur sunt duo testamenta. Gregorius: "Sacra Scriptura quasi speculum oculis mentis obicitur, ut interna facies anime uideatur. Ibi enim feda nostra et probra [nostra] conspicimus, quantum proficimus et quantum a [profectu] distamus." Mulieres in hiis speculis inspiciunt, idest, anime sancte de salute sua sollicite maculas deprehendunt in eis et abluunt. Et iste mulieres "cubant in hostio tabernaculi," quia toto desiderio suspirant ad ingressum regni. Et bene Sacra Scriptura dicitur speculum, quia fracto speculo multe apparent ymagines, sicut Scripture multe sunt exposiciones, quia "pertransibunt plurimi et multiplex erit sciencia," Danielis xii. Item in hoc speculo [apparet] Dei similitudo, vera caritas et uera humilitas, quid sit licitum et quid sit illicitum, quid uelit Deus et quid nolit. Ideo facies Dei dicitur Scriptura, Exodi [xxxiii fine]. Item mulier menstruata respiciens in speculo generat in eo maculam. Idem facit anima peccatrix respiciens Sacram Scripturam, "quoniam in maliuolam animam non introibit sapiencia," Sapiencie i. [Et] nota quod triplex est speculum. Primum est planum, in quo apparent res prout sunt. Ipsum est Sacra Scriptura; Iacobi i: In hoc speculo consideramus "uultum natiuitatis nostre," etc. Secundum est concauum, secularis sciencia scilicet, in / (f. 104va) [qua] omnia apparent transuersa, quia ipsa "[peruertit] semitas iudicii," Prouerbiorum xvii. Tercium est conuexum, in quo apparent ymagines eleuate, per quod [philosophia] figuratur, ut [mathematica] et methaphisica, que eleuant et inflant; Corinthiorum viii: "Sciencia inflat." Quintum per quod ignis accenditur est uas uitreum cum aqua solis radiis oppositum. Vas uitreum est Beata Uirgo plena [aqua] graciarum, per quam ignis diuine caritatis accensus est in [fidelium] ecclesiis. Apocalipsis iii: "Mare uitreum in circuitu sedis simile cristallo." "Mare uitreum" Uirgo Maria est, mare propter habundanciam graciarum; vnde et Mater Gracie

for just as the sea never lacks water, whether in drought or in rain, in winter or in summer, so does she never lack the fullness of mercy. Hence: "Through her we have safe access to God," as Bernard says. She is compared to glass because of the frailty of her sex, for although by nature it may be frail, through the strength of virtue it has been made firm. And as the sunbeam passes through glass and glass and sunbeam take on one color, so did the Son of God pass through her and draw from her our colors, that is, human frailties. She is said to be "like crystal," because in giving birth to her son she was found to be undefiled, just as light rays come from a crystal without hurting it. Dionysius: "As a crystal that is moistened and placed against the sun emits rays and sparks, so the Blessed Virgin, filled with the dew of heavenly grace, gave birth to a son." She is "round about the throne," because she intercedes for sinners throughout the space of all the lands. In the sixth way fire is lighted with a beryl, and better with one that is perforated than whole, as they say. The perforated beryl is Christ crucified, through whose wounds heavenly charity lights and illuminates us. As the Philosopher says, a stone comes from natural mud dried in the heat of the sun. So Christ, as to his human nature, comes from the Virgin's body purified by the Holy Spirit; "a burning wind from the desert has dried up her springs," Osee 13; that is, the Holy Spirit sent from heaven extinguished in her all disturbances of the sinful urge. Christ, therefore, was a beryl in the sending of the Holy Spirit, who appeared in fire. He was a pearl in his conception, for a pearl is conceived from heavenly dew in the seashell and is found in its flesh. He was steel in his passion—Isidore: "*Adamas,* 'steel,' is thus named as if it were *indomita vis,* 'untamed strength,'"—"when he set his face as a most hard rock," Isaias 50, that is, as if he made himself insensitive to pain. And as a steel magnet attracts iron, so has Christ drawn hard and obstinate men to the faith; John 12: "When I am lifted from the earth, I will draw all things to myself." He was a carbuncle in his resurrection because of the splendor of his immortality and future glory; as a sign of which "angels in white" appeared in his resurrection, at the end of Matthew.

Charity is likened to fire for many reasons, whether one speaks of the created or the uncreated kind. First, because fire lays low what is high, which can be seen in that, when fire falls on a house or castle, it reduces everything to ashes. Likewise charity lays low the proud, and it does so through the gift of fear; Gregory: "The heart's anchor is the weight of fear." Also, fire brightens

IW. 299 Bernardus *marg* E. **fragilitatis** stabilitatis I. 300 **quia . . . factus** que . . . facta JFGL. **natura** *om* E. 302 **transiit** transit EIW; transivit J. 305 Dyonisius *marg* E. 309 **sexto** quinto L. 310 **melius** cicius A; *om* H. **dicitur** dicunt JFGHL; dicit Tullius AW; dicit Basilius I. 312 **caritas superna** diuina gracia A. 313 Philosophus *marg* E. 314 **hominem** humanitatem J; homines G. 315 **Osee** *blank* E. 318 **que** qui E. 319 **concha marina** concha maris E; contaminata J; conca margarina H; conca maxima L. 320 Ysidorus *marg* E. 322 **insensibilem** *add* se JA. 323 **trahit** ***(2nd)*** traxit AFGHILW. 325 **resurreccione** transfiguracione I; crucifixione W. 327 **in resurrectione** uestiti A; in transfiguracione I; *om* W. **Matthei fine** *om* E. 329 **si** quia si FL. 331 Gregorius *marg* E. 335 Bernar-

dicitur, quia sicut mare nunquam caret aquis, nec in siccitate nec in pluuiis, nec tempore hyemis nec estatis, ita nec ipsa plenitudine pietatis. Vnde: "Securum habemus per ipsam accessum ad Deum," ut dicit Bernardus. Vitro conparatur racione fragilitatis sexus, quia licet [natura] sit fragilis, uirtutum robore factus est stabilis. Et sicut uitrum pertransit radius solis et fiunt uitrum et radius unius coloris, sic per eam Filius Dei [transiit] et nostros colores, idest humanos defectus, ex ipsa contraxit. "Similis cristallo" dicitur, quia filium gignendo incontaminata reperitur, sicut radii ex cristallo sine sui lesione oriuntur. Dyonisius: "Sicut cristallus madefacta et ad solem apposita radios et scintillas ex se producit, sic Beata Virgo rore superne gracie repleta / f. 104vb filium peperit." Ipsa est "in circuitu sedis," quia per uniuersa terrarum spacia intercedit pro peccatoribus. Sexto modo accenditur per berillum, et melius per perforatum quam per integrum, ut dicitur. Berillus perforatus est Christus crucifixus, per cuius uulnera nos accendit et illuminat caritas superna. Fit autem lapis ex ingenuo luto, ut dicit Philosophus, exsiccato calore solis. Ita Christus secundum hominem de corpore Virginis Spiritu Sancto purgato; "ventus enim urens de deserto exsiccauit uenas eius," [Osee] xiii; idest, Spiritus Sanctus missus de celo extinxit in ea omnes molestias fomitis. Christus igitur berillus fuit in Spiritus Sancti missione, qui apparuit in igne. Margarita fuit in concepcione, [que] ex rore celesti in concha [marina] concipitur et in eius carne inuenitur. Adamas fuit in passione—Ysidorus: "Adamas dicitur quasi indomita uis"—, "quando posuit faciem suam ut petram durissimam," Ysaie l, idest, quasi insensibilem fecit ad penam. Et sicut adamas trahit ferrum, ita duros et obstinatos trahit ad fidem; Iohannis xii: "Cum exaltatus fuero a terra, omnia traham ad meipsum." Carbunculus fuit in resurreccione propter splendorem immortalitatis et future glorie; in cuius signum apparuerunt "angeli in albis" in resurrectione, [Matthei fine].

Caritas conparatur igni propter plura, siue dicatur creata siue increata. / f. 105ra Primo, quia ignis alta humiliat, quod patet, si descendat super domum uel castrum, omnia incinerat. Ita caritas superbos humiliat, et hoc per donum timoris; Gregorius: "Anchora cordis pondus timoris." Item ignis tenebrosa illuminat; ita caritas

the darkness; thus, charity brings light to the blindness of envy, and it does so through the gift of knowledge, when it causes the envious to know and to love the good of his neighbor, for charity is the light of the mind, in Bernard's words; and 1 John 2: Love is "the true light." Further, fire softens what is hard, and charity softens the angry, which it does through the gift of counsel; Proverbs 27: "The good counsels of a friend are sweet to the soul." Further, fire makes heavy things light; thus, charity also lightens the slothful and lifts them from under the weight of their spirit, and it does so through the gift of understanding, when it gives them understanding and teaches them by which way one progresses to life, as the Psalm says. Further, fire warms what is cold; thus, charity through the gift of piety warms the greedy who are frozen and opens them up to their neighbors. Piety is profitable for this life and for that which is to come, Timothy 4. Fire also cooks raw meat and makes tasty what is tasteless; thus, charity quenches the pleasure of gluttony and gives a taste for heavenly things. Augustine: "Once the Spirit has been tasted, all flesh loses its taste." Finally, fire strengthens what is weak; this can be seen in the pot that is made firm in the fire. Thus, charity gives strength and resistance to those who are weak in the flesh, that is, the lustful, and it does so through the gift of strength; 1 Peter 5: "The God of all grace will confirm and establish you." Notice that the actions of the several gifts are here attributed to charity, because charity is "the mistress of the virtues," as Gregory says. Similarly does the Apostle, To the Corinthians 12, attribute the actions of the other virtues to charity when he says: "Charity believes all things, hopes all things, endures all things," because as we said earlier, charity informs the other virtues and gives them the power to merit reward.

Notice also that fire is kindled from wood; thus, the fire of love is kindled from the wood of the cross. This wood we must split up, that is to say, we must piece by piece remember the sufferings of the Crucified and thereby light the fire, that is love, in our hearts; Ecclesiastes 10: "He that cuts trees shall be wounded by them." And Leviticus 6: "The fire on the altar shall always burn, and the priest shall feed it, putting wood on it in the evening and the morning." The altar is our heart, as Gregory says, on which our longings and desires must be offered. The priest is not only the one who administers the sacraments, but any faithful if he lives a saintly life; Apocalypse 1: "He has made us a kingdom and priests to God." Therefore we must put wood on the fire mornings and evenings, that is, always think of Christ crucified and thank him for the gift of our redemption. Moreover, fire is well kept when it is hidden under ashes; thus, the fire of charity under the ashes of humility and of death. And so it is said in Micheas 1: "In the house of dust sprinkle yourselves with dust." Further,

dus *marg* E. 337 **xxvii** xxiiii E. 339 **et a . . . alleuiat** *om* L. **pondere** *add* peccati E. **spiritus** *add* sanctus E. 341 **Psalmus** *add* Intellectum tibi dabo et instruam te in uia qua gradieris I. 342 **sic . . . calefacit** *om* I. **per donum** *written twice* E. 343–44 **Pietas . . . iiii** *om* L. 344–45 **facit sapida** *om* G. 345 **ita** sic E; item H. 345–46 **celestium** celeste GIW. 346 Augustinus *marg* E. 347 **roborat** corroborat E. 348 **et** *add* luxuriosos *canc* E. 349 **v** ii E; fine JAGHIW. 350 **omnis** *written twice, the first canc* E. 352 Gregorius *marg* E. 353 **caritati** *om* F. 355 **ipsa est forma** format F. 357 **ligna** lignum E. 359 **Ecclesiaste** Ecclesiastici E. 360 **vi** v E; 8 L. 362 Gregorius *marg* E. 364 **uiuit** uiuat FGHILW. 365 **Deo** *add* nostro E; *om* H. 369 **Miche** *add* dicitur E. 370 **conspergite** *add* hoc eciam Iob 42: "Auditu

cecitatem inuidie, et hoc per donum sciencie, cum facit inuidum bona proximi cognoscere et amare, quia caritas lux mentis est, dicit Bernardus; et I Iohannis ii: Dilectio est "uerum lumen." Item ignis dura emollit, et caritas iracundos flectit, et hoc per donum consilii; Prouerbiorum [xxvii]: "Bonis amici consiliis anima dulcoratur." Item ignis grauia facit leuia; sic et caritas acidiosos leuigat et a pondere ° spiritus ° alleuiat, et hoc per donum intellectus, cum dat illi intellectum et instruit eum per quam uiam gradiatur ad uitam, ut dicit Psalmus. Item ignis frigida calefacit; sic caritas auaros congelatos per donum pietatis calefacit et dilatat ad proximos. Pietas autem ualet ad presentem et futuram uitam, Timothei iiii. Item ignis coquit cruda et insipida facit sapida; [ita] caritas delectacionem gule extinguit et desiderium celestium adducit. Augustinus: "Gustato Spiritu desipit omnis caro." Item ignis debilia [roborat]; patet de olla consolidata per ignem. Ita caritas infirmos carne, idest luxuriosos, facit / fortes et f. 105^{r}b
resistentes, et hoc per donum fortitudinis; I Petri [v]: "Deus omnis gracie confirmabit solidabitque." Et uide quod actus diuersorum donorum caritati hic attribuuntur, quia ipsa "magistra est uirtutum," ut dicit Gregorius. Ideo Apostolus Ad Corinthios xii actus aliarum uirtutum caritati attribuit dicens: "Caritas omnia credit, omnia sperat, omnia sustinet," quia ut predictum est ipsa est forma et ceteris dat efficaciam merendi.

Nota eciam quod ignis per ligna accenditur; sic ignis caritatis per [ligna] crucis. Que ligna debemus comminuere, idest, minutatim penas Crucifixi recolere et inde ignem, idest amorem, in cordibus nostris accendere; [Ecclesiaste] x: "Qui scindit ligna, uulnerabitur ab eis." Et Leuitici [vi]: "Ignis semper ardebit in altari, quem nutriet sacerdos subiciens ligna mane et uespere." Altare est cor nostrum, ut dicit Gregorius, in quo offerenda sunt uota et desideria. Sacerdos est non solum qui sacramenta dispensat, set quilibet fidelis si sancte uiuit; Apocalipsis i: "Fecit nos Deo ° regnum et sacerdotes." Ligna igitur debemus mane et uespere igni supponere, idest, Christum crucifixum iugiter recolere et pro beneficio redempcionis gracias agere. Item ignis bene custoditur cum cinere reconditur; sic ignis caritatis in cinere humilitatis et mortis. Ideo in Michee ° i: "In domo pulueris pul-

when green wood burns it weeps, just like Peter and Mary Magdalene; Lamentations 2: "Let tears run down like a torrent."

Charity is light. Ephesians 5: "You were heretofore darkness, but now are light in the Lord." This applies to charity given in justification. This is "the true light which now shines, because the darkness is passed," 1 John 1. Charity is light for several reasons. First, because it dispels the darkness of our mind; 1 Peter 1: "He has called us out of darkness into his marvelous light." Second, because light is infused into luminous bodies, according to Damascene, who says that the supercelestial bodies are vessels of light. Reason also teaches us the same, that light is not in a translucent body by the nature of that body, because in that case the eye would see in darkness; rather, light comes from the outside. When the image of an object is, by means of the intermediary luminous air, carried to the retina, which has the nature of a mirror in the middle of the eye, between the substance of air and water, then a visual impression occurs. In the same way, charity, which enlightens our soul so that it may know and love God, does not come to man from his own but from an extrinsic giver, that is, "from the Father of lights," James 1; nor would natural love be sufficient for man's salvation, because since that is bent back upon itself, it could never be lifted up toward God, as it cannot rise beyond itself except by added grace. Moreover, when a translucent body is infused with light, colors appear, according to the amount of light or the thickness of the translucent body, as when fire is mixed with water or air, and so forth. White and black, however, are the elements of the other colors. Thus, when charity is joined by and, as it were, mixed with our free will, meritorious works begin to appear, whose elements are nature and grace. Hence the Apostle in Corinthians 15 confesses that he does not labor by himself, but the grace of God with him. Also, light makes potential colors into actual ones; thus, charity makes the works of the other virtues meritorious. Therefore, it alone is said to reap reward, not because it alone deserves it, but because through it the merit of the other virtues is effected. In addition, light offers itself even to the blind eye, and it is not the light's fault that a blind man does not see; likewise it is not the fault of charity if someone remains in the darkness of sin. For the sun of justice is close by the gate of our mind with the light of his grace and knocks, "if any man shall open," Apocalypse 3.

auris audiui te; iccirco ago penitenciam in fauilla et cinere," idest in humilitate et asperitate, quia "oculus meus uidet te" crudelem ad uindictam. Et Iob 16: "Saccum consui super cutem meam." Per cutem et carnem peccata carnalia designantur, per saccum et cinerem uilitas et asperitas penitencie, que debet consui, idest inseparabiliter adherere tanquam vxor viro; ut Ysaie 53: "Alligata," etc.; Psalmus: "Beati quorum," etc. Nota: Tria fiunt de cinere que designant penitenciam: lessiua ad ablacionem, tegimen ignis ad conseruacionem, vitrum clarum per combustionem. Sic penitencia lauat sordes peccatorum—Ysaie 4: "Si abluerit," etc.—, et hoc cum aqua caritatis et gracie admiscentur, quia Corinthiorum 13: "Si tradidero corpus meum," etc., idest de se ipso cinerem faciens, "nichil," etc., quia non lauat tanquam cinis sine aqua *(next line cropped) marg, marked for insertion* J. 371 **Deduc** dedit GW. 374–75 **iustificacione** *add* inpii E; *add* item A. 376 **Est . . . caritas** et est caritas JFGHW; caritas est A; item caritas est L. 379 Damascenus *marg* E. 383 **differtur** defertur JAGH. 387 **homini** hominis A; bonum F; boni H; homo W. **seipso** *add* bonus W. 390 **posset** possit JFGILW. 391 **ex admixtione** cum exanimacione E; ex adiunccione F. 392 **paucitatem** paupertatem E. 395 **cooperatur** coaptatur J. 397 **Ideo** *corr from* Iob E. **xv** xvi E. 399 **actu colores** *om* EL; *marg*

uere uos con- / spergite." Item lignum uiride cum ardet, aquescit, ut Petrus et Magdalena; Trenorum ii: "Deduc quasi torrentem lacrimas." f. 105^{v}a

Caritas est lux. Ephesiorum v: "Fuistis aliquando tenebre, nunc autem lux in Domino." Hoc dicitur de caritate data in iustificacione °. Ipsa est "uerum lumen quod iam lucet, quia tenebre transierunt," I Iohannis i. Est autem caritas lux propter plura. Primo, quia depellit tenebras mentis; I Petri i: "Vocauit nos de tenebris in admirabile lumen suum." Secundo, quia lux infusa est corporibus luminosis, secundum Damascenum dicentem quod supercelestia corpora uasa luminis sunt. Et preterea racio docet hoc quod lux non est in dyaphano per naturam dyaphani, quia tunc uideret oculus in tenebris; vnde lux est ab extrinseco. Et cum differtur similitudo rei mediante aere lucido usque ad rethe grandinosum, quod naturam habet speculi in medio oculi inter naturam aeris et aque, tunc fit uisus immutacio. Hoc modo caritas, que animam illuminat ad Deum cognoscendum et amandum, non est homini a seipso set a datore extrinseco, idest a "Patre luminum," Iacobi i; nec sufficeret homini dilectio naturalis ad salutem, quia cum ipsa sit recurua in seipsam, nunquam erigeretur in Deum, cum non posset supra seipsam sine gracia superaddita. Item [ex admixtione] dyaphoni cum luce fiunt colores secundum multitudinem uel [paucitatem] uel fortitudinem ipsius dya- / phoni, ut cum ignis admiscetur aque uel aeri f. 105^{v}b etc. Album tamen et nigrum elementa sunt aliorum colorum. Ita cum caritas cooperatur et quasi admiscetur libero arbitrio, fiunt inde meritorie actiones, quarum elementa sunt natura et gracia. Ideo Apostolus Corinthiorum [xv] non dicit se solum facere opera, set graciam Dei cum illo. Item lux facit potencia colores [actu colores]; ita caritas opera ceterarum uirtutum facit meritoria. Ideo dicitur sola remunerari, non quia sola meretur, set quia per illam meritum aliarum ° [adinpletur]. Item lux offert se eciam oculo ceco, nec est defectus lucis quia cecus non uidet; similiter non [est] defectus caritatis quod aliquis in tenebris peccati manet. Sol enim iusticie presto est ad hostium mentis nostre per lucem gracie et pulsat, "siquis aperiat," Apocalipsis iii. Ideo sig-

I. 401 **meritum . . . adinpletur** merita aliarum adinplentur FL. **aliarum** *add* uirtutum EI. **adinpletur** inpletur E. 403 **est** *om* E. 404 **hostium** oculum GIW. 406

Hence we are expressly admonished, To the Hebrews 12: Look diligently "lest any man be wanting to the grace of God," which is to say that grace or charity of its own is not at fault, but sinful man when he rejects it after it is offered or drives it away after it has been given.

Charity is in the whole company of the virtues as the heart is in the joined total of the members of our body. For from the heart comes life, because in it lies the vital spirit; Proverbs 4: "Life issues out from it." This the Lord confirms when he says in Matthew 7: "The things which proceed out of the heart defile a man," that is, make him foul. On the same matter Bede says that the seat of the rational soul is in the heart. This should be understood according to its operations which belong to the activity of reason, because according to its substance it cannot have a location. Hence, the philosophers did not know its proper place in the body, as some said it was in the brain, others in the blood, and this can be conceded, on account of the different activities which belong more to the sensitive than the rational soul. As the heart thus is the principle of life in our body, so charity in the company of the virtues and their actions. Therefore, charity brings us from death to life; 1 John 3: "We have passed from death to life, because we love the brethren; and he that does not love, abides in death." Further, there are two ventricles or chambers in the heart. In one are the spirits, in the other blood, and each chamber draws from the other. Thus, in charity there are two chambers, discretion and compassion. Discretion considers the need of one's neighbor and by what spirit it is led, and "tries the spirits if they be of God," 1 John 4. For that reason, too, the gifts of "knowledge and piety" are joined together, Isaias 11, so that man may know how to commiserate and be merciful with discretion. In the second chamber of charity is the blood of compassion, for as by means of the blood our soul warms and nourishes the body—whence the soul of all flesh is said to be in the blood, Deuteronomy 12—, so does charity by means of compassion nourish our needy neighbor by giving him food and drink and warm him by clothing him; hence, Job 31: "If the fatherless has not eaten of my morsel and if he has not been warmed with the fleece of my sheep, let my shoulder fall from its joint," and so forth, as if he were saying: I have done both; I have fed the needy and have warmed him. Further, the heart of a stag turns into bone when he grows old, as the Philosopher says, because a bone grows in it. Thus, charity in many grows lukewarm and cold in the end, and what is cold hardens more readily, Matthew 10; and chapter 24: "The charity of many shall grow cold, because iniquity will abound." Moreover, according to the Philosopher the heart is the warmest part of our

Ad *om* GIW. **quis** quid JG. 408 **quando** *om* E; quando ⟨uel qui⟩ J; ipsam FL; quando ipsam AH. 409 **congerie** genere E; cognicione ⟨uel in serie⟩ J; serie *(canc)* congerie G. 411–12 **Hoc . . . Dominus** unde GIW. 413 Beda *marg* E. **idest inquinant** *om* GIW. 416 **est** *add* actus *canc* E. **situalis** spiritualis E; finalis ⟨uel situalis⟩ J; finalis H; statualis I. **ignorabant** ignorauerunt E. 422 **I . . . uitam** *om* A. 424 **uentriculi siue duo** *om* A. **duo** ***(2nd)*** *om* FL. **sunt** ***(2nd)*** est JFG; *om* A. 430 **sciat . . . misereri** *om* I. **discrete** discernere et FL; *om GW*. **conpati** pati E. 432 **et fouet** *om* F. 435 **vnde** *add* in E. 438 **foui . . . calefeci** *om* GIW. 438–39 **ossescit** os crescit E; algescit G. 439 Philosophus *marg* E. **ut** *om* EFGHL; sicut IW. 440 **tepescit** torpescit JL. 440–41 **et quod . . . indurescit** *om*

nanter dicitur Ad Hebreos xii: Videte "ne quis desit gracie Dei," quasi dicat, gracia uel caritas de se non deficit, set homo peccator [quando] repellit oblatam uel expellit iam datam.

Caritas est in [congerie] uirtutum sicut cor in coniunctione membrorum. Ex corde enim uita est, quia in ipso est spiritus uitalis; Prouerbiorum iiii: "Ex ipso uita procedit." Hoc attestatur Dominus Matthei vii dicens: "Que de corde procedunt coinquinant hominem," idest inquinant. Beda dicit de eodem quod sedes anime racionalis in corde est. Hoc intellige secundum suas operaciones que pertinent ad actus racionis, quia secundum substanciam non est [situalis]. Ideo philosophi [ignorabant] proprium locum eius in corpore, / ut quidam dicerent eam in cerebro, f. 106ra quidam in sanguine, et hoc posset concedi pro diuersis operacionibus que magis pertinent ad animam sensitiuam quam racionalem. Sicut igitur cor principium uite est in corpore, sic caritas in uirtutum et operum congerie. Vnde caritas transfert nos de morte ad uitam; I Iohannis iii: "Translati sumus de morte ad uitam, quoniam diligimus fratres; et qui non diligit, manet in morte." Item in corde sunt duo uentriculi siue duo thalami. In uno sunt spiritus, in altero est sanguis, et uterque thalamus haurit ex alterutro. Ita in caritate sunt duo thalami, discrecio et conpassio. Discrecio attendit que sit necessitas proximi et quo spiritu ducatur, et "probat spiritus si ex Deo sunt," I Iohannis iiii. Hac de causa eciam coniunguntur donum "sciencie et pietatis," Ysaie xi, ut homo sciat discrete [conpati] et misereri. In secundo uentriculo caritatis est sanguis conpassionis, quoniam sicut anima mediante sanguine calefacit corpus et fouet—et ideo dicitur anima omnis carnis esse in sanguine, Deuteronomi xii—, ita caritas mediante conpassione fouet proximum indigentem pascendo et potando et calefacit uestiendo; vnde ° Iob xxxi: "Si non comedit pupillus ex buccella mea et si non de uelleribus ouium mearum calefactus est, cadat humerus a iunctura," etc., quasi diceret: vtrumque feci; foui indigentem et calefeci. Item cor cerui / cum senescit, [ossescit], f. 106rb [ut] dicit Philosophus, quia os in eo crescit. Hoc est quod caritas multorum in fine tepescit et refrigescit, et quod frigidum est cicius indurescit, Matthei x; et xxiiii: "Refrigescet caritas multorum, quia habundabit iniquitas." Item cor est calidissima pars

body; wherefore it lies below the brain as the coldest member. Thus, charity is the most fervent of the virtues; it therefore burns more with love for heavenly things, desiring "to be dissolved and to be with Christ," Philippians 1. Out of its desire and fervor for heavenly things it does not fear worldly torment, as the Apostle testifies when he says: "Neither death nor life, nor things present, nor things to come shall separate us from the love of Christ," To the Romans 8. Through charity "the apostles went from the presence of the council rejoicing," Acts 5. Because of its future consolations charity does not think of its current tribulations. Therefore it is said of those who have charity, Deuteronomy 33: "They shall suck as milk the abundance of the sea"; that is, the world's afflictions will be sweet to them; and on Job 6, "Can an unsavory thing be eaten," and so forth, Gregory comments: "The ills of the world are sweet food through the love of heaven."

Charity is pure gold for four reasons. For its preciousness, for among all metals gold is more precious. So is charity among the virtues; therefore: "If a man should give all his substance, he could not buy it," end of Canticles. Further, he is indeed rich who owns a little gold, and the smallest amount of charity suffices for man's salvation; therefore, Apocalypse 3: "I counsel you to buy of me pure gold, that you may be made rich." But how to buy it if, as was said earlier, it cannot be bought? In reply we say that there are three states of charity: for charity is beginning, or progressing, or fulfilling. In the beginning state charity cannot be bought, because it is freely given, unless by "buying" one understands man's preparation that precedes, or perhaps almsgiving, through which someone who lives without charity obligates the poor and the Church to gain charity for him by their prayers, as Daniel said to Nebuchadnezzar: "Redeem your sins with alms," Daniel 4, for alms given after sin yield a reward in the giver, as Gregory explains on Job 15. But the increase and the fulfillment of charity are bought with good works—not that it grows in essence, since it is a simple habit, but rather in constancy, devotion, and deep-rootedness in merit and reward. Furthermore, gold weighs more than the other metals, because since it is purer, its parts are more closely knit. Thus, charity weighs more in its reward and merit; it is therefore called "the shekel of the sanctuary," Leviticus near the end, for beside its weight nothing in our works is acceptable. Next, if pure gold is broken, it shines as much inside as it does outside, and true charity is the same in a man's will as it appears in his deed. For it does not hesitate

IW. 442 **habundabit** habundauit AFL. 443 Philosophus *marg* E. **secundum Philosophum** secundum Plinium A; ut dicit Philosophus GIW. 444 **caritas** *om* EW. 446 **Christo** *add* ad E. 449 **Christi** *add* unde *canc* E. **Romanos** Corinthios E. 450–51 **Ipsa . . . tribulaciones** *om* F. 455 Gregorius *marg* E. 457 **omnia** *om* EHL. **preciosius** *add* est AGHW. 458 **inter** *add* omnes AGHW. 459 **Canticorum fine** *om* E; Corinthiorum fine F; Ecc fine L. 460 **caritas . . . sufficit** caritatis munera sufficiunt A. **minima** minutissima F. 463 **conparari** emi FL; operari G. 466 **habilitacio** abilitacio E; humiliacio JAH; humilitatem L. **forsitan** forsan E; *om* A. 468 **inpetrent caritatem** conparent caritatem uel inpetrent GIW. **sicut** sic E. **Daniel** dominus GIW. 470–71 **precium** premium FGL. 471 Gregorius *marg* E. **Augmentum** argentum E. 472 **emuntur** emitur EGIW. 473–74 **et radicacione** *om* FL. 474 **in** et EFL. 477 **fine** ii E. 479 **frangatur** frangitur EH. 482–83

corporis, secundum Philosophum; ideo supponitur cerebro tanquam frigidissimo membro. Ita [caritas] uirtutum est feruentissima; ideo magis ardet ad celestia, cupiens “dissolui et esse cum Christo,” ° Philippensium i. Ipsa enim ex feruore et desiderio celestium non timet mundanum supplicium, teste Apostolo qui ait: “Neque mors neque uita neque instancia neque futura separabunt nos a caritate Christi,” Ad [Romanos] viii. Per ipsam “ibant apostoli gaudentes a conspectu concilii,” Actuum v. Ipsa enim propter futuras consolaciones non reputat presentes tribulaciones. Vnde de habentibus eam dicitur Deuteronomi xxxiii: “Inundaciones maris quasi lac sugent”; idest, tribulaciones mundi eis dulcescent; et super Iob vi, “Nunquid potest comedi insulsum,” etc., Gregorius: “Mala seculi sunt dulces cibi pre amore celi.”

Caritas est aurum mundum propter quatuor. Propter preciositatem, quia inter [omnia] metalla aurum preciosius. Sic caritas inter uirtutes; vnde: “Si dederit homo totam substanciam suam, non posset conparare eam,” [Canticorum fine]. Item satis est diues qui sufficienciam habet auri, et caritas minima sufficit homini ad salutem; ideo Apocalipsis iii: “Suadeo tibi emere a me / aurum mundum, ut locuples fias.” Set qualiter emitur, cum su- f. 106^{v}a pra dicatur quod conparari non possit? Ideo dicendum tres esse status caritatis: est enim caritas incipiens, proficiens, et consumans. Quoad inicium non emitur, quia gratis datur, nisi dicatur “empcio” hominis [habilitacio] que precedit, uel [forsitan] elemosinarum largicio qua quis extra caritatem existens obligat pauperes et Ecclesiam, ut sibi inpetrent caritatem, [sicut] dixit Daniel ad Nabuchodonosor: “Elemosinis peccata tua redime,” Danielis iiii, quia in propria persona elemosina post peccatum est precium, Gregorius super Iob xv. [Augmentum] uero caritatis et consumacio [emuntur] bonis operibus—non quod ipsa crescat in essencia cum sit habitus simplex, set in constancia et deuocione et radicacione [in] merito et premio. Item aurum plus ponderat ceteris metallis, quia cum sit purius, habet partes magis consertas. Sic caritas plus ponderat in merito et premio; vnde ipsa dicitur “syclus sanctuarii,” Leuitici [fine], quia extra pondus ipsius nichil acceptabile in operibus nostris. Item aurum purum ita lucet intra si [frangatur] sicut extra, et uera caritas talis est in uoluntate qualis

within nor take offense without; Timothy 1: "The end of the commandment is charity, from a pure heart, and a good conscience, and an unfeigned faith." Lastly, gold is pulverized and thus more safely carried abroad; see above in the chapter on humility.

Charity is the tree of life in the middle of paradise, so that one may say of it: "She is a tree of life to them that lay hold on her; and he that shall retain her is blessed," Proverbs 3. In addition, it is the "great and strong tree" of Daniel 4, whose "height reached unto heaven, and under it dwell beasts, and in the branches thereof the fowls of the air; its leaves are most beautiful and its fruit exceeding much; therefore, in it is food for all." The great and strong tree is unsurpassable charity; its top reaches heaven because it directly contemplates God; the beasts underneath are active men, the birds in its branches the contemplative; its leaves are the words of doctrine, by which we are taught to love God and our neighbor, and they are "for medicine" to our souls, Ezechiel 47. Its fruit is our just reward; Wisdom 3: "The fruit of good labors is glorious." For the fruit of charity will be for us the meal of eternal refreshment. As Hesychius comments on Leviticus 25, "There shall be a sabbath of eternal resting," in the Gloss: "Of what we have done here we shall eat the fruit in the future." Also, this is the tree of which the Philosopher says that in it dwell doves for which a dragon lies in wait, and it always shuns the shade of this tree. The doves are the saints, guileless and innocent; Isaias 60: "As doves to their windows." Gregory: "'As doves to their windows' are those who long for nothing in this world, who without guile pass by all things and are not drawn to what they see with grasping zeal." Their opposite is the kite, who gasps with ravenous desire for everything his eyes catch. The dragon that lies in wait for the doves is our old enemy of Apocalypse 12, where he is called the "red dragon," because after sin he brings shame and in the end he draws us into the fire. The shade of this tree is penitence, which must rise out of love, not merely out of fear. This the dragon and all evil ones fear, as is shown in the Psalm: "They that dwell in the uttermost borders shall be afraid at your signs," that is, the wicked, when they come to the end of the world and the gate of hell, fear the signs of penitence. And Isaias 19: "The land of Judah shall be a terror to Egypt." "The land of Judah" is the life of a penitent; "Egypt" is the world or the sinners of the world, to whom the life of the saints is detestable. Or else, the shade of charity can be called Christ's penance, who suffered for us out of his great charity. His penance was small with regard to his love, but very great with regard to the weakness of his human nature, and it made our own penance efficacious, which without his would never be able to be sufficient; therefore: "Under his shadow

Item . . . humilitate *om* F. 485–86 **et . . . eam** *om* F. 486 **iii** *om* EH. 487 **Danielis iiii** *om* GIW. 488–90 **pulcherrima . . . inuincibilis** inuincibilia FL. 495 **est** sunt GIW; *om* F. 497 Esycius *marg* E. 498 Glossa *marg* E. **terre** eterne JFGILW; certe H. 500 **Philosophus** propheta E. 503 Gregorius *marg* E. 509–10 **debet** dicitur AH. 516 **penitencia** pena *corr from* penitencia E. **magna** maxima AGHW.

apparet in opere. Intus enim est sine scrupulo, et extra sine scandalo; Thymothei i: "Finis precepti est caritas de corde puro et consciencia bona et fide non ficta." Item aurum puluerizatur et ita securius transportatur; nota supra capitulo de humilitate.

Caritas est lignum uite in medio paradysi, ut / possit dici de f. 106vb ea: "Lignum uite est hiis qui apprehenderint eam; et qui tenuerit eam, beatus," Prouerbiorum [iii]. Preterea ipsa est "arbor fortis et magna," Danielis iiii, "cuius proceritas tangit celum, et sub ea habitant animalia, et in ramis eius uolucres celi; folia eius pulcherrima et fructus nimius; vnde esca uniuersorum in ea est." Arbor magna et fortis est caritas inuincibilis; cacumen eius tangit celum quia ipsa immediate contemplatur Deum; animalia subter eam sunt actiui, volucres in ramis sunt contemplatiui; folia eius sunt doctrine uerba, quibus erudimur ad dilectionem Dei et proximi, et ipsa sunt "in medicinam" animarum, Ezechielis xlvii. Fructus eius est merces retribucionis; Sapiencie iii: "Bonorum laborum gloriosus est fructus." Fructus enim caritatis erit nobis prandium eterne refectionis. Esycius super Leuitici xxv, "Sabbatum erit terre requiecionis," Glossa: "Eorum que hic gessimus in futuro fructum manducabimus." Item hec est arbor de qua dicit [Philosophus] quod in ea habitant columbe quibus insidiatur draco et semper fugit umbram arboris. Columbe sunt sancti simplices et innocentes; Ysaie lx: "Quasi columbe ad fenestras suas." Gregorius: "'Quasi columbe ad fenestras' sunt qui nichil in mundo concupiscunt, qui simpliciter omnia transeunt et ad ea que uident rapacitatis studio non trahuntur." Econtra miluus est qui ad ea que oculis considerat rapaci de- / siderio anhelat. Draco f. 107ra columbis insidians antiquus hostis est, Apocalipsis xii, vbi dicitur "draco rufus," quia post peccatum adducit uerecundiam et in fine trahit ad flammam. Vmbra huius arboris penitencia est, que debet fieri ex amore, non solum ex timore. Hanc timet draco et omnes mali, ut in Psalmo: "Qui habitant terminos, pauebunt a signis tuis," idest, mali positi in exitu mundi et in porta inferni timent signa penitencie. Et Ysaie xix: "Erit terra Iuda Egipto in pauorem." "Terra Iuda" uita penitentis est; "Egiptus" mundus siue mundi peccatores, quibus uita sanctorum est execrabilis. Vel umbra caritatis potest dici [penitencia] Christi, qui ex magna caritate pro nobis passus est. Vnde pena parua fuit respectu eius amoris, licet maxima respectu humane infirmitatis, et ipsa dedit efficaciam nostre penitencie, que sine illa nunquam posset suffi-

we shall live among the Gentiles," Lamentations at the end. Further, if my tree is planted in your orchard, it yields to me my own fruit as well as yours, that is, that which grows on your soil, and I shall be allowed by human laws to go through your field and harvest my fruit. Thus, if the tree of my charity is transplanted into your orchard, so that I truly love you in God and for God, your fruits will also be mine. Bernard: "A precious thing is charity, which makes other people's good our own; a most wicked thing is envy, which takes even our own good away from us." Gregory in his *Dialogue*: "We talk about virtues in vain, and, just as if we were placed among fruitbearing boughs, we smell the fruit but do not eat it."

Charity is the river of paradise, Genesis 2, whose four heads are the four objects of love, according to Augustine: first, that we love what is above us, that is, God; second, what is within us, that is, our own soul; third, what is beside us, that is, our neighbor's soul; and fourth, what is beneath us, that is, our own flesh.

Charity is the wedding garment without which no one is admitted to the heavenly banquet, Matthew 22, for "no one clothed with sackcloth," that is, with the shabby cloak of his sins, "might enter the king's court," Esther 4. This wedding garment is dyed of four colors, which are spoken of in Exodus 26. The first is violet, the color of air, named after a stone or a flower, which indicates heavenly desire which comes from charity. The second is purple, of the color of blood, which indicates martyrdom, in which the blood of his saints is offered to the Lord. The third is scarlet twice dyed, named after a flower, which is very red and indicates the twofold love. The fourth is fine twisted linen, a kind of pure white linen which is bleached with much work, just as chastity is acquired with great effort. And charity is rightly considered a garment, for it protects against the cold of faithlessness and the heat of lust, against pleasure that warms wrongly and fear that makes one wrongly humble. These two hold us back much from good achievements, and they are indicated in a Psalm: "Things set on fire and dug down," and so forth. Likewise, a garment hides the body's shamefulness; thus, charity hides the enormity of our sins, that they may not be counted for our punishment; James, near the end: "Charity covers a multitude of sins."

Charity is, further, like mortar, with which the living stones are bound together in the construction of the heavenly building, that is, the faithful in the unity of the Church, without which they are "as chaff set in high places, and plasterings made without cost," Ecclesiasticus 22, that is, not bound together

518 **infirmitatis** fragilitatis GIW. 521 **fine** *om* E. 523 **pertransire** *add* per E; transire FL. 526 Bernardus *marg* E. 527 **nostra** ***(1st)*** mea GIW. **est** autem J; res est AFH. 528 Gregorius *marg* E. 529 **positi** pomi E; poniti G. **odoramus** adoramus EGHI; ordoramus L. 532 Augustinus *marg* E. 533 **secundum** *add* ut di E. 534 **tercium** tercio EFGL. 534–36 **tercium . . . propriam** *after* non licet *line 538* G. 535 **quartum** quarto EFGL. 539 **palacium regis** aulam regiam GIW. 541–42 **aerei coloris** aereus FGL. 542 **sic** *om* E. 545 **flore** *add* sic GIW. 547 **et** que E. 548 **castitas** caritas JFL(?). **cum** *add* magna AIW. 549 **uestis** *add* nupcialis JA. 550 **contra . . . incendentem** *om* L. **incendentem** incedentem EF; accendentem AGW; ascendentem I. 554 **fine** ii E; *om* F. 556 **uiui** muri A. 557 **structura** fructu E. 559 **idest** *om* EAHL. 560–61 **temperatura** tempe-

cere; vnde: “Sub umbra eius uiuimus in gentibus,” Trenorum [fine]. Item arbor mea plantata in orto tuo michi communicat et fructus meos et tuos, scilicet qui de tuo solo nutriuntur, et licebit michi per leges humanas pertransire ° agrum tuum ut colligam fructum meum. Ita, si arbor caritatis mee transplantetur in orto tuo, ut uere te diligam in Deo et propter Deum, eciam fructus tui erunt mei. Bernardus: “Preciosa res est caritas, que aliena bona nostra facit; pessima est inuidia, que eciam nostra nobis fa- / cit aliena.” Gregorius in *Dyalogo*: “De uirtutibus uacui loqui- f. 107rb mur et quasi inter arbusta fructifera [positi] fructum [odoramus] nec manducamus.”

Caritas est fluuius paradysi, Genesis ii, cuius quatuor capita sunt quatuor diligendorum genera, secundum Augustinum: primum, ut diligamus quod supra nos est, idest Deum; secundum, ° quod intra nos est, idest animam propriam; [tercium], quod iuxta nos est, idest animam proximi; [quartum], quod subtus nos est, idest carnem propriam.

Caritas est uestis nupcialis sine qua nullus recipitur ad celeste conuiuium, Matthei xxii, quoniam “non licet indutum sacco,” idest uili peccatorum pallio, “intrare palacium regis,” Hester iiii. Fit autem hec uestis nupcialis ex quatuor coloribus, de quibus Exodi xxvi. Quorum primus est iacinctus, et est color aerei coloris a lapide uel flore [sic] dictus, in quo notatur celeste desiderium quod ex caritate est. Alius est purpura sanguinei coloris, in quo notatur martirium, in quo offertur Domino sanguis sanctorum suorum. Tercius est coccus bistinctus a flore dictus, qui ualde rubicundus est, et signat geminam dilectionem. Quartus est bissus retorta, que est genus lini candidissimi [et] cum magno labore candidatur, sicut castitas cum difficultate aquiritur. Et bene est caritas uestis, quia munit contra frigus infidelitatis et contra estum concupiscencie, contra cupiditatem male [incenden- / tem] et f. 107va contra timorem male humiliantem. Hec duo multum retardant bonum expediendum, et notantur in Psalmo: “Incensa igni et suffossa,” etc. Item uestis celat corporis turpitudinem; sic caritas peccatorum enormitatem, ne inputentur ad penam; Iacobi [fine]: “Caritas operit multitudinem peccatorum.”

Item caritas est quasi cementum, quo ligantur lapides uiui in [structura] celestis edificii, idest, fideles in unitate Ecclesie, sine qua sunt “tanquam palee in excelso posite et sicut cementa sine inpensa posita,” Ecclesiastici xxii, [idest], non ligata per calcem et

with lime and gravel according to the mason's craft. Untempered mortar does not bind the stones in a wall; thus, the praise and flattery of the wicked does not solidify the pile of good works without charity, even if by lying it should render them glittering. This the Lord says in Ezechiel 13: "Son of man, say to them that daub the wall without tempering that it shall fall." Similarly, charity is the pitch with which the boat of Peter is caulked, that is, the Church of the faithful, which is tossed about by the waves of afflictions but does not sink; so Gregory declares in commenting on Job 9, "The turning about of Arcturus," etc. Further, charity is nourishment for the souls of the faithful. Therefore, whoever is cut off from the body of the Church is not kept alive by this food. The nurse of every good is grace, which is the same as charity; Wisdom 16: "Grace that nourishes all," etc. But a member that is cut off does not share in it; 1 John 2: "They went out from us, but they were not of us." Augustine in his own work: "As a bad fluid comes out of the body—add: and is not of the body—, thus the wicked from the body of the Church; therefore, they dry up without spiritual growth."

Since earlier we said that charity is either created or uncreated, after discussing created charity, which belongs entirely to man, we now turn to that charity which is at once created and uncreated, which is the love of Christ as a human being for men, "because he has first loved us," 1 John 4. His love appears in many things. First in his predestination; Habacuc 1: "I have loved Jacob," that is, I have preelected him, "I have hated Esau," that is, rejected him. However, the cause of eternal election lies not in our merits, but in the generosity of God's will alone; Ephesians 1: "He chose us in his charity before the foundation of the world," and so forth. Rejection, however, that is, the withdrawal of grace or the provision of punishment, is caused by men's evil deeds. Second, his love appears in his creation, in which he wanted to share his exceedingly great goodness with his creatures. Hence, in Book I of the *First Philosophy*: "The beginning of all things is love and desire." And Boethius in the *Consolation*:

> No external causes impelled you to make this work from chaotic matter.
> Rather it was the form of the highest good, existing within you.

Third, in the giving of grace; Isaias 43: "Since you became honorable in my eyes, I have loved you, says the Lord." Fourth, in his sharing our nature; Jeremias 31: "I have loved you with an everlasting love; therefore have I drawn

rancia E. 563 **reddant** reddunt E. **reddant . . . Dominus** ostendant GIW. 564 **liniunt** linient EIW: sinunt G. 567 Gregorius *marg* E. **super** *om* EFGLW. **Arcturi** artari EF; *om* J; artaui A; arthuri GIW; auari H. 570 **est *(2nd)*** *om* E. 573 Augustinus *marg* E. **set** que E; quia AHILW; qui G. **in originali** *om* FL. 574 **sic** *add* nec JAGHILW; *add* uero F. 575 **uegetacione** *add* de caritate creata et increata *rubr* J; *add* de caritate increata *rubr* I. 576 **alia *(2nd)*** *add* est E. 577 **dicto de creata** *om* FL. 578 **et** *add* de EFH. 580 **sua dilectio** *om* FL. **Abacuc i** Malachie i F; Abacuc i ⟨uel Malachie⟩ J. 581 **idest *(2nd)*** *add* predestinando JG. 582 **electionis** electioni E; dileccionis AH; elacionis L. 582–83 **liberalitate** libertate JFL; uoluntate I. 583 **uoluntatis** libertatis I. **i** v E. 585 **inproperacionis** preparacionis JFGHILW. **merita** *om* FL. 587 **suam** sue AH; s GILW. 588 **Philosophie** Ephesiorum E; *om* A; prophecie GW. 589 Boecius *marg* E. **in Consolacionibus** *om* E. 590 **non** nec E. **pepulerunt** pupugerunt GIW; *add* uel pupugerunt A. 594–95 **Quarto . . . communicacione** *om* L. 595 **communicacione** circumscisione GW;

sabulum secundum artem cementarii. Cementa enim sine [temperatura] non ligant murum; ita laus et adulacio inpiorum non solidant sine caritate congeriem operum, etsi menciendo nitidam [reddant]. Hoc dicit Dominus, Ezechielis xiii: “Fili hominis, dic ad eos qui [liniunt] absque temperatura murum quod casurus sit.” Item caritas est bitumen quo ligatur nauicula Petri, idest credencium Ecclesia, que fluctibus tunditur tribulacionum set non submergitur; dicit Gregorius [super] Iob ix, “girum [Arcturi],” etc. Item caritas est nutrimentum animarum fidelium. Vnde qui a corpore Ecclesie abscinditur, hoc nutrimento non uegetatur. Omnium enim bonorum gracia nutrix est, que et caritas [est]; Sapiencie xvi: “Omnium nutrici gracie,” etc. Membrum uero abscisum illa non communicat; I Iohannis ii: “Ex nobis prodierunt, [set] ex nobis non / erant.” Augustinus in originali: “Sicut malus f. 107vb
humor exit de corpore—et de corpore non est, suple—, sic mali de corpore Ecclesie; ideo exsiccantur sine spirituali uegetacione.”

Quia dictum est supra quod caritas alia creata, alia ° increata, dicto de creata, que est puri hominis, dicendum est de increata et ° creata simul, que est Christi hominis ad homines, “quoniam ipse prior dilexit nos,” I Iohannis iiii. Apparet autem sua dilectio in multis. Primo in predestinacione; Abacuc i: “Iacob dilexi,” idest predestinaui, “Esau odio habui,” idest reprobaui. Tamen eterne [electionis] non est causa in meritis, set in sola liberalitate diuine uoluntatis; Ephesiorum [i]: “Elegit nos in caritate ante mundi constitucionem,” etc. Reprobacionis uero, idest gracie subtractionis uel pene inproperacionis, mala hominum merita sunt causa. Secundo apparet sua dilectio in creacione, qua uoluit summam bonitatem suam creature communicare. Vnde I *Prime* [*Philosophie*]: “Principium omnium amor et desiderium.” Et Boecius [in *Consolacionibus*]:

> Quem [non] externe pepulerunt fingere cause
> Materie fluctuantis opus uerum insita summi
> Forma boni.

Tercio, in gracie apposicione; Ysaie xliii: “Ex quo honorabilis factus es coram me dilexi te, dicit Dominus.” Quarto, in nostre nature communicacione; Ieremie xxxi: “[In] caritate perpetua di-

you, taking pity on you." Fifth, in his passion; Apocalypse 1: "He has loved us and washed us from our sins in his own blood." Sixth, in letting us take part in his name, so that after Christ we are called Christians; 1 John 3: "Behold, what manner of charity God has bestowed on us, that we should be called and should be the sons of God." Seventh, in the protection of grace; John 14: "If anyone loves me, my Father will love him, and we will come to him and will make our abode with him"; that means, protect us. Eighth, in his chastizing us in this life; Apocalypse 3: "Such as I love, I rebuke and chastize." Ninth, in giving us temporal goods; Canticles 2: "His left hand is under my head," says the bride, that is, the abundance of temporal goods, which is the blessing of the left hand. But it seems that Gregory contradicts this. For he says that the temporal wealth is a sure sign of eternal rejection and not, therefore, a sign of love. You should reply to this that in wicked men who abuse God's good gifts, wealth is a sign of rejection, and it is out of great mercy that they receive their reward in worldly goods, because they shall have no future part with the elect. In good men, however, it is a sign of love, so that they can carry out by deed the good they have conceived in their will. This is the opinion of Augustine when he comments on the verse: "If riches abound," and so forth. Tenth, in our glorification, where love is consummated; John 13: "Having loved his own, he loved them unto the end," that is: to the end that they might share eternal life with him, or else unto the end, namely into his death, which was the way to life.

Christ loved us with sweet love in his incarnation; therefore, the Church sings that "The heavens have been made to flow with honey"; and Proverbs 8: "His delights were to be with the children of men." He also loved us with wise love, namely in sharing our weaknesses, for as Gregory says: "He took the cluster of grapes but avoided the thorn," that is, he took upon him our nature but avoided sin. This is stated in Hebrews 4, that "he has been tempted in all things like as we are, without sin." Further, he loved us with persistent love, namely into eternal life, John 13. Also, he loved us with strong love, so that he refused neither pain nor death; at the end of Canticles: "Love is strong as death." In addition, he loved us from his whole heart, according to the commandment given to man, in Matthew 22, for he even offered his heart, in so far as he was man, to be pierced by the lance, so that he might draw us gently to love. Jeremias 48: "My heart shall sound for Moab like pipes." "Moab" means from the father and denotes sinners, who are from their father the devil through their sin, John 8;

assumpcione I. **in** *om* EGHILW; *interl* J. 596 **Quinto** quarta L. 597 **nos** ***(2nd)*** *om* JAFGIW. **Sexto** quinto L. 599–634 **ut . . . suo** etc F. 600 **Septimo** sexto L. 602 **Octauo** septimo L; quarto G. 604 **Nono** octauo L. 605 **dicit sponsa** *om* GW; etc I. 606 Gregorius *marg* E. 610 **eis** *om* EW. 613 Augustinus *marg* E. 614 **Decimo . . . dilectionis** *after* uitam, *line 617, as* nono L. **est** *om* EH. 616 **cum eo** tandem J. **perciperent** participent AGI. 617 **que . . . uitam** *om* GIW. 618 **Christus** decimo L. 619 **et** *add* in EAH. 620 **Dilexit nos eciam** *om* GIW. 622 Gregorius *marg* E. **spinam cauit** spina caruit AI. 623 **cauit culpam** caruit culpa AI. **Hoc . . . dicitur** vnde GIW. 625 **dilexit nos** *om* GIW. 626 **dilexit nos** *om* GIW. 627 **fine** *om* EH. **dilexit nos** *om* GIW. 631 **interpretatur** *om* GIW. 635 **optulit** *add* et de-

lexi te; ideo attraxi te miserans." Quinto, in passione; Apocalipsis i: "Dilexit nos et lauit nos in sanguine suo." Sexto, / in nominis f. 108ra sui participacione, ut a Christo dicamur Christiani; I Iohannis iii: "Videte qualem caritatem dedit nobis Deus ut filii Dei nominemur et simus." Septimo, in gracie conseruacione; Iohannis xiiii: "Siquis diligit me, Pater meus diliget eum, et ad eum ueniemus et mansionem apud eum faciemus"; hoc est conseruare. Octauo, in presenti castigacione; Apocalipsis iii: "Ego quos amo arguo et castigo." Nono, in temporalium largicione; Canticorum ii: "Leua eius sub capite meo," dicit sponsa, idest temporalium habundancia, que est benedictio sinistre. Set contra hoc uidetur dicere Gregorius. Dicit enim quod eterne reprobacionis indicium est habundancia temporalium, non igitur signum dilectionis. Et dicas quod in malis qui Dei donis abutuntur signum est reprobacionis, et ex summa misericordia est quod premiantur in temporalibus, quia non est [eis] pars futura cum electis. In bonis autem signum est dilectionis, ut possint explere in opere bonum conceptum in uoluntate. Sentencia est Augustini, ibi: "Diuicie si affluant," etc. Decimo, in glorificacione, ubi [est] consumacio dilectionis; Iohannis xiii: "Cum dilexisset suos, in finem dilexit eos," idest: hoc fine ut cum eo perciperent uitam eternam, uel in finem, idest, in mortem, que fuit uia ad uitam.

Christus dilexit nos dulciter in incarnacione; vnde canit Ecclesia quod "melliflui facti sunt celi"; et ° Prouerbiorum viii: "Delicie eius esse cum filiis hominum." Dilexit nos eciam sapienter, in infirmitatum nostrarum participacione, quia ut dicit Gregorius: "Botrum sumpsit et spinam cauit," idest, / assumpsit na- f. 108rb turam et cauit culpam. Hoc est quod dicitur Hebreorum iiii quod "temptatus est per omnia pro similitudine absque peccato." Item dilexit nos perseueranter, quia ad uitam eternam, Iohannis xiii. Item dilexit nos fortiter, ut nec penam nec mortem repelleret; Canticorum [fine]: "Fortis est ut mors dilectio." Item dilexit nos toto corde, iuxta preceptum homini datum, Matthei xxii, quia eciam cor suum in quantum homo lancee opposuit perforandum, ut nos alliceret ad diligendum. Ieremie xlviii: "Cor meum ad Moab quasi tibia eris sonabit." "Moab" interpretatur ex patre et peccatores signat qui sunt ex patre dyabolo per culpam, Iohannis

for them Christ's love should sound most sweetly, which was so great that he did not spare his heart for us. He further loved us with his whole soul, for he offered his dear soul for our redemption; Jeremias 12: "I have given my dear soul," and so forth. And he loved us with his whole mind; whence he made a sign on himself to remember us by, as is shown in his keeping his wounds, so that he may show what he has suffered for man. Isaias 49: "Can a woman forget her infant?" and so forth, "and if she should forget, yet will I not forget you." And he gives the reason: "Behold, I have graven you in my hands."

Thus it is manifest that Christ loved us in seven manners, the first four of which are taken from blessed Bernard, the following three from the Gospel. Also manifest is the greatness of his love, from the ten benefits mentioned above. Therefore, we are obligated to love him for all these benefits and in the same manner in which he has loved us. For charity is the way in which he came to us and in which we shall go to him; therefore, it is the "more excellent way," To the Corinthians 13. Hence we must love him with sweet love, so that for his love all earthly love may grow paltry for us which is full of bitterness and gall. But to fools some things dyed with gall appear golden; just as according to Boethius in his *Consolation* all earthly happiness is shot through with bitterness. On the other hand, the love of Christ is "sweeter than honey and the honeycomb," and it is sweet not only to the taste, when through the gift of *sapientia* we taste how "sweet the Lord is," but also in our memory; Ecclesiasticus 49: "The memory of Josiah shall be as sweet as honey in every mouth." Likewise the memory of Jesus; Bernard: "He is a song of joy in my heart, honey in my mouth, and a tune in my ear"; and at the end of Osee: "His memorial shall be as the wine of Libanus." Behold, how his remembrance is a joy to our mind. With sweet love did the bride love him who said, Canticles 2: "Tell my beloved that I languish with love"; therefore, "stay me up with flowers, compass me about with apples." "Flowers" are the virtues of the saints, such as the lilies of virgins, the roses of martyrs, and the violets of confessors; sweet-smelling "apples" are their examples, by whose sweet smell we are drawn to the love of heavenly things. In these things the soul that languishes for Christ is stayed up that she may not falter on her way. In addition, blessed Anselm also loved him with sweet love when, addressing the Son with his Glorious Mother, he spoke: "Let my heart always languish with your love, let my soul melt, let my flesh fail me. Would that the bowels of my soul burned with the sweet fire of your love, so that my fleshly bowels may dry up."

He must also be loved with a wise love, not something else in his place. For many turn the love of God to themselves and the love of their neighbor to their

dit AH. 636–37 **dilexit nos** *om* GIW. 637 **infixit** fixit FHL. 640–41 **causam** *add* quare A; *add* quare non uult obliuisci nostri GIW. 643 Bernardus *marg* E. **sequentes** residui GIW. **ab** de FL. 644 **eciam** enim E; *om* I. 645 **decem** *om* AGHIW. 646 **eisdem** ***(1st)*** hiis GIW. **et . . . modis** *om* J. 649 **igitur** *om* AH; ergo W. 651 **fatuis** facius E. 652 Boecius *marg* E. 657 Bernardus *marg* E. 658 **fine** *om* E. 666 Anshelmus *marg* E. **ipsum** eum AFGILW. **beatus** *om* E; pater G. 667 **continuo** gratissimo G. 668 **Utinam** ut EF; nunc W. 669 **feruore** fauore E; flore G. **exardescant** inardescant GIW. **ut** et E. 671 **eo** *add* Romanorum i f mutauerunt veritatem dei in mendacium *marg* J. 672 **seipsos** *add* Apostolus erunt in nouis-

viii; quibus dulcissime sonare debet tanta Christi dilectio, ut pro nobis non parceret eciam cordi suo. Item dilexit nos ex tota anima, quia dilectam animam suam optulit in nostram redempcionem; Ieremie xii: “Dedi dilectam animam meam,” etc. Item dilexit nos tota mente; vnde nostri memoriam infixit in se, ut patet in cicatricum reseruacione, ut ostendat quid pertulit pro homine. Ysaie lix: “Nunquid obliuisci potest mulier infantem suum?” etc., “et si illa oblita fuerit, ego non obliuiscar te.” Et dicit causam: “Ecce in manibus meis descripsi te.”

Sic patet quod septem modis dilexit nos Christus, quorum primi quatuor sumuntur a beato Bernardo, tres sequentes ab Ewangelio. Patet [eciam] magnitudo sue di- / f. 108va lectionis in suprapositis decem beneficiis. Vnde nos tenemur ei ad dilectionem pro eisdem omnibus et eisdem modis quibus nos dilexit. Caritas enim uia est qua ipse uenit ad nos et qua nos ituri sumus ad ipsum; vnde hec est “uia excellencior,” Ad Corinthios xiii. Debemus igitur ipsum diligere dulciter, ut pro eius amore uilescat nobis omnis amor terrenus amaritudine et felle plenus. Set quedam felle tincta [fatuis] apparent aurea; sic omnis terrena felicitas amaritudine respersa est, secundum Boecium in *Consolacionibus*. Econtra amor Christi dulcior “super mel et fauum,” et non solum dulcis est in gustu, cum per donum sapiencie degustatur quam “dulcis est Dominus,” set eciam in memoria; Ecclesiastici xlix: “Memoria Iosie in omni ore quasi mel indulcabitur.” Ita et memoria Iesu; Bernardus: “Ipse est iubilus in corde, mel in ore, melos in aure”; et Osee [fine]: “Memoriale eius sicut uinum Lybani.” Ecce quod eius memoria est anime leticia. Dulciter amabat eum sponsa que dicebat Canticorum ii: “Nunciate dilecto quia amore langueo”; ideo “fulcite me floribus, stipate me malis.” “Flores” sunt sanctorum uirtutes, ut lylia uirginum, rose martirum, viole confessorum; “poma” odorifera sunt eorum exempla, quorum odore trahimur ad amorem celestium. In hiis fulcitur languens anima pro Christo ne deficiat in uia. Preterea dulciter amabat ipsum [beatus] Anshelmus, / f. 108vb qui Filium cum Matre Gloriosa alloquens sic ait: “Vestro continuo amore langueat cor meum, liquefiat anima mea, deficiat caro mea. [Utinam] sic uiscera anime mee dulci [feruore] uestre dilectionis exardescant, [ut] uiscera carnis mee exarescant.”

Item diligendus est sapienter, non aliud pro eo. Multi enim dilectionem Dei conuertunt in seipsos et dilectionem proximi in

own, those who love the world and what is in it and become God's enemies, because "the friend of this world becomes an enemy of God," James 4. Man's love of God should be so great that either he is alone in man's heart, as is the case in the perfect, or he is the highest, as is the case with good active men, who, even if they love other things besides God, still place his love before everything else.

He must also be loved with strong love, so that we are prepared to love him as he has loved us. And how he has loved us, John expresses: "God so loved the world as to give his only begotten Son," John 3. Just as he gave his soul for us, so should we give our souls for him and for one another and cling to him with such a fervent spirit that no affliction of this life or worry of the world can draw us away from him. An example of the strongest love is the desire to suffer for Christ. Hence blessed Jerome cites the example of the young dog who finds blood from a wounded animal and pursues it so vigorously that neither thorns nor briars nor winding ditches make it turn back. Jerome: Thus should a Christian be steadfastly intent upon the Crucified, that he may overcome all obstacles which are in his way until he comes to him. The Apostle intimates the way we should run, Hebrews 10: "He has dedicated for us a new way in the blood of his Son." As long as this blood was still fresh and warm in the hearts of his believers, an immense crowd hastened to him, passing through fire and sword; but now that blood has grown cold and the sweet smell of his ointments, that is, of heavenly desires, has faded, and the *asa fetida* of sins dulls the heart's sense of smell. *Asa fetida* is a kind of gum of disagreeable smell. Moreover, when the hawthorn is in bloom, dogs lose their sense of smell; thus, men forfeit the smell of God's sweetness in the midst of temporal wealth. Ezechiel 8: "Behold, they put a branch to their nose." To put a branch to one's nose is to seek the flower of this world with so much love that the love of God is forgotten. In contrast to this, if the love of God "has once taken hold of our mind, it cuts it completely off from the love of the world"; so Gregory says in commenting on the verse of Canticles, "Love is strong as death." Seneca: "It is an honorable disgrace to die for a good cause."

God also must be loved with persistent love, for "he that shall persevere to the end," in his love, "he shall be saved," Matthew 24. Some are friends of one hour, who love their own profit and not their friend, and more God's gifts than

simis diebus homines seipsos amantes *marg* J. 674 **quia . . . constituitur** *om* FL. 676 **solum** solus JAFHL. **sit ut** sicut AH. 678 **preponunt** *add* Gregorius quicquid preter deum propter seipsum et preter proximum propter deum mens decepta elegerit uere dileccionis metas excedit *marg* J. 679 **ut** *om* JA. 680 **dilexit *(2nd)*** dilexerit E. **exponit** *add* iii dicens AH. 681–82 **Iohannis iii** *om* AH. 683 **ipso** Christo FIL. 686 Ieronimus *marg* E. 687 **reperiens** respiciens J. 689 Ieronimus *marg* E. **Ieronimus** *om* JF. 692 **Iniciauit** iniciant J; insinuauit L; nunciauit W. 695 **sanguis ille** *om* GIW. 696 **deficit** defecit AW; *corr from* defecit L. **asa** anima AGHIW. 698 **gumme fetentis** summe fetens J; anime fetentis I. 704 Gregorius *marg* E. **occidit** recedit J; subuertit AH; occiditur L. 705 Seneca *marg* E. 708 **usque in finem** *om* E. 709 **horarii** honorarii JA; *add* auari F; horum W. 710 **et** set E. 712 Se-

suos, qui diligunt mundum et que in eo sunt et inimici Dei constituuntur, quia "amicus huius mundi inimicus Dei constituitur," Iacobi iiii. Tanta debet esse hominis dilectio ad Deum ut uel ipse solum sit in corde, ut est in perfectis, uel summus sit, ut est in bonis actiuis, qui etsi alia preter ipsum diligant, eius tamen amorem omnibus preponunt.

Item diligendus est fortiter, ut parati simus diligere ipsum sicut ipse dilexit nos. Et qualiter [dilexit] Iohannes exponit: "Sic Deus dilexit mundum ut Filium suum vnigenitum daret," Iohannis iii. Sicut igitur ipse animam suam pro nobis posuit, et nos pro ipso et pro adinuicem debemus animas ponere, et tam feruenti spiritu ipsi adherere, ut nulla uite molestia uel seculi angustia possit nos retrahere. Exemplum firmissime dilectionis est desiderium passionis pro Christo. Vnde beatus Ieronimus ponit exemplum de catulo qui reperiens sanguinem bestie uulnerate tam fortiter insequitur quod nec spinis nec uepribus uel fouearum anfractibus reuocatur. Ieronimus: Ita Christianus indesinenter Cruci- / fixo intendat, ut omnia pretereat que occurrunt scandala f. 109[r]a
donec ad ipsum perueniat. Viam autem qua curramus insinuat Apostolus, Hebreorum x: "Iniciauit nobis uiam nouuam in sanguine Filii sui." Dum iste sanguis fuit recens et calidus in cordibus credencium, infinita turba per ignem et gladium transiens currebat ad ipsum; set sanguis ille iam refriguit et odor ungentorum deficit, idest celestium desideriorum, et asa fetida peccatorum olfactum cordis inficit. Est autem asa quoddam genus gumme fetentis. Preterea cum floret spina, perdunt canes olfactum; ita homines odorem diuine dulcedinis ad habundanciam temporalium. Ezechielis viii: "Ecce isti applicant ramum ad nares." Ramum ad nares applicare est florem mundi tanta delectacione insequi ut in obliuionem cedat amor Dei. E contrario autem est quod si dilectio Dei "mentem semel ceperit, a dilectione mundi funditus occidit"; dicit Gregorius de illo uerbo Canticorum, "Fortis est ut mors dilectio." Seneca: "Honesta turpitudo est mori pro bona causa."

Item diligendus est perseueranter, quia "qui perseuerauerit [usque in finem]," in dilectione sua, "hic saluus erit," Matthei xxiiii. Quidam sunt horarii amici, qui diligunt suum commo-

the giver. Of them is said in Ecclesiasticus 6: "There is a friend a companion at the table, but he will not abide in the day of distress." But Seneca says: "He is not a friend who does not share both fortunes," that is to say, unless he loves you in adversity as well as in prosperity. Tullius: "Friendship means to want and not to want the same thing in good days and bad." Many are like the cricket or the cuckoo, who only sing in summer and are still in winter. In this fashion do those love who give praise in prosperity and grumble in adversity. On the contrary, Ecclesiasticus: "He that is a friend loves at all times."

God must further be loved "from one's whole heart," Matthew 22; Augustine: "That is to say, with one's whole intellect" without error. And this corresponds to the Wisdom of the Father, that is, the Son, so that we may truly understand what is written of him and have the right attitude about his mysteries, which is the essence of right belief, so that we may not incur the reproach leveled at the Pharisees who were blind in their intellectual pride, Matthew 22: "You err, not knowing the Scriptures, nor the word of God." Jerome: "Today, many adopt the Pharisees' arrogance," add: when they trust their erring mind and an apparent reason more than the sense of the Holy Spirit; and thus "they will be proven," not wise but "foolish" in their teaching, Jeremias 10. He loves with his whole intellect who has true understanding and right belief.

Moreover, God must be loved from one's whole soul; Augustine: "That is to say, with one's whole will" without opposition, add: so that we desire nothing opposed to his commandments or prohibitions. Augustine *On the Psalms*: "Will what God wills, lest you be bent." And understand that we must conform ourselves to his will only in our acts of mercy, where we are taught always to assume the best because we do not know the truth of the saints and the equity of justice. But in acts of justice we must not imitate God, because it is often possible for us to want what is opposed to his will, since in many things we do not know what is true and what is just. For example, it is possible for me, in my pious wish, to want my father to live, whom God for a just reason wants to die, and it is possible for me to want him to be saved, whom God in just reward wants to be condemned. Even though the objects of our wills may be opposed to each other, our wills are not, because misery and ignorance on my part excuse what justice carries out in him. And because we conform ourselves to him in our will, and thus love him with our whole soul, we honor the Holy Spirit, who is called Will and Goodness by Augustine in his book *On the Trinity*—Goodness in so far as he communicates his goods, Will in so far as he is the efficient cause that anything exists.

neca *marg* E. 714 Tullius *marg* E. 715 **idem** *om* JAFHL. 715–16 **cicade** philomene G. 717 **et *(1st)*** qui FL. 718 **Econtra** *add* in E. 720 Augustinus *marg* E. 721 **hoc** *om* E; hic A. 722 **ipso** eo JF. 726 Ieronimus *marg* E. **Ieronimus** ideo JF. 729 **probabuntur** conprobantur J. 730 **qui . . . intelligit** *om* E. 731 Augustinus *marg* E. **ex** *om* EFHL. **Augustinus** *om* AH. 733 Augustinus *marg* E. 736 **docemur** docetur AGHLW. 737 **et *(1st)*** *om* EL. 741 **racione** uoluntate E. 742 **de** deus JA. 743–44 **uoluntates** uoluntas EI; uolentes L. 745–746 **et . . . diligimus** *om* E. 746 **anima** uoluntate F. **Spiritum Sanctum** ipsum s GW; ipsum I. 747 Augustinus *marg* E. 748 **Bonitas . . . Voluntas** *om* L. **dona** bona AFH; bona ⟨uel dona⟩ J. 748–49 **Voluntas . . . efficiens** *om* H. 750 Augustinus

dum, non amicum, [et] magis dona Dei quam datorem. De talibus dicitur Ecclesiastici vi: “Est amicus socius mense, set non permanet in die necessitatis.” Set / dicit Seneca: “Amicus non est f. 109rb qui particeps utriusque fortune non est,” idest, nisi diligat in aduersitate sicut in prosperitate. Tullius: “Amicicia est idem uelle et idem nolle in prosperis et in aduersis.” Multi similes sunt cicade et cucullo, qui solum cantant in estate et silent in hyeme. Sic illi diligunt et laudant in prosperis et murmurant in aduersis. Econtra ° Ecclesiasticus: “Omni tempore diligit qui amicus est.”

Item diligendus est “ex toto corde,” Matthei xxii; Augustinus: “Idest, toto intellectu” sine errore. Et [hoc] respondet Sapiencie Patris, idest Filio, ut uere intelligamus que de ipso scripta sunt, et bene de secretis eius senciamus, in quibus consistit recta fides, ne inproperetur nobis quod obiectum est Phariseis cecis ex superbia intellectus, Matthei xxii: “Erratis nescientes Scripturas neque uerbum Dei.” Ieronimus: “Multi assumunt sibi hodie de supercilio Phariseorum,” suple: magis credentes erranti intellectui et apparenti racioni quam sensui Spiritus Sancti; et ideo non sapientes set “fatui probabuntur” in doctrina sua, Ieremie x. Toto intellectu diligit [qui uere intelligit] et recte credit.

Item diligendus est [ex] tota anima; Augustinus: “Idest, tota uoluntate” sine contrarietate, suple: ut nichil uelimus contrarium preceptis eius uel prohibicionibus. Augustinus *Super Psalmos*: “Hoc uelis tu quod Deus uult, alioquin curuus es.” Et intellige quod conformari debemus uoluntati sue tantum in operibus misericordie, / in quibus docemur semper meliorem partem suppo- f. 109va nere eo quod ignoremus [et] sanctorum ueritatem et equitatem iusticie. In operibus uero iusticie non debemus eum imitari, set possumus uelle contrarium multociens, eo quod in multis ignoremus quid uerum et quid iustum sit. Vnde possum uelle patrem meum uiuere pia uoluntate quem ipse iusta [racione] uult mori, et possum uelle istum saluari quem ipse de iusticia meritorum uult dampnari. Et licet uolita sint contraria, non tamen [uoluntates], quia in me excusant miseria et ignorancia quod in eo exequitur iusticia. Et in eo quod uoluntate ei conformes sumus, [et sic tota anima eum diligimus,] Spiritum Sanctum honoramus, qui Uoluntas et Bonitas dicitur in libro Augustini *De Trinitate,* set Bonitas in quantum dona sua communicat, Voluntas in quantum efficiens causa est ut aliquid sit.

And we must also love God "from our whole mind"; Augustine: "That is to say, in our whole memory" without forgetting. Indeed, we must continually remember him through whom we have all good things together, some now, others in the future. Through him we have our being and our being good, as Augustine states, and our becoming better in the future. And in Acts 17: "In him we live and move and are." And if these things are to be retained in our memory, we must recall them often, for "thought and recollection keep memories alive," as is said in book III of *On the Soul*. And among all other benefits we should recall most of all the benefit of our salvation, because it is greater than all others in its effects. For although all of Christ's merits are equal with respect to the habit of our virtues—for as Gregory says: According to the merit of his soul, Christ did not have whereby he could be of help—, yet with respect to its effect on our virtues and their fruit, his passion is greater than his incarnation; and thus it is said: "To be born would do no good, had it not been for the good of being redeemed."

Christ's passion, then, must be remembered for six reasons. First, in order to have the love of Christ, who loved us so much that he gave us not only his gifts but himself; Galatians 1: "Who gave himself for our sins, that he might deliver us from this present wicked world." And Bernard: "This is what draws us so violently and binds us so closely: the cup you drank, o good Jesus!" Second, it helps us to avoid ingratitude, lest we be unmindful of such a great benefit; Bernard: "He could have redeemed us in a different way but he did not want to, for he preferred his own suffering to your ingratitude." Third, for the sake of imitating him; 1 Peter 4: "Christ having suffered in the flesh, be you also armed with the same thought, so that you should follow his steps," and so forth. Fourth, in order to awaken penitence, which is prefigured in Machabees 6: "They showed the elephants the blood of grapes and mulberries to provoke them to fight." Elephants are chaste and strong penitents turning toward the tree of the cross. Just as the elephant sleeps leaning against a tree which, in its absence, men nearly cut through the middle, so that when the elephant leans against it and falls down, they capture and kill it, so the enemy of penitence, the devil, cuts through penitence and pierces it, so that a man who leans on it may fall from grace; and this is shown in Osee 7: "Strangers have devoured his strength." The dragon also ties up the elephant's legs with its tail so that it falls; thus, the old serpent ties up the penitent and "sets up his tail like a cedar," Job

marg E. 751–52 **memorari** *add* eius AFH. 753 **spe** specie EG. 753–54 **et . . . sumus** *om* L. 754 Augustinus *marg* E. **ut . . . sumus** *om* G. 754–55 **Et . . . sumus** *om* IW. 758 **III** in libro E. 759 **inter cetera** *om* F. **maius** manifestius AFH. 760 **merita** merito AH; mandata L. **essent** sint AFH; erunt I. 761 Gregorius *marg* E. **iuxta** *om* AW; quoad F. 764 **Nichil** *add* nobis JF. 765 **passio** *add* Christi J *(interl)* AF. 766 **solum** tantum AGIW. 767 Bernardus *marg* E. 772 Bernardus *marg* E. 772–73 **Potuit . . . Tercio** *om* L. 773 **Tercio** item GIW. 775 **Quarto** item GIW; tercio L. 776 **quod figuratur** *om* GIW. 778 **Elephanti uel** *om* JAF. 779 **crucis** cruci AH; *add* se E. 780 **quod** quam JAFHI. **homines** *corr from* hominis E. 780–81 **secantes** sarrientes J *(marg corr)* AGHIL; seruantes W. 783 **et hoc dicitur** unde GIW. 785 **in** *om* EAH. **in pedibus** *om* F. **cum** in E; et AH: *om* FGILW. 786 Gregorius *marg* E. 786–87 **Gregorius . . . insidiatur** *om* L.

Item debemus eum diligere eciam tota mente; Augustinus: "Idest, tota memoria" sine obliuione. Et merito continue memorari debemus per quem omnia bona simul habemus, alia in re, alia in [spe]. Per ipsum habemus quod sumus et quod boni sumus, ut dicit Augustinus, et quod meliores futuri sumus. Et in Actuum xvii: "In ipso uiuimus, mouemur, et sumus." Et si ista debeant memoriter retineri, oportet eorum sepius recordari, quia "meditaciones in reminiscendo memoriam saluant," ut / dicitur f. 109^{v}b [III] *De anima*. Et inter omnia beneficia maxime recolendum est beneficium recreacionis, quod inter cetera in effectu maius est. Licet enim omnia merita Christi quoad habitum uirtutum essent equalia—quia ut dicit Gregorius: Non habuit Christus iuxta anime meritum quo posset proficere—, quoad effectum tamen uirtutum et earum fructum maior est passio quam incarnacio; et sic dicitur: "Nichil nasci profuit nisi redimi profuisset."

Et est passio memoranda propter sex. Primo propter dilectionem Christi habendam, qui in tantum dilexit nos ut non solum sua daret nobis set eciam seipsum; Galatarum i: "Dedit semetipsum pro peccatis nostris, ut nos eriperet de hoc presenti seculo nequam." Et Bernardus: "Hoc est quod uehemencius nos allicit et arcius nos astringit: calix quem bibisti, o bone Iesu!" Secundo ualet ad ingratitudinem uitandam, ne immemores simus tanti beneficii; Bernardus: "Potuit aliter redimere set noluit, quia maluit cum iniuria sui quam cum ingratitudine tui." Tercio propter imitacionem; I Petri iiii: "Christo passo in carne, et uos eadem cogitacione armamini, vt sequamini uestigia eius," etc. Quarto propter excitacionem penitencie, quod figuratur Machabeorum vi: "Ostenderunt elephantibus sanguinem uue et mori ad acuendum eos in prelium." Elephanti uel elephantes sunt penitentes casti et fortes arbori crucis / ° inclinantes. f. 110^{r}a Sicut elephas dormit incumbens arbori, quod homines eo absente fere per medium secantes elephantem ibi incumbentem et ruentem conprehendunt et interficiunt, ita hostis penitencie dyabolus secat eam et penetrat, ut homo illi innitens a gracia deficiat; et hoc dicitur Osee vii: "Comederunt alieni robur eius." Draco eciam stringit elephantem [in] pedibus [cum] cauda sua ut ruat; sic serpens antiquus penitentem qui "stringit caudam suam quasi cedrum," Iob xl. Gre-

40. Gregory: "His tail is set up when he lies in wait for a man's ending." Therefore, the penitent is shown the blood of grapes and mulberries that he may be aroused to fight, that is, to do penance. Christ was a mulberry when he wanted to die for the wretched and his dried-up blood turned black like the juice of a mulberry. He was a grape when he was placed "upon the lever" of the cross, Numbers 13; from it wine is pressed into the cup of the Church. In the fifth place we should remember his passion in order to keep away the devil. Exodus 12: The blood of a lamb put on the side posts and the upper doorpost kept away the slayer of Egypt. The upper doorpost in the house of the soul is reason, whose two side posts are intellect and will; to put the blood of a lamb on them is to recollect, understand, and love Christ's passion, and thereby to keep away the slayer. Sixth, in order to resist sin; Hebrews 12: "Think diligently upon him that endured such opposition from persecutors. For you have not yet resisted unto blood." And notice that these things are to be remembered in order to carry out deeds and to render thanks, and this is to love God with our whole mind. And it corresponds to the person of the Father in the Trinity, according to Augustine, for just as our memory is the dwelling place of visual images, so is the Father the well-spring of the other persons. But there are many things which take away his memory. The first is the sleep of sin; Romans 13: "It is now the hour for us to rise from sleep." The second is the infirmity of evil desires; Corinthians 11: "There are many infirm and weak." Of these two it is said in book II of *On the Soul*: "Our mind is veiled by sickness or sleep." The third is the "care" which "chokes up the word," Matthew 13. The fourth is "the sorrow of the world" which "works death," 2 Corinthians 7. The fifth is worldly prosperity; Genesis 40: "The chief butler, when things prospered with him, forgot Joseph." Hence, his memory cannot be better kept than by often recalling the things that were mentioned above.

Now we turn to the love of our neighbor. Deuteronomy 6: "You shall love your neighbor as yourself; and the same in Matthew 5. Such love consists in the two rules of natural law, namely: "As you would that men should do to you, do you also to them in like manner," Luke 6; the second is in Tobias 4: "Never do to another what you would not have done to you." Our neighbor must be loved in three manners: in our desire, word, and good deed, that is, in heart, mouth, and action. By desire we understand our good will or affection with which I am obligated to desire his good, and this the Lord indicates when

788 **proponitur** preponitur E; apponitur AFH; proponuntur GW. 789 **Morus** mortuus AFGH. 790–91 **pro . . . mori** *om* W. 791 **factus** *om* E. **fuit positus** positus fuit E. 792 **vnde** vue E. 793 **Quinto** quarto L. **cohibicionem** cohabitacionem EJ. 794 **exterminatorem** exterminacionem E. 795 **sunt** *add* racio *canc* E. 796 **et affectus** *om* W. 797 **exterminatorem** exterminacionem E. 798 **Sexto** quinto L. 800 **contradictionem** *add* hoc est E; *add* et sequitur GIW. 803 **Et hoc** hoc eciam E. 804 Augustinus *marg* E. **specierum est** prima est in anima E. 809 **autem** *om* E. 810 **egritudine** *om* E. 810–11 **Tercium . . . xiii** *follows as* Quartum *after* Corinthiorum vii *(812)* L. 811 **Quartum** tercium L. 811–12 **Quartum . . . vii** *exchanged with the following* (Quintum . . . Ioseph) GW. 814 **melius** *om* EG. **memoria** *add* Christi EAH. 815 **predictorum** preteritorum J. **recordari** *add* de dilectione proximi *rubr* EJI. 817 **idem** *om* EAF. 819–20 **uultis . . . fieri** *om* I. **alia est in** *om* G. 822 **et** *om* EI. 824 **idest . . . teipsum** *om* IW. **id** *add* ad E. 826

gorius: "Cauda eius stringit cum fini hominis insidiatur." Ideo penitenti sanguis uue et mori [proponitur] ut ad pugnandum, idest ad penitendum, excitetur. Morus fuit Christus qui uoluit mori pro miseris, cuius sanguis induratus ad similitudinem liquoris mori niger [factus] est. Vua [fuit positus] "in uecte" crucis, Numeri xiii; [vnde] uinum in calicem Ecclesie expressum est. Quinto propter [cohibicionem] dyaboli. Exodi xii: Sanguis agni in postibus et superliminari prohibuit [exterminatorem] Egipti. Superliminare in domo anime racio est, cuius duo postes sunt intellectus et affectus; quos sanguine agni intingere est passionem Christi recolere, intelligere, et diligere, et ita [exterminatorem] prohibere. Sexto propter resistenciam contra peccatum; Hebreorum xii: "Recogitate eum qui talem a persecutoribus sustinuit contradictionem.° Nondum enim usque ad sanguinem restitistis." Et nota / f. 110rb quod ista memoranda sunt ad operis inplecionem et ad graciarum actionem, et hoc est diligere ipsum tota mente. [Et] hoc respondet persone Patris in Trinitate, secundum Augustinum, quia sicut memoria mansio [specierum est], ita Pater aliarum personarum origo. Sunt autem plura que tollunt eius memoriam. Primum est sompnus peccati; Romanorum xiii: "Hora est iam nos de sompno surgere." Secundum est infirmitas concupiscencie; Corinthiorum xi: "Multi infirmi et inbecilles." De hiis duobus dicitur II *De anima*: "Velatur [autem] intellectus [egritudine] uel sompno." Tercium est "sollicitudo" que "suffocat uerbum," Matthei xiii. Quartum est "tristicia seculi" que "mortem operatur," II Corinthiorum vii. Quintum est prosperitas temporalis; Genesis xl: "Pincerna oblitus est ipsius Ioseph succedentibus prosperis." Non potest igitur [melius] memoria ° saluari quam predictorum sepius recordari.

Sequitur de dilectione proximi. Deuteronomi vi: "Diliges proximum tuum sicut teipsum"; et Matthei v [idem]. Hec dilectio consistit in duabus regulis iuris naturalis, hiis scilicet: "Prout uultis ut faciant uobis homines, et uos facite illis," Luce vi; alia est in Thobie iiii: "Non facias alii quod tibi non uis fieri." Et est tribus modis diligendus proximus: voto, uerbo, et beneficio, idest corde, ore, [et] opere. In uoto notatur uoluntas bona siue desiderium quo teneor ei desiderare bonum, et hoc notat Domi-

he says, "as yourself," that is, to the same end as yourself, namely to eternal life; not however with equal intensity, though with the same habit of love, for just as there is an order in the degrees of love, so is there in its intensity. About this love in the heart the Apostle says, Philippians 1: "God is my witness, how I long after you all in the bowels of Jesus Christ." Likewise our neighbor is to be loved in word, so that you should instruct, correct, comfort, and pray for him; at the end of Thessalonians: "Rebuke the unquiet, comfort the feebleminded," etc. And again he is to be loved in good deeds; near the end of Galatians: "Bear you one another's burdens," etc.; the Gloss: Those bearing others' burdens are those who give one another counsel and aid.

And so that none may be excused from loving his neighbor, it is said in Ecclesiasticus 17: "God gave to everyone commandment concerning his neighbor." Augustine on the same: "By the name of 'neighbor' everyone is understood." This the Lord teaches in the Gospel, Matthew 5: "If you remember that your brother has anything against you." By the name 'brother' every man is understood, because all have the same father in the flesh, Adam, and in the spirit, God; Malachias 2: "Have we not all one father?" And Boethius in his *Consolation*: "There is one father of all things." By "brother" we therefore understand great and small, faithful and pagan, and even woman, who is included in the term "neighbor." Therefore, if you have hurt your brother, either by hating him against the Law—Leviticus 19: "You shall not hate your brother in your heart"—, or in word, namely by reproach or backbiting—because "the lips of a fool intermeddle with strife," Proverbs 18—, or through doing him some damage by stealing his money or withholding his own—for all damage is to be made good to the owner, Exodus 22—, or in hurting his body by striking him "with the fist wickedly," Isaias 58, or in hurting his soul by provoking him to sin—as "the mouth of a fool provokes quarrels," Proverbs 18—, or by giving him a bad example—as those who "proclaim abroad their sin and do not hide it," Isaias 3—: if you have hurt your neighbor by any of these, "leave your offering before the altar and go first to be reconciled to your brother," Matthew 5. Thus, God commended the love of our neighbor much when, in order to reestablish it, he would have his sacrifice interrupted.

Since by "neighbor" every man is understood, as Augustine says, the name of "neighbor" also includes our enemies. The Lord shows this explicitly when he says: "But I say to you, love your enemies," Matthew 5. Our friends we must love in God, according to Augustine, and our enemies for God; add, our

quia . . . dileccionis *om* E. 830 **ores** or-res E. **fine** ii E; 5 F. 832 **fine** *om* E; 6 F. 833 Glossa *marg* E. **Alter** *om* AFH. 834 **sibi** *om* E. 836 Augustinus *marg* E. **Mandauit** *add* deus AFH. **proximo** *add* suo AGIW. 838 **in Ewangelio** *om* FGIW. **v** *om* E. 841 **scilicet** *om* EGIW. **et** *om* EGHILW. 842 Boecius *marg* E. 849 **rapiendo** capiendo AW. 851 **percuciens** percuciendo FI. Ysaie lviii *om* E. 854 **iii** *om* EW. 858 **intermitti** pretermitti FH. 859 Augustinus *marg* E. 861 **dicit** dixit GIW. 863 Augustinus *marg* E. **ut . . . Augustinus** *om* L. 865 **idest . . .**

nus cum dicit, "sicut teipsum," idest, ad id ° / quod teipsum, f. 110va scilicet ad uitam eternam; non tamen equali motu, licet eodem habitu dilectionis, [quia sicut est ordo in gradibus dileccionis,] ita in eius motibus. De dilectione cordis dicit Apostolus Philippensium i: "Testis est michi Deus quomodo cupiam uos omnes in uisceribus Iesu Christi." Item diligendus est uerbo, ut instruas, corripias, consoleris, et ores pro eo; Thessalonicensium [fine]: "Corripite inquietos, consolamini pusillanimes," etc. Item diligendus est beneficio; Galatarum [fine]: "Alter alterius onera portate," etc.; Glossa: Alter alterius onera portantes sunt consilium et auxilium [sibi] inuicem inpendentes.

Et ne quis posset excusari a dilectione proximi, dicitur Ecclesiastici xvii: "Mandauit unicuique de proximo." Augustinus ad idem: "Nomine 'proximi' omnis homo intelligitur." Hoc docet Dominus in Ewangelio, Matthei [v]: "Si recordatus fueris quia frater tuus habet aliquid aduersum te." Et nomine 'fratris' intelligitur omnis homo, quia omnes eundem patrem habent carnalem, [scilicet] Adam, [et] spiritualem, Deum; Malachie ii: "Nonne unus pater omnium nostrum?" Et Boecius in *Consolacionibus*: "Vnus rerum pater est." "Frater" igitur intelligitur maior uel minor, fidelis uel infidelis, uel eciam mulier, que nomine "proximi" intelligitur. Si igitur fratrem leseris, aut odio habendo contra Legem—Leuitici xix: "Non oderis fratrem tuum in corde tuo"—, aut uerbo, scilicet obiurgando uel detrahendo—quia "labia stulti inmiscent se rixis," Prouerbiorum xviii—, aut dampno peccunie rapiendo uel detinendo quod suum est—quia omne dampnum restituendum est domino / rei, Exodi xxii—, aut lesione corporis f. 110vb percuciens "pugno inpie," [Ysaie lviii], aut lesione anime prouocando ad peccatum—sicut "os stulti iurgia prouocat," Prouerbiorum xviii—, aut prauo exemplo—sicut illi qui "peccata sua predicant nec abscondunt," Ysaie [iii]—: si aliquo istorum proximum leseris, "relinque munus ante altare et uade prius reconciliari fratri tuo," Matthei v. Valde commendauit Deus dilectionem proximi, cum propter ipsam reformandam uoluit suum sacrificium intermitti.

Quia nomine "proximi" intelligitur omnis homo, ut dicit Augustinus, sub nomine "proximi" cadunt eciam inimici. Quod expressius ostendit Dominus cum dicit: "Ego autem dico uobis, diligite inimicos uestros," Matthei v. Amicos debemus diligere in Deo, ut dicit Augustinus, et inimicos propter Deum; amicos su-

friends in God, that is, those who already are in the state of charity, and our enemies for God, that is, for the sake of his commandment, or else so that they may become friends. Moreover, we must love in them what God loves in them, that is, what he has planted in their nature, not what vice has deformed, as Augustine says. And Gregory: "The wicked are to be loved in what they are, not in what they do." What the Lord says in Matthew 5: "It was said to them of old: you shall hate your enemy," however, was never expressed in the Law but comes from the tradition of the Scribes and Pharisees. The sign of hatred is permitted in the Law, but never the rancor of the mind, as when the Lord gave his permission to subdue the infidels, Deuteronomy 7: "You shall make no league with them," etc., and chapter 20: "You shall slay them with the edge of the sword," etc. Expound this as follows: As a law I establish that "you shall hate," that is, you shall act as if you hated by pursuing them, by punishing "eye for eye, tooth for tooth," Exodus 21, and by withdrawing benefits and fellowship, so that perhaps your enemies may be converted to the faith. But the Lord abolished these things when he said: "But I say to you: love your enemies." And the Lord commanded three things concerning the love of our enemy, as against threefold harm; the first kind of harm belongs to the heart, such as hatred and rancor, and against it he says, "love." The second pertains to the mouth, such as insult and quarrel, and against it he says, "pray for them that persecute and calumniate you." The third is harm in deed, and against it the Lord says, "do good to them that hate you." And how this should be done is taught in To the Romans 12 and Proverbs 25: "If your enemy is hungry, give him to eat; if he thirsts, give him to drink." Take this to mean, with bodily as well as spiritual food. Then follows: "For doing this, you will heap coals of fire upon his head." These coals of fire set the cold aflame, and they signify the fire of charity. The head of the inner man is the mind itself; the reason for this is touched upon by the Gloss on Leviticus 6, for as the head governs the members, so does the mind rule our actions. The meaning, then, is: By doing this good deed you will kindle him to charity, and if this does not happen, it will grow into hellfire for him, first because he hates, and second because he scorns your charitable deed. And since among all the commandments that about loving our enemies is the most wonderful, the Lord adds a word about the reward of such love: "That you may be the children of God," and so forth, add: adopted through grace and imitators by example, for he himself continually does good to his worst enemies, making "his sun to rise upon the good and the bad." For he grants all

ipsi *om* I. 867 Augustinus *marg* E. **in natura** innatum E. 868 Gregorius *marg* E. **eo quod** quantum E. 870 **nunquam** non tamen JG. 874–75 **et . . . etc** *om* F. 876 **facies** A *ends.* 878 **xxi** xxii EF. **comunionem** *add* reddendo *canc* E. 880 **precepit** precipit FHL. 882 **quarum** *om* GIW. 884 **pro persequentibus** pro sequentibus E; *om* I. 887 **xxv** xxxv E; 22 F. 888 **eciam** *om* FGIW. 889 **Sequitur** *om* FHW. **eius** *add* etc, *then text missing to Chapter IV, line 1* L. **qui** que FH. 890 **accendunt** accenderunt E. **quas** quos HW. 892 Glossa *marg* E. 894 **accendens** accendes FI; accendit G. **accrescit** accrescat J; accrescet HIW; attrectent G. 895 **primo** priori E. 909–10 **diligunt . . . benefactores** hoc faciunt F. 912 Tullius

ple in Deo, idest qui iam sunt in caritate, et inimicos propter Deum, idest propter eius preceptum uel ut ipsi amici fiant. Preterea debemus diligere in eis quod in illis diligit Deus, idest, quod [in natura] plantauit, non quod uicium deformauit, ut dicit Augustinus. Et Gregorius: "Mali diligendi sunt in [eo quod] sunt, non in eo quod faciunt." Quod autem dicit Dominus in Matthei v: "Dictum est antiquis: odio habebis inimicum," nunquam fuit in Lege expressum set ex tradicione Scribarum et Phariseorum. Signum tamen odii permissum est in Lege, nunquam rancor animi, ut cum permisit Dominus expugnare infideles, Deuteronomi vii: "Non inibis cum eis fedus," etc., et xx: "Percucies eos in ore gladii," etc. / f. 111^{r}a Secundum hoc ita expone: Pro statu legis dico "odio habebis," idest facies ac si odires persequendo, talionem reddendo ut "oculum pro oculo, dentem pro dente," Exodi [xxi], beneficia et comunionem subtrahendo, ut sic forsitan conuertantur ad fidem. Set ista eliminauit Dominus cum dixit: "Ego autem dico uobis: diligite inimicos uestros." Et tria precepit Dominus circa dilectionem inimici contra triplicem iniuriam; quarum prima est cordis, ut odium uel rancor, contra quam dicit "diligite." Secunda est oris, ut contumelia uel rixa, contra quam dicit "orate [pro persequentibus] et calumpniantibus uos." Tercia est operis, contra quam dicit "benefacite hiis qui uos oderunt." Et qualiter hoc debeat fieri docetur Ad Romanos xii et Prouerbiorum [xxv]: "Si esurierit inimicus tuus, ciba illum; si sitierit, potum da illi." Hoc intellige alimento corporali et eciam spirituali. Sequitur: "Hoc enim faciens prunas congeres super capud eius." Prune sunt carbones ardentes qui frigidos [accendunt], per quas ardor caritatis intelligitur. Capud autem interioris hominis est ipsa mens; cuius racio tangitur in Glossa Leuitici vi, quod sicut capud regit membra, ita mens actiones. Est igitur sensus: Tali beneficio accendens ipsum ad caritatem, uel si non, accrescit ei ad materiam gehenne, [primo] quia odit, secundo quia opus caritatis contempnit. Et quia inter omnia mandata mira- / f. 111^{r}b bilius est illud quod est de diligendis inimicis, ideo additur de retribucione huius dilectionis: "Vt sitis filii Dei," etc.: adoptiui suple per graciam et imitatores per exemplum, quia ipse continue benefacit inimicis suis pessimis, faciens "solem suum oriri super bonos et malos."

worldly prosperity to infidels, to the faithless Jews, and to false Christians, in order to teach us to love our enemy; Deuteronomy 10: "He loves the stranger and gives him food and raiment." "Stranger" he calls any servant of the demons out of those named above, yet in him he still loves what is his and hates what is foreign.

We must love our enemy for several reasons. First because it pleases God much, who admonishes us so urgently to love our enemy. We rarely read that he spoke about loving one's friend, because that we do naturally, for "even the publicans and sinners" love their friends and benefactors, Matthew 5 and Luke 6. Second, because our enemies have greater need, and the needy should be given help. Tullius: "Help must be given more promptly to those who are in great misery, unless perhaps they deserve their misery." Third, because in loving our enemy we are mindful of God's love, who prayed for his enemies and those who crucified him, saying: "Father, forgive them," etc. In this he gave us a marvelous remedy against envy, praying for those who nailed his feet and hands on the gibbet; Job 26: "God's obstetric hand brought forth the winding serpent." The serpent of envy is taken out of one's heart when one recalls the love of the Crucified for his enemies. Fourth, because we gather for ourselves a great profit of merit because of the difficulty of such love. Jerome: "Difficulty increases merit"; and in the *Ethics*: "Art and virtue are concerned with what is difficult." Fifth, because our enemies open for us the gates of paradise through the tribulations they cause us, for "through many tribulations we must enter into the kingdom of heaven," Acts 14. Sixth, because they increase our patience, which grows in tribulation; therefore: "The Lord left the nations that by them he might instruct Jerusalem," Judges 3, which indicate the rivals and persecutors of the just. Seventh, because the wicked are like hedges that keep us from entering evil as long as we fear their abuses and taunts, in order that we may not suffer their scratches, if we should by any chance commit some evil; Ecclesiastes 10: "He that breaks a hedge, a serpent shall bite him." For this reason, sometimes the tongue of one cursed old woman in the parish restrains people from sinning more than all the prohibitions given by the Church. Eighth, because through the love of one's enemy the envy of the devil is utterly confounded, through which "death came into the world," Wisdom 2. Hence, as he is overthrown by humility, so is he wounded by love. Further, we are constrained to love our enemy on account of Christ's love, because Christ died for us while we were still his enemies, so that through his death he might reconcile

marg E. **calamitosos** calamitosis E. 913 **calamitate** calamite E. 914 **memores** meliores H. **et** eciam E. 915 **orauit** exorauit FGHIW. 916 **fixerunt** affixerunt FGHIW. 921 Ieronimus *marg* E. **auget** accumulat FGHI; accelerat W. 922 Philosophus *marg* E. 923 **per** *marg* E. 923–24 **tribulaciones . . . per** *om* F. **quas . . . tribulaciones** *om* H. 924 **oportet** *add* nos GHIW. 925 **xiiii** *written twice, the second canc* E. 927 **Ierusalem** Israel FIW; *om* H. 929 **timemus** pacienter tolleramus ⟨et timemus⟩ J; pacienter tolleramus G. 932 **in parochia** *om* GIW. 938 **per**

Incredulis enim et perfidis Iudeis et falsis Christianis omnem concedit temporis prosperitatem, ut doceat nos diligere inimicum; Deuteronomi x: “Amat peregrinum et dat ei uictum et uestitum.” “Peregrinum” uocat aliquem ex predictis seruum demoniorum, in quo tamen diligit quod suum est et odit quod alienum est.

Diligendus est inimicus propter plura. Primo, quia multum placet Deo, qui tam sollicite ammonet de inimico diligendo. Raro enim legitur sermonem fecisse de dilectione amici, quoniam naturaliter hoc facimus, nam publicani et peccatores diligunt amicos et benefactores, Matthei v et Luce vi. Secundo, quia inimici magis indigent, et indigentibus conferendum est beneficium. Tullius: “Prompcior debetur benignitas in [calamitosos], nisi forte sint [calamitate] digni.” Tercio, quia in dilectione inimici memores sumus dilectionis Dei, qui pro inimicis [et] crucifixoribus orauit dicens: “Pater, dimitte illis,” etc. In quo mirum dedit inuidie remedium, orans pro illis qui pedes eius et manus fixerunt ad patibulum; Iob xxvi: “In manu / Domini obstetricante eductus f. 111va
est coluber tortuosus.” Coluber enim inuidie a corde educitur cum dilectio Crucifixi ad suos inimicos recolitur. Quarto, quia magnum beneficium meriti nobis accumulamus propter difficultatem huiusmodi dilectionis. Ieronimus: “Difficultas auget meritum”; et in *Ethicis*: “Ars et uirtus circa difficilia.” Quinto, quia portas paradysi nobis aperiunt per tribulaciones quas ingerunt, quia “per multas tribulaciones oportet intrare in regnum celorum,” Actuum xiiii. Sexto, quia pacienciam in nobis augent, que dilatatur in tribulacione; vnde: “Dominus reliquit gentes in quibus erudiret Ierusalem,” Iudicum iii, que signant iustorum emulos et persecutores. Septimo, quia mali sunt tanquam sepes, ne ad malum transeamus dum timemus eorum conuicia et obprobria, ne si forte malum faciamus, morsus eorum paciamur; Ecclesiaste x: “Qui dissipat sepem, mordebit eum coluber.” Vnde plus cohibet a malo quandoque in parochia lingua unius uetule maledicte quam omnes prohibiciones Ecclesie. Octauo, quia per dilectionem inimici maxime confunditur inuidia dyaboli, per quam “intrauit mors in orbem terrarum,” Sapiencie ii. Vnde sicut humilitate prosternitur, ita dilectione uulneratur. Item ex dilectione Christi ualde artamur ad dilectionem inimici, quia cum adhuc

us to God, Romans 5. And Chrysostom: "If it were just that you should hate your enemies, God would have never received you, his enemy, from the Gentiles into his love, he who for his enemies gave his own Son into death, who adopted his enemy as his son and made him a co-heir with his Only-begotten Son."

The punishment for envy is the worm of conscience, not only in hell but also in this life, since here the envious suffers pain at other people's well-being; at the end of Isaias: "Their worm shall not die"; the Gloss: "Just as envy torments him now, so his conscience will torment him then." Another punishment of envy will be sorrow, for even now the envious man grieves at another man's prosperity, as Gregory and the Philosopher declare. And his grief will be like the grief of those "who have lost hope," and so forth, Thessalonians 4, for "when the wicked man is dead, there shall be no hope any more." The third punishment will be his dread of the future torment, because already now the successes of other people make him fear that he might lose the favor of this world. Gregory: "When he is damned, he will fear not only what he already endures, but the infinite sufferings which he sees coming to his fellow man." This is what the Lord threatens sinful Israel with, Deuteronomy 28: in the hostile land "the Lord will give you a fearful heart, and languishing eyes, and a soul consumed with pensiveness. You will fear day and night, and your life will be as it were hanging before you."

mortem *om* GIW. 939 **Crisostomus** Co E. 940 **fuisset** fuit FGHW. 941 **dilectionem** *add* quia E. **proprium** propriis E. 943 **constituit** *add* de pena inuidie *rubr* J. 945 **quia** qui FGHW. 946 Glossa *marg* E. **fine** *om* E; ultimo F. 948–49 **quia . . . tristicia** *om* F. 948 **tristatur** tristabitur E. 949 Gregorius Philosophus *marg* E. 952 **quia** qui E. 953 Gregorius *marg* E. 954 **quod** quia E. 955 **futura** *om* GIW.

inimici essemus, pro nobis mortuus est, ut per mortem / nos f. 111^{v}b Deo reconciliaret, Romanorum v. Et [Crisostomus]: "Si iustum fuisset inimicos odire, Deus te ex Gentibus inimicum nunquam in suam suscepisset dilectionem, ° qui pro inimicis [proprium] Filium tradidit in mortem, qui inimicum suum in filium adoptauit et coheredem Unigenito suo constituit."

Pena inuidie est vermis consciencie, non solum apud inferos set eciam in presenti, quia hic dolet de aliorum prosperitate; Ysaie [fine]: "Vermis eorum non morietur"; Glossa: "Sicut nunc stimulat inuidia, ita tunc stimulabit consciencia." Preterea alia eius pena erit tristicia, quia nunc eciam [tristatur] de prosperitate aliena, ut dicit Gregorius et Philosophus. Et erit tristicia talis qualis est eorum "qui spem non habent," etc., Thessalonicensium iiii, quoniam "mortuo homine inpio nulla erit ultra spes." Tercia pena erit pauor futuri supplicii, [quia] eciam nunc per aliorum successus timet perdere gloriam mundi. Gregorius: "Non tantum timebit dampnatus [quod] iam sustinet, set infinita mala que in proximo futura uidet." Hoc est quod comminatur Dominus Israeli peccanti, Deuteronomi xxviii: in terra hostili "dabit tibi Dominus cor pauidum et oculos deficientes et animam merore consumptam. Timebis die ac nocte, et erit uita tua quasi pendens ante te."

IV

ON MEEKNESS AND PATIENCE

Next we deal with meekness and patience, which are the remedies for anger. Though these two are opposed to one and the same vice, they are yet two different virtues, as is shown in their separate acts which correspond to separate habits. Meekness consists in suppressing inner motions, so that these may not arouse anger; patience lies in sustaining external vexations, that these may not inflict anger. Jerome: "A meek person hurts no one, a humble one scorns no one." Therefore, humility yields to every injury. And it is obvious that meekness is next kin to humility. Now, mildness, a word that is not in use, is the same as meekness, but they differ in their actions, because meekness suppresses motions that come from anger and make us want to inflict harm—Gregory: "Each time we restrain turbulent motions in us with the virtue of meekness, we make an attempt to return to the likeness of God"—; whereas mildness represses violent motions that compel us to loud outcries—Isidore: "*Mitis,* 'a mild person,' is said to suffer injuries as if he were *mutus,* 'mute.'" Chrysostom counts "Blessed are the mild" and "Blessed are the meek" as one virtue and says: "A meek person does not provoke evil, nor is he provoked by evil, nor does the cause of sin prevail against him, nor does ever any cause of sin arise from him for someone else; but he would rather suffer harm than do it, for unless a man is reconciled to suffering some harm, he can never be without sin." And Chrysostom defines meekness as follows: "Meekness is the calmness of a mind which cannot easily be vexed by the evils it suffers nor be provoked to inflict evils." It renders to none evil for evil, but on the contrary renders good, as is said near the end of Thessalonians.

Mansuetus, "the meek person," means *ad manum suetus,* "accustomed to being at someone's hand," that is, humble, obedient, and manageable. The Philosopher: "Man is an animal meek by nature." The meek person is like the hawk which, when it is shown raw meat, comes to one's hand and feeds there; thus a person who looks at the reddened flesh of Christ and thereby grows meek. But the Lord complains of the opposite situation in Proverbs 1: "I have called and you have refused, I have held out my hand and there was none who would look." And Isaias 65: "I have held out my hand all day to a people with-

IV *om all MSS.* 1 **De . . . paciencia** *rubr* EJ; de mansuetudine *rubr* FHW; *om* GL; de mansuetudine vel paciencia *rubr* I. 4 **quibus . . . habitus** *om* W. 5–6 **prouocent . . . iram** *om* I. 7 Ieronimus *marg* E. 8 **Vnde . . . iniurie** *om* F. 9–10 **Mititudo . . . mansuetudo** *om* H. 12 Gregorius *marg* E. 15 Ysidorus *marg* E. **turbidos insurgentes** insurgentes turbidos *marked for reversal* E. 16 Crisostomus *marg* E. 16–17 **numerat** *add* Matthei vi (*marg*) I. 19–20 **nec . . . peccati** *om* L. 19 **ex eo** *om* JFGW. **nascitur** irascitur JFG. 22 Crisostomus *marg* E. 25–26 **set . . . fine** *om* L. 25 **ut** *add* ad E. 26 **fine** *om* E; 5 FW. 28 Philosophus *marg* E. 30 **ad** *om* E. **accedit** attendit E. 31 **et** *om* FLI; ex G. 32 **conqueritur Dominus** *om*

[IV]

DE MANSUETUDINE ET PACIENCIA

Sequitur de mansuetudine et paciencia, que sunt remedia ire. Et licet uni uicio obuient, tamen di- / f. 112ra uerse sunt uirtutes, ut patet per proprios actus quibus proprii respondent habitus. Set mansuetudo est in reprimendo motus interiores ne iram prouocent; paciencia est in sustinendo molestias exteriores ne iram ingerant. Ieronimus: "Mansuetus neminem ledit, humilis neminem contempnit." Vnde humilitas cedit omni iniurie. Et patet quod proxima cognata humilitatis est mansuetudo. Mititudo uero, quod nomen in usu non est, idem est quod mansuetudo, set in opere differunt, quia mansuetudo reprimit motus ad supplicia inferenda ex ira—Gregorius: "Quociens turbulentos motus insurgentes sub mansuetudinis uirtute restringimus, tociens ad similitudinem Dei redire conamur"—; mititudo uero reprimit motus turbidos insurgentes ad conuicia—Ysidorus: "Mitis dicitur suscipiens iniurias quasi mutus." Crisostomus pro una uirtute numerat "Beati mites" et "Beati mansueti" et dicit: "Mansuetus est qui nec irritat malum, nec irritatur a malo, nec aduersus eum preualet causa peccati, nec aduersus alterum aliquando ex eo nascitur causa peccati; set magis contentus est iniuriam pati quam facere, nam nisi contentus fuerit homo ut ei noceatur, nunquam potest esse sine peccato." Et diffinit Crisostomus mansuetudinem sic: "Mansuetudo est tranquillitas mentis que / f. 112rb nec illatis malis exasperari nec ad inferenda facile prouocari potest." Nulli enim malum pro malo reddit, set e contrario bonum, ut ° Thessalonicensium [fine].

Dicitur autem mansuetus quasi ad manum suetus, idest, humilis, obediens, et tractabilis. Philosophus: "Homo est animal mansuetum natura." Mansuetus similis est accipitri, qui ostensa carne rubea [ad] manum [accedit] et inde se reficit; sic qui carnem Christi rubricatam attendit et inde mansuescit. Set e contrario conqueritur Dominus, Prouerbiorum 1: "Vocaui et rennuistis, extendi manum meam et non erat qui aspiceret." Et Ysaie lxv:

out faith," and so forth. Likewise, mild and tamed animals are to help men and to provide food and clothing, but wild beasts are fierce and rage against men with their teeth and horns. The same applies to meek and to angry people. And it is marvelous that wild beasts are more easily tamed than angry people; as in James 3, where the Gloss speaks of a tame serpent which came to the table of a prince for its daily allowance. Also, Isidore says that a wild bull when it is tied to a fig tree becomes tame; much more assuredly should an angry or proud person become mild at the tree of the cross, which is a fig tree because of its fruit, but a prickly juniper because of its painfulness. Proverbs 27: "He who guards the fig tree shall eat its fruit." The fruit of the cross is threefold. First, Christ himself, the fruit of the Virgin's womb. The second is penance; Isaias 27: "This is the whole fruit, that his sin be taken away," that is, man's sin, through penance. The third is eternal reward; Wisdom 3: "The fruit of good works is glorious." Further, there are some animals which never become tame. Such is the wild boar, which never accepts any discipline, as is stated in book I of *On Animals*. An angry or haughty person is rightly compared to a wild boar, because he cannot be tamed by meekness; and of such people Ezechiel 2 says: "They are children of a hard face and untameable heart." Further, the boar fights with its teeth; so does an angry man in his striving; Proverbs 30: "A generation which instead of teeth has a sword." Further, it gnashes its teeth to indicate its wrath; so do angry and proud men; the Psalm: "They have gnashed their teeth over me." In addition, the boar gets roused by the barking of a puppy and becomes enraged; just so does an angry man get provoked by a word even before it has been spoken; Ecclesiasticus 19: "A fool goes into labor at the hearing of a word," which is to say: he suffers anxieties because he does not answer at once. Likewise, the boar wounds the dogs that pursue it, and an angry person hurts those who correct him; whence: "He who teaches a scoffer does harm to himself," Proverbs 9; and 29: "The man who with a stiff neck scorns anyone that corrects him will come to sudden ruin." This is the boar that destroys his master's vineyard, that is, who disturbs the community of saints or the congregation of the good. In contrast, meekness maintains concord and nourishes it. Meekness is the soft pillow on the bed of conscience, on which our soul rests in safety; Ecclesiasticus 10: "My son, keep your soul in meekness." It is the

FHL. 35 **domita** domestica J. 36 **et *(1st)*** ad E. 37 **est** *om* ELW. 38 **ferarum** animalium FH. **melius** facilius FH. 39 Glossa *marg* E. **ut** *om* FGHLIW. 41 Ysidorus *marg* E. 42 **mansuescit** mansuesceret JL; mansuescat G; mansuescet W. 43 **iracundus uel** *om* FH. 44 **iuniperus** impiis *interl* J; *om* H; in viperis W. 51 **Et . . . est** ut FH. **aper** asper, *with* s *canc* E. 52 Philosophus *marg* E. **I** principio L; libro W. **animalibus** *add* iracundus est aper siluestris FH. 54 **dicitur** *om* FGHLI. **facie** ceruice FGH. 59 **indignatur** dedignatur F; dedignatur ⟨uel indignatur⟩ J. 60 **prolatum** *om* E. 61 **sustinet** patitur FH. 66 **exterminat** exterminauit E. **turbat** perturbat J; conturbat FH; tardat G. 67 **sanctorum** sanctam EJ. **uel . . . congregacionem** *om* FH. 68 **retinet . . . nutrit** rerum concordiam nutrit FH. 69–70

“Expandi manus meas tota die ad populum non credentem,” etc. Item animalia micia et domita hominibus sunt ad iuuamentum, ad uictum, [et] uestitum, immicia uero rapida sunt et dentibus et cornibus in homines seuiunt. Idem dicendum [est] de mansuetis et iracundis. Et quod mirabile est, ferarum natura melius domatur quam hominum iracundia; ut Iacobi iii, vbi refert Glossa de quodam serpente domito qui ad mensam cuiusdam principis cottidianam querebat annonam. Item dicit Ysidorus quod si taurus siluester ligatus fuerit ad arborem fici, mansuescit; multo forcius homo iracundus uel superbus mitescere debet ad arborem crucis, que ficus est racione fructus, set aspera iuniperus racione penalitatis. Prouerbiorum xxvii: / “Qui seruat ficum, comedet fructus [f. 112va] eius.” Fructus crucis triplex est. Primus ipse Christus, fructus uteri uirginalis. Secundus est penitencia; Ysaie xxvii: “Hic est totus fructus, ut auferatur peccatum eius,” idest, hominis per penitenciam. Tercius est retribucio eterna; Sapiencie iii: “Bonorum laborum gloriosus est fructus.” Item quedam animalia sunt que nunquam mansuescunt. Et talis est aper agrestis, qui nunquam recipit disciplinam, ut in I *De animalibus*. Iracundus uel superbus bene conparatur apro, quia per mansuetudinem domari non potest; et de talibus dicitur Ezechielis ii: “Filii dura facie et indomabili corde sunt.” Item aper pugnat dentibus; sic iracundus contencionibus; Prouerbiorum xxx: “Generacio que pro dentibus gladium habet.” Item frendet dentibus in signum ire; sic iracundi et superbi; Psalmus: “Frenduerunt super me dentibus suis.” Item ad uocem catuli excitatur et multum indignatur; sic iracundus ad uerbum nondum [prolatum] prouocatur; Ecclesiastici xix: “A facie uerbi parturit fatuus,” quasi dicat: angustias sustinet quod non statim respondet. Item aper uulnerat canes insequentes, et iracundus affligit corripientes; vnde: “Qui erudit derisorem, ipse sibi iniuriam facit,” Prouerbiorum ix; et xxix: “Viro qui corripientem dura ceruice contempnit, repentinus superueniet interitus.” Hic est aper qui [exterminat] uineam Domini, / idest turbat [f. 112vb] [sanctorum] societatem uel bonorum congregacionem. Econtra mansuetudo retinet concordiam et nutrit. Mansuetudo est mollis culcitra in lecto consciencie, in qua requiescit anima cum securitate; Ecclesiastici x: “Fili, in mansuetudine serua animam tuam.”

anointing which makes the head of our inner man, that is, our mind, smooth and supple. Hence a person who fasts is told to anoint his head and wash his face, Matthew 6, because penitential practices sometimes can interfere with one's patience and meekness. Therefore, the Lord tells the penitent to anoint his head, which Augustine in his book *On the Lord's Sermon on the Mount* explains as follows: "Anointing refers to joy, washing to purity."

Further, meekness is praiseworthy for many reasons. First, because the Lord himself assumes the task of teaching it and places it at the beginning of his lesson; Matthew 11: "Learn from me, because I am mild and of humble heart." Second, because God's pleasure is said to rest in it, together with faith, which is the first gift of grace; Ecclesiasticus 1: "Meekness and faith are a pleasure to him." Third, because meekness deserves men's love; Ecclesiasticus 3: "My son, do your works in meekness, and you will be loved above all glory." Fourth, because meekness deserves to be a leader; therefore, Moses, the mildest of men, became the leader of the twelve tribes, Numbers 12. Fifth, because meekness is the mother of holiness; in Ecclesiasticus 45 it is said of the holy man: "In faith and gentleness God has made him holy." Sixth, because the Lord takes his rest in meekness; for this virtue is "the flowery bed of the bride," Canticles 1. Seventh, because meekness is promised to receive an inheritance, as in the Psalm: "The meek shall inherit the earth." This is literally true, because the meek are more acceptable in human society. Or else it applies to the "earth" of our free will; Proverbs 15: "He who remains quiet under outcries possesses his heart"; this is the meek person who keeps the "land" of his heart under his control. Or else the passage can refer to the "land" of the living, in which the just have their share, which is called "land" because it is stable and an eternal dwelling-place. In a fourth way the quoted passage may refer to the "earth" of our body, which in this life is mortal but in the future will live forever, when Christ will "make the body of our lowness like to the body of his glory," Philippians 3.

The effects of meekness are as follows. First, it prepares us for our correction; the Psalm: "Meekness will come upon us and we shall be corrected." Second, it raises us up; the Psalm: "He will raise up the meek in their salvation." Third, it makes us rich; the Psalm: "The meek shall inherit the earth." Fourth, it blesses, that is, it makes us blessed; Matthew 5: "Blessed are the meek," and so forth. Fifth, it teaches us; Isaias 61: "He has sent me to teach the meek."

securitate sanctitate ⟨uel . . . securitate⟩ J; saturitate GW. 71 **Preterea** *om* JFH; propterea I; item L. 73 **vi** *om* E. 75 Augustinus *marg* E. **penitenti** *om* FH; penitentem W. **ungere** *add* capud JFW. **Augustinus** *add* in EW. 78 **commendatur** commendabilis est E. 88 **xlv** xl E. **dicitur** *om* FH. 90 **est** *om* E. 92 **ut in** *om* FGHILW. 93–94 **conuersacione** conseruacione E; conuersione J. 97 **qua** quo E; que W. 98 **mansionis** beatitudinis FH; mansuetudinis GILW. 100–101 **configurabit Christus** configurat Christus E; configurabitur H. 103 **Superuenit** *corr from* superueniet E. 106 **beat idest** *om* FGHILW. **beatos** beatum E; bonos HI(?). 107 **Quintus** *add* est EJ. **lxi** xli E; 6 H. 108 **misit** *corr from* mitesit E. 109 **Septimus**

Preterea ipsa est unctio que capud hominis interioris, idest mentem, lenit et emollit. Ideo precipitur ieiunanti ut ungat capud suum et faciem lauet, Matthei [vi], quia penitencia solet quandoque turbare pacienciam et mansuetudinem. Ideo precipit Dominus penitenti ungere, quod exponit Augustinus ° libro *De sermone Domini in monte* sic: "Vngere pertinet ad leticiam, lauare ad mundiciam."

Item mansuetudo [commendatur] a pluribus. Primo ex eo quod magisterium eius ascribit sibi Dominus et ordinat eam in principio lectionis; Matthei xi: "Discite a me, quia mitis sum et humilis corde." Secundo, quia in ipsa cum fide, que est prima gracia, dicitur esse Dei beneplacitum; Ecclesiastici i: "Quod beneplacitum est illi, mansuetudo et fides." Tercio, quia ipsa dilectionem hominum meretur; Ecclesiastici iii: "Fili, in mansuetudine opera tua fac, et super omnem gloriam diligeris." Quarto, quia illa meretur principatum; vnde Moyses mitissimus hominum factus est princeps duodecim tribuum, Numeri xii. Quinto, quia ipsa est mater sanctitatis; Ecclesiastici [xlv] dicitur de uiro sancto: "In fide et lenitate sanctum / f. 113ra fecit illum." Sexto, quia in ea requiescit Dominus; ipsa enim [est] "lectulus floridus sponse," Canticorum i. Septimo, quia ipsi promittitur hereditaria possessio, ut in Psalmo: "Mansueti hereditabunt terram." Quod uerum est ad litteram, quia mansueti magis sunt accepti in [conuersacione] hominum. Uel de "terra" liberi arbitrii; Prouerbiorum xv: "Qui acquiescit increpacionibus, hic possessor est cordis"; hic est mansuetus, qui "terram" cordis sui subicit sibi. Vel de "terra" uiuencium, in [qua] est porcio iustorum, que "terra" dicitur racione stabilitatis et eterne mansionis. Quarto exponitur de "terra" corporis nostri, quod in presenti mortale est, in futuro uiuet in eternum, quando "corpus humilitatis nostre" [configurabit] Christus "corpori claritatis sue," Philippensium iii.

Effectus mansuetudinis sunt isti. Primus, quod instruit correpcionem; Psalmus: "Superuenit mansuetudo et corripiemur." Secundus, quia exaltat; Psalmus: "Exaltabit mansuetos in salutem." Tercius, quia ditat; Psalmus: "Mansueti hereditabunt terram." Quartus, quod beat, idest [beatos] facit; Matthei v: "Beati mites," etc. Quintus °, quod instruit; Ysaie [lxi]: "Ad annun-

Sixth, it arms us against anger; Proverbs 15: "A soft answer breaks wrath." Seventh, it makes us joyful; Isaias 31: "The mild in the Lord shall increase their joy." Eighth, it saves us; James 1: "Accept with meekness the ingrafted word, which can save your souls." Ninth, it causes us to be loved; that is, it brings us love; Ecclesiasticus 3: "Do your works in meekness, and you shall be loved above the glory of men." Tenth, it softens people; Ecclesiasticus 6: "A sweet word softens your enemies." Eleventh, it increases the gifts of grace; 2 Kings 22: "My meekness has multiplied me."

Meekness has three degrees, according to Jerome. The first is that man reflects on what he does not have, for if he is rich in one bodily or spiritual good, he lacks a hundred others; and if he should say he is rich and needs nothing, Apocalypse 3, yet he is "pitiful and unhappy, blind and naked." Pitiful he is in his birth, unhappy in his death. Augustine in the first book of his *Confessions*: "What can be more pitiful than an unhappy wretch unaware of his own sorry state?" Gregory in the *Moralia*: "He is poor because he has not the riches of virtues; blind, because he sees not the poverty which he is suffering; naked, because he has lost his first garment." These things are said of man after his fall from grace. The second degree is to reflect on what he has from others; Corinthians 4: "What do you own that you have not received? Why do you boast as if you had not received?" The third degree is to reflect that one can lose what one has, for "unless one holds himself diligently in the fear of the Lord, one's house will quickly be overthrown," Ecclesiasticus 27. And Osee 6: "The thief has come in to steal, the robber is outside." The "thief" encourages sin and is our concupiscence which engages in secret thefts, for "we judge it when we ourselves are deceived," as is said in *Ethics*. The "robber from outside" is our ancient foe, experienced in wiliness and zealous in his mischief.

We have spoken of meekness, which represses inner motions toward anger; now we turn to patience, which suffers external hardships that arouse anger. Gregory defines it as follows: "Patience is the virtue which suffers external ills with equanimity and is not bitten with pain against the person who inflicts those ills." The Philosopher: "Patience is the virtue that bears with equanimity the onslaught of affronts and of all adversity." Patience is commendable for many things. First, because it makes us like God and makes us his children, that

add quod EF. 111 **Octauus** *add* quod EF. 116 **graciarum** *add* suple E. 118 Ieronimus *marg* E. 119 **quod** ut JFGHLW. 121 **et nullius egeat** *om* FH. 121–22 **et *(2nd)* . . . est** *om* FH. 123 Augustinus *marg* E. **Augustinus I Confessionum** I Confessionum Augustinus E. 124 Gregorius *marg* E. **Moralibus** *add* in moribus E. 127 **graciam** graciam *canc* peccatum J. 128 **habes** est E. 132–33 **latrunculus** latrunculos E; etc FL; *om* G; latens I. 133–35 **Fur . . . Latrunculus** fur spolians et latro F. 135 Philosophus *marg* E. 136 **malicia** *add* de paciencia *rubr* EJFI; de uirtute paciencie *rubr* W. 139 Gregorius *marg* E. **sic** *om* E. 140 **mala** *bona FHW; bona mala I. **aduersus** contra FG. 141 Philosophus *marg* E. **morderi** moueri FGHI(?). 142 **omnis** omnes GHW. 144 **spirituales** spirituales ⟨speciales

ciandum mansuetis misit me." Sextus, quia armat contra iram; Prouerbiorum xv: "Responsio mollis frangit iram." Septimus, ° letificat; Ysaie xxxi: "Addent mites in Domino leticiam." Octauus, ° saluat; Iacobi i: "In mansuetudine suscipite insitum uerbum, quod potest saluare animas uestras." / Nonus, adama- f. 113rb
tur; idest amorem meretur; Ecclesiastici iii: "In mansuetudine opera tua fac, et super hominum gloriam diligeris." Decimus, mitigat; Ecclesiastici vi: "Verbum dulce mitigat inimicos." Vndecimus, auget dona graciarum; ° II Regum xxii: "Mansuetudo mea multiplicauit me."

Tres sunt gradus mansuetudinis secundum Ieronimum. Primus est quod homo cogitet quid non habeat, quia si in uno bono corporali uel spirituali habundat, in centum deficit; et si dicat quod diues sit et nullius egeat, Apocalipsis iii, est tamen "miser et miserabilis, cecus et nudus." Miser est in ortu, miserabilis in obitu. [Augustinus, I *Confessionum*]: "Quid miserius misero non miserenti seipsum?" Gregorius in *Moralibus* °: "Pauper, quia uirtutum diuicias non habet; cecus, quia nec paupertatem quam patitur uidet; nudus, quia primam stolam perdidit." Et sunt hec dicta de homine lapso post graciam. Secundus gradus est attendere quod ab alio habet; Corinthiorum iiii: "Quid [habes] quod non accepisti? Quid gloriaris quasi non acceperis?" Tercius est attendere quod perdere potest quod habet, quia "si non instanter tenuerit se quis in timore Domini, cito subuertetur domus eius," Ecclesiastici xxvii. Et Osee vi: "Ingressus est fur spolians, [latrunculus] foris." "Fur" est fomes siue concupiscencia que occulta exercet latrocinia, quia "non indecepti iudicamus illam," dicitur in *Ethycis*. "Latrunculus fo- / ris" est antiquus hostis expertus in f. 113va
astucia et diligens in malicia.

Dictum est de mansuetudine, que reprimit motus interiores ad iram; dicendum est de paciencia, que tolerat molestias exteriores iram concitantes. Que [sic] diffinitur secundum Gregorium: "Paciencia est aliena mala equanimiter perpeti et aduersus eum qui mala ingerit nullo dolore morderi." Philosophus: "Paciencia est uirtus contumeliarum et omnis aduersitatis inpetus equanimiter portans." Paciencia est in multis commendabilis. Primo, quia assimilat nos Deo et filios eius constituit, idest spirituales imita-

is, his spiritual imitators; Matthew 5: "Blessed are the peacemakers, for they will be called children of God." The Almighty himself, who can destroy the entire world with one nod, still desires to bear in patience our transgressions and his injuries; Isaias 30: "God waits that he may have pity on us; therefore, by sparing us he will be exalted." This is why the Church says that he shows his omnipotence most by sparing and having mercy, that is, in so far as "he overlooks the sins of men for the sake of their repentance," as in Wisdom 11. For he takes pity but remains unchanged, because he cannot be hurt by any pain, according to Augustine, *Confessions* I. Thus, although his is the task of punishing who carries out just trial and strict vengeance, he would rather spare his enemies, so that he might teach us to bear ourselves patiently in our unjust sufferings. Moreover, patience makes us especially like Christ, who showed perfect patience by his word and example, so that "when he was reviled, he did not revile; when he suffered, he did not threaten; but he delivered himself to him who judged him unjustly," 1 Peter 2. Patience is also a special sign of God's servants; 2 Corinthians 6: "Let us in all things show ourselves as God's servants in much patience." Further, in the praise of the effects of charity, which this virtue achieves through other virtues, charity is first said to be "patient," Corinthians 13. Patience also conquers the enemy, according to the saying:

> A noble way of victory is patience. He wins
> Who suffers. If you want to win, learn to suffer.

Moreover, patience saves man in temptation; Apocalypse 3: "Because you have kept the word of my patience, I too will keep you in the hour of temptation." Patience makes a man proven and perfect; Romans 5: "Patience works trials." Patience also crowns man for his deserts; James 1: "Blessed is the man who suffers temptation, for," and so forth; and Romans 2: "God will render to those who according to patience in good work [seek] glory and honor, [eternal life]." Further, the deserved punishment to which we are bound urges us to practice patience. We are bound to a fourfold punishment. The first is due to original sin; Ecclesiasticus 40: "A heavy yoke is on the children of Adam from the day they leave their mother's womb." The second is due to actual sin; Proverbs 5: "Each one is tied down with the cords of his sins." The third we derive from

corr⟩ J; speciales IW. 147 **iniurias** *add* pacienter GW. 152–53 **ut . . . sauciatur** *om* L. 152 **xi** ix E; 2 F; 5 H. **incorruptibilis** in corruptibilibus EF; incorruptibilius GHW. 153 Augustinus *marg* E. 153–54 **Propterea** preterea EFG; *om* L. 154 **districtio** discrecio JGW. 155 **mauult** uult E. 156 **nos** *om* E. **assimilat** assimilatur E; alat W. 158 **maledixit** maledicebat HIW; *om* F. 165 **solet dici** *dicit Philosophus L; solet dicere W. 173–74 **Reddet** reddit E. 174 **operis** operantur E; *om* FL. 176 **uirtutem paciencie** pacienciam FHL. **autem** enim FGHILW. 180 **sci-**

tores; Matthei v: "Beati pacifici, quoniam filii Dei uocabuntur." Ipse enim Omnipotens, qui uno nutu potest totum mundum delere, adhuc uult pacienter nostras transgressiones et suas iniurias sustinere; Ysaie xxx: "Expectat Deus ut misereatur nostri; propterea exaltabitur parcens nobis." Hoc est quod Ecclesia dicit quod omnipotenciam suam parcendo maxime et miserando manifestat, idest, in eo quod "dissimulat peccata hominum propter penitenciam," ut Sapiencie [xi]. Ipse enim miseretur [incorruptibilis] eo quod nullo dolore sauciatur, Augustinus, I *Confessionum*. [Propterea] cum eius sit punire cuius est examen iusticie et districtio uindicte, [mauult] tamen hostibus suis parcere, ut doceat nos in iniuriis pacienter agere. Item paciencia specialiter [nos assimilat] Christo, qui tam perfectam docuit pacienciam / f. 113vb uerbo et exemplo, "qui cum malediceretur non maledixit; cum pateretur non comminabatur; set tradidit se iudicanti iniuste," I Petri ii. Item paciencia est speciale signum ministrorum Dei; II Corinthiorum vi: "In omnibus exhibeamus nos sicut Dei ministros in multa paciencia." Item in commendacione effectuum caritatis, quos ipsa efficit per alias uirtutes, primo dicitur "caritas paciens est," Corinthiorum xiii. Item paciencia uincit hostem, secundum quod solet dici:

Nobile uincendi genus est paciencia. Vincit
Qui patitur. Si uis uincere, disce pati.

Item paciencia seruat hominem in temptacione; Apocalipsis iii: "Quia seruasti uerbum paciencie mee, et ego te seruabo ad horam temptacionis." Item paciencia probatum et perfectum reddit hominem; Romanorum v: "Paciencia probacionem operatur." Item paciencia coronat hominem pro meritis; Iacobi i: "Beatus uir qui suffert temptacionem, quoniam," etc.; et Romanorum ii: "[Reddet] Deus hiis qui secundum pacienciam boni [operis] gloriam et honorem." Item ipsa obligacio pene qua tenemur incitat nos ad uirtutem paciencie. Obligamur autem pena quadruplici. Prima debetur peccato originali; Ecclesiastici xl: "Graue iugum super filios Adam a die exitus ex uentre matris eorum." Secunda debetur peccato actuali; Prouerbiorum v: "Funibus peccatorum suorum quisque constringitur." Terciam contrahimus ex miseriis in

the miseries into which we fall, hunger, thirst, disease, and death; Thessalonians 3: "Let no one be moved in these tribulations, knowing that we have been appointed unto them." The fourth is the pain through which we must come to share in the sufferings of Christ; 1 Peter 4: "Christ having suffered in the flesh, be you also armed with the same thought"; Bernard says: "It is not fitting that under a head crowned with thorns the members should lie in delicate rest," by which he means: the members must share the pains of their head, unless they are separated from the whole or dead. Further, we are compelled to bear ourselves patiently in the hardship of present suffering in order to avoid even greater suffering to come, because in comparison with eternal pain any present affliction is a consolation. Thus Job 7: "This may be my comfort, that afflicting me with sorrow," and so forth. A further reason for patience can be derived from reflecting on past sins; Job 33 speaks of the afflicted person, admonishing him to be patient, and says: "His flesh is wasted with punishments, let him return to the days of his youth"; in other words: let recalling his guilt lessen the weight of his suffering. In addition, the examples of the saints invite us to be patient, "who were cut asunder and were stoned and were put to death by the sword," Hebrews 11. Therefore has Job 8 enjoined us to investigate the remembrance of our fathers diligently, and in Jeremias 6 the Lord commands us to inquire about old paths which may be the good way, and to walk in it. "Path" is the life of the saints, which is the harder, straighter, purer, and shorter way; Isaias 26: "The path of the just man is straight, his road is right to walk in." Of these paths we find examples if we meditate on Jerome's sack and cribble-bread, on Benedict's thorn-bush, on the mat of Eulalius, the tears of Arsenius, the nakedness of the Egyptian woman, the devotion of Mary Magdalene. In these lies the way to patience. Further, the lightness of our present punishment arms us to be patient; 2 Corinthians 4: "For that which is momentary and light of our tribulation will be a weight of glory," and so forth. Also the shortness of this punishment; 1 Peter 1: "If now you must be for a little time made sorrowful." And the low price of this punishment, for "there is one who buys much for a modest price," Ecclesiasticus 21. Penitential suffering in this life frees from eternal punishment; in contrast, eternal punishment will be most grievous. "Hell is so hot," says Augustine in his book *On the Morals of the Church,* "that even if the whole ocean flowed into it, it would not cool a bit." This is not beyond belief, because Greek fire, which is man-made, is stronger than water. In addition, it will be perpetual, for "their worm will not die and their fire will not be extinguished," Isaias at the end. It is also useless, for "whether [it lasts for] ten or a

entes sciens E; etc L. 185 Bernardus *marg* E. 186 **pena** penam JIL. **debent** deberet E. 187 **mortua** *add* set Philosophus manus abscisa non est manus et sic non est membrum *marg* J. 188 **sequentis** sequens E. 190 **michi** *om* E. 191 **ut . . . dolore** et afflic *(corr to* afflig ?) in *(canc)* dolore m *added interl above* in E. 197 **Ideo** sancto, *corr to* Dominus *marg* E. 198 **viii** *corr from* iiii E. 200–201 **et ambulare . . . et *(1st)*** *om* W. 201 **rectior** curtior G. **conpendiosior** ponderosior W. 203 Exempla *marg* E. **saccum** sanctum *canc*, saccum *marg* E. 204 **mattulam** sactulam J; uarculam G; uactulam HL; uaculam I; maceriam(?) W. **mattulam Eulalii** *om* EF. 205 **Arsenii** Arthemii E; acerui W. **hiis** *add* semitis FGH. 207 **Id** ad EW. 207–8 **Id . . . etc.** id momentaneum et leue tribulacionis nostre Matthei xi iugum enim meum suaue est et honus meum leue J; id quod in presenti est etc. FL; id momentaneum G; id momentaneum et leue HIW. 208 **Et** item J; uel G; secundo ILW. 209–10 **si . . . redimat** amat F. 209 **Et** uel G; tercio ILW. 210–11 **precio . . . eternam** *om* W. 211 **absoluit** abluit E. 212 Augustinus *marg* E. **libro De** in libro de E; in FGHLW; libro iii in I. 217 **fine** *om* E; ultimo JFGL. 218 **accusacio** excusacio

quas incidimus, famem, sitim, infirmitatem, et mortem; Tessalonicensium iii: "Nemo moueatur in istis tribulacionibus [scientes] quia in hiis positi sumus." / f. 114ra Quarta est qua debemus fieri participes pene Christi; I Petri iiii: "Christo passo in carne uos eadem cogitacione armamini"; Bernardus: "Non decet sub spinato capite membra delicata requiescere," quasi diceret: pena capitis [debent] membra participare, nisi sint diuisa a toto uel mortua. Item uitacio maioris pene [sequentis] conpellit nos pacienter agere in angustia pene presentis, quia omnis presens afflictio conparacione pene eterne est consolacio. Ideo Iob vii: "Hec [michi] sit consolacio [ut affligens me dolore]," etc. Item ex respectu peccatorum preteritorum sumitur materia paciencie; Iob xxxiii loquitur de tribulato monens ad pacienciam et dicit: "Consumpta est caro eius a suppliciis, reuertatur ad dies adolescencie sue," quasi diceret: magnitudinem pene alleuiet memoria culpe. Item exempla sanctorum inuitant nos ad pacienciam, "qui secti sunt, lapidati sunt, in occisione gladii mortui sunt," Hebreorum xi. [Ideo] precepit Iob viii diligenter inuestigare patrum memoriam, et Ieremie vi precipit Dominus interrogare de semitis antiquis, que sit uia bona, et ambulare in ea. "Semita" est sanctorum uita, quia arcior est uia et rectior et mundior et conpendiosior; Ysaie xxvi: "Semita iusti recta est, rectus callis eius ad ambulandum." De hiis semitis patet in exemplis si recogitemus saccum Ieronimi / f. 114rb et panem cribrarium, vepres Benedicti, [mattulam Eulalii,] lacrimas [Arsenii], nuditatem Egipcie, deuocionem Magdalene. In hiis uia est ad pacienciam. Item pene presentis leuitas armat nos ad pacienciam; II Corinthiorum iiii: "[Id] momentaneum et leue tribulacionis nostre erit glorie pondus," etc. Et pene breuitas; I Petri i: "Modicum nunc si oportet contristari." Et pene utilitas, quia "est qui multa redimat modico precio," Ecclesiastici xxi. Pena penitencialis in presenti [absoluit] eternam; econtra pena futura erit grauissima. "Tam feruens," dicit Augustinus ° libro *De moribus Ecclesie*, "est gehenna quod, si totum mare influeret, neque ad modicum refrigeraret." Et non est hoc incredibile, quia ignis Grecus quem homo conficit preualet aque. Preterea erit eciam perpetua, quia "uermis eorum non morietur, et ignis non extinguetur," Ysaie [fine]. Est eciam inutilis, quia "siue decem siue

hundred or a thousand years, among the dead there is no accusing of life," Ecclesiasticus 41, that is, they are punished but not purified, nor is the remembrance of their sins of any help there except to increase their punishment, for as Jerome says on Isaias 24: "After this life the remembrance of past pleasures will be matter for torments." It further endows us with patience that our present pains are nothing in comparison with our glory; Romans 8: "The sufferings of this time are not worthy to be compared with the glory to come that will be revealed in us." Likewise the subsequent joy inspires us; Ecclesiasticus 1: "A patient man shall bear for a time, and afterwards joy shall be restored to him."

Examples of patience. Patience is a fortified castle, in which we rest most secure from the enemies' assaults. It is "the tower of David, built with bulwarks," Canticles 4. It is, further, the chest in which the treasure of virtues is kept. Luke 21: "In your patience you shall possess your souls." To possess one's soul is to keep it unmoved in tribulation with the help of patience and to rule over its motion from the stronghold of the virtues, according to Gregory. But when the chest breaks, the treasure is lost. The same is true of the treasure of virtues when patience is overcome. It is also the shield of Christ's champions. Thus, when Job was violently assaulted by the fiend, he protected himself with this shield against the heavy attacks from all sides and said: "The Lord gave, and the Lord has taken away; as it has pleased the Lord, so is it done"; Gregory: "The warrior caught in the heat of battle everywhere raises up his shield of patience." Further, when Job says, "Naked came I out of my mother's womb," Gregory comments: "He recalls his poverty in order to remain patient." In addition, any purgative medicine has some bitter scammony in its ingredients; thus, patience is intermingled with the bitterness of tribulations, and yet it is very good for one's health. Therefore, Jeremias 15 says: "I made a boast of the presence of your hand, Lord, for you have filled me with bitterness" (or "with agitation," in another reading), as if he were saying: though it is a bitter drink for those who endure tribulation, yet it heals their souls. Therefore, in Wisdom 3 it is said of the saints: "They have been afflicted in few things, in many they shall be well rewarded." Patience is also an eyesalve, which first irritates the eye and then heals it; Apocalypse 3: "Anoint your eyes with eyesalve," etc. What this eyesalve should be like and how it is prepared can be seen above, in the chapter on Christ the physician. Further, patience is a furnace in which the cho-

E. 219 **xli** xl EH; xi LW. **idest** *om* JIL; *add* ibi FGH. 219–21 **nec . . . xxiiii** et I. 221 Ieronimus *marg* E. **ut dicit** *om* FGHLW. 223 **pene** *om* E. 225 **huius . . . nobis** ad futuram gloriam JIW; *om (quotation abbreviated)* FGHL. 229 **insultibus** infestacionibus J. 230 **Item** *om* EFGI. 231 **thesaurus** *add* domini *canc* E. 234 Gregorius *marg* E. 235–36 **Idem . . . uincitur** *om* GW. 239 **est** *add* ibi dicit E. 240 Gregorius *marg* E. 242 Gregorius *marg* E. 243–44 **purgatiua** *om* E. 244–45 **amaritudine** *add* passionum uel E. 246 **Ideo dicit** *om* FGHILW. 247–48 **uel . . . littera** *om* FIL. 248 **tribulacionem** *corr from* tribulacionum E. 249 **animarum** animorum EH. 251 **Item** *om* EFG. **que** quod J*(corr)* FLW. 254–55 **pur-**

centum siue mille anni, non est apud inferos [accusacio] uite," Ecclesiastici [xli], idest, puniuntur set non purgantur, nec ualet ibi recordacio peccatorum nisi ad augmentum suppliciorum, quia ut dicit Ieronimus super Ysaie xxiiii: "Post hanc uitam recordacio preteritarum deliciarum erit materia cruciatuum." Item animat nos ad pacienciam quod omnes [pene] presentes nulle sunt conparate ad gloriam; Romanorum viii: "Non sunt condigne passiones huius temporis ad futuram gloriam que reuelabitur in nobis." Item animat nos / sequens iocunditas; Ecclesiastici i: "Vsque ad f. 114va tempus sustinebit paciens, et postea reddicio iocunditatis."

Exempla paciencie. Ipsa est castrum munitum, in quo tutissime quiescimus ab hostium insultibus. Ipsa est "turris Dauid edificata cum propugnaculis," Canticorum iiii. [Item] ipsa est archa, in qua seruatur thesaurus uirtutum. Luce xxi: "In paciencia uestra possidebitis animas uestras." Animam possidere est ipsam in tribulacione seruare per pacienciam immobilem et motibus eius ex arce uirtutum inperare, secundum Gregorium. Set cum archa frangitur, thesaurus amittitur. Idem de thesauro uirtutum, cum paciencia uincitur. Item ipsa est scutum atletharum Christi. Vnde cum Iob uehementissime inpugnaretur ab hoste, isto clipeo muniuit se undique ad graues insultus dicens: "Dominus dedit, Dominus abstulit; sicut Domino placuit, ita factum est"; ° Gregorius: "Bellator certaminum feruore deprehensus ubique paciencie clypeum opponit." Preterea ubi dicit, "Nudus egressus sum de utero matris mee," ibi dicit Gregorius: "Reducit paupertatem ad memoriam ut seruet pacienciam." Item medicina [purgatiua] aliquid recipit de amarissima scamonia; ita paciencia amaritudine ° tribulacionum respersa est, et tamen ualde sanatiua est. Ideo dicit Ieremie xv: "Gloriatus sum a facie manus tue, Domine, quoniam amaritudine replesti me" (uel "commocione," / alia littera), quasi diceret: licit amara sit pocio tribulacionem pa- f. 114vb cientibus, tamen curacio est [animarum]. Ideo dicitur de sanctis, Sapiencie iii: "In paucis uexati, in multis bene disponentur." [Item] ipsa est collirium, que prius turbat oculum et sanat postmodum; Apocalipsis iii: "Collirio inunge oculos tuos," etc. Et quale debeat esse hoc collirium et qualiter factum, uide supra in capitulo de Christo medico. Item ipsa est fornax, in qua [purgan-

sen are purified like gold and silver. And notice that in the furnace alloys are mixed together with lead so that the foreign matter may be separated out. Thus, the weight of tribulation is added in the trial of this virtue, so that whatever is base in our soul may be eliminated by the boiling lead of persecution. But notice that if there is too much rust in the gold or silver, or another alloy, then the lead is consumed by the fire and the gold is not purified. Thus, if in the furnace of tribulation someone fails because of the added rust of sin, patience does not effect any cleansing in him; Jeremias 6: "The bellows have failed, the lead is consumed in the fire, the founder has melted in vain, their wicked deeds are not consumed," as if he were saying: in these the virtue of patience has failed. Moreover, patience is a frying pan in which the elect are burned so that they may become lighter and more pleasing to God. For fried food is lighter and tastier; for its earthly liquids which cause it to be heavy and bitter are made to evaporate. Thus, tribulation strips man of his earthliness and renders him acceptable to God if he has patience; the Psalm: "My bones are grown dry like cinder" (a different reading has: "they have been fried as in a frying pan"). The Lord's "bones" are holy and robust men who carry the burden of the Church's body and lie hidden in the mass of flesh; yet they are filled with the marrow of devotion and holy meditation. But "cinder in the frying pan" are those who grow dry in tribulation without patience. For cinder is what is left of the flesh after it has been burned in the flame. Further, man endures burning and cutting so that his flesh may be healed. The poet:

If you want your body to heal,
You must suffer fire and steel.

Much more readily should we bear with adversity, so that we may heal our soul. Therefore Augustine, on "Rebuke me not, o Lord, in our indignation," verse 2, prayed: "Burn here, cut there!" Patience is, furthermore, the armor of the saints; Canticles 4: Upon the tower of David, which is patience, hangs "all the armor of valiant men." And Ambrose: "My weapons are my jaws."

We have said that patience is directed against external vexations; therefore it should be known that external vexation is of four kinds, and four kinds of patience are necessary. External vexation consists in verbal insult, in bodily torment, in the loss of goods, and in forced service. Against all of these, we are taught fourfold patience by our heavenly master in Matthew 5. He taught pa-

gantur probantur E. 256 **adulteratis** adulterinis J. 259 **consumatur** eliminatur J. **Set** et JFHLW. 262 **rubiginem** tribulacionem J. 262–63 **paciencia . . . efficit** *om* W. 263 **Defecit** deficit EIW; *om* G. 268 **sunt** *add* delectabiliora JG. 270 **hominem** hominum E. **exuit** exuitur E; exit F. 276 **Cremium . . . illud** idest W. 278 Poeta *marg* E. **curet** *corr from* curat E; curat W. 279 **pacieris** paciaris E. 281 Augustinus *marg* E. **super** *add* Psalmum FH. 282–84 **Ex . . . sunt** *om* G. 284 Ambrosius *marg* E. **sunt** *add* de paciencia *rubr* J. 286 **sciendum** *add* est FGIL. 287–88 **uerborum** *add* idest E. 288 **angaria** angustia JFILW. 289 **a** in E. 289–90 **quad-**

tur] electi ad similitudinem auri uel argenti. Et nota quod plumbum admiscetur metallis adulteratis in fornace, ut aliena materia separetur. Ita pondus tribulacionis apponitur in exercicio huius uirtutis, ut si quid uiciosum in anima sit, ebullienti plumbo persecucionis consumatur. Set nota quod cum rubigo preualet in auro uel argento uel metallum adulterinum, tunc plumbum consumitur ab igne et aurum non purgatur. Ita cum quis in fornace tribulacionis propter ammixtam rubiginem culpe deficit, paciencia in ipso nullam purgacionem efficit; Ieremie vi: "[Defecit] sufflatorium in igne, consumptum est plumbum, frustra conflauit conflator, malicie eorum non sunt consumpte," quasi diceret: defecit in eis uirtus paciencie. Item ipsa est frixorium in quo uruntur electi ut leuiores fiant et Deo delectabiliores. Frixa enim leuiora sunt et sapidiora; euaporantur enim in eis humores terrestres, / qui sunt causa ponderositatis et amaritudinis. Ita tribulacio f. 115ra [hominem] a terrenitate [exuit] et acceptum Deo reddit, si paciencia assit; Psalmus: "Ossa mea sicut cremium aruerunt" (alia littera: "sicut in frixorio frixa sunt"). "Ossa" Domini sunt uiri sancti et robusti, qui pondus portant corporis Ecclesie et latent in multitudine carnalium; inplentur tamen medullis deuocionis et sancte meditacionis. "Cremium" uero "in frixorio" fiunt qui in tribulacione sine paciencia arescunt. Cremium uero est illud quod relinquitur de carne post ustionem flamme. Item homo patitur ustionem et sectionem ut curet carnem. Poeta:

Ut corpus redimas, ferrum [pacieris] et ignem.

Multo forcius pacienda sunt aduersa, ut curemus mentem. Ideo orauit Augustinus super "Domine, ne in furore," ii: "Hic ure, hic seca." Item ipsa est armatura sanctorum; Canticorum iiii: Ex turre Dauid, que est paciencia, dependet "omnis armatura forcium." Et Ambrosius: "Arma mea maxille mee sunt."

Dictum est quod paciencia est contra molestias exteriores; ideo sciendum quod quadruplex est exterior molestia, et necessaria quadruplex paciencia. Molestia exterior est in contumelia uerborum, ° in cruciatu corporum, in dampno rerum, in angaria operum. Contra hec omnia [a] celesti magistro docetur [quadruplex] paciencia, Matthei v. Pacienciam ad uerba docuit qui tot

tience in the presence of verbal attacks when he endured without murmur so many insults, contradictions, invectives, and taunts, as for instance when they said to him: "You are a Samaritan, you have a devil," John 8, and again: "He casts out devils by the prince of devils," Luke 11, and again: "Behold a man that is a glutton and a drinker of wine, a friend of publicans and sinners," Luke 7. On all these occasions he did not curse or threaten punishment or voice a reproach. Therefore, in this it is especially manifest that he was the son of David, who said of his enemy that reproached him and flung insults at him: "Let him alone that he may curse as the Lord has bidden him, perhaps the Lord may look upon my affliction and may render me good for the cursing of this day," 2 Kings 16. Moreover, when at the beginning of his passion he was accused by many, he did not answer but set a guard to his mouth when the sinners stood against him. And Jerome tells us the reason, in his comment on Matthew 26, "But Jesus held his peace," in the Gloss: "He knew that whatever he said would be twisted into a false accusation." Just as he knew that it was written: "If a wise man contends with a fool, whether he be angry or laugh, he shall find no rest," Proverbs 29. Such patience makes man an angel, as it was said to David, who stands for Christ especially in his meekness and patience, 2 Kings 14: "Even as an angel of the Lord, so is my lord the king, that he is neither moved with blessing nor cursing." Also, he who swells up or strives against insults that are flung at him is like the scorpion, which when stepped upon puts out its sting and hurts those that have stepped on it. Scorpions are people who curse and insult, who at the beginning of their speech put on a pleasant face, but in the end they curse and strive so much more sharply. Nonetheless, scorpions cannot harm anyone except those who do not bear God's sign on their forehead, Apocalypse 9, that is, those who lack the virtue of patience. Likewise, he who replies to insults with harsh words is like a dog that bites a stone thrown to him. Indeed, he is even more foolish than a dog, who withdraws when it sees the stone; but man, the harsher a word is, the more firmly does he retain it in his heart and the harder does he grind it with his teeth. In this he is worse than the devil, who asked that stones be made bread, Matthew 4. Man in contrast wants that the bread of correction or instruction be turned into stones; Hilary: "Those make bread from stones who endure harsh words with meekness"; and Gregory: "Even when we can resist, let us turn aside the wrath of the proud with humility. For it is more honorable to flee from injury in silence than to triumph over it in kind." For insults and scorn make us humble and help us

ruplex *om* E. **quadruplex . . . qui** *om* F. 291 **contradictiones tot conuicia** uicia E. 294 **demonia** demones E; etc I. 297 **Vnde** *marg* E; *om* J. 298 **fuisse** esse GILW. **filius** *om* E. **exprobranti** exprobrante E. 299 **obicienti** obiciente E; dicenti G. **maledicat** *add* michi E. 304 Ieronimus *marg* E. 305 Glossa *marg* E. **xxvi** xvi *and* x *added in marg* E. 306 **in** ad E. **enim** *om* E. 311 **est** *om* E; es L. 318 **Dei** crucis GIW. **ix idest** xxi E; 91 G. **uirtutem** uirtutes E. 321 **est** *om* EL. 323 **est** *om* EL. 324 **correpcionis** correctionis JFW. 325 Hylarius *marg* E. **efficiunt** conficiunt L; efficiuntur W. 326 Gregorius *marg* E. 328–29 **Gloriosius . . . superare** *om* L. 328 **iniuriam** iram E; murmura G. 329–30 **humiliant** illuminant

contumelias, tot [contradictiones, tot conuicia], tot obprobria sine murmure susti- / [f. 115^{r}b] nuit, vt cum diceretur ei: “Samaritanus es tu, demonium habes,” Iohannis viii, et iterum: “In principe demoniorum eicit [demonia],” Luce xi, et iterum: “Ecce homo deuorator et bibens uinum, amicus publicanorum et peccatorum,” Luce vii. In omnibus hiis nec maledicta inuexit, nec penam comminatus est, nec obprobria intulit. Vnde in hoc apparet specialiter fuisse [filius] Dauid, qui de inimico [exprobranti] et conuicia [obicienti] dicebat: “Dimitte eum ut maledicat ° iuxta preceptum Domini, si forte respiciat Dominus afflictionem meam et reddat michi bonum pro maledictione hac hodierna,” II Regum xvi. Preterea in preludiis passionis sue accusatus in multis non respondit, set posuit custodiam ori suo, cum consisterent peccatores aduersus eum. Et Ieronimus dicit racionem, super Matthei xxvi ibi: “Iesus autem tacebat,” Glossa: “Sciens quecumque dixisset retorqueri [in] calumpniam.” Sciuit [enim] esse scriptum: “Vir sapiens si cum stulto contenderit, siue irascatur siue rideat, non inueniet requiem,” Prouerbiorum xxix. Talis paciencia facit hominem angelum, sicut dictum est ad Dauid, qui specialiter Christum signat in mansuetudine et paciencia, II Regum xiiii: “Sicut angelus Domini, sic [est] dominus meus rex, ut nec benedictione nec maledictione moueatur.” Item qui ad contumeliam illatam intumescit uel contendit, similis est scorpioni, qui cum calcatur aculeos exerit et calcantes ledit. Scorpiones sunt / [f. 115^{v}a] maledicentes et contumeliosi, qui in principio sermonis blandiuntur facie, set acrius tamen maledicunt uel contendunt in fine. Nec possunt tamen scorpiones nocere nisi illis qui carent signo Dei in fronte, Apocalipsis [ix, idest], qui non habent [uirtutem] paciencie. Item qui dura uerba ad contumelias respondet, similis est cani mordenti lapidem sibi proiectum. Immo stulcior cane [est], qui cum lapidem percipit recedit; homo uero quanto uerbum durius est, tanto illud corde retinet firmius et dentibus conterit durius. In hoc peior [est] dyabolo, qui peciit lapides panes fieri, Matthei iiii. Iste uero uult panem correpcionis siue instructionis in lapides conuerti; Hylarius: “Panes de lapidibus efficiunt, qui dura uerba cum mansuetudine suscipiunt”; et Gregorius: “Eciam cum resistere possumus, iram superbiencium humiliter declinemus. Gloriosius enim est [iniuriam] tacendo fugere quam respondendo superare.” Contumelie enim et obprobria nos humiliant et ad cognicionem proprie infirmitatis [multum] iuuant.

much to recognize our own weakness. The same author: "He who could go out of himself through praise returns to himself when he is struck by insults." Moreover, he is very foolish who blows into the fire or puts wood in it when he knows he will be burned by it; the same holds for him who gives a harsh answer to words of insult. Hence Ecclesiasticus 8: "Strive not with a man that is full of tongue, and heap not wood upon his fire." Likewise, scoffers sometimes attack even more willingly those who willingly engage in strife, just like the man who pulls a puppy by its ears because it snaps and barks all about him; Proverbs 26: "As he that takes a dog by the ears, so is he that passes by in anger and meddles with another man's quarrel." Moreover, whoever replies to harsh words with patience has an excellent defense around his castle, which in French is called *hurdiz*; for when soft material is spread over a castle's bulwarks, the blows from rocks and engines will lose their destructive force. Similarly: "A mild answer breaks wrath, but a harsh word stirs up fury," Proverbs 15. Further, when solid bodies clash, fire is generated, and when harsh words clash, wrath and indignation; hence it is said above: "A harsh word stirs up fury," and so forth.

In the face of harsh words one must take upon oneself the patience of Sara, the daughter of Raguel, who when she was assaulted with grievous abuse, took refuge to prayer and said: "I beg, o Lord, that you loose me from the bond of this reproach," and so forth, Tobias 3. Further, in order that verbal strife may stop, it is necessary that one of the striving parties either yield or be removed. But a proud man smarts when he appears as the loser; Gregory on Job 8: "Proud people scorn keeping a modest silence, lest it be thought that they are keeping quiet out of ignorance." And yet, "he is hateful" to men "who is bold in speech," Ecclesiasticus 20. And although one should be patient vis-à-vis insults, yet on occasion the folly of quarrelsome people may be rebutted with good reason; and this is meant by "answering a fool according to his folly, lest he imagine himself to be wise," Proverbs 26, that is, by a shrewd answer you may evade the wrangling of a fool. Sometimes it is a good thing, too, to withdraw from verbal fighting, because "it is an honor for a man to separate himself from quarrels," Proverbs 20. The Lord also taught this when "he went aside from the multitude standing in the place," John 5, for through his presence there might have arisen a quarrel over the man healed on the Sabbath. A certain hermit, in the *Lives of the Fathers,* forgot this truth when after a long quiet and extended silence he presented himself in the assembly of brethren, and as some-

FGHIW. 330 **multum** *om* E. 331 Idem *marg* E. 331–32 **Idem . . . redit** *om* L. 332 **in** *om* JGHL. 334 **viii** *add* dicitur EH. 336 **libencius** libenter E; *om* L; libencium W. 341 **circa** contra FL. **hurdiz** hurdeto E. 345 **corporum** coporum E. 346–47 **ideo . . . supra** Prouerbiorum xv GILW. 348 **Sare filie** vnde Sara filia E. 349 **que** *om* E. 351 **possit** posset JGHW. 353 Gregorius *marg* E. 354 **moderanter** modaciter E; moderaciter JGIW; mordaciter F. 358–59 **et . . . suam** *om* L. 359 **iuxta** secundum E; etc F. 360 **elidas** euadas L. 361 **bonum est** *om* L. 365 Exemplum *marg* E. **doctrine** *add marg* non, *marked for insertion after* doctrine E. 367 **diuturnum** diutinum JGHILW. **se** *marg* E. **congregacione** congregacio-

Idem: "Qui exire foras per laudes potuit, repulsus contumeliis ad se redit." Item ualde stultus est qui in ignem exsufflat et ligna apponit unde comburendum se nouit; sic qui ad uerba contumeliosa respondet duriora. Ideo Ecclesiastici viii ° : "Non litiges cum homine linguato, et non strues ad ignem illius ligna." Item illos qui libenter contendunt, irrisores / f. 115vb quandoque [libencius] inpetunt, sicut qui catulum per aures dilaniat eo quod hinc inde mordet et latrat; Prouerbiorum xxvi: "Sicut qui apprehendit auribus canem, sic qui transit inpaciens, admiscebitur rixe alterius." Item qui duris uerbis pacienter respondet, optimum munimentum circa castrum suum habet, quod Gallice dicitur [hurdiz]; quia cum mollia in propugnaculis castri substernuntur, ictus lapidum et machinarum a lesione prohibentur. A simili: "Responsio mollis frangit iram, et sermo durus suscitat furorem," Prouerbiorum xv. Item ex collisione solidorum [corporum] generatur ignis, et ex collisione durorum uerborum ira et indignacio; ideo dicitur supra: "Sermo durus suscitat furorem," etc.

Item ad dura uerba sumenda est paciencia [Sare, filie] Raguelis, [que] cum grauissimis opprobriis inpeteretur, fugit ad subsidium oracionis dicens: "Peto, Domine, ut de uinculo inproperii huius absoluas me," etc., Thobie iii. Item ad hoc quod possit contumelia sedari, necesse est alterum contendencium uel cedere uel subtrahi. Set superbus dolet uictus uideri; Gregorius super Iob viii: "Contempnunt superbi [moderanter] reticere, ne credantur ex inpericia tacuisse." Et tamen "odibilis est" hominibus "qui procax est ad loquendum," Ecclesiastici xx. Et quamuis ad contumelias habenda sit paciencia, racionabiliter tamen refelli potest quandoque litigancium stulticia; et hoc est "respondere stulto [iuxta] / f. 116ra stulticiam suam, ne sibi uideatur sapiens," Prouerbiorum xxvi, idest, per prudentem responsionem elidas stulti cauillacionem. Item aliquando bonum est subtrahere se a uerbis contumelie, quia "honor est homini qui se separat a contencionibus," Prouerbiorum xx. Hoc eciam docuit Dominus quando "declinauit a turba constituta in loco," Iohannis v, quia per eius presenciam futura esset contencio pro sanato in sabbato. Huius doctrine oblitus fuit quidam solitarius in *Uitas Patrum*, qui post multam quietem et diuturnum silencium presentauit se in congregacione

one else spoke against him with abuse, he withdrew in shame and berated himself for appearing in public. Said he: "What did you want among people?" We also read of blessed Francis that, when he heard that reproaches and insults were leveled against him, he used to say: "Such it is fitting for the son of Pietro di Bernaduno to hear." Moreover, sometimes it is good to dissemble in the face of people's quarrels and mockery, as Saul did, Kings 10: When he noticed that he was being despised by his fellows, "he dissembled as though he did not hear." In contrast, an overly sensitive person who marks and weighs every single word is like a stick standing rigid in a stream, on which every piece of rubbish gets stuck which is carried along by the running water. This is so because a stick resists and does not yield to the stream; whereas a reed that bends does not get soiled by any such rubbish. The same is true of him who is personally offended by every single contradiction or insult that other people direct against him and fights battles in his heart. Therefore says Ecclesiasticus 41: "It is not good to keep all shamefacedness." Likewise, striving that experiences pain at being overcome or at losing honor comes from pride. Therefore says Seneca: "Do not quest for glory and it will not hurt you if you are without it." Chrysostom: "Whoever longs for the glory of heaven does not fear shame on earth, and the more one delights in people's praise, the more one is saddened by their reproach. He who gets exalted by praise, gets depressed by censure; where one looks for honor, one fears embarrassment. But he who only looks for honor before God does not fear being embarrassed in the face of men."

Patience at the loss of possessions was shown by Christ when he allowed himself to be stripped of his own garments, Matthew 27, as was said by Isaias 53: "He shall be dumb as a lamb before his shearer." For when a lamb is shorn, it does not murmur or complain, nor does it defend itself with teeth and hoofs, but instead surrenders its wool in meekness. Christ showed the same type of patience in his despoiling. Hence he is well called a lamb. For he is "the lamb which was slain from the beginning of the world," Apocalypse 13, that is, his slaying was prefigured in the lamb which Abel offered, Genesis 4, and which Moses offered up, all through the Law; it is for that lamb, too, that Isaias prayed in chapter 16: "Send forth, o Lord, the lamb," and so forth. To this lamb John pointed with his finger, John 1. These are the examples which Gregory gives in his commentary on Job 38: "Will you be able to join together

nem JFGHIW. 370 Exemplum *marg* E. **homines** *om* E. 371 **beato** sancto J. **cum audiret** ad GW. 371–72 **et . . . inferri** *om* G. 372–73 **dicebat . . . Bernaduno** *om* W. 372 **decet** decent E. 373 **Bernaduno** bono animo J; Bernardo F; Bernadiuono G; Bernadumo HI. 375–76 **scrupulosus** scisipulosus E; scrapulosus G. 378 **trahuntur** contrahuntur FHIW; colliguntur et contrahuntur G. 382–83 **reuerenciam** irreuerenciam FGHILW. 384 Seneca *marg* E. 385 Crisostomus *marg* E. **et non** quoniam E. 389–90 **ibi . . . apud** *om* W. 390 **hominum** *add* de paciencia rerum *rubr* J. 391 **cum se** in se cum E. 394 **Agnus . . . tondetur** *om* H. 397 **expoliacione** spoliacione JGLW. **Ideo . . . enim** qui GIW. 399–400 **Genesis . . . obtulit** *om* W. 403 **xxxviii** xxxvi E. 404 **etsi** et E. **tempore** opere ⟨uel . . . tempore⟩ J; opere IW. 405–6 **Vniuersitas . . . interpellat** *om*

fratrum, et cum a quodam probrose contradiceretur, cum uerecundia recessit, seipsum ualde increpans quod in publicum processit. Dicebat enim sic: "Quid inter [homines] uoluisti?" Legitur eciam de beato Francisco quod cum audiret increpaciones et obprobria sibi inferri, dicebat: "Talia [decet] audire filium Petri de Bernaduno." Item quandoque bonum est dissimulare ad contenciones uel irrisiones hominum, sicut fecit Saul, Regum x: Videns se contempni a suis, "dissimulauit se audire." Homo uero [scrupulosus] qui singula uerba notat et ponderat similis est palo fixo in fluuio, in quo omnes sordes colliguntur que per aquam fluentem trahuntur. Et hoc est quod palus resisit et fluctui non obedit; arundinem uero que se inclinat nichil de predictis sordibus inquinat. Simile est de illo qui ad singulorum / f. 116^{r}b contradictiones uel contumelias congregat iniquitatem sibi et in corde constituit prelia. Ideo dicit Ecclesiasticus xli: "Non est bonum omnem reuerenciam obseruare." Item ex superbia est contencio, que dolet uinci uel honorem perdere. Ideo dicit Seneca: "Non queras gloriam [et non] dolebis cum inglorius fueris." Crisostomus: "Qui gloriam celi optat, obprobrium non timet in terra, et quantum quis de laude hominum letatur, tantum de eorum obprobrio tristatur. Nam quem laus extollit, uituperacio deprimit; vbi quis querit gloriam, ibi timet confusionem. Set qui querit tantum gloriam apud Deum, non timet confundi in conspectu hominum."

Pacienciam ad dampna rerum exhibuit Christus [cum se] propriis denudari permisit uestimentis, Matthei xxvii, sicut per Ysaiam predictum fuit, liii: "Quasi agnus coram tondente se obmutescet." Agnus enim cum tondetur neque murmurat neque conqueritur, nec dentibus nec unguibus se defendit, set cum mansuetudine lanam tradit. Eandem formam paciencie exhibuit Christus in sua expoliacione. Ideo bene dicitur agnus. Ipse enim est "agnus occisus ab origine mundi," Apocalipsis xiii, idest prefiguratus occidi in agno quem obtulit Abel, Genesis iiii, et quem obtulit Moyses, in Lege per totum; pro quo eciam rogauit Ysaias xvi: "Emitte agnum, Domine," etc. Hunc agnum Iohannes digito demonstrauit, Iohannis I. Hec sunt exampla Gregorii super Iob [xxxviii] / f. 116^{v}a ibi: "Nunquid coniungere uales micantes Pleiades," idest, sanctos coniunctos fide [etsi] non tempore.

the shining Pleiades?" that is, the saints, who are joined in faith, if not in time. For all saints together foretell the Lamb, whom the Church invokes every day. According to Isidore, *agnus,* "lamb," is derived from *"agnon,"* meaning pious, and the pity of this Lamb appears openly in his incarnation, passion, and redemption, whose sacrifice is our redemption; Corinthians 5: "The pasch sacrificed for us is Christ." Or else *agnus,* "lamb," derives from *"agnoscendo,"* acknowledging, for he acknowledged his Father through his obedience, "becoming obedient unto death," Philippians 2. He also acknowledged his mother through sharing the same flesh, which he indicated by saying: "Woman, behold your son," John 19. He acknowledged us through his inner pity; for "he knew who are his," Second Letter to Timothy 2. Because of this threefold acknowledgement we invoke the Lamb three times in the Mass. And notice that although a lamb is shorn, yet its wool grows again. Thus, when man is stripped of his temporal goods, he is renewed in spiritual ones; therefore, the Apostle commands us to put off our former way of life and be made new in the spirit of our mind, Ephesians 4. A serpent, too, casts off its skin and revives, and so does the eagle after it has cast off its feathers. This was understood by those who in early times spurned the world and by the early fathers of the Church, who by their voluntary poverty took off the fleece of worldly possessions, of whom Canticles 4: "Your teeth are as flocks of sheep that are shorn, which have come up from the washing." And well are they called "teeth," because made hard through patience they also rose above [*read*: ate up? cut off?] the flesh by the purity of their life, ground food for the soul by expounding the Scriptures and preaching the word of God, Isidore. The front teeth were the apostles, the eye teeth the scholars, the molars Enoch and Elijah. All these are compared to flocks of shorn sheep because they became poor of their own will, and therefore they "come up from the washing," that is, they are cleansed from sin.

Furthermore, those do us a great service who take temporal goods from us; Proverbs 11: "The fool shall serve the wise." They take from us what is dangerous to us. A father takes away from his beloved child a knife or any other tool with which the child could hurt himself, and a nurse takes a coin away from her baby, so that it may not choke itself. In this way God allows our temporal goods to be taken from us so that he may remove their dangers at the same time, because "gold and silver has destroyed many," Ecclesiasticus 8; and 31:

F. 405 **Agnum** *om* E. 406 Ysidorus *marg* E. **autem** enim EL; quod G. 408 **et** *om* E; in IL. **redempcione** immolacione GIW. 410 **agnus** *om* E. 417–18 **Ita . . . renouatur** *om* IW. 418 **in** *om* E. 420 **reuiuiscit** reiunescit E; iuuenescit J; reiuuenescit GHL; reiunscit(?) W. 421 **cognouerunt** recognouerunt EF; nouerunt L. 422 **primitiui** primum J; primi F; primitiue I. 423 **paupertatem** uoluntatem et paupertatem J; uoluntatem F. 426 **excedebant** excedant W; *all others have* excedebant: *error for* exedebant *or* excidebant? 427 **uerbum Dei** *om* GIW. 428 Ysidorus *marg* E. **Ysidorus** *add* Dentes dicuntur Grece stontes, et inde Latinum nomen habent uel trahere uidentur. Horum primi preciores [*sic*] dicuntur, quia omne quod accipitur ipsi prius incidunt. Sequentes canini uocantur, quorum in dextera maxilla et duo in sinistra sunt. Et dicti canini quia in similitudine canorum (!) existunt, et canis ex ipsis ossa frangit. Sicut et homo quod non possunt prioris precedere illis tradunt ut confringatur. Ultimi sunt molares qui concisa a prioribus atque confructu subigent et molunt atque immasserant. Vnde et maiorales uocantur J, *the section from* sicut et

Vniuersitas enim sanctorum [Agnum] prenunciat, quem Ecclesia cottidie interpellat. Dicitur [autem] agnus secundum Ysidorum ab "agnon," quod est pium, et manifeste apparet pietas huius Agni in incarnacione, passione, [et] redempcione, cuius immolacio nostra est redempcio; Corinthiorum v: "Pasca nostrum immolatus est Christus." Vel dicitur [agnus] ab "agnoscendo," quia ipse agnouit Patrem per obedienciam, "factus obediens usque ad mortem," Philippensium ii. Agnouit matrem per carnis substanciam, quod innuit cum dixit: "Mulier, ecce filius tuus," Iohannis xix. Agnouit nos per internam pietatem; "nouit enim qui sunt eius," II Ad Thymotheum ii. Propter istam trinam agnicionem ter in Missa inuocamus Agnum. Et nota quod licet agnus tondeatur, lana tamen renouatur. Ita cum homo exuitur temporalibus, renouatur [in] spiritualibus; ideo precipit Apostolus deponere pristinam conuersacionem et renouari spiritu mentis, Ephesiorum iiii. Serpens eciam pellem abiciens [reuiuiscit], et aquila postquam plumas abiecerit. Hoc [cognouerunt] qui primo mundum calcauerunt et primitiui doctores Ecclesie, qui per spontaneam paupertatem exuti sunt temporalium uellere, de quibus Canticorum iiii: "Dentes tui sicut greges tonsarum, que ascenderunt de lauacro." Et bene uocantur illi "dentes," quia duri / per f. 116vb
pacienciam excedebant eciam carnem per uite mundiciam, terebant cibum animarum Scripturas exponendo et uerbum Dei predicando, Ysidorus. Dentes incisores fuerunt apostoli, canini bene litterati, molares Enoch et Helyas. Omnes isti tonsarum gregibus conparantur, quia sponte depauperantur, et per hoc ascendunt de lauacro, idest mundantur a peccato.

Item multum nobis seruiunt qui temporalia a nobis auferunt; Prouerbiorum xi: "Qui stultus est seruiet sapienti." Ipsi auferunt ° nobis periculum nostrum. Pater enim aufert dilecto filio suo cultellum uel aliud instrumentum quo ledi poterit, et nutrix aufert paruulo nummum, ne se strangulet. Ita permittit Deus auferri temporalia, ut auferat simul pericula, quia "multos perdit aurum et argentum," Ecclesiastici viii; et xxxi: "Multi dati sunt

homo *to the end marked* vacat *in margin.* 432 **a nobis** *om* FGIW. 433 **auferunt** *add* a EG. 434 **nostrum** *om* IW. **dilecto** *om* FIW. 435 **uel . . . instrumentum** *om* FGIW. 437 **perdit** perdidit HIL. 438 **et xxxi** *om* GHIW. 439 **simul** finium E; a

"Many have been brought to fall for gold." Further, thieves of our temporal goods carry off also the cares and worries of our mind. In Ecclesiastes 2 it is said of a greedy person that "all his days are full of sorrows and miseries," whence "even at night he does not rest in his mind." Augustine in *The Lord's Sermon on the Mount*: "You love greed with pain, but God is loved without pain. You have filled your coffers and lost peace; you have acquired gold and lost your sleep." Likewise, those who take these things from us bring us rest; Isaias 14: "The poor rest with confidence." In addition they bring us safety; Jerome: "A poor man sleeps more safely in his straw than a rich man in his purple." They also leave us unburdened so that we may follow the giant on his run, that is, Christ, who has a twofold nature; Gregory: "He who has taken a burden from me, has made me light to run more swiftly"; Bernard: "Peter, you have done well in leaving all things. For with a burden on you, you could not follow the runner." Moreover, Abraham "numbered for himself lightly armed servants of his house," Genesis 14. Thus Christ numbers for himself those stripped of temporal goods and "children of them that have been shaken," that is, of the poor apostles, that they may be unburdened to run the way of the commandments. Further, those who seize our temporal goods free us from the bonds of the devil, for "they that will become rich fall into," and so forth, Timothy near the end; Bernard: "He himself has put snares in gold and silver and said, 'Who will see them?'" In addition, those who seize our temporal goods prepare our way to heaven; Isaias 62: "Make the road plain and pick out the stones" (the Septuagint has "cast out"). They offer as our gift before God what they take from us, if we endure this in patience, give thanks, and pray for them, together with those of whom is said in Hebrews 10: "You took with joy the theft of your goods."

This patience the Lord taught us not only by his example, as we saw above, but also by his word. Matthew 5: "If a man will contend with you in judgment and take away your coat, let go your cloak also to him." The cloak signifies temporal goods, because it covers neither head nor feet but only the middle of the body; neither are temporal goods born with us, nor are they buried with us; Job 1: "Naked came I out of my mother's womb, and naked shall I return thither," that is, to the mother of all. Moreover, a cloak is always open on one side, and the desire for temporal goods always feels that something is wanting; Jerome: "A greedy person even lacks an obolus." This is why Giezi removes the

filiis ⟨uel simul⟩ J; scilicet G. 440 **Dicitur . . . cupido** *om* FGIW. **de cupido** *om* E. 441 **et** uel E. 441–42 **vnde . . . requiescit** *om* F. 442 Augustinus *marg* E. **De** *written twice, the first canc* E. 447 Ieronimus *marg* E. **Ieronimus** solucio G; Iere IW. 448 **purpura** pupura E. 450 Gregorius *marg* E. 451 Bernardus *marg* E. **me** *om* EHL. **Bernardus** *add* ad Petrum E. **Petre** *add* Petre GHILW. 452 **oneratus** onustus ⟨vel oneratus⟩ J; onustus HIL; onustius W. 456 **qui . . . rapiunt** raptores FGIW; qui temporalia a nobis auferunt L. 458 Bernardus *marg* E. **fine** *om* EI; vi.f. J; 6 F. **laqueos** *add* suos FHIW; in nos G. 459–60 **qui . . . temporalia** *om* FGIW. 461 **Septuaginta . . . proicite** *om* L. **habent** hunc E; hinc *corr from* habent(?) J; habet I. 463 **de . . . si** et G. **nobis** *add* que *canc* E. 463–64 **et . . . dicitur** *om* W. 464 **cum . . . dicitur** *om* FGI. 466 **docuit** *om* E. 466–67 **non . . . uerbo** uerbo et exemplo FGIW. 467–68 **in iudicio** in iudicium J; *om* FGILW. 469 **figurantur** *om* FGIW; signantur L. **tegit** tangit E. 471–72 **egressus . . . omnium** etc FGILW. 472 **matrem** matres E. **omnium** *add* Thy. vi: nichil intulimus etc *interl* J. 473 **et** hoc est quod E. 474 Ieronimus *marg* E. 475 **obolo** obulo E. 476 **pre-**

in auri casus." Item raptores temporalium rapiunt [simul] curas et sollicitudines mencium. Dicitur enim [de cupido], Ecclesiaste ii, quod "cuncti dies eius doloribus [et] erumpnis pleni sunt," vnde "nec per noctem mente requiescit." Augustinus *De sermone Domini in monte*: "Amas auariciam cum labore, sine labore amatur Deus. Inplesti archam, perdidisti securitatem; acquisiuisti aurum, perdidisti sompnum." Item qui hec auferunt, quietem conferunt; Ysaie xiiii: "Pauperes homines fiducialiter requiescunt." Adducunt / eciam securitatem; Ieronimus: "Securius dormit pauper in f. 117ra
palea quam diues in [purpura]." Item expeditos nos reddunt ut gygantem currentem sequamur, idest, Christum duplicem naturam habentem; Gregorius: "Qui onus michi abstulit, ad currendum cicius [me] expediuit"; Bernardus ° : "Petre, bene omnia reliquisti. Non enim poteras oneratus sequi currentem." Preterea Abraham "numerauit sibi uernaculos expeditos," Genesis xiiii. Ita Christus numerat sibi temporalibus exutos et "filios excussorum," idest pauperum apostolorum, ut sint expediti ad currendam uiam mandatorum. Item qui temporalia nobis rapiunt, a nexibus dyaboli nos absoluunt, quia "qui uolunt diuites fieri, incidunt," etc., Thymothei [fine]; Bernardus: "Ipse posuit laqueos in argento et auro et dixit, 'Quis uidebit eos?'" Item qui rapiunt temporalia, parant nobis iter ad celestia; Ysaie lxii: "Planum facite iter et eligite lapides" (Septuaginta [habent] "proicite"). Item ipsi exennia nostra deferunt ante Dominum, si pacienter sustineamus de hiis que nobis auferunt, si gracias agamus et pro eis oremus cum illis de quibus dicitur Hebreorum x: "Rapinam bonorum uestrorum cum gaudio suscepistis."

Item hanc pacienciam [docuit] Dominus non solum exemplo, ut supra, set eciam uerbo. Matthei v: "Si quis uult tecum in iudicio contendere et tunicam auferre, da ei / et pallium." Bene per f. 117rb
pallium figurantur temporalia, quod nec capud nec pedes [tegit], set medium corporis; nec temporalia nobiscum nascuntur nec nobiscum sepeliuntur; Iob i: "Nudus egressus sum de utero matris mee, et nudus reuertar illuc," idest, in [matrem] omnium. Preterea pallium ex una parte semper est apertum, [et] cupiditas temporalium semper habet defectum; Ieronimus: "Auarus eciam indiget [obolo]." Hoc est quod Gezi ammouet Sunamitem a pedibus

Shunammitess from the feet of Elisha, 4 Kings 4. "Giezi" means seeing what is broken off, that is, the avaricious person or the lover of temporal goods, who always discerns some future need as he imagines. "The Shunammitess" means wretched or captive; that is the avaricious person's soul, which greed keeps away from contemplating God. "Elisha" means my God's salvation or my God who saves, from whom the defective love of temporal goods keeps away our mind. It is truly called defective because at the time when they are most needed temporal goods are not found, which are so avidly desired. Therefore "the cloak is lost on the day of cold weather," Proverbs 25. This is the cloak by which the shameless lady tried to hold back Joseph. "Joseph" means growing or increasing, that is, making progress in the virtues. The shameless lady is the glory of this world, which sometimes impedes our progress in the virtues because of its desire for temporal goods. But the hem of the cloak gets torn when one's love of possession is frustrated. According to Isidore the "hem" is the border of a garment, that is the *tache*; or according to Paschasius it is a torn part of the cloak, as the Gloss says on Lamentations 4. This is the cloak with which Jael covered Sisera, and after he had drunk milk, she killed him with a hammer and nail, Judges 4. "Jael" means climbing and signifies the glory of the world. "Sisera," that is, the exclusion of joy, signifies the lover of this world who is excluded from the delight of paradise. He is wrapped in a cloak as long as he is surrounded by an abundance of worldly goods. He is given milk to drink as long as he delights in the false love of these goods. A nail is driven into his brain when his soul is forced by the sting of death to leave. He is struck with the hammer when he is condemned by the Judge's sentence and handed over to eternal punishment; Proverbs 19: "Striking hammers for the bodies of fools." Therefore, the cloak is left behind in the hand of the shameless lady, so that by scorning the goods and honors of the world we may partake of the glory of heaven, for they who leave all things behind and follow the naked Christ are promised eternal riches, Matthew 19. In addition, we should not only patiently endure the theft of our temporal goods, but even voluntarily give them to the thieves. And that is perfect. The Lord has invited us to do this when he commanded that he who takes away our coat should also be given the cloak, Matthew 5. There is the example of a hermit: When thieves came to him and took away his donkey and put all his food and what was necessary for his life on the animal, he called after the one who drove off the donkey and said: "Have the

ruptum prerupium E; principium W. 481 **defectiuus** defectiui s E; defectus G. 482 **defectiuus** defectus FG; defectuus G. **tempore** ipse E; ipsi L. 485 **quo** quod E. 486 **retinere** *add* cum E; *add* eciam H. **interpretatur** idest G; *om* IW. 488 **in *(2nd)*** *om* E. 489 **lacinia** lasciuia EFG; lascinia L. 490 **rescinditur** recinditur ⟨uel restringitur⟩ J; restringitur FGIW; frangitur L. **lacinia** lasciuia EFG; lascinia L. 490–91 **tache** cache J; cliche L; chache W. 491 Ysidorus Pascasius *marg* E. 492 Glossa *marg* E. **Trenorum** Thymothei E. 492–93 **Iahel** Iohel EJI; Iael FHLW; Iahel G. 493 **Cisaram** Cisuram E; Ciseram H. **interficit** interfecit JW. 494 **Iahel** Ioel E; Iohel J; Iael FHLI; Iabel W. 495 **Cisara** Cisura E; Cisera H. 495–96 **Cisara . . . mundi** *om* F. 495 **amatorem** amatores E. 496 **excluditur** excluduntur E; exclusus dicitur L. 496–97 **pallio . . . quamdiu** *om* H. 497 **rerum** *om* E. 500 **dampnatur** condempnatur JL. 504–5 **quia . . . eterne** sicut promittitur talibus G. 504 **nudum** *om* E; mundum I. 507 **inuitauit** incitat E. 508 **precepit** precipit E. **dari** *add* et JFW. 509 Exemplum *marg* E. 510 **suum** *om* E; eius FGIW. 510–11 **cetera** eius E; *om* JFG. 512 **scuticam** scuticiam E; scu-

Helizei, IIII Regum iiii. “Gezi” interpretatur [preruptum] uidens, hoc est, auarus siue amator temporalium, qui semper preuidet defectum ut sibi uidetur. “Sunamitis” interpretatur misera uel captiua; hec est anima auari, quam ammouet cupiditas a contemplacione Dei. “Helyseus” enim interpretatur Dei mei salus, uel Deus meus saluans, a quo penitus remouet animum [defectiuus] amor temporalium. Et uere defectiuus dicitur, quia [tempore] maxime necessario non inueniuntur temporalia, que tam auide diliguntur. Et hoc est quod “pallium amittitur in die frigoris,” Prouerbiorum xxv. Hoc est pallium [quo] nititur inpudica domina retinere ° Ioseph. “Ioseph” interpretatur accrescens siue augmentans, idest, in uirtutibus proficiens. Inpudica domina est mundi gloria, que prouectum in uirtutibus quandoque retinet [in] temporalium concupiscencia. Set [lacinia] pallii frangitur cum amor habendi rescinditur. Et est [“lacinia”] hora uestis, / (f. 117^{v}a) idest tache, secundum Ysidorum; uel secundum Pascasium pars pallii fracta, Glossa super [Trenorum] iiii. Hoc est pallium sub quo [Iahel] operit [Cisaram] et lacte potatum malleo et clauo interficit, Iudicum iiii. [“Iahel”] interpretatur ascendens et signat gloriam mundi. [“Cisara”], idest exclusio gaudii, significat [amatorem] mundi, qui [excluditur] ab amenitate paradysi. Qui tamdiu pallio inuoluitur, quamdiu [rerum] habundancia circumdatur. Lacte potatur dum eorum falso amore delectatur. Clauus cerebro infigitur dum aculeo mortis anima egredi conpellitur. Malleo percutitur cum sentencia Iudicis dampnatur et eterne pene deputatur; Prouerbiorum xix: “Mallei percucientes stultorum corporibus.” Relinquitur igitur pallium in manu inpudice domine, ut contemptis mundi opibus et honoribus participes efficiamur celestis glorie, quia omnia relinquentibus et Christum [nudum] sequentibus diuicie promittuntur eterne, Matthei xix. Item non solum pacienter ferre debemus rapinam temporalium, set eciam sponte conferre raptoribus. Et hoc est perfectum. Ad hoc [inuitauit] Dominus cum auferenti tunicam [precepit] dari pallium, Matthei v. Exemplum de quodam solitario: Ad quem cum uenissent raptores et asinum [suum] abegissent et ei omnia uictualia sua et [cetera] uite necessaria inposuissent, clamauit post illum qui abegit asinum suum dicens: / (f. 117^{v}b) “Insuper et [scuticam] tene,” idest flagel-

whip too," that is, the scourge needed to goad animals on. Another hermit gave his vegetables to a thief, so that in this way he might perhaps keep him from stealing. Further, we should endure the theft of temporal goods in patience, because through that we have an opportunity to come to Christ. This is clearly prefigured in Absalom and Joab, 2 Kings 14. For Joab did not want to come to Absalom until the latter set fire to his field and thus forced him to come. Thus, many are forced to come in their poverty who delay and are listless while they are prosperous; Gregory: "He turns more quickly to the Lord who has nothing in this world wherein he takes delight." Notice that all men must leave temporal goods, either in actual possession or in their loving attachment, as the perfect do, or in their love alone, as good men in the active life do, who are "as having nothing, and possessing all things," 2 Corinthians 6. And these leave all things behind, that is, their love of all things, or else they leave all things behind when they put the love of God first. Ambrose on Luke 14 draws another distinction by saying: "He who has, renounces; he who distributes, leaves behind." This is true according to the primary meaning of the two verbs; nonetheless, they can be used interchangeably. And notice the reasons why all things are to be left behind: First of all, because it is God's counsel; Matthew 19: "If you want to have a treasure in heaven, go," and so forth; "but the Pharisees and the lawyers despised the counsel of God against themselves," Luke 7. It is a wonder that a safe counselor, who in all things knows what is more profitable, is not believed. One believes a physician when one wants to recover one's health, and a lawyer when one wants to obtain one's inheritance. Further, all things ought to be left behind in order to unburden oneself; Bernard: "The way is narrow and steep; since it is narrow, let us grow slim through humility; since it is steep, let us lighten ourselves through poverty." Further, in order to adhere to God thoroughly; for it is necessary to cast all things off or to subject them, as was said earlier. Therefore, "to renounce" and "to leave behind" are synonymous. The fourth reason is that we may show that God alone is sufficient; if we have him, we have all things, as is said of Tobias 9. And Jerome says: "He is very greedy indeed who is not contented with God." The fifth reason is that we may repay Christ in kind, who left his family and his possessions and himself for our sake; Jeremias 12: "I have forsaken my house, I have left my inheritance," and so forth. The sixth reason is that we may have eternal life, about

ciam W. 513 Exemplum *marg* E. **animalium** asini JFGI. **olera** omnia FGHIW; oscula L. 514–15 **pacienter . . . quam** per rapinam temporalium FIW. 515 **quam** *marg* E. **occasionem** *corr from* occisionem (?) E. 515–16 **Quod . . . Ioab** *om* G. 518 **suum** *marg* E. 519 **multi** *om* E. 519–20 **qui . . . prosperitate** *om* L. 520 Gregorius *marg* E. 525 **Et** vel E. 525–26 **idest . . . relinquunt** *om* F. **relinquunt** *add* omnia JIW. 526 Ambrosius *marg* E. **xiiii** *om* E; 24 F. 528–29 **Et . . . adinuicem** *om* E. 529 **adinuicem** inuivem J. 530 **xix** *om* E; 10 L. 533 **est** *om* JFGIW. **tuto** *om* E; tanto JLW; tuo H. 534–35 **recuperandum . . . hereditatem** *om* H. 535 **consequendam** adquirendam FGI. 535–36 **Item . . . propter** *om* G. **relinquenda sunt** *om* FIL. 536 Bernardus *marg* E. 537 **arta** ardua E. **per** propter E. 538–39 **alleuiemus . . . quia** *om* G; *see at 541–42*. 538–39 **ut . . . adhereamus** *om* FI. 541–42 **Item . . . quo** alleuiemus nos per paupertatem quia G; item F; item quia IW. 542 **habito** *add* deo FGIW. **sicut . . . de** *om* FGIW. 542–43

lum ad instigacionem animalium. Alius heremita dedit olera sua cuidam furi, si forte sic posset a furto cohiberi. Item pacienter debemus ferre rapinam temporalium, per quam occasionem habemus ueniendi ad Christum. Quod bene figuratur in Absalone et Ioab, II Regum xiiii. Noluit enim uenire Ioab ad Absalon priusquam agrum suum succenderet et ita uenire conpelleret. Ita [multi] conpelluntur uenire in paupertate qui tardant et torpent in prosperitate; Gregorius: "Cicius ad Deum conuertitur qui non habet in mundo unde delectetur." Et nota quod necesse est omnibus relinquere temporalia, aut possessione aut affectione sicut faciunt perfecti, aut affectione tantum ut boni actiui, qui sunt "tanquam nichil habentes et omnia possidentes," II Corinthiorum vi. [Et] isti relinquunt omnia, idest amorem omnium, vel relinquunt cum amorem Dei preponunt. Ambrosius super Luce [xiiii] aliam facit differenciam dicens: "Renunciat habens; relinquit distribuens." [Et hoc uerum est secundum primam significacionem uerborum; sumuntur tamen pro adinuicem.] Et nota quare relinquenda sunt omnia: Primo, quia Dei consilium est; Matthei [xix]: "Si uis habere thesaurum in celis, uade," etc.; "Pharisei tamen et legis periti spreuere consilium Dei in seipsis," Luce vii. Et mirum est quod non creditur [tuto] consiliario qui per omnia nouit quid magis expedit. Creditur medico propter sanitatem recuperandam, et aduocato propter hereditatem consequendam. Item relinquenda sunt propter expedicionem; / Bernardus: "Via arta est et f. 118[r]a
ardua; quia [arta] est attenuemus nos [per] humilitatem; quia ardua, alleuiemus nos per paupertatem." Item, ut Deo penitus adhereamus; quia aut oportet omnia abicere aut subicere, ut predictum est. Ideo "abrenunciare" uel "relinquere" dicuntur equiuoce. Item quarta causa est ut solum Deum sufficientem ostendamus; quo habito habentur omnia, sicut dicitur de Thobia, ix. Et Ieronimus ait: "Satis est auarus, cui non sufficit Deus." Item quinta racio est, ut Christo uicem rependamus, qui reliquit [suos] et sua et seipsum [propter nos]; Ieremie xii: "Reliqui domum meam, dimisi hereditatem," etc. Item sexta racio est, ut ui-

Thobia ix *om* F. 543 Ieronimus *marg* E. **Et . . . ait** *om* GI. 544 **Item . . . qui** *om* FW; deus G. **item . . . est** item IL. 545 **suos** suas E. **propter nos** *om* E. 546–48 **Item . . . etc.** *om* FGIW. 546 **sexta . . . est** *om* L. 548 **dixit** dicit JL. **etc.** *add* de

which Peter presented his question when he said: "Behold we have left all things," and so forth.

Now we turn to patience in bodily injury. This is more perfect than the other two kinds, which concern external matters. Christ showed this patience above all in his passion when he allowed himself to be bound, scourged, beaten with fists, spat on, and crucified; Isaias 50: "I have given my body to the strikers and my cheeks to them that plucked them; I have not turned away my face from them that rebuked me and spat upon me," and so forth; and chapter 53 in its entirety treats of this patience. He also has invited us to it by his word, saying in Matthew 5: "If anyone strikes you on one cheek, turn to him," etc. But it seems that the Lord went against his own teaching when, being struck on the cheek, he said: "Why do you strike me?" John 18. To that objection you might say that while it was just that the Lord should reproach this evil-doer, he was still ready to turn his other cheek, whence he did not go against his own teaching. The Lord reproached the one who struck him for two reasons, namely, that he might point out the injury done by the evil-doer and the innocence of so great a ruler. Therefore, you may expound "turn the other cheek" as: be prepared to turn it, because it is not fitting to expose ourselves to risks in violent acts, but rather to bear inflicted injuries in patience. With this Jerome agrees in commenting on Jonas, "Cast me into the sea," and so forth, in the Gloss: "It is not our business to reach for death, but willingly to accept it when it is inflicted." This seems to be contradicted by Judges 5: "Who have willingly offered your lives," and so forth; and in the same chapter: "You who of your own good will offered yourselves to danger, bless the Lord!" With respect to this objection you must distinguish whether an injury is general or personal. If it is general and affects the whole Church, in that it constitutes a danger to faith or failure in justice, a man may and must offer himself willingly, as did Eleazar when he saw the demanded offense against the divine Law, 2 Machabees 6. But if the injury is personal, and especially if it affects an everyday object, not a spiritual one, then it was not necessary to get involved, but one may withdraw oneself for reasons of place, time, cause, and person. And thus do we understand the words of Matthew 10: "If they have persecuted you in one city, flee to another." This is the flight of caution or protection, and it is good; of which Christ sometimes availed himself when he escaped out of the hands of his ene-

paciencia in lesione *rubr* J; *add* de paciencia in lesione proprii corporis *rubr* W. 549 **Et hec** que FGIW. 550 **que . . . exterioribus** *om* G. 551 **se** *om* E. **ligari** *add* et FGILW. 552 **colaphyzari . . . crucifigi** et huiusmodi FGIW; etc L. 555 **traditur** *om* FGIW. 555–56 **Ad . . . uerbo** *om* FW; et GI. 556 **dicens** *om* FGIW. 557 Questio *marg* E. 557–58 **percussus** percucienti FGIW. 558 Solucio *marg* E. **Set** *om* FGIW. 559 **malefactorem** maledictionem E; malefactores W. 560 **tamen** *om* JFGHLW. **alteram** aliam FGILW. 560–61 **vnde . . . obuiauit** *om* FGILW. 561 **ferientem** malefactorem FGILW; ferventem H. 562 **malefactoris** maledictionis E. 563 **alteram** alteri E. 564 **in factis** interfectoribus FGILW; interfectis H. 565–66 **Cui attestatur** *om* FGILW. 566 Ieronimus *marg* E. 567 Glossa *marg* E. 568 Questio *marg* E. **accipere** excipere FGIL. 569–70 **animas . . . uos** *om* F. 570 Solucio *marg* E. 571 **aut** uel GILW. **personalis** particularis FILW; temporalis G. 571–72 **tocius** tangit corpus E. 573 **potest . . . debet** debet homo

tam eternam habeamus, propter quam mouit Petrus questionem cum dixit: “Ecce nos reliquimus omnia,” etc.

Sequitur de paciencia in lesione proprii corporis. Et hec est perfectior duabus ceteris, que sunt de rebus exterioribus. Hanc exhibuit Christus precipue in sua passione permittens [se] ligari, flagellari, colaphyzari, conspui, et crucifigi; Ysaie l: “Corpus meum dedi percucientibus, et genas meas uellentibus; faciem meam non auerti ab increpantibus et conspuentibus,” etc.; et liii per totum traditur de hac paciencia. Ad hanc eciam inuitauit uerbo, Matthei v, dicens: “Siquis te percusserit in una maxilla, prebe,” etc. Set huic doctrine uidetur Dominus obuiare cum percussus in maxillam dixit: “Quid me cedis?” Iohannis xviii. Set ad hoc dicas quod licet Dominus [malefactorem] iuste redargueret, ad prebendam tamen alteram maxil- / f. 118rb lam paratus fuit, vnde doctrine sue non obuiauit. Et redarguit Dominus ferientem duplici de causa, scilicet ut pateret iniuria [malefactoris] et innocencia tanti inperatoris. Expone igitur sic: “Prebe [alteram],” idest, esto paratus ad prebendum, quia in factis atrocibus non oportet discrimini nos offerre, set iniurias illatas pacienter sustinere. Cui attestatur Ieronimus super Ionam ibi: “Mittite me in mare,” etc., Glossa: “Non est nostrum mortem arripere set illatam libenter accipere.” Set contra uidetur Iudicum v: “Qui sponte obtulistis animas uestras,” etc.; et in eodem: “Qui propria uoluntate obtulistis uos discrimini, benedicite Domino!” Ad hoc distinguas utrum iniuria sit generalis aut personalis. Si generalis est et [tocius] Ecclesie, in qua uersatur periculum fidei uel defectus iusticie, potest homo et debet se sponte offerre, sicut fecit Eleazarus uidens irritacionem legis diuine, II Machabeorum vi. Si autem iniuria sit personalis, et maxime si sit rei familiaris, non de spiritualibus, non necesse est se ingerere, set subtrahere se potest quis pro loco et tempore et causa et persona. Et sic intelligitur [illud] Matthei x: “Si uos persecuti fuerint in una ciuitate, fugite in aliam.” Hec est fuga cautele [uel] tutele et bona, qua Christus quandoque usus est declinans manus inimicorum [suorum], Io-

FGILW. 574 **irritacionem** irreccionem G; irrisionem L; imitacione W. 575 **personalis** particularis FILW. 577 **illud** *om* EFGIW. 579 **uel** et E; siue FGHILW. 580 **quandoque** *om* FGILW. **suorum** *om* E. 581 **timiditatis** tarditatis

mies, John 10. Another kind of flight is that of fearfulness, and it is evil, as when "the hireling sees the wolf coming and flees," John 10. Likewise, when the Lord taught us to offer our cheek to him who strikes it, why did he order to buy swords when he was already close to his passion, Luke 22? From this the canon derives its authority which allows clerics to bear arms in a dangerous locality; for it permits to oppose force with force, at the same moment and with the same weapons. To this objection you should say that there are different commandments according to the kind and need of the occasion, as we read in Esther 11 and in Distinctio 12, *The Holy Roman Church Knows*. You should also say that the Lord ordered to buy swords more for the spiritual meaning than for his defense, namely, in order to show that he could have saved himself by earthly power if he had wanted it, were it not that he had come to die of his own will, and further to show that there is a twofold hierarchy of the Church, clerical and lay, and that those who disdain the spiritual sword are to be struck with the material one. And notice that the Church has only the spiritual sword for its use, but the material one to give in charge, which it hands over to the prince when it anoints him. For this reason Peter is reprehended for using the sword, Matthew 26: "Put up your sword into its place." In addition, the swords were brought to him to indicate Christ's regal power, and that the miracle of healing the ear might convert his enemies, and that he might show that two testaments suffice, according to the Gloss. With respect to the canon that permits clerics to oppose force with force: it does however not allow to inflict violence but ward off other people's mischief; this is done more by great fear than by love. Nonetheless, the weapons of the perfect are their cheeks, as Ambrose says. Therefore, the Lord, while he patiently let himself be struck on the cheek, struck the Philistines with a jawbone, Judges 15, that is to say, he overcame his adversaries in patience, he who will still give them palms on their cheeks; Osee 11: "I will be to them as one who takes off the yoke," etc. (the Septuagint reads: "I will be like a man who gives blows upon their cheeks.")

How efficacious patience in bodily suffering is can be seen in Christ, who through patiently suffering his passion brought redemption to mankind. The efficacy of this virtue can also be seen in a certain hermit; when a madman struck him on the cheek and he turned the other, a defeated demon went out and exclaimed as follows: "I have been overcome by mere patience. Through it alone I have lost the vessel which I have firmly possessed for a long time!" Likewise, a religious in his death devoutly kissed the hands of his enemy who had

E; tumiditatis H. 584 **Preterea** *corr* E; propterea FI; idem W. 585 **clericos** *om* JW; clerico FGHI. 586 **instanti** est F; *om* G; tempore L; loco W. 587 **ad hoc** *om* E. **qualitate** quantitate JF. **et necessitate** *om* E. 588–89 **Hester . . . Distinctione** Hebr 9 F. 589 **Dic . . . quod** sic ergo E. 591 **scilicet** *om* EI. **quod** *add* sola E. 595 **esse gladio** *om* E; gladio HL. 596–97 **committendum** comminandum E. 599 **Preterea** propterea FI. 601 **curate hostes** hostis sui curare E. 602 Glossa *marg* E. **clericis** *om* FGILW. 605 Ambrosius *marg* E. **arma . . . maxilla** maxime non sunt arma concessa uel eciam permissa E. 608 **est** erat E. 609–10 **Osee . . . eorum** *om* F. **etc. . . . alapas** *om* G. 610 **homo** *om* E. 611 Exemplum *marg* E. 613 Exemplum *marg* E. 614 **arrepticius** arreptiuus E. **maxilla** maxillam E. 615 **alteram** ateram E. 617 Exemplum *marg* E. **firmiter** *om* JL. 618 **manus** *add*

hannis x. Alia est fuga [timiditatis] mala, ut cum "mercennarius uidet lupum uenientem et fugit," Iohannis x. Item cum Dominus docuerit dare / maxillam percucienti, quare precepit emere gladios, proximus iam passioni, Luce xxii? (f. 118va) Preterea, inde trahit auctoritatem canon permittens clericos ferre arma in loco periculoso; permittit enim uim ui repellere in eodem instanti et in eisdem armis. Set dicas [ad hoc] quod pro qualitate [et necessitate] temporum est diuersitas preceptorum, sicut legitur Hester xi et xii Distinctione, *Scit sancta Romana Ecclesia*. [Dic igitur quod] propter significacionem precepit Dominus emere gladios plus quam propter defensionem, ut ostenderet [scilicet] quod ° potestate terrena se liberasset si uellet nisi sponte mori uenisset, et ut duplicem gerarchiam Ecclesie ostenderet, clericalem scilicet et laicalem, et ut contempnentes spiritualem gladium ostenderet feriendos [esse gladio] materiali. Et nota quod solum spiritualem gladium habet Ecclesia ad utendum, materialem uero ad [committendum], quem principi tradit cum ipsum inungit. Vnde Petrus reprehenditur quod gladio utebatur, Matthei xxvi: "Conuerte gladium tuum in locum suum." Preterea allati sunt illi gladii ad significandam regiam potestatem Christi, et ut miraculum auris [curate hostes] conuerteret, et ut duo testamenta sufficere ostenderet, secundum Glossam. Quod autem clericis permittit canon uim ui repellere: non tamen concedit vim inferre set aliorum maliciam cohibere; quod magis fit per terrorem quam per amorem. Perfectis tamen / [arma sunt maxille], ut dicit Ambrosius. (f. 118vb) Vnde Dominus pacienter ferens maxillam percuti, in maxilla strauit Philisteos, Iudicum xv, idest, paciencia uicit aduersarios qui tamen adhuc daturus [est] palmas in maxillas eorum; Osee xi: "Ero eis quasi exaltans iugum," etc. (Septuaginta: "Ero quasi [homo] dans alapas super maxillas eorum").

Quante efficacie sit uirtus paciencie in penis corporis patet in Christo, qui per pacienciam passionis fecit redempcionem humani generis. Patet eciam in quodam heremita efficacia huius uirtutis; quem cum percuteret quidam [arrepticius] in [maxilla] et ille [alteram] offerret, uictus demon exiuit et huiusmodi uocem emisit: "In sola paciencia uictus sum. Hac sola amisi uas quod diu firmiter possedi!" Item quidam religiosus moriens osculabatur

taken everything from him and often beaten him severely, saying: "These hands which have beaten me lead me to paradise." Further, a juggler lets himself be heavily beaten for money or a small reward. Much more readily do the patient give their bodies over to torments for God's sake, because "though in the sight of men they suffered torments, their hope is full of immortality," Wisdom 3. A truly patient man is like a bear, who feeds and grows stout on blows. For the Psalmist says to the Lord: "For I am ready for scourges," and so forth. A truly patient man is also like a fool, who lets himself be beaten and treated with shame for the sake of food and drink. Such foolishness for Christ is the greatest wisdom; Corinthians 3: "If any among you seems to be wise," and so forth. Further, a truly patient man is like a salamander, who lives in the fire; so does he live in tribulation, to whom the Lord promises comfort and help, Isaias 33: "When you shall walk through the fire, I shall be with you," and so forth. Also, there is a certain very fine cloth of silk which, if it gets soiled, cannot otherwise be cleaned than in very hot fire; so does God boil his own in bodily pain "as silver," Isaias 48. For this reason, the martyrs who endure harsh bodily tortures fly off completely purified. In his book *On the One Baptism* Augustine says of Victorinus the martyr that if anything remained in him to be purified, it was cut out by the knife of his passion. And Haymo comments on the Epistle to the Hebrews: "After their death the martyrs receive their glory at once, in whom nothing remains to be purified for which glory should be delayed." Further, diseased flesh which cannot be healed by a poultice or a plaster is sometimes healed by cautery; thus a spiritual sickness by bodily pain; Gregory on Job 12: "Our flesh is nourished by delights, but our soul draws its strength from bitterness." Moreover, a person who suffers bodily pains is either to be damned or to be saved. If damned: in case he has suffered hardships in this life, he will better know how to bear pain which he is used to; but if he is to be saved, his comfort will be so much more pleasing to him after the suffering, on which Isaias in his last chapter: "As a child that his mother caresses, so will I comfort you," and so forth. Also, after suffering, rest will be more welcome, of which Ecclesiasticus at the end: "I have labored a little, and have found much rest." From these things it is manifest that in every case it is better to be afflicted here than to indulge in delights. And that was "the knowledge of the saints," Wisdom 10, of

cuiusdam FGHIW. 620 Exemplum *marg* E. **ducunt** ducent E. 623–24 **ad . . . est** etc FIW. **ad . . . Item** *om* G. 623 **quia** *om* E. 623–24 **quia . . . est** *om* L. 625 **Dicit enim** *om* FGILW. 626 **Quoniam** *om* FGILW. 627 **uerus paciens** *om* FGILW. 628–29 **Et . . . sapiencia** *follows after the quotation* sapiens etc FGILW. 629 **est** *add* paciencia *canc* E. **uidetur** uult GLW. 630 **verus paciens** *om* FGILW. 630–31 **sic . . . auxilium** *om* FGIW. 633 **cum** *om* E. 634 **aliter** *om* E. 634–35 **corporali** temporali ⟨uel corporali⟩ J; temporali F; materiali L. 635 **excoquit** extorquet E; ex quo quid J. 636 **Inde est quod** unde FGILW. **duros . . . sustinentes** *om* FGILW. 637 Augustinus *marg* E. 639 Haymo *marg* E. **fuit** fuerit JFHLW. **est** fuit GILW. 642 **potuit** *add* quandoque FGILW. 643 **spiritualem** spiritualiter E. 644 Gregorius *marg* E. **xii** 2 F; xi GIL. 647 **dura** *om* E; angustias FGILW. **sciet** *add* in futuro FGILW. 648 **gracior** graciosior FGHILW. 650 **eciam** *om* E; et JH. **de qua** *om* FGILW. 651 **Ecclesiastici fine** Ec-

deuote manus aduersarii sui qui omnia ei abstulerat et grauiter eum sepe uerberauerat dicens: "Manus iste que me uerberauerunt [ducunt] me in paradysum." Item ioculator aliquis permittit se percuti grauiter propter nummum uel paruum emolumentum. Multo forcius ueri pacientes tradunt corpora sua propter Deum ad supplicia, [quia] "etsi coram homine tormenta passi sunt, spes illorum immortalitate plena est," Sapiencie iii. Item uerus paciens similis est urso qui ictibus nutritur / et incrassatur. Dicit enim f. 119ra Psalmista Domino: "Quoniam ego in flagella paratus sum," etc. Item uerus paciens similis est stulto, qui pro cibo et potu permittit se percuti et uiliter tractari. Et talis stulticia pro Christo summa est sapiencia; Corinthiorum iii: "Siquis uidetur inter uos sapiens," etc. Item verus paciens similis est salamandre, que uiuit in igne; sic ille in tribulacione, cui promittit Deus solacium et auxilium, Ysaie xxxiii: "Cum transieris per ignem tecum ero," etc. Item est quedam uestis serica tenuissima, que [cum] fedatur, non [aliter] abluitur nisi in igne feruentissimo; ita in pena corporali [excoquit] Dominus suos "quasi argentum," Ysaie xlviii. Inde est quod martires duros corporum cruciatus sustinentes omnino purgati euolauerunt. Augustinus in libro *De unico baptismo* dicit de Victorino martire quod, si quid in eo purgandum fuit, falce passionis resectum est. Et Haymo super Epistolam ad Hebreos: "Martiribus post mortem statim gloria datur, in quibus nichil purgandum est per quod gloria differatur." Item carnem infirmam, quam non potuit curare fomentum siue emplastrum, quandoque curat cauterium; sic pena corporis [spiritualem] morbum; Gregorius super Iob xii: "Caro delectacione pascitur, anima uero amaritudinibus uegetatur." Item ille qui patitur penas corporis aut est dampnandus aut saluandus. Si damp- / nandus: si in f. 119rb presenti [dura] sit passus, melius sciet asuetos ferre labores; si uero saluandus, multo gracior erit ei consolacio post penam, de qua Ysaie ultimo: "Quomodo si mater blanditur, ita et ego consolabor," etc. Erit [eciam] requies accepcior post laborem, de qua [Ecclesiastici fine]: "Modicum laboraui et inueni multam requiem." Ex hiis apparet quod omni casu melius est hic affligi quam deliciis uti. Et hec fuit "sciencia sanctorum," Sapiencie x,

which Bernard says: "The wisdom of the saints is, to be tormented in time and to enjoy glory in eternity."

Now we turn to patience in forced service. Forced service is the imposition of bodily service that is not owed on the very person of somebody; additional service lies in other things, such as horses, donkeys, or something of that nature. To patience of this kind the Lord has called us when he says, in Matthew 5: "If anyone forces you to go a thousand steps, go with him another two thousand," add: that is to say, be prepared to go according to the time or the usefulness of the material good involved, because in matters that are against God one must not yield to anyone in such situations. The interlinear gloss indicates this in commenting on the words "a thousand steps," and so forth: "That is, a Sabbath's journey," and this is taken from Acts 1, as if the gloss were saying: in such things as do not disturb the Sabbath of our mind, that is, that are lawful, we should submit to forced service, in unlawful ones not. Therefore, those sin grievously who break the Sabbath by ordering or carrying out work for temporal gain or profit. And by "Sabbath" you should understand every solemn feast day. The celebration of the Sabbath of the Law was transferred to Sunday when Christ's resurrection occurred. For by resting in the grave through the Sabbath he put an end to the Sabbath of the Law, as Isidore says. Further, they who break the Church's Sabbath are worse in this respect than the Jews, who observe the Sabbath of the Law so strictly that they do not even kindle a fire on it on which they may cook their food, Exodus 35. In addition, such people do not deserve help from God or the saints, whose holy days they break by their irreverence; Proverbs 20: "It is ruin for a man to charm the saints." And "to charm" means to pursue, as it were, with one's vows, or to cheat someone of the holy things which one owes as it were by promise, that is, under a firm obligation. Such people, moreover, deserve eternal suffering, as in the Psalm: "They shall suffer forever"; or at the end of Lamentations: "They will be threatened by their necks, and the weary will not be given rest." Further, such people sometimes suffer temporal death with Nicanor, whose head and hand with the shoulder were cut off, and his tongue was given piecemeal to the birds, because he did not keep the Sabbath, 2 Machabees near the end. For he said: "If there is a mighty one in heaven who commanded the Sabbath-day to be kept, I too am mighty on earth and command to take arms and do the king's business." Likewise, if the Lord commanded to stone him who gathered sticks on the Sabbath of the Law, Numbers 15, much more will that person have to be punished who breaks the spiritual Sabbath which has been bought

clesiasticus EGL; Ecclesiastici 51 F. 653 **sciencia** uita FGLW. 654 Bernardus *marg* E. **de qua dicit** *om* FGLW; de qua I. **sanctorum** *om* FILW. 655 **gloriari** *add* de paciencia ad angarias *rubr* J; *add* de paciencia ad angarias operum *rubr* I; *add* de paciencia in angariis operum *rubr* W. 658–59 **perangaria . . . cum** *om* FGLW. 659 **dixit** dicit J; de hac FGLW; *om* I. 662 **sunt** fiunt FGIW. 663 Glossa *marg* E. **innuit** *add* Glossa E. 664 **sabbati** saltim GH. 665 **i** *om* E. **Glossa** *om* **non** nunc E. 668 **precio uel** *om* FGILW. 670 **dominicam** dominicum E. 672 **enim om** EF. 673 Ysidorus marg E. **Item** *om* FGILW. 675 **ignem succendant** ignis accendatur L. 676 **ipsi** *om* FGILW. 677 **xx** *om* E. 677–78 **deuotare** deuorare JGHILW. **deuotare . . . tanquam** etc. F. 678 **Et . . . tanquam** idest GILW. **deuotare** deuorare JH. **persequi** prosequi JF. 679–80 **idest . . . obligacione** *om* FGILW. 679 **legitima** firma JH. 680 **tales** *om* FGILW. **ut in** *om* GILW. 680–81 **ut . . . et** *om* F. 681 **fine** *om* EGH; 4 F; 5 L. 684 **sua** *om* EL. 685 **fine** *om* EL; ultimo F. 688 **illum** eos FIL; illos W. **collegit** collegerunt FIW; colligunt L. 689 **die . . . sabbati** sabbato FILW. 689–90 **puniendus . . . soluit** puniendi sunt qui soluunt

de qua dicit Bernardus: “Sapiencia sanctorum est temporaliter cruciari et eternaliter gloriari.”

Sequitur de paciencia ad angarias operum. Et est angaria operum coactio seruicii corporalis indebiti in propria alicuius persona; perangaria uero est in rebus aliis, ut equo uel asino uel aliquo tali. Ad huiusmodi pacienciam inuitauit Dominus cum dixit Matthei v: “Siquis angariauerit te mille passus, uade cum illo alia duo milia,” suple: idest, esto paratus ad eundum pro tempore uel rei familiaris utilitate, quia in hiis que contra Deum sunt, nulli in talibus est obtemperandum. Et hoc innuit ° interliniaris ibi, “Mille passus,” etc.: “Idest, sabbati habens iter,” et sumitur de Actibus [i], quasi diceret [Glossa]: In hiis que [non] inpediunt sabbatum mentis, idest in licitis, obtemperandum est in angaria operis, in illicitis non. Vnde grauiter peccant qui sabbatum soluunt precipiendo uel exequendo pro temporali precio uel commodo. / Et per “sabbatum” intellige omne festum sollempne. f. 119va Celebritas enim legalis sabbati in diem [dominicam] fuit translata, quando in ipsa resurrectio Christi fuit facta. Quiescens [enim] in sepulcro per sabbatum, finem inposuit legali sabbato, ut dicit Ysidorus. Item qui soluunt sabbatum Ecclesie, in hoc peiores sunt Iudeis, qui tam arte seruant sabbatum Legis ut nec in eo ignem succendant quo alimenta sibi coquant, Exodi xxxv. Item ipsi demerentur auxilium Dei et sanctorum quorum festa irreuerenter soluunt; Prouerbiorum [xx]: “Ruina est hominis deuotare sanctos.” Et est “deuotare” tanquam ex uoto persequi, vel defraudare ea que debentur tanquam ex uoto, idest legitima obligacione. Item tales merentur laborem eternum, ut in Psalmo: “Laborabunt in eternum”; et Trenorum [fine]: “Ceruicibus minabuntur et lassis non dabitur requies.” Item tales quandoque cum Nichanore incurrunt temporalem perdicionem, cuius capud et manus cum humero abscisa sunt, et lingua [sua] particulatim auibus data, quia non reuerebatur sabbatum, II Machabeorum [fine]. Dixit enim: “Si est potens in celo qui inperauit agi diem sabbati, et ego sum potens in terra qui inpero sumi arma et negocia regis inpleri.” Item, si Dominus precepit illum lapidari qui collegit ligna in die legalis sabbati, Numeri / xv, multo forcius puniendus f. 119vb est qui soluit spirituale sabbatum quod Christi morte redemptum

with Christ's death. On workdays, however, such forced service is meritorious, if it is done with patience, otherwise not, for as Augustine says in his book *On True Innocence*: "We gain no merit from our sufferings unless they are shaped by patience." Further, we are invited to accept forced service by the example of him who carried the cross on his own shoulder, as in John 19: "And he went forth bearing his own cross," and so forth. Isaias had foretold this in chapter 9: "His leadership is on his shoulder," and so forth, that is, the cross by which he overcame the prince of darkness and won his leadership. This was prefigured in Isaac, who carried the wood for the burnt offering on his shoulders, Genesis 22. This the Lord indicated expressly when he spoke to Job about the devil's power, which was to be overcome by the cross, Job 40: "Will you perhaps bore through his jaw with a buckle?" A buckle is an ornament of the arm, hanging down from the shoulder, according to Isidore, and it typifies Christ's cross, which he carried on his shoulder and arm, with which he bored through the throat of Behemoth and struck a way for the captive prey. We, too, must carry the cross of penance with Simon of Cyrene after Jesus, Luke 23; though this cross is carried in forced service, it must not be carried in mental anguish. "Simon" must carry it, that is, the obedient one, and "of Cyrene," that is, the heir, to whom is owed a lasting inheritance which he merits for his purity of life. Amos 1: "The people of Syria shall be carried away to Cyrene." "Syria" is interpreted as sublime and signifies the peak of life, which is to be carried away to Cyrene, that is, to the eternal inheritance.

Patience in temptation the Lord taught us when, attacked by the fiend with a threefold temptation, he defended himself not with weapons but with Scripture and patience. Elsewhere, he also taught patience in temptation when, in the agony of his death, he took refuge in prayer and submitted himself totally to his Father's will, as is shown at the end of the Gospel. This patience is praised in James 1: "Blessed is the man that endures temptation," and so forth, that is, who gets the upper hand over temptation and casts it down. But it seems that temptation is evil, because the just man prays that he may be delivered from it, and the Gloss on Matthew 4 says: "Temptation is food for the devil," and so forth. To the first objection you should say that the just man prays to be delivered from temptation in the sense that he may not be overcome by it; for it is a virtue to suffer and not be led astray, as the Wise Man says. To the second objection you should reply that the devil's food is the delight or consent in temp-

FILW. 692 Augustinus *marg* E. **aliter . . . ait** *om* G. **Augustinus** *add* in E. 693 **De uera innocencia** *om* H. 694 **informentur** informemur JFILW. **nos** *om* E. 695 **sicut in** *om* FGL. **baiulans** baiolans E. 697 **Factus est** *om* GILW. 699 **Hoc . . . in** unde G. 700 **Hoc . . . ostendit** unde G. 700–701 **loquens ad** *om* E. 701 **de . . . Iob** *om* H. 702 **perforabis** perforabis ⟨uel perforabit⟩ J; perforabit ILW. 703 Ysidorus *marg* E. 704 **portauit** portabat E. 705 **captiuam** *om* FILW. 707 **portare . . . portetur** *om* G. **xxiii** xiii E. 711 **populus Syrie** post Syna E. 711–12 **Syria . . . Cyrenen** *om* G. 713 **hereditatem** *add* de paciencia ad temptacionem *rubr* J. 714 **temptacionem** temptaciones FHIL. 716–17 **Alias . . . temptacionem** item G. 718–19 **ut . . . commendat** *om* G. 720 **etc.** idest subtus fert FGIW; *add* idest subtus fert HL. 721 Questio *marg* E. **prosternit** sternit FL; substernit GI; decernit W. 722 Glossa *marg* E. **et** *om* EHLW. 723 Solucio *marg* E. 725 Solucio *marg* E. 727 **pena uel** penale E. 728–29 **ut . . . Apostolus** *om*

est. In diebus uero operis angaria huiusmodi est meritoria si sit cum paciencia, aliter uero non, quia ut ait Augustinus ° libro *De vera innocencia*: "Passionibus non meremur nisi paciencia informentur." Item ad angariam operum exemplo [nos] inuitat qui proprio humero tulit patibulum, sicut in Iohannis xix: "Exiuit ergo [baiulans] sibi crucem," etc. Hoc predixerat Ysaias ix: "Factus est principatus super humerum eius," etc., idest crux per quam principem tenebrarum deiecit et principatum obtinuit. Hoc figuratum est in Ysaac, qui humeris suis tulit lingna holocausti, Genesis xxii. Hoc signanter ostendit Dominus [loquens ad] Iob de potestate dyaboli per crucem vincenda, Iob xl: "Nunquid perforabis armilla maxillam eius?" Armilla est ornamentum brachii ab humero dependens, secundum Ysidorum, et figurat crucem Christi quam [portauit] in humero et brachio, per quam fauces Behemoth perforauit et predam captiuam excussit. Et nos debemus crucem penitencie cum Symone Cyreneo post Iesum portare, Luce [xxiii]; que licet portetur in angaria operis, non est tamen portanda in angaria mentis. Hanc debet portare "Symon," idest obediens, et "Cyreneus," idest hereditarius, cui debetur hereditas mansura quam meretur uite mundicia. Amos i: "Transferetur [populus Syrie] Cyrenen." "Syria" interpretatur subli- / mis f. 120ra
et signat uite eminenciam, que transferenda est ad Cyrenen, idest ad eternam hereditatem.

Pacienciam ad temptacionem docuit Dominus quando triplici genere temptacionum ab hoste inpulsus non armatura se defendit set Scriptura et paciencia. Alias eciam docuit pacienciam contra temptacionem cum factus in agonia mortis confugit ad subsidium oracionis et se totum commisit uoluntati Patris, ut patet in fine Ewangelii. Hanc pacienciam commendat Iacobus i: "Beatus uir qui suffert temptacionem," etc., hoc est quando temptatus preualet temptacioni et prosternit eam. Set uidetur quod temptacio mala sit, eo quod iustus ab ea liberari petit, [et] Glossa super Matthei iiii dicit: "Temptacio est cibus dyaboli," etc. Ad primum dic quod iustus petit liberari a temptacione, idest non superari; virtus enim est pati et non deduci, ut dicit Sapiens. Ad secundum dicas quod delectacio uel consensus in temptacione cibus eius est,

tation, not its hardship or trial, in which lies matter for virtues. And notice that, as the Apostle says in Corinthians 10, temptation "brings much profit"; for God does not allow us to be tempted above what we are able. For like an eagle he constrains the strength of our prey. For an eagle restrains prey with its claws before its young until they can overcome it for themselves. Thus the Lord represses the enemy's strength until the faithful is able to resist. Gregory on Job 2, "But yet save his life," and so forth: "God does not altogether unbind the enemy lest he strike on all sides and break our faith." From this it appears how fragile we are to withstand, how prone to sin, we who now hardly fight with the bound enemy with whom, when he will have been loosed in the end of the world, the saints will have to fight in whose comparison we are as good as nothing, as Augustine says in book XX of *The City of God,* where he deals with the verse from Apocalypse 20: "And when the thousand years are finished, Satan shall be loosed," and so forth. And it should be noted that the Apostle says: "Let no temptation take hold on you but such as is human." This is human temptation according to Augustine, to understand things differently from the way they are, though one may do so with good intention. But angelic perfection is not to think differently from the way things are. Whereas it is diabolical persumption to think differently from the way things are without wanting to be corrected. And notice that temptation brings forth many good fruits. It produces self-knowledge; Ecclesiasticus 34: "What does he know who has not been tried?" Also, compassion for one's fellow man, for through it man understands his neighbor's character, Ecclesiasticus 31. Further, temptation kindles prayer; Isaias 26: "Lord, they have sought you in distress," and in the Psalm: "In my trouble I cried to the Lord," and so forth. It also arouses the protection of humility; 2 Corinthians 12: "Lest the greatness of the revelation," and so forth. Further, it cleanses from sin; Ecclesiasticus 27: "The furnace tries the potter's vessels," and so forth. It also generates hope of divine consolation and reward; Judith 8: "They passed through many tribulations, remaining faithful," and so forth, as many examples there show. In addition, it renders man acceptable to God; Tobias 12: "Because you were acceptable to God," and so forth. And to the winner it gives the crown; James 1: "When he has been proved," and so forth.

Patience in bodily infirmity the Lord has taught us when he took upon himself our infirmities, as he foretold in Isaias 53: "Surely he has borne our infirmities," and so forth. And Luke 12: "I am straitened by two things"; the

FGILW. 730–31 **conprimit** opprimit E. 732 **unguibus** *om* E. 734 Gregorius *marg* E. 736 **fragiles sumus** simus debiles E. 738 **uix** uere E. 739 **sancti** *add* in FL. **quasi** *om* EL. 740 Augustinus *marg* E. 742–43 **dicit . . . est** *om* FGILW. 743–44 Augustinus *marg* E. **Augustinum** *add* est FGILW. 744 **bono animo** homo FG; homo animo L. 745 **est** *om* E. 745–46 **quam . . . habet** *om* F. 746 **se habet** *add* ⟨uel quam res est⟩ J; est GHL. 747–48 **multiplex . . . enim** temptacio G. 753 **Ad . . . clamaui** *om* E. 756–57 **et retribucionis** *om* G. 757 **Iudith** Iudicum EH. 758–59 **sicut . . . reddit** *om* G. 758 **plura** plurimi E; multa L. **exempla** per exemplum E. 759–60 **Item . . . coronam** et G. 760 **Cum . . . etc.** beatus uir qui suffert temptacionem etc F. **etc.** *add* de paciencia ad corporalem infirmitatem *rubr* J. 763 **ex duobus** etc F; donec perficiatur ille zelus

non [pena uel] exercicium, in quibus est materia uirtutum. Et nota quod temptacio “magnum facit prouentum,” ut dicit Apostolus, Corinthiorum x; non enim permittit Deus nos temptari supra id quod possumus. Ipse enim ad similitudinem aquile [conprimit] fortitudinem prede nostre. Aquila enim stringit predam coram pullis suis [unguibus] donec possint eam sibi subicere. Ita reprimit Dominus inimici fortitudinem donec possit fidelis resistere. Gregorius super Iob ii, / f. 120rb “Verumtamen animam illius serua,” etc.: “Non penitus relaxat Deus hostem ne undique feriens frangat fidem.” Apparet ex hiis quam [fragiles sumus] ad resistendum, quam proni ad peccandum, qui modo cum hoste ligato [uix] dimicamus, cum quo iam soluto in fine seculi pugnaturi sunt sancti, quorum conparacione [quasi] nichil sumus, ut dicit Augustinus, XX *De ciuitate Dei*, tractans illud uerbum Apocalipsis xx: “Cum consummati fuerint mille anni, soluetur Sathanas,” etc. Et nota quod dicit Apostolus: “Temptacio uos non apprehendat nisi humana.” Et est humana temptacio, secundum Augustinum, aliter sapere quam res se habet, licet bono animo hoc faciat. Angelica autem perfectio [est] non aliter suspicari quam res se habet. Dyabolica uero presumpcio est aliter suspicari quam res se habet et nolle corrigi. Et nota quod multiplex est prouentus cum temptacione. Ipsa enim operatur sui ipsius cognicionem; Ecclesiastici xxxiiii: “Qui non est temptatus, quid scit?” Item, proximi conpassionem, quia per ipsam intelligit homo que sunt proximi sui, Ecclesiastici xxxi. Item, oracionis excitacionem; Ysaie xxvi: “Domine, in angustia requisierunt te,” et Psalmo: [“Ad Dominum cum tribularer clamaui,”] etc. Item, humilitatis custodiam; II Corinthiorum xii: “Ne magnitudo reuelacionum,” etc. Item, peccati purgacionem; Ecclesiastici xxvii: “Vasa figuli probat fornax,” etc. Item operatur spem diuine consolacionis et retribucionis; [Iudith] viii: “Per multas tribulaciones transierunt / f. 120va fideles,” etc., sicut [plura] ibidem probant [exempla]. Item Deo reddit acceptum; Thobie xii: “Quia acceptus eras Deo,” etc. Item uictori reddit coronam; Iacobi i: “Cum probatus fuerit,” etc.

Pacienciam ad corporalem infirmitatem docuit Dominus cum nostras infirmitates suscepit, sicut predixit Ysaias liii: “Vere langores nostros ipse tulit,” etc. Et Luce xii: “Coartor ex duobus”;

Gloss explains: "Since Christ had no cause for suffering in himself, he was tormented by our afflictions." Which and of what kind the infirmities were that Christ took upon himself from us, Cassiodorus shows when he says: "O great infirmity that the fountain of life should thirst, the bread hunger, strength become infirm, and life die!"

Bodily infirmity is good for many things; and therefore it should be borne with patience, so that the patient man may say with Jeremias 10: "Truly this is my own infirmity, and I will bear it," and Micheas 1: "She is become infirm unto good that dwells in Maroth" (or "in bitterness," as another version has it). The first good which derives from it is that man turns back to himself and through sickness of the body attains to health of his soul; Gregory comments on Job 5, "He wounds and he cures": "The soul which used to lie dead to its salvation is made alive by a wound." The second good is humility; there is an example in Antiochus, Machabees 9, who, having been subdued in his great pride by his unbearable stench, began to come to self-knowledge. The third is an increase of patience; Jeremias 10: "I will bear it," and so forth. The fourth is the preservation and strengthening of our virtues; 2 Corinthians 12: "When I am weak, then I am stronger," and so forth, that is, with respect to the virtues; this should be understood of the guarding and strengthening of our virtues. The fifth is the purification of our soul; Ecclesiasticus 31: "A grievous sickness makes the soul sober." The sixth is paying the penalty that is owed on account of our sins which cannot be paid in this life; whence Ecclesiasticus 20: "There is he who buys much for a small price," add: of temporal sickness. The seventh is divine consolation; the Psalm: "According to the multitude of my sorrows in my heart, your comforts have given joy to my soul"; Gregory: "Consolation is measured out according to the weight of the affliction." The eighth is that it increases reward and merit; Gregory: "Those who suffer much on earth receive a great reward in heaven." The ninth is that in his infirmity man condemns his previous pleasures; Job 33: "He rebukes by sorrow in the bed, and he makes all

animarum cruciat me donec redempcio animarum fiat L. 764 Glossa *marg* E. 765 **angebatur** *add* doloribus et E. 765–68 **Que . . . moreretur** *om* G. 765 **fuerunt** fuerint E. 765–66 **infirmitates** *corr from* iniquitates E. 766 Cassiodorus *marg* E. 768 **et . . . moreretur** *om* FGILW. **moreretur** *corr from* mordetur E. 769 **Et . . . est** et est infirmitas corporis pacienter G. 771 **portabo** portabit E. **Infirmata** infirmitas E. 771–72 **in bonis** ita bonum E; in bonum GHL; bonum W. 772 **siue** necnon E. 772–73 **siue . . . est** *om* F. 773–74 **Primum . . . et** *om* G. 773 **homo** *add* per eam FILW. 774 **corporis** *om* E. 775 Gregorius *marg* E. 777 **exemplum de Anthiocho** de Anthiocho dicitur E. 778 **qui** quod E. 779 **deductus** deuictus J; deiectus FILW. **cognicionem** agnicionem JGH. 780–81 **augmentum . . . est** *om* L. 782–83 **scilicet . . . uirtutes** *om* EH; quoad uirtutes JL. 782–85 **scilicet . . . Sextum** *om* G. 783 **hoc . . . corroboracione** *om* L. 784 **Quintum** quartum L. **depuracio** sobrietas J; depurgacio F; deputacio H. 785 **Sextum** quintum L. 785–86 **est . . . que** ad solucionem pene debite que pro peccatis suis quoad uirtutes G. 787–88 **precio . . . egritudinis** *om* G. 787 **suple** *add* precio E. 788 **Septimum** sextum L. **Septimum . . . consolacio** ad diuinam consolacionem O. 790 Gregorius *marg* E. 791 **Octauum** septimum L.

Glossa: “Cum non haberet in se Christus unde doleret, nostris tamen angebatur ° erumpnis.” Que et quales [fuerunt] infirmitates quas a nobis suscepit Christus ostendit Cassiodorus dicens: “Magna infirmitas ut fons uite sitiret, panis esuriret, uirtus infirmaretur, et uita moreretur.”

Et ualet infirmitas corporis ad plura; ideo pacienter est ferenda, ut dicat paciens cum Ieremia x: “Plane hec infirmitas mea est, et [portabo] illam,” et Michee i: “[Infirmata] est [in bonis] que habitat in Marath” ([siue] “in amaritudinibus,” alia littera est). Primum bonum quod inde prouenit est quod homo redit ad seipsum et per egritudinem [corporis] uenit ad sanitatem mentis; Gregorius super Iob v, “Ipse uulnerat et medetur”: “Mens uiuificatur ex uulnere, que mortua iacebat in salute.” Secundum bonum est humilitas; [exemplum] de Anthiocho °, Machabeorum ix, [qui] per intoleranciam fetoris sui ex graui deductus superbia cepit ad cognicionem sui uenire. Tercium est augmentum pa- / ciencie; (f. 120^{v}b) Ieremie x: “Portabo illam,” etc. Quartum est conseruacio uirtutum et corroboracio; II Corinthiorum xii: “Cum infirmor, tunc forcior sum,” etc., [scilicet quoad uirtutes]; hoc intellige de custodia uirtutum et corroboracione. Quintum est depuracio anime; Ecclesiastici xxxi: “Infirmitas grauis sobriam facit animam.” Sextum est solucio pene debite pro peccatis que non posset peragi in hac uita; vnde Ecclesiastici xx: “Est qui multa redimat modico precio,” suple: ° temporalis egritudinis. Septimum est diuina consolacio; Psalmus: “Secundum multitudinem dolorum meorum in corde meo consolaciones tue letificauerunt animam meam”; Gregorius: “Iuxta pondus afflictionis dispensatur mensura consolacionis.” Octauum est quod auget meritum et premium; Gregorius: “Multa pacientibus in terris multa merces est in celis.” Nonum est quod in illa dampnat homo precedentes uoluptates; Iob xxxiii: “Increpat per dolorem in lectulo et omnia ossa eius marcessere facit.” Deci-

791–92 **Octauum . . . meritum** ad meriti et premii augmentum G. 792 Gregorius *marg* E. **multa** *corr from* multis E. 793–94 **multa . . . uoluptates** ad dampnacionem precedencium multa merces est in celis voluptatum G. 793 **Nonum** octauum L. 795–96 **Decimum** nonum L. **Decimum . . . mortis** ad mortis me-

his bones to wither." The tenth is that infirmity urges us to think of death; Machabees 1: Antiochus "fell in his bed and recognized that he would die." A sickness unto death is a peremptory summons—while sickness that is not fatal is dilatory—and warns us to make peace with the Lord and to obtain grace from our judges, that is, from the poor and the saints, who "will sit on twelve seats judging the twelve tribes of Israel." The eleventh is that infirmity is the consummation of the virtues; 2 Corinthians 12: "Power is made perfect in infirmity," that is, in the patient suffering of infirmities, for according to Gregory strengths increase when weaknesses are put on the scale. The twelfth is that infirmity is a sign of God's love; John 11: "Behold: Lazarus, whom you love, is sick." Likewise, the dearer his wares are to a merchant, the more ropes are they tied up with. Thus Christ, the wisest merchant, who came in search of precious pearls and gave himself so that he might buy them, the dearer they are to him, the stronger the ties which he puts onto them; Ezechiel 27: "Precious riches were wrapped up with cords," and Job 12: "He girds the loins of kings with a cord." For the cords of infirmity are strong bonds of chastity. In contrast, those whose cords of liberty and license are loosened often go slack in illicit pleasures; this the Lord indicated when he spoke to Sion, Isaias 33: "Your ropes are loosened and will be of no strength." "Sion" means watch-tower and signifies the soul created to know and love God. Likewise, wild and untamed animals are usually made tame with fetters and whips; thus the Lord tames through sicknesses those who rebel against him, that they may not offend God, or harm themselves, or hurt their neighbors.

All these things urge the infirm to suffer patiently. This is what the Lord says to Ezechiel, 4: "Behold, I have encompassed you with bonds; you shall not turn yourself from one side to the other." Further, a father in the *Lives of the Fathers* spoke as follows to his disciple when the latter was sick: "Do not grieve on account of sickness and toil of the body. The height of religion is to give thanks in sickness. If you are iron, you lose rust through fire; but if you are gold, you are tried through fire and progress from great things to greater ones." Also, the Lord "himself has borne our infirmities and carried our sorrows," Isaias 53. He literally bore the defects of human weakness, when he had no causes of infirmity from the good constitution of his own nature; or else "he has borne," that is, he took away, sickness from the sick as a physician, not that he

moriam habendam G. 796 **admonet** conscia est E. 797 **Antyochus** Alexander F. **decidit** cecidit E. 798–99 **non . . . dilatoria** *om* F. 799 **monet** ammonet E. 800 **conparanda** conparando E; operanda G. 800–801 **et sanctorum** *om* FILW. 802 **Undecimum** decimum L. 802–3 **Undecimum . . . uirtutum** ad consumacionem uirtutum G. 804 Gregorius *marg* E. 804–5 **idest . . . Gregorium** Gregorius G. 805 **dum** dicit E. **Duodecimum** undecimum L. 805–6 **Duodecimum . . . ipsa** *om* G. 808 **pluribus . . . funibus** funiculos apponit forciores G. **uinciuntur** cinguntur F. 810–11 **quanto . . . forciores** etc G. 810 **tanto** *add* sibi E. 812 **et** *om* E. 814 **et . . . relaxantur** laxantur et licencie E. 816 **Ysaie** *om* E. 817–18 **interpretatur . . . creatam** anima secundum nominis interpretacionem G. 818 **et *(2nd)*** *om* E. 819 **uinculis et** *om* FL; eciam W. 823 **iiii** iii E. 824 Exemplum *marg* E. 827 **ut** *om* E. **quis . . . agat** *om* E. 828 **aurum** *add* es E. **probatus** probaris E; probaris et F. 829 **Dominus ipse** *om and see lines 838–40* G. 830 **nostros** *add* ipse E. **liii** *corr from* lxiii E. 834 Haymo *marg* E. **Exposicio**

mum est quod ipsa [admonet] de memoria mortis; Machabeorum i: Antyochus "[decidit] in lectum et cognouit quod moreretur." Egritudo enim usque ad mortem est citacio peremptoria—non ad mortem uero est dilatoria—et [monet] de facienda pace cum Domino et gracia assessorum [conparanda], idest, pauperum et sanctorum qui "sedebunt super sedes duodecim iudicantes duodecim tribus Israel." Undecimum est quod infirmitas est consumacio / uirtutum; II Corinthiorum xii: "Uirtus in infirmitate f. 121ra perficitur," idest in paciencia infirmitatum, quia secundum Gregorium crescunt forcia [dum] pensantur infirma. Duodecimum est quod ipsa est signum amoris Dei; Iohannis xi: "Ecce Lazarus quem amas infirmatur." Item quanto merces sunt mercatori cariores, tanto pluribus uinciuntur funibus. Ita Christus mercator sapientissimus qui uenit preciosas margaritas querere et seipsum dedit ut conpararet eas, quanto sibi cariores sunt, tanto ° apponit funiculos forciores; Ezechielis xxvii: "Gaze preciose obuolute sunt funibus," [et] Iob xii: "Renes regum fune precingit." Funes enim infirmitatis forcia sunt uincula castitatis. Econtra illi quibus funes libertatis [et licencie relaxantur], sepe per illicita desideria resoluuntur; quod innuit Dominus loquens ad Syon, [Ysaie] xxxiii: "Laxati sunt funiculi tui et non preualebunt." "Syon" interpretatur specula et signat animam ad Dei cognicionem et dilectionem creatam. Item seua animalia [et] indomita solent uinculis et uerberibus domari; ita Dominus rebelles per egritudines sibi domat ne Deum offendant uel sibi noceant uel proximos ledant.

Hec omnia monent infirmos ut pacienter ferant. Hoc est quod dicit Dominus ad Ezechielem [iiii]: "Ecce circumdedi te uincu- / lis; non conuertes te a latere in latus." Item quidam senex in *Ui-* f. 121rb *tas Patrum* discipulo suo infirmanti sic locutus est: "Non contristeris ex infirmitate uel plaga corporis. Summa enim religio est [ut] in infirmitate [quis gracias agat]. Si ferrum es, eruginem per ignem amittis; si uero aurum °, per ignem [probatus] a magnis ad maiora procedis." Item Dominus "ipse languores nostros tulit et dolores nostros ° portauit," Ysaie liii. Ad litteram pertulit defectus humane infirmitatis, cum ex bonitate sue conplexionis non habuit causas infirmitatis; vel "tulit," idest abstulit,

might receive it in himself but that he might heal. This is the interpretation of Haymo, and he calls "infirmities" original sin. For *langor*, "infirmity," is *longus angor*, "long anguish," and original sin from the beginning induced a sickness, namely the death of body and soul; Ecclesiasticus 10: "A prolonged anguish is troublesome to the physician." By "sorrows" you should understand actual sins. For the heavenly physician brought not only the remedy of patience for bodily infirmities, but also the remedy of penance for spiritual ones. Further, it is reported of a virgin in Wales that, when she was so much infected with severe leprosy that she lost her nose and eyes and her whole body swelled up with pustules like a tree with a knotty bark, she said that she was much afraid that she might be unworthy of God's love because he did not inflict as much pain on her as she was able to bear with her last breath. Moreover, we should not forget the patience of Job who, when he was so diseased that he was stricken with a very grievous ulcer from the sole of his foot to the crown of his head, yet did he not sin with his lips but said: "If we have received good things at the hand of the Lord, why should we not receive evil," and so forth. Also, the future immortality of our bodies encourages us to bear infirmities, when "God shall bind up the wound of his people and shall heal the stroke of their wound," Isaias 30. For then "he shall give for earth flint, and for flint torrents of gold," Job 22. "Earth" is our weak and infirm flesh, which will become incapable of suffering like flint if at this time it bears its torments in patience. "Torrents of gold" are the joys of heaven. Gold denotes a precious substance, a torrent, abundance. Just as fish rejoice in a brook where they have water and light on all sides, so the saints rejoice in joy.

Patience in the face of the world's contempt and scorn the Lord showed when he was spat upon, his face veiled, and his beard plucked, because "he gave his cheeks to those that plucked them," Isaias 50; and also when he was mocked as they cried, with bended knees, "Hail, King of the Jews," John 19. To this very day does he show patience with those that mock him. For bad priests mock him when they treat the sacraments of the Church scornfully; Ecclesiastes 10: "For laughter they make bread and wine." Under this twofold form is the sacrament of the Eucharist. Evil clerics and evil religious also mock him when they have the sign but not what it signifies; Proverbs 3: "He shall scorn the scorners." Wicked overseers and stewards of the rich scourge him, as is pre-

sentencia E. 838–40 **Celestis . . . penitencie** *after* Item, *line 829* G. 840 Exemplum *marg* E. 840–49 **Item . . . autem etc.** *om* G. 842 **oculis** oculi E. 843 **uorticibus** corticibus JFW. 846 **tantum** *corr from* tanta E. 848 **percuteretur** torqueretur E. **nec** non E. 857–58 **undique . . . claritatem** *om* G. 858 **sic . . . gaudio** *om* W. **exultant** exultabunt FIL; *om* G. 859 **exhibuit** ostendit E. 860 **conspuicione** conspiracione G. **uelacione** velamine JFGHIW. 861 **suas** *om* E. 861–62 **in . . . flexis** irrisorie L. **irrisione** illusione J; passione I. 866 **sacra-**

ut medicus infirmitatem ab egroto, non ut in se acciperet, set ut curaret. [Exposicio] est Haymonis, et uocat "languores" originale peccatum. Languor enim est longus angor, et peccatum originale ab inicio morbum induxit, idest mortem corporis et anime; Ecclesiastici x: "Languor prolixior grauat medicum." Per "dolores" intellige peccata actualia. Celestis igitur medicus non solum contra corporales infirmitates tulit medicinam paciencie set eciam contra spirituales medicinam penitencie. Item narratur de quadam uirgine in Wallia quod cum tantum esset infecta asperrima lepra ut naso priuaretur et [oculis] et totum corpus intumesceret pustulis sicut arbor nodosa uorticibus, dixit quod ualde time- / bat se indignam Dei amore, eo quod non tantam infligeret ei f. 121va penam quantam cum extremo spiritu posset sustinere. Item non est obliuioni tradenda paciencia Iob, qui cum in tantum infirmaretur ut a planta pedis usque ad uerticem capitis ulcere pessimo [percuteretur], [nec] peccauit tamen labiis suis set dixit: "Si bona suscepimus de manu Domini, mala autem," etc. Item ad infirmitates tolerandas inuitauit nos futura corporum immortalitas, quando "alligabit Deus uulnus populi sui et percussuram plage eius sanabit," Ysaie xxx. Tunc enim "dabit pro terra silicem, et pro silice torrentes aureos," Iob xxii. "Terra" est caro nostra fragilis et infirma, que tanquam silex inpassibilis est futura, si modo pacienter portat supplicia. "Torrentes aurei" sunt gaudia celi. In auro notatur preciosa substancia, in torrente habundancia. Sicut enim exultant pisces in fluuio undique habentes aquam, undique claritatem, sic exultant sancti in gaudio.

Pacienciam ad despectum mundi et uilitatem [exhibuit] Dominus in conspuicione, in faciei uelacione, in barbe depilacione, quia "genas [suas] dedit uellentibus," Ysaie l; et eciam in irrisione, cum genibus flexis dicerent, "Aue, Rex Iudeorum," Iohannis xix. Et adhuc cottidie ostendit pacienciam illusoribus suis. Illu- / dunt enim ei mali sacerdotes sacramenta Ecclesie contemp- f. 121vb tibilia facientes; Ecclesiaste x: "In risum faciunt panem et uinum." In hac duplici specie est sacramentum Eucharistie. Illudunt eciam ei mali clerici et mali religiosi habentes signum et non signatum; Prouerbiorum iii: "Illusores ipse deludet." Item flagellant eum mali prepositi et senescalli diuitum, quod in Pylato

figured by Pilate, who scourged the Lord, Matthew 27. "Pilate" means hammerer, and those are hammerers of the poor. Likewise, perjurers, flatterers, and liars spit on him, who make their king to pass "as froth upon the face of the earth," Osee 10. Those make their king to pass who call Christ to witness in their perjury and lies. Also, the soldiers who crucified him still kill him in his members when they break the flesh of the poor as "in a pot," Micheas 3. Yet in all these things does the Lord patiently bear his injury, so that he may invite us to be patient.

In addition, Isaiah foresaw his patience in face of the world's contempt when he said: "We have seen him as one despised, as it were a leper and one struck by God," Isaias 53. He became "the most abject of men," as it is said in the same chapter. And others seek to be the first among the people, wanting "the first chairs in the synagogue and salutations in the market place," and so forth, Matthew 23. What further strengthens us against the world's contempt is the baseness or humiliation of his passion. For as the Lord knew that man would not otherwise return to glory except through humility and through worldly disgrace, after a little glory on Palm Sunday he bore a great amount of shame on the day of his sufferings. For there he was received in solemn procession as the Lord, but here he was led with scorn to the gallows like a thief. There, garments were spread before his feet, but here he was stripped of his clothes and despoiled. There, branches and flowers were prepared, but here the awesome wood of the cross. There he was greeted, here mocked at. There adored, here spat upon. There, "blessed is he who comes in the name of the Lord," here, "ah, he who destroys the temple of the Lord." There the children shout, "Hosanna"; here the faithless Jews, "Crucify!" Thus, great was the humility of his birth, but incomparably greater the humility of his passion. For he was born at night but crucified in midday. He was born in a small and unknown town, but crucified in the capital of the kingdom where he had preached and worked miracles and was known to almost everyone. In his birth wrapped in swaddling clothes, in his passion naked. In his birth lying between the beasts in his crib, in his passion hanging on the gallows between thieves. Born in an inn, crucified on the brow of a hill. There in the company of Joseph and Mary, but here before "a great crowd that had gathered for the feast day." There

mentum *add* ecclesie *canc* E. 873 **Osee x** omnes enim E. 876 **membris suis** tenebris E. 877 **lebete** lebetem E. 880 **ad . . . Ysaias** preuidit Ysaias ad contemptum mundi E. 884 **primas** prima E; *om* FGILW. **synagogis** synagoga E. 886 **sue** *add* dilectionis *canc* E. 887 **rediturum** redempturum E; redditurum HI. 889–90 **penarum suarum** petrarum scissarum G. 892 **ante** *om* E. 895 **irrisus** derisus E; irsutus W. **irrisus . . . hic** *om* I. **Ibi *(2nd)*** *add* clamatur E. 896 **vath** vach E. **destruit** destruis JFH. **Dei** domini JF; *om* GL. 901 **et *(1st)*** ubi E. 902 **erat** fuerat FLW; fuit I. 904 **appensus** suspensus FG. 910 **crucem** *add* omni E. 912 **et** *add* ad E.

flagellante Dominum figuratur, Matthei xxvii. "Pilatus" interpretatur malleator, et tales sunt pauperum malleatores. Item conspuunt eum periuri, adulatores, et mendaces, qui transire faciunt regem suum "tanquam spumam super faciem terre," [Osee x]. Quasi spumam regem suum transire faciunt qui Christum peierando uel menciendo testem inducunt. Item adhuc occidunt eum in [membris suis] milites crucifixores qui concidunt carnes pauperum tanquam "in [lebete]," Michee iii. Et in omnibus hiis Dominus pacienter tolerat iniuriam suam, ut nos inuitet ad pacienciam.

Item eius pacienciam [ad contemptum mundi preuidit Ysaias] cum dixit: "Vidimus eum quasi despectum, quasi leprosum et a Deo percussum," Ysaie liii. Ipse factus est "nouissimus uirorum," ut dicitur in eodem capitulo. Et alii querunt priores esse in populo, querentes "[primas] kathedras in [synagogis] et salutaciones in foro," etc., Matthei / xxiii. Item armat nos ad pacienciam f. 122^{r}a
contra mundi despectum uilitas siue abieccio sue passionis. Sciens enim Dominus non aliter esse [rediturum] hominem ad gloriam quam per humilitatem et mundi ignominiam, post modicam gloriam in die Palmarum magnam portauit confusionem in die penarum suarum. Ibi enim cum sollempni processione tanquam Dominus est susceptus, hic uero cum irrisione tanquam latro ad patibulum est deductus. Ibi uestimenta [ante] pedes eius proiecta sunt, hic uero uestimentis nudatus est et spoliatus. Ibi parati sunt rami et flores, hic uero horrida ligna crucis. Ibi est salutatus, hic [irrisus]. Ibi adoratus, hic consputus. Ibi ° "benedictus qui uenit in nomine Domini," hic "[vath] qui destruit templum Dei." Ibi clamatur "Osanna" a pueris; hic "crucifige" a perfidis Iudeis. Vnde magna fuit humilitas natiuitatis, set inconparabiliter maior fuit humilitas passionis. Natus est enim de nocte, set crucifixus in meridie. In parua ciuitate et ignota est natus, set in capite regni est crucifixus, vbi predicauerat [et] miracula fecerat et fere omnibus notus erat. Item in natiuitate pannis inuolutus, in passione exutus. In natiuitate inter animalia reclinatus in presepio, in passione inter latrones appensus in patibulo. Natus in diuer- / sorio, f. 122^{r}b
crucifixus in montis supercilio. Illic presentibus Ioseph et Maria, hic uero coram "turba multa que conuenerat ad diem festum." Il-

adored by the wise men, here cudgeled from the palace of Pilate to Calvary. There tenderly played with, here cruelly torn to pieces. And because he bore these things patiently, he has given us the very model of patience, for "having joy set before him, he endured the cross, despising the shame," Hebrews 12. He became, as it were, unfeeling towards suffering and reproach. Thus the words of Ezechiel 3 are those of the Father to the Son: "I have made your face like an adamant and like flint." Christ was a flint in suffering pain, an adamant in drawing to penance. And it was necessary that all these things should happen first in the head, for the health of the members. For cautery is done on a healthy limb so that the diseased one may be healed; Bernard: "The head hurts, and cautery is done on the arm; the kidneys hurt, and it is undertaken on the shin." Therefore, as the entire body was decaying, the searing iron was placed on our head, "by whose stripes we are healed," 1 Peter 2. It was absolutely necessary for us that Christ should thus suffer for our sake, so that from the hewn rock and the hole of the pit the life-giving waters should abound for us, Isaias 51, for when this rock had been struck, the abundance of grace flowed forth to us, the blood of redemption and the water of baptism, the richness of grace and the knowledge of the Scriptures. Then "the floodgates of heaven were opened," Genesis 7. Then the sackcloth was torn so that the price of our salvation might appear; the Psalm: "You have cut my sackcloth." Then the "sealed-up fountain" was broken open, Canticles 4, so that the faithful might have drink. And in all that has been mentioned, Christ's lowness is our humility; Bernard: "The more abject he has been for my sake, the dearer he is to me," and Jerome: "The more humiliating the things are which he suffered for me, the more do I owe him."

And notice that in the world's scorn and contempt the saints find treasures of gold and silver that are hidden in sand, Deuteronomy 33. For sand is scorned by the eyes and trodden down by the feet. Thus is the life of saints contemptible to the world, but at the time of retribution it is found to yield praise and glory; Gregory: "The more despicable a just man is to the world, the more precious he is to God and the angels." For this reason David received the Amelekite when he was weary and scorned by his army, in the next-to-the-last chapter of the Book of Kings, which Gregory explains in his *Moralia*: "Our savior, who is truly strong of hand (which is the meaning of 'David'), often turns those whom he find despised by worldly glory to his own love; he feeds them, because he refreshes them with the knowledge of his word; he made him a guide on his way, because he makes him his preacher." Behold, not only Christ's lowness encourages us to suffer humiliation, but also the gaining of a reward in the future life and in this. In addition, all things that make us humble encourage

Patris *om* E. 914 **Christus** *om* E. 917 Bernardus *marg* E. 920 **nobis** ***(1st)*** *om* FILW. 921 **et** *add* de E. **laci** lancee E; icti G; *om* I. 926 **nostre** *om* FILW. 926–28 **Tunc . . . Et** *om* F. 927 **Canticorum** Ecclesiastici E; Matthei G. **potus** *om* E. 929 Bernardus *marg* E. **michi** *om* E; pro me G. 930 Ieronimus *marg* E. 932–33 **inueniunt** inuenerunt JL. 934 **enim** *om* EL. 936 Gregorius *marg* E. **inuenitur** inuenietur JFHL. 938 **est** ***(1st)*** *om* EW. **recepit** recipit E. 939 **exercitu** *add* iam E. 940 Gregorius *marg* E. 941 **quod** qui et E. **quod . . . dicitur** *om* FG. **dicitur** *om* EHILW. 945 **uilitatem paciendam** pacienciam G. 946 **et** eciam E. 946–47 **Preterea . . . nos** ***(1st)*** eciam G. 947 **que nos humiliant** *om* **F. nos** ***(2nd)*** illos

lic a magis adoratus, hic a pretorio Pylati usque ad Caluariam fustigatus. Ibi dulciter tractatus, hic crudeliter laceratus. Et per hoc quod hec pacienter sustinuit, nobis formam paciencie tradidit, quia "proposito sibi gaudio sustinuit crucem, ° confusione contempta," Hebreorum xii. Tanquam insensibilis enim factus est ad penas et ° obprobria. Ideo uerba [Patris] ad Filium sunt hec Ezechielis iii: "Vt adamantem et silicem dedi faciem tuam." Silex fuit [Christus] in paciendo iniuriam, adamas trahendo ad penitenciam. Et necesse fuit omnia hec precedere in capite pro membrorum salute. In sano enim membro fit cauterium ut sanetur infirmum; Bernardus: "Dolet capud et in brachio fit coctura; dolent renes et fit in tibia." Ita pro tocius corporis putredine cauterium infixum est in nostro capite, "cuius liuore sanati sumus," I Petri ii. Et fuit nobis pernecessarium ita pro nobis pati Christum, ut de cisa petra et ° cauerna [laci] redundarent nobis uitales fluuii, Ysaie li, quia hac petra percussa fluxit ad nos graciarum habundancia, sanguis redempcionis et aqua baptismatis, copia graciarum et sciencia Scripturarum. Tunc "aperte sunt catharacte celi," Genesis vii. Tunc concissus est saccus ut pa- / teret precium (f. 122va) nostre salutis; Psalmus: "Concidisti saccum meum." Tunc enim "fons signatus" est diruptus, [Canticorum] iiii, ut fieret [potus] credentibus. Et in omnibus supradictis Christi uilitas est nostra humilitas; Bernardus: "Quanto pro me uilior, tanto [michi] carior," et Ieronimus: "Quanto sunt humiliora que pro me passus est, tanto illi amplius debeo."

Et nota quod sancti in uilitate et in abiectione mundi inueniunt thesauros auri et argenti, qui in harena sunt absconditi, Deuteronomi xxxiii. Harena [enim] oculis est despicabilis, pedibus conculcabilis. Ita uita sanctorum mundo est contemptibilis, set inuenitur in laudem et gloriam in tempore retribucionis; Gregorius: "Iustus quanto mundo est uilior, tanto Deo et angelis [est] preciosior." Hoc est quod Dauid [recepit] puerum Amalechite iam lassum et ab exercitu ° contemptum, Regum penultimo, quod exponit Gregorius in *Moralibus*: "Redemptor noster ueraciter manu fortis ([quod] 'Dauid' [dicitur]) nonnunquam quos despectos a mundi gloria inuenit in suum amorem conuertit; cibo pascit, quia uerbi sciencia reficit; ducem itineris elegit, quia suum predicatorem facit." Ecce quod non solum inuitat nos ad uilitatem paciendam uilitas Christi, set eciam retribucio premii [et] in futuro et in presenti. Preterea ad hanc pacienciam inuitant

us to have this patience. What these are can be found in the chapter on humility.

There are three kinds of patient people: Christ in his innocence, the penitent thief, and the blaspheming thief. If a just man suffers without guilt, he follows Christ, and this is the true patience of a Christian, to suffer innocently for justice's sake, for which we are commanded to "fight even unto death," Ecclesiasticus 4; and 1 Peter 2: "For this is thankworthy, if for conscience towards God a man endures sorrows, suffering wrongfully." By conscience towards God is meant that in which God gives testimony to the truth, when a patient person knows himself to be innocent and fears God's punishment; Gregory: "The just man sighs under the rod, for he does not know for what offense he is being punished." The thief on the right hand suffered for his guilt, yet he repented on the cross and was converted, and he recognized Christ on the cross whom he had not recognized when he was free. Such is the man who has been justified after his sin, who has been corrected with lashes, who on the cross of tribulation recognizes what offense he has given to his Creator and how vast his crime has been. Such a person often becomes more humble than anyone else and ready for good works. Sophonias, at the end: "From beyond the river of Ethiopia, my suppliants." The black Ethiopians are those who after the rivers of vices are cleansed in the gulf of their tears, and thus the caldrons are changed into phials, Zacharias, last chapter, and the vessels of wrath and disgrace into vessels of glory, Romans 9. This is what Isaias says, 11: "Edon and Moab shall be under the rule of their hand," that is, of the apostles, to whose preaching and precepts those nations were subject, just as the truly penitent subject themselves totally to the rules of the Church. For they say in their hearts with Micheas 7: "I will bear the wrath of the Lord, because I have sinned against him"—by "wrath" understand temporal punishment, because when God is spoken of as angered or moved, the antecedent is put instead of the consequence, for it is from such an emotion that one usually inflicts punishment on evildoers. The thief on the left hand signifies those who murmur in their pain, who are like a pot cracking in the furnace, for whom tribulation does not cleanse their present life but increases the pain in the future, as is shown in the Gloss on Jeremias 5. The same is shown in an example: children who cannot be chastized by words or with a rod are usually undressed and flogged with a switch; Augustine in book I of the *Confessions*: "The rod is followed by greater torments." Thus people who are not corrected by means of temporal punishment, are kept for the eternal; therefore, in Jeremias 1 first the switch is seen, then the caldron. The

E. 947–48 **Vide . . . humilitate** que in capitulo de humilitate sunt G; *om* I. 952 **scilicet** sua HW. 953 **agonizari** agonizare FGILW. 954 **quis** aliquis E; *om* F. 955 **Consciencia . . . Dei** conscienciam dei dicit E; consciencia pacientis iniuste dicitur consciencia dei JW. 957 Gregorius *marg* E. 958 **qua** *add* causa E. 959 **cruce** ecclesia E. 960 **cognouerat in** cognouit E. 961 **cruce** ecclesia E. 962 **recognoscit** recognouit J; cognouit F; cognoscit GILW. **offensam sui Creatoris** suum creatorem F. 963 **ceteris** aliis FILW. 964 **fine** ultimo EILW; 3 F; fieri G. **Ultra** *om* E. 965 **Nigri** vltra J. **sunt** *om* FGHILW. 965–66 **mundantur** emundantur E. 966 **ita** *om* FILW. 967 **Zacharie** *om* E. **fine** *om* EL; 9 fine J; ultimo F. 968 **est** *om* EW. 971 **in . . . suo** *om* FILW. 973 **temporalem** corporalem *canc* temporalem *marg* J; corporalem uel temporalem F; temporalem uel corporalem GILW. 977 **presentis** *add* turb *canc* E. 977–78 **purgacio . . . sequentis** *om* W.

nos omnia que [nos] humiliant. Vide / que sint illa in capitulo de humilitate. f. 122vb

Tria sunt genera paciencium: Christus innocens, latro penitens, et latro blasphemans. Quia iustus sine culpa patitur, Christum imitatur, et hec est uera paciencia Christiani, pro iusticia scilicet innocenter pati, pro qua precipitur "usque ad mortem agonizari," Ecclesiastici iiii; et I Petri ii: "Hec est enim gracia, si propter conscienciam Dei sustinet [quis] tristicias, paciens iniuste." [Consciencia dicitur Dei] in qua Deus testimonium perhibet ueritati, cum paciens nouit se innocentem et timet punientem; Gregorius: "Iustus ingemiscit in uerbere, quia ignorat pro qua ° feriatur ulcione." Latro dexter pro culpa passus est, tamen in [cruce] conpunctus et conuersus, et Christum cognouit in cruce quem non [cognouerat in] sua libera potestate. Talis est iustificatus post culpam, flagellis emendatus, qui in [cruce] tribulacionis recognoscit offensam sui Creatoris et immanitatem sui sceleris. Et talis frequenter fit ceteris humilior et ad opera bona paracior. Sophonie [fine: "Ultra] flumen Ethyopie inde suplices mei." Nigri Ethyopes sunt qui post flumina uiciorum [mundantur] gurgite lacrimarum, et ita lebetes transmutantur in phyalas, [Zacharie fine], et uasa ire et contumelie in uasa glorie, Romanorum ix. Hoc [est] quod dicit Ysaias xi: "Ydumea et Moab preceptum manuum eorum," idest apostolorum, quorum pre- / di- f. 123ra cacioni et preceptis ille gentes subiecte sunt, sicut uere penitentes preceptis Ecclesie omnino se subiciunt. Dicunt enim in corde suo cum Michea vii: "Iram Domini portabo, quia peccaui ei"—vt "iram" dicas penam temporalem, quia cum dicitur Deus iratus uel commotus, antecedens ponitur pro consequenti, quia ex affectione tali solet pena peccantibus infligi. Latro sinister signat murmurantes in pena, qui sunt tanquam olla crepans in fornace, quorum tribulacio non est uite presentis purgacio set pene sequentis accumulacio, ut patet in Glossa super Ieremie v. Idem patet per exemplum: [pueri] qui uerbis non castigantur [nec] ferulis, solent exui et uirgis uerberari; Augustinus I *Confessionum*: "Ferulis maiora supplicia succedunt." Sic qui temporali pena non corriguntur, eterne reseruantur; vnde Ieremie [i] primo uidetur uirga,

switch is present discipline, the caldron future hell. Such pain did Pharaoh experience, who though often scourged grew more hardened and was finally drowned in the Red Sea.

Patience is of three kinds. The first is that of a donkey, who suffers because it is necessary; he notices that he has committed a crime and has deserved punishment. This is why "Issachar the strong ass bowed his shoulder to carry," Genesis 49. The second is that of a mercenary, who suffers because it is gainful. But this kind of patience is twofold. One exists for the sake of temporal pay, which receives its reward here, Matthew 6, and Osee 10; "Ephraim is a heifer taught to love to tread out corn." Gregory: "As a heifer that is used to the labors of treading out corn often, even when it is untied, returns to its usual work without compulsion, so the mind of vicious people which is devoted to serving the world busies itself in earthly sweat, even if it may lawfully rest," and it does so because it expects some vile gain. The other sort of this kind of patience suffers for the sake of eternal reward, which says: "Let your voice cease from weeping, for there will be a reward for your work," Jeremias 31; and Bernard: "If work frightens you, let its reward encourage you." But from this it may seem that the charity of the saints is mercenary because it serves for the sake of created glory and not for the sake of God alone. To this objection you should reply that the charity of the saints places created glory, which consists in the gifts, as an end beneath another end in its reward, and it places God as the ultimate end, to whom alone one should adhere for his own sake, as Augustine says. The third kind of patience is that of free will, which suffers because it pleases, and which after the example of Christ "endures the cross with joy," Hebrews 12.

The reward for patience is the inheritance of glory; Matthew 5: "Blessed are the peacemakers, for they shall be called children of God." And if natural children and first-born, it follows that they are heirs, Galatians 4. "Natural" you should understand not by their natural propagation but by their natural condition, which has its beginning from the first principle that establishes nature. Peacemakers are makers of peace. Hence no one is patient unless peace is in him. Therefore we must say something about peace.

Peace is manifold, as Augustine teaches in book XVII of *The City of God,* first [or: chapter one] defining peace thus: "Peace is the ordered tranquillity of minds that are agreed in the good." In the same book he defines: "The peace of the body consists in the duly proportioned arrangement of its parts." Again: "The peace of the irrational soul is the harmonious repose of the appetites."

979 **pueri** puerorum EW. **nec** *om* E. 980 Augustinus *marg* E. 982 **i** *om* E. 983 **secundo** deinde FILW. 984–85 **Hanc . . . et** *om* I. 984 **penam** *om* E. 985 **Rubro** *om* FILW. 988 **supponit** supposuit ⟨uel supponit⟩ J; supposuit L. 992 Gregorius *marg* E. 993 **triture** triturare E; trituire G. **assueta eciam** associata et E. **ad usum** non usu E. 994 **laboris** *add* eciam E. 995 **liceat** libeat EJHILW. 996 **emolumentum** emolimentum E. **patitur** *om* E. 998 Bernardus *marg* E. 999 Questio *marg* E. 999–1001 **sit . . . sanctorum** *om* F. 1001 Solucio *marg* E. 1004 Augustinus *marg* E. 1006 **xii** xiii E; 15 L. 1011 **naturante habet** parente habuit F. 1012 **paciens** paciencia E. 1013 **Vnde . . . est** *om* G. **est** *add* diffinicio pacis *rubr* W. 1014 Augustinus *marg* E. **XVII** *add* vel 19 *interl* J; 19 F; XXVII I. 1016 Idem *marg* E. 1017 **Ibidem** *om* FGW. 1017–18 **Ibidem . . . appeticionum** *om* EJ; *text from* H. **irracionalis** racionalis GW. 1018 Idem *marg* E. **ordinata . . . appeticionum** ordinacio appetituum F. **requies** *om* LW. 1018–19 **Ibidem . . . consensio** *om* I. 1019 **cogni-**

secundo olla. Virga est presens disciplina, olla est sequens iehenna. Hanc [penam] pertulit Pharao qui sepe flagellatus magis induratus est et tandem in Mari Rubro submersus.

Est autem triplex paciencia. Prima est asinaria, que patitur quia oportet; que attendit se commisisse culpam et meruisse penam. Hoc est quod "Ysachar asinus fortis supponit humerum ad portandum," Genesis xlix. Secunda est mercennaria, que patitur quia expedit. Set hec duplex. Alia enim est pro mercede tem- / porali, que hic recipit remuneracionem, Matthei vi, et Osee x: f. 123rb "Effrayn docta uitula diligere trituram." Gregorius: "Sicut uitula [triture] laboribus [assueta eciam] relaxata plerumque [ad usum] laboris ° non conpulsa reuertitur, ita prauorum mens mundi seruiciis dedita, eciam si uacare [liceat], terrenis sudoribus occupatur," et hoc quia uile [emolumentum] expectat. Alia [patitur] pro mercede eterna, que dicit: "Cesset uox tua a ploratu, quia erit merces operi tuo," Ieremie xxxi; et Bernardus: "Si labor te terret, merces inuitet." Set uidetur ex hoc quod caritas sanctorum sit mercennaria ex quo seruit pro gloria creata et non solum pro Deo. Et dicas ad hoc quod caritas sanctorum gloriam creatam, que consistit in dotibus, ponit tanquam finem sub fine in sua remuneracione, et Deum ponit tanquam finem ultimum, cui soli propter se est inherendum, ut dicit Augustinus. Tercia paciencia est uoluntaria, que patitur quia placet, que exemplo Christi "cum gaudio sustinet crucem," Hebreorum [xii].

Remuneracio autem paciencie est hereditas glorie; Matthei v: "Beati pacifici, quoniam filii Dei uocabuntur." Et si filii naturales et primogeniti, sequitur quod heredes, Galatarum iiii. Et intellige "naturales" non per nature propagacionem set per eius condicionem, que a primo naturante habet principium. Pacifici uero sunt pacem facientes. Vnde / non est [paciens] nisi in quo est pax. f. 123va Vnde de pace aliquid dicendum est.

Est autem pax multiplex, ut docet Augustinus XVII *De ciuitate Dei*, primo diffiniens pacem sic: "Pax est concordancium in bono mencium ordinata tranquillitas." In eodem: "Pax corporis est ordinata temperancia parcium." [Ibidem: "Pax anime irracionalis est ordinata requies appeticionum."] Ibidem: "Pax anime ra-

Again: "The peace of the rational soul is the harmony of knowledge and action. Peace between body and soul is a well-ordered life and health." The same in the same chapter: "The peace of mortal man is the well-ordered obedience of faith to eternal law. Peace between man and man is well-ordered concord." Again: "Domestic peace is the well-ordered concord between those of the family who rule and those who obey." In the same place: "The peace of the celestial city is the perfectly ordered and harmonious enjoyment of God and of one another. Peace among all things is the tranquillity of order. Order, however, is the distribution which allots things equal and unequal each its own place." In the same book you will find many other definitions.

And notice that in one way peace is a virtue or fruit, in so far as it makes peaceful all the motions of the virtues; and thus it can be said to be in the rational faculty. In another way, peace is the end of all virtues and directly gives the soul rest in the highest good; and thus peace is the seventh in the catalogue of virtues. But notice that some peace is evil, some is good. Evil peace is the restlessness of a settled mind, and this makes a truce with the sins and does not fight them. Of it is said in Wisdom 14: "Whereas they live in a great war of ignorance, they call so many and so great evils peace." This is temporal peace, of which is said in Luke 19: "And in this day, the things that are to your peace." One kind of peace is the peace of heart in those that are on their pilgrimage here on earth, another is the eternal peace in those that for ever live in their heavenly home. Of the former the Lord says in John 15: "Peace I leave with you," as if he were saying: let him who can, receive it. Of the latter he says: "My peace I give to you." After this peace, no disturbance follows. And since it cannot be lost, it is well called a gift. For a gift is something given which cannot be returned, as the Philosopher says. But temporal peace is given, yet not a gift.

And notice how diligently peace must be kept, which especially makes us like God, since God's Only Son is called peace, as Chrysostom says; and in chapter 2 of the letter to the Ephesians: "He is our peace." Further, through peace God dwells in us; thus: "His place is in peace." This is prefigured in that Solomon built the temple for the Lord, 2 Kings 6. But David, a warrior, is prevented from building, 1 Paralipomenon 28. And this because "the Lord is not the God of dissension, but of peace," Corinthians 14. Further, the special bequest which Christ made to the apostles when he was about to leave them concerned peace, and he who impedes a bequest incurs excommunication.

cionis cogitacionis E; agnicionis L. 1019–20 **cognicionis . . . ordinata** *om* G. 1020 Idem *marg* E. 1020–25 **Idem . . . invicem** *om* G. 1020–22 **Pax . . . concordia** *om* FL. 1022 **Ibidem** *om* EL. 1024 **Ibidem** *om* E. **ordinatissima** ordo ueracissima FLW. 1025 **concordatissima** concordissima JL. 1027–28 **Alias . . . multas** *om* EH. 1030 **est pacificans** pacificat *corr* E. 1030–31 **potest . . . esse** est FGILW. 1032–33 **septima** *om* E; alia G; vna I. 1033–34 **Set . . . bona** *om* G. 1034–38 **Pax . . . tibi** *after* donum, *line 1045* G. 1034 **et** *om* EG. 1035 **cum** in E. 1037 **est** *om* E. 1038–39 **pectoris** *add* bona JFILW. 1044 Philosophus *marg* E. **irredibilis** incadibilis E. **ut . . . Philosophus** secundum Philosophum FGILW. 1046 **quam** quod FHW. 1047 Crisostomus *marg* E. **assimilat** seruat E. **Dei** *om* E. 1048 **Ephesios** Philippenses FGILW. **est** *om* EH. 1048–49 **pacem** ipsam FGILW. 1049 **vnde** *add* Psalmus E. 1050 **templum** domum FL. 1053 **speciale** spirituale E. 1054 **apostolis** discipulis FG. 1055–56 **Vnde . . . sunt** *om* G. 1056 **xxviii** *corr*

cionalis est ordinata [cognicionis] actionisque consensio. Pax corporis et anime est ordinata uita et salus." Idem in eodem: "Pax hominis mortalis est ordinata in fide sub eterna lege obediencia. Pax hominum communiter est ordinata concordia." [Ibidem:] "Pax domus est ordinata inperandi obediendique concordia cohabitancium." [Ibidem:] "Pax celestis ciuitatis est ordinatissima et concordatissima societas fruendi Deo et inuicem. Pax omnium rerum est tranquillitas ordinis. Ordo uero est rerum parium dispariumque sua cuique tribuens loca disposicio." [Alias diffiniciones inuenies ibi multas.]

Et nota quod pax uno modo est uirtus siue fructus, secundum quod pax [est pacificans] omnes motus uirtutum; et sic potest dici esse in vi racionali. Alio modo est pax finis omnium uirtutum et inmediate quietat animam in summo bono; et sic est pax [septima] in cathalago uirtutum. Set nota quod alia est pax mala, alia bona. Pax mala est conposite mentis inquietacio, [et] ista habet treugas [cum] peccatis / et non inpugnat ea. De qua Sapiencie f. 123^{v}b
xiiii: "Viuentes in magno insciencie bello tot et tam magna mala pacem appellant." Et hec [est] pax temporis, de qua Luce xix: "Est quidem in hac die que ad pacem sunt tibi." Alia est pax pectoris peregrinantibus in uia, alia pax eternitatis permanentibus in patria. De prima dicit Dominus Iohannis xv: "Pacem relinquo uobis," quasi dicat: qui potest eam capere, capiat. De secunda dicit: "Pacem meam do uobis." Post illam non sequitur turbacio. Et quia ipsa amitti non potest, bene dicitur donum. Donum enim est dacio [irredibilis], ut dicit Philosophus. Pax temporis uero datum est et non donum.

Et nota quam diligenter pax sit seruanda, que specialiter nos Deo [assimilat], cum pax dicatur [Dei] Unigenitus, ut dicit Crisostomus; et Ad Ephesios ii: "Ipse [est] pax nostra." Item per pacem nos inhabitat Deus; vnde °: "In pace factus est locus eius." Hoc figuratur per hoc quod Salomon edificat templum Domini, II Regum vi. Dauid autem uir bellator ab edificio prohibetur, Paralypomenon xxviii. Et hoc quia "non est Dominus Deus dissensionis set pacis," Corinthiorum xiiii. Item [speciale] legatum Christi quod fecit apostolis recessurus ab eis fuit de pace, et qui legatum inpedit excommunicacionem incurrit. Vnde tur-

Therefore, those who disturbed the peace among their brethren were excommunicated; Ecclesiasticus 28: "The whisperer and the double-tongued, let him be accursed; for he has troubled many that were at peace." Moreover, peace is the keeping of the heart; Philippians 4: "The peace of God, which surpasses all understanding, keep your hearts and your minds." In addition, it brings spiritual gladness; Colossians 3: "Let the peace of Christ rejoice in your hearts," and Proverbs 12: "Joy follows them that take counsels of peace." It also makes a covenant with the Lord; Isaias 54: "The covenant of my peace shall not be moved." Also, it is the seed of all good; James 3: "The fruit of justice is sown in peace," that is, the reward of justice, which is given to just deeds, is sown in peace, because for peace of the heart, which is the seed of virtue, is given eternal peace, which is the harvest. Again, the Apostle shows how necessary peace is, as he often wrote to his disciples: "Grace to you and peace." "Grace," that is, the remission of sin; "peace," that is, tranquillity of mind. Further, when the Lord sent out his disciples to preach, he gave them as a law to offer peace to each one, Matthew 10: "First say, 'Peace be to this house.'" Similarly in the Mosaic Law, according to Deuteronomy 20, before a city was to be stormed, it was first to be offered peace. This the Lord commanded in both testaments, that is, first to offer peace, as if binding all other virtues "in the bond of peace," Ephesians 4. The priest intimates the same thing when in the Mass he asks for peace after all the other petitions. Further, the Son of God himself came not merely to make but to become peace, Ephesians 2: "He is our peace," and so forth. And the peace which he made by his death he first announced to his disciples after his resurrection; Luke, last chapter: "Peace be to you." This peace the bishop, Christ's special representative, announces when he turns around toward the people. Further, peace is the rest and support of the city above; whence the Psalmist speaks to heavenly Jerusalem: "Who has placed peace in your borders," and Isaias 32: "My people shall sit in the beauty of peace." In contrast, within the confines of hell are pain and discord. Moreover, the heavenly bodies themselves admonish us to have peace, such as Saturn, the sun, and the rest, which do not change their order or slow down their motion. And the very heaven turns with sweet harmony in peace. The poet: "Great things keep peace, discord perturbs the smallest of things." Again, peace leads us to Christ; Isaias 55: "You shall go out with joy, and be led forth with peace." This peace must be bought at a very high price; Augustine: "Throw away your money and buy yourself peace and a tranquil heart."

We must have peace with all, as the Apostle admonishes in Romans 12:

from xxviiii E. 1062 **xii** vii E. 1064 **Item . . . boni** *om* G. 1065–66 **idest . . . seminatur** *om* F. 1066 **in** neque sine E. 1066–67 **in . . . datur** *om* W. 1067–70 **Item . . . tranquillitas** *om* G. 1077–78 **Item . . . fieri pax** ideo dominus qui est pax uera G. 1079 **Et . . . quam** item quod pacem E. **per** post FILW. 1080 **fine** dicitur E; ultimo F; *om* L. 1082 **quiecio** quietacio JFHILW. 1083 **ad . . . dicit** *om* G. 1086 **supercelestia** supracelestia JH; celestia FGILW. 1087 **motum** locum E. 1088 **in pace** *om* E. 1089 Poeta *marg* E. **magna** magnam EJFGI. **minimas** minimos E; nummos F; minima G; minimis W. 1090 **perturbat** perturbant EFL. 1091–92 **Valde . . . pax** unde G. 1092 Augustinus *marg* E. 1094 **Pax . . . Apostolus** et G. **omnibus** *add* hominibus FILW. **sicut . . . Apostolus** *om* L. 1094–95 **sicut . . . omnibus** *om* H. 1097 **Amaritudo . . . contricionis**

bantes fraternam pacem excommunicati sunt; Ecclesiastici xxviii: "Su- / surro et bilinguis, sit ille maledictus; multos enim turbauit f. 124ra pacem habentes." Item pax est custodia cordis; Philippensium iiii: "Pax Dei que exsuperat omnem sensum custodiat corda uestra et intelligencias uestras." Item ipsa adducit leticiam spiritualem; Colossensium iii: "Pax Dei exultet in cordibus uestris," et Prouerbiorum [xii]: "Qui pacis ineunt consilia, sequetur eos gaudium." Item ipsa iungit fedus cum Domino; Ysaie liiii: "Fedus pacis mee non mouebitur." Item ipsa est semen omnis boni; Iacobi iii: "Fructus iusticie in pace seminatur," idest, merces iusticie que iustis operibus datur [in] pace seminatur, quia pro pace pectoris, que semen est uirtutis, datur pax eternitatis, que est messis. Item quam necessaria sit pax ostendit Apostolus scribens sepius discipulis suis: "Gracia uobis et pax." "Gracia," idest remissio peccati; "pax," idest mentis tranquillitas. Item Dominus mittens discipulos ad predicandum, legem dedit eis pacem ostendere singulis, Matthei x: "Primum dicite, 'Pax huic domui.'" Similiter in Lege, Deuteronomi xx, expugnande ciuitati primo offerenda fuit pax. Hoc precepit Dominus in utroque testamento, primo scilicet offerre pacem, tanquam concludens omnes alias uirtutes "in uinculo pacis," Ephesiorum iiii. Idem innuit sacerdos in Missa post omnes peticiones rogans pacem. Item ipse Filius Dei non / solum f. 124rb uenit pacem facere set eciam fieri pax, Ephesiorum ii: "Ipse est pax nostra," etc. [Et pacem quam] fecit per mortem primo annunciauit discipulis post resurrectionem; Luce [fine]: "Pax uobis." Hanc annunciat episcopus specialis Christi uicarius conuersus ad populum. Item ipsa est quiecio et stabilimentum superne ciuitatis; vnde Psalmista ad celestem Ierusalem dicit: "Qui posuit fines tuos pacem," et Ysaie xxxii: "Sedebit populus meus in pulcritudine pacis." Econtra, fines gehenne sunt dolor et discordia. Item ipsa supercelestia corpora monent nos ad pacem, ut Saturnus, sol, et cetera, qui ordinem non mutant et [motum] non retardant. Ipsum eciam celum, quod cum dulci armonia [in pace] uersatur. Poeta: "Pacem [magna] tenent, [minimas] discordia rerum [perturbat]." Item ipsa perducit ad Christum; Ysaie lv: "In leticia egrediemini et in pace deducemini." Valde caro precio emenda est ista pax; Augustinus: "Proice peccuniam et eme pacem tibi et cor tranquillum."

Pax cum omnibus habenda est, sicut monet Apostolus, Romanorum xii: "Cum omnibus hominibus pacem habentes."

"Have peace with all men." We must have peace first with God, which is reestablished through contrition of heart. For the bitterness of contrition which is known only to God makes amends for sensual delight, and thus peace is made; Isaias 38: "Behold, in peace is my bitterness most bitter." There is, as it were, a debate between God's justice and his mercy on account of the sinful soul, Isaias 27. Justice threatens punishment and asks: "Shall I march against it in battle?" Mercy advocates forgiveness and asks: "Or rather, shall I take hold of my strength?" And the Lord answers them: "It shall make peace with me, it shall make peace with me"; the former refers to contrition, the latter to confession. Furthermore, through confession peace is reestablished with the Church, whom one causes dishonor by committing sin; Isaias 57: "I created the fruit of the lips, peace," and Job 22: "Be at peace, and thereby you shall have the best fruits." Again, the peace between soul and body is reestablished through groaning within and without; of this in the Psalm: "I roared with the groaning of my heart," and Job 3: "As of overflowing water, so is my roaring." When the lion roars, the other beasts stop still. Thus, all movements of carnal lust are slowed down at the roaring of a truly penitent person. This is what Job says, chapter 5: "The beasts of the earth shall be at peace with you," that is, fleshly stirrings grow quiet at the roaring of penance; and he adds: "And you shall know that your tabernacle will be in peace," that is, your body, which is frail, changeable, and at last to be dissolved. In addition, peace must be reestablished with our neighbor through satisfaction, that is, by restoring things taken from him and by appeasing those that have been hurt; Romans 14: "Let us follow after the things that are of peace," among one another and towards all. Peace with one's neighbor is above all kept by the two rules of natural law. The first is Tobias 4: "Do not do to another what you do not want to have done to you"; the second, Luke 6: "As you would that men should do to you, do you also to them." Further, peace between man and his guardian angel is reestablished through obedience and humility. For the angels are very humble, which is shown in that they serve the lowest sinners. They are also very obedient, for they serve at his beck. They rejoice with us over our peace and feel grief with us at our distress; Isaias 33: "The angels of peace shall weep bitterly"; that is, they have cause for weeping when we sin and abandon their counsels. In addition, when we make peace with God, we must send an embassy beforehand, so that we might ask for "conditions of peace," Luke 14. And besides the things which have been men-

amando enim contricionem F; *om* G. 1098 **uoluptatis** uolumptatis E; *om* G. 1099 **amarissima** *add* nota quod FGILW. 1099–1100 **disceptacio** deceptacio FHI; decepcio GLW. 1100 **pro . . . peccatrice** *om* FILW. 1102–3 **In . . . querit** *om* H. 1102 **spondet** respondet E. 1104 **Dominus** *om* FI. 1105–6 **confessionem** satisfaccionem FL. 1106 **quam quis** quamuis FLW; quando I. 1107 **peccando** *add* conteritur E. 1108 **et *(1st)*** *om* E. 1109 **inter** in E; *om* J. 1110 **de quo** unde E. 1111 **et** *om* E. **iii** xxx E. 1112–13 **figunt gressum** fugiunt gressum E; signat gradum G. 1115 **tibi idest** ibi enim E; idest J. 1115–16 **quiescunt** quiescent E. 1116 **et sequitur** *om* EGH. **pacem** *om* E. 1118 **pax** *om* JHIW. **reformanda** *om* E. 1119 **xiiii** xviii E; iiii ⟨vel 18⟩ J. 1121 **potissime** *om* E; potentissime G; cotidie W. **legis** iuris E; *om* H. 1122 **Non . . . fieri** quod ab alio oderis fieri etc FL. 1130 **facienda pace**

Primo habenda est pax cum Deo, que reformatur per cordis contricionem. Amaritudo enim contricionis que soli Deo nota est satisfacit pro delectacione [uoluptatis], et sic fit pax; Ysaie xxxviii: "Ecce in pace amaritudo mea amarissima." Quasi quedam disceptacio fit pro anima pecca- / trice inter Dei iusticiam et eius mi- f. 124va
sericordiam, Ysaie xxvii. Iusticia comminatur penam, vnde et querit: "In prelio gradiar super eam?" Misericordia [spondet] ueniam, vnde et querit: "An pocius tenebo fortitudinem meam?" Et respondet sibi Dominus: "Faciet pacem michi, pacem faciet michi"; primum refert ad contricionem, secundum ad confessionem. Item reformatur pax cum Ecclesia, quam quis scandalizat peccando, ° per confessionem; Ysaie lvii: "Creaui fructum labiorum pacem," [et] Iob xxii: "Habeto pacem et per hoc habebis fructus optimos." Item pax [inter] animam et carnem reformatur per gemitum interiorem et exteriorem; [de quo] in Psalmo: "Rugiebam a gemitu cordis mei," [et] Iob [iii]: "Tanquam inundantis aque, sic rugitus meus." Cum leo rugit, cetera animalia [figunt] gressum. Sic ad rugitum ueri penitentis retardantur omnes motus carnalis uoluptatis. Hoc est quod dicit Iob v: "Bestie terre pacifice erunt [tibi," idest] carnales motus ad rugitum penitencie [quiescunt]; [et sequitur:] "Et scies quod [pacem] habebit tabernaculum tuum," idest corpus fragile et mobile et in fine dissoluendum. Item pax [reformanda] est cum proximo per satisfactionem, scilicet restituendo ablata et lesos pacificando; Romanorum [xiiii]: "Que pacis sunt sectemur," inuicem et in omnes. Pax ad proximum [potissime] custoditur in duabus regulis [legis] naturalis.
/ Prima est Thobie iiii: "Non facias alii quod non uis tibi fieri"; f. 124vb
secunda, Luce vi: "Prout uultis ut faciant uobis homines, et uos facite illis." Item inter hominem et angelum custodem pax reformatur per obedienciam et humilitatem. Angeli enim ualde humiles sunt, quod patet quia uilissimis peccatoribus seruiunt. Sunt eciam ualde obedientes, quia ad nutum ministrantes. Isti congaudent nostre paci et condolent nostro discrimini; Ysaie xxxiii: "Angeli pacis amare flebunt"; idest, causam fletus habent cum peccamus et consiliis eorum dissentimus. Item in [facienda pace] cum Deo premittenda est legacio ut rogemus "ea que pacis sunt," Luce xiiii. Et preter ea que dicta sunt, ut est contricio et confes-

tioned, namely contrition and confession and so forth, there are two other messengers to be sent, namely prayer and alms. Almsgiving leads us with an armed hand and protects us; Ecclesiasticus 29: "Better than the shield and the spear it shall fight for you," and so forth. It also prepares the way for those who direct their course to God; Proverbs 18: "A man's gift enlarges his way, and before princes," that is, the holy angels and saints, "it makes him room." But prayer presents one's business before the Highest Judge; Augustine in *On the Psalms*: "Prayer enters before God as if it were a person and conducts our business at a place that our flesh cannot reach." That it completes its business is stated in Job 33: "It will pray to the Most High, and he will be gracious to it." If however tears go with it, they will wrench mercy from him; Origen: "Pure tears have such power that they rule even over the Most High."

After treating the question with whom we must be united in peace, we now consider from whom we should be disunited, that is, what beings we should not communicate with. First, from our own flesh, in order that Delilah may be made tame so that she should not deceive Samson, Judges 16. For that reason the Apostle took care to chastize his body and bring it into subjection, Corinthians 9. For it often happens that we do not overcome our fleshly stirrings because we do not tame Delilah through penance; Isaias 26: "We have not wrought justice on the earth, therefore the inhabitants of the earth have not fallen." By "justice" we mean penance, because it is a species of justice and is justly owed for our sins. "The inhabitants of the earth" are our fleshly stirrings, which rule over fleshly people in the whole world. Secondly, we should be dissociated from the devil, so as to avoid "the spirits of wickedness in the high places," Ephesians, last chapter. This is prefigured in Jeremias 21, where it is said: "He that will flee over to the Chaldeans that besiege you shall live, and his life shall be to him as a spoil." The "Chaldeans" are thought to stand for fierce demons, that is, those that have no pity on anyone. Fleeing to them is falling into sin. But if one wants to live and have peace, "his life will be as a spoil," that is, that he may deliver it with force and speed from the mouth of the lion; Proverbs 6: "Deliver yourself as a doe," and so forth. Spoil is taken by three: by fire, by a beast, and by a thief. Third, we must be dissociated from the world, so that it may not seduce us with its false peace and instill in us idle worries and harmful occupations. "For no man being a soldier to God entangles himself with secular business," 2 Timothy 2. With this Jethro reproaches Moses when he is too burdened with the care of the people, Exodus 18: "You are spent with foolish labor, you alone cannot bear it." But many people, for the sake of ambi-

faciendo pacem E. 1132 **Et . . . sunt** *om* FL. 1136 **xviii** xvi E; 34 F. 1137 **idest** *add* ante FHL. 1138 **et** *om* JI. 1139 Augustinus *marg* E. 1139–40 **Psalmos** Psalmum E. 1144 Origenes *marg* E. 1145 **Altissimo** *add* de quibus habenda est pax *rubr* J; *add* a quibus habenda est pax *rubr* W. 1146 **dicendum est** sequitur FL; sequitur uidere IW. 1147 **communicemus** comunicamur E; *add* uel coniungamur JL; *add* uel ut coniungamur IW. 1147–48 **carne propria** carnibus propriis E. 1148 **Sampsonem** Sapsonem E; sapiens G; assumpcione W. **xvi** vi E; xv W. 1149–50 **et . . . redigens** *om* F; etc L. 1151 **per** *written twice* E. **penitenciam** paciencian *corr to* penitenciam *marg* J; *om* F; paciencian HW. 1157 **fine** ii E; 6 F; *om* L. 1158 **qui** quoniam E. 1159 **uiuet** undique E; *om* J; viuent H. 1164 **igne** *add* a E. 1165 **et** a E; *om* FIL. **et . . . pax** *om* G. **predone** leone J. 1166 **seducat** seducatur J; *om* FILW. **vanas** *add* enim E; varias F. **ingerat** ingerit EI. 1167 **enim** autem E; *add* predone G. 1168 **inproperat** imperat FILW; sperat G. **in** de FILW. 1171 Gregorius *marg*

sio, etc., alii duo nuncii mittendi sunt, scilicet oracio et elemosina. Elemosina deducit in manu armata et protegit; Ecclesiastici xxix: "Super scutum et lanceam pugnabit pro te," etc. Preterea ipsa parat uiam tendentibus ad Deum; Prouerbiorum [xviii]: "Donum hominis dilatat uiam eius et ante principes," idest angelos et sanctos, "spacium ei facit." Oracio autem proponit negocium in conspectu Summi Iudicis; Augustinus *Super* [*Psalmos*]: "Oracio quasi quedam persona ad Deum intrat et negocium peragit quo caro peruenire nequit." Quod autem negocium perficiat dicit Iob xxxiii: / "Deprecabitur Altissimum et placabilis f. 125ra erit ei." Si uero lacrima assit, misericordiam extorquebit; Origenes: "Tante efficacie sunt pure lacrime, quod eciam inperant Altissimo."

Dicto cum quibus debemus habere pacem, dicendum est a quibus, idest, ne illis [communicemus]. Et primo a [carne propria], ut dometur Dalila ne [Sampsonem] decipiat, Iudicum [xvi]. Hoc enim cauebat Apostolus corpus suum castigans et in seruitutem redigens, Corinthiorum ix. Sepe enim contingit quod idcirco carnales motus non uincimus quia Dalilam per penitenciam non domamus; Ysaie xxvi: "Iusticiam non fecimus in terra, ideo non ceciderunt habitatores orbis." "Iusticiam" dicimus penitenciam, quia species est iusticie et iuste debetur pro peccatis. "Habitatores orbis" sunt motus carnis, qui per totum orbem dominantur carnalibus. Secundo habenda est pax a dyabolo, ut uitemus "spirituales nequicias in celestibus," Ephesiorum [fine]. Hoc signatur Ieremie xxi, vbi dicitur: "Qui transfugerit ad Caldeos [qui] obsident nos [uiuet] et erit ei anima sua quasi spolium." "Caldei" interpretantur feroces demones, scilicet qui nullius miserentur. Ad eos fugit qui in peccatum incidit. Set si uult uiuere et pacem habere, "erit ei anima sua quasi spolium," idest, ut uiolenter et festinanter eruat illam de o- / re leonis; Prouerbiorum vi: "Eruere f. 125rb quasi damula," etc. A tribus aufertur spolium: ab igne, ° bestia, [et] predone. Tercio habenda est pax a mundo, ne falsa pace seducat, vanas ° curas et noxias [ingerat] occupaciones. "Nemo [enim] militans Deo inplicat se negociis secularibus," II Thymothei ii. Hoc inproperat Ietro Moysi nimis grauato in cura populi, Exodi xviii: "Stulto labore consumeris, non potes solus

tion, take upon themselves cares which are too much for them; Job 26: "The giants groan under the waters"; Gregory: "They groan under the weight of people as long as they crave for honor." Thus Ecclesiasticus 11 says to the point: "My son, do not meddle with many matters"; a wise man puts an end even to honorable activities.

We have spoken of the remedy for anger. Now we must speak of its punishment. A special punishment for anger is the harshness and bitterness of conscience itself. "The wicked shall be angry with himself, he gnashes his teeth and pines away," as the Psalmist says. And again: "The Lord shall trouble them in their wrath," and so forth. They will grow so angry at themselves that they would rather not be or kill themselves; Apocalypse 8: "On that day man will seek death, and it will fly," and so forth; Bernard: "Then they will ardently desire what they now ardently hate."

E. 1171–73 **Gregorius . . . gemunt** *om* F. 1173 **dicitur . . . xi** dicit Ecclesiasticus EIW. 1174 **ponit** inponit E. **in** *om* E. **honestis** *add* de ira *rubr* J; *add* de pena ire *rubr* H. 1175 **Dictum est** dicto FIL. 1177–78 **ut . . . Psalmista** *om* FGILW. 1181 Bernardus *marg* E. **Bernardus** *om* FGILW.

sustinere." Set multi ambicionis causa curas suscipiunt ad quas non sufficiunt; Iob xxvi: "Gigantes gemunt sub aquis"; Gregorius: "Dum honorem appetunt, sub pondere populorum gemunt." Ideo signanter [dicitur Ecclesiastici xi]: "Fili, ne in multis sint actus tui"; sapiens [ponit] finem eciam [in] rebus honestis.

Dictum est de remedio ire. Dicendum est de eius pena. Erit autem specialis pena ire ipsa asperitas consciencie et amaritudo. "Irascetur enim peccator sibi, dentibus suis fremit et tabescit," ut dicit Psalmista. Et iterum: "Dominus in ira sua conturbabit eos," etc. In tantum uero irascentur sibi quod uellent non esse uel mortem sibi inferre; Apocalipsis viii: "In illa die desiderabit homo mori, et fugiet mors," etc.; Bernardus: "Tunc uehementer desiderabunt quod hic uehementer oderunt."

V

ON OBEDIENCE

After the chapter on humility and patience follows one on obedience, for humility is the mother of obedience, just as pride is the mother of disobedience; but patience is the nurse of obedience. Humble people easily submit themselves, patient people are easy to guide, and these two make a person obedient. Now, obedience is defined in a variety of ways: sometimes with respect to the person who commands, sometimes with respect to him who obeys, sometimes with regard to both, and sometimes with regard to the thing that is commanded. With respect to both, the following definition is given: "Obedience is the virtuous carrying out of a just command by a mind that takes counsel." This definition is put together from the book by Bernard entitled *On Commandment and Dispensation.* Another definition considers only the part of the obeying person: "Obedience is the free denial of one's will for the sake of discipline." With respect to what is commanded, obedience is defined as follows: "Compliance with a just demand." And notice that just as Simon, whose name means obedient, is the prince of the apostles, obedience is the mistress of the virtues; Gregory: "Obedience plants the virtues and guards them after planting." This virtue did the master of virtues teach us who "became obedient unto death," Philippians 2, so that our obedience should be unto death, "unto" meaning including. And it is no wonder that our will should draw us to such a pledge, since the necessity of dying draws us to death. Therefore: "As we have borne the image of the earthly," that is, of Adam, who sinned and therefore of necessity had to die, as is stated in Corinthians 15, so "let us bear also the image of the heavenly," that is, of Christ, who died for us out of free will, as he himself testifies in John 10: "I have the power to lay down my life." In these things it is apparent to what extent obedience must be given, namely unto death.

To whom we must show obedience, Peter teaches in his First Epistle, chapter 2: "Obey your prelates, not only the good, but also the froward." This the Lord teaches us by his example, being subject not only to Mary and Joseph, Luke 2, but also to Pilate, as is clear when he said: "You would not have any power against me," and so forth, John 19. In addition, he obeyed even the devil

V *om all MSS.* 1 **De obediencia** *rubr* EJHI; *om* FGL; *illeg* W. 2 **Post . . . paciencia** *om* G. 3–4 **sicut . . . inobediencie** *om* H. 3 **superbia** *add* mater F. 5 **faciunt** *add* obedienciam idest F; *add* obedienciam et G; *add* obedienciam uel LW. **obedientem** obedienciam I. 7–8 **quandoque *(1st)* . . . utriusque** *om* FLW. 10 Bernardus *marg* E. **beati** *om* JFGILW. 11 **est** dicitur E. 13 **diffinitur** *om* FL. 14 Gregorius *marg* E. 19–20 **Philippensium . . . mortem** *om* E. 20 **est** *om* E; non H. 21 **trahat** trahit E; retrahat L. 23 **Ade . . . ideo** *om* F. 23–25 **ex . . . morientis** *om* I. 27 **extendi** ostendi JW; excerceri F; contendi G. 30 **solum** tantum

[V]

DE OBEDIENCIA

Post capitulum de humilitate et paciencia sequitur de obediencia, quia humilitas est mater obediencie, sicut super- / f. 125^{v}a bia inobediencie; paciencia uero est nutrix obediencie. Humiles uero sunt subiectibiles, pacientes uero suadibiles, et hec duo faciunt obedientem. Diffinitur autem obediencia pluribus modis: quandoque ex parte precipientis, quandoque ex parte obsequentis, quandoque ex parte utriusque, quandoque ex parte eius quod precipitur. Ex parte utriusque datur ista: "Obediencia est animi deliberantis honesta iuste iussionis execucio." Hec colligitur ex libro beati Bernardi qui [est] *De precepto et dispensacione.* Alia datur ex parte obsequentis tantum: "Obediencia est pro discipline studio proprie uoluntatis uoluntaria abnegacio." Aliter diffinitur penes illud quod precipitur: "Obediencia est iuste rei obtemperancia." Et nota quod sicut Symon, qui interpretatur obediens, est princeps apostolorum, ita obediencia magistra uirtutum; Gregorius: "Obediencia uirtutes inserit, insertasque custodit." Hanc uirtutem docuit magister uirtutum "factus obediens usque ad mortem," [Philippensium ii, ut nostra obediencia sit usque ad mortem,] "vsque" inclusiue. Nec [est] mirum si ad talem obligacionem nos [trahat] uoluntas, cum ad mortem nos pertrahat moriendi necessitas. Vnde: "Sicut portauimus ymaginem terreni," idest Ade peccantis et ideo morientis ex necessitate, ut Corinthiorum xv, ita "portemus ymaginem celestis," idest Christi pro nobis morientis ex libera uoluntate, ut ipse testatur Iohannis x: "Potestatem habeo / f. 125^{v}b ponendi animam meam." In hiis apparet quantum debeat extendi obediencia, scilicet usque ad mortem.

Quibus autem exhibenda sit obediencia docet Petrus in Canonica prima, secundo capitulo: "Obedite prepositis uestris, non [solum] bonis set eciam discolis." Hoc exemplo docuit Dominus non solem Marie et Ioseph subiectus, Luce ii, set eciam Pylato, quod patet cum dixit: "Non haberes in me potestatem," etc., Iohannis xix. Preterea ipsi dyabolo quodammodo obediuit cum se

in a certain way, when he permitted himself to be taken, that is led, into the mountain and upon the pinnacle of the temple, Matthew 4. Other examples, too, encourage us to be obedient. In every creature there is an element of obedience, so that things may happen to it that God wants, when he wants, and as he wants, as Augustine comments on Genesis; and in his book *On the Creed*: "Material potency is the first principle in a creature," that is, its natural obedience. Further, all higher creatures obey him, they move and stand at his beck; the Philosopher says: "All things shall stand at his beck." And near the end of Jeremiah's Letter: "The sun and the moon and the stars, as they are bright and are sent forth for profitable uses, are obedient"; and Baruch 3: "The stars were called and they said, 'Here we are.'" Intermediate creatures, too, obey him; Jeremiah in his Letter, near the end: "The lightning and the spirit that blows in every country," that is, wind and clouds, "do what is commanded them"; and Job 37: "The clouds spread their light and illuminate everything whithersoever the will of him that governs them shall lead them." Also the lower creatures obey him, because "he has set the sea bars and doors so that they may break its waves," Job 38; and Matthew 8: "The sea and the winds obey him." Again, it is a wonder that man, a worm, does not obey another man, while the wild beasts do so. For David subjugated the lion and the bear, Kings 17. Also, a single man ruled an elephant in battle, which has such a large body and unbending joints; Machabees 6: "In a wooden tower on the elephant, the master of the beast." Moreover, a young boy ties up and looses a large and strong war-horse, and he lets it loose and bridles it at his will. Poisonous snakes, too, obey man; Isaias 11: "The weaned child shall thrust his hand into the den of the basilisk." Furthermore, how great the obedience of the sons of Rechab was, that at their father's bidding they would not taste wine as long as they journeyed far from their homeland, is clearly seen in Jeremias 35.

Three things are required for perfect obedience. First it must be voluntary; Bernard: "A truly obedient person gives his wanting and not-wanting, so that he may say, 'My heart is ready, my heart is ready for anything you may command me to do.'" Further, it must be swift, so that whatever is commanded be done at once, if possible. Thus, Abraham rose at night to obey the Lord, Genesis 22. And the *Lives of the Fathers* report of someone who at the call of his superior rose at once and left the circle of the letter O unfinished. Further, obedience must be complete, so that all things be done that are bidden; at the end of Exodus: "Moses did all that the Lord had commanded." As a fourth condi-

E. 31 **Luce ii** *om* FILW. 34 **supra** super FL. 35 Exempla *marg* E. 36 **omni** *add* enim FILW. **de ea** de eo E; *om* FILW. 37 Augustinus *marg* E. 38–39 **et . . . obediencia** *om* F. 40 **mouent** mouentur E. 40–41 **eius . . . nutum** *om* EW. 40 **Philosophus** Plato in Thimeo G. 41 Ieronimus *marg* E. **eius** conditoris FILW. **Et** *add* in E. **Ieremie** Ieronimi EJFGH. 42 **et sidera** *om* FL. 43–44 **obaudiunt . . . media** *om* F. 43 **et *(1st)*** *om* E. 44 **Epistula** *om* E. **Ieremie** Ieronimi F. **fine** *om* EFL. 45 **spirat** spirant JGHI. 48 **duxerit** dixerit E; direxit L. 49 **hostia** hostes EH. 51 **homini** *om* E; ei JG. 52 **obediant** obediunt JFGILW. **Dauid** deus E. 53 **xvii** xvi J; 15 FILW; 42 G; *blank* H. **unus** uermis EI. **rexit** regit JFGL. 54 **et** *om* E. 55 **In . . . bestie** turres lignee super uniuersas bestias et super eas machine et super singulas etc FL. 56 **puer** prouer E. **et *(2nd)*** *om* EG. 59 **mittet** mittit E. **filiorum** *om* E; filii L. 60 **gustarent** gustaret E; gustabant G. 60–61 **duraret . . . a** peregrinaret in E. 63 Bernardus *marg* E. 64 **Paratum** *add* est JGHW. **meum *(1st)*** *add* deus E. **paratum cor meum *(2nd)*** *om* FILW. 64–65 **paratum . . . cita** *om* G. 65 **fiat** faciat E. 66 **si . . . sit** *om* FILW. 67 Exemplum *marg* E. **xxii** xii E; xxi JIW. 69 **statim** *om* FGILW. 70 **fiant** statim faciat E. 71 **Quarto** quarta EJH;

in montem et supra pinnaculum templi assumi permisit, idest deduci, Matthei iiii. Item inuitant nos exempla ad obedienciam. In omni creatura est materia obediencie, ut fiat de [ea] quod uult Deus et quando uult et prout uult, ut dicit Augustinus super Genesim; et in libro *De symbolo*: “Potencia materie est primum in creatura,” idest, naturalis eius obediencia. Item omnia superiora obediunt ei, [mouent] et stant ad nutum eius; [Philosophus: “Omnia stabunt ad nutum eius.”] Et ° Epistula [Ieremie] in fine: “Sol et luna et sidera, cum sint splendida et emissa ad utilitates, obaudiunt”; [et] Baruch iii: “Stelle uocate sunt et dixerunt, ‘Assumus.’” Item media obediunt ei; [Epistula] Ieremie [fine]: “Fulgur et spiritus qui in omni regione spirat,” idest uentus et nubes, “perficiunt quod inperatum est eis”; et Iob xxxvii: “Nubes spargunt lumen et lustrant cuncta quocumque gubernantis uoluntas [duxerit] adesse.” Item inferiora obediunt ei, quia ipse / (f. 126ra) “posuit mari uectes et [hostia], vt confringant tumentes fluctus suos,” Iob xxxviii; et Matthei viii: “Mare et uenti obediunt ei.” Item mirum est quod homo uermis non obedit [homini] cum seua animalia obediant ei. [Dauid] enim leonem et ursum subiecit sibi, Regum xvii. Item [unus] homo rexit elephantem in bello, qui est tam magni corporis [et] in iuncturis inflexibilis; Machabeorum vi: “In lignea turre super elephantem magister bestie.” Item [puer] ligat et soluit magnum dextrarium et fortem [et] laxat et cohibet ad nutum suum. Item serpentes uenenosi obediunt homini; Ysaie xi: “Infans ab ubere in cauernam reguli manum [mittet].” Item quanta fuerit obediencia [filiorum] Rachab ut ad preceptum patris sui non [gustarent] uinum quamdiu [duraret peregrinacio a] terra sua patet in Ieremie xxxv.

Tria exiguntur ad perfectam obedienciam. Primo ut sit uoluntaria; Bernardus: “Bonus obediens dat suum uelle et suum nolle, ut possit dicere, ‘Paratum cor meum, ° paratum cor meum ad omnia que iusseris facere.’” Item debet esse cita, ut statim [fiat] quod precipitur, si possibile sit. Vnde Abraham de nocte surrexit ut obediret Domino, Genesis [xxii]. Et de quodam legitur in *Vitas / (f. 126rb) Patrum* quod statim ad preceptum superioris relicto semicirculo huius littere O statim surrexit. Item debet esse integra, ut [fiant] omnia que precipiuntur; Exodi ultimo: “Fecit Moyses

tion may be added that obedience should be persevering, which is indicated in the tail of the sacrificial beast that is offered with the ear, Leviticus 22; by the ear we understand obedience, by the tail perseverance. One also usually adds that obedience should be discreet, so that one never commits anything evil for the sake of obedience, even if sometimes good actions may be omitted. Augustine: "The rule of obedience should be kept in such a way that you do not agree with good men in evil things, and do not contradict evil men in good things." The Canon, too, says that one must never give obedience against the law of faith or of the Church.

From these things it is apparent what obedience should be like, for in the preceding we have spoken of how much and to whom it should be given. In addition, man must obey his superior, because we read that higher things have obeyed man. For the sun obeyed Joshua so that one day became two, as it were, Josue 10. Sedulius:

> Still stood the sun at Gibeon, high in the midst of heaven.

We also read there that the Lord obeyed the voice of a man. So did the sky obey Elijah's voice that it did not rain on the earth for three years and six months. Further, we should obey our superiors, so that God may obey our prayers. Hebrews 12: "We shall obey the father of spirits and live"; Augustine comments on the same text: "As much as we shall have been obedient to our fathers, so much will God obey our prayers."

According to Bernard there are three kinds of obedience: of a dog, of a hawk, and of the ass. A dog's obedience is that which only knows its own friends and obeys those by whom it has been or will be advanced. For a dog fawns on those it knows, but those it does not know, it barks and bares its teeth at. Such are people who submit themselves only to their friends, while for others they have brawls and quarrels; of whom it is said in Philippians 3: "Beware of dogs, beware of mutilation!" A hawk's obedience is given only for some temporal reward. He looks at the prize but not at his merit. *Accipiter,* "the hawk," is thus called from *accipere,* "to snatch." Paul accused the ministers of being such, in 2 Corinthians 11: "For you suffer it if a man takes," and so forth. Such people are ministers of their brothers and of the monastery, not by the Lord's command but by their lust for gain. Whence the Lord, ignoring such men, asks in Job 39: "Does the hawk grow feathered at your command, spreading its wings to the south?" The hawk sheds its feathers every year when the

item quartum F; *om* G; quartum IW. **sit** *om* EG. 72 **hostie** *om* E; bestie GL. 73 **xxii** xii E; xxi J. 74–75 **licet . . . bona** *om* GL. 75 Augustinus *marg* E. 75 **Sic** dixit E. 77 **eciam** enim JG. 79–80 **Ex . . . exhiberi** *om* G. 79 **qualis** in quibus E; qualiter J. 79–80 **quia . . . debeat** *om* J. 80 **dicebatur** dictum est FILW. 80–81 **Item . . . superiori** debemus autem obedire superioribus G. 80 **bene** *om* E. 81–82 **obedisse** obediuisse E. 82 **obediuit** *om* E. 82–83 **ut . . . x** *om* L. 83 **Sedulius** *om* EH. 85–86 **uoci . . . obediuit** *om* F. 88 **oracionibus nostris** nobis E; oracionibus I. 89 Augustinus *marg* E. **spirituum** superum EG. 92–133 **Est . . . fine** *after* capitulo *(line 159)* G. 93 **asinina** asinaria ILW. 94–95 **per . . . promouendus** *om* F. 96 **rictum** ictum E; ritum F. **solum** solis GH; solis *marg for* suis J. 98 **concisionem** concisiones JIW; malos operarios FL. 104 **xxxix** xxix E; 33 F. 105 **tuum** *om* E. 106 **pennas** *marg for* alas *canc*

omnia que precepit Dominus." [Quarto] potest addi ut [sit] perseuerans, quod notatur in cauda [hostie] oblata cum aure, Leuitici [xxii]; in aure obediencia, in cauda perseuerancia. Solet eciam addi ut sit discreta, ut nunquam fiant mala pro obediencia, licet quandoque intermittantur bona. Augustinus: "[Sic] modus obediencie tenendus est ut bonis in malo non consencias et malis in bono non contradicas." Dicit eciam Canon quod nunquam obediendum est contra statum fidei uel Ecclesie.

Ex hiis apparet [qualis] debet esse obediencia, quia in supradictis dicebatur quantum debeat et quibus exhiberi. Item [bene] debet homo obedire suo superiori, quia legimus superiora [obedisse] homini. Sol enim [obediuit] Iosue ut fieret una dies quasi duo, Iosue x. [Sedulius:]

Sol stetit ad Gabaon medii cacumine celi.

Legitur eciam ibidem quod Dominus obediuit uoci hominis. Item celum obediuit Helye uoci ut non plueret super terram annis tribus et mensibus sex. Item debemus obedire superioribus, ut Deus obediat [oracionibus nostris]. Hebreorum xii: "Obtemperabimus patri [spirituum] et uiuemus"; ibi Augustinus: "Quanto obedientes fuer- / imus patribus nostris, tanto obediet Deus ora- f. 126va
cionibus nostris."

Est autem triplex obediencia secundum Bernardum: alia est canina, alia accipitris, alia asinina. Canina est illa que solum nouit suos familiares et eis obtemperat per quos promotus est uel promouendus. Canis enim notis blanditur, ignotis uero latratum et [rictum] dencium ostendit. Tales sunt qui solum familiaribus subiecti sunt, ad alios uero rixas et dissensiones inueniunt; de quibus Philippensium iii: "Videte canes, uidete concisionem!" Obediencia accipitris est que solum propter temporale emolumentum obedit. Lucrum enim respicit, non meritum. Accipiter enim ab accipiendo dicitur. Pro talibus redarguit Paulus prelatos, II Corinthiorum xi: "Sustinetis enim si quis accipit," etc. Tales non ex precepto Domini set ex cupiditate lucri ministri sunt fratrum et monasterii. Vnde tales ignorans Dominus querit a Iob [xxxix]: "Nunquid ad preceptum [tuum] plumescit accipiter expandens alas suas ad austrum?" Accipiter singulis annis pennas proicit

south wind has grown hot, and those people change their allegiance every year that they may climb higher. "Feathers" refers to temporal goods, "south" to abundance, "wings" to the sight and devotion that is directed to earthly things and not to God. For greedy people in the cloisters are like the bat, which walks on its wings because it lacks front legs. People walk on their wings when they turn their sight and devotion down to earthly things, and so they are impure, Leviticus 11. An ass's obedience accepts everything that is laid on it and carries it patiently. It says to the Lord: "I am become as a beast before you," and so forth. Once a man of great learning and reputation came to a monastery and, putting on the religious habit, made the following resolution: "Let us assume you are an ass"; and this resolution he kept very well. When later on he was asked by his brethren how he obeyed in such patience and humility, he told them of his resolution and edified his audience greatly. A man of perfect obedience is well compared to an ass, who carries dung as willingly as flowers; thus a truly obedient person is indifferent to burdens whether they are hard or soft. Therefore we read in Genesis 49: "Issachar, a strong ass lying down between the borders, saw rest," and so forth. "Issachar" means reward and indicates an obedient man, who for the great reward in heaven obeys man under God; of this reward is said in Matthew 5: "Your reward is very great in heaven." He is fittingly an ass, who is always ready for the burden, as was said before. He "lies down between the borders" when he withdraws from the world because he scorns it, being kept by the burden of his flesh on this side of heaven, and is thus lifted by the spirit "between the earth and the heaven," Ezechiel 8. He also realizes that "rest is good" after labor; whence he willingly labors a little in order to gain much rest, Ecclesiasticus near the end. He also sees that "the land is excellent," that is, the promised bliss, which is called "land" because of its stability and its fruit of reward. Its fruits in this life are groans and sighs; Augustine in book IV of the *Confessions*: "Sweet fruit is plucked from bitterness: groaning, weeping, and pain." That land "flows with milk and honey, as may be known by its fruits; but it has very strong inhabitants," Numbers 13. That land flows with the honey of Christ's divinity and the milk of his mankind; whence: "How sweet our homeland is can be tasted in advance in our longing for it; for, if it is sweet to weep for it, it is much sweeter to taste its joys," as Bernard says. And Romans 11: "If the first fruit is holy, so is the lump"; the

E. 110 **enim** *om* EG. 112 **ambulant** ambulat FILW. 113 **declinant** declinat FLW; inclinat I. 114 **asinina** asinaria ILW. 115 **Domino** Psalmista Domino JI; Dauid FL; Dominus G. 116 Exemplum *marg* E. 117–18 **posicionem** proposicionem E; positum FGI. 118–19 **positum** posicionem E. 120 **positum suum** posicionis modum E. 122 **sicut et** quam J; sicut FGILW. 123 **dura** duriora FILW. 124 **accubans** accumbens E; etc F; a te W. 127 **copiosa** multa F. 128–29 **predictum** dictum FGILW. 130 **detentus** detentum E. **ita** *om* E; tamen L. 132–33 **vnde . . . laborat** *om* F. 133 **fine** *om* EGL; 6 F. 134 **Videt** vidit E. **Videt . . . promissa** item quia obediens habebis pro mercede terram optimam idest beatitudinem promissam G *(see at 92)*. 135 **terra** *om* E. **pro fructu** hoc cum profectu E. 136 Augustinus *marg* E. 137 **IIII** *add* libro E; xlix W. 139 **potest** possit JFH; *om* G. 140 **diuinitatis** deitatis EW. **humanitatis** humilitatis HW. 141 **sit patria** *om* E. 143 **ut** *om* EFGILW. 144 **prelibacio . . . massa** *om* F. 146–47

cum auster incaluerit, et tales singulis annis obediencias mutant ut ad maiora conscendant. In “plumis” intelliguntur temporalia, in “austro” habundancia, in “alis” contemplacio et deuocio / f. 126vb que terrenis exhibentur et non Deo. Claustrales [enim] cupidi similes sunt uespertilioni, que ambulat super alas cum pedibus anterioribus careat. Super alas ambulant qui contemplacionem et deuocionem ad terrena declinant, et tales immundi sunt, Leuitici xi. Obediencia asinina est que omnia suscipit iniuncta et portat cum paciencia. Hec dicit Domino: “Vt iumentum factus sum apud te,” etc. Vnde uir quidam magne litterature et magni nominis ueniens ad claustrum et habitum religionis induens talem fecit [posicionem]: “Ponatur te esse asinum”; et optime seruauit [positum]. Requisitus tandem a fratribus suis qualiter tam pacienter et humiliter obediret, [positum suum] eis indicauit, et audientes multum edificauit. Homo perfecte obediencie bene conparatur asino, qui tam libenter portat fimum sicut et flores; sic bonus obediens ad dura et mollia est indifferens. Hoc est quod legitur Genesis xlix: “Ysachar asinus fortis [accubans] inter terminos uidit requiem,” etc. “Ysachar” interpretatur merces et uirum obedientem signat, qui pro multa mercede in celis homini sub Deo obtemperat; de qua Matthei v: “Merces uestra copiosa est in celo.” Iste bene est asinus, qui semper paratus est ad onus, ut pre- / f. 127ra dictum est. “Inter terminos accubat” recedens a mundo per eius contemptum, mole carnis [detentus] citra celum, et [ita] eleuatus est per spiritum “inter terram et celum,” Ezechielis viii. Intelligit eciam quod “requies sit bona” post laborem; vnde libenter modicum laborat, ut multam requiem acquirat, Ecclesiastici [fine]. [Videt] eciam quod “terra sit optima,” idest beatitudo promissa, que [“terra”] dicitur racione stabilitatis sue et [pro fructu] retribucionis. Fructus eius in uia sunt gemitus et suspiria; Augustinus IIII ° *Confessionum*: “Dulcis fructus de amaritudine carpitur: gemere, flere, et dolere.” Terra illa “fluit lacte et melle, ut ex suis fructibus cognosci potest; set cultores habet fortissimos,” Numeri xiii. Terra illa fluit melle [diuinitatis] et lacte humanitatis Christi; vnde: “Quam dulcis [sit patria] pregustatur per eius desideria; quia si dulce est flere pro illa, multo magis gaudere de illa,” [ut] dicit Bernardus. Et Romanorum xi: “Si prelibacio sancta est,

"first fruit" is our longing, the "lump" the prize itself, for whose sake the saints willingly "bow their shoulders to carry," they keep down their heart and bear everything that is brought upon them, Ecclesiasticus 2. But notice that that land "has very strong inhabitants," strong in mind and upright in tribulation. But carnal people do not live in this land but desire to return to Egypt, Numbers 11. For they say they cannot suffer such things, since their flesh is not of brass, Job 6. Therefore, through their great fear of the penance undertaken by saints they are excluded from the promised land. And so they choose their lot on their side of the Jordan, on its eastern shore, Numbers 32; that is, they choose their happiness in this life and think little of future bliss. This is what the children of Ruben and of Gad do. "Ruben" means the son of vision and signifies the clergy; "Gad" means girt and signifies the knights. These two "have very much cattle," sheepfolds and stalls for cattle; thus they look for nothing on the other side of the Jordan, as is shown in the same chapter.

The good that comes from obedience is shown in many examples. First in the supreme obedience of Christ, by which he gained the glorious resurrection for himself and for us; Philippians 2: "For which cause God has exalted him," that is, for the good of obedience in his passion. Further, Peter in obeying the Lord's voice walked upon the waters, Matthew 14. Moses in obeying the Lord's voice brought forth waters from the rock, Numbers 20; yet the Lord reproached him because he ascribed this deed in part to himself. Moreover, Maurus, the disciple of blessed Benedict, out of obedience ran upon water without knowing it, so that he might save his fellow disciple Placidus from drowning. Again we read of another in the *Lives of the Fathers* that as he watered a dry tree at the bidding of his elder every day, and the water was so far away that he went in the morning and came back in the evening, after three years the tree, which had so far been dry, bore fruit, and the elder called it the fruit of obedience. Another story in the *Lives of the Fathers* has it that when someone asked for the habit of religious life, the abbot of the monastery wanted to test his obedience and ordered him to enter a burning furnace. As he did so, the fire went out, just as it happened to the three young men of Daniel 3. In the same book we read of John, the disciple of Abbot Paul, a man of great obedience, that at the abbot's bidding he had bound a very fierce lioness and brought her to him. When the abbot saw that, he wanted to humble his disciple and said: "Son, you have brought me a silly dog." John released the lioness and let her go.

It may seem that obedience is not meritorious. For Augustine says: "The

omne . . . est omnia que sibi applicita sunt E. 150 **enim** *add* se FGH. 150–51 **illorum** eorum JFGILW. 155 **filii** *om* FL. 155–56 **uisionis** visitacionis FILW. 156 **clericos** diuites *corr from* clericos J. 158 **Iordanem** *add* regionem FLW. 159 **capitulo** *add* est . . . Ecclesiastici *(lines 92–133)* G. 160 Exempla *marg* E. 161 **qua** que E. 163 **in passione** *om* L. 165 **obediens . . . Domini** *om* FGILW. 166 **tamen** *om* FL. **Dominus** *om* E. 166–67 **quia . . . ascripsit** quod partem sibi ascribit E. 167 **beati** sancti E. 169 **submersione** subuersione E. 171–72 **aqua . . . rediret** *om* E. 172–73 **lignum . . . aridum** de ligno prius arido F. 173–77 **Item . . . Danielis iii** *om* G. 175 **experiri** probare F. 177 **est** fuit E. 178 **abbatis** *om* FILW. 179 **ligauerat** ligauerit E. 180 **duxerat** duxerit EHIW. 183 Questio Augustinus *marg* E. 183–200 **Uidetur . . . uoluntate** *om*

et massa"; "prelibacio" est desiderium, "massa" ipsum premium, propter quod sancti libenter "supponunt humerum ad portandum," deprimunt cor suum, et sustinent [omne quod sibi applicitum est], Ecclesiastici ii. Set nota quod terra illa "fortissimos habet cultores," fortes mente et sustinentes in tribulacione. Carnales uero terram istam non colunt set in Egiptum re- / dire uolunt, f. 127rb Numeri xi. Dicunt enim non posse pati talia, cum non caro illorum sit enea, Iob vi. Vnde ad penitenciam sanctorum perterriti a terra promissionis sunt exclusi. Ideo eligunt sortem suam citra Iordanem in orientali plaga, Numeri xxxii; idest, in presenti uita eligunt sibi felicitatem, futuram paruipendentes beatitudinem. Hoc faciunt filii Ruben et Gad. "Ruben" interpretatur filius uisionis et signat clericos; "Gad" interpretatur accinctus et signat milites. Isti duo "habent peccora multa," caulas ouium et stabula iumentorum; ideo nichil querunt trans Iordanem, ut in eodem capitulo.

Bona obediencie multis probantur exemplis. Primo per summam obedienciam Christi, [qua] sibi et nobis meruit gloriam resurrectionis; Phylippensium ii: "Propter quod Deus exaltauit eum," idest propter bonum obediencie in passione. Item Petrus obediens uoci Domini ambulauit super aquas, Matthei xiiii. Moyses obediens uoci Domini de petra produxit aquas, Numeri xx; quem tamen [Dominus] reprehendit [quia pro parte sibi ascripsit]. Item Maurus, [beati] Benedicti discipulus, propter obedienciam nesciens currebat super aquam, ut Placidum condiscipulum suum a [submersione] eriperet. Item legitur de alio in *Vitas Patrum* quod cum rigasset lignum aridum ad preceptum senioris per singulos dies et tam / longe distaret [aqua ut uadens f. 127va mane rediret] uespere, post tres annos tulit fructum lignum prius aridum, quem uocauit senex fructum obediencie. Item legitur in *Vitas Patrum* quod cum quidam peteret habitum religionis, uolens pater monasterii eius obedienciam experiri, precepit ei ut intraret fornacem ardentem. Quod cum faceret, ignis extinctus est, sicut et tribus pueris factum [est], Danielis iii. Item legitur in eodem de Iohanne discipulo Pauli abbatis, qui fuit uir magne obediencie, quod ad preceptum patris [ligauerat] leenam ferocissimam et ad illum [duxerat]. Ille hoc uidens et discipulum humiliari uolens dixit: "Fili, canem fatuum adduxisti michi." Quam soluit et abire concessit.

Uidetur quod obediencia non sit meritoria. Dicit enim Au-

less a service is owed, the more pleasing it is." But the works of obedience are absolutely owed; therefore they appear less pleasing and less meritorious. Furthermore, Jerome says that services done under compulsion do not please. But the works of obedience are done under compulsion; therefore, and so on. To this you should say that the works of obedience are meritorious for two reasons: first, because through obedience we stifle our self-will; and second, because through obedience we are made similar to God's will. When Augustine says: "The less a service," and so forth, he compares the works of precept with those of counsel. Even if he declares the works of counsel to be more pleasing, yet he does not deny that works of precept are meritorious. As to what Jerome says about services done under compulsion, we must take this to refer to such works as are done without the assent of our will. Now, the works of obedience, though they are owed because of the obligation that comes from a vow, yet they are not owed with respect to the freedom that is exercised in making a vow. Therefore Augustine comments on the Psalm "Vow and pay": "To make a vow is of the will; to pay, of necessity." And Anselm says in his book *Why God Became Man*: "Nobody must be said to lead a holy life out of necessity, but rather out of his free will with which he has made a vow."

Further, it may seem that obedience is a general virtue, just as disobedience is a general vice; Ambrose: "Sin consists in disobedience to the divine commandments." In addition, every virtue is directed toward fulfilling a commandment; but fulfilling a commandment is obedience, according to Gregory; therefore it appears that obedience comprises every virtue. To this one should say that obedience is both general and special. As a general virtue it is the fulfilling of commandment, and thus it is the same as justice in general; but justice refers to the person who commands or the thing that is commanded, whereas obedience refers to the person who carries out the command. Obedience as a special virtue is different, whose act consists in wanting to fulfill what has been commanded, and in fulfilling it one way or the other. This virtue does not have a special external act. It is likewise not a theological virtue, because it does not immediately refer to God but rather to a command, just as chaste or reverential fear does not immediately refer to God but rather to being separated from him, which the just person fears above all else; he does not fear God with the fear of pain, since he has no cause for offense.

And again it is sometimes asked whether obedience should have anything of its own. It may seem that it should not. Gregory: "It is not obedience which has anything of its own." And Bernard: "A truly obedient person gives his

IW. 185 **Set . . . debita** *om* L. 186 Ieronimus *marg* E. 187 **placent** *add* deo E. 187–88 **Set . . . etc.** *om* L. 188 Solucio *marg* E. 189 **opera obediencie** *om* EG. 191 Augustinus *marg* E. **Tanto** *om* E. 192–93 **Et licet . . . consilii** *om* H. 193 **negat** *add* tamen ea J. **Quod** *add* autem E. 194 Ieronimus *marg* E. 195 **admiscetur** admiscentur E. 197 Augustinus *marg* E. 199 Anshelmus *marg* E. **libro** in libro E; secundo JH; in G. 201 Questio *marg* E. 202 Ambrosius *marg* E. 204 **ad inplecionem** in adinplecione E. 205 Gregorius *marg* E. **quod** *add* ipsa JH. 206 Solucio *marg* E. 207 **adinplecio** ad inplecionem EJ. 208 **parte** *add* rei E. 210 **preceptum est** precipitur E. 210–11 **et . . . inplere** *om* F. 212 **est *(2nd)*** *om* E; cum G. 217 Questio *marg* E. 218 Gregorius *marg* E. 218–19 **Videtur . . . Et** *om* W. 219 Bernardus *marg* E. **Et** *om* E; eo I. 220 **etc.** ut possit dicere paratum

gustinus: “Tanto seruicia sunt graciora quanto magis sunt indebita.” Set opera obediencie omnino sunt debita; quare uidentur minus graciora et minus meritoria. Preterea dicit Ieronimus quod seruicia coacta non placent °. Set opera obediencie sunt coacta; quare, etc. Et dicendum quod duplici de causa sunt meritoria [opera obediencie]: primo quia per illam mactamus propriam uoluntatem; secundo quia per illam assimilamur diuine uoluntati. Et quod dicit Augustinus: “[Tanto] sunt graciora,” etc., ipse conparat opera precepti ad opera consilii. Et licet dicat illa graciora que sunt consilii, non negat / esse meritoria que sunt precepti. Quod f. 127vb
° dicit Ieronimus de coactis seruiciis, intellige de hiis quibus non [admiscetur] assensus uoluntatis. Opera enim obediencie, licet sint debita ex obligacione uoti, sunt tamen indebita quoad libertatem uouendi. Vnde Augustinus super Psalmum “Vouete et reddite”: “Vouere est uoluntatis; reddere necessitatis.” Ideo dicit Anshelmus ° libro *Cur Deus homo*: “Nemo sancte uiuere dicendus est ex necessitate, set ex libera qua uouit uoluntate.”

Item uidetur quod obediencia sit uirtus generalis, sicut inobediencia est uicium generale; Ambrosius: “Peccatum est inobediencia diuinorum mandatorum.” Et preterea omnis uirtus est [ad inplecionem] mandati; inplecio uero mandati est obediencia, secundum Gregorium; quare uidetur quod omnem uirtutem conplectatur. Et dicendum quod est obediencia generalis et specialis. Generalis est [adinplecio] mandati, et ipsa est idem quod iusticia generalis; set iusticia ex parte ° precipientis uel rei precepte, obediencia ex parte obsequentis. Alia est obediencia specialis, cuius actus est uelle inplere quod [preceptum est] et sic uel sic inplere. Et hec non habet actum specialem exteriorem. Item ipsa non est uirtus theologica, quia non [est] immediate in Deum set in preceptum, sicut timor castus siue reuerencialis non est in Deum immediate set in separacionem ab ipso, quam precipue ti-
/ met iustus; Deum enim non timet timore pene, cum non habeat f. 128ra
causam offense.

Item solet queri an obediencia aliquid de suo debeat habere. Videtur quod non. Gregorius: “Nulla est obediencia que aliquid habet de suo.” [Et] Bernardus: “Bonus obediens dat suum uelle

wanting and his not wanting," and so forth. Hence, it appears that perfect obedience keeps nothing of its own for itself. But on the other hand it appears that, if obedience is a meritorious virtue, it contains the cooperation of free will; and therefore of necessity it does keep something of its own for itself. To this must be said that obedience acts differently in prosperity and in adversity. In both cases one must draw a further distinction. Prosperity is of two kinds. One refers to goods of the body, in which obedience must not keep anything of its own; Gregory: "If a command brings with it success in this world or a higher place, the person who obeys and thereby acquires these goods loses the merit of obedience if he pants for these goods of his own desire." But in the prosperity of the soul, that is in meritorious acts, obedience can have something of its own. Thus, Isaiah offered himself willingly to the work of preaching, chapter 6: "Lo, here am I, send me." And what Isaiah offered out of obedience, that Jeremiah excuses himself for out of perfect humility. The same distinction one must draw with regard to adversity. For there are some ills in which obedience has nothing of its own, so that it may not withdraw from its good intention, as in reproaches and in temporal losses for Christ's sake; hence the Apostle counted all things as a loss that he might gain Christ, Philippians 3. There is another kind of adversity, such as physical suffering, in which obedience may have something of its own, for since nature is bent in upon itself, as Tullius says, it naturally has pity for itself. This is clearly seen in Christ who, though perfectly disposed with respect to his natural being, nevertheless said: "My soul is sorrowful even unto death." And the Apostle Thomas journeyed unwillingly to India, yet did he not lose his merit, because natural fear shrinks back from pain, which obedience cannot wholly exclude.

There is also the question whether one must obey bad prelates. The Gospel seems to say so, Matthew 23: "Whatsoever they say, do," and 1 Peter 2: "Be subject to your masters," and so forth. But on the other hand it appears that when an evil prelate does not obey God, he does not deserve obedience from the lowest creature. And one of the holy fathers said: "Do I obey him who does not obey God?" To that you should reply that we must obey them for the sake of their order and of their office, not because of their merit. In addition, as long as the Church bears with them, we must obey them in what belongs to their office. But two things belong to their office, expounding God's commandments and administering the sacraments. In these one may not oppose anyone, except if he is cut off from the Church. For the Canon says that all those must be toler-

cor meum deus paratum cor meum ad omnia J; *the same abbreviated* FHILW. 221 Contra *marg* E. **reseruat** debet reseruare FIW; reseruet GH. 221–23 **Set . . . seruari** *om* W. 222–23 **et . . . seruari** *om* E. 223 Solucio *marg* E. **seruari** reseruari FGHILW. 225 **distinguendum** distinguitur E; distingue J; distinguis G. 226 Gregorius *marg* E. 229 **anhelat** *add* item E. **prosperitate** prosperitatibus EFGIL. 230 **in** *om* E. **actibus** accionibus FGHIL; *illeg* W. 231–32 **Ecce . . . me** *om* I. 232 **obtulit** *add* se EF. 232–33 **Ieremias excusat** etc excusatur E. 233 **distingue** distinguendum est E; distinguitur ⟨vel distingue⟩ J. 234 **obediencia** obediens. E. 235 **a . . . proposito** homo a precepto E. 235–36 **rerum iacturis** similibus E. 236 **reputauit** putauit E. 239 Tullius *marg* E. 240 **conpatitur** conparatur EL; componitur F. 245 Questio *marg* E. 245–46 **Quod uidetur** uidetur EHW; quod sic uidetur FL; videtur quod sic GI. 247 Contra *marg* E. 248 **quia** quod E. **prelatus** *om* JFILW. 248–49 **obedienciam** *om* FLW. 250 Solucio *marg* E. **Nunquid** numquam JFGHLW. **dicas** dicendum E. 253 **pertinent. Ad kathedram** *om* H.

et suum nolle," etc. Vnde uidetur quod perfecta obediencia nichil de se sibi reseruat. Set contrarium uidetur quod cum ipsa sit uirtus meritoria, habet secum cooperacionem liberi arbitrii; [et ita necesse est aliquid de se sibi seruari.] Dicendum quod aliter se habet obediencia in prosperis, aliter in aduersis. Vtrobique tamen [distinguendum]. In prosperis, quia duplex est prosperitas. Vna est corporis, in qua nichil debet habere de suo; Gregorius: "Cum huius mundi successus precipitur, cum locus superior inperatur, is qui ad hec percipienda obedit obediencie sibi meritum euacuat, si ad hec ex proprio desiderio anhelat." ° In [prosperitate] anime, idest [in] actibus meritoriis, potest habere aliquid de suo. Vnde Ysaias sponte obtulit se ad predicandum, vi: "Ecce ego, mitte me." Et quod Ysaias obtulit ° ex obediencia, [Ieremias excusat] ex humilitate perfecta. Similiter [distingue] in aduersis. Sunt enim quedam aduersa in quibus [obediencia] nichil habet de proprio ne reuocetur [a bono proposito], ut in conuiciis et [rerum iacturis] pro Christo; vnde Apostolus omnia [reputauit] detrimentum ut Christum lucrifaceret, Phylippensium iii. Alia sunt aduersa, ut cruciatus corporum, in qui- / bus potest aliquid habere f. 128^{r}b de suo, quia cum natura sit in seipsam recurua, ut dicit Tullius, naturaliter sibi [conpatitur]. Patet in Christo optime disposito secundum naturalia, qui tamen dixit: "Tristis est anima mea usque ad mortem." Et Thomas apostolus inuite perrexit ad Yndos, nec tamen meritum euacuauit, quia timor naturalis penam formidauit, quem obediencia excludere non potest.

Item queritur an obediendum sit malis prelatis. [Quod] uidetur ex Ewangelio, Matthei xxiii: "Que autem dicunt, facite," et I Petri ii: "Obedite prepositis uestris," etc. Contrarium uidetur [quia] ex quo malus prelatus non obedit Deo, demeretur obedienciam minime creature. Et quidam de sanctis patribus dixit: "Nunquid illi obedio qui Deo non obedit?" Ad hoc [dicas] quod obediendum est eis racione ordinis et officii, non racione meriti. Et preterea dum tolerat eos Ecclesia, obediendum est eis in hiis que ad kathedram pertinent. Ad kathedram uero pertinent duo, exposicio preceptorum Dei et dispensacio sacramentorum. In hiis nulli contraire licet nisi precisus fuerit ab Ecclesia. Dicit enim

ated whom the Church bears with. And just as prelates demand obedience from their subjects, so must they give it to their superiors, as is decreed in Distinction 83: "Those who do not obey their bishops are for no reason to be considered clerics or priests," but rather "criminal and reprobate." Gregory also says that it shows great pride, wanting to be obeyed and not wanting to obey. Again, as the *Hierarchy* of Dionysius makes plain, the lower and intermediate angels obey the higher ones. The lower stars obey the higher ones in certain influences. Also the fierce bull, which rules over the cattle, naturally obeys the lion. And in the order of nature all lower creatures owe obedience to the higher ones.

255 **contraire . . . Ecclesia** contradicere G. 257 **prelati** *om* E. 258 **suis** *om* E. **ut** *om* E. **Distinctione** *add* iii FG. 260 Gregorius *marg* E. **eciam** enim JL; *om* F. 261 **sibi obtemperari** obtemperare E. 262 **et medii** *om* EFILW. 263 **Dyonisii** *add* et FILW.

Canon quod omnes illi tolerandi sunt quos tolerat Ecclesia. Et sicut [prelati] exigunt obedienciam a subditis, ita debent exhibere [suis] superioribus, [ut] LXXXIII Distinctione: “Nulla racione clerici aut sacerdotes habendi sunt” set “rei et reprobi qui suis episcopis non obediunt.” Dicit / eciam Gregorius quod magna f. 128^{v}a
superbia est uelle [sibi obtemperari] et nolle obtemperare. Item angeli minores [et medii] obediunt maioribus, ut patet in *Ierarchia* Dyonisii. Stelle inferiores obediunt superioribus in quisbusdam effectibus. Item thaurus ferox qui armento preest naturaliter leoni obedit. Et de ordine nature omnia inferiora obedienciam debent superioribus.

VI

ON STRENGTH

In the fourth place follows the remedy for sloth, which is the virtue of strength. According to the Philosopher, strength is that virtue which holds in check all assaults of the spirit. Or else: "Strength is the considered accepting of risks and the longlasting bearing of hardships." Thus according to Tullius. Otherwise, according to Augustine in his book *Whence Evil Comes*: "Strength is the state of mind by which we scorn all inconveniences." The office of this virtue is to undertake difficult things, as the Wise Man says. For it raises and strengthens the soul, whereas sloth depresses and weakens it. Therefore Isaias 35 invites us to use the remedy of strength: "Strengthen the feeble hands and confirm the weak knees. Say to the fainthearted, 'take courage.'" Hence, those who receive consolation of the spirit renew their strength. Isaias 40: "They shall renew their strength," and so forth. Gregory: "They are eager in spiritual work who once were strong in the flesh."

This virtue has five species: great-heartedness, confidence, composure, high-mindedness, and constancy. Great-heartedness is the voluntary and reasonable undertaking of difficult things. And it is necessary to have this virtue against sloth so that the latter may not swallow a person through sadness or break him through despair. Judas Maccabeus was great-hearted as he was prepared in all things to die in body and soul for his compatriots, 2 Machabees in the end. It is very useful to be great-hearted, because our body weighs us down a good deal, drawing us to pleasures and sorrows. Whence: "The corruptible body is a load upon the soul"; and 2 Esdras 4: "The strength of the bearer of burdens is decayed, for the rubbish is too much"; that is, the strength of the spirit is weakened because it is borne down by the weight of the body. Holy men, because of their great-heartedness, are likened to the lion, Proverbs 28: "The just, bold as a lion, shall be without dread." The saints are also like the great-hearted son of Aeacus, for as he stood firm against the raging waves, according to the poet, so do they stand against the world's afflictions. Deuteronomy 33: "They shall suck as milk the abundance of the sea," that is, to the

VI *om all MSS.* 1 **De fortitudine** *rubr* EHI; de remedio accidie *rubr* J; remedia contra accidiam idest de virtute fortitudinis *rubr* W; *om* FGL. 2 **Quarto loco** *om* FGL. 3 Philosophus *marg* E. 4 **retundens** recondens E; recundans H; recludens G. 5 **ita** ista J; hec FL; *om* I. 6 Tullius Augustinus *marg* E. **aliter** vel aliter FILW. 8 **Huius uirtutis** hec uirtus E. 9 **accidia** accendit F. **econtra . . . eam** contrahit FL. 10 **remedium** uirtutem G. **fortitudinis** accidie J. **inuitat** *add* dominus ad fortitudinem J. **xxxv** *add* dicens E. 11 **Confortate** confotate E. 13 **xl** *om* E. 14 Gregorius *marg* E. **student** *add* forciores esse F. 15 **fuerunt** fuerant JGHIW; erant FL. 16–17 **fiducia . . . constancia** securitas magnificencia constancia fiducia E. 18 **racionalis** racionabilis JFIW. 22 **fine** *om* EGL; 8 F. 23 **habere . . . animum** esse magnanimum E. 24 **tristicias** debilitates E. 25–26 **Debilitata . . . quia** *om* E. 27 **Viri** vnde E. 27–28 **Viri sancti** virorum sanctorum quidam L. 29 **xxviii** 24 FG; xxviii vel 24 J. **terrore** pauore E. 30 **sancti** *om* FILW. **sicut** *add* ille GHIW. 31 Poeta *marg* E. **ruentes** rugientes E; tuentes W. 33 **seculi** *add* ita

[VI]

DE FORTITUDINE

Quarto loco sequitur de remedio accidie, idest de uirtute fortitudinis. Et est fortitudo secundum Philosophum uirtus omnes inpetus animi [retundens]. Vel aliter: "Fortitudo est periculorum considerata suscepcio et laborum diuturna perpessio." Ita secundum Tullium. Aliter secundum Augustinum in libro *Vnde malum*: "Fortitudo est affectio qua omnia incommoda contempnimus." [Huius uirtutis] est aggredi forcia, ut dicit Sapiens. Ipsa enim eleuat animam et roborat, accidia econtra deprimit eam et debilitat. Ideo ad remedium fortitudinis inuitat Ysaias xxxv °: "[Confortate] manus dissolutas et genua debilia roborate. Dicite pusillanimis, 'confortamini.'" Vnde qui consolacionem spiritus recipiunt, fortitudinem suam mutant. Ysaie [xl]: "Mutabunt fortitudinem suam," etc. Gregorius: "Quia student in spirituali opere qui dudum fortes fuerunt in carne."

Huius uirtutis quinque sunt species: magnanimitas, [fiducia, securitas, magnificencia, / constancia]. Magnanimitas est difficilium f. 128^{v}b spontanea et racionalis aggressio. Et oportet magnum animum habere contra accidiam, ne ipsa absorbeat hominem per tristiciam uel frangat per desperacionem. Magnum animum habuit Iudas Machabeus, qui paratus erat per omnia corpore et animo mori pro ciuibus suis, II Machabeorum [fine]. Multum expedit [habere magnum animum], quia ualde aggrauat nos corpus nostrum trahens ad delectaciones et [tristicias]. Vnde: "Corpus quod corrumpitur aggrauat animam"; et II Esdre iiii: "[Debilitata est fortitudo portantis quia] humus nimia est"; idest, fortitudo spiritus lassatur quia pondere corporis grauatur. [Viri] sancti pro magno animo conparantur leoni, Prouerbiorum xxviii: "Iustus quasi leo confidens absque [terrore] erit." Item sancti sunt similes magnanimo Eacidi, quia sicut stabat contra [ruentes] undas, secundum poetam, sic illi contra mundi tribulaciones. Deuteronomi xxxiii: "Inundaciones maris quasi lac sugent," idest mala seculi [fiunt] sanctis dulces cibi pre amore celi,

saints the world's ills become sweet food for their love of heaven, as Gregory says in commenting on Job 6, "Can an unsavory thing be eaten?" and so forth. The life of the wicked is like a torrent which with many waves, that is, distress, floods the life of the saints. A torrent is a winter stream which dries up in summer. Thus the life of the wicked is to be dried up in the fire of judgment. Gregory: "When the sun of heavenly constraint blazes, it turns the joy of the wicked into drought." Of such people Job complained when he was beset by their vexations, Job 6: "They have passed by me as the torrent that passes swiftly in the valleys." They pass in the valleys because from the valley of sin they go to the valley of punishment. In order to resist that assault, we stand in need of great-heartedness.

Confidence is the certain hope to carry to its end a task one has undertaken. The Apostle calls us to this virtue in Hebrews 5: "Let us go with confidence to the throne of his glory, that we may obtain mercy," and so forth. We should have much confidence that he who gave us a good beginning will help us to the end, "he who works in us both to will and to accomplish," Philippians 2. "To will" I call meritorious, because "to will is present to us," Romans 8. We ought to place our trust and hope most forcefully in him through whom anything good is begun, advanced, and brought to completion. Therefore, Proverbs 3: "Have confidence in the Lord with all your heart." For the heart's anguish or the world's trouble cannot prevail where the power of such a helper is present. Bernard: "However fiercely affliction might rage, do not think yourself abandoned but remember that it is written, 'I am with him in tribulation.'" Moreover, he sees our afflictions who alone "considers hardship and pain." He "will look into the causes of everyone," Job 35. Further, he is ready to come to the aid of the afflicted. In proof of which Stephen, as he was being stoned, saw him "standing," Acts 7. He saw the one standing that he knew to be ready to help. Furthermore, we should trust in the help of the saints, for in God alone is our trust of reward, lest we be contrary to Jeremias 17: "Cursed be the man who trusts in man." This trust refers to our reward. The Jews, however, receive this curse because they place their trust of salvation in the Messiah as a pure human being; it is against them that the prophet inveighs. But it is help that we hope for from the merits and prayers of the saints; thus says Job 5: "Turn to some of the saints." Likewise, the afflicted should place their hope in the help of the Church, for as she once prayed for Peter when he was in chains—Acts 12:

J. **fiunt** fuerunt E; sunt F. 34 Gregorius *marg* E. **vi** *om* E. 35 **etc.** *om* J; *add* quod non est sale conditum etc I. **qui** que E. 36 **est** *om* EIW. 38 Gregorius *marg* E. **iudicii** incendii E. 39 **incanduerit** incaluerit F. 40 **conqueritur** *om* E. **eorum . . . Iob** *om* H. **conpressus** oppressus FGILW. 41 **me sicut** siciam E. **torrens** *add* qui J. **raptim . . . conuallibus** etc FL. 42 **transeunt** transierunt E. 43 **tendunt** transeunt F; *om* L. 45 **Fiducia** secunda est fiducia que FILW. **perducendi** producendi EH. 50 **dico** dicit E. 50–51 **quoniam uelle** quia naturale vel quoniam velle J; quoniam naturale FHILW; quia naturale G. 53 **iii** *corr from* xiii *and add* dicitur E. 55 **auxiliatoris** *add* primo *preceded by paragraph mark* E (*cf.* 58). 56 Bernardus *marg* E. 57 **te** *add* esse GIW. 58 **Preterea** secundo E; *om* F. **afflictiones** tribulaciones FILW. 59 **causas** curas F. 62 **vii** vi E; ii G; *add* glossa J. 64 **fiducia est** ponenda est fiducia FIL. **Maledictus** *add* homo FIW. 65 **premii** salutis I. 69 **Item**

ut dicit Gregorius super Iob [vi] ibi, "Nunquid commedi potest insulsum?" etc. Malorum uita est tanquam torrens, [qui] multis undis, idest angustiis, sanctorum uitam obruit. Et [est] torrens fluuius hybernalis qui in estate siccatur. Talis est malorum uita igne [iudicii] ex- / [f. 129ra] siccanda. Gregorius: "Cum sol superne districtionis incanduerit, reproborum leticiam in siccitatem uertit." De talibus [conqueritur] Iob eorum molestiis ualde conpressus, Iob vi: "Preterierunt [me sicut] torrens raptim transit in conuallibus." In conuallibus [transeunt] quia de ualle peccati ad uallem supplicii tendunt. Vt contra tantum inpetum resistamus, magnanimitate indigemus.

Fiducia est certa spes [perducendi] ad finem rem inchoatam. Ad hanc inuitat nos Apostolus, Hebreorum v: "Adeamus cum fiducia ad tronum glorie eius, ut misericordiam consequamur," etc. Multum debemus confidere quod iuuet nos in finem qui bonum dedit principium, "qui operatur in nobis et uelle et perficere," Philippensium ii. "Velle" [dico] meritorium quoniam "uelle adiacet nobis," Romanorum viii. In ipso potissime ponenda est fiducia et spes per quem bonum inchoatur, promouetur, et consumatur. Ideo Prouerbiorum iii °: "Habe fiduciam in Domino ex toto corde tuo." Non enim potest preualere cordis angustia uel mundi molestia ubi tanti auxiliatoris ° presens est potencia. Bernardus: "Quantumcumque seuiat tribulacio, non putes te derelic- / [f. 129rb] tum set memento esse scriptum, 'cum ipso sum in tribulacione.'" [Preterea] ipse uidet afflictiones qui solus "laborem et dolorem considerat." Ipse "singulorum causas intuetur," Iob xxxv. Preterea ipse paratus est succurrere tribulatis. In cuius signum "stantem" uidit illum Stephanus inter lapides, Actuum [vii]. Stantem uidit quem paratum ad succursum cognouit. Item in sanctis habenda est fiducia suffragii, quia in solo Deo fiducia est premii, ne sit contrarium Ieremie xvii: "Maledictus qui confidit in homine." Hoc dicitur de fiducia premii. Iudei uero hanc maledictionem incurrunt, qui in Messya puro homine fiduciam salutis ponunt; contra quos inuehitur propheta. Spem uero suffragii ponimus in sanctorum meritis et oracionibus; ideo dicit Iob v: "Ad aliquem sanctorum conuertere." [Item] in suffragiis Ecclesie ponenda est spes afflictorum, que sicut quondam orauit

"Prayer was made without ceasing by the Church unto God for him"—, so does she ask daily for the troubled and the captives: "Deliver Israel, O God, from all its tribulations."

Composure means not to be afraid of the inconveniences that lie before us and accompany the task we have begun. Such composure springs from three things. From purity of heart, for "a composed mind is like a continual feast," Proverbs 15. From fulfilling the commandments; 2 Paralipomenon 17: "The heart of Josaphat took courage for the ways of the Lord." For courage is born from composure; and "the ways of the Lord" are his commandments, in which we travel towards life. Composure also springs from voluntary poverty, just as fear and sadness spring from wealth. Isaias 14: "The poor shall rest with confidence." And Gregory in his *Morals*: "It is a wonderful composure of our heart not to seek what belongs to others but to be content with what is sufficient for each single day." From which composure rises everlasting rest, for from good and peaceful thoughts we pass on to eternal joy. In contrast, the wicked are harassed, here in their desires and there in torments.

High-mindedness is carrying difficult and noble things to the end. God's high-mindedness is his power, which does great and marvelous things; Ecclesiasticus 43: "His magnificence is wonderful." But our own high-mindedness has respect to the end in our work, which is the most powerful of causes, for whose sake the others are set in motion. Yet it often happens that something is begun well but becomes deprived of its proper end. Isidore: "Many have begun, but few bring things to an end." This is shown in Judas, who began well and ended badly. It is shown in the disciples who turned back, John 6, and in others who put their hand to the plow and look back, Luke 9. We read of a hermit who, after sitting in his cell for thirty years, suffered accidia in the Lord's fetters and was overcome by his temptation, so that he wanted to return to the delights of the world. And as he climbed up the wall of his dwelling in order to open up a place to get out, his feet slipped and a nail pierced his throat near his chin, and so he died hanging from the wall. To such an end does sloth lead, through overpowering sadness or despair! Consider the example of Judas, near the end of Matthew, and of Achitophel, 2 Kings 17. Therefore Bede says in his commentary on Luke: "We must always mourn, for we do not know what end we are coming to." Thus, many fail to reach the proper end because they withdraw

om E. 71 **xii** vii E. 71–72 **sine intermissione** .s. E. **sine . . . eo** etc FGL. 72 **ita** ideo E. 72–73 **pro** ***(2nd)*** **. . . dicit** canimus in psalmo F; et captiuis L. 75 **Securitas** tercia est securitas que FILW. **est** *add* uirtus J. 78 **Ex** et F; item ex ILW. 81 **tendimus** *add* Matthei 19: "Siuis ad uitam ingredi, serua mandata." Eciam si non peccasset, homo ad hoc teneretur, quia Ecclesiaste 12: "Mandata eius obserua," hoc est, omnis homo, glossa: idest ad hoc factus *marg* J. **eciam** autem J; *om* FGILW. 82 **securitas** audacia FL. 83 Gregorius *marg* E. 89 **Magnificencia** quarta est magnificencia que FILW. 90 **magna et** *om* E. 92 **potissima** potencia F. 94 Ysidorus *marg* E. **frustrari** *add* acriores in principio etc *marg* J. 95 **paucorum** *add* ut F; *add* quod G. 96 **Patet** *add* eciam FG. 97 **et** ***(1st)*** *om* E. 98 Exemplum *marg* E. **aspiciunt** respiciunt J; *om* FG. **Legitur** item legitur FL. **qui** quod JFGHLW. 99 **acciadiatus** *add* est JF. 100 **Domini et** deinde JGIW. **uictus** devictus FGILW. **lasciuiam** lasciua E. 101 **ut** et E. 103 **ille pendebat** pendens E. **mortuus** *add* est E.

pro Petro in uinculis—Actuum [xii]: "Oracio fiebat [sine intermissione] ab Ecclesia ad Deum pro eo"—, [ita] cottidie pro afflictis et captiuis dicit: "Libera, Deus, Israel ex omnibus tribulacionibus suis."

Securitas est incommoditates imminentes et rei inchoate affines non formidare. Ista securitas ex tribus nascitur. Ex cordis mundicia, quia "secura mens quasi iuge conuiuium," Prouerbiorum xv. / Ex inplecione mandatorum; II Paralypomenon xvii: f. 129^{v}a "Cor Iosaphat sumpsit audaciam propter uias Domini." Audacia enim ex securitate nascitur; "vie" autem "Domini" sunt precepta, quia per illa ad uitam tendimus. Item ex spontanea eciam paupertate nascitur securitas, sicut ex habundancia timor et tristicia. Ysaie xiiii: "Pauperes homines fiducialiter requiescunt." Et Gregorius in *Moralibus*: "Mira quippe securitas cordis est aliena non querere set uniuscuiusque diei sufficiencia contentum manere." Ex qua uidelicet securitate perhennis nascitur requies, quia a bona et tranquilla cogitacione ad gaudia eterna transitur. Econtra reprobi et hic fatigantur in desideriis et illic in tormentis.

Magnificencia est difficilium et preclarorum consumacio. Dei uero magnificencia est sua potencia faciens [magna et] mirabilia; Ecclesiastici xliii: "Mirabilis magnificencia eius." Nostra uero magnificencia finem respicit in opere, que est potissima causarum, propter quam mouentur cetere. Set sepe contingit rem bene inchoari et debito fine frustrari. Ysidorus: "Incepisse est multorum, ad finem uero perduxisse paucorum." Patet in Iuda, qui bene inchoauit et male consumauit. Patet in discipulis retro auersis, Iohannis vi, [et] in aliis qui mit- / tunt manum ad aratrum et f. 129^{v}b aspiciunt retro, Luce ix. Legitur de quodam heremita qui cum sedisset clausus in cella sua per triginta annos accidiatus in uinculis Domini et temptacione uictus, uoluit ad [lasciuiam] mundi reuerti. Et cum ascendisset parietem domus [ut] locum egressionis frangeret, pedibus suis labentibus clauus gutturi eius obuius mento eius infixus est, et [ille pendebat] de pariete mortuus °. Ad talem finem trahit accidia per nimiam tristiciam uel desperacionem! Exemplum de Iuda, Matthei [fine], et de Achitophel, II Regum xvii. Ideo dicit Beda super Lucam: "Semper lugere debemus, quia quo fine terminandi simus nescimus." Ideo enim multi

from their good resolution. Sophonias 3: "They rose early and corrupted all their thoughts," that is, they began well but ended badly; they started to build, but did not want to finish, Luke 14. Such are some members of religious orders who in the first year of their religious life are angels, in the second men, and in the third devils occupied about earthly affairs and distracted by many cares. Hence we should recall what is said in Deuteronomy 33: "As the days of your youth, so shall also your old age be"; that is, your religious fervor should be as strong in death as it was in your novitiate. Someone in the *Lives of the Fathers* taught another who wanted to enter the religious life: "Keep your pilgrimage every day as you do on the first day when you enter their community, and do not become confident."

Constancy is the mind's stability that is firm and persevering in its resolve. It is of four kinds. One is of the heart, so that a person may be "nothing wavering in faith. For a double-minded man is inconstant in all his ways," James 1. The second kind is of the mouth, so that "it should not be 'it is' and 'it is not' with a person," 2 Corinthians 1; and that "in all works the true word and steady counsel may go before," Ecclesiasticus 37. Another kind is constancy of mien; Christ always had that. As the Gloss comments on Isaias 42, "He shall not be sad nor troublesome": "He always preserved a calm mien; which the philosophers falsely boast of Socrates." But the opposite seems to be the case when we read that Christ wept over the city, Luke 19, and over Lazarus, John 11; that he further seems to have been angry when he cast out from the temple those who were selling and buying there, John 2; and in Ecclesiastes 8 we read about Christ: "The Most Mighty will change his face." To this you should reply that Christ did always keep the calmness, that is, stability, of his mien. For he did not tear his face or gesticulate, as do those who are brought to a mourning and "roar and cry at the feast when one is dead," Epistle of Jeremias 2. The fourth kind of constancy is in one's action, so that a person does not approve of again what he has formerly condemned, or the reverse. Galatians 2: "If I build up again the things which I have destroyed, I make myself a prevaricator." This means, to build up Jericho again and receive the curse, Josue 7. Into just as many kinds can one divide inconstancy. For many are like a reed that is shaken by the wind, Matthew 11. They are "children tossed to and fro who are carried about with every wind of doctrine," Ephesians 4. They are more changeable

105 **fine** *om* EFGL. 106 Beda *marg* E. 111 **Tales** nota tales FL. 112 **regulares** claustrales F; religiosi I; seculares L. **conuersionis** *add* sue FILW. **sunt** ***(2nd)*** *om* FILW. 113 **sunt** *om* FILW. 115 **iuuentutis** *add* tue FIL. 115–16 **senectus tua** senectutis tue EGL. 117 Exemplum *marg* E. 118 **ingredieris** ingrederis ELW. 119 **non** tunc J. 121 **Constancia** quinta est constancia que FILW. 122 **Et est quadruplex** est autem constancia quadruplex FILW. **Alia est** *om* FILW. 125 **opera** *om* E. 127 Glossa *marg* E. **est** *om* EL. **constancia** *om* FG. 127–28 **quam . . . turbulentus** quod F. 129 **falso** philosopho EIL; *om* F. 130 Questio *marg* E. **Christus** Christum JFGILW. 131 **super Lazarum** similiter FILW. 132 **quod** et FG. **uidetur** *add* fuisse E. **et ementes** *om* JHIW. 133 **et** *add* in E. **Ecclesiaste viii** Ecclesiastico E. **de Christo** *om* E. 134 Solucio *marg* E. **commutabit** mutabit EFG; *illeg* W; *add* et E. 136 **dilaniauit** dilatauit E. 137–38 **Epistula Ieremie** epistula Iude IW; Iude FGL. 141 **maledictionem** maledictum E. 142 **vii** viii JGHILW; 4 F. 142–43 **Et . . . Matthei ix** *om* F. 143 **paruuli** *om* FL. 147 **superficies** *add* de

deficiunt a fine debito quia recedunt a bono proposito. Sophonie iii: "Consurgentes diluculo corruperunt omnes cogitaciones suas," idest, bene inchoabant set male terminabant; ceperunt edificare, noluerunt consumare, Luce xiiii. Tales sunt quidam regulares qui primo anno conuersionis sunt angeli, secundo sunt homines, tercio sunt demones terrenis negociis occupati, multis curis distracti. Ideo reuocandum est ad memoriam quod dicitur Deuteronomi xxxiii: "Sicut dies / [f. 130ra] iuuentutis, ita et [senectus tua]"; idest, ut tanta sit religio in obitu quanta fuit in nouiciatu. Quidam in *Vitas Patrum* docuit quendam uolentem ingredi religionem dicens: "Sicut in prima die quando [ingredieris] ad eos, sic custodi peregrinacionem tuam omni die, et non assumas fiduciam."

Constancia est stabilitas animi firma et in proposito perseuerans. Et est quadruplex. Alia est cordis, ut sit homo "nichil in fide hesitans. Duplex enim animo inconstans est in omnibus uiis suis," Iacobi i. Alia est oris, ut "non sit apud hominem 'est' et 'non,'" II Corinthiorum i; et ut "ante omnia [opera] precedat uerbum uerax et consilium stabile," Ecclesiastici xxxvii. Alia [est] constancia uultus; quam semper tenuit Christus. Glossa super Ysaie xlii ibi, "Non erit tristis neque turbulentus": "Semper tenuit equalitatem uultus; quod de Socrate [falso] gloriantur philosophi." Contrarium tamen uidetur quod legitur Christus fleuisse super ciuitatem, Luce xix, et super Lazarum, Iohannis xi; quod eciam uidetur ° iratus eiciens uendentes et ementes de templo, Iohannis ii; et ° [Ecclesiaste viii] legitur [de Christo]: "Potentissimus faciem eius [commutabit]." ° Ad hoc dicas quod semper habuit equalitatem uultus, idest stabilitatem. Non enim [dilaniauit] uultum nec gestum mutauit, sicut conducti ad luctum qui / [f. 130rb] "rugiunt clamantes in cena mortui," Epistula Ieremie ii. Quarta est constancia operis, ut que homo prius dampnauit non iterum approbet, nec e contrario. Galatarum ii: "Si que destruxi iterum reedifico, preuaricatorem me constituo." Hoc est Iericho reedificare et [maledictionem] incurrere, Iosue vii. Et tot modis dicitur inconstancia. Multi enim sunt similes arundini que uento agitatur, Matthei xi. Hii sunt "paruuli fluctuantes qui circumferuntur omni uento doctrine," Ephesiorum

than the water's surface which obeys every breeze, as it is said of the impious, Job 24: "He is light over the face of the water," that is, lighter than its surface.

Special remedies against sloth are the following. The continual working of the Creator; what he created in the beginning and put in order, he is still keeping in existence and ruling. Therefore, the Son of God says in John 5: "My Father works until now, and I also work." Further, the continuing care of Christ. This is shown in his vigils, fasting, prayers, preaching, healing, and many travels. Hence "he is always carefully set to his work," Ecclesiasticus 38. Further, the untiring ministry of the angels who never cease from serving or praising their Creator. Isaias 6: They always cry, "holy, holy, holy," and so forth, and Apocalypse 4: "They do not rest day and night, saying: 'Holy, holy, holy, Lord, God Almighty.'" This passage speaks of the holy animals, by which we understand the angels, who have rational life. The same is taught by the continual motion of the heavens and the stars, which neither stops nor slows down but is for us "for signs and for seasons, for days and years," Genesis 1, that is, for the distinction between all those. Likewise the elements are in continual motion with respect to generation and corruption—in their parts, not in the whole. Near the end of Wisdom: "The elements are changed in themselves, as in an instrument the sound of the quality is changed"; that is, they alternately act and are acted upon at the will of the Maker, as in music the sound is changed at the will of the singer. Hence the Philosopher says that the elements are put in motion just like instruments. Furthermore, animals that are given over to our uses are working continually; even on a slender provision of food they yield us grain, but for themselves stubble and straw. And how is the Lord going to feed us if we do not work? Anselm: "Who would feed cattle that does not give as much profit as it eats?" 2 Thessalonians 3: "Who does not work shall not eat." Moreover, work was imposed on the first sinner as his penance; Genesis 3: "In the sweat of your face," etc. Thus, "the valiant woman has not eaten her bread idle," Proverbs, near the end. Also, we can learn good habits from small animals, as Seneca writes. And in Proverbs 6 it is said: "Go to the ant, o sluggard," as if to say: observe the animal which has such a small body and yet does so much work, so that you may wake up from your sluggishness. In addition, the bee has such a small body, yet such great skill and zeal that in its honeycomb it appears so subtle in separating wax and honey. Ecclesiasticus 11: "The bee is small among flying things," and so forth. The same is taught by the long efforts of the saints. Jerome comments on the words "Rest a little," and so forth, of Mark 6: "Long are the efforts of the saints and short their rest"; add: in the pres-

speciebus contra accidiam *rubr* J. 148 **Specialia** spiritualia EFG. **Operacio** opera E. 149 **disposuit** *add* et JI. 152 **in** ***(3rd)*** et FGL; *om* J. 153 **in** ***(1st)*** **. . . multis** *om* FILW; et multis aliis G. 155 **indefessum** indefestum E. 157–58 **etc. . . . sanctus** ***(3rd)*** *om* E. 157–59 **et . . . Omnipotens** *om* F. 159 **Deus** *om* E. 160 **uitam** uocem JL. 162 **tempora** *add* et JFL. 165 **fine** *om* EL; 19 FI. 167 **agunt** agitur E. **nutum Factoris** iussum conditoris J. 168 Philosophus *marg* E. **cantoris** creatoris GL. 169 **animalia** alia J. 171 **illis** istis F; vel GHW. 172 Anshelmus *marg* E. **operibus** laboribus J. 175 **etc.** uesceris pane tuo JIW. 176 **Ideo** secundo E; item JFL. 177 **fine** *om* EL; ultimo F. 178 Seneca *marg* E. 179 **quasi** et J; idest F; quasi dicat ILW. 183 Ieronimus *marg* E. 183–84 **longus . . . etc.** *om* JG. 184

iiii. Hii sunt mobiliores quam superficies aque que omni aure obedit, sicut dicitur de inpio, Iob xxiiii: "Leuis est super faciem aque," idest plusquam eius superficies.

[Specialia] remedia contra accidiam sunt hec. [Operacio] continua Conditoris; que ab inicio creauit et disposuit, adhuc conseruat in esse et regit. Vnde Filius Dei dicit Johannis v: "Pater meus usque modo operatur, et ego operor." Item continua sollicitudo Christi. Patet in vigiliis eius et ieiuniis, in oracionibus, in predicacionibus, in curacionibus, in itineribus multis. Vnde "semper in sollicitudine positus est propter opus suum," Ecclesiastici xxxviii. Item [indefessum] ministerium angelorum, qui nunquam cessant ab officio nec a laude Conditoris. Ysaie vi: Semper clamant, "sanctus, sanctus, sanctus," [etc., et Apocalipsis iiii: "Non habent requiem die ac nocte dicencia: 'sanctus, sanctus, sanctus,] Dominus [Deus] Omnipotens.'" De sanctis animalibus ibi loquitur, per que angeli intelliguntur / uitam racionalem habentes. f. 130va
Item idem docet continuus motus celi et siderum, qui nec deficit nec languescit set est nobis "in signa et tempora, dies et annos," Genesis i, idest ad distinctionem omnium istorum. Item elementa in continuo motu sunt quoad generacionem et corrupcionem—secundum partes et non secundum totum. Sapiencie [fine]: "In se elementa conuertuntur, sicut in organo qualitatis sonus immutatur"; idest, mutuo [agunt] et paciuntur ad nutum Factoris, sicut in musica mutatur sonus pro uoluntate cantoris. Ideo dicit Philosophus quod elementa mouentur ut organa. Item animalia usibus nostris deputata in continuo labore sunt; eciam cum tenui dieta nobis cedunt grana, illis stipula et palea. Et qualiter pascet nos Dominus sine operibus? Anshelmus: "Quis pascit pecus quod non tantum prodest quantum consumit?" II Thessalonicensium iii: "Qui non laborat non manducet." Item labor primo peccanti pro penitencia iniungitur; Genesis iii: "In sudore uultus tui," etc. [Ideo] "mulier fortis panem ociosa non commedit," Prouerbiorum [fine]. Item ab exiguis animalibus possumus trahere mores, ut dicit Seneca. Ideo dicitur Prouerbiorum vi: "Vade ad formicam, o piger," quasi: uide animal tam parui corporis et tanti laboris, ut a torpore exciteris. Preterea apis tam parui est corporis
et tante artis et sollicitudinis, / ut in fauo tam subtilis appareat in f. 130vb
separacione cere et mellis. Ecclesiastici xi: "Breuis in uolatilibus est apis," etc. Item idem docet longus labor sanctorum. Ieronimus super [Marci] vi, "Requiescite pusillum," etc.: "Longus la-

ent life, because in the future it will be very long, when God's people will rest "in wealthy rest," Isaias 32. A similar remedy is the performance of good works. Timothy 4: "Exercise yourself unto godliness." The good kind of solicitude takes away idleness and prevents sin. Thus Romans 12: "In solicitude not slothful." But solicitude is of two sorts. One belongs to forethought, which the Apostle is speaking about; the other goes with worrying, and it is forbidden in the Gospel of Matthew 6: "Be not solicitous for tomorrow," and so forth. To the same end avails prayer, which is an offering to God, comfort for the soul, the obtaining of forgiveness, and the confounding of our enemy. The Lord taught us to resort to prayer in temptation and tribulation, Luke 22, when "being in an agony he prayed the longer"; and in Luke 6 "he passed the whole night in prayer." But many are like Saul, who in time of war cast away his weapons and threw himself upon his sword. Thus acts a slothful person when he flees from prayer and sharpens his distress like a sword or lance with which to pierce his soul. Another remedy is to read Holy Scripture, as the Wise Man intimates in Wisdom 8: "She will be a comfort in my care and grief"; she, that is, Scripture. Thus, one of the holy fathers says: "Reading and prayer strengthen the mind." Gregory: "When we pray, we speak with God; when we read, God speaks with us." And you can infer from this that he who neither reads nor prays rarely speaks with God or God with him; and thereby increases slothful sadness. Another help is conversing with the good. Thus Ecclesiasticus 6: "Stand in the multitude of ancients that are wise, and join yourself from your heart to their wisdom, that you may hear every discourse of God." "Ancients" he calls those who are older and more discreet among the people, whose speech is edification, as the Apostle commands in Thessalonians 5: "Comfort one another and edify one another."

Marci Matthei EGL. 187 **bonorum** *om* ILW. 188 **teipsum** te E. 189 **Ideo** *om* JF. 190 **Est autem** et est E; et H. 191 **prouidencie** *marg, to replace* prudencie *canc* E. **Apostolus** *add* hic J*(interl)*G. 191–92 **in ewangelio** *om* FGL. 192–93 **in crastinum** *om* FILW. 193–94 **et . . . consolacio** *om* F. 195 **docuit** *add* nos *interl* J. **fugere** confugere GHILW. 198 **sua** *om* FIW; *add* in JG. 202 **mei hec** *om* E. 204 Gregorius *marg* E. 207 **inde accrescit** ideo crescit J. **accidiosa** *apparently corr from* accidioso E; accidioso FGILW. **eciam** *om* FGILW. 208 **collocucio** societas E; collocucio ⟨uel collacio⟩ J. **Ideo** *om* EW. 209 **prudencium** *om* E.

bor sanctorum et breuis requies"; suple: in presenti, quia in futuro erit longissima, vbi quiescet populus Dei "in requie opulenta," Ysaie xxxii. Item ad idem ualet exercicium bonorum operum. Thymothei iiii: "Exerce [teipsum] ad pietatem." Bona sollicitudo tollit ocium et inpedit peccatum. Ideo Romanorum xii: "Sollicitudine non pigri." [Est autem] sollicitudo duplex. Vna est prouidencie, de qua dicit Apostolus; alia est curiositatis, que in Ewangelio prohibetur, Matthei vi: "Nolite solliciti esse in crastinum," etc. Item ad idem ualet oracio, que est Dei oblacio et anime consolacio et uenie inpetracio et hostis confusio. Ad hanc docuit Dominus fugere in temptacione et tribulacione, Luce xxii, quando "factus in agonia prolixius orabat"; et in Luce vi "erat pernoctans in oracione." Set multi sunt similes Sauli qui proiecit arma sua tempore belli et incubuit super ensem suum. Hoc facit accidiosus fugiens oracionem et acuens suam angustiam quasi gladium et lanceam qua transfigat animam suam. Item ad idem ualet leccio Sacre Scripture, quod innuit Sapiens, Sapiencie viii: "Hec erit allocucio cogitacionis et tedii / [mei"; hec,] idest Scrip- f. 131ra
tura. Ideo dixit quidam de sanctis patribus: "Mentem solidant leccio et oracio." Gregorius: "Cum oramus, cum Deo loquimur; cum legimus, Deus loquitur nobis." Potes igitur inferre quod qui neque legit neque orat, raro loquitur cum Deo uel Deus cum illo; et inde accrescit tristicia accidiosa. Item ualet eciam ad idem bonorum [collocucio. Ideo] Ecclesiastici vi: "In multitudine presbiterorum [prudencium] sta et sapiencie illorum ex corde coniungere, ut omnem narracionem Dei possis audire." "Presbiteros" uocat seniores et discreciores in populo quorum sermo edificacio est, sicut precipit Apostolus, Tessalonicensium v: "Consolamini inuicem et edificate alterutrum."

VII

ON MERCY AND PITY

In the fifth place follows the remedy for avarice, which is mercy or pity; and these are one and the same virtue, except that mercy is in one's affection, pity in the deed. Mercy is defined by the Philosopher as follows: "Mercy is the virtue through which one's mind is moved over the misfortune of afflicted people." But pity is threefold. The first kind is called *theosebia,* that is, worship of God, according to Augustine, *On the Trinity*. The second kind stands for the works of mercy; Timothy 4: "Exercise yourself unto pity." The third is the veneration or obedience or kindness that we owe our parents, which the Philosopher describes as follows: "Through pity we render service and diligent care to those who are joined by blood and are devoted to our country."

The Lord taught us mercy by his words in Matthew 5: "Blessed are the merciful," that is, those whose heart is made miserable by another person's want, as Bernard explains; those are the ones who understand their neighbors' need from their own disposition, Ecclesiasticus 31. The Lord also taught this virtue by his example, when he gave us not only what belonged to him but himself. Galatians 1: "He gave himself for our sins, that he might deliver us from this wicked world." This lesson the Apostle had in mind when he said: "I most gladly will spend and be spent myself for your souls," near the end of 2 Corinthians.

Mercy is commendable for many reasons. First because as God created out of his goodness, so he restored out of mercy. That he created out of goodness is clear from the definition of the good: "The good spreads or communicates its own being," as Augustine says in his book *On the Nature of the Good*. And Boethius in the *Consolation* speaks of the Creator as follows:

> No external causes impelled you to make this work from chaotic matter,
> rather it was the form of the highest good.

And the Philosopher: "The beginning of all things is love and desire." From these words can be seen that as he created out of goodness, so did he restore from mercy; Titus 2: "According to his mercy he saved us." Further, mercy

VII *om all MSS.* 1 **De . . . pietate** *rubr* EH; de remedio auaricie *rubr* JIW; *om* FGL. 2 **Quinto loco** quinto E; *om* FGL. 3 **siue** *et FGHILW. **sunt** est J. 4 Philosophus *marg* E. 6 **autem** *om* JF. 7 Augustinus *marg* E. **Trinitate** ciuitate dei F. 10 Philosophus *marg* E. 15 Bernardus *marg* E. 16 **proximorum** proximi E. 18–19 **pro . . . Cuius** *om* L. 19 **seculo** seruitute J; presenti seculo I. 25 **enim** *om* E; autem F. 26 Augustinus Boethius *marg* E. **Augustinus** *add* in E. 26–30 **Et . . . boni** *om* F. 28 **pepulerunt fingere** pepulerint figere E; repulerunt ⟨vel pepulerunt⟩ fingere J. 32 **sicut** *marg* E. 33 **ii** *om* E; 3 F; 5 G. 35 Augustinus

[VII]

DE MISERICORDIA ET PIETATE

Quinto [loco] sequitur de remedio auaricie, idest de misericordia siue pietate; et sunt eadem uirtus, set misericordia est in affectu, pietas in effectu. Misericordia sic diffinitur a Philosopho: "Misericordia est uirtus per quam mouetur animus super calamitate afflictorum." Pietas autem triplex est. Prima dicitur theosebia, idest cultus Dei, secundum Augustinum *De Trinitate*. Alia sumitur pro operibus misericordie; Thymothei iiii: "Exerce teipsum ad pietatem." Tercia est ueneracio siue obsequium siue beneficium debitum parentibus, quam sic describit Philosophus: "Pietas est per quam sanguine iunctis et patrie beniuolis officium et diligens tribuitur cultus."

Misericordiam / docuit Dominus uerbo, Matthei v: "Beati f. 131rb misericordes," idest, ob alienam indigenciam miserum cor habentes, secundum Bernardum; tales enim sunt qui ex seipsis necessitatem [proximorum] intelligunt, Ecclesiastici xxxi. Docuit eciam illam exemplo, non solum dans nobis sua set eciam seipsum. Galatarum i: "Dedit semetipsum pro peccatis nostris, ut nos eriperet a seculo nequam." Cuius leccionem memoriter tenuit Apostolus cum dixit: "Libenter inpendam et superinpendar pro animabus uestris," II Corinthiorum ultimo.

Misericordia in multis est commendabilis. Primo quia sicut Deus ex bonitate creauit, ita ex misericordia recreauit. Quod autem creauit ex bonitate, patet ex boni diffinicione: "Bonum [enim] est diffusiuum sui esse uel communicatiuum sui," sicut dicit Augustinus ° libro *De natura boni*. Et Boecius in *Consolacionibus* de Creatore sic loquitur:

> Quem non externe [pepulerunt fingere] cause
> Materie fluitantis opus, verum insita summi
> Forma boni.

Et Philosophus: "Principium omnium, amor et desiderium." Ex hiis patet quod sicut ex bonitate creauit, sic ex misericordia recreauit; Ad Thytum [ii]: "Secundum suam misericordiam saluos

bent the heavens and drew God down from heaven, as Augustine says; add: from heaven into the Virgin's womb, from the cross into the sepulcher. But his soul it drew into hell. Of this mercy is written in Jeremias 31: "I have loved you with an everlasting love, therefore have I drawn you, having mercy on you"; and 2, where the Lord speaks to the assembly of the first believers: "I have remembered you, having mercy on your youth and the love of your espousals." In this can be seen that it was mercy which bound him to our forefathers, which has now united him in the flesh with the Church of the Gentiles. Likewise, mercy sold the Redeemer himself for the redemption of the prisoners, so that it might be said of her what is written in Wisdom 10: "She forsook not the just when he was sold but delivered him from sinners." Though this applies literally to Joseph, yet his selling prefigured the selling of Christ, which Zacharias 11 foretold: "They weighed for my price thirty pieces of silver." Further, just as mercy has bought the miserable ones back, so does it protect them from both sin and punishment; Lamentations 3: "Many are the mercies of the Lord, that we are not consumed." Further, not only the earth but also heaven needs mercy; whence the Psalm says: "O Lord, your mercy is in heaven." But this seems to be contradicted by Anselm when he says that where there is no misery, no one needs mercy; but it is certain that in heaven there is no misery; therefore, and so forth. And the Gloss on Leviticus 25, "There shall be a sabbath of resting," comments: "In the future, the commandments of the Gospel will cease." But those commandments deal mostly with mercy; therefore, etc. And Augustine says in his book *On Charity*: "Take away those who are miserable, and the works of mercy will cease." To this objection you may reply that heaven does not need that kind of mercy which mitigates or dispenses with regard to pain or guilt, because no one in heaven will be "uncircumcised or unclean," and so forth, Isaias 52. But it does need that mercy which maintains and preserves, so that because of its condition it may not fall into nothingness. According to Augustine and John Damascene, "everything that could be created can be changed back, that is, by its nature it is capable of changing into non-being." Furthermore, mercy has the highest power of judgment. For as it were it overrules justice and makes satisfaction for sinners. Therefore it takes upon itself, so to speak, the amends for the sins which it forgives. James, near the end: "Mercy exalts itself above judgment." In addition, it is the porter, or much rather the keeper of God's inn, who prepares a chamber for each guest. Ecclesiasticus 16: "Mercy shall make a place for every man according to the merit of his works

marg E. 36–37 **De hac misericordia** *om* E. 38–39 **vbi . . . dicens** *om* GL. 40–42 **Vbi . . . Gentibus** *om* G. 41 **que** qui J. 42 **per . . . eum** per carnem induit eam E; per caritatem unitur J. 43–44 **ut . . . legitur** *om* G. 44 **posset** possit FHILW. **Hec** *om* E. 45 **dereliquit** derelinquit JGI. 48–51 **Item . . . consumpti** *om* G. 49–50 **Trenorum** Ecclesiastici FIL. 52 **vnde** ut in JHILW; *om* FG. 53 **Set . . . uidetur** *om* L. 53–55 **Set . . . etc.** *om* F. 53 **hoc . . . quod** ***(2nd)*** *om* G. 54–55 **set . . . miseria** *om* EIL. 55 Glossa *marg* E. **xxv** *om* E. 56 **mandata** uerba J. 57 Augustinus *marg* E. 57–58 **Augustinus** *add* in E. 59 Solucio *marg* E. 60 **siue dispensante** *om* FILW. 61 **ibi** *om* E. 63 Augustinus Damascenus *marg* E. **in** ad J. 64 **est** *om* JGHI; *add* tendere F. 66 **et** *om* E. 68 **fine** *om* EL; ultimo G; 2 F. 73 **sic** sicut E. 74 **et conparat** ita eciam sperat E. **et conparat . . .**

nos fecit." Item misericordia celos inclinauit et Deum de celo deposuit, ut dicit Augustinus; suple: de celo in Uirginis uterum, de cruce in sepulcrum. Animam uero deposuit in abyssum. [De hac misericordia] Ieremie xxxi: "Caritate perpetua dilexi te, ideo attraxi te miserans te"; et ii, vbi alloqui- / f. 131^{v}a tur Dominus ecclesiam primorum fidelium dicens: "Recordatus sum tui, miserans adolescenciam tuam et caritatem desponsacionis tue." Vbi apparet quod misericordia copulauit eum antiquis patribus, que modo per carnem [uniuit eum] Ecclesie de Gentibus. Item misericordia ipsum Redemptorem uendidit pro redempcione captiuorum, ut posset de ea dici quod legitur Sapiencie x: "[Hec] venditum iustum non dereliquit set a peccatoribus liberauit illum." Licet hoc ad litteram conueniat Ioseph, tamen eius uendicio Christi uendicionem prefigurauit, de qua predixit Zacharie xi: "Appenderunt precium meum triginta argenteis." Item sicut misericordia redemit, sic ipsa miseros custodit et a peccato et a supplicio; Trenorum iii: "Misericordie Domini multe, quia non sumus consumpti." Item non solum terra set eciam celum indiget misericordia; vnde Psalmus: "Domine, in celo misericordia tua." Set contra hoc uidetur quod dicit Anshelmus, quod ubi non est miseria, nullus indiget misericordia; set in celo constat quod nulla est miseria, ergo, etc. Et Glossa super Leuitici [xxv] ibi, "Sabbatum requiecionis erit": "In futuro cessabunt mandata ewangelica." Set illa potissime sunt de misericordia; quare, etc. Et Augustinus ° libro *De caritate*: "Tolle miseros, et cessabunt opera misericordie." Ad hoc dicas quod celum non indiget misericordia relaxante siue dispensante circa penam uel culpam, / f. 131^{v}b quia nullus [ibi] "incircumcisus uel immundus," etc., Isaie lii. Indiget tamen misericordia continente et saluante, ne de sua condicione tendat in nichilum. Secundum Augustinum et secundum Damascenum "omne creabile uertibile, idest, de sui natura possibile est ad non esse." Item misericordia habet supremam iudiciariam potestatem. Ipsa enim quasi inperat iusticie [et] pro peccatoribus satisfacit. Vnde quasi in se suscipit emendas culparum quas remittit. Iacobi [fine]: "Superexaltat misericordia iudicium." Item ipsa est hostiaria, immo custos hospicii Dei, que singulis parat mansionem. Ecclesiastici xvi: "Misericordia faciet locum unicuique secundum

and according to the understanding of his pilgrimage"; that is to say: as he understands that he is a pilgrim, so does he recognize that he is miserable and has mercy for his neighbor and acquires a reward and prize for himself. Moreover, that mercy puts itself against justice is manifest in Christ's passion. In his justice the Father threatened mankind, and out of mercy the Son offered his body to the blow, just as one holds up one's hand or arm against a person that tries to strike. The Son is the Father's hand, for through the Son the Father has performed all his works. And the Son is called arm because in him the Father's strength is shown and his enemy is thrown down. Moreover, by means of the arm the hand is connected to the body, and by means of the Son we are connected to the Father, we who are the work of his hand. The Son is quite properly the Father's arm, because in him the bloodletting was undertaken, which is the purging of the whole body, that is, the Church. In bloodletting the arm is bared, bound, spat on, and cut open; and all these things were done to the Son. Isaias 52: "The Lord has prepared his arm in the sight of all the nations." This is the arm which received the blow and healed us with his bruises, Isaias 53. In addition, mercy shares in all the losses or injuries or trials of our neighbors, because it feels and suffers with all men, 2 Corinthians 12. Out of deepest mercy were these words spoken: "Who is weak, and I am not weak?" Mercy is ready to sustain all trials and sufferings for its neighbor. It bears fruit more easily in the most barren soil, for in rich humus it produces sterility, that is to say, it bears fruit in the poor, but among the rich it chokes. Thus Luke 14: "When you make a feast, call the lame," and so forth. Also, mercy has a special keeper of its goods, the Lord himself, who says: "Lay up to yourselves treasures in heaven, where neither rust nor the thief," and so forth, Matthew 6. In contrast, what is kept by men gets either stolen or ruined or lost in some other way. Further, mercy makes the Highest One himself our debtor; Proverbs 19: "He that has mercy on the poor lends to the Lord." It also assures the forgiveness of sins. He who forgives all has all forgiven; Luke 6: "Forgive, and you shall be forgiven." In contrast, the wicked servant is convicted because, while all his debt was forgiven, he had no mercy on his fellowman, Matthew 18.

Notice that God's mercy is manifold. One kind forgives; Luke 6: "Forgive, and you shall be forgiven." Another kind spares or mitigates the debt that is owed; Lamentations 3: "Many are the mercies of the Lord, that we are not con-

premium *om* FL. 75 **opponit** opposuit E. **opponit se** opponitur W. **manifestum est** monstratum est F; ut patet G; manifestum H. 76 **generi** *om* E. 77 **corpus** *marg, to be inserted for* se patri *canc* E. 78 **opponere** obicere F. 80 **Preterea** item FL. 82 **qui** quia JF. **manus** manuum J; *om* F. 83 **minucio idest** *om* L. 85 **ligatur** *om* E. **Filio** in Filio JFILW. 87 **liuore** uulnere G. 89 **siue** et E. 92–93 **Ipsa . . . proximo** *om* I. 93 **proximo** Christo FL. **melius** *om* E; mens I. 94 **pingui** fertili J. **sterilitatem** subtilitatem E. 96 **uoca** *add* pauperes JI. **specialem** spiritualem E. 97 **custodem** custodiam E. **ipsum** Christum F. 99 **uero** nec E. 103 **Qui** quia EL. 105 **Econtra** Mt. E. 106 **habuit** habet J. 108–9 **ignoscens** enim

meritum operum suorum et secundum intellectum peregrinacionis ipsius"; idest: secundum quod intelligit se peregrinum, secundum hoc cognoscit se miserum, et [sic] habet misericordiam ad proximum, [et conparat] sibi meritum et premium. Item quod misericordia [opponit] se iusticie manifestum est in Christi passione. Pater de iusticia comminatus est humano [generi], et Filius de misericordia obiecit corpus ferienti, sicut solet aliquis manum uel brachium opponere percucienti. Filius enim est manus Patris, quia per ipsum cuncta operatus est. Et brachium dicitur, quia in ipso fortitudo Patris ostenditur et hostis prosternitur. Preteraea mediante brachio adheret manus corpori, et mediante Filio adheremus nos Patri, qui opus manus eius sumus. Item / bene est Fi- f. 132ra
lius brachium Patris, quia in ipso facta est minucio, idest purgacio tocius corporis, quod est Ecclesia. Brachium enim nudatur, [ligatur,] conspuitur, uulneratur; et hec omnia facta sunt Filio. Ysaie lii: "Parauit Dominus brachium suum in oculis omnium gencium." Hoc est brachium quod ictum suscepit et suo liuore nos sanauit, Ysaie liii. Item misericordia communicat omnibus detrimentis [siue] dampnis siue periculis proximorum, quia omnibus condolet et omnibus conpatitur, II Corinthiorum xii. Ex intima misericordia dictum est illud: "Quis infirmatur et ego non infirmor?" Ipsa enim omnia pericula et tormenta parata est sustinere pro proximo. Item ipsa in terra macerrima [melius] fructificat, quia in pingui humo [sterilitatem] parit, idest fructificat in pauperibus, suffocatur in diuitibus. Ideo Luce xiiii: "Cum facis conuiuium, uoca claudos," etc. Item misericordia [specialem] habet [custodem] bonorum suorum, ipsum Dominum qui dicit: "Thesaurizate uobis thesaurum in celis ubi nec erugo neque fur," etc., Matthei vi. Que [uero] ab hominibus custodiuntur, aut furantur aut corrumpuntur aut alio modo subtrahuntur. Item misericordia ipsum Altissimum facit debitorem; Prouerbiorum xix: "Feneratur Domino qui miseretur pauperi." Item ipsa habet securitatem remissionis peccatorum. [Qui] enim omnia dimittit, omnia dimittuntur ei; / Luce vi: "Dimittite, et dimittetur uobis." f. 132rb
[Econtra] seruus nequam redarguitur, quia cum omne debitum sit ei dimissum, nullam habuit misericordiam ad proximum, Matthei xviii.

Et nota quod multiplex est Dei misericordia. Alia est [ignoscens]; Luce vi: "Dimittite, et dimittetur uobis." Alia est parcens siue relaxans de pena debita; Trenorum iii: "Misericordie Domini

sumed." Another kind corrects; Wisdom 12: "When we are judged, we hope for your mercy," and so forth. Another one intercedes; Hebrews 7: "He makes intercession for us," and so forth. It even interceded for enemies, when it spoke: "Father, forgive them," and so forth. Another kind comes to assistance in our needs; Ecclesiasticus 35: "The mercy of God is beautiful in the time of affliction."

Mercy also calls us to penance; Proverbs 1: "I called, and you refused." It waits for penance and suspends judgment; Isaias 30: "God waits, that he may have mercy on us; therefore shall he be exalted sparing us." Mercy also "overlooks sins because of our penitence," Wisdom 12. For these reasons mercy is said to have bowels—Luke 2: "Through the bowels of the mercy of our God"—, for in the bowels vile matter is retained until it is expelled, and God's mercy bears with our vileness until it is improved or punished. It also promises grace to him who returns; Jeremias 3: "Return to me, and I will receive you." However, Gregory says that "he who promises the penitent grace does not promise him the morrow."

Many things invite us to be merciful. First the mercy of God, which is endless; whence it is also said to be greater than all his works; as in the Psalm: "His mercies," and so forth. Moreover, it is directed not only to his friends but also to his enemies. For "he makes his sun to rise upon the good and the bad," Matthew 5, and Ecclesiasticus 18: "The compassion of man is toward his neighbor; but the mercy of God is upon all flesh." Chrysostom: "Blessed are the merciful, etc. Not only is he merciful who has compassion for the orphan and the widow. Such mercy is quite often found even among those who do not know God. But he is merciful who has compassion for his own enemy and does him good after the Lord's commandment: 'Do good to them that hate you,' etc." Further, he gives abundantly, James 1, and upbraids no one; but others give few things and upbraid much, Ecclesiasticus 20. And how abundantly God gives is manifest: He gives temporal goods for their necessary uses; he gives goods in time, that is, virtues, so that we might gain merit; and he gives goods above time, that is, eternal goods, as our reward. In addition, his mercy will never fail, nor can it be exhausted by our miseries; Isaias 54: "The mountains and hills shall be moved, but my mercy shall not fail." In contrast, our own mercy "is as

innocens E; innocens H. 117 **Item ipsa** ipsa eciam E; item misericordia F; ipsa ILW. 118 **Ipsa** *add* eciam E. 120 **Item ipsa** ipsa eciam E; ipsa FGL. 121 **penitenciam** misericordiam J. 122 **ii** xii E; 5 G. 124–25 **corigantur uel puniantur** corrigamur uel puniamur E. 126 Gregorius *marg* E. **dicit . . . quod** Gregorius L. 127–28 **promittit** *add* de misericordia *rubr* J. 130 **et** *om* E. 131 **vnde** ut in JH; *om* FGILW. **Miseraciones** misericordia FILW. **eius** tue E. **etc.** *add* Ecclesiastici 5: "Secundum magnitudinem eius sic misericordia eius cum ipso est." Set magnitudinis eius non est finis; ergo infinita G. 132 **set . . . inimicos** *om* F. **Facit** fecit E. 135 **Crisostomus** Mt E; *om* L. 137 **et** aut FIW. 138 **Deum** *marg* E. **proprii** *om* EL. 139–42 **Benefacite . . . det** *om* G. 141–42 **alii . . . inproperant** *om*

multe, quia non sumus consumpti." Alia est corripiens; Sapiencie xii: "Cum de nobis iudicatur, speramus misericordiam tuam," etc. Alia est intercedens; Hebreorum vii: "Interpellat pro nobis," etc. Ista intercessit eciam pro inimicis cum dixit: "Pater, ignosce illis," etc. Alia est subueniens in neccessitatibus; Ecclesiastici xxxv: "Speciosa misericordia Dei in tempore tribulacionis."

[Item ipsa] uocat ad penitenciam; Prouerbiorum i: "Vocaui et rennuisti." Ipsa ° expectat ad penitenciam et suspendit sentenciam; Ysaie xxx: "Expectat Deus ut misereatur nostri; propterea exaltabitur parcens nobis." [Item ipsa] "dissimulat peccata propter penitenciam," Sapiencia xii. Hiis de causis dicitur misericordia habere uiscera—Luce [ii]: "Per uiscera misericordie Dei nostri"—, quia intra uiscera continentur turpia donec emittantur, et misericordia Dei tolerat feda nostra donec [corigantur uel puniantur]. Item ipsa reuertenti promittit ueniam; Ieremie iii: "Reuertere ad me, et ego suscipiam te." Dicit tamen Gregorius quod "qui penitenti ueni- / am spondet, diem crastinum non promit- f. 132va
tit."

Multa inuitant nos ad misericordiam. Primo misericordia Dei, que est infinita; vnde [et] maior dicitur omnibus operibus suis; vnde Psalmus: "Miseraciones [eius]," etc. Preterea ipsa non solum est ad amicos set eciam ad inimicos. [Facit] enim "solem suum oriri super bonos et malos," Matthei v, et Ecclesiastici xviii: "Miseracio hominis circa proximum suum; misericordia autem Dei super omnem carnem." [Crisostomus]: "Beati misericordes, etc. Non tantum ille misericors est qui miseretur pupilli et uidue. Hec enim misericordia sepius inuenitur eciam apud illos qui non cognoscunt Deum. Ille uero misericors est qui [proprii] inimici miseretur et benefacit ei iuxta preceptum Domini: 'Benefacite hiis qui oderunt uos,' etc." Item ipse dat habundanter, Iacobi i, et nulli inproperat; [alii uero pauca dant et multa inproperant,] Ecclesiastici xx. Et quam habundanter det, patet: Dat enim bona temporis ad usus necessarios; dat bona in tempore, idest uirtutes, pro meritis consequendis; dat bona supra tempus, idest eterna, in precium remuneracionis. Item sua misericordia nunquam deficiet nec nostris miseriis exhauriri potest; Ysaie liiii: "Montes et colles commouebuntur, misericordia autem mea non

a morning cloud and as the dew that goes away in the morning," Osee 6. For a cloud and the dew are dispersed by a light breeze; thus, our mercy is quickly troubled or completely dispersed by the wind of anger or envy. The examples of the saints, too, urge us to be merciful. Blessed Martin divided his cloak; blessed Lawrence distributed the Church's money and gave it to the poor, and was not afraid of the glowing coals and the gridiron. Of blessed Anselm we also read that his almoner, having given alms twice on the same day to a poor man who changed his appearance, and then catching him a third time, asked the archbishop whether he should give him alms or not. Anselm, filled with mercy, replied: "Give. Perhaps it is the Lord, tempting me." We also read about the bishop of Nola, as Gregory reports in his *Dialogue,* that when he had exhausted his means in the works of mercy, he sold himself into captivity in order to buy the captive son of a widow. Whereupon the merciful Lord freed him and, with many other prisoners, reinstalled him in his former position. Similarly, the bishop of Charotae, having drained his means in works of mercy, secretly stole what he might give the poor. As he was accused of theft he said: "For the just man there is no law. For I do not rob this person of what belongs to him, but I give back to that what belongs to him." But notice that Jerome says that the privileges of the few must not become a general custom. We further read in the *Lives of the Fathers* of someone who had a gospel book that was much needed by the brethren for their reading, and as he read in it one day the words of Matthew 19, "If you will be perfect, go and sell," and so forth, he sold his book and gave the money to the poor." When he was asked by his brethren why he had done that, he replied: "I have sold the word that told me to sell everything and give it to the poor." If only those would attend to this who take such great pains to produce superfluous deluxe books, with gold letters and covers of silk or satin, made more for showiness and elegance than for edification and usefulness, and they might find some use in what we read of certain people in the Acts of the Apostles, 19: "Many of them who had followed curious arts brought together their books and burnt them before all." Nature itself also invites us to be merciful and compassionate. For when one member is hurt, the spirit and humors of the other members quickly move to the painful spot. Thus should our pity and compassion hasten to those who are in pain and tribulation,

E. 145 **precium** premium J. 149 **Osee vi** *om* E. 150 **uel** *add* superbie uel F. 152 Exempla *marg* E. 154 **dedit pauperibus** *om* FL. **neque craticulam** FL; in craticula IW. 155 **eciam** *om* EJ; autem H. 156 **in *(2nd)* . . . mutato** *om* L. 157 **ab eodem** *om* I. **archiepiscopo** episcopo E. 159 **Nolano** Volano J; Ionalo G; Nonalo H; beato Valerio I; beato Nicholao F; Nicholao LW. 160 Gregorius *marg* E. **episcopo . . . Dyalogo** *om* FLW. 162 **redimendo** inde redempto J. 163–64 **cum . . . restituit** alios multos captiuos proprio officio restituit F. 164 **Charotarum** Charetarum JGHIW; Carecarum L; Cathecarum F. 165 **reprehensus** deprehensus JFILW. 167–68 **Nota . . . consuetudinem** *om* L. 168 Ieronimus *marg* E. 168–69 **non . . . consuetudinem** etc G. 168 **sunt** *om* EGH. 169 **consuetudinem** consequenciam JFHIW. 170 **ewangelicum** euangelii J. 174 **uendidi** inueni E. 175 **qui** *add* habent FILW. 176 **sericis** purpureis F. 177 **conscribere** scribere JFILW. 178–79 **et . . . eis** quibus credo G. 184 **accurrunt** accedunt J. **et *(2nd)*** *om* EFILW. 186 Gregorius *marg* E. **Redemptoris** creatoris J. 187 **nostri** *om*

deficiet." Econtra nostra misericordia "quasi nubes matutina et quasi ros mane pertransiens," [Osee vi]. Nubes enim et ros a modico uento disperguntur; sic nostra misericordia uento ire / uel f. 132vb inuidie aut cito turbatur aut omnino dispergitur. Item ad misericordiam nos prouocant sanctorum exempla. Beatus Martinus diuisit clamidem; beatus Laurencius Ecclesie peccuniam dispersit et dedit pauperibus, non formidauit carbones neque craticulam. Legitur [eciam] de beato Anshelmo quod cum elemosinarius suus bis in die dedisset egeno in diuersam personam mutato, cum tercio esset ab eodem deprehensus, quesiuit ab [archiepiscopo] an tali conferret an non. Qui plenus misericordia respondit: "Da illi. Forsitan Dominus est et temptat me." Legitur eciam de Nolano episcopo, sicut refert Gregorius in *Dyalogo,* quod cum esset exhaustus in operibus misericordie, seipsum uendidit in captiuitatem pro captiuo filio uidue redimendo. Vnde et Dominus misericors eum liberauit et cum multis aliis captiuis proprio officio eum restituit. Item Charotarum episcopus in operibus misericordie exhaustus clam rapiebat que pauperibus daret. Vnde reprehensus tanquam de furto ait: "Iusto nulla lex posita est. Non enim illi quod suum est surripio, set isti quod suum est reddo." Nota tamen quod dicit Ieronimus, quod priuilegia paucorum non [sunt] trahenda in consuetudinem. Item legitur de quodam in *Vitas Patrum* quod cum haberet codicem ewangelicum fratribus le- / gen- f. 133ra tibus satis necessarium et legeret in eo quadam die illud Matthei xix: "Si uis perfectus esse, vade et uende," etc., uendidit ipse codicem suum et dedit pauperibus. Requisitus a fratribus quare hoc fecisset, respondit: "Verbum [uendidi] quod precepit omnia uendi et dari pauperibus." Vtinam hoc attenderent qui libros sumptuosos et superfluos cum aureis litteris et uelamentis sericis uel bissinis tam diligenter conscribere student, magis ad ostentacionem et curiositatem quam ad edificacionem et utilitatem, et esset eis utile quod de quibusdam in Actibus Apostolorum legitur, xix: "Multi ex eis qui erant curiosa sectati contulerunt libros et conbusserunt coram omnibus." Item ad misericordiam et conpassionem nos inuitat ipsa natura. Vno enim membro uulnerato, spiritus et humores aliorum membrorum ad locum dolentem accurrunt. Sic nostra pietas et conpassio ad dolentes [et] in tribula-

since we are members of each other, Corinthians 12; and Gregory: "We do not otherwise become members of our Redeemer than by clinging to God and having pity on our neighbor." Also the nature of irrational animals teaches us to have mercy. For the stork provides its weak and infirm parents with what they need. The same can be found to be true of fierce wolves. For someone has reported that he saw two wolves leading a blind female between them. Therefore, let human pitilessness and the tyrants' cruelty blush, which neither feel compassion for other people nor deserve mercy.

Many causes compel us to be merciful. First is the imitation of God, who is so merciful that he, as it were, suffers with us when he cannot be compassionate with our miseries; Isaias 1: "Ah, I will comfort myself over my adversaries." Before his vengeance he gives an expression of his pain, whereby he shows how great his compassion is. This is prefigured in David, 2 Kings 9, when after being anointed king and made strong in his kingship, he asked if anyone was left over from the house of Saul toward whom he should show mercy. "Saul" means abusing or striving and indicates our ancient enemy, who, by abusing his natural goods and striving for a superior place, came to a fall. Of his house are those who live in mortal sin, toward whom David, that is, Christ, nonetheless wants to show mercy, as he patiently waits for their penitence. And we should imitate him in his works of mercy, not his works of justice, for only he knows the amount of guilt and pain, he who cannot be deceived by either the quality of a sin or the disposition of the sinner, as Origen says in his comment on Numbers. The second reason for being merciful is that we ourselves may obtain mercy; Osee 10: "Sow justice in truth, and reap in the mouth of mercy." To sow justice is to perform the works of mercy to which we are obligated by justice. To reap in the mouth of mercy is to receive a pleasing reward when it will be said: "Come, you blessed of my Father," etc., Matthew 25. The third reason is that we may be mindful of our own need. Seneca: "He that is merciful towards the unfortunate is mindful of himself." The fourth is that we may obey the Gospel; Luke 6: "Be merciful as," and so forth. The fifth is the fulfillment of the natural precept; Tobias 4: "According to your ability be merciful; if you have much," and so forth. But man-made law seems to contradict this, as in Exodus 23: "You shall not have mercy on a poor man in judgment." But the solution to this objection lies in the following verse, because one must not have

E. 188 **irracionalis** irracionabilis JGI; irracionabilium FL. **natura . . . misericordiam** *om* L. 189 **necessaria** *om* FL. 190 **rapidissimis** rapacissimis FL; rapadissimis H. **enim** *om* EF. **qui** quidam quod JF; quod H. 191 **cecam ferentes** circumferentes E. **inter se** *om* E. 194 **Cause** item E. **plures** *add* raciones E. 196 **quod** *marg* E. **pro** *om* GILW. **miseriis** *add* non *interl* E. 199 **ix** xx E; *om* GW. 203 **cuius** eius JGH. 204 **in** *add* peccato EI. 208 **qualitas** quantitas J. 209 Origenes *marg* E. 209–10 **Secunda . . . est** item G; *thus consistently for reasons 2–12, with reversal of 6 and 7 and omissions.* 210 **Osee x** omnes enim E. 213 **gratam retribucionem** graciam retribucionis JG. **recipere** percipere HIW; percipietis G. 215 Seneca *marg* E. **nostre** misericordie E; *om* F. 215–16 **in calamitosos** *om* E; in calamitate J; in calamitos H. 216 **Quarta** *add* racio FILW. 216–17 **Quarta . . . obediamus** *om* G. 217 **Quinta** *add* racio FW. 219 Questio *marg* E. **ei** *om* E. 220 Solucio *marg* E. 221 **in *(2nd)* . . . non** non ea de causa JFGHILW. **non** *marg* E. 225 Tullius

cione positos accurrat, cum simus alter alterius membra, Corinthiorum xii; et Gregorius: “Non aliter membra Redemptoris [nostri] efficimur, nisi inherendo Deo et conpaciendo proximo.” Item irracionalis natura animalium docet misericordiam. Cyconia enim parentibus infirmis et debilibus necessaria ministrat. Idem eciam legitur de lupis rapidissimis. Retulit [enim] qui uidit duos lupos u- / nam lupam [cecam] ferentes [inter se]. Erubescat ergo f. 133rb humana inpietas et tyrannorum crudelitas qui nec hominum miserentur nec misericordiam merentur.

[Cause] conpellentes nos ad misericordiam sunt plures °. Prima est Dei imitacio, qui in tantum est misericors quod quasi condolet nobis quod pro nostris miseriis misereri non potest; Ysaie i: “Heu, consolabor super hostibus meis.” Ante uindictam premittit notam doloris, ut ostendat magnitudinem sue conpassionis. Hoc figuratur in Dauid, II Regum [ix], qui iam unctus in regem et corroboratus in regno quesiuit si superesset aliquis de domo Saul cum quo faceret misericordiam. “Saul” interpretatur abutens uel peticio, et antiquum hostem signat qui bonis naturalibus abutens et excellenciam petens casum inuenit. De cuius domo sunt qui in ° mortali existunt, cum quibus tamen Dauid, idest Christus, uult facere misericordiam, quos pacienter expectat ad penitenciam. Et nos debemus imitari ipsum in operibus misericordie, non in operibus iusticie, quia ipse solus nouit quantitatem culpe et pene, quem nec fallit peccati qualitas nec peccantis affectus, ut dicit Origenes super Numeri. Secunda racio est ut misericordiam consequamur; [Osee x]: “Seminate in ueritate iusticiam, et metite in ore misericordie.” Iusticiam / seminare f. 133va est opera misericordie exercere ad que tenemur de iusticia. In ore misericordie metere est gratam retribucionem recipere, cum dicetur: “Venite, benedicti Patris,” etc., Matthei xxv. Tercia racio est ut [nostre] necessitatis memores simus. Seneca: “Qui [in calamitosos] misericors est, sui meminit.” Quarta est ut Ewangelio obediamus; Luce vi: “Estote misericordes sicut,” etc. Quinta est inplecio precepti naturalis; Thobie iiii: “Prout potueris, esto misericors; si multum,” etc. Contraria tamen uidetur [ei] lex positiua, Exodi xxiii: “Non misereberis pauperis in iudicio.” Set solucio est in sequenti littera, quia in ea causa non miserendum est

mercy on a poor man in a case where "one would stray from the truth" or where one would support him in his error. What must be supported in the poor is their natural needs, not their sin. Therefore says Ecclesiasticus 12: "Give to the just, and do not receive the sinner"; add: that you should share in his sin. And Tullius says that "our kindness to the unfortunate must be prompt, unless they deserve their misfortune." The sixth reason is that we may lay up a treasure in heaven. For there is the proper storehouse of mercy; Matthew 6: "Lay up to yourselves treasures in heaven," and so forth. This can also be found in the history of blessed Lawrence: "The goods you are looking for, the hands of the poor have carried them to the treasure in heaven." The seventh reason is that we may preserve our human nature in those that are like us, as we naturally love it in them; Job 5: "Visiting your kind you shall not sin." The eighth is that we put those who receive our kindnesses under an obligation to us. Therefore the Psalm says: "Take a psalm," and so forth. "Psalm" comes from *psallin,* that is, to touch, and indicates a good deed. Therefore those who receive benefices are told: "Receive pious gifts and pay back with the help of your prayers." The ninth is that we render to the Lord in turn, "giving to the Most High according to his gift," Ecclesiasticus 35. This is what those who are grateful for God's kindnesses do. They say to him: "What we have received from your hand we have given you," Paralipomenon at the end. The tenth reason is that we escape his threat; James at the end: "Judgment without mercy to him that does not do mercy." The eleventh is that we may put the giver of all things under an obligation to us; Proverbs 19: "He that has mercy on the poor lends to the Lord." And the twelfth is that we may receive his blessing; Proverbs 22: "He that is inclined to mercy shall be blessed."

Another definition of mercy is: "Mercy is a compassionate and calm respect in one's mind and its sympathetic bending down towards the unfortunate." *Pietas* is the worship offered to God, which results in love of our neighbor; or else, it is the attitude of helpfulness that comes from the sweetness of a kind heart and from grace. Another definition was given earlier. Indulgence is forgiving another person's guilt, based on self-knowledge. Compassion is when a sympathetic heart is afflicted by someone else's suffering. All these virtues are closely related to mercy and are dear daughters of charity.

Mercy is a tree whose root is compassion, whose leaves comforting words,

marg E. **peccato** peccatori G; *om* FL. **calamitosos** calamitis E. 226 **prompcior** proximior FL. **debetur** debet esse J; est L. 227 **Sexta** *reverse reasons 6 and 7* G; *add* racio FILW. **est** *om* E. 228 **vi** *om* E. 230 **celestes thesauros** celum FIL. 231 **Septima** *add* racio FIL. 231–32 **consimilibus** similibus FL. 232 **naturaliter** *om* FL. 233 **Octaua** *add* racio FL. 234 **obligamus** obligamur E. **Vnde** *add* in EH; *om* I. 237 **suffragia** suffragium JFGHIW. **suffragia oracionis** opera caritatis L. **Nona** *add* racio FW. 238 **uicem** inuicem EG. 239 **suum** *om* E; eius F. 241 **fine** *om* E; ultimo G; 29 F; 20 L. **Decima** *add* racio I. 242 **fine** *om* EL; ultimo G; 2 F. 243 **Vndecima** *add* racio W. 243–45 **Vndecima . . . pauperi** *om* G. 245 **Duodecima** *add* racio W. 252 **affectio** effectio E. **Aliter . . . supra** *om* FL. 253 **Conpassio est** conpassione *(part of preceding sentence)* E. 258 **respectus** affectus F. 259–60

pauperi "ut quis a uero deuiet" uel ipsum in errore foueat. Fouenda est enim natura in pauperibus, non culpa. Ideo dicitur Ecclesiastici xii: "Da iusto, et ne receperis peccatorem"; suple: ut peccato communices. Et Tullius dicit quod "in [calamitosos] prompcior debetur benignitas, nisi forte sint calamitate digni." Sexta [est] ut in celo thesaurizemus. Ibi enim est proprium depositorium misericordie; Matthei [vi]: "Thesaurizate uobis in celo," etc. Hoc eciam legitur in hystoria beati Laurencii: "Facultates quas requiris in celestes thesauros manus pauperum deportauerunt." Septima est ut speciem nostram saluemus in nostris consimilibus, sicut eam in nostro consimili naturaliter diligimus; / Iob f. 133vb v: "Visitans speciem tuam non peccabis." Octaua est quia recipientes beneficia nobis [obligamus]. Vnde ° Psalmo: "Sumite psalmum," etc. "Psalmus" dicitur a psallin, quod est tangere, et signat bonam operacionem. Dicitur igitur beneficia recipientibus: "Accipite opera pietatis et rependite suffragia oracionis." Nona est ut [uicem] Domino reddamus, "dantes Altissimo secundum datum [suum]," Ecclesiastici xxxv. Hoc enim faciunt grati beneficiis Dei. Dicunt enim ei: "Que de manu tua accepimus, dedimus tibi," Paralypomenon [fine]. Decima est ut comminacionem uitemus; Iacobi [fine]: "Iudicium sine misericordia ei qui non facit misericordiam." Vndecima est ut datorem omnium obligemus nobis; Prouerbiorum xix: "Feneratur Domino qui miseretur pauperi." Duodecima est ut benedictionem consequamur; Prouerbiorum xxii: "Qui pronus est ad misericordiam benedicetur."

Alia est diffinicio misericordie: "Misericordia est clemens et equalis racionis dignacio et in afflictos conpassibilis animi inclinacio." Pietas est cultus Deo exhibitus, erga proximum operans caritatem; vel pietas est ex benigne mentis dulcedine et gracia auxiliatrix [affectio]. Aliter diffinitur supra. Indulgencia est alieni reatus remissio ex sui consideracione descendens. [Conpassio est] per quam ex proximi dolore condolenti animo quedam generatur afflictio. / Omnes iste uirtutes cognate sunt misericordie et cario- f. 134ra res filie caritatis.

Misericordia est arbor, cuius radix conpassio, folia uerba consolacionis, flores pii respectus, dulces auditus, et huiusmodi,

whose blossoms tender looks, sweet attention, and the like, whose fruit kind deeds, whose sap a charitable disposition, and whose foliage the seven bodily works of mercy. Mercy is further the wellspring of paradise, Genesis 2. Its seven streams can be called the seven works of mercy. This is the well of oil which, according to some, sprang from the earth at the coming of our Savior. Mercy is likewise Jacob's ladder, Genesis 28, whose two sides are heartfelt compassion and active generosity, whose rungs are the seven works of mercy; the base of this ladder is that a person begins with himself, its length is perseverance, and its top that all things are done for the sake of God and the reward of eternal life. Further, mercy is oil. Isidore: *"oleos"* in Greek is mercy in Latin. For oil floats on top of all other liquids. It does not mix with any juice other than what is similar to itself, that is, the mucous sap of the hollyhock. Similarly, the works of mercy are better not only than the works of the world and the flesh, but also than those of the other virtues, as is written about God most merciful: "His tender mercies are over all his works." Therefore, the Gloss on the Gospel says that mercy alone accompanies the dead—not that the soul will not carry the other virtues with it, but because the works of this particular virtue are of the greatest help to the dead. And thus it says in the Epistle for the dead, from Apocalypse 14: "Their works follow them," that is, not simply the reward or retribution for their works, as some say, but the very works which they performed while alive obligate the Church to pray for the departed. Oil also gives light, for it is the fuel for fire. Thus the works of mercy give light to the soul on its way toward its home. Therefore the prudent virgins, that is, wise souls, take oil in their vessels, Matthew 25. Oil also refreshes; thus the works of mercy are a refreshment for the soul. Hesychius comments on Leviticus 25: "In the future we shall eat the fruit of the works we have done here." In addition, when oil is poured into fire, it makes it burn more fiercely; thus the works of mercy kindle the fervor of love. This is why Nehemiah had the sacrifice be sprinkled with thick water, and a great fire was kindled, 2 Machabees 1. The thick water is oil; for any liquid shares in the special nature of water, as the Philosopher declares. Moreover, oil heals the shattered members; thus mercy heals souls that are weakened by sin. This is why Ecclesiasticus 17 says that almsgiving "strengthens those that faint in patience." Oil is also good

opera ***(2nd)*** operaciones J. 260 **exterioris** exteriores J; *om* FG; *add* que sic possunt intelligi: Vestio, poto, cibo, tectum do, uisito, soluo, quo defunctus eget non tua cura neget. De primo Ysaie 58: "Cum uideris nudum," etc. De secundo et tercio Prouerbiorum 55 [23] et Iob 31: "Si comedi bucellam [meam solus]," etc. De quarto Romanorum 13: "Hospitalitatem nolite," etc. De quinto Ecclesiastici 7: "Non te pigeat uisitare." De sexto Prouerbiorum 24: "Erue eos," etc. De septimo Ecclesiastici 7: "Mortuo non prohibeas," etc. FL; *text from* L; F *variants in square brackets*; F *omits* Non . . . Ecclesiastici 7. 261 **Septem** vnde E; sunt F; *om* L. 267 Ysidorus *marg* E. **et . . . eterne** *om* G. 268 **oleos** oleon E. 269 **Nulli** nullo E. **suco** fluctui F; succui L. 270 **idest . . . pinguedini** *om* E. 271 **carnis** caritatis E. 272–73 **sicut . . . Deo** *om* G. 273 **Deo** *add* Psalmus JG. **Ideo** item J; ut FILW; unde G. 274 Glossa *marg* E. 275 **quin** quod F; quia GI. **quin . . . deferat** quod non comitentur E. 276 **huius** eius E; *om* W. 276–77 **defunctis** *add* et E. 277 **Ideo . . . mortuis** *om* G. 280 **uiuentes . . . defunctis** *om* F. **iam** animabus J; *om* GW. 283 **sumunt** sumpserunt J; ponunt F. 285 Glossa *marg* E. **Esicius** esurienti. Glossa E. 287 **feruorem** ignem FL. 288 **perfundi** profundi JFGI. 290 **liquabile** liquibile ⟨uel liquabile⟩ J; liquibile FL. 291 Philosophus *marg* E. 293 **confirmat** infirmat GH; consumat I. 295 **sacre** *om* E. 298 **sacris** sanctis FGLW; *om* I.

fructus opera pietatis, humor interior caritas, frondes septem opera misericordie exterioris. Item misericordia est fons paradysi, Genesis ii. [Septem] eius riuuli septem eius opera possunt dici. Hec est fons olei qui secundum quosdam erupit de terra in ortu Saluatoris. Item misericordia est scala Iacob, Genesis xxviii, cuius duo latera sunt conpassio cordis et largitas operis, interscalaria septem eius opera; profundum huius scale est ut homo a se incipiat, longitudo eius perseuerancia, altitudo ut omnia fiant pro Deo et premio uite eterne. Item misericordia est oleum. Ysidorus: ["oleos"] Grece, misericordia Latine. Oleum enim aliis liquoribus superenatat. [Nulli] enim suco miscetur nisi sibi simili [idest muscilagini malue, idest eius pinguedini]. Similiter opera misericordie non solum operibus mundi et [carnis], set eciam aliarum uirtutum operibus excellunt, sicut dicitur de misericordissimo Deo: "Miseraciones eius super omnia opera eius." Ideo dicit Glossa super Ewangelium quod sola misericordia est comes defunctorum—non [quin anima deferat] secum habitus aliarum uirtu- / tum, set quia opera [huius] uirtutis maxime prosunt defunctis. f. 134rb ° Ideo dicitur in Epistula de mortuis, Apocalipsis xiiii: "Opera illorum secuntur illos," idest, non solum merces uel retribucio operum, ut quidam dicunt, set eciam ipsa opera que fecerunt uiuentes obligant Ecclesiam orare pro iam defunctis. Item oleum illuminat, quia pabulum ignis est. Sic opera misericordie illuminant animam ad uiam patrie. Ideo prudentes uirgines, idest anime sapientes, sumunt oleum in uasis suis, Matthei xxv. Item oleum reficit; sic opera misericordie sunt refectio anime. [Esicius] super Leuitici xxv: "Eorum que hic fecimus, in futuro fructum manducabimus." Item oleum infusum igni magis ardere facit; sic opera misericordie accendunt feruorem caritatis. Hoc est quod Neemias aqua crassa fecit sacrificium perfundi et accensa est flamma magna, II Machabeorum i. Aqua crassa oleum est; omne enim liquabile specialem habet naturam aque, ut dicit Philosophus. Item oleum medetur membris conquassatis; sic misericordia animabus per peccatum debilitatis. Hoc est quod dicitur Ecclesiastici xvii quod elemosina "confirmat deficientes sustinere." Item oleum ualet ad distemperandum colores quibus so-

for mixing the dyes with which sacred temples are commonly painted. Sacred temples are the faithful souls; Corinthians 3: "The temple of God is holy, which you are." The dyes are the virtues, which through the works of mercy become more brilliant to the eye. And notice that, just as in holy places one depicts the passions and miracles of the saints, so in unclean hearts is depicted the "likeness of creeping things," that is, of the envious or the proud, and "the abominations of living things," that is, of lechers, and "all the idols" of the greedy; Ezechiel 8: "Dig in the wall, and you will see these abominations." In addition, oil quenches fire on a stone but kindles it on wood; thus, mercy quenches the fire of lust in a stony heart. Of this speaks Ecclesiasticus 29: "Do not hide your money under a stone"; the Gloss comments: under a hardened and stony heart. About the quenching: Ecclesiasticus 3 says that as water quenches fire, so almsgiving quenches sin. Wood, which is the proper fuel for a fire, symbolizes a person who is well disposed to receive and to be subject unto grace. Such wood "the fire of the Lord consumed," 3 Kings 18. Oil also preserves tools from rust. The soul's rust is the corruption of sin. Whence Ecclesiasticus 12 says of the wicked: "As a brass pot his wickedness rusts." Moreover, the *History of Jerusalem* reports that oil quenches Greek fire; thus, mercy quenches the fire of hell. Therefore, the words of Isaias 43 tell a person who has mercy: "When you walk through the fire, the flame will not burn you." Oil also makes things mild and soft; thus, mercy makes the judge mild and softens his heart. Matthew 6: "Anoint your head and wash your face." To anoint the head is to soften Christ through the works of mercy or to gladden one's soul. Therefore Augustine says in his book *On the Lord's Sermon on the Mount*: "Anointing refers to gladness, washing to purity." Furthermore, when before an incision the vein is rubbed with oil, it lets blood more easily; and through works of mercy one achieves purgation more readily. Hence Ecclesiasticus 7: "Purify yourself with your arms," that is, with your works of mercy, through which sin is let as blood is through the arm. Also, things fried in oil become lighter; and works of mercy make lighter because they cancel the punishment for sins. Proverbs 15: "By mercy sins are purged away." Oil further has its lightness from the air, its density from earth; thus, mercy is made lighter by the hope of reward and becomes heavier from performing good deeds. This is why the spouse is found to be black but beautiful, Canticles 1; and Luke 10, although Martha was heavy with grief in her solicitude, yet she drew comfort from the Lord's presence. Mercy is the companion of every good work. Therefore, the commandment was given

299–300 **depingitur similitudo** depinguntur similitudines E; depinguntur similitudo H. 300 **idest** est E. **inuidorum** immundorum FI. 300–304 **in . . . ignem** *om* FL. 305–6 **De . . . corde** *follows after* peccatum *line 308* FL. 305 **quo** lapideo corde FL. 305–7 **Non . . . Ecclesiastici iii** *om* G. 306 Glossa *marg* E. 309 **figuratur** signatur JGHIW; significatur F. **dispositus** disposicio E. 311 **ferramenta** erramentum J; ferramentum FILW. 312 **eramentum** ferramentum FW. 316 **ardebit te** nocebit te nec ardebit J; nocebit te F. 319 **mitigare** imitari E. 320 Augustinus *marg* E. **Augustinus** *add* in E. 322 **peruncta** uncta FGILW. 323 **et** sic E. **consequitur** consequetur FLW; H *ends here.* 324 **Ideo** item J; vnde F; *om* G. 325 **minuitur peccatum** muniuntur F; minuuntur L. 328 **misericordiam** penitenciam E; penam FL; fidem et misericordiam G *and source.* 331 **legitur** loquitur FL; *om* W. **nigra** *add* sum JFLW. 333 **Domini est consolata** dei valde est consolata FGILW; domini est quieta vel consolidata J. **Item cum** quia in J; item quia cum FIL. **opere** *om* FL. 334 **siue** sit E. 336 **crux** opera J. 337 **marti-**

lent [sacre] edes depingi. Sacre edes sunt anime fide- / les; f. 134va Corinthiorum iii: “Templum Dei sanctum est, quod estis uos.” Colores sunt uirtutes que per opera misericordie lucidiores sunt in ostensione. Et nota quod sicut in locis sacris solent depingi passiones et miracula sanctorum, ita in cordibus immundis [depingitur “similitudo] reptilium,” [idest] inuidorum uel superborum, et “animalium abhominacio,” idest luxuriosorum, et “uniuersa ydola” auarorum; Ezechielis viii: “Fode parietem, et uidebis abhominaciones istas.” Item oleum extinguit ignem in lapide, accendit in ligno; sic misericordia extinguit ignem concupiscencie in lapideo corde. De quo Ecclesiastici xxix: “Non abscondas peccuniam sub lapide”; Glossa: sub duro et lapideo corde. De extinctione: Ecclesiastici iii, sicut aqua extinguit ignem, ita elemosina extinguit peccatum. In ligno autem, quod est debita materia ignis, figuratur [dispositus] ad graciam et subiectibilis ei. Talia ligna “uorat ignis Domini,” III Regum xviii. Item oleum seruat ferramenta a rubigine. Rubigo anime est corrupcio culpe. Vnde de iniquo dicitur Ecclesiastici xii: “Sicut eramentum eruginat nequicia illius.” Item dicitur in *Hystoria de Ierusalem* quod oleum extinguit ignem Grecum; sic mi- / sericordia infernale incen- f. 134vb dium. Vnde habenti misericordiam dicitur illud Ysaie xliii: “Cum transieris per ignem, flamma non ardebit te.” Item oleum mitigat et mollificat; sic misericordia mitigat iudicem et emollit animum. Ideo Matthei vi: “Vnge capud tuum et faciem tuam laua.” Caput ungere est Christum [mitigare] per opera misericordie uel ipsam animam letificare. Vnde Augustinus ° libro *De sermone Domini in monte*: “Vngere pertinet ad leticiam, lauare ad mundiciam.” Item uena fleubotomata peruncta oleo facilius emittit sanguinem; [et] per opera misericordie consequitur quis faciliorem purgacionem. Ideo Ecclesiastici vii: “Propurga te cum brachiis,” idest cum misericordie operibus, per que minuitur peccatum sicut sanguis per brachium. Item res oleo frixe leuiores sunt; et opera misericordie alleuiant, quia penam peccatorum remittunt. Prouerbiorum xv: “Per [misericordiam] purgantur peccata.” Item oleum leuitatem habet ex aere, grossiciem ex terra; sic misericordia ex spe mercedis alleuiatur, ex exercicio operum turbatur. Hoc est quod sponsa legitur nigra set formosa, Canticorum i; et Luce x, licet Martha ex sollicitudine sit turbata, tamen ex presencia Domini est consolata. Item cum omni opere bono comes misericordia. Ideo preceptum est Leuitici ii quod omnis oblacio [siue]

in Leviticus 2 that every offering, whether from the frying pan or the gridiron or the oven, should be anointed with oil. The oven symbolizes the world's affliction, the frying pan the cross of penance, and the gridiron the suffering of martyrdom. All these are burned without oil; that is, they become dry and lose their meritoriousness, unless mercy accompanies them.

Mercy has five species, which are derived from the Gospel. The first is to give; Luke 6: "Give, and it shall be given to you." The second is to lend, as in the same chapter: "Lend, hoping for nothing thereby." The third is to pardon, as in the same: "Forgive, and you shall be forgiven." The fourth is to show compassion, as the Lord taught when he wept over the city, Luke 19, and on another occasion over Lazarus, John 11. And compassion, by which one gives of oneself, is greater than an external bestowing by which one gives of one's possession, as Gregory says. The fifth species is correction; Matthew 18: "If your brother offends against you, rebuke him between," and so forth; the Gloss: lest he lose face if he were rebuked in public. From such a work of mercy sometimes follows the bond of friendship; Proverbs 28: "He that rebukes a man shall afterward find favor with him, more than he that by a flattering tongue deceives him."

rii martirum E; martiris I. 338 **misericordia** *add* de speciebus misericordie *rubr* J; *add* quinque species misericordie *rubr* F; *add* species misericordie *rubr* I; *add* set nota quod G. 339–40 **que . . . colliguntur** *om* G. **colliguntur** habentur J. 341 **ut . . . capitulo** Luce 6 FGL. 342 **ut in eodem** ut in eo E; Luce 6 FGL; ut eodem IW. 345 **maior** interior E. **per . . . seipso** *om* G. 346 Gregorius *marg* E. **quam** et E. **per . . . suo** *om* G. **Gregorius** *add* qui dat elemosinam de suo dat conpaciens seip-sum dat G. 348 Glossa *marg* E. 351 **postea** pocius E; *om* FL.

de sartagine / siue de craticula siue de clybano, oleo fit lita. In clybano intelligitur mundi tribulacio, in sartagine crux penitencie, in craticula [martirii] pena. Omnia ista cremantur sine oleo; idest, arida fiunt et sine merito, nisi assit misericordia. f. 135ra

Quinque sunt species misericordie que ex Ewangelio colliguntur. Prima est dare; Luce vi: “Date et dabitur uobis.” Secunda est commodare, ut in eodem capitulo: “Date mutuum, nichil inde sperantes.” Tercia est condonare, ut in [eodem]: “Dimittite, et dimittetur uobis.” Quarta est conpati, quam Dominus docuit flens super ciuitatem, Luce xix, et iterum flendo super Lazarum, Iohannis xi. Et est conpassio [maior] per quam dat de seipso [quam] exterior largicio per quam dat de suo, ut dicit Gregorius. Quinta est correpcio; Matthei xviii: “Si peccauerit in te frater tuus, corripe eum inter,” etc.; Glossa: ne publice correptus uerecundiam perdat. Et ex tali opere misericordie solet quandoque sequi fedus amicicie; Prouerbiorum xxviii: “Qui corripit hominem, graciam [postea] inueniet apud eum magis quam ille qui per lingue blandimenta decipit.”

VIII

ON ABSTINENCE

In the sixth place follows the remedy for gluttony, that is, abstinence, which is of two kinds, one general, the other specific. Abstinence in general is the restraint of all illicit impulses, just as Galen says that abstinence is medicine for all diseases that come from excess. This type of abstinence, which flees all illicit things, is greater than the one that restrains one's appetite for food, of which Ecclesiasticus 3 says: "A heart which has understanding will abstain from sins." "Which has understanding" can be taken with an active or a passive meaning, namely, it understands itself, or it is understood by God. Such a heart abstains from illicit things. Abstinence in the specific sense is "not to anticipate the time set for a meal." It especially restrains the impulses of gluttony. But it seems as if this were not a virtue. For Jerome comments on Matthew: "Justice lies neither in eating nor in abstaining." And if there is no justice in abstinence, there is no other virtue in it either, since justice is virtue in general. Further on the same point, we do not gain merit from our natural sufferings; but abstinence is a suffering and affliction of our nature; therefore it will not be meritorious. And Isaias 58 says: "It is not such a fast as I have chosen, for a man to afflict his soul," and so forth. This shows that bodily abstinence is of little or no value. To this you should reply as Augustine does in his book *On True Innocence,* that "we do not gain merit from our natural sufferings unless they are shaped by patience." Therefore, the withdrawal of food is not meritorious unless it is done voluntarily out of love, as when someone abstains in hope of the meal he will have in the future glory. For many fast who gain no merit thereby: as when the sick fast for the sake of health, the poor because of their poverty, the misers in order to fill their purses. But these are fed with the flesh of the dragon, that is with sins, which are the food of the devil, as in the Psalm: "You have given the dragon to be meat for the people of the Ethiopians." The people of the Ethiopians is the assembly of sinners, for whom the devil's delight, that is, unclean deeds, become their food.

One must abstain from several things. First from eating too much, "lest if you eat much, you are hated," Ecclesiasticus 31. And in the same chapter: "Exceed not, lest you offend." Boethius in the *Consolation*: "Nature is satisfied with

VIII *om all MSS.* 1 **De abstinencia** *rubr* EFI; de remedio gule *rubr* J; *om* GL; remedia gule *rubr* W. 2 **Sexto loco** sexto E; *om* FL. **de *(1st)* . . . abstinencia** capitulum de abstinencia scilicet de remedio gule I. 3 **quia** *om* JFGL. 4 Galienus *marg* E. 5 **medicina** inedia F. **morborum** membrorum F; membrorum vel morborum L. **qui ex** que JF. 6 **fiunt** fit F; sunt L. **fugit** fugat W. 7 **iii** *add* dicitur E. 8–10 **a . . . abstinet** *om* F. 8 **intelligibile** *add* dupliciter JILW. 10 **abstinet** abstinebit IE; abstinebit se L. 11 **terminum** *add* tempus *marg* J; terminum *corr from* tempus F. 12 Questio *marg* E. **enim** *om* FGIL. 14 **Et** set FGIL. 15 **ad** *om* JGILW. 16 **erit** est FL. 18–19 **corporalis . . . nulla** nulla sit uirtus abstinencia corporalis G. 19 Solucio *marg* E. 21 **informentur** informemur JFIW. 24 **merentur** *add* ut JG. 24–25 **pro penuria** pre penuria uel pro premio E. 25 **auari** aurari E; auarus W. **augenda** implenda uel augenda FL. 26 **que** qui J. 29 **cibum** *add* uel potest dici quod est duplex passio siue pena, scilicet in quantum est ab inferentibus illata non est meritoria, quia est a mala uoluntate; ipsa tamen in quantum illata passio, est a gracia et meritoria *marg* J. 32 Boecius *marg* E. **Noli** *corr from* Nole E. **nimius** nimium comedens E. **ne** *add* forte JFL. 33 **Natura** *add* humana E. 34 **moderata** *add*

[VIII]

DE ABSTINENCIA

Sexto [loco] sequitur de remedio gule, idest de abstinencia, que duplex est, quia alia generalis, alia specialis. / Generalis est chohi- f. 135rb bicio omnium motuum illicitorum, sicut dicit Galienus quod abstinencia est medicina omnium morborum qui ex superfluitate fiunt. Et ista abstinencia que [fugit] omnia illicita maior est illa que temperat ab esca, de qua Ecclesiastici iii °: "Intelligibile cor abstinebit se a peccatis." Et dicitur "intelligibile" actiue uel passiue, idest, quod se intelligit uel a Deo intelligitur. Tale cor abstinet ab illicitis. Specialis abstinencia est "statutum prandendi terminum non preuenire." Hec specialiter refrenat motus gule. Set uidetur quod ista non sit uirtus. Dicit enim Ieronimus super Mattheum: "Nec in manducando nec in abstinendo est iusticia." Et si iusticia non est in abstinencia, ergo nec aliqua uirtus, cum iusticia sit uirtus generalis. Item ad idem, passionibus non meremur; set abstinencia est passio et afflictio nature; quare non erit meritoria. Et Ysaie lviii: "Non est tale ieiunium quod elegi, hominem affligere animam suam," etc. Vnde uidetur quod corporalis abstinencia modica sit uel nulla. Ad hoc dicas sicut dicit Augustinus in libro *De uera innocencia* quod "passionibus non meremur nisi paciencia informentur." Vnde ipsa priuacio alimentorum non est meritoria nisi assit uo- / luntas caritate informata, f. 135va ut cum quis abstinet spe refectionis que erit in gloria. Ieiunant enim multi qui non merentur: infirmi pro sanitate, pauperes [pro penuria], [auari] pro bursa augenda. Isti tamen uescuntur carne draconis, idest peccatis, que sunt cibus demonis, ut in Psalmo: "Dedisti draconem escam populis Ethyopum." Populus Ethyopum est congregacio peccatorum, quibus delectaciones demonum, idest immunda opera, cedunt in cibum.

Est autem abstinendum a pluribus. Primo a superfluitate cibi, "vt non cum manduces multum, odio habearis," Ecclesiastici xxxi. Et in eodem: "Noli esse [nimius] ne offendas." Boecius in *Consolacionibus*: "Natura ° paucis contenta est." Ad litteram:

little." Which means literally: The body's health lies in moderate abstinence, since our natural heat by itself is sufficient to burn and digest our food. Second, one must abstain from overly refined food. Bernard: "What does it matter from what sort of food excrement is made?" Many rich people seem to belong to the household of him whose "food is dainty," Habacuc 1, which is interpreted as referring to the devil, who is nourished with the deeds of overindulgent people. Third, one must abstain from wantonness, so that one eats "for refreshment and not for riotousness," Ecclesiastes 10. Fourth, from greediness; Ecclesiasticus 37: "Be not greedy in any feasting." Fifth, one must abstain from anticipating a mealtime, for "woe to the land whose princes eat in the morning," Ecclesiastes 10.

Even the animals without reason teach us abstinence. The eagle does not fly in search of prey until after the sun has risen and the day is under way. Further, there is no bird, however small, that does not rise aloft after daybreak and sing the praise of its Creator before it looks for food on the ground. Thus Deuteronomy 26: "After adoring the Lord your God you shall feast in all good things." That is what Job says, 3: "Before I eat, I sigh." Moreover, only the pig, among all other animals, looks for food immediately after daybreak; and piggish people are those who look for food for their body before their divine work or prayer, while the sinner is not worthy of the food he eats, as Augustine remarks. Consider the properties of the pig treated in the chapter on gluttony above. Also the owl, which is hateful to all other birds, sings at night and feeds at night; to which may be compared those people who by day are not satisfied in their gluttony and drunkenness unless they are also given the night to have their pleasure. Therefore: "They that are drunk, are drunk in the night," Thessalonians 5. Furthermore, at night the owl stays around graves; so do such people stay around the graves of their lust, that is, gluttony and lechery, Numbers 11. At the "graves of their lust" were those destroyed who longed for meat. Also, among the soothsayers the cry of an owl was the sign of future mourning. So the poet has it: "The ugly bird is the messenger of grief to come." Likewise the song of such people is the sign of mourning; Proverbs 14: "Mourning takes hold of the end of joy."

Abstinence has seven companions, that is, those that together with abstinence form the species of temperance, which are eight: modesty, shamefacedness, abstinence, propriety, restraint, sparingness, soberness, and chasteness.

refectio uel E. 35 **sufficit** non sufficit J; facit FILW. 36 Bernardus *marg* E. 37 **Multi** etc E. 40 **leccacitate** uoracitate J; edacitate F; laucitate G; bocacitate L. 41 **luxuriam** luxuriandum JFG. 42–43 **abstinendum est** *om* FGILW. 45–46 **Item . . . diei** *om* G. 45 **eciam** *om* JFIL. 47 **aurore** diei E. 48 **canat** cantet FLW; cantat I. 49 **querat** sumat J; sumat uel querat FL. 50–51 **Antequam . . . suspiro** *om* W. 51 **cetera** omnia JG. 51–52 **animancia** animalia E. 53 **diuinum** diurnum JFGL; diutinum I. **siue oracionem** sine oracione J. 54 **uescitur** uescatur JFGI. 55 Augustinus *marg* E. 56 **aliis** *om* E. **auibus** *add* est JFLW. 57 **gula et ebrietate** *om* E. 58 **non** *add* sufficienter E. 62 **desiderabant** *add* ut quilibet dicat cum Iob spiritus meus attenuabitur J. 64 Poeta *marg* E. **Poeta . . . luctus** *om* F. **Fedaque** feda quod E. **istorum** illorum JFL. 65 **cantus . . . luctus** spiritualiter G. 67 **idest . . . ipsa** quia ipse E; idest *(corr)* quot cum ea J; et F; que cum ipsa I; idest quot sunt ipse L; W *illeg.* 70 **cultum** sensum J. 71 **faciens** facere E. 72 **medium** medium

Sanitas est corporis moderata ° abstinencia, cum calor naturalis per se sufficit coquere et digerere alimenta. Secundo abstinendum est a preciositate ciborum. Bernardus: “Quid refert ex quibus cibariis conficiantur stercora?” [Multi] diuites uidentur esse de eius familia cuius “cibus est electus,” Abacuc i, quod de dyabolo exponitur, qui delicatorum actibus pascitur. Tercio abstinendum est a leccacitate, ut homo uescatur “ad reficiendum, non ad / luxuriam,” Ecclesiaste x. Quarto ab auiditate; Ecclesiastici f. 135^{v}b
xxxvii: “Noli auidus esse in omni epulacione.” Quinto abstinendum est a temporis anticipacione, quia “ue terre cuius principes mane comedunt,” Ecclesiaste x.

Item eciam irracionabilia docent nos abstinenciam. Vnde aquila non uolat ad predam nisi orto sole et post processum diei. Item non est tam parua auicula que post ortum [aurore] in altum non ascendat et laudem Creatori canat, priusquam in terra alimenta querat. Ideo in Deuteronomi xxvi: “Adorato Domino Deo tuo, epulaberis in omnibus bonis.” Hoc est quod Iob ait iii: “Antequam comedam, suspiro.” Item solus porcus inter cetera [animancia] post auroram diei cicius querit cibum; et porcini homines sunt qui ante laborem diuinum siue oracionem alimenta corporis querunt, cum peccator non sit dignus pane quo uescitur, ut dicit Augustinus. Et nota proprietates porci supra capitulo de gula. Item bubo omnibus [aliis] auibus odiosa de nocte cantat et de nocte pascitur; cui conparantur qui de die [gula et ebrietate] non ° saciantur nisi uoluptatibus explendis eciam nox accomodetur. Vnde: “Qui ebrii sunt, nocte ebrii sunt,” Tessalonicensium v. Preterea bubo de nocte adheret sepulcris; ita isti sepulcris concupiscencie, idest gule et luxurie, Numeri xi. Ad / “sepulcra f. 136^{r}a
concupiscencie” sue consumpti sunt qui carnes desiderabant. Item clamor bubonis apud augures fuit signum futuri luctus. Poeta: “Feda[que] uolucris uenturi nuncia luctus.” Et istorum cantus signum est luctus; Prouerbiorum xiiii: “Extrema gaudii luctus occupat.”

Comites autem abstinencie sunt septem, [idest quot cum ipsa] sunt species temperancie, que sunt octo: modestia, verecundia, abstinencia, honestas, moderancia, parcitas, sobrietas, pudicicia.

Modesty consists in keeping our apparel, movements, and all our behavior in the middle between deficiency and excess; that is to say, modesty teaches us the mean in the stirrings of our sensuality that pertain to food and sex, just as prudence teaches the mean in general in all our actions, as the *Ethics* says that "prudence examines the mean." Modesty is counted among the fruits of the spirit, Galatians 5, for it teaches us that virtuous acts lie in the mean. But this kind of modesty is identical with prudence. Shamefacedness is the virtue by which the open brow blushes at its mistakes. Because of its bashfulness it sometimes even trembles at proper things. But gluttons and lechers lack modesty because they do not blush at what is excessive in their behavior. Both faults are touched upon in Isaias 56: "The most impudent dogs," which means, without shamefacedness, "never had enough," that is, without modesty. Yet shamefacedness differs from sensitiveness in so far as shamefacedness is afraid to do evil, whereas sensitiveness is afraid to hear it. Therefore John Damascene: "Sensitiveness is fear in the expectation of some reproach"; and this is a very good affect. Of abstinence we have spoken earlier. Propriety consists in not seeking sumptuous dishes and in not bestowing one's care upon overly elegant food preparation. But this definition of propriety is a special one, referring to one's appetite. Another one is general and applies also to one's actions; it goes as follows: "Propriety is a suitable and becoming expediency in all things and actions." This virtue was lacking in him who "feasted sumptuously every day," wherefore "he was buried in hell," Luke 16. Restraint is to hold back an excessive appetite for food with the rule of reason. It is a bridle in eating; and worthless is the squire who forgets to put the bit on the horse sent to fodder. Gregory: "We should eat what our need requires, not what our lust to eat prompts us to." Sparingness means not to exceed the right measure of eating. But some people eat sparingly, not in order to avoid gluttony but for the sake of avarice, who "do not have their fill of bread, but are depressed at their own table," Ecclesiasticus 14. Soberness means to restrict the impulse of going to extremes. But this is the general kind. Such soberness as is opposed to drunkenness rules our desire for drink without totally omitting what we need; Ecclesiasticus 31: "Sober drinking is health to soul and body." Chasteness means to tame insolence with the control of reason. Seneca: "No one has at once been obedient to both lust and reason." How lust springs from drunkenness may be found above, in the chapter on drunkenness.

⟨uel modum⟩ J. 73 **medium** medium ⟨uel modum⟩ J. 74 Philosophus *marg* E. 76 **hec** in hoc J. 78 **frons** sors FGL. **falsis** *om* J; factis FI; superfluus G. **pudiciciam** prudenciam FI. 79 **ebriosi** *add* eciam E. 80 **nesciunt** *add* et E. **carent** *om* JGIW. 85 Damascenus *marg* E. 86 **et . . . passio** *om* L. 87 **honestas** *add* uero JW. 88 **in** *om* JFGLW. **apparatu** appetitui F; appetitu GL. 93 **Moderancia** modestia E. 94 **reuocare** *refrenare F. 95 **frenum** frem E; freni G. **prebendario** predendario E. 96 Gregorius *marg* E. 99–100 **Ecclesiastici** Iob FL. 100 **inpetum** inpetus JF. 101 **contraria** *add* est EJ. 103 **corpori** corporis JFL. 104 Seneca

Est autem modestia cultum et motum et omnem nostram occupacionem ultra defectum et citra excessum [faciens] sistere; idest, modestia docet medium in motibus sensualitatis qui sunt ad gulam et luxuriam, sicut prudencia docet medium communiter in omnibus agendis, prout dicitur in *Ethicis* quod “prudencia inspectrix est medii.” Modestia uero inter fructus spiritus nominatur, Galatarum v, quia actus uirtutum docet sistere in medio. Set hec modestia communicat cum prudencia. Verecundia est uirtus qua frons ingenua falsis erubescit. Hec propter sui pudiciciam quandoque eciam pauet honestatem. Set gulosi et ebriosi ° modestia carent quia medium nesciunt, ° uerecundia carent quia de superfluitate non erube- / scunt. Vtrumque tangitur Ysaie lvi: f. 136rb
“Canes inpudentissimi,” ecce quod sine uerecundia, “nescierunt saturitatem,” ecce quod sine modestia. Differunt tamen uerecundia et erubescencia quia uerecundia timet malum committere, erubescencia timet audire. Vnde Damascenus: “Erubescencia est timor in expectacione conuicii”; et est optima hec passio. De abstinencia dictum est supra. Honestas est nec lauciores cibos querere nec in nimio apparatu operam dare. Set hec diffinicio honestatis specialis est, que est in appetitibus. Alia est generalis, que est eciam in actionibus; que sic potest diffiniri: “Honestas est quarumlibet rerum seu actionum conueniens et decens utilitas.” Honestate caruit qui “cottidie splendide comedit,” vnde “in inferno sepultus fuit,” Luce xvi. [Moderancia] est nimium appetitum ciborum racionis inperio reuocare. Ipsa est frenum in edendo; et malus est armiger qui frenum in [prebendario] obliuiscitur. Gregorius: “Edenda sunt que necessitas exigit, non que libido edendi suggerit.” Parcitas est mensuram refectionis non excedere. Set est qui parcit auaricie non gule, qui “non saciatur pane indigens, set in tristicia est super mensam suam,” Ecclesiastici xiiii. / Sobrietas est excessuum inpetum cohibere. Set hec est f. 136va
generalis. Sobrietas vero contraria ° ebrietati libidinem potus temperat et necessitatem non excludit; Ecclesiastici xxxi: “Sanitas anime et corpori sobrius potus.” Pudicicia est moderamine racionis petulanciam domare. Seneca: “Nemo simul libidini et racioni paruit.” Qualiter uero libido de ebrietate [nascitur] patet supra, capitulo de ebrietate.

[VIII]

Christ taught the virtue of abstinence, first by his example of fasting for forty days and forty nights; second by his word when he said, "Blessed are they that hunger and thirst," and so forth, Matthew 5. To hunger and thirst after justice is to want to fulfill all of God's commandments. "Justice" is here taken in general because it ranges through all individual commandments. In this way, "they that hunger" are those who truly abstain, to whom repletion is promised, "for they shall have their fill"; and in Isaias 49: "They shall not hunger nor thirst any more."

Now, it might seem that the saints have their spiritual fill also in this life. John 6: "I am the bread of life; he that comes to me shall not hunger." And the Gloss comments on Luke 9: "He will not hunger who has received the food of Christ, that is, Christ as his food, as by metonymy." But the opposite seems to be true of both kinds of repletion. That in the present life is contradicted by Ecclesiasticus 24: "They that eat me shall yet hunger." Future repletion is seemingly denied by Ecclesiasticus 42: "Who shall be filled with beholding God's glory?"—the interrogative form implies a negation, as if the writer said: no one. The Psalm: "Seek his face evermore," on which Augustine comments: "As our love grows, so grows the search for what has been found." And so there seems never to be full repletion in heaven. To the first objection you should reply that in this life a spiritual hunger continues, because the Bread of Life is received under a different form; thus our soul is only half filled. But since it desires this meal before all others, it accepts it as filling and deems the foretaste a complete meal. To the objection about the repletion in heaven you must reply that they are said to hunger there in the sense that they will desire more and more. Gregory: "They enjoy and do not become sated; they desire what they already have, so that they may have it more fully." And this is meant in Augustine's "As our love grows," and so forth. Not that love grows in heaven, but the extension of the delight and desire does that is in it.

"Hunger" is of several kinds. One is a lack or weakness in our nature; according to the Philosopher, this is the appetite for hot and dry things. Another kind is the burning of concupiscence; Ambrose: "Every lust suffers hunger for itself." Another is the glowing heat of avarice; Ecclesiastes 5: "A covetous man will not be satisfied with money." The fourth is the desire for the future glory; Matthew 5: "Blessed are they that hunger and thirst after justice," and so forth. The first kind of hunger is natural to man, the second to the devil, the third to the toad, and the fourth to the pilgrim.

But abstinence is commendable for many reasons. First because it tames our

marg E. 104–6 **Seneca . . . ebrietate** *om* L. 105 **nascitur** nascatur E. 110 **et sitire** sitire et E. 111 **Dei** *marg* E. **que** eo quod E. 112 **ueri** uiri uere J. 115 **eciam** tamen FL. **sanctis** *om* E. **sacietas** ebrietas J. 117 Glossa *marg* E. 118 Questio *marg* E. **ut sit ypalage** *om* E. 119 **que** qui EJGW. 122 **interrogacio** interrogatiua E. 123 Augustinus *marg* E. 124 **inuenti** inuenta EFGL; intuenti I. **inquisicio** adquisicio F. 125 Solucio *marg* E. 126 **forma** specie J. 126–27 **percipitur** sumitur L. 128–29 **pre . . . refectionem** *om* G. 128 **sacietate** saturitate E. 129 Solucio *marg* E. **illud** aliud JI. 130 **dicuntur** diffinitur E; dicitur FILW. 132 Augustinus *marg* E. 133–34 **delectacionis** dileccionis GIW. 135 **Est autem** et est JW. **multiplex** triplex G. 136 Philosophus *marg* E. 137 Ambrosius *marg* E. **ardor** *om* E; defectus siue languor nature idest ardor G. 139 **Quarta** alia F. **glorie** gule G. 139–40 **Matthei v** *om* JFILW. 141 **secunda** *add* hominis, *canc* E. 142 **plura** multa FIL. 143 Augustinus *marg* E. 144–45 **Gregorius . . . roboratur** *om*

Virtutem abstinencie docuit Christus, primo exemplo quadraginta diebus et quadraginta noctibus ieiunando; secundo uerbo cum dixit, “Beati qui esuriunt et sitiunt,” etc., Matthei v. Et est esurire iusticiam [et sitire] inplecionem omnium mandatorum Dei desiderare. Et sumitur hic “iusticia” generaliter [que] in omnibus preceptis est distributa. Hoc modo “esurientes” sunt ueri abstinentes quibus promittitur saturitas, “quoniam ipsi saturabuntur”; et in Ysaie xlix: “Non esurient neque sicient amplius.”

Videtur eciam quod in presenti sit [sanctis] sacietas spiritualis. Iohannis vi: “Ego sum panis uite; qui uenit ad me non esuriet.” Et Glossa super Luce ix: “Non esuriet qui accepit cibum Christi, idest Christum in cibum, [ut sit ypalage.]” Set contrarium uidetur utrique sacietati. Illi [que] est in presenti obuiat illud Ecclesiastici xxiiii: “Qui edunt me adhuc esurient.” Future autem sacietati / f. 136vb obuiat illud Ecclesiastici xlii: “Quis saciabitur uidens gloriam Dei?”—[interrogacio] innuit negacionem, quasi diceret: nullus. Psalmus: “Querite faciem eius semper”; ibi Augustinus: “Crescente amore crescit [inuenti] inquisicio.” Et ita nunquam uidetur in patria plena sacietas. Et dic ad primum quod in presenti esuries spiritualis est, quia Panis Uite sub aliena forma percipitur; ideo anima semiplene reficitur. Quia tamen hanc refectionem pre omnibus desiderat, eam pro [sacietate] sibi reputat et prelibacionem estimat refectionem. Ad illud de sacietate patrie dic quod [dicuntur] ibi esurire, idest magis ac magis desiderare. Gregorius: “Fruuntur nec fastidiunt; desiderant quod habent ut plenius habeant.” Et sic intelligitur illud Augustini, “Crescente amore,” etc. Non quod crescat caritas in patria, set extensio delectacionis et desiderii quod est in illa.

Est autem multiplex “esuries.” Alia est defectus siue languor nature; hec secundum Philosophum est appetitus calidi et sicci. Alia est [ardor] concupiscencie; Ambrosius: “Omnis uoluptas esuriem sui patitur.” Alia est estus auaricie; Ecclesiaste v: “Auarus non inplebitur peccunia.” Quarta est desiderium glorie; Matthei v: “Beati qui esuriunt et sitiunt iusticiam,” etc. Prima fames est hominis, secunda demonis, tercia / f. 137ra bufonis, quarta uiatoris.

Est autem abstinencia commendabilis propter plura. Primo quia domat carnem; Augustinus: “Carnem uestram domate absti-

flesh; Augustine: "Tame your flesh by abstinence from food and drink." Second because it strengthens our spirit; Gregory: "What wears away our flesh strengthens our spirit." Third because it conquers the vices; Isaias 30: "The Lord overthrows his enemies with timbrels and harps and great battles." By the "timbrels" we understand abstinence or mortification of the flesh, by "harps" prayer, and by "great battles" the works of mercy; and with all these are the vices overthrown. Fourth because it increases our almsgiving; Isaias 58: "Deal your bread to the hungry," and so forth. Jerome: "Give to the poor what you were going to eat if you did not fast, so that your fast may not bring gain to your purse but fullness to your soul." Fifth because it prolongs life; Ecclesiasticus 37: "He who abstains will add to his life." Sixth because it preserves one's health; Ecclesiasticus 31: "Sober drinking is health to soul and body." And Galen, when he was asked what might be the best medicine, answered, "Abstinence." Take this to refer to diseases that come from excess. Seventh because it helps our prayer; Tobias 12: "Prayer is good with fasting." Eighth because it disposes our soul to receive the Holy Spirit; according to Acts 2, the Holy Spirit was sent to the disciples as they were fasting. Ninth because it merits divine consolation, while it is taken away from or denied to those who receive their consolation from elsewhere. Bernard: "Divine consolation is very delicate, which is not given to those who accept any other kind."

As discreet abstinence is praiseworthy, so indiscreet abstinence is reprehensible. Ambrose: "God wants to be served prudently, not that his servants should grow weak through excessive abstinence and then have to seek help from the doctors. Moderation is in order, so that, if possible, the task one has begun may progress step by step, rather than be hindered through lack of considerateness." Such indiscreet abstinence is blameworthy for several reasons. First because it is the daughter of a proud desire to be exceptional. Luke 18: "I am not as the rest of men," and so forth; Bernard: "He is giving thanks, not because he is good but because he is unique." Further, its first sister is presumption, and the Lord "humbles them that presume of themselves and glory in their own strength," Judith 6. Its second sister is the show of holiness, against which Jeremias 2: "Why do you endeavor to show your way good," and so forth. The third is hypocrisy; Matthew 6: "Sad hypocrites, they disfigure their faces, that," and so forth. Also, it ruins the citizen and gladdens the enemy; that is, it destroys our nature and nourishes the devils, whereas Gregory teaches the opposite when he says: "Our enemy must be thus overthrown that the citizen is

F. 148 **carnis** corporis L. **mortificacio** maceracio FL. 149 **in** de J; *om* FGILW. 151 Ieronimus *marg* E. 154 **adiciet** prolongat E. 156 Galienus *marg* E. **quid** que JI. 157 **in . . . ex** de E. 160 **discipulis** *add* et orantibus FIL. 161 **quia** quod E; *om* G. 162 **quia** que FILW. 162–63 **aliunde . . . negatur** *om* G. **uel negatur** spiritus sanctus E. 163 Bernardus *marg* E. 163–64 **que . . . alienam** non enim facile conceditur habentibus alienam F. 166 Ambrosius *marg* E. **Ambrosius** *add* super illud modico uino utere etc G. 168 **requirant** requirat E; inquirant J; requisitus L. 169 **prouehatur** promoveatur L. 169–70 **per . . . minuatur** etc E; per inconsideracionem minuatur J. 170 **Ipsa** preterea J; indiscreta abstinencia F. **Ipsa . . . est** est enim indiscreta abstinencia G. 172 Bernardus *marg* E. 174 **et** *add* de FGL. 175 **ostentacio** ostensio GW. 177 **exterminant** *add* enim E. 178 **perimit** pertrahit E. 180 Gregorius *marg* E. 181 **contrarium** *om* FGL; *add* scilicet

nencia esce et potus." Secundo quia roborat spiritum; Gregorius: "Vnde caro atteritur, inde spiritus roboratur." Tercio quia expugnat uicia; Ysaie xxx: "Dominus expugnat hostes in tympanis et cytharis et bellis precipuis." In "tympanis" intelligitur abstinencia siue carnis mortificacio, in "citharis" oracio, in "bellis precipuis" misericordie opera; et in hiis omnibus expugnantur uicia. Quarto quia auget elemosinam; Ysaie lviii: "Frange esurienti panem tuum," etc. Ieronimus: "Quod manducaturus eras si non ieiunares, da pauperibus, ut ieiunium tuum non sit marsupii lucrum set anime saturitas." Quinto quia prolongat uitam; Ecclesiastici xxxvii: "Qui abstinens est, [adiciet] uitam." Sexto quia conseruat sanitatem; Ecclesiastici xxxi: "Sanitas anime et corporis, potus sobrius." Et Galienus, requisitus quid esset summa medicina, respondit, "Abstinencia." Et hoc intellige [in morbis ex] superfluitate. Septimo quia iuuat oracionem; Thobie xii: "Bona est oracio cum ieiunio." Octauo quia disponit animam ad Spiritus Sancti suscepcionem; Actuum ii ieiunantibus discipulis missus / est f. 137ʳb
Spiritus Sanctus. Nono [quia] meretur diuinam consolacionem, quia aliunde consolacionem recipientibus subtrahitur [uel negatur]. Bernardus: "Delicata est diuina consolacio, que non conceditur admittentibus alienam."

Sicut discreta abstinencia est laudabilis, ita indiscreta est reprobabilis. Ambrosius: "Prudenter uult Deus sibi seruiri, non ut nimietate abstinencie debiles fiant et post medicorum suffragia [requirant]. Temperandum est enim, ut si fieri potest ceptum officium gradatim prouehatur pocius quam [per inconsideranciam minuatur]." Ipsa pluribus de causis est uituperabilis. Primo quia filia est superbie singularis. Luce xviii: "Non sum sicut ceteri hominum," etc.; Bernardus: "Gracias agit non quia bonus est, set quia solus." Item prima soror sua presumpcio est, et Dominus "de se presumentes et sua uirtute gloriantes humiliat," Iudiht vi. Secunda soror est sanctitatis ostentacio, contra quam Ieremie ii: "Quid niteris bonam ostendere uiam tuam," etc. Tercia est ypocrisis; Matthei vi: "Ypocrite tristes, exterminant ° facies suas ut," etc. Item ipsa [perimit] ciuem et letificat hostem, idest, naturam destruit et demones reficit, cum contrarium do-

nourished." It further makes God an offering from stolen goods, whereas he himself says the opposite, that he "hates robbery and the holocaust," Isaias 61. Indiscreet abstinence commits robbery when it deprives nature of its necessary sustenance, when it robs it of food and sleep and other necessary contributions. Moreover, it takes from God what is his, when because of its lack of strength and excessive weakening of the body it withholds payment of the owed service. Therefore says Jerome: "The servant of God must eat and drink in such a way that he is able to read, pray, and sing psalms."

The punishment for gluttony is hunger; Isaias 9: "Everyone shall eat the flesh of his own arm." And thirst; Luke 16, about the rich man who feasted sumptuously, who asked for a drop of water, and so forth. Further, gnashing of teeth, Matthew 8; the Gloss comments: "Because they rejoiced in their voracity." And the memory of past delights; Isaias 24: "The drink shall be bitter," and so forth. Jerome: "After this life the memory of bygone delights will be matter for torments."

E. 182 **lxi** xli E; xli ⟨uel lxi⟩ J. 184 **dum . . . sompnum** *om* L. 184–85 **necessarie** nature F (*and perhaps* GIL); necessaria tributa vel necessitati attributa J. 185 **per** *om* E. 186 **ministerii** ministerio E. 187 Ieronimus *marg* E. 188 **psallere** *add* de pena gula *rubr* J. 190 **sitis** *om* E. 191 Glossa *marg* E. 192 **gaudebant** gaudebat FL. **precedencium** presencium G. 193 Ieronimus *marg* E. **xxiiii** *add* cum gaudio non bibit uinum FL.

ceat Gregorius dicens: “Sic expugnandus est hostis ut nutriatur ciuis.” Item ipsa offert Deo de rapina, cum ipse dicat contrarium, ° quod “odio habeat rapi- / nam in holocaustum,” Ysaie [lxi]. f. 137va Rapinam committit indiscreta abstinencia dum subtrahit nature necessaria alimenta, dum rapit cibum et sompnum et cetera necessarie tributa. Item ipsa aufert Deo quod suum est, dum [per] inpotenciam et nimiam corporis debilitatem debiti [ministerii] subtrahit pensionem. Ideo dicit Ieronimus: “Ita debet seruus Dei commedere et bibere, ut possit legere, orare, et psallere.”

Pena gule est fames; Ysaie ix: “Vnusquisque carnem brachii sui uorabit.” Et [sitis]; Luce xvi, de epulone qui guttam aque peciit, etc. Item stridor dencium, Matthei viii; Glossa: “Quia de edacitate gaudebant.” Item memoria deliciarum precedencium; Ysaie xxiiii: “Amara erit pocio,” etc. Ieronimus: “Post hanc uitam recordacio preteritarum deliciarum materia erit cruciatuum.”

IX

ON CONTINENCE

In the seventh place follows continence, which is the remedy for lechery. According to Tullius, continence is the virtue by which desire is ruled under the guidance of our judgment. But this definition is of continence in general. Another is of continence in the strict sense: "Continence is the virtue which restrains illicit stirrings toward carnal lust." In the same fashion is there a general and a specific chastity. Chastity in general is that which in all actions keeps a proper moderation. But in the specific sense it is the virtue which restrains illicit stirrings, which is the more meritorious, the more forcefully it restrains the inciting force of carnal desire. Continence or chastity has three parts: chasteness in spouses, continence in widows, and integrity in virgins. This division is not one of a genus into its species, but rather one of accidental qualities. For it is an accidental quality whether continence is in virgins or in spouses, for "if a virgin should marry, she does not sin," Corinthians 7, but in either state she is said to be continent and chaste.

First we must speak of chasteness in spouses, whose protection is marriage. Thus, "matrimony is so named as if it were the *munium,* that is office, of a *mater*; for the office of matrimony can be seen more obviously in the mother than in the father." It is she who carries more burdens of married life; for she is weighed down in her pregnancy, troubled in childbirth, and full of cares in rearing her offspring. Marriage is "the lawful assembly of man and woman which preserves their individual life," as in *Causa* XXVII, question 2. Or else: "Marriage is the joining of male and female, the sharing of life together, and the partaking of divine and human law," *Digest,* "On the Usage of Wedlock."

Marriage is praiseworthy for several reasons. First, because God established it. Second, because he wanted to be born from it. Third, because he was present at a wedding in order to sanctify it. Fourth, because he endowed it with several good effects, as is shown in these verses:

Marriage cleanses and makes fruitful,
  Changes and unites,
Is made worthy by its author,
  Time, and law, and place.

IX *om all MSS.* 1 **De continencia** *rubr* EJFI; *om* GL; remedia luxurie *rubr* W. 2 **Septimo loco** *om* FL; septimo G. 3 Tullius *marg* E. **est** *interl* E. 4 **Set . . . generalis** *om* G. 6 **Eodem** eo EG. 7–8 **agendis** *om* E. 9 **restringens** stringens GL. 10 **carnalis** *om* FL. **fomitis** concupiscencie W; comitis I. **incentiuum** *incendium E. 11 **partes** species F; species uel partes J. 11–15 **pudicicia . . . casta** *om* G. 12 **uirginalis** *uidualis E; uirginalis aut coniugalis J. 13 **Accidit** aut E. 14 **sit** *add* uidualis *canc* E. **etsi** et *with* si *add marg* E; si J. 15 **statu** casu FL. 16 **pudicicia** continencia FL. 16–17 **munimentum** monimentum E. 17 **dicitur** *om* E. 18 **munium** municio E; munimen F. **enim** *om* E. 19 **matrimonii** matronum E; uiuencium J. **ipsa** *add* mater W. **copule** copula JFI. 21–25 **legittima . . . nupciarum** *om* G. 22 **coniunccio** associacio . . . uel coniunctio I. **consuetudinem** sollicitudinem F. 22–23 **ut . . . ii** *om* F. 23–25 **Uel . . . nupciarum** *om* E. 24 **coniunctio** *om* FL. **communis** omnis FIL; W *illeg.* 25 **communicacio** coniunctio FIL; W *illeg.* **ff. . . . nupciarum** *om* F. **ritu** iure I. 26 **pluribus de causis** propter plures causas FIL; W *illeg.* **pluribus . . . Primo** *om* G. 27 **illo** *add* deus G. 28 **interfuit** interesse uoluit G. 31 **Pollens** pellens FL. **auctore** auctor E. **loco** *add* se

[IX]

DE CONTINENCIA

Septimo loco sequitur de continencia, que est remedium luxurie. Et est continencia secundum Tullium per quam cupiditas consilii gubernacione regitur. Set hec est diffinicio generalis. Alia est continencie specialis: "Continencia est uirtus reprimens motus illicitos ad carnalem concupiscenciam." [Eodem] modo est castitas generalis et specialis. Castitas generalis est que in omnibus [agendis] honestam tenet temperiem. Specialis uero est uirtus / motus f. 137vb restringens illicitos, que tanto meretur amplius, quanto ualidius carnalis fomitis reprimit [incentiuum]. Continencie siue castitatis tres sunt partes: pudicicia coniugalis, continencia uidualis, integritas [uirginalis]. Et non est ista diuisio generis in species, set magis accidentis in accidencia. [Accidit] enim continencie quod sit uirginalis aut coniugalis, quia "etsi uirgo nubat, non peccat," Corinthiorum vii, set in utroque statu dicitur continens et casta.

De pudicicia coniugali primo dicendum est, cuius [munimentum] est matrimonium. Ideo "[dicitur] matrimonium quasi matris [munium], idest officium; magis [enim] apparet officium [matrimonii] in matre quam in patre." Et ipsa coniugalis copule plura subit onera; est enim in conceptu grauida, in partu anxia, in educatu sollicita. Est autem matrimonium "legittima uiri et mulieris coniunccio, indiuiduam uite consuetudinem retinens," ut XXVII, questio ii. [Uel aliter: "Matrimonium est maris et femine coniunctio, consorcium communis uite, divine et humani iuris communicacio," ff., "De ritu nupciarum."]

Matrimonium est commendabile pluribus de causis. Primo quia Deus illud instituit. Secundo quia de illo nasci uoluit. Tercio quia nubciis sanctificandis interfuit. Quarto quia plures bonos effectus eidem contulit, ut patet in hiis uersibus:

Coniugium mundat, fecundat, mutat, et unit
Pollens [auctore], tempore, lege, loco.°

Marriage cleanses from fornication. Thus, the Apostle demonstrates in Ephesians 6: as Christ has sanctified his Church, washing it with the bath of water so that it may have no spot or wrinkle, thus he has also cleansed the marital union. It makes the Church bear fruit by its offspring, for this is the final cause of marriage, the raising of offspring to the worship of God, as Augustine says in his book *The Value of Marriage*. And the Lord spoke to those who stepped out of the ark: "Increase and multiply," Genesis 9. It changes mortal to venial sin, that is, what now is venial sin or no sin at all would be mortal if it were not made blameless by marriage. Thus, virgins are supported by the soft marriage bed according to Gregory, so that they may not come to ruin. It unites minds and bodies; hence: "They shall be two in one flesh," Genesis 2, that is to say: in one fleshly union, or in one offspring which they engender, or because neither of them has power over himself. It is further made worthy by virtue of its author, God; also by the time of its establishment, that is, before sin; by the law, for it was established under the law of nature; and by the place, that is, paradise.

Although matrimony is praiseworthy, yet is its practice sometimes reprehensible. Otherwise it would not be written that "Asmodeus," that is, a devil contrary to God, rules in those "who in such manner receive matrimony as to shut out God from their mind and to give themselves to their lust," Tobias 6. Such men, according to Jerome, are adulterers with their spouses, not husbands, and do not seek offspring but their own lust. And such sometimes fall with Herod from adultery into murder, Matthew 14; that is, as they do not seek offspring but their pleasure, they procure poisons to cause sterility or to kill the child after it has been conceived or is already alive. Spouses should be fearfully aware that our first parents, though they were created by God and joined together in paradise, had as their first child Cain, a man of envy and a murderer, and born to damnation, whence he was also "cursed" by God "upon the earth," Genesis 4. Let spouses further be aware that "there is a time and opportunity for every business," Ecclesiastes 8. Therefore, even if man has feet, he nonetheless does not always run, or even if he has teeth, he does not always eat; the same holds true of sexual intercourse and other conjugal practices. Furthermore, irrational animals have certain times assigned for carnal intercourse. But man, when he becomes servant to his flesh, is less reasonable than wild animals and observes neither times nor hour nor manner; he does not "ask the beasts of the land or the birds of the air," that he may learn wisdom, Job 12. In addition,

Christo E; *add* exposicio I; *add* exposicio versuum W. 35 **hec** *om* E. 35–36 **finalis matrimonii** fidelis L. 36 Augustinus *marg* E. **dicit** ait E. 36–37 **Augustinus** *add* in E. 38 **multiplicamini** *add* etc E. **Mutat** commutat G. 39–40 **idest . . . ueniale** *om* I. 39 **nunc** non G; *om* W. **non** nunc F. 40–41 **excusaretur** extergeretur E. 42 Gregorius *marg* E. **Vnit et** unum sint in F. 43 **carne vna** una vita L. 45 **item a** *om* E; a W. 46 **peccatum** E *apparently began to write* tempus *and then changed to* peccatum; *add* est JW. 49 **non** enim E; *om* I. 50 **Deo contrarius** de supernis E. 51 **suscipiunt** contrahunt E. 52 Ieronimus *marg* E. 53 **non *(1st)*** ut E; *om* W. **non mariti** *om* J. 54 **quandoque** frequenter G. 56 **ut** *om* E. **formatum** mortuum FL. **puerum** puerperium JG. 57 **siue** uel E. **extinguant** extinguunt E; extinguat G. 59–60 **dampnacioni** in dampnacionem E. 62 **etsi** et E. **homo** *om* FW. **habet** habeat JFILW. 63 **currit** currendum est F; currendum IL. 63–64 **commedit** commedunt E; comedendum IL. 66 **carnis** *add* et JFGIW. 68 **addis-**

Mundat a fornicacione. Vnde exemplum Apostoli Ad / f. 138ra Ephesios vi: sicut Christus sanctificauit Ecclesiam mundans lauacro aque ut non habeat maculam neque rugam, sic et mundauit copulam coniugalem. Fecundat Ecclesiam prole, quia [hec] est causa finalis matrimonii, multiplicacio prolis ad cultum Dei, ut [dicit] Augustinus ° libro *De bono coniugii*. Et Dominus egressis de archa dixit: "Crescite et multiplicamini," ° Genesis ix. Mutat mortale peccatum in ueniale, idest quod nunc est ueniale uel quod non est peccatum fieret mortale, nisi per matrimonium [excusaretur]. Ideo molli thoro coniugali excipiuntur uirgines, secundum Gregorium, ne cadant in interitum. Vnit et mentes et corpora; vnde: "Erunt duo in carne vna," Genesis ii, idest: in una carnali copula, uel in una prole procreanda, uel quia neuter habet potestatem sui ipsius. Item commendatur ab auctore, Deo; [item a] tempore, quia ante peccatum institutum; lege, quia sub lege naturali institutum est; loco, quia in paradyso.

Licet matrimonium sit commendabile, tamen eius officium est quandoque uituperabile. Aliter [non] diceretur "Asmodeus," idest demon [Deo contrarius], dominari hiis "qui ita coniugium [suscipiunt] ut Deum a mente sua excludant et libidini uacent," Thobie vi. Item tales secundum Ieronimum adulteri sunt suarum coniugum [non] mariti, non querentes prolem set libidinem. Et tales quandoque / f. 138rb cum Herode cadunt ab adulterio in homicidium, Matthei xiiii; idest, quia non querunt prolem set uoluptatem, venena sterilitatis procurant, uel [ut] formatum puerum [siue] iam animatum [extinguant]. Item ualde timeant coniuges quod primi parentes a Deo creati et in paradyso copulati primogenitum suum Cayn inuidum et homicidam ediderunt [dampnacioni], vnde et a Deo "maledictus est super terram," Genesis iiii. Item attendant coniuges quod "omni negocio tempus est et oportunitas," Ecclesiaste viii. Vnde [etsi] homo habet pedes, non tamen semper currit, vel etsi dentes, non tamen semper [commedit]; sic de operibus carnis et aliis officiis coniugii. Item animalia irracionabilia habent tempora asignata carnali commixtioni. Homo uero seruus carnis stulcior est brutis, nec tempus nec horam nec modum attendit; non "interrogat iumenta terre nec uolatilia celi" ut addiscat sapienciam, Iob xii. Item obseruanda sunt

spouses should observe the right times, because of various dangers for their offspring, for the sins of parents sometimes result in grave punishment for their children; otherwise we would not be born as "children of wrath," Ephesians 2. Therefore, Jerome comments on Isaias 65 that from their parents' intercourse at an improper time are born children that are lepers, hunchbacks, monsters, or have other defects of nature. How serious the sin of adultery and what its punishment is, can also be found above in the chapter on lechery.

One woman is joined to one man for several reasons, as Augustine teaches in his book *The Value of Marriage*. The first is that it is a symbol for the union between Christ and the Church; Ephesians 6: "This is a great sacrament, in Christ and in the Church." The second, because "the head of the woman is the man," Corinthians 11, and if one woman were to have several husbands, she would, so to speak, have several heads, and that would be a monstrous marriage. Likewise, one woman could not obey several husbands at one and the same time, for if "no one can serve two masters," Matthew 5, much less so four or five. Further, peace and concord could hardly subsist among several husbands, since each would claim his own right to rule. Whence Damascenus proves by this argument that it is impossible that there are several gods, because they would disagree in ruling the universe. In addition, one could not tell after conception whose offspring it was nor to whom the inheritance belonged. And also, the wife would be loved less by each individual husband because she would be common to several.

How husbands should comport themselves towards their wives in patience and reverence, the Lord has taught us in his work of creation, when he formed woman from the rib and not from any other part—not from the head, not from the foot, so that he might teach that she should be man's companion, not his ruler nor his slave. Hence the verse:

From Adam's rib is given his wife and enemy.

How husbands should act towards their wives is further taught by the Apostle in Ephesians 6: "Husbands, love your wives as your own bodies," and also "as Christ loves the Church"; the Gloss explains: He died for her, and so should you for your wives, if necessary. We should notice, however, how this comes to be and for what reason. For many are cruel to their wives and irresponsible toward their own children, like the ostrich which "is hardened against his young ones, as though they were not his," Job 39. They are also like the *lamia*, an owl, which tears its young ones to pieces; and it therefore has its name, as if it were *lania*, from *laniare*, "to rend to pieces," as Isidore says.

cat discat J; *om* G. 71 Ieronimus *marg* E. **nasceremur** nascerentur GW; nascerentur vel nasceremur J. 73 **gypposi monstruosi** *om* G. 74–75 **Item . . . luxuria** *om* G. 74 **et . . . eius** *om* L. **pena eius** pene sequentes JFI; W *illeg*. 76 **docet** *dicit J; W *illeg*. 77 **unionis** in nomine G. 79 **Secunda** *add* est F. 80–81 **quasi . . . et** *om* G. 82 **obedire** *satisfacere E. **si** *om* JFGIW. 83 **multo . . . quinque** *om* G. 84 **plures** multos F. **et concordia** *om* G. 85 Damascenus *marg* E. 86–87 **regimine** regione FL. 87 **uniuersi** *om* E. 89 **uxor** *om* FILW. 90 **Qualiter** item qualiter FL. **habeant** debeant habere G. **uiri ad uxores** *canc and marked* vacat *and corr to* uxores ad uiros *in marg* E. **uxores** mulieres uxores F. **in . . . reuerencia** *om* G. 91 **cum** dum E. 91–93 **cum . . . ancillam** *om* G. 93 **non *(2nd)*** uel EW; neque L. 94 Versus *marg* E. **versus** *om* GW. 96 **Item** *om* G. **qualiter** *add* eciam E. **docet Apostolus** *om* G. 98 Glossa *marg* E. **eciam** *om* G. **dilexit** *om* F. 101 **in** eciam JLW; et I; *om* F. 101–2 **duratur** induratur JF. 103 **sunt** *om* E. 104 Ysidorus *marg* E. 105 **Item** *om* JGILW. **mulieres** uxores G. **docet Petrus** docet F; docetur

tempora coniugibus propter uaria pericula fetus, quia peccata parentum quandoque redundant in penam paruulorum; aliter non nasceremur "filii ire," Ephesiorum ii. Vnde dicit Ieronimus super Ysaie lxv quod ex copula parentum tempore non debito generantur leprosi, gypposi, monstruosi, uel alios defectus nature passi. Item quam graue sit peccatum adulterii et que pena eius, patet supra capitulo de luxuria.

/ Item una uni coniungitur pluribus de causis, ut docet Au- f. 138va
gustinus libro *De bono coniugii*. Prima est figura unionis Christi et Ecclesie; Ephesiorum vi: "Sacramentum hoc magnum est, in Christo et Ecclesia." Secunda, quia "uir est capud mulieris," Corinthiorum xi, et si una haberet plures uiros, quasi plura haberet capita et esset matrimonium monstruosum. Item non posset una simul et semel pluribus [obedire], quia si "nemo potest duobus dominis seruire," Matthei v, multo minus quatuor uel quinque. Item inter plures uix staret pax et concordia, cum quilibet uendicaret equale ius dominandi. Vnde per hoc medium probat Damascenus inpossibile plures esse deos, quia discordarent in regimine [uniuersi]. Item non posset agnosci cuius esset suscepta proles, nec ad quem pertineret hereditas. Item minus diligeretur uxor a singulis, eo quod esset communis pluribus.

Qualiter se habeant [uiri ad uxores] in paciencia et reuerencia docuit Dominus in opere creacionis, [cum] de costa formaret mulierem et non de parte alia—non de capite, non de pede, ut doceret esse uiri sociam, non dominam, [non] ancillam. Vnde versus:

Ex Ade costis illi datur uxor et hostis.

Item qualiter ° se habeant uiri ad uxores docet Apostolus
Ephesiorum vi: "Viri, diligite uxores uestras / ut corpora uestra," f. 138vb
et eciam "sicut Christus dilexit Ecclesiam"; Glossa: Mortuus est pro illa, ita et uos pro uxoribus vestris, si opus sit. Videndum tamen quomodo fiat hoc et qua de causa. Multi enim crudeles sunt uxoribus suis et inpii in propriis filiis, similes strucioni qui "duratur ad filios suos tanquam non sint sui," Iob xxxix. Similes eciam [sunt] lamie que laniat catulos suos; vnde a laniando nomen habet, quasi lania, ut dicit Ysidorus.

Now, how wives should comport themselves towards their husbands is taught by Peter, 1 Peter 3: in obedience, in service, that they may be modest in spirit, irreproachable in appearance, "whose adorning let it not be the plaiting of hair or the wearing of gold; but as the holy women adorned themselves, being in subjection to their own husbands." Also, a wife should strive how "she may please her husband," Corinthians 7, not how she may lay the devil's snares for those who look at her, Isaias 42: "They are all the snare of young men." In their smile, their look, their gesture, and their dress they "allure unstable souls," 2 Peter 2; that is, they secretly deceive them; or more properly, they lure them with their painted skin, "having their eyes full of adultery." Other noteworthy things you can find in the chapter on lechery.

Many people often ask whether one can have sexual intercourse in marriage without sin. It seems that one cannot. Gregory: "Such carnal pleasure is not without sin." But all intercourse in marriage is accompanied by pleasure; therefore it is not without sin. Further, the Apostle says in Corinthians 7, when he allows spouses to have intercourse: "But I speak this by indulgence, not by commandment." But "indulgence" relates to sin; therefore such intercourse seems to be sinful. In addition, Origen declares: "In marital intercourse the Holy Spirit is not present." But "the spirit of discipline will only flee the deceitful," Wisdom 1; therefore, there is sin in such an act. Furthermore, Corinthians 6: "They shall be two in one flesh." Augustine: "There the soul becomes totally fleshly." But from this it appears that the rational soul is perverted because she is now under the rule of the flesh, as is said in the book *On Property*. Furthermore, such an act is not without shame, which is a natural perturbation due to sin; therefore, it does not appear to be without sin. And finally, Augustine in his *City of God*: "Every sin comes from lust." But every sex act comes from lust; therefore, and so forth. Against these arguments, Augustine: "Intercourse with one's own wife is entirely without sin." Likewise Bede: "If there were any stain in marriage, the Lord would never have hallowed it by his presence and the first of his miracles." Further, matrimony is a sacrament of the New Law, hence it confers grace of its own power; but sin never does such a thing; therefore, there can be no sin in matrimony. To solve this question, one must understand that one can have intercourse with one's wife for four reasons: in order to engender offspring, or to pay one's debt, or to avoid incontinence, or to satisfy one's lust. In the first case, intercourse can be meritorious; in the second and third likewise, although some venial sin accompanies it; in the

G. 106 **obediencia** *add* et FI. **in spiritu** *om* GI. 107 **capillatura** capillata E. 109 **propriis** suis E. **debet . . . placeat** debent uxores qualiter uiris suis placeant G. **suo** proprio E; suis G. 110–11 **iniciat** iniciant G. 111 **in uisu** *om* JG; *after* in gestu F. 113 **per** *om* E. **fucatam** fuscatam FW. 116 Questio *marg* E. 117 Gregorius *marg* E. 118 **commixtio coniugalis** commixtio carnalis coniugalis E; carnalis commixtio G; coniunccio coniugalis W. 119 **Apostolus** Glossa *canc*, Apostolus *marg* E. 121–22 **inperium** *add* Origenes E. 122 Origenes *marg* E. 123 Origenes *marg* E. 124 **adest** est E; eiusdem I. **fugit** effugiet E. 126 Augustinus *marg* E. 128 **ut . . . proprio** *om* L. **De proprio** proprii idest V Topicorum W. 130 Augustinus *marg* E. **uidetur** *add* esse FGL. 131 **est *(1st)*** fit FL. **talis** *om* FLW. 132 Contra Augustinus *marg* E. 133 Beda *marg* E. **peccato** culpa JGW. **Si in nupciis** *om* G. 137 **in matrimonio** matrimonium E; in modo F. 138 Solucio *marg* E. **erit** est FGILW. **sciendum** dicendum I. 139 **procreande** creanda G. 141 **in . . . similiter** in secundo similiter et in tercio J. 141–42 **comitetur** committatur J; con-

Item qualiter se habeant mulieres ad uiros suos docet Petrus I Petri iii: In obediencia, in officio, ut sint modeste in spiritu, irreprehensibiles in habitu, "quarum non sit [capillatura] aut circumdacio auri; set sicut sancte mulieres ornabant se subiecte uiris [propriis]." Item studere debet uxor qualiter "uiro [suo] placeat," Corinthiorum vii, non qualiter laqueos dyaboli aspicientibus iniciat, Ysaie xlii: "Laqueus iuuenum omnes." In risu, in uisu, in gestu, in habitu "pelliciunt animas instabiles," II Petri ii; idest, latenter decipiunt; vel magis proprie [per] pellem fucatam alliciunt, "oculos eciam habentes plenos adulterio." Et alia notabilia vide capitulo de luxuria.

Solet queri a pluribus an sine peccato possit actus copule coniugalis exerceri. Videtur quod non. Gregorius: "Illa carnalis delectacio non est sine culpa." Set omnis commixtio ° coniugalis
/ est cum delectacione; ergo non est sine culpa. Item Apostolus f. 139ra
Corinthiorum vii, cum permittit coniuges uti opere carnali, dicit: "Hoc autem dico secundum indulgenciam, non secundum inperium." ° "Indulgencia" autem est respectu peccati; quare illud uidetur esse peccatum. Item Origenes: "In opere coniugali non [adest] Spiritus Sanctus." Set "spiritus discipline non [fugit] nisi fictum," Sapiencie i; ergo peccatum in hoc opere est. Item Corinthiorum vi: "Erunt duo in carne una." Augustinus: "Anima tota ibi fit carnalis." Set ex hoc uidetur anima racionalis peruersa, quia iam illi a carne inperatur, ut habetur libro *De proprio*. Item ille actus non est sine erubescencia, que est naturalis confusio peccati; vnde non uidetur sine peccato. Item Augustinus *De ciuitate Dei*: "Ex libidine est omne peccatum." Set omnis actus talis est ex libidine; ergo, etc. Contra, Augustinus: "Coitus cum propria uxore omnino sine peccato est." Item Beda: "Si in nupciis esset aliqua macula, Dominus nunquam sua presencia et suorum signorum iniciis eas consecrasset." Item matrimonium est sacramentum Noue Legis, ergo de suo effectu confert graciam; hoc autem nunquam facit peccatum; quare [in matrimonio] nullum erit peccatum. Ad hoc sciendum quod quatuor de causis cognoscitur uxor: aut causa prolis procreande, aut debiti reddendi, aut incontinencie uitande, aut libidinis explende. In primo casu potest esse meritorium; / in secundo et tercio similiter, licet comite- 139rb

fourth case one has to distinguish whether one sleeps with one's wife with marital love, even if lustfully; in this case it still is only a venial sin. But if one's lust is so great that one could not distinguish between one's wife and another woman, then it is a mortal sin. As to Gregory's saying that such lust is not without sin, this applies to our third and fourth case, for venial sin is hardly absent from any of these cases because of the accompanying corruption. As to the Apostle's "by indulgence," and so forth, one must distinguish between one kind of indulgence meaning concession, which is about good things, and another kind meaning permission, which is about evils. As to Origen's "In the marital act the Holy Spirit is not present," and so forth, one should say that the grace of the Holy Spirit is not given on the ground of this act, but because of the meritorious intention by which one intends to obey the Law and increase God's worship. As to Augustine's "There the soul becomes flesh," this is said because of reason's being violently flooded by sensuality; but if reason lets itself voluntarily be swallowed up by sensuality, then indeed it becomes perverted. As to Augustine's "That act is not without shame," one should say that "shame" does not always stand for sin, but sometimes it is a punishment and sometimes a virtue, as was said earlier. As to Augustine's "Every sin comes from lust," and so forth: this statement, however, cannot be turned around, so as to read "all lust is sin," because lust is sometimes the natural appetite which would have been in Adam even if he had not sinned; however, it would then not have been a disordered appetite, as it would have been under the control of reason.

Continence in widowhood is the virtue which turns away from human embraces and draws itself up into those of God. It is praiseworthy for many things. First, because it makes a widow adhere more closely to God. Corinthians 7: "If her husband has died, a woman is freed from the law of her husband"; and then "she finds the occasion to be free for God," as Augustine says about Victorinus, in book VIII of his *Confessions*. Further, a widow is entrusted to God's grace to rule her. Therefore, after Joseph's death the Blessed Virgin was entrusted to John, whose name means grace, John 19. This virtue also helps to tame one's flesh; Judith 8: "Judith, a widow, the daughter of Merari, wore haircloth upon her loins." It further helps towards gaining purity of the flesh, for those who bestow their care on pleasure have "a spotted garment," Epistle of Jude. Such people have their garment dyed with the blood of a kid, Genesis 37; "the blood of a kid" is the life of a lecherous person. Widowhood further renders prayer acceptable; whence: "The cry of a widow's tears goes up to heaven," Ecclesiasticus 35. And it earns the spirit of prophecy; Luke 2: "Anna, a widow,

comitetur FLW; communicetur G. 142 **est** *add* scilicet E. 143 **suam** *add* uxorem E. 144 **sit** est GL. **discerneret** discernat JI; decerneret F; disceret G. **utrum** inter E. **suam** *add* cognosceret ⟨uel cognoscat⟩ J. 145 Gregorius *marg* E. 145–46 **illa . . . non** nulla libido E. 147 **istorum casuum** *om* F; casu ILW. **comitantem** concomitantem JFLW. 149 **concessionis** FGIL *and source*; confessionis EW; confessionis ⟨uel concessionis⟩ J. 149–50 **que . . . bonis** et F; *om* LW. 152 **gracia . . . Sancti** Spiritus Sanctus FL; Spiritus Sanctus idest gracia G. 156–57 **Augustini** *om* E. 157 **actus** *add* ille JFG. 160 **ex libidine** *om* E. 162 **fuisset** fuit JFL. 162–63 **non . . . inordinatus** set tamen ordinatus E. **non . . . subiectus** *om* G. 163 **subiectus** *add* de continencia uiduali *rubr* J; *add* continencia uidualis *marg* I. 164 **et** *om* F. 165 **laudabilis** commendabilis J. 166 **proximius** promcius F; *om* I. 168 Augustinis *marg* E. 169 **Victorino** *add* confessore libro E. **viii** vii E. 171 **est** *written twice* E. 174 **maculatam** maculosam E. 176 **est** *add* feda JGW. 177 **acceptam** *add* esse J; *add* deo GL; *add* domini W. 178 **ascendit** ascendunt E. 180

tur ueniale. In quarto distinguendum est ° utrum maritali affectu cognoscat suam °, quamuis libidinose; adhuc est ueniale. Si uero tanta sit libido quod non discerneret [utrum] suam an alienam, mortale est. Quod uero dicit Gregorius quod [illa] libido [non] est sine culpa, in tercio casu et quarto locum habet, vel quia uix in aliquo istorum casuum propter comitantem corrupcionem deest ueniale. Ad illud Apostoli "secundum indulgenciam," etc., distingue quod est indulgencia [concessionis], que est de bonis, alia permissionis, que est de malis. Ad illud Origenis "In actu coniugali non adest Spiritus Sanctus," etc., dicendum quod ex tali actu non datur gracia Spiritus Sancti, set pro meritoria intencione qua intendit Legi obedire et cultum Dei ampliare. Ad illud Augustini "Anima ibi fit caro," hoc dicitur propter uehementem depressionem racionis a sensualitate factam; si tamen a sensualitate uoluntarie absorbetur, iam fit peruersa. Ad illud [Augustini] "Non est actus sine erubescencia," dic quod "erubescencia" non est semper pro culpa, set quandoque est pena et quandoque uirtus, ut supra dictum est. Ad illud Augustini "Omne peccatum [ex libidine]," etc.: non tamen conuertitur quod "omnis libido sit peccatum," quia libido quandoque est naturalis appetitus qui fuisset in Adam eciam si non peccasset; [non tamen inordinatus], / quia racioni subiectus. f. 139va

Continencia uidualis est uirtus humanos declinans et in diuinos se colligens amplexus. Hec propter plura laudabilis est. Primo quia absolutam a uiro proximius facit adherere Deo. Corinthiorum vii: "Si dormierit uir, liberata est mulier a lege uiri"; et tunc "inuenit occasionem uacandi Deo," sicut dicit Augustinus de Victorino, ° *Confessionum* [VIII]. Item uidua commendatur diuine gracie regenda. Vnde Beata Virgo mortuo Ioseph commendata est Iohanni, qui interpretatur gracia, Iohannis xix. Item ualet ad carnem edomandam; Iudiht viii: "Iudiht uidua filia Merari posuit cilicium super lumbos suos." Item ualet ad carnis mundiciam, quia uoluptati dantes operam "[maculatam]" habent "tunicam," Epistula Iude. Hii enim habent tunicam tinctam sanguine hedi, Genesis xxxvii; "sanguis hedi" est uita luxuriosi. Item ipsa facit acceptam oracionem; vnde: "Exclamacio lacrimarum uidue [ascendit] ad celum," Ecclesiastici xxxv. Item ipsa meretur

a prophetess," and so forth; the Gloss: "She had reached this height through long chastity and long fasting, that she should receive the spirit of prophesying." In addition, widowhood nourishes Christ, which is foreshadowed in the widow who fed Elijah, 3 Kings 17. The Apostle, too, hints at the same when in Timothy 5 he praises a widow that is filled with the works of mercy, who "has followed every good work." Continence further deserves to be fed by the Lord; therefore, the priest Abimelech allowed the young men that were clean from women to eat of the holy bread, Kings 21. But only the pure and holy are allowed to eat from the table of the Lord. Thus Hebrews at the end: "We have an altar, whereof they have no power to eat who serve the tabernacle." "The tabernacle" is our movable and portable body, which has to be carried "till we come to the place of setting it up," Numbers 10. And the place of setting it up is wherever the soul leaves the body and goes up to heaven. Continence or chastity is further a precious vessel in which are aromatic spices, such as purity of the mind, cleanness of heart, modesty in bearing, propriety in dress, abstinence in food and drink, shamefastness in mien, and discretion in word and deed. This vessel is symbolized in the ointment box of Magdalene, whose aroma fills the wide space of the Church. Chastity is also the soul's wall which protects its possessions of virtues and merits and keeps off its bodily and spiritual enemies, that is, vices and the devils. For this wall the Church prays: "Lord, surround us with your unconquerable wall." The foundation of this wall is chasteness of the flesh; its building blocks are the works of penance, such as fasts, vigils, hard work, and mortification; its mortar is the grace of God; its ramparts the guarding of the five senses. Chastity is also a precious treasure without price on earth. Ecclesiasticus 26: "No price is worthy of a continent soul." And near the end of Proverbs: "Man does not know the price thereof," that is, of a chaste woman, for "from the uttermost coasts is her price"; that is, the rewards of chastity are the dowries of heavenly glory; for heaven is the farthest point in our changeable dwelling. Chastity is further a girdle of virtues, just as a belt draws up garments so that they may not gather mud, because unless chastity is present, the garments of the other virtues are deemed ugly. Therefore, continence in widowhood, which in a large sense includes the conversion of any sinner after his fall, is symbolized by the leather girdle of the Baptist, Matthew 3, and by the leather girdle of Elijah, 4 Kings 1. Or else, the leather girdle is chasteness in marriage, which engages in the act of the flesh without yielding to corruption. In contrast, continence in widowhood is a linen

Glossa *marg* E. **hoc culmen** hunc cultum E. 184 **operibus misericordie** misericordia J. **opus** *om* E. 187–88 **De . . . sanctificatis** *om* JL. 189 **fine** *om* EJFL; ultimo G. 190 **tabernaculo** *add* de thabernaculo E. 191 **mobile** immobile G; mortale L. 194 **siue castitas** *om* FGL. 196 **habitu** ritu F. 197 **figuratur** frangitur L. 198 **odor** *om* I. 199–200 **meritorum** premeritorum F. 200 **idest . . . demones** *om* W. 202 **muri** *add* muri *canc* E. 203 **penitencie** misericordie GW. **ieiunia** *add* et oraciones G. **et** *om* E. 207–8 **Prouerbiorum fine** Iob 28 FL; procul G. 208 **fine** *om* E. 209–10 **premium** premia J; precium F. 210 **mutabilis** inuisibilis L. 211 **zona** cingulum F. **stringit** cingit J; stringens L. 212 **contrahant** trahant E. 213 **uestes uirtutum** uirtutes J. 215 **Baptiste . . . zona *(2nd)*** *om* W. 215–16 **Baptiste . . . zona** que F. 216 **Vel** *add* in E. 218 **enim** uero FIL. 219 **tunditur** tenditur F. 219–20 **laborioso** longo J. 220 **est . . . lineum**

spiritum prophecie; Luce ii: “Anna uidua prophetissa,” etc.; Glossa: “Longa castitate longisque ieiuniis ad [hoc culmen] peruenerat, ut spiritum prophetandi acciperet.” Item ipsa / pascit f. 139vb Christum, quod figuratur in uidua que pauit Helyam, III Regum xvii. Hoc eciam innuit Apostolus, Tymothei v, commendans uiduam operibus misericordie plenam que “omne [opus] bonum secuta est.” Item continencia meretur eciam pasci a Domino; vnde pueris mundis a mulieribus permisit Achymelech sacerdos commedere de panibus sanctificatis, Regum xxi. De mensa uero Domini non licet commedere nisi mundis et sanctificatis. Vnde Hebreorum [fine]: “Habemus altare de quo commedere non licet hiis qui tabernaculo ° deseruiunt.” “Tabernaculum” est corpus nostrum mobile et portabile, quod tamdiu portandum est “donec perueniatur ad erectionis locum,” Numeri x. Et est locus erectionis vbicumque anima corpus deserit et celum ascendit. Item continencia siue castitas est quoddam preciosum uas in quo sunt species aromatice, ut puritas mentis, mundicia cordis, modestia in gestu, honestas in habitu, abstinencia in cibo et potu, verecundia in uultu, discrecio in uerbo et facto. Hoc uas figuratur in alabastro Magdalene, cuius odor inplet latitudinem Ecclesie. Item castitas est murus anime conseruans possessiones uirtutum et meritorum, arcens hostes corporales et spiritales, idest uicia et demones. Pro quo muro orat Ecclesia: “Muro tuo inexpugnabili circumcin- / ge nos, Domine.” Huius muri fundamentum est pudicicia carnis; f. 140ra lapides opera penitencie, ut ieiunia, uigilie, labores, [et] discipline; cementum est gracia Dei; eius propugnacula quinque sensuum custodia. Item castitas est quidam preciosus thesaurus, cuius estimacio non est in terris. Ecclesiastici xxvi: “Omnis ponderacio non est digna continentis anime.” Et Prouerbiorum [fine]: “Nescit homo precium eius,” idest caste mulieris, quia “ab ultimis finibus precium eius”; idest, dotes celestis glorie sunt premium castitatis; celum enim est ultimus terminus mutabilis habitacionis. Item castitas est cingulum uirtutum, sicut zona stringit uestimenta ne [contrahant] lutum, quia nisi assit castitas, fede reputantur cetere uestes uirtutum. Continencia igitur uidualis, que large conplectitur conuersionem cuiuslibet penitentis post lapsum, figuratur in zona pellicea Baptiste, Matthei iii, et in zona pellicea Helye, IIII Regum i. Vel ° zona pellicea est coniugalis pudicicia que carnali uacat operi, non tamen subcumbit corrupcioni. Zona uero linea est uidualis continencia. Linum enim longo la-

girdle. Linen is beaten and woven and blanched with much labor; and such continence is acquired with laborious effort. This girdle is the linen loincloth which Jeremiah hid by the river Euphrates and it rotted, Jeremias 13. The loincloth's rotting by the Euphrates signifies that the life of continent people becomes corrupted through too great a wealth of temporal goods. Gregory comments on Job 40, "Gird up your loins like a man," as follows: "The wealth of temporal goods loosens the continence of one's loins." And Bernard: "Chastity is endangered among pleasures, humility among riches, pity in business, truth in much talking, and charity in this evil world." Chastity in virgins is a girdle of gold, which is twofold, according to Corinthians 7: that a virgin "may be holy both in body and in spirit." Virginity of the flesh is symbolized by the golden girdle of the angel who was girt at the loins, Daniel 10; virginity of the spirit, by the golden girdle of the angel who was girt about the breast, Apocalypse 1. The Lord taught us continence of the flesh when he said: "Let your loins be girt," Luke 12. Gregory: "We gird our loins when we restrain fleshly lust with continence. Men have lust in their loins, women in their navel." Thus, the strength of Behemoth is said to lie "in his loins and in the navel of his belly," Job 40; for through those lustful parts the enemy enters the soul's fortifications, as if it were through its weaker places, and kindles in them the fire of carnal desire, which is "a fire that devours to destruction," Job 31; Lamentations 4: "He has kindled a fire," and so forth. The enemy also finds some of his retinue inside our castle, who prepare his way even as far as our heart. Therefore Gregory: "And so he is overcome with greater difficulty because he is strengthened against us by parts of our own being." Continence of the spirit the Lord taught us when he said: "Blessed are the clean of heart," and so forth, Matthew 5. Cleanness of heart is the mind's eye with which God is seen in this life, and this vision may be called the illumination of faith. Augustine: "Faith is the mind's illumination to see God." Or else, cleanness of heart means not to be bitten by the delight of former sins, not to incline to the desire of future evil, and not to be stained by present temptation. But since few people have all these qualities, Proverbs 20 asks: "Who can say, 'My heart is clean?'" "Who" indicates rareness, not impossibility.

This cleanness has several good effects. The Lord indicates the first when he says: "For they shall see God." God is seen in this life in four ways, by means of two natural things and two gifts of grace. The two natural things are our intel-

debet habere linum E. 221–22 **Ieremias . . . Lumbare** Ieremie 30 F. 221 **fluuium** *om* E. 221–22 **et . . . Eufraten** *om* G. 222 **Eufraten** fluuium F. 223 Gregorius *marg* E. 224 **Accinge** accingere E. 225 Bernardus *marg* E. 226 **humilitas** humanitas J; *om* W. 226–27 **negocio** negociis E. 227 **caritas . . . nequam** *om* FLW. 229 **mente** nomine E. 229–30 **carnis** corporis J. 230–31 **renes . . . ad** *om* FGL. 233 Gregorius *marg* E. **Lumbos** *add* enim E. 235–36 **Ideo . . . umbilico** *om* L. 237 **quia per illa** per illa enim E. 238 **infirmiores** inferiores FL. 239 **perdicionem** perdendum E. 240 **iv** *om* E; ii JI. 241 **faciunt** faciant E. 242 Gregorius *marg* E. **quia** *add* quia E. **de nostro** demon FL. 246 Augustinus *marg* E. 247 **Deum** *om* E. 249 **presenti** presente EF. 252 **Quis . . . inpossibilitatem** *om* E; quis (*blank*) notat inpossibilitatem G. **raritatem** largitatem W. 255 **in**

bore tunditur et texitur et candidatur; et hec continencia laborioso exercicio acquiritur. Hec zona [est lumbare lineum] quod abscondit Ieremias iuxta [fluuium] Eufraten et conputruit, Ieremie xiii. Lumbare / iuxta Eufraten conputrescere est superhabundancia f. 140rb temporalium uitam corrumpi continencium. Gregorius super Iob xl, "[Accinge] sicut uir lumbos tuos," ibi: "Habundancia temporalium dissoluit continenciam renum." Et Bernardus: "Periclitatur castitas in deliciis, humilitas in diuiciis, pietas in [negocio], ueritas in multiloquio, caritas in hoc seculo nequam." Zona aurea est castitas uirginalis, que est duplex, ut Corinthiorum vii: vt sit uirgo "sancta [mente] et corpore." Virginitas carnis figuratur in zona aurea angeli precincti ad renes, Danielis x; virginitas mentis in zona aurea angeli precincti ad pectus, Apocalipsis i. Continenciam carnis docuit Dominus cum dixit: "Sint lumbi uestri precincti," Luce xii. Gregorius: "Lumbos ° precingimus cum carnis luxuriam per continenciam coartamus. Viris enim luxuria in lumbis est, feminis in umbilico." Ideo fortitudo Behemoth dicitur esse "in lumbis eius et in umbilico uentris eius," Iob xl; [quia] per illa ° loca luxurie tanquam per partes infirmiores intrat hostis municiones anime et succendit in eis ignem concupiscencie, qui est "ignis ad [perdicionem] deuorans," Iob xxxi; Trenorum [iv]: "Succendit ignem," etc. Inuenit eciam in castris nostris de satellitibus suis, qui [faciunt] illi aditum eciam usque ad cor nostrum. Vnde Gregorius: "Ideo difficilius uincitur, quia / ° de nostro contra nos roboratur." Continenciam mentis f. 140va docuit Dominus cum dixit: "Beati mundo corde," etc., Matthei v. Et est mundicia cordis oculus mentis quo uidetur Deus in presenti, que uisio potest dici fidei illuminacio. Augustinus: "Fides est mentis illuminacio ad uidendum [Deum]." Uel mundicia cordis est preteritarum culparum delectacione non morderi, uoluntate futuri mali non inclinari, [presenti] temptacione non pollui. Set quia omnes istas condiciones habent pauci, ideo queritur Prouerbiorum xx: "Quis potest dicere, 'mundum est cor meum?'" ["Quis" raritatem notat, non inpossibilitatem.]

Et sunt plures effectus huius mundicie. Primum notat Dominus cum dicit: "Quoniam ipsi Deum uidebunt." Videtur autem Deus in uia quatuor modis, per duo naturalia et per duo gratuita.

lect and the mirror of creation. Jerome comments on Matthew: "Our intellect is the mind's eye." Of the second, Romans 1: "The invisible things of God," and so forth. The two gifts of grace are faith and mental illumination, as the Philosopher says: "Illumination comes from the practical and speculative intellect by the agency of the highest intelligence." Just as in the process of physical sight three things are necessary, namely, the eye's transparency, intermediary light, and the instrument's turning to what is visible, so are three things required in the vision of God. Transparency, which is cleanness of heart; whence: "Blessed are the clean of heart." Intermediary light is grace itself; for as light is seen because of its splendor, so God is discerned in this life by means of a certain inner illumination of the soul, when the soul makes a ladder of itself by which it climbs beyond itself, as Gregory says. Nor is this astonishing, since the agent intellect, when it actively perceives, "turns entirely away from the body," as Augustine says in his book *On the Immortality of the Soul.* Turning the instrument to what is visible means turning the soul's total desire towards the Father of Lights, according to Isaias 51: "Lift up your eyes to heaven," and so forth. Another effect of this cleanness is that it earns infusion of grace. Therefore, the Church sings on Pentecost that the Holy Spirit found the hearts of the disciples as clean vessels and gave them charismatic gifts. Another effect is that it deserves the grace of prayer and of preaching. Proverbs 22: "He that loves cleanness of heart, for the grace of his lips shall have the king for his friend"; that is, he has Christ as his friend who cleanses his heart so that he may be devout in prayer and fruitful in preaching. Cleanness of heart further deserves a clean mansion in heaven. The Psalm: "Who shall ascend into the mountain of the Lord? The innocent in hands and clean of heart." How attentively and incessantly this cleanness must be prayed for, the Psalmist taught when he said: "Create a clean heart in me, o God." And well does he say "create," which means to make out of nothing, because grace, by whose power cleanness exists, is created out of nothing, that is, after nothing, and is given without merits. Or else, "creating" means the purging of the heart, for an unclean heart is, so to speak, nothing; Proverbs 10: "The heart of the wicked is worth nothing." Therefore, when it is cleansed, it is, so to speak, created anew.

Several things help to preserve continence. The first is guarding our heart; Proverbs 4: "With all watchfulness keep your heart." Abba Agathon: "Man is a

uia *om* F. 256 **intellectiua** intelligencia EFL; intellectiua, *and marg* intelligencia J. 257 Ieronimus *marg* E. **De** *add* duobus *canc* E. 259 Philosophus *marg* E. 260 **Fiunt** sunt FGL. **irradiaciones** tradiciones EFGLW. 261 **a** *om* E. 265 **media** *add* que E. 267 **qua** et EG. 268 Gregorius *marg* E. **Nec** fiet E. 269 **auertitur** conuertitur E. 270 Augustinus *marg* E. **anime** *add* Augustinus: Quis est iste super caput anime mee? Per ipsam animam meam ascendam ad ipsum G. 279 **habet** habebit E. **sit** *om* E. 281 **munda mansio** mundicia mansionis J. 283 **attente . . . assidue** attente F; *om* L. 285–86 **de . . . idest** *om* E. **quia . . . creata** *om* F. 286 **data** dare E. 289 **Vnde . . . creatur** *om* G. **nouo** nichilo FL. **creatur** *add* de hiis que seruant continenciam *rubr* J. 290 **ad conseruacionem continencie** continere E. 292 Agaton *marg* E. 294–95 **corrupcio . . . corporis** corrupto totum corpus

Duo naturalia sunt [intellectiua] potencia et speculum creature. Ieronimus super Mattheum: "Intellectus est oculus mentis." De secundo Romanorum i: "Inuisibilia Dei," etc. Duo gratuita sunt fides et spiritualis illuminacio iuxta Philosophum dicentem: "Fiunt autem [irradiaciones] ex parte intellectus practici et speculatiui [a] suprema intelligencia agente." Et sicut in uisione corporali tria sunt necessaria, vt dyaphoneitas oculi, lux media, conuersio instrumenti ad uisibile, ita in ista uisione exiguntur tria. Dyaphoneitas, que est mundicia cordis; vnde: "Beati mundo corde." Lux me- / dia ° est ipsa gracia; vnde sicut lux suo f. 140vb splendore uidetur, ita Deus quadam interna illuminacione anime in uia cognoscitur, cum anima de seipsa facit scalam [qua] se supergreditur, ut dicit Gregorius. [Nec] hoc mirum, quia intellectus agens, cum actu intelligit, omnino "a corpore [auertitur]," ut dicit Augustinus libro *De immortalitate anime*. Conuersio instrumenti ad uisibile est totum desiderium anime in Patrem Luminum conuertere, iuxta illud Ysaie li: "Leuate in celum oculos uestros," etc. Alius effectus huius mundicie est quod meretur gracie infusionem. Vnde canit Ecclesia in Penthecoste quod Spiritus Sanctus inuenit corda discipulorum receptacula munda et tribuit eis carismatum dona. Alius effectus est quod meretur graciam orandi et predicandi. Prouerbiorum xxii: "Qui diligit cordis mundiciam, propter graciam labiorum habebit amicum regem"; idest, Christum [habet] amicum qui mundat cor suum ut [sit] deuotus in oracione et fructuosus in predicacione. Item mundicie cordis debetur munda mansio celestis. Psalmus: "Quis ascendet in montem Domini? Innocens manibus et mundo corde." Item quam attente et quam assidue petenda sit hec mundicia docuit qui dixit: "Cor mundum crea in me, Deus." Et bene dixit "creare," idest [de nichilo facere, quia gracia per quam est mundicia ex nichilo est creata, idest] post nichilum, et eciam sine meritis [data]. Vel quedam "creacio" est cordis purgacio, quia cor immundum est quasi nihilum; Prouerbiorum x: "Cor stultorum / pro nichilo." f. 141ra Vnde cum mundatur, quasi de nouo creatur.

Plura sunt que faciunt [ad conseruacionem continencie]. Primum est custodia cordis; Prouerbiorum iiii: "Omni custodia serua cor tuum." Abbas Agathon: "Homo est arbor, custodia

tree, guarding his body is its foliage, and guarding his heart its fruit." And it is well that the heart should be guarded, for just as the whole body's life comes from it, so from it also comes the whole body's corruption. Thus, the Psalm says well: "My heart has been inflamed, and my reins have been changed," etc. Gregory in his *Morals* calls the ancient serpent "slippery"; that is, he calls the devil a "worm of the loins," because as soon as his first suggestion is not warded off, he suddenly slips into the core of one's heart without being perceived. The second is watching one's body. Ecclesiasticus 7: "Do you have daughters? Have a care to their body." And understand here the body with its five senses, for death usually enters through the windows, Jeremias 9. Gregory in his *Morals*: "He who rules the senses of his body badly, opens his bright windows to blind darkness." The third is moderation in food and drink, as the Church prays:

Let scarcity in food and drink
Wear thin our flesh's pride.

For abstinence preserves chastity, just as abundance of food calls forth lust; on Leviticus 3, where "the caul of the liver with the two little kidneys" are commanded to be burned, Hesychius comments that "in the liver is the seat of heat, the beginning of lust, and the desire for food." For the liver gives operative power to the kidneys. Thus, Augustine says in *On True Innocence*: "I have never seen a continent person whom I did not see abstain." The fourth is to avoid women, for just as it is difficult to walk on hot coals without burning one's footsoles, or to hide fire in one's bosom without burning one's clothes, "so he that goes in to his neighbor's wife is not clean when he has touched her," Proverbs 6. And Jerome in his book *On the Value of Solitude*: "The prime temptation of clerics is to dwell with women." Therefore Canon XVIII, question ii, *We determine*, says that "dwelling with women often introduces adultery." Therefore, it is forbidden in Distinction xxxii, *Your guest-chamber*. The fifth is chastizing our flesh; Galatians near the end: "They that are Christ's have crucified their flesh, with the vices and concupiscences." The sixth is meditating on Christ's passion; Hebrews 12: "Think diligently upon him, etc., for you have not yet resisted unto blood." The seventh is thinking of our death; Gregory: "The living flesh cannot be better tamed than by meditating on what it will be like when it is dead." The eighth is the vileness and ugliness and anguish of sin; the Gloss on

corrumpitur J; corrupto tocius corporis corrupcio FGIW. 296 Gregorius *marg* E. 297 **lubricum** lustricum (?) E. 299 **intima** menia L. 300 **vii** vi E. 302 Gregorius *marg* E. **ix** *om* E. 303–4 **luminis** *om* FL. 308 **enim** *om* E. 309 **iecoris** *marg* E. 310 Esycius *marg* E. 312 Augustinus *marg* E. 313 **Non** vix J. 315 **ut . . . comburantur** et non comburi FL. 316–17 **mulierem** uxorem J. 317 **est** erit JFILW. 318 Ieronimus *marg* E. 320 **questio ii Diffinimus** *om* F. 321–22 **Ideo . . . Hospitalis** *om* FL. 322 **xxxii** xxxiii E. **Hospitalis** hospiciolum J. **castigacio** edomacio JFILW. 323 **fine** *om* EL; 5 F; ultimo G. 325 **xii** ii E. 326 Gregorius

corporis folia, custodia cordis fructus." Et bene custodiendum est cor, quia sicut ex ipso est uita tocius corporis, ita ex ipso corrupcio tocius corporis. Ideo bene dicit Psalmus: "Inflammatum est cor meum, et renes mei commutati sunt," etc. Gregorius in *Moralibus* uocat antiquum serpentem "lubricum"; idest, dyabolum uocat "uermem lumborum," quia dum eius prime suggestioni non resistitur, repente totus ad intima cordis dum non sentitur illabitur. Secundum est custodia corporis. Ecclesiastici [vii]: "Filie tibi sunt? Serua corpus illarum." Et intellige corpus cum quinque sensibus, quia mors solet ingredi per fenestras, Ieremie [ix]. Gregorius in *Moralibus*: "Qui male regit sensus corporis, fenestras luminis aperit ad tenebras cecitatis." Tercium est modestia cibi et potus, sicut orat Ecclesia:

Carnis terat superbiam
Potus cibique parcitas.

Abstinencia [enim] seruat castitatem, sicut superfluitas prouocat libidinem; Leuitici iii, vbi precipitur adolere "reticulum iecoris cum renunculis," dicit Esycius quod "in iecore est sedes caloris, inicium / desiderii, et appetitus gule." Iecur enim renibus uim f. 141rb
operacionis ministrat. Ideo bene Augustinus dicit, *De vera innocencia*: "Non uidi continentem quem non uidi abstinentem." Quartum est uitacio mulierum, quia sicut difficile est ambulare super prunas ut plante non comburantur, aut abscondere ignem in sinu ut uestimenta non ardeant, "sic qui ingreditur ad mulierem proximi sui non est mundus cum tetigerit eam," Prouerbiorum vi. Et Ieronimus libro *De bono solitudinis*: "Prima temptamenta clericorum sunt cohabitaciones mulierum." Ideo dicit Canon XVIII, questio ii, *Diffinimus*, quod "cohabitacio mulierum sepe intercipit adulterium." Ideo prohibet eam Distinctio [xxxii], *Hospitalis*. Quintum est castigacio carnis; Galatarum [fine]: "Qui Christi sunt, carnem suam crucifixerunt cum uiciis et concupiscenciis." Sextum est memoria passionis Christi; Hebreorum [xii]: "Recogitate eum, etc., nondum enim usque ad sanguinem restitistis." Septimum est memoria mortis; Gregorius: "Non potest melius domari caro uiua quam cogitare qualis erit mortua." Octauum est uilitas et feditas et anxietas peccati; Glossa su-

Exodus 6: "Nothing is harder than serving the devils in works of the flesh." The ninth is the eternity of punishment; Gregory: "What delights us is momentary; what torments us, eternal." The tenth is considering our reward, for "the undefiled will have fruit in the visitation of holy souls, and the eunuch," that is, the continent, "will be given a precious gift," Wisdom 3.

He who makes a vow of continence dedicates a temple to the Lord. For the Lord wants "that the temple of his habitation should be in us," 2 Machabees 14. Hence, the soul of a just man is God's temple, as in Corinthians 3. In this temple should be depicted images of the saints as examples for imitation, such as the obedience of the angels, who serve God at his beck, as they see him towering above them, as Dionysius says. Also the faith of the patriarchs should be depicted in it: "Abraham believed," and so forth, Genesis 15. Further, the constancy of the prophets, who did not hide a word out of fear of death. Ecclesiasticus 49: "Twelve prophets strengthened Jacob and redeemed themselves"; that is, they set their souls free because they proclaimed to the people their crimes. Further, the poverty of the apostles, in whose person Peter says, "Behold, we have left all things," Matthew 19. Further, the patience of the martyrs, who "were stoned, were cut asunder," Hebrews 11. Further, the longing of the confessors, in whose person the spouse of Canticles 5 says: "Tell my beloved that I languish with love." Further, the chastity of the virgins, namely that "happy is the barren and undefiled," Wisdom 3. Notice that God's dwelling place in us should be dedicated like a real church building. First the pagan filth must be thrown out so that the ornaments of the saints can be put in. This will be done by Judas, that is, confession; Machabees 4: "Judas and his brethren said, 'Behold, our enemies are discomfited; let us go up now to cleanse the holy places and to repair them.'" In the dedication of a church four things are to be observed. First, the change of usage. Dedication means to change something from common usage to the use of God; thus: "Who has yielded his members to serve uncleanness and iniquity, let him now yield them to serve justice unto sanctification," Romans 6. The second is renewal, after former sin has been laid aside; Ephesians 4: "Put off, according to former conversation, the old man, and be renewed in the spirit of your mind." The third is the raising of songs. Esdras 3: In dedicating the temple "one could not distinguish the voice of the shout of joy from the noise of the weeping of the people." Thus, in spir-

marg E. 330 **seruire** deseruire JFIL. Gregorius *marg* E. 331 **est** *add* id E. **Decimum** *add* est JFILW. 332 **quia** *om* E. 332–34 **incoinquinati . . . electum** *canc*, electi *interl* J. 333 **idest continenti** *om* GL. 337 **est** *om* E. **vt** unde E; *om* FGILW. 340 Dyonisius *marg* E. **supra** super E. **imminentem** inuicem FI; in mente L. 341 **in eo** *om* E. 343 **uerbum** uerbis FI; *om* L. 347 **nos** *om* E. 353 **habitacio** ecclesia F. 364 **Tercium** quartum E. 365 **agnoscere** cognoscere FGL. 366 **fletus** flentis F. 368 **est** *om* EG. 368–69 **innouacione** nouacione E.

per Exodi vi: "Nichil durius quam demonibus in operibus carnis seruire." Nonum est perpetuitas supplicii; Gregorius: "Momentaneum est ° / quod delectat; eternum quod cruciat." Decimum f. 141va consideracio premii, [quia] "incoinquinati habebunt fructum in respeccione animarum sanctarum, et spadoni," idest continenti, "dabitur donum electum," Sapiencie iii.

Vovens continenciam dedicat templum Domino. Vult enim "templum habitacionis sue fieri in nobis," II Machabeorum xiiii. Vnde templum Dei [est] anima iusti, [vt] Corinthiorum iii. In hoc templo debent depingi sanctorum ymagines ad exemplum et imitacionem, ut obediencia angelorum qui Deo ministrant ad nutum, prout ipsum uident [supra] se imminentem, ut dicit Dyonisius. Item depingatur [in eo] fides patriarcharum: "Credidit enim Abraham," etc., Genesis xv. Item constancia prophetarum, qui timore mortis non tacuerunt uerbum. Ecclesiastici xlix: "Duodecim prophete corroborauerunt Iacob et redemerunt se"; idest, animas suas liberauerunt, quia scelera sua populo annunciauerunt. Item paupertas apostolorum, in quorum persona dicit Petrus: "Ecce [nos] reliquimus omnia," Matthei xix. Item paciencia martirum, qui "lapidati sunt, secti sunt," Hebreorum xi. Item desideria confessorum, in quorum persona dicit sponsa, Canticorum v: "Nunciate dilecto quia amore langueo." Item castitas uirginum, scilicet quod "felix et sterilis et incoinquinata," Sapiencie iii. Et nota quod ad similitudinem materialis templi dedicanda est / in f. 141vb nobis habitacio Dei. Primo sunt eiciende spurcicie gencium, ut inferantur ornamenta sanctorum. Et hoc faciet Iudas, idest confessio; Machabeorum iiii: "Dixit Iudas et fratres eius, 'Ecce contriti sunt inimici nostri; ascendamus nunc mundare sancta et renouare.'" In dedicacione quatuor sunt notanda. Primum est usus mutacio. Dedicacio enim est separacio ab usibus communibus ad usum Dei; ita: "Qui exhibuit membra sua seruire immundicie ad iniquitatem, ita exhibeat ea seruire iusticie in sanctificacionem," Romanorum vi. Secundum est innouacio deposita uetustate peccati; Ephesiorum iiii: "Deponite uos secundum pristinam conuersacionem ueterem hominem, et renouate spiritum mentis uestre." [Tercium] est canticorum exultacio. Esdre iii: In dedicacione templi "non poterat quisquam agnoscere uocem clamoris letan-

itual dedication there should be the voice of joy in hope of forgiveness, and the voice of weeping in sorrow for one's sin and fear of punishment. The fourth is the banquet of holy celebration, because following upon such a renewal the penitent is worthy of spiritual food. That is what the Apostle says in Corinthians 11: "Let a man prove himself, and so let him eat of that bread and drink of the chalice." Three things are carried out by the bishop, namely, the aspersion, the anointing, and the inscription. The aspersion symbolizes the refreshment of the saints from the hardships of the world; Jeremias 6: "You shall find refreshment for your souls." The anointing symbolizes the soothing of our minds from the sufferings of this misery. This is that "unction which teaches us of all things," John 2. The inscription symbolizes the salvation of the elect, against the fear of damnation, for those inscribed in the king's or prince's register are usually safe. And this inscription is made in the sand and in the lowest place, because more of the poor will be written in the book of life than of the rich; for to the former will be said: "Rejoice and exult, for your names are written in heaven," Luke 10. Ambrose explains this in his *Exameron* as follows: "This name is the sum of somebody's good qualities which is not to be found in someone else." The inscription is the correspondence of the place with that name. And two alphabets are written down, namely the Latin and the Greek, because only these two peoples believe; for of the Hebrews it is spoken: "Let them be blotted out of the book of the living, and with the just let them not be written." Other things are as it were the material for the dedication such as, the salt of wisdom, the wine of spiritual joy, the chrism of grace, the fire of doctrine, the ashes of meditation on death, the water of tears, the incense of devotion, and the procession of solicitude in good works. The first day of the dedication symbolizes Christ's union with the militant Church, the octave, with the triumphant Church, when it will be said: "Behold, the tabernacle of God with men, and he will dwell with them," Apocalypse 21. But many dedicate "a statue of gold" with Nebuchadnezzar, Daniel 3, such as those who on account of some bodily or spiritual grace become haughty in pride. They make Jerusalem "the habitation of strangers," Machabees 1, they make of God's temple a temple of the devil and convert the church into a pantheon, which is the dwelling-place of all the devils; in which the idol of Venus is painted through lechery, that of Bacchus through drunkenness, of Mercury through covetousness, of Mars through discord, the likeness of poisonous snakes through envy, and the abominations of vile passions which "it is a shame to speak of," Ephe-

369–70 **dicit Apostolus** dicitur FILW; *om* G. 373 **vi** v E. 374 **refrigerium** *marg corr from* requiem *canc* E; requiem FIL. 377–78 **quia . . . securi** *om* F. 377 **matricula** cartula G. 378 **inscripcio** descripcio FL. 379 **imo** primo FL; uno GW. 380 **et exultate** *om* JFGLW; in domino I. 381 Ambrosius *marg* E. 383 **Scripcio . . . congruencia** scripta autem congruenta E. 387 **dedicacionis** dictacionis E. 388 **lux doctrine** *om* J. 390 **coniunctionem** communionem F. 393 **plures** *add* sunt qui E. 395 **propter** per E. **graciam** gloriam F. **aliquam** *om* FILW. 398 **habitaculum** habitacio J. 400 **ebrietatem** gulam F. **cupiditatem** *corr from* cupidititatem E; auariciam G. 401 **uenenatorum** uenatorum GI. **inuidiam** immundiciam L. 401–2 **abhominaciones ignominiosarum** habitacio ignominiarum E. 404 **multas** *add* de uirginitate *rubr* JFI. 405 **carnis** *om* E; mentis I. 406

cium et uocem fletus populi." Ita in dedicacione spiritali fit uox leticie pro spe uenie, et uox fletus pro reatu culpe et timore pene. Quartum [est] sacre celebracionis refectio, quia facta tali [innouacione], dignus est penitens spirituali cibo. Hoc est quod dicit Apostolus Corinthiorum xi: "Probet seipsum homo, et sic de pane illo edat et de calice bibat." Fiunt autem tria ab episcopo, scilicet aspersio, inunccio, / inscripcio. Aspersio signat refrigerium f. 142ra sanctorum contra labores mundi; Ieremie [vi]: "Inuenietis refrigerium animabus uestris." Inunctio est animorum mitigacio contra dolores huius miserie. Hec est "unctio que docet nos de omnibus," Iohannis ii. Inscripcio est electorum predestinacio contra timorem dampnacionis, quia scripti in matricula regis uel principis solent esse securi. Et fit hec inscripcio in sabulo et in imo loco, quia de pauperibus plures scribentur in libro uite quam de diuitibus; hiis enim dicitur: "Gaudete et exultate, quia nomina uestra scripta sunt in celis," Luce x. Quod exponit Ambrosius in *Exameron*: "Hoc nomen est collectio bonorum alicuius, quam non est in alio reperire." [Scripcio autem est congruencia] loci ad tale nomen. Et scribitur duplex alphabetum, scilicet Latinum et Grecum, quia iste due gentes tantum credunt; de Hebreis enim dicitur: "Deleantur de libro uiuencium et cum iustis non scribantur." Alia sunt tanquam materia [dedicacionis], vt sal sapiencie, vinum spiritualis leticie, crisma gracie, lux doctrine, cinis memoria mortis, aqua lacrimarum, thus deuocionis, circuitus sollicitudo boni operis. Prima dies dedicacionis signat coniunctionem Christi cum Ecclesia militante, octaua cum triumphante, quando dicetur: "Ecce tabernaculum Dei cum hominibus, et habitabit cum eis," Apocalipsis xxi. Set plures ° / ° dedicant "statuam f. 142rb auream" cum Nabuchodonosor, Danielis iii, vt illi qui [propter] graciam aliquam corporalem aut spiritualem eleuantur in superbiam. Isti faciunt Ierusalem "habitacionem exterorum," Machabeorum i, de templo Dei templum dyaboli, et ecclesiam conuertunt in pantheon, quod est habitaculum omnium demoniorum; in quo depingitur ydolum Veneris per luxuriam, Bachi per ebrietatem, Mercurii per cupiditatem, Martis per discordiam, similitudo reptilium uenenatorum per inuidiam, [abhominaciones ignominiosarum] passionum quas "turpe est dicere," Ephesiorum

sians 5. Thus it is said in Ezechiel 8: "Dig in the wall, and you will see many abominations."

Virginity is integrity of the flesh, which has no merit unless the mind remains uncorrupted. "Virginity" is so called from *viror genitus,* "innate strength," that is, the beauty we have from our birth. A "virgin" is so called by syncope from the word *virago,* as if she were just like Eve, made from *vir,* "man," while she was uncorrupted. According to Augustine, virginity is "the perpetual contemplation of incorruption in our corruptible flesh."

Many things recommend virginity. First, because it is the spouse of Christ; 2 Corinthians 11: "I have espoused you, a virgin, to one husband," etc. This is also prefigured in the marriage of the high priest, Leviticus 21: "He shall take a virgin unto his wife, not a widow or one that is divorced," and so forth. Further, virginity gave birth to Christ; Isaias 7: "Behold, a virgin shall conceive," and so forth; and Isaias at the end: "Before she was in labor, she brought forth," and so forth. In addition, virginity feeds Christ; Canticles 2: "He feeds among the lilies." Gregory: "He feeds among the lilies who takes delight in the sweet-smelling and pure white life of the saints." Christ was literally fed with the milk of the Blessed Virgin; with a little milk he was fed, and so forth. Virginity also brings one close to God; Wisdom 6: "Incorruption brings near to God," as is shown in John, who leaned "on the breast of the Lord" at the Last Supper, John 13. Further, it makes us rich with celestial fruit. Therefore, the promise of Deuteronomy 28: "Blessed shall be the fruit of your womb," applies especially to the Blessed Virgin, who made a vow of virginity first; and likewise Wisdom 3: "Happy is the barren and the undefiled; she shall have fruit in the visitation of holy souls." Although she is fruitful in natural offspring, she was yet barren with regard to lustful acts. Virginity further enjoys a single life on earth; Jerome: "To live in the flesh outside the flesh is angelic, not human." Through virginity has been restored what was lost; Jerome: "The chasteness of womanly virtues has restored what was lost"; and Anselm: "Through the son of the Glorious Virgin, what was in hell rejoices in its freedom, and what is in the world is happy in its being restored." Virginity further reveals mysteries, as is shown in Joseph, Genesis 40, and in the three young men of Daniel 1. It also strengthens the mind, as is seen, Judith 15, in the words of the priest Joachim to Judith: "Your heart has been strengthened because you have loved chastity." And it adorns the soul with the garments of the virtues; Apocalypse 16: "Blessed is he that keeps his garments," and so forth. In addition, virginity follows the Lord with both feet; Apocalypse 14: "They are virgins and follow the Lamb," etc. Further, it is honored in several ways; Gregory: "Virginity is not only hon-

uiror uigor E. 408 **quia** quasi EIW; *om* F; quasi dicat L. 409 Augustinus *marg* E. 416 **fine** *om* ELW; 66 F; ultimo G. 417–20 **Item . . . etc.** *in line 415 before* Item J. 418 Gregorius *marg* E. 419 **Beate** beatissime FILW. 421 **vt** quod J; *om all others.* 423 **xiii** xxxiii E; *om* G. 424 **emisit** promisit E. 429 Ieronimus *marg* E. 429–30 **Item . . . humanum** *om* G. 431 Ieronimus *marg* E. 431–32 **Ieronimus . . . et** *om* G. 432 Anshelmus *marg* E. 432–33 **Uirginis** uirginitatis EW. 433 **erant** *om* E. 441 Gregorius *marg* E. **honoratur** honorat FGILW. 442 **eciam an-**

v. Ideo dicitur Ezechielis viii: "Fode parietem, et uidebis abhominaciones multas."

Uirginitas est [carnis] integritas, que nullum habet meritum nisi mens fuerit incorrupta. Et dicitur "uirginitas" quasi [uiror] genitus, idest decor nobiscum natus. "Virgo" dicitur per syncopam ab hoc nomine uirago, [quia] hec est talis qualis fuit Eua de uiro facta dum esset incorrupta. Secundum Augustinum virginitas est in carne corruptibili perpetua incorrupcionis meditacio.

Multa commendant uirginitatem. Primo quod ipsa est sponsa Christi; II Corinthiorum xi: "Despondi uos uni uiro virginem," etc. Hoc est eciam figuratum in coniugio summi sacerdotis, Leuitici xxi: "Virginem ducet uxorem, non uiduam aut repudiatam," etc. Item ipsa genuit Christum; Ysaie / f. 142va vii: "Ecce uirgo concipiet," etc.; et Ysaie [fine]: "Antequam parturiret, peperit," etc. Item ipsa pascit Christum; Canticorum ii: "Pascitur inter lylia." Gregorius: "Inter lylia pascitur quia in odorifera et candida sanctorum uita delectatur." Et ad litteram pastus est lacte Beate Virginis; paruo lacte pastus est, etc. Item ipsa facit esse Deo proximum; Sapiencie vi: "Incorrupcio facit esse proximum Deo," vt patet de Iohanne, qui "supra pectus Domini" in cena recubuit, Iohannis [xiii]. Item fructu celesti ditatur. Vnde Beate Virgini, que primo uotum uirginitatis [emisit], specialiter conuenit illa promissio Deuteronomi xxviii: "Benedictus fructus uentris tui"; et Sapiencie iii: "Felix sterilis et incoinquinata; habebit enim fructum in respectione animarum sanctarum." Et licet ipsa sit fecunda in prole nature, fuit tamen sterilis in opere concupiscencie. Item celibe uita gaudet in terris; Ieronimus: "In carne preter carnem uiuere angelicum est, non humanum." Item per ipsam restaurata sunt perdita; Ieronimus: "Pudicicia muliebrium uirtutum restaurauit perdita"; et Anshelmus: "Per filium Gloriose [Uirginis], et que in inferno [erant] se letantur liberata, et que in mundo sunt se gaudent restaurata." Item ipsa reuelat misteria, vt patet de Ioseph, Genesis xl, et de tribus pueris, Danielis i. Item mentem corroborat, ut Iudiht xv, / f. 142vb verba Ioachin pontificis ad Iudiht: "Confortatum est cor tuum eo quod castitatem amaueris." Item ornat animam uestibus uirtutum; Apocalipsis xvi: "Beatus qui custodit uestimenta sua," etc. Item Dominum sequitur gemino pede; Apocalipsis xiiii: "Virgines enim sunt et sequuntur Agnum," etc. Item multipliciter honoratur; Gregorius: "Virginitas honorabilis non solum Deo set eciam angelis constat amabi-

orable before God but also lovable to the angels." It moreover quenched the fire around the young men of Daniel 3, soothed wild beasts, and cooled boiling oil, as is seen in Agatha and others. Virginity is placed higher than marriage; Jerome *Against Jovinian*: "The Church does not condemn marriage but places it lower than virginity; it does not set it aside but puts it in its proper place." Virginity further fills heaven; Jerome again: "Marriage fills the earth, virginity paradise." Moreover, it offers the first-fruits to God; Apocalypse 14: "These were purchased from among men, the first-fruits to God," and so forth. Jerome in the same book: "If virgins are the firstfruits, then widows and people who live continently in marriage are the after-firstfruits"; that is, in the second and third degree the formerly lost people could not be saved unless it offered such sacrifices of chastity to God; add: that is to say, some kind of continence. Virginity also adorns the victors; Apocalypse 3: "He who overcomes will be clothed in white garments"; and this refers to the undefiled. Further, it is counted as martyrdom; Lamentations 4: "Her Nazarites were whiter than snow, more ruddy than ivory," and so forth. Old ivory turns ruddy, and long-lasting chastity is equivalent to martyrdom. Ambrose: "Virginity is praiseworthy not because it is found in martyrs but because it makes martyrs." It crowns us in the end; Canticles 4: "Come from Libanus, come, you will be crowned." Virgins are compared to the violet-colored skins in the tabernacle, of which the uppermost cover was made, Exodus 26. And this for five reasons: because of their heavenly way of life, for violet is the color of the air; because of their likeness to angels; because of their mortification of the flesh; because of the highness of their rank; and because of their fight against the powers in the air.

It may seem that virginity is not a virtue, because a person who has one virtue, has them all; for Gregory says that the virtues fly in one flock; and many people have the virtues but they lack virginity. Further, Augustine: "If one does not observe continence in marriage, one need not fear damnation." So it seems that salvation exists without continence; therefore also without virginity, which is a species of continence. But without the virtues there is no salvation; therefore, virginity is not a virtue. Further, Corinthians 7: "If a virgin marries, she does not sin"; but no virtue is lost except through sin; therefore, virginity is not a virtue. The minor is proved by what Dionysius says, that when one thing comes into being, another fades away; this holds true of the virtues and the vices. In response: the term "virginity" is used ambiguously. In one way it

gelis hominibus J. 443 **in pueris** rapicis E. 444 **ut** *om* EIL; quod G; *illeg* W. 444–45 **Agatha . . . aliis** sanctis uirginibus G. 445 Ieronimus *marg* E. 445–46 **Iouinianum Ecclesia** ieiuniarum *and blank space* E. 447 Idem *marg* E. 448 **replent uirginitas** et uiduitas F. 449 **xiiii** *om* E. 450 Ieronimus *marg* E. 451 **post-primicie** primicie J; post primicias FIL. 453 **Deo** Christo JFGI; *om* W. 453–54 **suple . . . continencie** *om* I. 453 **aliquod** ad E. 454–55 **Item . . . inquinatis** *after* facit *(460)* FIL. 454 **ornat** honorat FL. 455 **uestietur** *written twice* E. **uestimentis** uestibus E. **inquinatis** coinquinatis E. 456 **Nazarei** *add* eius E. 457 **rubescit** erubescit GIL. 458 Ambrosius *marg* E. **martirio equipollet** pro martirio reputatur L. 459 **set** imo GILW. 460 **coronat** coronatur J. **iiii** viii E. 462 **operimentum** cooperimentum F. 463 **conuersacionem** conuersionem G; conuersionem ⟨uel conuersacionem⟩ J. 467 Questio *marg* E. 468 Gregorius *marg* E. **gregatim** congregatim EI. 469 Augustinus *marg* E. 471 **Sic** set I; *corr from* set J. 473–75 **Item . . . uirtus** *om* G. 474 **amittitur** amouetur J. 476 Dyonisius *marg* E. 477 Solucio *marg* E. **tenet** sic est E; iterum F; item et L. **Responsio** respondeo F. 478 **est** dicitur FL. 478–79 **sic . . . paruulis** sic non est virtus sicut

lis.” Item ipsa ignem extinguit [in pueris], Danielis iii, seuas bestias mitigauit, oleum feruens infrigidauit, [ut] patet in Agatha et in aliis. Item coniugio preponitur; Ieronimus *Contra [Iouinianum*: “Ecclesia] matrimonium non dampnat, set uirginitati subicit; non abicit set dispensat.” Item celum replet; idem ibidem: “Nupcie terram replent, uirginitas paradysum.” Item primicias offert Deo; Apocalipsis [xiiii]: “Hii empti sunt ex hominibus, primicie Deo,” etc. Ieronimus in eodem: “Si uirgines primicie sunt, ergo uidue et in matrimonio continentes sunt post-primicie”; idest, in secundo et tercio gradu nec prius perditus populus saluari poterit, nisi tales hostias castitatis obtulerit Deo; suple: idest [aliquod] genus continencie. Item uictores ornat; Apocalipsis iii: “Qui uicerit, uestietur [uestimentis] albis”; et loquitur de non [inquinatis]. Item pro martirio reputatur; Trenorum iiii: “Candidiores Nazarei ° niue, rubicundiores ebore,” etc. Ebur antiquum rubescit, et diuturna casti- / tas martirio equipollet. Ambrosius: “Non est f. 143^{r}a
laudabilis uirginitas quia in martiribus reperitur, set quia martires facit.” Item in fine coronat; Canticorum [iiii]: “Veni de Lybano, veni, coronaberis.” Item uirgines conparantur pellibus iacinctinis in tabernaculo, de quibus erat supremum operimentum, Exodi xxvi. Et hoc propter quinque: propter celestem conuersacionem, quia iacinctus habet aereum colorem; propter angelorum similitudinem; propter carnis mortificacionem; propter gradus altitudinem; propter potestatum aerearum inpugnacionem.

Uidetur quod uirginitas non sit uirtus, quia qui habet unam, habet omnes; dicit enim Gregorius quod uirtutes [gregatim] uolant; et multi habent uirtutes, qui uirginitate carent. Item Augustinus: “Si continencia in coniugio non seruatur, dampnacio non timetur.” Sic uidetur quod sine continencia sit salus; ergo sine uirginitate, que species est continencie. Sine uirtutibus autem non est salus; igitur ipsa non est uirtus. Item Corinthiorum vii: “Virgo si nubat, non peccat”; set nulla uirtus amittitur nisi per peccatum; ergo uirginitas non est uirtus. Probacio minoris patet per hoc quod dicit Dyonisius quod unius generacio est alterius corrupcio; [tenet] in uirtutibus et uiciis. Responsio: “virginitas” dicitur equiuoce. Vno modo est carnis integritas tantum, et sic

stands only for the integrity of the flesh, and thus it is not a virtue, since it exists in children before baptism. In another way it stands for the integrity of both mind and body, and is the same as the virtue of continence. But it has an additional characteristic, the integrity of the flesh, which is not necessary in a person who has all the other virtues, since it is not a virtue itself but only a quality of a virtue. And thus the solution of the first argument is manifest. To the second ("if one does not observe continence," and so forth), one should reply that in this context "continence" is not understood as a virtue but as abstinence from the sex act, with which marital chasteness can well coexist; therefore Augustine says that "damnation is not feared." With regard to the Apostle's saying that "a virgin does not sin when she marries," the Apostle speaks the truth, because she does not lose any virtue but changes the degree of her continence.

Also, the willingly corrupted flesh does not deserve the heavenly crown; however, if it has been violated against its will, it does deserve it, for as Augustine says in his book *On Lying*: "The body is not corrupted unless the mind is corrupted first." Also the corrupted mind which repents deserves the crown, but not the corrupted flesh, because the corruption of the mind can be restored, that of the flesh cannot. And therefore Jerome says that "while God can do all things, he cannot crown a corrupt virgin as if she were uncorrupted." But this is not a defect of his power, but rather of the potential matter in woman; just as it is not a defect of the sun that a blind man does not see, but rather of his natural power, which he lacks completely.

Jerome further says that "perfect penance restores all that has been taken away." Why, therefore, does it not restore virginity? Gregory also: "Very often a life that after sin burns with love becomes more pleasing to God than innocence that lies torpid in self-complacency." Against this, Amos 5: "The virgin of Israel is fallen, and she shall rise no more"; the Gloss: She will not attain to the degree of blessedness she would have reached if she had not sinned. Therefore, penance does not restore everything. In response: it restores virtues and merits, but not the state or physical beauty from which a virgin has fallen. And a person's state is of three kinds: innocence, which man possessed before the Fall; justice, which a baptized person has before he commits a sin; and justification, which the penitent possesses after his fall. These are listed in descending, not in ascending order.

Foolish virginity is not allowed to join the spouse but is excluded from the

in parvulis J; sic est uirtus in paruulis I. 480 **dicit integritatem** dicitur integritas FL. 485–86 **si . . . etc.** *om* FL. 485 **non** *add* seruatur *canc* E. 486 **cum cuius** quia cum eius E. 487 Augustinus *marg* E. **ideo** secundo E; ibi G; item I. 488 **Ad** ob E. 492 Augustinus *marg* E. **debetur** *marginal addition in different hand*: Legitur in uita Sancte Lucie virginis quod cum tortor precepit adduci lecatores qui corpus virginis inuite macularent, illa dixit: "Si me inuitam uiolaueris, castitas michi duplicabitur ad coronam." F. **Augustinus** *add* in E. 494 **animus** anima FIL. **menti** mente EGI. 495 **carni** carne JGILW. **reintegrari potest** redintegratur J. 496 Ieronimus *marg* E. **Et** *om* FG. **ideo** secundum quod E; *om* J. 498 **in . . . potencie** in potencia dei quin potest J. **set** *add* defectus J. **potencialis** penalis E. 501 Ieronimus *marg* E. 502 Gregorius *marg* E. 503 **amore** timore E; *om* G. 504 Questio *marg* E. 505 Glossa *marg* E. **uirgo** filia FIL; *illeg* W. 506 **quantam** quan E. 507 Solu-

non est uirtus, cum sit in paruulis ante baptismum. Alio modo dicit / integritatem mentis et corporis, et est idem quod uirtus f. 143^{r}b continencie. Superaddit tamen quoddam accidens, quod est carnis integritas, quam non est necesse habere omnem uirtutem habenti, cum non sit uirtus set accidens uirtutis. Et sic patet solucio primi. Ad secundum dicendum ("si continencia non seruatur," etc.) quod "continencia" non supponit ibi pro uirtute set pro abstinencia ab actu carnalis copule, [cum cuius] exercicio manere potest coniugalis pudicicia; [ideo] dicit Augustinus quod "dampnacio non timetur." [Ad] hoc quod dicit Apostolus quod "uirgo non peccat cum nubit," verum dicit, quia non perdit uirtutem set mutat gradum continencie.

Item corrupte carni uoluntarie non debetur aureola; tamen uim passe et inuite debetur, quia ut dicit Augustinus ° libro *De mendacio*: "Non corrumpitur corpus nisi prius corrumpatur animus." Item corrupte [menti] et penitenti debetur aureola, non corrupte carni, quia corrupcio spiritus reintegrari potest, carnis uero non. Et [ideo] dicit Ieronimus quod "cum omnia possit Deus, non potest de corrupta coronare incorruptam." Set hoc non est in eo defectus potencie set [potencialis] materie in muliere; sicut non est defectus solis quod cecus non uidet, set naturalis potencie qua omnino caret.

Item dicit Ieronimus quod "perfecta penitencia restituit omnia ablata." Quare ergo non uirginitatem? Item Gregorius: "Fit plerumque Deo gracior [amore] / ardens uita post culpam quam se- f. 143^{v}a curitate torpens innocencia." Contra, Amos v: "Cecidit, non adiciet ut resurgat uirgo Israel"; Glossa: Ad tantam beatitudinem non perueniet, ad quan[tam] si non peccasset. Ergo penitencia non omnia restituit. [Dicendum:] restituit uirtutes et merita, non statum uel decenciam a quibus uirgo cecidit. Et distinguitur status triplex: innocencie, que fuit hominis ante culpam; iusticie, que est baptizati ante lapsum; iustificacionis, que est penitentis post lapsum. In istis contingit descendere, nunquam ascendere.

Fatua uirginitas ad copulam sponsi non admittitur set a nup-

cio *marg* E. **Dicendum** responsio E. 508 **decenciam** descendenciam F. 509 **innocencie** munificencie G. **hominis** omnibus G. **culpam** peccatum vel culpam F. 511 **contingit** conuenit J. 512 **sponsi** sponse FL. 513 **excluditur** *om* E. **hoc**

wedding; and this because its lamp is extinguished, that is, its grace is lost, and its oil is poured out, because its good works lie dead. Foolish virginity has four attendants. The first is her corrupt will. Isidore: "A person who is a virgin in the flesh but not in mind will have no reward guaranteed." Therefore, being a virgin in the flesh is worth nothing if one is married in one's mind. However, this must be understood with some qualification in the cases of the Blessed Virgin and of John the Evangelist, who agreed to a marital life in common, but not to fleshly corruption; or in other words, their consent was conditional, given upon divine advice, whether God commanded one thing or the other, as can be found in Augustine, in his book *On Virginity*. The second attendant is arrogance of heart. Jerome: "Pride in virginity is the brothel, if not of men, at least of devils." The third is external glorying and seeking praise from the people. Gregory: "To ask for oil from one's neighbors is to seek the glory that is due to one's good deed from the testimony of another man's mouth." The Psalm says in contrast: "All the glory of the king's daughter is within." Gregory: "For if she were to seek her glory outside, she would not have that inward beauty which the king desires." The fourth attendant is physical wandering about; whence Dinah, once she had gone out, was ravished, Genesis 44. A foolish virgin is a relative to the daughter of Jephthah, Judges 11, who wandered about the mountains for two months bewailing her virginity. Thus, that virgin is foolish who wanders in wide open and pleasant spaces, that is, who dances about and sings, and offers her virginity for sale and, as it were, laments that she has kept it too long; and this happens in two months, that is, between Easter and the feast of John the Baptist, which are the season of wantonness. Against such wandering, Ecclesiasticus counsels, chapter 26: "On a daughter that turns not away set a strict watch, lest finding," and so forth. For to such the Lord says through Ezechiel, chapter 3: "Go in and shut yourself up in the midst of your house." Behold the rule for virgins: a secret place and silence. The Blessed Virgin was found in a secret room, not in the stadium; therefore did the angel when he came to her say: "Hail, full of grace," and so forth, Luke 1. One would be very stupid to carry a lighted lamp and expose it to the wind on the mountains or the press of crowds in the villages, for thereby one would either extinguish the light or break the vessel. The fragile vessel is a virgin's body, which can not be mended after it has been broken. Therefore it is unsafe to store a great treasure in an earthen vessel, 2 Corinthians 4. Foolish virginity is like an ear without grain, a lamp without oil, a purse without silver, a nut without kernel, a vat without wine, an eye without pupil, a body without soul, appearance without

om E. 513–14 **idest . . . amittitur** dimittitur FL. 516 Ysidorus *marg* E. **habebit** habet JG. 517 **repromissione** promissione J; retribucione G. **ideo** Ieronimus ILW; *add* Ieronimus G. 518 **pro** de F. 519 **Iohanne** *om* E. 522 Augustinus *marg* E. **Augustino** *add* in E. 523 Ieronimus *marg* E. 525 Gregorius *marg* E. 525–26 **Oleum a proximis** laudem a populo querere W. 528 **Gregorius** *om* E. **speciem** gloriam I. 529 **rex** dominus F. 530 **oppressa** corrupta I. 533 **circueundo** eundo E. 534–35 **deplangit** plangit FG; deplangit, *with* de *canc* J. 536 **beati** sancti FLW; *om* GI. **lasciuum** lasciuie E; lasciuium W. 537 **discursum** cursum F. 538 **Tali** illi E. 540 **tue** *add* et non egredieris in medio eorum et linguam adherere faciam palato tuo JGIW; *add* et ecce data sunt super te vincula et ligabunt te in eis et non egredieris de medio eorum et linguam tuam adherere faciam palato tuo et eris mutus nec quasi uir obiurgans FL. 542 **theatro** tecto F. 544 **eam** *om* E. **montibus** mensibus E. **turbarum** gencium vel turbarum I. 545 **uillis** uasis E. 546 **irreparabile** irrecu-

ciis [excluditur]; et [hoc] quia lampas extinguitur, idest gracia amittitur, et oleum effunditur, quia bona mortificantur. Fatua uirginitas quatuor habet pedissequas. Prima est corrupta uoluntas. Ysidorus: “Virgo carne non mente nullum habebit premium in repromissione.” Et ideo nichil prodest uirginitas carnis si mente quis nupserit. Hoc tamen caute intellige pro Beata Uirgine et [Iohanne] Ewangelista, qui consenserunt in coniugalem societatem, non in carnis corrupcionem; vel utriusque consensus fuit condicionalis, diuino consilio commissus, siue hoc iuberet siue aliud, ut haberi potest ab Augustino ° libro *De virginitate*. Secunda est cordis elacio. Ieronimus: “Superba uirginitas, etsi non hominum, tamen prosti- / f. 143vb bulum est demonum.” Tercia est exterior gloriacio et laudem querere a populo. Gregorius: “Oleum a proximis petere est gloriam boni operis a testimonio alieni oris inplorare.” Econtra Psalmus: “Omnis gloria filie regis ab intus.” [Gregorius:] “Quia si foris gloriam quereret, intus speciem quam rex concupisceret non haberet.” Quarta est corporalis euagacio; vnde Dyna egressa est oppressa, Genesis xliiii. Fatua uirgo est cognata filie Iepte, Iudicum xi, que circuiuit in montibus duobus mensibus plangens uirginitatem suam. Ita fatua uirgo est que in locis spaciosis et amenis [circueundo], idest coreas ducendo et cantando, uirginitatem uenalem exponit et quasi diu seruatam deplangit; et hoc duobus mensibus, idest a Pasca usque ad festum beati Iohannis Baptiste, in quibus solet esse [lasciuum] tempus. Contra hunc discursum dat Ecclesiasticus consilium, xxvi: “In filia non auertente se firma custodiam, ne inuenta,” etc. [Tali] enim dicit Dominus per Ezechielem, iii: “Ingredere et includere in medio domus tue.” Ecce regula uirginum: secretus locus et silencium. Beata Uirgo inuenta est in secreto cubiculo, non in theatro; vnde ingressus angelus ad eam dixit: “Aue, gracia,” etc., Luce i. Valde stultus esset qui portaret lampadem accensam, si exponeret [eam] uento in [montibus] aut pressure turbarum in [uillis], quia uel lucem extingueret uel / f. 144ra vas frangeret. Vas fragile est corpus uirginale post ruinam irreparabile. Vnde magnus thesaurus dubie reponitur in fictili uase, II Corinthiorum iiii. Fatua uirginitas est quasi spica sine grano, lampas sine oleo, loculus sine argento, nux sine nucleo, dolium sine uino, oculus sine pu-

reality, a flower without fruit, and a spouse without ornament. Eve was a foolish virgin, in her pride believing that she would become an equal to God in knowledge when the serpent said to her: "You will be as gods," and so forth; she was covetous, because not content with what had been given to her; she yielded to the devil's temptation, became inobedient to God's command, did not believe his words, looked at and touched and tasted what was forbidden, and drew her husband into disaster and shut paradise for us. In contrast, the Blessed Virgin was most humble, whence, "Behold the handmaid of the Lord"; she was obedient to the angel, whence, "Let it be done to me according to your word." Therefore, an angel was sent to Mary, but a serpent to Eve. In addition, Mary believed the trustworthy messenger; whence, "Blessed are you who have believed," Luke 1. She also never changed her mind from her original purpose; whence, "For I do not know man," that is, I do not intend to know. She also has opened paradise for us, as the Church sings: "Through you the gates of paradise have been opened for us," and so forth. Moreover, Eve has her name from *"eu,"* which means good, and *"a,"* which means without, because she lost all good when she gave her consent to sin. In contrast, Mary was addressed with *"Ave,"* that is, without the *vae* of pain and sin. For she was not troubled in childbirth as she was not violated in conception, according to Bernard. Furthermore, Eve in paradise ate but brought forth no fruit other than the beginning of labor and pain. Ecclesiasticus 25: "From the woman came the beginning of sin, and by her we all die." In contrast, Mary brought forth fruit in the Church, "whose fruit has loosed the bonds of our grief." She is further the city of the highest king; the Psalm: "Glorious things are said of you, o city of God." This is the "city that lies in a four-square," Apocalypse 1, whose four sides are the four cardinal virtues. From prudence she had three things: that she willingly listened to the angel, judged what she had heard, and responded to it with wisdom. From temperance also three: chasteness of the flesh, humility of the spirit, and modesty of speech. From fortitude, that she made her vow of virginity, kept it, and gave credence to such an enormous thing. From justice, that she rendered obedience to God, worship to the angel, and service to Elizabeth. These are the twelve stars on the head of the woman who "was clothed with the sun," Apocalypse 12. She is further the "great throne of ivory," 3 Kings 10, which "Solomon overlaid with the finest gold." Ivory betokens chastity, gold humility. And note that the gold covered the ivory, because humility is greater than chastity. Therefore Bernard says: "Even if you can only admire chastity in the Virgin, yet try to imitate her humility." Further, the Virgin took a part of

perabile F. 550 **corpus . . . anima** *om* G. 551 **Eua** *add* quia E. 552 **cum** cui FILW. 554 **precepto Dei inobediens** precepto dei non obediens J; deo inobediens G. **Dei** deo E. 557 **vnde** Luce i FL. 560 **fideli** fidei E. **fuit credula** credidit F. 562 **idest** *written twice* E. 563 **sicut** vnde E. 565 **quia** quasi JFL. 568 Bernardus *marg* E. **uiolata** uiciata E. 570 **Ecclesiastici xxv** Ecclesiaste xxxv E. 576 **libenter** diligenter JGI; prudenter FLW. **audita** *add* prudenter J. 579 **tam immense** tamen immensam E. **fidem** *add* rectam L. 582 **erat** est JG; fuit L. 585 **ebur texit** ebore texitur J. **excellit** precellit J. 586 Bernardus *marg* E. **Ideo . . . Bernardus** Ieronimus dicit F. 587 **nisi admirari** imitari E; admirari G.

pilla, corpus sine anima, apparencia sine existencia, flos sine fructu, sponsa sine ornatu. Item fatua uirgo fuit Eua, ° superba credens Deo parificari in sciencia, cum dixit serpens: "Eritis sicut dii," etc.; cupida, quia concessis non contenta; dyabolice temptacioni acquiescens, precepto [Dei] inobediens, verbis eius discredens, vetitum uidens, tangens, et gustans, et uirum suum trahens in interitum, clausit nobis paradysum. Econtra Beata Uirgo facta est humillima, vnde "Ecce ancilla Domini"; angelo obediens, vnde "Fiat mihi secundum uerbum tuum." Vnde ad Mariam angelus, ad Euam serpens est missus. Preterea Maria [fideli] nuncio fuit credula; vnde "Beata que credidisti," Luce i. Preterea animum nunquam mutauit a proposito; vnde illud "Quoniam uirum non cognosco," idest, me cognituram non propono. Ipsa eciam nobis paradysum aperuit, [sicut] canit Ecclesia: "Paradysi porte per te nobis aperte," etc. Item Eua dicitur ab "eu," quod est bonum, et "a," quod est sine, quia omni bono priuata / est cum consensit peccato. Econtra Marie dictum est f. 144rb
"Aue," idest sine ue pene et culpe. Non enim fuit anxia in partu que non est [uiolata] in conceptu, secundum Bernardum. Item Eua in paradyso commedit, sed fructum non peperit nisi inicium laboris et doloris. [Ecclesiastici xxv:] "Inicium peccati mulier, et per illam omnes morimur." Econtra Maria in Ecclesia fructum peperit, "cuius fructus nostri luctus relaxauit uincula." Item hec est ciuitas regis altissimi; Psalmus: "Gloriosa dicta sunt de te, ciuitas Dei." Hec est "ciuitas in quadro posita," Apocalipsis i, cuius quatuor latera sunt quatuor cardinales uirtutes. Ex prudencia habuit tria: quod angelum libenter audiuit, audita diiudicauit, ad ea sapienter respondit. Ex temperancia tria: pudiciciam carnis, humilitatem mentis, modestiam sermonis. Ex fortitudine uotum uirginitatis emisit, emissum tenuit, rei [tam immense] fidem adhibuit. Ex iusticia reddidit Deo obedienciam, angelo reuerenciam, Elyzabet obsequium. Ecce duodecim stelle in capite mulieris, que "amicta erat sole," Apocalipsis xii. Item ipsa est "thronus grandis ex ebore," III Regum x, quem "uestiuit Salomon auro fuluo nimis." In ebore castitas, in auro humilitas signatur. Et nota quod aurum ebur texit, quia humilitas castitatem excellit. Ideo dicit Bernardus: "Etsi non possis / in Uirgine castitatem f. 144va
[nisi admirari], saltem stude humilitatem imitari." Item ipsa de

each state of those who will be saved and left another part behind. From virginity she took its integrity and left its sterility; from marriage she took its fruitfulness, but not its ugliness; from widowhood she took continence, but not the bereavement of her husband, for she remained always bound to her celestial spouse. She is further the most noble vessel in which the aroma remains after the cordial has been taken out, as Bernard says. Thus, Ecclesiasticus 24: "Like the best myrrh," and so forth. She is quite deservedly called Mother of Mercy who bore mercy itself in her womb, whose sweet odor she retains in her mind.

She is also a cedar, as the loftiest member of the Church. Bernard: "In heaven he presented his mother with a unique glory, whom on earth he was solicitous to preserve with a unique grace." A cedar is sweet-smelling, which symbolizes her face; Luke 1: "All generations shall call me blessed." A cedar lasts for a long time, in which the constancy of faith in the Virgin is symbolized, who on Holy Saturday stood alone in faith. Hence the Church celebrates her office on that day. Further, a cedar is not injured by the moth, which indicates her chaste cleanness; whence: "You are inviolate, spotless, and chaste, O Mary." The sap of the cedar preserves things from rot; thus, meditating on her from the corruption of sin. Therefore, we should run in the odor of her ointments, that is, in meditating on her virtues, Canticles 1. Further, the smell of the cedar puts snakes to flight; and her invocation frightens the devils when it is said: "Protect us from our enemy." Moreover, she is a cypress, which is a medicinal tree, and she brings healing to bodies and souls. Bernard: "Mary opened her breast of mercy, so that all might accept from her fullness: the sick healing, the sad comfort." A cypress does not cast off its beautiful foliage, nor does Mary ever cast off her virginity: a virgin she was before giving birth, a virgin thereafter. The beams in the temple were made of cedar, and Mary strengthened the Church on Holy Saturday, as was said earlier; Canticles 1: "Our rafters are of cypress trees," for in her constancy and devotion our faith is strengthened. A cypress cannot rot, and Mary is free of sin; Augustine in his book *On Virginity*: "When we speak about sin, I will not make mention of her." She is also a palm, which is the sign of victory, because in virtue and grace she has passed all women; at the end of Proverbs: "You have surpassed them all." She also defeated the devils; therefore the Lord told the serpent, Genesis 3: "She will crush your head"; and in Canticles 6: she is "terrible as an army set in array."

588 **saluandorum** *om* E. 589 **assumpsit** sumpsit E. 590 **non** reliquid EL. 591 **desolacionem** dissolucionem FIL. 593 Bernardus *marg* E. **electuarium** balsamum L; liquorem . . . uel electuarium I. 596 **retinet** retinuit F. 598 Bernardus *marg* E. **suam** *om* E. **dotatus** donatus ⟨vel donaturus⟩ J; decoraturus F; dotatur G; donaturus IW; dotaturus L. 602 **Parasceuem** ascensionem in crucem et passionem F; asscencionem L. 603 **Vnde . . . die** *om* G. 604–5 **mundicia** integritas FL. 605 **integra** intacta E; *om* L. 606 **conseruat res** reseruat E. 607 **unguentorum** unguenti FW. 609 **cum** vnde E; cui L. 610 **protege** *add* Bernardus: "Non tantum timent hostes aciem paratam ad prelium, quantum maligni spiritus Marie nomen et patrocinium." J. 611 Bernardus *marg* E. 612 **sinum** sinus FL. 616–17 **predictum est** dicitur F; dictum est L. 619 Augustinus *marg* E. 622–23 **Prouerbiorum . . . uniuersas** *om* L. 622 **fine** *om* EF; ultimo G. 622–23 **Tu . . . uniuersas** multe filie congregauerunt diuicias etc FIW. 623 **Item** *om* E. **ipsa** *add* eciam E. 624 **dixit** ostendit F; dicit

quolibet statu [saluandorum] aliquid assumpsit, aliquid reliquid. De uirginitate [assumpsit] integritatem, reliquid sterilitatem; de coniugio fecunditatem, [non] feditatem; de uiduitate continenciam, non uiri desolacionem, quia celesti sponso semper coniuncta fuit. Item ipsa est uas nobilissimum, in quo relinquitur odor post extractum electuarium, ut dicit Bernardus. Ideo Ecclesiastici xxiiii: "Quasi mirra electa," etc. Merito igitur dicitur Mater Misericordie, que ipsam misericordiam portauit in uentre, cuius odorem retinet in mente.

Item ipsa est cedrus, quia excellentissimum membrum Ecclesie. Bernardus: "Matrem [suam] in celestibus singulari dotatus est gloria, quam in terris curauit singulari preuenire gracia." Cedrus est odorifera, in quo notatur eius fama; Luce i: "Beatam me dicent omnes generaciones." Cedrus diu durat, in quo notatur constancia fidei in Virgine, que in sabbato post Parasceuem sola stetit in fide. Vnde eius officium celebrat Ecclesia tali die. Item cedrus non leditur a tinea, in quo figuratur castitatis eius mundicia; vnde illud: "Inuiolata, [integra], et casta es, Maria." Item resina cedri [conseruat res] a putredine; ita eius memoria a peccati corrupcione. Ideo currendum est in odore unguentorum eius, idest in memoria uirtutum eius, Canticorum i. Item o- / [f. 144vb] dor cedri fugat serpentes; et eius inuocacio terret demones [cum] dicitur: "Tu nos ab hoste protege." Item ipsa est cypressus, que est arbor medicinalis, et ipsa medetur corporibus et animabus. Bernardus: "Misericordie sinum aperuit Maria, ut de eius plenitudine accipiant uniuersi: eger curacionem, tristis consolacionem." Cypressus uenustatem come non deponit, nec ipsa aliquando castitatem: virgo ante partum, uirgo post partum. Trabes in templo fiebant de cedro, et ipsa Ecclesiam roborauit in sabbato, ut predictum est; Canticorum i: "Laquearia nostra cypressina," quia eius constancia et deuocione roboratur fides nostra. Cypressus est inputribilis, et ipsa a peccato immunis; Augustinus libro *De uirginitate*: "Cum de peccato agitur, nullam uolo de ipsa fieri mencionem." Item ipsa est palma, que est signum uictorie, quia uirtute et gracia uincit omnes mulieres; Prouerbiorum [fine]: "Tu supergressa es uniuersas." [Item] ipsa ° uincit demones; vnde dixit Dominus serpenti, Genesis iii: "Ipsa conteret capud tuum";

She also overcame her son in the prayers of the poor. This is foreshadowed by his giving up his spirit on the cross with his head inclined toward her. Her standing in the middle between the cross and the north further indicates that she is the mediatrix of sinners; Canticles 7: "Your stature is like a palm tree," as if to say: you thus stand at the right hand because whatever you ask for you will receive. A palm tree is narrow below and wide above; similarly, Mary was a poor woman on earth, but a queen in heaven. Thus it is well said in Canticles 3: "Who is she that goes up by the desert as a pillar of smoke of aromatic spices?" For a pillar of smoke is contracted below, but further up it becomes ever wider. A palm tree is green with longlasting leaves; this symbolizes the perseverance of virginity. It is a tree whose leaves have medicinal uses, Ezechiel 47. A palm tree is sweet in its fruit, that is, in its dates; thus is virginity in the examples of holy life; Canticles 7, she has kept all fruits for her beloved, that is, the works of her youth and of her age. It brings fruit a hundredfold; thus, Mary bore Christ in her perfect age, Luke 1: "Blessed is the fruit of your womb." She is a rose born of thorns, that is, of the Jews; 2 Kings 23: "Transgressors shall be plucked up from the earth as thorns." A rose is red; thus is she in her charity, interceding for sinners. Canticles 4: "Your lips, o spouse, are as a scarlet lace." Scarlet is a red flower or wool dyed in it, which signifies the fervor of her love. In addition she is white in her virginity; Canticles 4: "You are all fair, my love, and," and so forth. She is also sweet-smelling through her good reputation; Canticles 7: "The odor of your mouth like pomegranates." Moreover, rose oil cools, even if it is moderately warm; and meditating on her cools the incitements of the flesh. Canticles 4: "Your shoots are a paradise of pomegranates." Pomegranates bring coolness to the feverish; so do her shoots, that is, meditations about her. Likewise, the taste of a rose is, as it were, a mixture of bitter and sweet. And she is bitter in her name, because "Mary" means the bitter sea; but she is sweet in her whole way of life, even sweeter in her glory, and sweetest in her interceding for sinners. Therefore, Canticles 5: "I have eaten the honeycomb with my honey," which indicates her sweetness. Further, a rose shrinks swellings, and Mary's humility shrinks the swellings of pride; therefore she is called "our little sister," Canticles near the end, for among all others she is the humblest. Further, juice from the rose heals eyes, and Mary's entire way of life heals the eyes of our mind, "that we may behold" and follow; as in Canticles 6: "The daughters of Sion saw her," and so forth. She is the olive tree of

LW. 625 **ipsa** *om* EG. 628 **media** *om* F. 631 **inferius** interius E. 633 **dicitur** queritur FGIL. 636 **hoc** quo FL. 637–42 **Ipsa . . . tui** *om* F. 637 **folia** *add* utilia E. 638 **pomis** fructu L. 640 **idest** et E. **et senectutis** *om* G. 641 **etate** caritate GLW. 645 **Vitta coccinea** fauus distillans J. 646 **uel . . . tinctum** *om* E. **filum** linum FI; lilium L. 647 **Item** *add* ipsa E. 650 **rosaceum** rosatum JL; rosarum G. 653 **refrigerant** infrigidant JFILW; infrigerant G. 654 **idest . . . Item** *om* G. 655 **tanquam** tamen cum aqua J. 656 **amarum** *om* FL. 657–58 **intercessione** remissione; *add* peccatorum *canc* E. 659 **sedat** *corr from* sedet E. 660 **tumores** tumorem JFILW. **vnde** *add* bene FILW. 661 **fine** *om* EL; ultimo FG. **ceteras** omnes E. 663 **ut . . . sequamur** *om* FL. **vnde** vt E; *om* FGILW. 665 **Michee**

et in Canticorum vi: quod [ipsa] "terribilis est ut castrorum acies ordinata." Item ipsa uincit filium in peticionibus pauperum. Hoc figuratum est cum in cruce inclinato capite ad illam emisit spiritum. Figuratur eciam in hoc quod ipsa stat media inter crucem et aquilonem quod ipsa sit mediatrix peccatorum; Canticorum vii: "Statura tua / assimilata est palme," quasi: ideo stas a dextris quia f. 145^{r}a quidquid postulaueris optinebis. Palma eciam [inferius] est stricta, superius lata; ita ipsa paupercula in terris, regina in celis. Ideo bene dicitur in Canticorum iii: "Que est ista que ascendit per desertum sicut uirgula fumi ex aromatibus?" Virgula enim fumi in imo contrahitur, superius uero magis ac magis dilatatur. Palma diuturnis uiret foliis; in hoc notatur perseuerancia uirginitatis. Ipsa est arbor cuius folia ° sunt in medicina, Ezechielis xlvii. Palma suauis est in pomis, idest in dactilis; sic ipsa in exemplis sancte conuersacionis; Canticorum vii, omnia poma seruauit dilecto suo, [idest] opera iuuentutis et senectutis. Centenaria fert fructum; sic ipsa in perfecta etate genuit Christum, Luce i: "Benedictus fructus uentris tui." Ipsa est rosa nata de spinis, idest de Iudeis; II Regum xxiii: "Preuaricatores quasi spine euellentur de terra." Item rosa rubet; sic ipsa per caritatem, intercedendo pro peccatoribus. Canticorum iiii: "Vitta coccinea labia tua, sponsa." Coccus est flos rubicundus [uel filum ex eo tinctum], in quo notatur feruor caritatis illius. Item ° albescit per uirginitatem; Canticorum iiii: "Tota pulcra es, amica," etc. Item odorifera est per bonam famam; Canticorum vii: "Odor oris tui sicut malorum punicorum." Item oleum rosaceum infrigidat, / licet tem- f. 145^{r}b perate sit calidum; et eius memoria refrigerat carnis incentiua. Canticorum iiii: "Emissiones tue paradysus malorum punicorum." Mala punica refrigerant febricitantes; sic nos eius emissiones, idest meditaciones de ipsa. Item sapor rose amarus est et dulcis tanquam mixtus. Et ipsa est amara in nomine, quia "Maria" interpretatur amarum mare; dulcis uero in tota conuersacione, dulcior in glorificacione, dulcissima in peccatorum [intercessione]. Vnde Canticorum v: "Comedi fauum cum melle meo," in quibus notatur eius dulcedo. Item rosa sedat tumores, et humilitas Marie tumores superbie; vnde appellatur "paruula soror nostra," Canticorum [fine], quia inter [ceteras] humillima. Item liquor eius medetur oculis, et eius tota conuersacio oculis mentis nostre, "ut intueamur" et sequamur; [vnde] Canticorum vi: "Viderunt eam filie Syon," etc. Ipsa est oliua arbor pacis, quia

peace, for he was born from her who "is our peace," Ephesians 2; and Micheas 5: "There will be peace when he will set his foot on the mountain," and so forth. Also, from her flows the oil of mercy, whence she is called Mother of Mercy. She is "the rock that poured out rivers of oil," Job 29. She is, further, a plane tree because of the breadth of her love towards God and towards herself and towards her neighbor; near the end of Canticles: "He set in order charity in me." Also because of its height, for she was raised above the choirs of angels. She is also the cinnamon, blackish in color as it were because of worldly tribulation and the passion of her son; Canticles 1: "I am black but beautiful; the sun has altered my color." Also slender in its twigs; thus Mary with respect to temporal goods, whence she fed her son with her needle in Egypt, as Jerome declares. She also was slender in body; Fulgencius: "Her body was not swollen and inflated, but delicate and transparent, so that it seemed to be an image of her inner being." Further, she is balsam because of the sweet smell of her good reputation; Canticles 1: "We will run to the odor of your ointments." Balsam gains fragrance from the heat of the sun; thus Mary from the love of her son, after the incarnation of him who is "the sun of justice," Malachias at the end. Balsam also floats on all liquids, and Mary surpasses all in virtues; Judith 13: "Blessed are you above all women on earth." Balsam further curdles with milk; so did Christ in her when the Virgin became a mother and he was nourished with her milk through whom not even a bird goes hungry. Moreover, woolen clothes steeped in balsam do not get dirty; likewise, people who follow Mary are not stained with any filth, whence the "steps of the prince's daughter" are said to be "beautiful in her shoes," Canticles 7, because she leads her followers on the way of cleanness. She is myrrh because of the bitter passion of her son; Luke 2: "Her own soul a sword shall pierce"; and Canticles 1: "A bundle of myrrh is my beloved to me." Myrrh is five cubits in height, and in the Virgin five distinctions are found, namely that she was a virgin, mother, spouse, martyr, and widow—a martyr, that is, in the death of her son. These five are symbolized in Solomon's scaffold with its five cubits in length and five in width, 2

Mach E; Mat G. 666 **calcauerit** incaluerit E; *om* L. **ex** *om* E. 667 **dicitur** *add* Nota proprietates alias olive. In radice habet amaritudinem, in quo notatur pena cordis. Jeremie 31: "Statue tibi speculam," etc. Prouerbiorum 14: "Cor quod novit amaritudinem," etc. Ysaie 38: "Recogitabo tibi omnes annos," etc. In cortice habet virorem continuum. Vnde Sa. "Ego sum oliva virens," in quo notatur perseverancia virtutis. Matthei 5: "Beati mundo corde." In fructu habet flexibilitatem, in quo notatur prompta obediencia. Hebreorum 13: "Obedite prepositis vestris." Arbor fructifera. Matthei 13: "Facite dignos fructus penitencie." Ministrat pabulum lumini per bonam vitam et doctrinam. Matthei 5: "Sic luceat," etc. Ministrat medicinam vulneri per auxilium et consilium. Ministrat refeccionem esurienti corporalem et spiritualem. Minstrat lenimen dolori mulcendo, fovendo, consolando. L. 669 **latitudinem** altitudinem IL. 670 **fine** *om* EFL; ultimo G. 671 **exaltata** *add* est FGIL. **Item** *om* EG. **ipsa est** Maria dicitur F. 673 **i** *om* E. **formosa** *add* quia E. 674 **decolorauit me sol** *om* FL. **virgis** substancia JF. 675 Ieronimus *marg* E. 676 Fulgencius *marg* E. 678 **Item** *om* EGIW. 681 **fragrat** flagrat E. 682 **Malachie fine** Mach E; *om* L. 684 **Item** *add* balsamum E. 685 **Christus** *om*

ex ipsa ortus est qui "est pax nostra," Ephesiorum ii; et [Michee] v: "Erit pax cum [calcauerit] in monte," etc. Item [ex] ipsa manat oleum misericordie, vnde et Mater Misericordie dicitur. Ipsa est "petra que fundit riuos olei," Iob xxix. Item ipsa est platanus propter latitudinem caritatis ad Deum et ad se et ad proximum; Canticorum [fine]: "Ordinauit in me caritatem." Item propter altitudinem, quia exaltata super choros angelorum. [Item] ipsa est cyna- / momum, quasi subnigra in colore pro mundi tribulacione f. 145va et filii passione; Canticorum [i]: "Nigra sum set formosa; ° decolorauit me sol." Item tenuis in virgis; sic ipsa in temporalibus, vnde filium suum pauit acu in Egipto, ut dicit Ieronimus. Item fuit eciam tenuis in substancia carnis; Fulgencius: "Non fuit corpus eius turgidum et inflatum, set subtile et perspicuum, ita ut interioris hominis uideretur esse simulacrum." [Item] ipsa est balsamum propter odorem bone fame; Canticorum i: "Curremus in odorem vnguentorum tuorum." Item balsamum ex calore solis magis [fragrat]; sic ipsa ex amore filii post incarnacionem eius qui est "sol iusticie," [Malachie fine]. Item balsamum superenatat aliis liquoribus, et ipsa omnes transcendit in uirtutibus; Iudiht xiii: "Benedicta tu pre omnibus mulieribus super terram." Item ° cum lacte coagulatur; sic [Christus in ipsa cum Uirgo mater efficitur et] eius lacte pastus est, per quem nec ales esurit. Item uestes lanee eo [infuse] non fedantur; sic qui ipsam sequuntur nullis sordibus inquinantur, vnde "pulcri" dicuntur "in calciamentis gressus filie principis," Canticorum vii, quia per uiam mundicie deducit sequentes se. Ipsa est mirra [propter] amaritudinem passionis filii; Luce ii: "Ipsius animam pertransibit gladius"; et Canticorum i: "Fasciculus mirre dilectus meus michi." Item mirra habet quinque cubitos in altitudine / et quinque insig- f. 145vb nia reperiuntur in Uirgine, scilicet quod fuit uirgo, mater, sponsa, martir, et vidua—martir scilicet in morte filii. Ista quinque figurantur in columpna Salomonis quinque cubitos habente longitudinis et quinque latitudinis, II Paralypomenon vi. Item

ILW. **Christus in** *canc* J. 684–85 **Christus . . . et** eciam ipsa cum ipsa mater efficitur Christus E. 685 **cum *(2nd)*** *canc* J; et *canc* I. **Uirgo** *add* et W. 687 **infuse** infuso E. 689–90 **quia . . . est** *om* G. 690 **mundicie** mundam JF. **deducit** ducit FILW. **propter** per E. 691–93 **passionis . . . Item** *om* I. 692 **et . . . michi** *om* L.

Paralipomenon 6. Myrrh is also like the hawthorn; so is Mary similar to the Jews in the flesh, but not in their infidelity; Canticles 2: "Like the lily among thorns, so is my love among the daughters." In addition, it keeps away worms and rot, and thinking of Mary's chastity keeps away carnal desires; therefore, "her lips drop choice myrrh," Canticles 5, because she was the first to make a vow of chastity as an example for her followers. Myrrh soothes inflammations, and Mary soothes the swellings of pride with the example of her humility. Furthermore, she is a gum tree, whose drop is clean when kept on the clean bark, but unclean when it flows down to the ground; likewise, grace that is given for her sake profits the pure and perishes in the unclean. The Psalm: "It will rejoice in its showers," and so forth, that is, make progress in the virtues. The sap of the gum tree is honeylike; so is also her prayerful speech for the salvation of mankind; Canticles 4: "Honey and milk," and so forth. She is a thick, resinous sap which has much strength of spirit and no softness of the flesh; therefore, at the end of Canticles: "I am a wall, and my breasts are as a tower." She is the wall which holds back the enemies and protects us; her breasts are a tower because they exhibit a mother's task when she prays for us. She is a fingernail, because she protects the fleshy parts from being hurt. This is shown in the Old Law where nobody could prevent God's wrath from hurting; Isaias 44: "There is none, o Lord, that rises and takes hold of you." This is shown in the flood, Genesis 6, and in the region of the five cities, Genesis 19. *Ungula* is further the same as *onycha aromatica*, an aromatic spice—*"onyx"* in Greek is *"ungula"* in Latin—, for this kind of plant looks like a human fingernail; and Mary is *onycha aromatica,* full of all virtues, as if she were seasoned with "all the powders of the perfumer," Canticles 3. She is the drop of perfume that sheds into the sand, that is, into spiritually dry people, not tears of grief but stirrings of affection; Canticles 4: "Your lips, my spouse, are as a dropping honeycomb." This drop heals hardenings of the body, and Mary soothes the anxieties of our heart and makes smooth what is rough. Therefore her name is said to be "oil that is poured out," Canticles 1, for oil softens what is hard and smoothes what is rough. She is further called *libanus*, "frankincense," because she bears fruit many times: once by giving birth to her son, many times by coming to our aid with her merits and prayers. Therefore: "Blessed is the fruit of your womb." Bernard: "Blessed in its sweet smell, blessed in its taste, blessed in its beauty." She also is the terebinth, small in self-esteem; whence: "Behold, the handmaiden," and so forth, even though she was the queen of heaven. She is further a vine because of her fruitfulness; Canticles 7: "Your breasts are like clusters of grapes"; two breasts, piety and mercy. Also because of her joyfulness; Bernard:

695 **martir *(2nd)* . . . filii** *om* L. 699–700 **sic . . . filias** etc JFL; *om* GIW. 700–701 **recogitata** cogitata E. 701 **distillant** stillant FGL. 703–4 **Item . . . ipsa** *om* G. 704 **ipsa** Maria F. 705 **immunda** immundam E; mundam J. 706 **mundis** immundis EG; in hominibus mundis F. **perit** parit E; pariter J; *om* I. 707–8 **proficiens** proficiemur E. 711–12 **vnde . . . turris** *om* L. 711 **fine** *om* E; ultimo FG. 713 **representant** representat EG; presentant JW. 714 **carnales** carnes ILW. 716 **xliiii** 64 GLW; lxx I. 717–18 **et . . . xix** *om* L. 717 **pentapoli** pentupos E. 719 **humani** *om* E. 722 **aromatica** amonica GLW. **harenas** hapenas E. 723 **siccos** *end of F, catchword* homines. **homines** humores J. **motus** ypotus E; *in a marginal repetition of the text* J *has* pocius. 725 **corporis** cordis E. **cordis angustias** corda E. 725–26 **et . . . lenit** *om* GILW. 726 **aspera** aspersa E. 726–27 **Ideo . . . lenit** *om* E; *marg* J. **Canticorum . . . lenit** *om* L. 729 **nobis** nunc E; pro nobis J; *om* IL. 730 Bernardus *marg* E. 732 **tamen** *om* JL. 734 **pietas et misericordia** opera pietatis et misericordie L. 735 Bernardus *marg* E. **letificatura est** le-

mirra est similis albe spine; sic ipsa Iudeis in carne, non in infidelitate; Canticorum ii: "Sicut lilium inter spinas, sic amica mea inter filias." Item uermes arcet et putredines, et eius castitas [recogitata] concupiscencias carnales; vnde "labia eius distillant mirram primam," Canticorum v, quia prima uouit castitatem ad exemplum sequencium. Item inflaturas sedat, et ipsa tumores superbie exemplo humilitatis sue. Item ipsa est storax, cuius gutta seruata in cortice munda est, fluens in terram [immunda]; et gracia per ipsam data proficit [mundis], [perit] in immundis. Psalmus: "In stillicidiis eius letabitur," etc., idest in uirtutibus [proficiens]. Item liquor storacis est melleus; sic sermo oracionis eius pro salute humani generis; Canticorum iiii: "Mel et lac," etc. Ipsa est galbanus cartillaginosa multum habens de robore spiritus, nichil de mollicie carnis; vnde Canticorum [fine]: "Ego murus, et ubera mea turris." Ipsa est murus hostibus resistens et nos defendens; vbera eius turris dum [representant] officium matris in postulacione pro nobis. Ipsa est ungula, quia carnales prohi- / bet a f. 146[r]a
lesione. Hoc enim patet in Ueteri Lege vbi nullus prohibuit iram Dei a lesione; Ysaie xliiii: "Non est, Domine, qui surgat et teneat te." Hoc patet in diluuio, Genesis vi, et in [pentapoli], Genesis xix. Item idem est ungula quod onicha aromatica—"onis" Grece, "ungula" Latine—, quia hec species ad similitudinem [humani] unguis formatur; et ipsa est onicha aromatica, omnium uirtutum odore plena, quasi condimento "vniuersi pulueris pigmentarii," Canticorum iii. Ipsa est gutta aromatica que stillat in [harenas], idest in siccos homines, non lacrimas doloris set [motus] affectionis; Canticorum iiii: "Fauus distillans labia tua, sponsa." Item hec gutta duricias [corporis] curat, et ipsa [cordis angustias] mitigat et [aspera] lenit. [Ideo dicitur nomen eius "oleum effusum," Canticorum i, quia oleum dura mitigat et aspera lenit.] Ipsa eciam dicitur lybanus, quia sepe fructificat: semel filium pariendo, sepe meritis et precibus [nobis] subueniendo. Vnde: "Benedictus fructus uentris tui." Bernardus: "Benedictus in odore, benedictus in sapore, benedictus in specie." Ipsa est terebintus, breuis sua reputacione; vnde: "Ecce ancilla," etc., cum tamen regina celi esset. Item est vitis propter ubertatem; Canticorum vii: "Vbera tua sicut botri uinee"; duo ubera, pietas et misericordia. Item propter

"Mary will gladden the city of God with her graceful song." This is what is spoken of in Exodus 16, that after passing the Red Sea Mary took a timbrel, together with the young women, and they sang to the Lord a song of victory; thus, when the world has come to an end and Pharoah is drowned, that is, when the enemy of the human race is overcome, Mary with the holy virgins will sing praises to the Lord. She is also a grapevine because of her power to inebriate, because whom she fills with her love, she alienates from the love of the world; Canticles 5: "Drink and be inebriated, my dearly beloved." This drunkenness is delight in God and forgetfulness of worldly desire, according to Augustine, *On Music,* book VI.

Mary is further the bush that gave forth flames but did not burn, Exodus 3; Bernard: "That is, Mary giving birth without suffering pain." She is also the rod of Aaron which blossomed without being watered, Numbers 17; Bernard: "Mary conceiving without knowing a man." She is the rod coming forth out of the root of Jesse, Isaias 11. This rod was graceful in its humility, whence "Behold, the handmaiden of the Lord"; flexible in its obedience, whence "Let it be done to me according to your word"; and the more flexible, the closer it was to its fruit, that is, to her childbirth. Therefore we, too, should be the more flexible, the closer we are to our reward. Moreover, the rod is in the middle between the root and the fruit; so is Mary between God and man. This is shown in her standing between the cross and the north, as was said earlier. The rod easily trembles, and Mary was afraid not only of man but also of the angel; whence, "she was troubled at his greeting." A rod carries the point that pricks the ox, the hook that catches the fish, and the lime that holds fast the bird; and Mary carried Christ who with his prudence tricked the devil, who is ox, fish, and bird, Job 40—an ox, because he is fed with hay and straw, that is, with the life of carnal persons; a fish, because he takes delight in the waters of lust; and a bird, because he lifts up the unsteadfast mind through vanity and curiosity. Mary is the fleece of Gideon, Judges 6. For the fleece sits over the flesh, from which it takes its origin. Bernard: "The fleece taken from flesh without wound of the flesh, what else does it signify than Christ who took flesh from the flesh of the Virgin without harm to her virginity?" Further, the fleece covers the flesh, and she protects us from our enemy; whence: "Protect us from our enemy." And when the fleece is rained upon or gets wet, it does not break; similarly Mary in her conceiving or giving birth; the Psalm: "He shall come down like rain upon the fleece." Moreover, clothes for people are made out of wool or fleece, and Mary clothed God with her flesh. Hence, 3 Kings in the end:

tificat E; letificand est L. 736 **dicitur** *add* in E. **xvi** xli E. 737 **sumpsit** sumet JFGI; sunt W. 737–38 **cantabant** cantabit J; cantabat I; cantavit L; cantat W. 743 **mundane** humane E. 744 Augustinus *marg* E. **VI** V E; V ⟨vel VI⟩ J. 746 Bernardus *marg* E. **iii** iiii E. 747 Bernardus *marg* E. **florida** *add* et E. 750 **vnde . . . fuit** *om* G. 751–52 **flexibilior . . . tanto** *om* L. 752 **fructui** fructus E. **tanto** *om* JG. 756 **eciam** *om* GILW. 757 **salutacione** sermone IL. 759 **retardat** *end of* G. 764 Bernardus *marg* E. 765–66 **sine . . . carne** *om* ILW. 768 **vnde . . . protege** *om* ILW. 771–72 **hominum . . . mutauit** *om* I. 772 **fine** *om*

iocunditatem; Bernardus: "Ipsa eleganciori cantu [letificatura est] ciuitatem Dei." Hoc est quod dicitur ° Exodi [xvi] quod transito Mari Rubro Maria sump- / (f. 146^{r}b) sit tympanum cum puellis et cantabant Domino canticum uictorie; ita finito mundo et Pharaone submerso, idest inimico humani generis deuicto, ipsa cum sanctis virginibus cantabit laudes Domino. Item uitis est propter inebriacionem, quia quos amore inbuit, ab amore mundi alienos facit; Canticorum v: "Bibite et inebriamini, karissimi." Et ista inebriacio est in Deo delectacio et [mundane] uoluptatis obliuio, secundum Augustinum, [VI] *Musice*.

Item ipsa est rubus flammas emittens et non ardens, Exodi [iii]; Bernardus: "idest Maria pariens et non dolens." Item ipsa est virga Aaron florida, ° non humectata, Numeri xvii; Bernardus: "Maria concipiens et uirum non cognoscens." Hec est uirga surgens de radice Iesse, Ysaie xi. Ista uirga fuit gracilis per humilitatem, vnde "Ecce ancilla Domini"; fuit flexibilis per obedienciam, vnde "Fiat michi secundum uerbum tuum"; et tanto flexibilior quanto [fructui] proximior, idest partui; ita nos tanto flexibiliores quanto remuneracioni proximiores. Item uirga est media inter radicem et fructum; sic ipsa inter Deum et hominem. Hoc patet in statura eius inter crucem et aquilonem, ut predictum est. Virga de facili tremit, et ipsa non solum hominem set eciam angelum timuit; vnde "Turbata est in salutacione eius." Item uirga / (f. 146^{v}a) portat aculeum qui pungit bouem, hamum qui capit piscem, viscum qui retardat auem; et ipsa portauit Christum qui prudencia sua decipit dyabolum, qui est bos et piscis et auis, Iob xl—bos, quia feno et palea pascitur, idest uita carnalium; piscis, quia delectatur in aquis uoluptatum; auis, quia uanitate et curiositate eleuat instabilem animum. Ipsa est uellus Gedeonis, Iudicum vi. Vellus enim carnem excedit de qua originem trahit. Bernardus: "Vellus sumptum de carne sine carnis uulnere, quid signat nisi Christi carnem assumptam de carne Uirginis sine detrimento uirginitatis?" Item uellus carnem tegit, et ipsa nos ab hoste protegit; vnde: "Tu nos ab hoste protege." Item cum uellus recipit pluuiam uel effundit, non frangitur; sic nec illa concipiendo uel pariendo; Psalmus: "Descendet sicut pluuia in uellus." Item de lana uel uellere fit uestis hominum, et ipsa carne uestiuit Deum.

"King Jehoshaphat changed his dress and went into the battle." "Jehoshaphat" means judgment and signifies Christ, who will judge the world; he changed his dress when he hid his divinity in human nature "and was found in habit as a man," Philippians 2, that is, having human nature united to himself, not put on like a dress, as some heretics have said. A fleece also can be folded together, which indicates obedience; and it is soft to the touch, which indicates patience. Mary is the "little cloud like a man's foot which arose out of the sea," 3 Kings 18. For a little cloud is drawn out of the sea by the sun's heat and is raised up high, and Mary, by a unique act of grace, was chosen from the world and raised high above the choirs of angels. For then "the spirit of God moved over the waters," Genesis 1, when he chose that steadfast one among changeable women. "Like a man's foot" is well said, too, for she gave birth to a man who did not know man. That was " the new thing the Lord created upon the earth," Jeremias 31: "A woman shall compass a man." Bernard: "A man in the fullness of senses, not in the corporality of his members." That was also prophesied by the pagans—by the astronomer Albumasar: "In the sign of Virgo the Virgin will be born, and she who did not know man will nurse a child." There is however another translation. Further, bitter water becomes sweet in a cloud, and human nature, which in Eve had become bitter, was made sweet in the Virgin. Therefore we sing at his birth: "Today throughout the whole world the heavens have begun to drop honey." Moreover, out of a little cloud which gave light to the world for three days the body of the sun was made, according to some saints; and from Mary the Savior's body was made, who is the "sun of justice," end of Malachias. Also, in a cloud the sunlight is tempered, which in its sphere is unbearable to the eye. This is true of the light of divinity in its incarnation, for "no man has seen God at any time" in his own form, John 1; and Exodus 33 at the end: "Man shall not see me and live." Further, no image would show in a mirror unless some lead were put on the back, because of the transparency of glass; neither would the mirror of eternity show us his beauty except by means of a human body, because of his immense brightness, since he is "the brightness of eternal light and the unspotted mirror," Wisdom 7. Also, in a cloud the sunrays are refracted, and in the Virgin the wrath of the Almighty is mitigated. This is shown in the heavenly bodies. For the sun passes from Leo to Virgo, from Virgo to Libra. In the Old Testament God was like a lion, raging fiercely

EL. 778–79 **in *(2nd)* . . . paciencia** Item suavissimum ad tangendum, et ipsa est mater tocius pietatis. Vnde Bernardus: "Quid de fonte pietatis procederet nisi pietas? Nonne si quis pomum in manu sua dimidia die tenuerit, reliqua parte diei pomi servabit odorem? Cuius igitur replevit viscera, illius pietatis affecit in quibus commensibus requievit. Nam tante replevit mentem quam ventrem, et cum ex utero processit ex anima non recessit." Item quia pluvia descendens in vellus mundat si quid mundandum repperit et cum aliquam sordem contrahit et quo ad quid sordidior fit vel exprimitur; sic Christus in Virgine descendens abstersit ab ea et ex qua induit carnem similem peccatrici L. **quo** *marg* E. 780 **III** IIII E. 787 Bernardus *marg* E. **Bernardus Virum** *om* IL. 788–89 **eciam . . . astronomo** autem in prophecia a Saba regina austri verificatur J. 789 **gentibus** gentili E. **a *(2nd)* . . . astronomo** *om* L. 791 **tamen** *om* ILW. 794 **que . . . illuminauit** sol *(marg)* mundum illuminat E. 797 **Malachie fine** Mach E; Mal L. 798 **sua** sui E. **rota** *add* in se E. 800 **et** *add* in E. **xxxiii fine** xxx E; 33 L. 801 **reluceret** relucet E; luceret L. 802 **esset** sit E. **uitri** uiri LW. **transparenciam** circumferenciam vel transparenciam L; apparenciam W. 805–6 **franguntur** frangunt E. 806 **Uirgine** Maria J. 815–16 **me-**

Vnde III Regum [fine]: “Rex Iosaphat mutauit habitum et ingressus est bellum.” “Iosaphat” interpretatur iudicium et signat
Christum, qui iudicaturus est mundum; qui habitum mutauit cum
diuinitatem in humanitate celauit “et habitu inuentus ut homo,”
Philippensium ii, idest in habendo sibi hominem unitum, non ut
uestem indutum, / sicut dixerunt quidam heretici. Item uellus est 146vb
conplicabile, in quo notatur obediencia; in tactu leue, in quo notatur paciencia. Ipsa est “nubecula parua quasi uestigium hominis
que ascendit de mari,” [III] Regum xviii. Nubecula enim calore
solis de mari attrahitur et in altum eleuatur, et hec singulari gracia de mundo est electa et super choros angelorum exaltata. Tunc
enim “spiritus Domini ferebatur super aquas,” Genesis i, cum istam elegit stabilem inter mutabiles feminas. Et bene dictum est
“quasi uestigium hominis,” quia uirum peperit que uirum non
cognouit. Hoc fuit “nouum quod fecit Dominus super terram,”
Ieremie xxxi: “Femina circumdabit uirum.” Bernardus: “Virum
plenitudine sensuum, non corpulencia membrorum.” Hoc eciam
a [gentibus] prophetatum est—a Balach tegni astronomo: “In
Uirginis signo nascetur Uirgo, lactabit puerum que non cognouit
uirum.” Alia tamen translacio est. Item aqua amara dulcescit in
nube, et humana natura in Eva amaricata dulcis facta est in Uirgine. Vnde in eius partu canitur: “Hodie per totum mundum
melliflui facti sunt celi.” Item ex nubecula [que mundum illumi-
nauit] per triduum factum est corpus solis, secundum aliquos
sanctos; et ex ista formatum est corpus Saluatoris, qui est “sol
iusticie,” [Malachie fine]. Item in nube temperatur lux solis, que
in [sua] rota ° est inconprehensibilis. Sic in car- / ne assumpta f. 147ra
lux diuinitatis, quia “Deum” in sua forma “nemo uidit unquam,”
Iohannis i; et ° Exodi [xxxiii fine]: “Non uidebit me homo et
uiuet.” Item in speculo non [reluceret] ymago nisi plumbum appositum [esset] propter uitri transparenciam; nec speculum eternitatis suam speciem nobis ostenderet nisi per corpus humanum
propter immensam claritatem suam, cum ipse sit “candor lucis
eterne et speculum sine macula,” Sapiencie vii. Item nube [fran-
guntur] solis radii, et in Uirgine mitigatur Omnipotentis ira. Hoc
figuratur in superioribus. Sol enim transit a Leone in Uirginem, a
Uirgine in Libram. In Ueteri Testamento fuit Deus quasi leo

and punishing his enemies, but in the Virgin's lap he became as mild as a unicorn, so much that he even went to the scales of the cross for his enemies. Furthermore, a cloud brings coolness to the earth and shelters vineyards and flowers from the heat; and this cloud God created "for a shade from the heat" of avarice and "from the whirlwind" of envy and "from the rain" of lechery, Isaias 4. In addition, Mary is the dawn, the messenger of light, Canticles 6; through her coming we receive eternal light. The dawn is in the middle between darkness and light; thus Mary between sinners and her son. Further, just as dawn leads forth the sun to the joy of those who dwell on earth, thus Mary brought forth Christ; therefore, in his coming the angel told the shepherds: "I bring you tidings of great joy," and so forth, Luke 2. Moreover, when dawn appears, wild animals, thieves, and devils go into hiding, because all the beasts of the forest range at night. Thus her coming disturbed the Jews and the devils; and so it is well said of her: "Terrible as an army set in array," Canticles 6. Also, at daybreak all the birds in the forest sing; thus, all the prophets foretold that the Savior would be born of the Virgin Mary. That is what is spoken of in Wisdom 17, that "a whistling wind, and among the spreading branches of trees the melodious voice of birds" were heard. The whistling wind is the Holy Spirit that impregnated Mary with its holy breath; the voice of the birds is the preaching of the prophets; and the spreading branches of the trees are their hidden meanings. Furthermore, Mary is the closed gate, the gate of the Church and window of heaven, for many follow her in marriage, few in virginity. She is also the "star risen out of Jacob," Numbers 24. She is the north star whom sailors follow, that is, those who bear the pains and dangers of the world. Bernard: "Do not turn your eyes away from the light of this star, unless you want to perish in the tempest." A star is large and seems little, and so she is little before the unbelievers but large before the angels, as she herself witnesses in Luke: "He that is mighty has done great things to me." Also a star has a great amount of form but little substance; and Mary has a great amount of grace but little temporal substance, as was said earlier. A star is a transparent body, and her body was delicate and transparent, so that it appeared as if it were the image of her inner being, as Fulgencius says. The north star moves very little, whence it is said to be immobile; and Mary was steadfast in faith, while the disciples ran away. For this reason her steadfastness is likened to a palm, because at that moment she earned the praise of victory. Also, a star is a luminous body, and Mary's glorious life brought light to the world. Mary is further the moon, which lights the darkness of the night, that is, of this mortal life, according to what the Philosopher says: "The moon is the eye of the night." By the moon

dium media IL; media uel medium J. 822 **et demones** *om* E. 823 **contra** circa E. 825 **predicauerunt** predixerunt L. 828 **flatu** flamine J. 830–32 **Item . . . uirginitate** *at end, after* spiritualem *(871)* J; *om* ILW. 834 Gregorius *marg* E. **Bernardus** Gregorius E. **Non** *marg* E. 835 **obrui** *add* mundi J; *add* mori in I. 837 **angelis . . . testante** deo et angelis J. 839 **temporali** corporali vel temporali L. 842 Fulgencius *marg* E. **dicit Fulgencius** *om* L. 843 **stabilis** *add* movente filio J. **retrocedentibus** recedentibus JIL. 846 **lucem dedit** lucet in L; uitam dedit

acriter seuiens et hostes puniens, set in gremio Uirginis mansuetus factus est uelut unicornis, in tantum ut eciam pro hostibus transiret in libram crucis. Item nubes refrigerat terram, vineas et flores ab estu protegit; et hanc nubem creauit Deus “in umbraculum ab estu” auaricie et “turbine” inuidie et “pluuia” luxurie, Ysaie iiii. Item ipsa est aurora, lucis prenuncia, Canticorum vi; per cuius ortum recipimus lumen eternum. Item aurora est medium inter tenebras et lucem; sic ipsa inter peccatores et filium. Item sicut aurora producit solem ad leticiam terram inhabitancium, sic ipsa genuit Christum; vnde in eius ortu dixit angelus
pastoribus: “An- / nuncio uobis gaudium magnum,” etc., Luce f. 147rb
ii. Item cum aparet aurora, absconduntur seua animalia, latrones, et demones, quia in nocte pertranseunt omnes bestie silue. Sic eius ortus turbauit Iudeos [et demones]; ideo bene dicitur: “Terribilis ut castrorum acies ordinata,” Canticorum vi. Item [contra] lucem aurore cantant omnes uolucres silue; sic omnes prophete predicauerunt nasci Saluatorem de Virgine Maria. Hoc est quod dicitur Sapiencie xvii quod auditus est “spiritus sibilans, et inter spissos arborum ramos suauis auium sonus.” Spiritus sibilans est Spiritus Sanctus Mariam sacro flatu inpregnans; sonus auium est predicacio prophetarum; spissi rami arborum sunt occulte sentencie eorum. Item ipsa est porta clausa, porta ecclesiastica et celi fenestra, quia multi sequuntur eam in coniugio, pauci in uirginitate. Item ipsa est “stella orta ex Iacob,” Numeri xxiiii. Ipsa est stella in polo sita, quam sequuntur nauigantes, idest penas et pericula mundi pacientes. [Bernardus]: “Non auertas oculos a fulgore huius syderis, si non uis obrui procellis.” Item stella magna est et uidetur parua, et ipsa parua est coram incredulis, magna coram angelis, ipsa testante Luce i: “Fecit michi magna qui potens est.” Item stella multum habet de forma, parum de materia; et ipsa multum de gracia, parum de temporali substancia, ut dictum
est supra. Item stella / est corpus perspicuum, et eius corpus sub- f. 147va
tile fuit et perspicuum, ut interioris hominis uideretur esse simulacrum, dicit Fulgencius. Item stella in polo parum mouetur, vnde dicitur immobilis; et ista in fide fuit stabilis retrocedentibus discipulis. Vnde in hoc assimilatur statura eius palme, quia tunc meruit laudem uictorie. Item stella est corpus luminosum, et eius uita gloriosa lucem dedit seculo. Item ipsa est luna tenebras noctis, idest huius uite mortalis, illuminans, iuxta quod dicit Philosophus: “Luna est oculus noctis.” Item per lunam habemus noti-

we can tell the time of month and year, and by Mary we can tell the time of grace and of the salvation of all things; Ecclesiasticus 43: "The moon is for a declaration of time," and so forth. Also, by the moon we know the feast days of the Old Law and the New, and with Mary the whole Church began its feasting, whereas Eve gave the beginning to labor, pain, and death; Ecclesiasticus 43: "From the moon is the sign of the festival day." Furthermore, the place which is directly beneath the moon is full of dew, as Ambrose says in the *Exameron*. Thus he who is subject and devoted to Mary abounds more than anyone else with the dew of grace; to indicate this, the Church has the Office of the Virgin: "Drop down dew, you heavens, from above," and so forth, Isaias 45. The moon also is queen over the waters, according to the Philosopher; and Mary is the queen of angels and men; Apocalypse 17: many waters, many peoples. In addition, the moon is the efficient cause that dew falls down; thus through Mary the dew of grace, which cools the burning of concupiscence; Ecclesiasticus 43: "The dew that meets the heat overpowers it." The moon also causes the sea to rise and fall, although there are other causes that go with it; and through Mary we rise to Christ, after fleeing from the depth of the sea, that is, the danger of this world. Bernard: "O man, you can safely rise up to God, for the mother before her son," and so forth. And the moon is the closest planet to the earth; so she is closer to sinners, because of her compassion. That is shown by her saying, when they were lacking wine at the wedding: "They have no wine," John 2. And if she obtained bodily joy for us from her son, much more so will she obtain spiritual joy.

Here ends the Summa of the Virtues.

I. 847 Philosophus *marg* E. 852 **festiuitatis** *add* in E. 855 Ambrosius *marg* E. 856 **qui illi** ille qui E. 861 **sic . . . ros** *om* I. 863 **efficit** facit JL; *illeg* W. 865 **ad Christum** *om* IL. 866 Bernardus *marg* E. 867 **quia** qui mediatorem cause tue L. 868 **peccatoribus** peccatoris E. 869 **conuiuis** conuiuii E; conuiuiis W. 870 **ii** *om* E. **et si nobis** si enim JW; si IL. 871 **magis** forcius ILW. **spiritualem** *add* Item . . . uirginitate *(see 830–32)* J; *add* Oracio cuiusdam religiosi: "Ave, Dei Patris venerabile templum. Ave, Dei Filii spirituale habitaculum. Ave, Spiritus Sancti insigne sacrarium. Ave, domina angelorum. Ave, mediatrix Dei et hominum. AmeN." IW; W *adds further*: Oracio beati Anselmi: "O Domina, porta vite, ianua salutis, via reconciliacionis, aditus recuperacionis, obsecro te per salvatricem tuam fecunditatem, fac ut per te mihi peccatorum venia et bene vivendi gracia concedatur, et usque in finem hic servus tuus Johannes sub tua proteccione custodiatur. Per Ihesum Christum filium Dominum nostrum. Amen." Oret mente pia pro dictatore Maria. 872 **Explicit . . . virtutum** *rubr* E; explicit de virtutibus *rubr* JI; *om* L; explicit *rubr* W.

ciam temporis mensium et annorum, et per ipsam cognoscimus tempus gracie et salutis uniuersorum; Ecclesiastici xliii: "Luna ostensio temporis," etc. Item per lunam cognoscuntur festa legalia et ewangelica, et per ipsam sumpsit inicium festiuitatis ° tota Ecclesia, quia inicium laboris et doloris et mortis dedit Eua; Ecclesiastici xliii: "A luna signum diei festi." Item locus qui perpendiculariter est sub luna multum habundat rore, ut dicit Ambrosius in *Exameron*. Sic [qui illi] subiectus est et deuotus habundat pre ceteris rore gracie; in cuius signum tale habet Ecclesia Uirginis officium: "Rorate celi desuper," etc., Ysaie xlv. Item luna est regina aquarum, secundum Philosophum; et ipsa est regina angelorum et hominum; Apocalipsis xviii: aque multe populi multi. Item luna est causa mouens ut descendat / ros; sic per ipsam ros f. 147vb
gracie qui refrigerat ardorem concupiscencie; Ecclesiastici xliii: "Ros obuians ardori humilem efficit eum." Item per lunam est accessus maris et recessus, licet alie sint concause; et per ipsam habemus accessum ad Christum fugientes maris profundum, idest mundi periculum. Bernardus: "O homo, securum habes accessum ad Deum, quia matrem ante filium," etc. Item luna est proximior planeta terre; sic ipsa [peccatoribus] conpassione. Hoc patet in eo quod indigentibus vino [conuiuis] dixit: "Vinum non habent," Iohannis [ii]. Et si nobis inpetrauit a filio leticiam corporalem, multo magis spiritualem.

Explicit Summa virtutum.

APPENDIX

The following section on the signs of humility, at the end of Chapter II, appears only in E, ff. 100–101. The entire passage is verbally taken from Peraldus, *Summa virtutum,* tract. V (de beatudinibus), pars iv (de humilitate), cap. 4 (de signis humilitatis), where it forms signs three to six, renumbered here as one to four.

Signa humilitatis multa sunt. Primum est amor uilitatis; Bernardus:
"Verus humilis uult uilis reputari, non humilis predicari. Gaudet de
contemptu sui. Hec sola sane superbos laudesque contempnit." De hoc
exemplum habemus II Regum v: "Ludam," inquit, "et uilior fiam." Et
in *Dyalogo* Gregorius de quodam parue stature, qui Constantinus
diceba- / tur, cum dixisset ei quidam quod nichil hominis haberet, pro- 101ra
tinus letus in amplexum eius ruit eumque ex amore nimio brachiis
constringere cepit et osculari magnasque gracias agere quod de se talia
iudicasset, dicens: "Tu solus es qui in me oculos apertos habuisti." De
Dauid legitur II Regum xvi: "Dimitte," inquit, "ut maledicat michi." Et
Actuum v: "Ibant apostoli gaudentes a conspectu concilii," etc. Humilitas ex propriis [*read*: opprobriis] pascitur, ut cibo proprio; Trenorum iii:
"Saturabitur obprobriis." Sicut se habet superbia ad gloriam, sic humilitas ad ignominiam. Humilitati ea sunt preciosa que alii essent uilia. Ipsa
sputum est abhominacionis [*Peraldus*: ipsa enim spiritum abominatio-
nis], et contemptus conuertit quasi in aurum et gemmas. Ipsa uilis uult
uideri aliis, sicut et uilis sibi uidetur, et quanto sibi est uilior, tanto est
Deo preciosior. Gregorius in *Moralibus*: "Tanto unaqueque anima preciosior fit in conspectu Dei, quanto pro amore Dei despectior fit ante
oculos suos." Gregorius: "Tanto fit quisque uilior Deo, quanto sibi preciosior, et tanto preciosior Deo quanto propter eum uilior."

Secundum est, si humilia officia quis libenter facit. De hoc exemplum habemus in Abygail, I Regum xv. Cum misisset Dauid ut eam du-
ceret in uxorem, ipsa ait: "Ecce famula tua sit in ancillam, ut [*add* lauet]
seruorum pedes Domini mei." In *Uitas Patrum* quidam senex perfectus
uirtutibus / orauit Dominum dicens: "Ostende michi, Domine, quid sit 101rb
perfectum anime, et faciam." Et dictum est sibi ut requireret consilium
a quodam alieno sene. Ille respondit ei per reuelacionem: "Vis facere
quecumque dico tibi?" At ille: "Volo." Et dixit: "Vade, pasce porcos."
Et fecit sic. Et cum alii uiderent quod pasceret porcos, dixerunt quod
factus esset fatuus. Et uisa eius humilitate reuocatus est ad locum suum.

Tercium est, si consilio aquiescit, sicut hoc quando aliquis non aquiescit consilio signum est superbie. Gregorius de non acquiescente consilio: "Si," inquit, "meliorem se non crederet, nequaquam consilium cunctorum sue deliberacioni postponeret."

Quartum est, si contumelias uel eciam correpcionem mansuete audit. Gregorius: "Qui gloriam non querit, contumeliam non sentit." Idem: "Non timet confundi in conspectu hominum qui solum gloriam querit apud Deum."

NOTES TO THE TEXT

The following notes are intended to identify the sources of quotations found in *Postquam*. It is most likely that the author of *Postquam* quoted his authorities at second hand; consequently, many quotations are not verbally identical with their original sources or are wrongly attributed. This is particularly true of quotations from "Augustine," which often come from such intermediaries as twelfth-century compilations, biblical commentaries, Peter Lombard, scholastic disputations, or Peraldus. I have tried to identify the original sources wherever possible. Biblical quotations are identified according to the Clementine edition of the Latin Vulgate, with the names of biblical books given in the form used by the Douay version and in their standard abbreviation. For works by classical authors I refer, wherever possible, to the divisions of books, chapters, and paragraphs or lines as they appear in the volumes of the Loeb Classical Library, without further identification of their modern editors and publication data. Medieval authors are cited according to standard recent editions, without further identification of modern editors and publication data. A "cf." before the source citation indicates that the cited source is verbally only similar to the quotation found in *Postquam*. In some instances I have suggested, with "perhaps," the probable patristic source that lies behind a quotation not verbally close to it.

The following abbreviated references are to series and works which are frequently cited in the notes:

CC	Corpus Christianorum. Series Latina. Turnhout: Brepols, 1954 ff.
CSEL	Corpus scriptorum ecclesiasticorum Latinorum. Vienna: F. Tempsky, 1866 ff.
PG	J.-P. Migne, ed. *Patrologiae cursus completus . . . Series Graeca.* 161 vols. Paris: J.-P. Migne (and successors), 1857–66.
PL	J.-P. Migne, ed. *Patrologiae cursus completus . . . Series Latina.* 221 vols. Paris: J.-P. Migne (and successors), 1844–64.
Anselm	F. S. Schmitt, ed. *S. Anselmi Cantuariensis Archiepiscopi Opera omnia.* 6 vols. Seckau, Rome, and Edinburgh: Thomas Nelson and Sons, 1938–61. Quoted by volume and page.
Auxerre	Guillaume d'Auxerre (Guillermus Altissiodorensis). *Summa aurea.* Paris: Nicolaus Vaultier & Durandus Gerlier, 1500. Reprint. Frankfurt/Main: Minerva G.m.b.H., 1964. Since the internal divisions of this work are extremely complicated and unclear in the printed edition, my citations are to folio and column (a–d).
Bernard	Saint Bernard of Clairvaux. *Opera.* Edited by J. Leclercq and H. Rochais. 7 vols. to date. Rome: Editiones Cistercienses, 1957–. Quoted by volume and page.
Bonaventure	Saint Bonaventure. *Opera omnia.* Edited by Patres Collegii a S. Bonaventura. 10 vols. in 11. Quaracchi: Collegium S. Bonaventurae, 1882–1902. Quoted by volume and column.
Decretum, Decretals	*Corpus iuris canonici.* Edited by Emil Friedberg. 2 vols. Leipzig: B. Tauchnitz, 1879. Reprint. Graz: Akademische Druck- und Verlagsanstalt, 1959. Quoted by volume and column.
Glossa	*Biblia Latina, cum glossa ordinaria Walafridi Strabonis aliorumque et interlineari Anselmi Laudunensis.* 4 vols. Strassburg: Adolf Rusch, 1481.
Hugh of St. Cher	Hugh of St. Cher. *Opera omnia.* 8 vols. Venice: Pezzana, 1732. Quoted by volume, folio, and column (a–d).
Isidore, *Etymologies*	Isidore. *Etymologiarum sive originum libri XX.* Edited by W. M. Lindsay. 2 vols. Oxford: Clarendon Press, 1911.
Legenda aurea	Jacobus a Voragine. *Legenda aurea.* Edited by Th. Graesse. 3rd ed. Breslau: Wilhelm Koebner, 1890. Reprint. Osnabrück: Otto Zeller Verlag, 1969.
Lombard, *Sententiae*	Peter Lombard. *Libri IV Sententiarum.* Edited by Patres Collegii S. Bonaventurae. 2nd ed. 2 vols. Quaracchi: Collegium S. Bonaventurae, 1916. Quoted by volume and page.

Lottin, *Psychologie*	Odon Lottin. *Psychologie et morale aux XIIe et XIIIe siècles*. 6 vols. Louvain: Abbaye du Mont César. Gembloux: J. Ducolot, 1942–60. Quoted by volume and page.
MDP	*Moralium dogma philosophorum*. Edited by J. Holmberg. Uppsala: Almqvist & Wiksells, 1929. Quoted by page and lines.
Peraldus, *Virtutes*	William Peraldus. *Summa virtutum*. The edition used is Gvillelmi Peraldi . . . summae virtvtvm ac vitiorvm tomus primvs (Lyons: Pierre Compagnon et Robert Taillandier, 1668). Citations are by *tractatus, pars*, and *caput*, followed by a reference to the pagination in this edition. Notice that the *Summa virtutum* has the following *tractatus*: I, Virtue in general; II, Theological virtues; III, Cardinal virtues; IV, Gifts of the Holy Spirit; V, Beatitudes.
Sarum Missal	*Sarum Missal*. Edited by J. Wickham Legg. Oxford: Clarendon Press, 1916.
Vincent	Vincent of Beauvais. *Speculum naturale* and *Speculum doctrinale*. Vols. 1 and 2 of *Vincenti Burgundi Speculum quadruplex*. Douai: Baltazaris Belieri, 1624. Reprint. Graz: Akademische Druck- und Verlagsanstalt, 1964–65.
Walther, *Proverbia*	Hans Walther. *Proverbia sententiaeque latinitatis medii aevi*. 6 vols. Göttingen: Vandenhoeck & Ruprecht, 1963–67. Quoted by entry number.

NOTES TO CHAPTER I

16. This quotation may be vaguely suggested by *Timaeus* 42A, ed. J. H. Waszink, in *Plato latinus*, ed. Raymund Klibansky, vol. 4 (London: Warburg Institute, 1962), p. 37.

24–27. The two etymologies for *politica* occur in Alanus of Lille, *De virtutibus et de vitiis et de donis Spiritus Sancti*, in Lottin, *Psychologie*, 6:50.

26. See Aristotle, *Ethica Nicomachea* II.1 (1103a–b).

35–36. Isidore, *Etymologiae* IV.vi.4.

52–53. See Aristotle, *Ethica Nicomachea* II.6 (1106b). Medieval Latin translations read *simpliciter*, which explains the strange adverbial form *indivisibiliter*.

55–56. Sallust, *De Catilinae coniuratione* I.6.

56–57. Prov. 4:25.

58–59. Boethius, *De consolatione Philosophiae* II, pr. i, 15 (CC 94:41). When MS E writes the title out, it uses the plural form *Consolaciones*, a practice shared by other manuscripts (JFW), though not consistently.

60. Cf. Aristotle, *Ethica Nichomachea* II.6 (1106b), though the *translatio antiqua* gives *coniectatrix* for *inspectrix*, and the phrase is used for virtue in general, not prudence.

62–69. This relation between justice, temperance, and fortitude derives from *MDP*, p. 8, ll. 15–19.

72–73. Geoffrey of Vinsauf, *Poetria nova*, ll. 44–45; ed. Edmond Faral in *Les Arts poétiques du XIIe et du XIIIe siècle* (Paris: Honoré Champion, 1924), p. 198.

80–82. This authority is often

quoted by scholastic theologians and attributed to Bede; see Lottin, *Psychologie*, 3: 158, 160, and 163, for references to Jean de la Rochelle, Odo Rigaud, and Bonaventure. It also appears in Peraldus, *Virtutes* III.i.2 (p. 188).

89–90. Augustine, *De libero arbitrio* I.xiii.27 (CC 29:228).

91. *MDP*, p. 7, ll. 18–19; from Cicero, *De inventione* II.liii.160.

92. Lombard, *Sententiae* III.xxxiii.1 (2:697).

93. Cf. Augustine, *De Genesi contra Manicheos* II.x.14 (PL 34:203–4).

94. Augustine, *De libero arbitrio* II.x.29 (CC 29:257).

95. Augustine, *De civitate Dei* XIX.iv.4 (CC 48:666).

96. Cf. Augustine, *De musica* VI.37 (PL 32:1183).

97. Lombard, *Sententiae* III.xxxiii.3 (2:698).

98. Augustine, *De musica* VI.55 (PL 32:1191).

99–100. Cf. Augustine, *Expositio quarumdam propositionum ex Epistula ad Romanos* 49 (PL 35:2073).

106. Augustine, *De libero arbitrio* I.xiii.27 (CC 29:228).

107–8. *MDP*, p. 7, line 19; from Cicero, *De inventione* II.liii.160.

110–11. Deut. 6:1.

112–13. Heb. 13:17.

114–15. See Luke 6:31.

116. See Ecclus. 31:18.

119. Exod. 22:18.

126. Augustine, *De libero arbitrio* I.xiii.27 (CC 29:228).

127–28. *MDP*, p. 7, line 20; from Cicero, *De inventione* II.liv.163.

129–30. Cf. *Glossa ordinaria* on Matt. 15:34 (PL 114:140), from Bede, *In Matthaei Evangelium expositio* III.15 (PL 92:77).

131–32. See Augustine, *De musica* VI.50 (PL 32:1189).

133. For a similar phrase, see below, VI.8.

134–35. Augustine, *De libero arbitrio* II.x.29 (CC 29:257).

136–37. Lombard, *Sententiae* III. xxxiii.1 and 3 (2:697–98).

137. Augustine, *De musica* VI.51 (PL 32:1189).

138. Lombard, *Sententiae* III.xxxiii.3 (2:698).

142–43. Augustine, *De libero arbitrio* I.xiii.27 (CC 29:228).

143–44. *MDP*, p. 7, ll. 21–22; from Cicero, *De inventione* II.liv.164.

146. Rom. 8:1–4.

147. Augustine, *De musica* VI.50 (PL 32:1189).

149. Lombard, *Sententiae* III.xxxiii. 3 (2:698).

150. Augustine, *Enarrationes in Psalmos*, Ps. 83, 11 (CC 39:1158).

150–51. This definition is attributed to "Arialdus" in Jean de la Rochelle, *Tractatus de divisione multiplici potentiarum animae*, ed. Pierre Michaud-Quantin (Paris: J. Vrin, 1964), p. 166, and derived from Bede, *In Matthaei Evangelium expositio* III.15 (PL 92:77).

153. Lombard, *Sententiae* III.xxxiii. 3 (2:698).

154. Augustine, *De musica* VI.55 (PL 32:1191).

159–60. James 1:17.

164. With regard to the form *theologice* here and in the following lines, notice that in the text E consistently contracts to *theo*[ce] or *theolo*[ce]. J reads *theologicas* at 161 and contracts as E elsewhere.

171. Cf. Jean de la Rochelle, *Tractatus* (as at I.150–51), p. 162, based on Augustine, *Epistula 120* 8–10 (PL 33:456–57).

172–73. Heb. 11:1.

178–79. See Lombard, *Sententiae* III.xxvi.1 (2:670–71), from Hugh of St. Victor, *Summa sententiarum* I.2 (PL 176:43).

181–82. Cf. Gregory, *Homiliae in Hiezechihelem prophetam* II.x.17 (CC

142:392). See also *Legenda aurea*, p. 855.

182–83. See Lombard, *Sententiae* III.xxvii.2 (2:673), from Hugh of St. Victor, *De sacramentis* XIII.6 (PL 176:528ff.).

184–85. Perhaps a conflation of William of St. Thierry, *De contemplando Deo* VII.14 (PL 184:375) and *De natura et dignitate amoris* II.4 (PL 184:383).

185. See Augustine, *De civitate Dei* XV.22 (CC 48:488).

209–11. See Lombard, *Sententiae* II.xxvii.5 (2:446), based on Augustine, *De libero arbitrio* II.18–19 (CC 29:268–73), and *Retractationes* IX.6 (PL 32:598).

229–30. Perhaps based on Aristotle, *Metaphysica* IV.v.19–20 (1010a).

240. Cf. Augustine, *Epistula 217* V.16 (PL 33:984).

243. Perhaps from Cicero, *De officiis* I.xviii.60.

249. 1 Cor. 3:9.

251. Augustine, *Sermo 169* XI.13 (PL 38:923).

252–53. See above, ll. 238–39.

257. See above, l. 240.

261. Rom. 1:7; and *Glossa* on Rom. 1:7, interlinear.

266. 1 Cor. 12:4.

270. Ecclus. 20:13.

273–75. 1 Pet. 4:10.

280. Perhaps Augustine, *Enarrationes in Psalmos*, Ps. 149, 10–11 (CC 40:2184–85).

281. John 1:16.

283. Zach. 4:7.

288. Lam. 3:44.

290–91. Isa. 44:22.

293–94. Job 37:21.

296. Osee 13:3.

298. Hab. 2:4.

298–99. Cf. Augustine, *Sermo 168* 2–3 (PL 38:912–13).

302–3. Wisd. 16:14.

304–5. John 5:35.

305–6. Cf. Bernard, *In Nativitate S. Joannis Baptistae* 5 (5:179). For the etymology of *Ioannes*, see *Legenda aurea*, p. 56.

307–8. Col. 1:3.

308–9. Cf. *Glossa* on Col. 1:3, interlinear.

310–11. Col. 3:16.

313–14. Wisd. 16:25.

317. John 1:16.

321–22. See Gen. 2:10.

323. Ecclus. 24:35.

324–25. Cf. Matt. 4:23.

327. Jer. 31:22. The manuscripts other than E continue the quotation: "Femina circumdabit virum," in various forms.

330–31. Isa. 2:10.

331–32. See Apoc. 2:4–11.

334–35. Bitter sea water becomes sweet by filtering through earth: see Vincent, *Speculum naturale* V.12 (col. 315). Vincent's source is probably Priscianus, *Ad Cosdroe*, ed. F. Duebner, in Plotinus, *Enneades* (Paris: Firmin Didot, 1855), p. 573, ll. 22–25.

337–38. Exod. 15:25.

341–42. Job 21:33.

343–45. Cf. Gregory, *Moralia* XV. lx.71 (PL 75:1118–20).

353. Jer. 6:16. The scribe of E was thinking of Matt. 11:29, "invenietis requiem animabus vestris."

354. Esther 10:6 or 11:10.

356–57. Zach. 13:1.

359–60. John 4:13.

360–62. For the images of Christ as *fons indeficiens* and Mary as *canalis* and *aquaeductus*, see Bernard, *Sermo in Nativitate Beatae Virginis Mariae* 3 (5:276–77).

363–64. Ibid., 4 (5:277).

366–67. Cf. John 6:52ff.

369–71. Cf. Augustine, *Epistula 187* VIII.26 (PL 33:841).

371–72. Cf. Lombard, *Sententiae* IV.iv.5 (2:770), but without the fish image.

373–74. 1 Tim. 4:14.

375–76. James 5:14–15.

378–79. Ecclus. 35:4.

380–82. See 1 Cor. 7:14.

384. Ecclus. 4:25.

388–89. See Matt. 14:1–11.

390–91. See *Primo*, f. 67ᵛb (on gluttony and Herod) and f. 72ᵛa (on how lechery springs from gluttony).

392. See Acts 5:1–11.

394. Ecclus. 20:17.

394–95. Prov. 12:16.

396–97. See 2 Kings 10:4.

399–400. James 4:6.

400–401. Ecclus. 20:13.

401–4. Cf. Bernard, *Super Cantica* LIV.9 (2:108).

406. Ecclus. 4:25.

407–8. See Exod. 33: 4, 17.

410–11. Luke 1:30.

413–14. Evidently the intended passage is Ecclus. 17:18, which reads *signaculum* instead of *sacculus*.

417–18. Prov. 31:30.

418–19. The thought occurs in Augustine, *De civitate Dei* XV.22 (CC 48:487–88).

419–20. Ps. 32:16.

421. 1 Cor. 12:9.

422–23. Prov. 25:10.

423–26. See Luke 16:19–25.

428–30. Boethius, *De consolatione Philosophiae* I, pr. i, 9 (CC 94:2).

NOTES TO CHAPTER II

5–8. On the relative order of virtues, see Alanus of Lille, *De virtutibus* II.3, in Lottin, *Psychologie*, 6:81; and Peraldus, *Virtutes* II.iv.1 (p. 145). For charity as the "magistra uirtutum" see Gregory, *Moralia* XXIII.xiii.24 (PL 76:265).

8. Heb. 11:1.

9. See *Glossa ordinaria* on Heb. 11:1 (PL 114:663).

11. A favorite quotation of this author. Gregory has only the idea: "omnes quippe virtutes in conspectu conditoris vicaria ope se sublevant," *Moralia* XXI.iii.7 (PL 76:192), which became the basic passage for scholastic discussions of the interconnection of the virtues; see Lottin, *Psychologie,* 3:197–252.

12–14. Gregory, *Homiliae in Evangelia* I.vii.4 (PL 76:1103).

14–15. Ps.-Bernard, *Sermo* "Ecce nos reliquimus omnia" (PL 184:1132).

17–18. Bernard, *De gradibus humilitatis et superbiae* I.2 (3:17).

18–20. Also in Peraldus, *Virtutes* V.iv.1 (p. 455), attributed to Augustine.

23. Matt. 16:24 and parallel in Mark 8:34.

24–25. Gregory, *Moralia* XXXIII.vi. 13 (PL 76:678).

27–29. 2 Kings 6:16, 23.

31-32. Prov. 29:22.

36. Matt. 5:3.

36–37. Ps.-Chrysostom, *Opus imperfectum in Matthaeum*, hom. IX (PG 56:680).

41. Ecclus. 6:2.

43. Job 15:13.

44–45. Col. 2:18.

46–47. Job 36:19.

47–49. See Gregory, *Moralia,* XVI. xxxii.39 (PL 76:1141).

51–52. Ecclus. 2:5.

54. Benedict, *Regula* VII.56 (CSEL 75:50).

55–56. Ecclus. 32:11.

62–63. Prov. 18:13.

65. Luke 17:10.

66–67. See Matt. 23:5.

67. Soph. 3:11.

69. See Lev. 13:45.

70–72. Cf. Gregory, *Moralia* XXVI. xl.72 (PL 76:391).

74–75. Rom. 12:10.

76. Luke 14:10.

78–79. James 3:17.

80–81. *Glossa* on Matt. 3:11, marginal.

81–84. The three degrees of humility also appear in *Glossa* on Matt. 3:15, and in Peraldus, *Virtutes* v.iv.5 (p. 471).

84–85. Matt. 3:15. For the reference to the Gloss, see the preceding note.

86–88. The idea occurs in Gregory, *Moralia* IV.xxviii.54 (PL 75:664–65), IX.xxxii.50–51 (PL 75:885–87), XXI.xv.22–24 (PL 76:203–4), and elsewhere.

92–93. Ecclus. 7:16.

94–95. Ecclus. 13:24.

97. Prov. 29:23.

101. Not Ecclus. 10 but Tob. 4:14.

101–4. The quotation is not from Gregory but Augustine, *Sermo 304*, iii–iv.3 (PL 38:1396).

107–8. Ps. 21:7.

111–12. 2 Kings 23:8.

119. Ps. 84:12.

120. Isidore, *Etymologiae* x.115.

124–25. 1 Pet. 2:24.

127–28. Luke 1:78.

129–31. Luke 4:22.

134–35. Isa. 49:6.

137. Gen. 2:7.

138–39. Job 13:12.

141. Mich. 6:14.

145. Job 30:19.

147–48. Isa. 30:14.

149. Gregory, *Regula pastoralis* III.14 (PL 77:72).

149–50. Job 20:2.

151–52. Gen. 8:21.

152–53. Gal. 6:1.

153–54. Cf. Bernard, *Sermo de Adventu Domini VI* 1 (4:196).

155–56. Prov. 24:16.

156–57. Osee 13:9.

159–60. Ps. 77:39.

161–62. Cf. Bernard, *Sermo De altitudine et bassitudine cordis*, formerly *De diversis*, Sermo XXXVI.3–4 (5:215–16).

163–64. Job 33:27.

165. Eccles. 9:1.

168–69. Job 16:23.

170–71. Eccles. 2:16.

171–72. Boethius, *De consolatione Philosophiae* II, m. vii, 13 (CC 94:34).

172–73. Horace, *Odes* I.iv.13–14.

175. Luke 1:48.

180–81. Ps. 45:5.

182. Ps. 64:14.

183–84. Gregory, *Moralia* XIX.xxi.34 (PL 76:119).

185–86. Cf. Isa. 11:2.

187–88. Ps. 135:23.

189–91. See *Vitae patrum* III.124, V.26, and VII.6 (PL 73:784, 959, and 1036).

191–93. See *Vitae patrum* V.XV.3 (PL 73:953).

194–95. Luke 18:14.

195–96. Dan. 4:14.

201–2. Gal. 6:1.

207. Isa. 59:10.

211–12. Virgil, *Aeneis* VI.126–31.

214. 1 Kings 14:13.

217–18. Prov. 30:28.

222–23. See Matt. 11:25.

225. The saying derives from Diogenes Laertius and is quoted, for example, by Cicero, *Academica posteriora* I.xii.44, and (with the *puteus* image) Lactantius, *Divinae institutiones* III.xxviii.13 (CSEL 19:266).

226–27. Luke 10:39.

227–28. *Glossa ordinaria* on Luke 10:39 (PL 114:287).

228. Gregory, *Moralia* XXIII.xvii.31 (PL 76:269).

232–33. Isa. 37:31.

234–35. Job 18:16.

238–39. Cant. 7:1.

242–43. Ezech. 21:22.

244–45. See Luke 14:28.

250–51. See Dan. 3:39.

251–52. Ecclus. 3:20.

253–55. Matt. 18:3.

259. Exod. 13:13.

260–61. Gregory, *Moralia* XXVII.xviii.38 (PL 76:421).

262–63. 1 Tim. 6:8.

264. Ecclus. 29:30.

265. Ps. 24:21.

267. Lev. 19:18.

268. The quotation may have been suggested by Seneca, *De ira* II.xxxii. 2–3.

270–71. Ecclus. 18:21.

274. See John 6:41 ff.

276–77. Jer. 11:19.

285–86. Prov. 12:27.

288. Gen. 18:27.

290. Ps. 11:7.

291–93. See Isidore, *Etymologiae* XVI.xix.2.

295. Mich. 6:14.

297. Job 19:12.

298–99. Gregory, *Homiliae in Evangelia* I.xi.1 (PL 76:1115).

303–4. 1 Pet. 1:7.

305–6. Gen. 1:16.

310–11. Ps. 106:5.

311–14. Ps. 141:4.

316. 1 Cor. 4:7.

321–22. Gregory, *Moralia* XXXV.v. 6 (PL 76:753).

324. Gregory, *Registrum epistolarum* 11.64 (PL 77:1195).

327. Isidore, *Etymologiae* X.115.

329. 2 Cor. 11:29.

333–34. Gal. 5:24.

336. Zach. 6:12.

337–38. Rom. 11:36.

340. Isa. 26:19.

341–42. Ecclus. 43:24.

346–47. Job 42:5–6.

349–50. 1 Kings 15:17.

353–54. Ecclus. 18:6.

354–55. Phil. 3: 13, 12.

358–59. Cf. Isidore, *Etymologiae* X.118.

361–62. Ecclus. 19:23.

363–64. *Glossa ordinaria* on Ecclus. 19:23 (PL 113:1203).

365. Not from Bernard but Pseudo-Jerome (Pelagius), *Epistula 1, Ad Demetriadem* 20 (PL 30:34).

366. Bernard, *In Assumptione beatae Mariae, Sermo 2* 5 (*Opera,* 5:235).

369–70. Gregory, *Moralia* XV.vi.7 (PL 75:1084).

371–72. See Dan. 14:6.

373. Matt. 23:27.

374. See Matt. 7:15.

376. Walther, *Proverbia,* no. 21158.

377–78. Job 8:11.

379. Cf. Gregory, *Moralia* VIII.xlii. 66 (PL 75:841).

380. 2 Cor. 11:14.

381–82. See Luke 14:34–35.

384–85. See 3 John 9.

386–87. Cf. *Glossa ordinaria* on 3 John (PL 114:706).

390–91. Jer. 2:11.

391–92. Cf. Isidore, *Etymologiae* VIII.xi.14.

394–95. Jer. 10:15.

398–99. Job 20:25.

399. See 1 Kings 6.

402–3. See Bernard, *De gradibus humilitatis et superbiae* (5).

405–6. Isa. 14:12.

406. Luke 10:18.

407–8. Job 20:25.

409. Isa. 13:8.

NOTES TO CHAPTER III

8. Cf. Lombard, *Sententiae* II. xxvii.5 (1:446); see also *Postquam* I.209–11.

9–10. The opinion that charity is the Holy Spirit was expressed by Lombard, *Sententiae* I.xvii (1:113–17), and was rejected by Schoolmen who affirmed that charity is a natural habit; see for instance Peter the Chanter, *Verbum abbreviatum* 95 (PL 205:273), and Auxerre, f. 138d.

14–15. Augustine states that charity is a fundamental condition for any merit, for example, in *De sermone Domini in monte* I.v.13 (CC 35:14); *In Joannis Evangelium* IX.8 (CC 36:95); and ibid., LXXXVII.1 (544).

20. 2 Tim. 4:8.

23. Cf. I Cor. 13:8.
26. Augustine, *Confessiones* I.3.
28. I John 4:8.
29–30. Perhaps based on Augustine, *In Joannis Evangelium* IX.8 (CC 36:94–95), and *Enarrationes in Psalmos*, Ps. 103, Sermo ii.3 (CC 40:1493).
30–31. Augustine, *De doctrina Christiana* III.x.16 (CC 32:87).
31. Augustine, *De Trinitate* XV.xvii. 28 (CC 50:502).
33–34. I John 3:1.
37–38. John 15:13.
40. Rom. 5:5.
48. Augustine, *De civitate Dei* XV.22 (CC 48:488).
49–50. Cf. Augustine, *Enarrationes in Psalmos*, Ps. 103, Sermo i.9 (CC 40: 1482); quoted as here in Lombard, *Sententiae* III.xxxi.1 (2:690).
51–52. Cf. Augustine, *In Epistolam Iohannis*, tract. v.7 (PL 35:2016).
53–54. John 13:35.
57. See *Postquam* I.184–85.
58–59. Cf. Lombard, *Sententiae* III.xxvii.2 (2:673), from Hugh of St. Victor, *Summa de sacramentis* II.xiii.6 (PL 176:528).
60–62. A similar thought occurs in Bernard, *De gradibus humilitatis et superbiae* II.3 (3:18).
62–66. Gregory, *Epistolae* IX.108 (PL 77:1035).
68–69. Cf. Gregory, *Homiliae in Evangelia* II.xxvii.1 (PL 76:1205).
72–73. Perhaps Augustine, *Sermo 265* viii.9 (PL 38:1223).
90–91. A scholastic commonplace based on Augustine, *De Trinitate* XI.vi. 10 (CC 50:346).
94–95. Based on Augustine, *In Epistolam Iohannis* VIII.4 (PL 35:2038).
100. I John 4:8.
107–8. I Cor. 13:6.
109. Cf. Augustine, *De verbis Domini*, Sermo IX (*Sermo 70*), iii.3 (PL 38:444).
109–10. Matt. 22:40.
114. The image ("lata ut Oceanus") appears in Petrus Cantor, *Verbum abbreviatum* 95 (PL 205:274).
114–15. Ps. 118:96.
116. Rom. 13:10.
117–18. Cf. Gregory: "Numquam est Dei amor otiosus," in *Homiliae in Evangelia*, II.xxx.2 (PL 76:1221).
120. I Cor. 13:8.
122. I John 4:16.
123–24. Eph. 4:3.
124–25. Col. 3:14 and Augustine, *Contra Cresconium Donatistam* II.xiii.16 (PL 43:476).
127. Eph. 4:2.
128–29. Cant. 6: 3, 9.
130–31. Matt. 12:25.
131–32. Jth. 15:4.
132–34. The fable is told by Avianus, *Fabulae* 18, "De quatuor iuvencis et leone"; Leopold Hervieux, ed., *Les Fabulistes latins*, vol. 3 (Paris: Firmin-Didot, 1894), pp. 274–75.
137–38. Ps. 4:7.
142–43. I John 2:11.
146–47. Lev. 27:25.
148–50. Job 28:15.
155. Ecclus. 43:10.
158. See above, ll. 62–63.
160. Ps. 38:4.
166. I Pet. 1:17.
167–68. Gregory, *Moralia* XXV.i.1 (PL 76:319).
169–70. I Cor. 9: 22, 19.
171. Gregory, *Moralia* VI.XXXV.54 (PL 75:759).
175. I Cor. 15:8.
175–76. Cf. Petrus Comestor, *Historia scholastica*, on Genesis, vi (PL 198: 1060); from Macrobius, *Commentarius in Somnium Scipionis* I.xx.32, ed. J. Willis (Leipzig: Teubner, 1963), p. 84.
179–80. Isa. 60:22.
183–84. I Cor. 13:7.
185. Cant. 8:7.
187–88. Cant. 5:14.
191–92. Ecclus. 31:18.
193. I Cor. 13:4.
193–94. The etymology appears also in Joannes Balbus, *Catholicon*

(Mainz, 1460; reprint ed., Farnborough, Hants.: Gregg International Publishers, 1971).

195–96. I John 3:17.

198. Cant. 8:6.

198–99. Isidore, *Etymologiae* III.lxvi. 2, giving nineteen years, however.

203–4. Ecclus. 24:32.

215–16. Jer. 23:24.

220. Cant. 5:10.

224–27. Ps.-Chrysostom, *Opus imperfectum in Matthaeum*, hom. XIII (PG 56:703).

229–30. Cf. Jer. 5:25.

231. Cf. Luke 12:49.

234–35. Luke 9:6; cf. Matt. 10:5ff.

237–38. John 20:21.

238–39. Zach. 12:6.

241. Gregory, *Homiliae in Hiezechihelem prophetam* I.xi.7 (CC 142: 172).

242–43. Abdias 18.

254. Zach. 9:16.

256–57. Jer. 51:20.

264–65. Exod. 38:8.

266–69. Gregorius, *Moralia* II.i.1 (PL 75:553).

275. Dan. 12:4.

278. Cf. Exod. 33:20.

279–80. See Aristotle, *De insomniis* 2 (459b); Pliny, *Historia naturalis* VII. xv.64.

280. Wisd. 1:4.

284. James 1:23.

286. Prov. 17:23.

290. I Cor. 8:1.

293–94. Apoc. 4:6.

298–99. Arnaud de Bonneval, *De laudibus Beatae Mariae Virginis* (PL 189: 1726), based on Bernard, *Sermo in Nativitate Beatae Mariae Virginis* (5:275–88).

305–8. This precise comparison appears in a sequence attributed to Adam of St. Victor, "De Nativitate Domini," stanzas 7–8; see G. M. Dreves and C. Blume, eds., *Analecta hymnica* (Leipzig: O. R. Reisland, 1886–1922), 54:154.

312–13. Cf. Vincent, *Speculum naturale* VII.80 (col. 476); perhaps based on Pliny, *Historia naturalis* XXXIV.xxxvii.135.

314–15. Osee 13:15.

320–21. Isidore, *Etymologiae* XVI. xiii.2.

321–22. Isa. 50:7.

324–25. John 12:32.

326–27. John 20:12.

331–32. Gregory, *Moralia* VI. xxxvii.58 (PL 75:762).

334. See above, l. 140.

335. I John 2:8.

337–38. Prov. 27:9.

340–41. See Ps. 31:8.

343–44. I Tim. 4:8.

346–47. Thus also quoted by Peraldus, *Virtutes* V.2 (p. 451), and by Auxerre, fols. 139b and 159b. Elsewhere the latter attributes the quotation to Gregory: fol. 181b; similarly, *Legenda aurea*, p. 330. The sentence occurs almost verbatim in Bernard, *Epistola 111* 3 (7:285).

349–50. I Pet. 5:10.

351–52. See above, ll. 62–63.

353–54. I Cor. 13:7.

359–60. Eccles. 10:9.

360–61. Lev. 6:12.

361–63. See Gregory, *Moralia* XXV. vii.15 (PL 76:328).

364–65. Apoc. 1:6.

369–70. Mich. 1:10.

371–72. Lam. 2:18.

373–74. Eph. 5:8.

375–76. I John 2:8.

377–78. I Pet. 2:9.

380. See John Damascene, *De fide orthodoxa* II.7 (PG 94:887–88).

388. James 1:17.

397–98. I Cor. 15:10.

398–99. See Aristotle, *De anima* III. 5 (430a).

405. Apoc. 3:20.

406. Heb. 12:15.

411. Prov. 4:23.

412–13. Matt. 15:18.

413–14. Cf. Bede, *In Matthaei Evan-*

gelium expositio III.xv (on Matt. 15:18; PL 92:75).

422–23. 1 John 3:14.

428. 1 John 4:1.

429. Isa. 11:2.

432–33. Deut. 12:23.

435–37. Job 31:17–22.

438–39. Vincent, *Speculum naturale* XVIII.43 (col. 1350), mentions a bone in the left part of the heart of a hart, which is medicinal.

441–42. Matt. 24:12.

442–43. Cf. Pliny, *Historia naturalis* XI.lxix.181.

445–46. Phil. 1:23.

448–49. Rom. 8:38.

449–50. Acts 5:41.

452–53. Deut. 33:19.

454. Job 6:6.

455. Cf. Gregory, *Moralia* VII.xv.18 (PL 75:775).

458–59. Cant. 8:7.

461–62. Apoc. 3:18.

469. Dan. 4:24.

470–71. Cf. Gregory, *Moralia* XII. li.57 (PL 75:1013).

477. Lev. 27:25.

481–82. 1 Tim. 1:5.

483. See *Postquam* II.280–304.

485–86. Prov. 3:18.

486–89. Dan. 4:8–9.

494. Ezech. 47:12.

495–96. Wisd. 3:15.

497–98. Lev. 25:4.

498–99. *Glossa ordinaria* on Lev. 25:4 (PL 113:368).

499–501. This tree is described in Vincent, *Speculum naturale* XX.30 (col. 1477), who quotes as his authority "Iorath." See further Nicole Bozon, *Contes moralisés*, ed. L. T. Smith and P. Meyer (Paris: Société des Anciens Textes Français, 1889), no. 116a and pp. 276–77.

502. Isa. 60:8.

503–5. Gregory, *Homiliae in Evangelia* I.v.4 (PL 76:1094–95).

506–7. Apoc. 12:3.

511–12. Ps. 64:9.

513–15. Isa. 19:17.

520. See Lam. 4:20.

526–28. The thought that love makes the goods of others our own occurs in Gregory, *Regula pastoralis* III.10 (PL 77:63).

528–30. Gregory, *Dialogi* III.37 (PL 77:313).

531. See Gen. 2:10ff.

532–36. Cf. Augustine, *De doctrina Christiana* I.xxiii.22 (CC 32:18).

537–38. Matt. 22:11.

538–39. Esther 4:2.

541. Exod. 26:31.

550–51. Cf. Bonaventure, *In Sententias* III.xxxi, art. i, qu. 1, 3: "Omne peccatum ortum habet vel ex timore male humiliante, vel ex amore male incendente" (3:674). Later, Bonaventure says, "ex amore male inflammante" (3:675).

552–53. Ps. 79:19.

555. Not James but 1 Pet. 4:8.

558–59. Ecclus. 22:21.

563–65. Ezech. 13:11.

565–67. Cf. Gregory, *Moralia* IX. xi.13 and XXIX.xxxi.72 (PL 75:866 and 76:517).

567. Job 38:31; cf. Job 9:9.

571. Wisd. 16:25.

572–73. 1 John 2:19.

573–75. The comparison of wicked people to evil bodily fluids occurs in *Glossa* on 1 John 2:19, marginal.

579. 1 John 4:10.

580–81. Not from Habacuc but Mal. 1:2–3.

583–84. Eph. 1:4.

588. Aristotle, *Metaphysica* I.4 (984. b.24).

590–92. Boethius, *De consolatione Philosophiae* III, m. ix, 4–6 (CC 94:52).

593–94. Isa. 43:4.

595–96. Jer. 31:1.

597. Apoc. 1:5.

599–600. 1 John 3:1.

601–2. John 14:23.

603–4. Apoc. 3:19.

604–5. Cant. 2:6.

607–8. Cf. Gregory, *Homiliae in Evangelia* II.xl.6 (PL 76:1307), and *Regula pastoralis* III.26 (PL 77:99–101).

608–13. Perhaps based on Augustine, *Enarrationes in Psalmos*, Ps. 144, 18 (CC 40:2101).

613. Ps. 61:11.

615. John 13:1.

618–764. The following schema of seven qualities which Christ's love for us has, and which our love for God should have, is an expansion of Matt. 22:37 (recalling Deut. 6:5) and a pattern developed by Bernard (*dulciter, fortiter, prudenter*) in *Super Cantica*, Sermo XX (1:114–21), and *De diversis* XXIX and XCVI.6 (6. 1: 210–14, and 360). *Perseveranter* appears as a synonym for *fortiter* in Peraldus, *Virtutes* II.iv.5 (p. 163).

619. Paulinus of Aquileia, *Carmina* XI.ii.1, ed. Ernst Duemmler, in Monumenta Germaniae historica, Poetae latini aevi Carolini, vol. 1 (Berlin: Weidmann, 1881), p. 144.

620. Prov. 8:31.

624. Heb. 4:15.

625. Cf. John 13:1–8.

627. Cant. 8:6.

628. Matt. 22:37.

630–31. Jer. 48:36.

632. See John 8:44.

636. Jer. 12:7. "Soul," *anima*, here and in the preceding sentence of course has the meaning of "life."

639–41. Isa. 49:15–16.

643–44. See note above, on ll. 618–764.

645. For the "ten benefits," see III.121–50.

648. 1 Cor. 12:31.

651–52. Cf. Boethius, *De consolatione Philosophiae* II, pr. iv, 20 (CC 94: 25).

653. Ps. 18:11.

655. Ps. 24:8 and 1 Pet. 2:3.

656. Ecclus. 49:1–2.

657–58. Bernard, *Super Cantica* XV. 6 (1:86).

658–59. Osee 14:8.

660–61. Cant. 5:8.

661. Cant. 2:5.

667–70. Anselm, *Oratio* 7 (3:24).

674. James 4:4.

680–81. John 3:16.

692–93. Heb. 10: 20, 19.

700–701. Ezech. 8:17.

703–4. Gregory, *Moralia* X.xxi.39 (PL 75:942–43).

705. Cant. 8:6.

705–6. The "Seneca" quotation appears in Publilius Syrus, *Sententiae* H.5, ed. Wilhelm Meyer (Leipzig: Teubner, 1880), p. 33.

707–8. Matt. 24:13.

711–12. Ecclus. 6:10.

712–13. Reference to a short tale in which a "philosopher" says these words in response to someone's claim that a certain poor man is a friend of a wealthy person. See Peraldus, *Virtutes* II.iv.2 (p. 150) and II.iv.15 (p. 180). In medieval works the saying is attributed to various philosophers (Socrates, Theophrastus) and was apparently contained in a collection of *proverbia* ascribed to Seneca.

714–15. For the "Tullius" quotation, cf. Sallust, *De Catilinae coniuratione* XX.4.

718–19. Not Ecclus. but Prov. 17: 17.

720. Matt. 22:37.

721. Notice that the expansions ("sine errore") of the Augustinian gloss ("idest toto intellectu") to the biblical text ("ex toto corde"), here and in ll. 731–32 and 751, appear in Innocent III, *Sermo de uno martyre* (PL 217:616–17) and are repeated by Auxerre, f. 140c–d, later Schoolmen, and Peraldus, *Virtutes* II.iv.5 (p. 163).

725–26. Matt. 22:29.

729. Jer. 10:8.

731–32. See note on l. 721.

734. Cf. Augustine, *Enarrationes in Psalmos*, Ps. 32, Enarr. ii, sermo i, 2–4 (CC 38:247–50).

746–47. Cf. Augustine, *De Trinitate* x (CC 50:311–32), and *De civitate Dei* XI.28 (CC 48:347–49).

751. See note on l. 721.

755. Acts 17:28.

757. Not in *De anima* but rather in Aristotle, *De memoria et reminiscentia* I (451a).

764. From the "Exultet" of the Easter Vigil service; see *Sarum Missal*, p. 118, ll. 29–30.

767–69. Gal. 1:14.

769–70. Bernard, *Super Cantica* XX. 2 (1:115).

772–73. Cf. Bernard, *Super Cantica* XI.7 (1:58).

774–75. 1 Pet. 4:1.

777–78. 1 Mach. 6:34.

784. Osee 7:9.

784–85. This property of the dragon appears in Pliny, *Historia naturalis* VIII.xi.32 and VIII.xii.33.

786. Job 40:12.

787. Cf. Gregory, *Moralia* XXXII. xix.33–34 (PL 76:655–57).

791. Num. 13:24.

793–4. See Exod. 12:7ff.

799–801. Heb. 12:3–4.

803–5. Cf. Augustine, *De Trinitate* x (CC 50:311–32).

807. Rom. 13:11.

808. 1 Cor. 11:30.

809–10. Aristotle, *De anima* III.iii (429a).

810–11. Matt. 13:22.

811–12. 2 Cor. 7:10.

813–14. Cf. Gen. 40:23.

816–17. Matt. 5:43. Cf. also Lev. 19:18.

818–19. Luke 6:31.

820. Tob. 4:16.

828–29. Phil. 1:8.

831. 1 Thess. 5:14.

832–33. Gal. 6:2.

836. Ecclus. 17:12.

837. Augustine, *De disciplina Christiana* III.3 (CC 46:210); *Enarrationes in Psalmos*, Ps. 25, sermo ii.2 (CC 38: 143); and elsewhere.

838–39. Matt. 5:23.

841–42. Mal. 2:10.

843. Boethius, *De consolatione Philosophiae* III, m. vi, 2 (CC 94:46).

846. Lev. 19:17.

847–48. Prov. 18:6.

849–50. See Exod. 22:12.

851. Isa. 58:4.

852. Prov. 18:6.

853–54. Isa. 3:9.

855–56. Matt. 5:24.

859. See above, l. 837.

861–62. Matt. 5:44.

862–63. This commonplace appears verbally not in Augustine but in Gregory, *Homiliae in Evangelia* II. xxvii.1 (PL 76:1205).

866–68. For the idea, cf. Augustine, *Enarrationes in Psalmos*, Ps. 25, ii.2 (CC 38:143).

868–69. For the Gregory quotation, cf. Augustine, *De doctrina Christiana* I.xxvii.28 (CC 32:22), and *De civitate Dei* XIV.vi (CC 48:421).

870. Matt. 5: 21, 43.

874–75. Deut. 7:2 and 20:13.

877. Exod. 21:24.

880. Matt. 5:44.

887–89. Rom. 12:20 and Prov. 25: 21.

891–92. *Caput* is glossed as *mens* in *Glossa* on Lev. 21:5 and on Rom. 12:20, interlinear.

898. Matt. 5:45.

900. Matt. 5:45.

903. Deut. 10:18.

909–10. See Matt. 5:46 and Luke 6:33.

912–13. Cicero, *De officiis* II.xviii. 61–62, quoted in *MDP*, p. 17, ll. 10–11.

915. Luke 23:34.

916–17. Job 26:13.

922. Aristotle, *Ethica Nicomachea* II.3 (1105a).

922–25. Acts 14:21.

926–27. Judges 3:1.

931. Eccles. 10:18.

934–35. Wisd. 2:24.

937–39. Rom. 5:10.

939–43. Ps.-Chrysostom, *Opus imperfectum in Matthaeum,* hom. XIII.43 (PG 56:702).

946. Isa. 66:24.

946–47. See *Glossa ordinaria* on Isa. 66:24 (PL 113:1316).

948–49. Cf. the definition of envy given in *Primo*, f. 12[r]b: "tristicia de prosperitate alicuius [vicini]." See John Damascene, *De fide orthodoxa* II.14 (PG 94:932), and Gregory, *Moralia* V.xlvi.84 (PL 75:727), and *Regula pastoralis* III.x (PL 77:63).

950. 1 Thess. 4:13.

951. Prov. 11:7.

953–56. For the notion that suffering in hell is increased by the damned soul's seeing the suffering that will befall his relative or neighbor, see Gregory, *Homiliae in Evangelia* II.xl.8 (PL 76:1308–9).

956–59. Deut. 28:65–66.

NOTES TO CHAPTER IV

12–14. Gregory, *Moralia* V.xlv.78 (PL 75:723).

15–16. Isidore, *Etymologiae* X.168.

17–22. Ps.-Chrysostom, *Opus imperfectum in Matthaeum,* hom. IX.4 (PG 56:681).

24–25. 1 Thess. 5:15.

27. Cf. "quasi manu adsuetus" in Isidore, *Etymologiae* X.168.

28–29. Aristotle, *De interpretatione,* 11 (20b); commonly cited in scholastic literature.

32–33. Prov. 1:24.

34. Isa. 65:2.

38–39. See James 3:7–8.

39–41. See *Glossa ordinaria* on James 3:7 (PL 114:676).

41–42. See Isidore, *Etymologiae* XVII.vii.17.

45–46. Prov. 27:18.

47–48. Isa. 27:9.

49–50. Wisd. 3:15.

51–52. See Aristotle, *Historia animalium* I.i (488b).

54–55. Ezech. 2:4.

56–57. Prov. 30:14.

58. Ps. 34:16.

60–61. Ecclus. 19:11.

63–64. Prov. 9:7.

64–66. Prov. 29:1.

66. Cf. Ps. 79:14.

68–70. The image of the pillow also occurs in Hugh of St. Cher's gloss on Matt. 5:4 (6:15d).

70. Ecclus. 10:31.

72–73. See Matt. 6:17.

76–77. Augustine, *De sermone Domini in monte* II.xii.42 (CC 35:135).

78–92. These seven points are very similar to the commentary on Matt. 5:4, *Beati mites,* in Hugh of St. Cher (6:16a).

80–81. Matt. 11:29.

82–83. Ecclus. 1:34.

84–85. Ecclus. 3:19.

86–87. See Num. 12:3.

89. Ecclus. 45:4.

90. Cant. 1:15.

92. Ps. 36:11.

95. Prov. 15:32.

100–101. Phil. 3:21.

103. Ps. 89:10.

104–5. Ps. 149:4.

105–6. Ps. 36:11.

106–7. Matt. 5:4.

107–8. Isa. 61:1.

109. Prov. 15:1.

110. Isa. 29:19.

111–12. James 1:21.

113–14. Ecclus. 3:19.

115. Ecclus. 6:5.

116–17. 2 Kings 22:36.

121–22. Apoc. 3:17.

123–24. Augustine, *Confessiones* I. 13.

124–26. Gregory, *Moralia* XXXIV. iii.6 (PL 76:720).

128–29. 1 Cor. 4:7.

130–31. Ecclus. 27:4.

132–33. Osee 7:1.

134. Aristotle, *Ethica Nicomachea* II. 9 (1109b).

140–41. Gregory, *Homiliae in Evangelia* II.xxxv.4 (PL 76:1261–62).

141–42. See *MDP*, p. 30, ll. 9–10.

145. Matt. 5:9.

148–49. Isa. 30:18.

150. From the Collect for the Eleventh Sunday after Trinity; *Sarum Missal*, p. 183.

151–52. Wisd. 11:24.

152–53. Cf. Augustine, *Confessiones* I.4.

158–59. 1 Pet. 2:23.

161–62. 2 Cor. 6:4.

163. 1 Cor. 13:4.

166–67. See Walther, *Proverbia*, no. 16974.

169–70. Apoc. 3:10.

171. Rom. 5:4.

172–73. James 1:12.

173–75. Rom. 2:6–7. The complete quotation is: "[Deus] reddet . . . iis quidem, qui secundum patientiam boni operis gloriam et honorem et incorruptionem quaerunt, vitam aeternam."

177–78. Ecclus. 40:1.

179–80. Prov. 5:22.

182–83. 1 Thess. 3:3.

184–85. 1 Pet. 4:1.

185–86. The quotation also appears in Hugh of St. Cher on Gen. 25, *At illa tollens* (1:32c), but here attributed to Jerome.

190–91. Job 6:10.

193–94. Job 33:25.

196–97. Heb. 11:37.

198. See Job 8:8.

199–200. See Jer. 6:16.

201–2. Isa. 26:7.

203–5. For *cibarius* [*sic*] *panis*, see Jerome, *Epistulae* LII.6, XLIII.3, and LII.12 (CSEL 54: 425, 320, and 435). The *vepres* of Saint Benedict are mentioned in his biography in *Legenda aurea*, p. 205. The *mattula* of Eulalius, as a sign of his patience and humility, appears in *Vitas Patrum* III.29 (PL 73:757). For the references to Arsenius and (Mary) the Egyptian, see *Legenda aurea*, pp. 808 and 247.

207–8. 2 Cor. 4:17.

209. 1 Pet. 1:6.

209–10. Ecclus. 20:12.

216–17. Isa. 66:24.

217–18. Ecclus. 41:7.

221–22. Jerome, *In Esaiam* VIII.xxiv. 7/13 (CC 73:318).

224–25. Rom. 8:18.

226–27. Ecclus. 1:29.

229–30. Cant. 4:4.

231–32. Luke 21:19.

232–34. See Gregory, *Moralia* V. xvi.33 (PL 75:697).

238–39. Job 1:21.

240–41. Gregory, *Moralia* III.x.17 (PL 75:608).

241–42. Job 1:21.

242–43. Cf. Gregory, *Moralia* II. xvii.30 (PL 75:570).

246–47. Jer. 15:17. The Vulgate has *comminatione*, whereas Jerome reads *amaritudine*: *In Hieremiam* III.58 (CC 74:151).

250. Wisd. 3:5.

252. Apoc. 3:18.

253–54. See *Primo*, f. 4[v].

263–65. Jer. 6:29.

271–72. Ps. 101:4. For the *alia littera*, see Peter Lombard, *Commentarius in Psalmos*, on Ps. 101:4 (PL 191:907). It stems from Augustine, *Enarrationes in Psalmos*, Ps. 101, sermo ii, verse 4 (CC 40:1428).

279. Ovid, *Remedia amoris*, l. 229.

281–82. Ps. 6:2. The Augustine quotation is cited by Peter Lombard, *Commentarius in Psalmos*, on Ps. 6:2 (PL 191:105), and attributed to Augustine.

282–84. Cant. 4:4.

289–90. Perhaps Matt. 5: 9–11 and 38–42.

292–93. John 8:48.

293–94. Luke 11:15.

294–95. Luke 7:34.

299–301. 2 Kings 16:10.

302–4. See Matt. 26:59–63.

305. Matt. 26:63.

305–6. Jerome, *In Evangelium Matthaei* IV (CC 77:260).

307–8. Prov. 29:9.

311–12. 2 Kings 14:10.

317–18. See Apoc. 9:4.

323–24. See Matt. 4:3.

325–26. Cf. Hugh of St. Cher on Matt. 4, *Si filius Dei es* (6:12).

327–29. Gregory, *Homiliae in Evangelia* I.xviii.4 (PL 76:1152–53).

334–35. Ecclus. 8:4.

338–39. Prov. 26:17.

343–44. Prov. 15:1.

347. Prov. 15:1.

350–51. Tob. 3:15.

354–55. Gregory, *Moralia* VIII. xxxvi.59 (PL 75:838), on Job 8:1.

355–56. Ecclus. 20:5.

358–59. Prov. 26:5.

362. Prov. 20:3.

363–64. John 5:13.

370–73. See Thomas de Celano, *Vita prima sancti Francisci Assisiensis*, ed. Patres Collegii Sancti Bonaventurae (Quaracchi, 1926), p. 58 = *Vita I*, pars i, cap. xix, par. 53.

374–75. 1 Kings 10:27.

382–83. Ecclus. 41:20.

385–90. Cf. Ps.-Chrysostom, *Opus imperfectum in Matthaeum*, hom. XII.12 (PG 56:684).

391–92. See Matt. 27: 28 and 35.

393–94. Isa. 53:7.

398. Apoc. 13:8.

399. See Gen. 4:4.

400. For instance, Exod. 29:38ff.

401. Isa. 16:1.

401–2. See John 1:29.

402–4. See Gregory, *Moralia* XXIX. xxi.69 (PL 76:515–16), on Job 38:31.

406–7. Isidore, *Etymologiae* XII.i. 12.

407. Notice that Latin *pietas* means both "piety" and "pity" in modern English, depending on whether the object of respect is the Deity or one's fellow man.

409–10. 1 Cor. 5:7.

410. Isidore, *Etymologiae* XII.i.12.

411–12. Phil. 2:18.

413. John 19:26.

414–15. 2 Tim. 2:19.

415–16. See the canon of the Mass; *Sarum Missal*, p. 225. The symbolic explanation of *agnus* developed in ll. 410–15 is based on William Durandus, *Rationale divinorum officiorum* (Lyons, n.p., 1568), p. 198.

418–19. Eph. 4:22.

424–25. Cant. 4:2.

426. *Excedebant*: Prof. A. G. Rigg suggests that this may simply be a misspelling of *exedebant*, "they ate up." But this type of misspelling would be quite unusual in E and the better manuscripts. A different possibility is *excidebant*, "they cut off," in light of Isidore's attributing to the front teeth the act of *praecidere, incidere,* or *concidere*.

428. Cf. Isidore, *Etymologiae* XI.i. 52. The passage is reproduced in J; see variants. The moralization in ll. 428–29 does not appear in Isidore.

433. Prov. 11:29.

437–38. Ecclus. 8:3.

438–39. Ecclus. 31:6.

441–42. Eccles. 2:23.

443–45. Augustine, *In Epistulam Johannis*, tract. X.4 (PL 35:2056).

446. Isa. 14:30.

453. Gen. 14:14.

454–55. Ps. 126:4.

457–58. 1 Tim. 6:9.

460–61. Isa. 62:10.

464–65. Heb. 10:34.

467–68. Matt. 5:40.

471–72. Job 1:21.

475–76. See 4 Kings 4:27.

484. Prov. 25:20.

485–86. See Gen. 39:12.

490–91. The gloss *hora uestis* does not seem to occur in Isidore's *Etymologiae* or *Quaestiones in Genesim*, on

Gen. 39:12. But it appears, as *hora vestimenti*, in the *Derivationes* of Hugutio of Pisa; see *Summa Britonis*, ed. Lloyd W. Daly and Bernardine A. Daly (Padua: Editrice Antenore, 1975), 1:367.

491–92. Cf. Paschasius, *Expositio in Lamentationes Jeremiae* IV (PL 120: 1221).

492–93. See Judges 4:17–21.

501. Prov. 19:29.

504–5. See Matt. 19:29.

508. See Matt. 5:40.

509–13. For similar stories in which a hermit gives thieves an object they had overlooked, see Frederic C. Tubach, *Index Exemplorum* (Helsinki: Suomalainen Tiedeakatemia, 1969), nos. 4810 and 3364.

513–14. A thief who robs a hermit's vegetables appears in *Historia Lausiaca* VIII.54 (PL 73:1165). The author's intention could of course have been *omnia*, not *olera*; but the latter is the *difficilior lectio*.

516–18. See 2 Kings 14:29–33.

520–21. Gregory, *Homiliae in Evangelia* II.xxxvi.7 (PL 76:1269–70).

524. 2 Cor. 6:10.

531. Matt. 19:21.

531–32. Luke 7:30.

542. Cf. Tob. 10:5.

545–46. Jer. 12:7.

548. Matt. 19:27.

552–54. Isa. 50:6.

556–57. Matt. 5:39.

558. John 18:23.

563. Matt. 5:39.

566. Jon. 1:12.

567–68. Jerome, *In Ionam* 1.12 (CC 76:390).

568–69. Judges 5:2.

569–70. Judges 5:9.

573–74. See 2 Mach. 6:18–20.

578–79. Matt. 10:23.

579–80. See John 10:39.

581–82. John 10:12.

583–84. See Luke 22:36.

585–87. The substance of this reference appears in Thomas de Chobham, *Summa confessorum* VII.via.6; ed. F. Broomfield (Louvain and Paris: Nauwelaerts, 1968), pp. 426–27; see also p. 442. The phrase *vim vi repellere* is from *Digest* IX.ii.45; see *Corpus iuris civilis*, ed. Paul Krueger et al., 16th ed. (Berlin: Weidmann, 1954), 1:162.

588. Cf. Esther 9:20–28.

588–89. *Decretum*, dist. XII, c. 3 (1: 27–28).

593–94. Matt. 26:52.

600–602. See *Glossa ordinaria* on Luke 22:38 (PL 114:340).

606–7. Judges 15:15.

609. Osee 11:4.

613–17. The story occurs verbatim in Petrus Cantor, *Verbum abbreviatum* 114 (PL 205:300–301). A similar story can be found in *Vitae Patrum* V.14 (PL 73:956–57).

617–20. Cf. *Vitae Patrum* V.xvi.19, III.74, VII.2 (PL 73: 973, 773, 1029).

623–24. Wisd. 3:4.

626. Ps. 37:18.

629–30. 1 Cor. 3:18.

632. Isa. 43:2.

635. Isa. 48:10.

637–39. See Augustine, *De unico baptismo* XIII.22 (PL 43:606); but this is said of Saint Cyprian.

644–45. Gregory, *Moralia* X.xxiv. 42 (PL 75:944), on Job 11:20.

649–50. Isa. 66:13.

651–52. Eccles. 51:35.

653. Wisd. 10:10.

654–55. Bernard, *De diversis,* Sermo XXI.2 (6.1:169).

660–61. Matt. 5:41.

664. *Glossa ordinaria* on Matt. 5:41.

665. See Acts 1:12.

671–73. Cf. Isidore, *Etymologiae* VI. xviii.18.

674–75. See Exod. 35:3.

677–78. Prov. 20:25.

681. Ps. 48:9.

681–82. Lam. 5:5.

683–85. See 2 Mach. 15.

686–88. 2 Mach. 15:5.

688–89. See Num. 15:32–36.

693–94. Cf. Augustine, *De continentia* XII.26 (PL 40:367).

696. John 19:17.

697. Isa. 9:6.

699–700. Gen. 22:6.

701–2. Job 40:21.

702–3. Cf. Isidore, *Etymologiae* XIX. xxi.16.

706–7. See Luke 23:26.

710–11. Amos 1:5.

714–16. See Matt. 4:1–11.

717–19. See Matt. 26:36–44.

719–20. James 1:12.

728. 1 Cor. 10:13.

729–30. See ibid.

734–35. Job 2:6.

735–36. Cf. Gregory, *Moralia* III. xxix.57 (PL 75:627).

737–39. See Augustine, *De civitate Dei* XX.8 (CC 48:713).

741. Apoc. 20:7.

742–43. 1 Cor. 10:13.

743–47. Augustine, *De Baptismo contra Donatistas* II.v.6 (PL 43:130).

749. Ecclus. 34:9.

750–51. Ecclus. 31:18.

752. Isa. 26.16.

753. Ps. 119:1.

754. 2 Cor. 12:7. The sentence continues: "extollat me, datus est mihi stimulus carnis meae angelus satanae, qui me colaphizet."

755–56. Ecclus. 27:6.

757–58. Jth. 8:22.

759. Tob. 12:13.

760. James 1:12.

762–63. Isa. 53:4.

763. Luke 12:50.

764–65. *Glossa ordinaria* on Luke 12:50 (PL 114:300).

770–71. Jer. 10:19.

771–72. Mich. 1:12. The Vulgate has *in amaritudinibus*, whereas Jerome reads *in Maroth: In Michaeam* I.i.10/15 (CC 76:430).

775. Job 5:18.

776. Gregory, *Moralia* VI.XXV.42 (PL 75:752).

777–79. See 2 Mach. 9.

780. Jer. 10:19.

782. 2 Cor. 12:10.

784–85. Ecclus. 31:2.

787. Ecclus. 20:12.

788–90. Ps. 93:19.

790–91. Gregory, *Moralia* XXXV. xii.22 (PL 76:761).

792–93. The thought occurs, for example, in Gregory, *Moralia* VIII.vii. 12 (PL 75:808–9).

794–95. Job 33:19.

797. 1 Mach. 1:6.

801–2. Matt. 19:28.

803–4. 2 Cor. 12:9.

804–5. For the idea, see Gregory, *Moralia* V.xvi.33 and VII.xiv.17 (PL 75:697 and 775).

806–7. John 11:3.

811–12. Ezech. 27:24.

812. Job 12:18.

816. Isa. 33:23.

823–24. Ezech. 4:8.

824–29. *Vitae Patrum* VII.XX.1 (PL 73:1044–45).

829–30. Isa. 53:4.

834. Cf. Haymo, on Isaiah 53:4 (PL 116:989).

837. Ecclus. 10:11.

848–49. Job 2:10.

851–52. Isa. 30:26.

852–53. Job 22:24.

861. Isa. 50:6.

862. John 19:3.

865–66. Eccles. 10:19.

868. Prov. 3:34.

869–70. See Matt. 27:26.

873. Osee 10:7.

877. Mich. 3:3.

881–82. Isa. 53:2.

882–83. Isa. 53.3.

884–85. Matt. 23:6.

895–96. Matt. 21:9.

896. Matt. 27:40.

897. Matt. 21:9; Luke 15:13.

906. John 12:12.

910–11. Heb. 12:2.

913. Ezech. 3:9.

917–18. Bernard, *In Circumcisione*, sermo III.3 (4:284).
919. I Pet. 2:24.
921–22. Isa. 51:1.
924–25. Gen. 7:11.
926. Ps. 29:12.
927. Cant. 4:12.
933. See Deut. 33:19.
937–38. Gregory, *Moralia* XVIII. xxxviii.59 (PL 76:70).
938–39. See I Kings 30.
940–44. Gregory, *Moralia* v.xli.73 (PL 75:721).
947–48. See *Postquam* II.98–173, 197–356.
952–53. Ecclus. 4:33.
953–55. I Pet. 2:19.
957–58. Perhaps Gregory, *Moralia* VII.ii–vi.2–6 (PL 75:767–69).
964–65. Soph. 3:10.
966. See Zach. 14:20.
967. See Rom. 9:22.
968–69. Isa. 11:14.
972. Mich. 7:9.
980–81. Augustine, *Confessiones* I. xix.30.
982–83. See Jer. 1:11ff.
984–85. See Exod. 5–14.
988–89. Gen. 49:15.
991. See Matt. 6:2.
992. Osee 10:11.
992–96. Gregory, *Moralia* XX.XV. 39 (PL 76:160).
997–98. Jer. 31:16.
998–99. Bernard, *De consideratione* II.vi.12 (3:419).
1005–6. Heb. 12:2.
1008. Matt. 5:9.
1008–9. Gal. 4:7.
1015–28. The following definitions are from Augustine, *De civitate Dei* XIX.13 (CC 48:678–79).
1032–33. The reference is to the position of peace in the list of beatitudes, see Matt. 5:9.
1036–37. Wisd. 14:22.
1038. Luke 19:42.
1040–41. John 14:27.
1042. Ibid.
1043–44. Aristotle, *Topica* IV.4 (125a).
1047. See Ps.-Chrysostom, *Opus imperfectum in Matthaeum*, hom. IX (PG 56:682).
1048. Eph. 2:14.
1049–50. Ps. 75:3.
1050–51. See 3 Kings 6.
1051–52. See I Par. 28:3.
1052–53. I Cor. 11:33.
1053–54. See John 20:19, etc.
1057–58. Ecclus. 28:15.
1059–60. Phil. 4:7.
1061. Col. 3:15.
1062. Prov. 12:20.
1063–64. Isa. 54:10.
1065. James 3:18.
1069. Rom. 1:7, etc.
1072. Matt. 10:12.
1073–74. Deut. 20:10.
1075–76. Eph. 4:3.
1076–77. Perhaps referring to the petition "Dona nobis pacem" at the end of the third "Agnus Dei"; *Sarum Missal*, p. 225.
1078–79. Eph. 2:14.
1080–81. Luke 24:36.
1083–84. Ps. 147:14.
1084–85. Isa. 32:18.
1089–90. Lucan, *De bello civili* II. 272–73.
1090–91. Isa. 55:12.
1095. Rom. 12:18.
1099. Isa. 38:17.
1099–1105. See Isa. 27:4–5.
1107–8. Isa. 57:19.
1108–9. Job 22:21.
1110–11. Ps. 37:9.
1111–12. Job 3:24.
1114–15. Job 5:23.
1116–17. Ibid.
1120. Rom. 14:19.
1122. Tob. 4:16.
1123–24. Luke 6:31.
1129. Isa. 33:7.
1131. Luke 14:32.
1135. Ecclus. 29:16–18.
1137–38. Prov. 18:16.
1140–41. Not from Augustine but

Cassiodorus, *Expositio psalmorum*, on Ps. 87:3 (CC 98:795); repeated in *Glossa ordinaria* (PL 113:990).

1142–43. Job 33:26.

1146–47. The two topics: *cum quibus debemus habere pacem* and *a quibus*, are similarly treated in Petrus Cantor, *Verbum abbreviatum* 111 (PL 205:295–96).

1148. See Judges 16.

1149–50. 1 Cor. 9:27.

1152–53. Isa. 26:18.

1156–57. Eph. 6:12.

1158–59. Jer. 21:9.

1163–64. Prov. 6:5.

1167. 2 Tim. 2:4.

1169–70. Exod. 18:18.

1171. Job 26:5.

1172–73. Gregory, *Moralia* XVII. xxi.31 (PL 76:25).

1173–74. Ecclus. 11:10.

1174. *Sapiens ponit*, etc.: see Juvenal, *Saturae* VI.444.

1177. Ps. 111:10.

1178. Ps. 20:10.

1180–81. Apoc. 9:6.

NOTES TO CHAPTER V

4–6. The affiliation of obedience derives from Petrus Cantor, *Verbum abbreviatum* 122 (PL 205:314).

9–10. Bernard, *De praecepto et dispensatione* (3:253–94) furnishes the elements of this definition.

12–13. Cf. Vincent, *Speculum doctrinale* IV.40 (col. 323), attributed to "Auctor."

17. Gregory, *Moralia* XXXV.xiv.28 (PL 76:765).

18–19. Phil. 2:8.

22–24. 1 Cor. 15:49.

26. John 10:18.

29–30. Heb. 13:17 and 1 Pet. 2:18.

31. Luke 2:51.

32. John 19:11.

33–35. See Matt. 4.

35–38. The *potentia obedientialis* of created things is a scholastic refinement of Augustine's teaching that by being created all creatures carry out (or can carry out) God's will; see for instance *De Genesi ad litteram*, V.xxiii. 44–45 (PL 34:337–38).

42–43. Bar. 6:59.

43–44. Bar. 3:34–35.

45. Bar. 6:60.

46–48. Job 37:11.

48–50. Job 38:10.

50. Matt. 8:27.

52–53. 1 Kings 17:36.

55. 1 Mach. 6:37.

58–59. Isa. 11:8.

59–61. See Jer. 35:1–11.

66–67. Gen. 22:3.

67–69. See *Vitae Patrum* III.143, V.xiv.5 (PL 73: 788, 948–49).

70–71. Exod. 40:14.

72. Lev. 22:23.

77–78. Cf. *Decretum* causa XXV, qu. i (1:1007–12).

82–83. Josue 10:13.

84. Sedulius, *Paschale carmen* I.163 (CSEL 10:28).

86–87. See 1 Kings 17:1ff.

88–89. Heb. 12:9.

89–91. Perhaps based on Augustine, *De opere monachorum* XVII.20 (PL 40:564–65).

98. Phil. 3:2.

102. 2 Cor. 11:20.

105–6. Job 39:27.

113. See Lev. 11:27.

115–16. Ps. 72:23.

124–25. Gen. 49:14.

127–28. Matt. 5:12.

131. Ezech. 8:3.

132. Gen. 49:15.

132–33. Ecclus. 51:35.

134. Gen. 49:15.

137–38. Augustine, *Confessiones* VI.5.

138–39. Num. 13:28–29.

143–44. Rom. 11:16.

145–46. Cf. Gen. 49:15.

146–47. See Ecclus. 2: 2 and 4.

149. See Num. 14:2ff.

150–51. See Job 6:11–12.

152–53. See Num. 32:19.

157. Num. 32:1.

162–63. Phil. 2:9.

163–64. See Matt. 14:28–31.

165–67. See Num. 20:11.

167–69. See Gregory, *Dialogi* II.7 (PL 66:146).

169–73. See *Vitae Patrum* v.xiv.3 (PL 73:948).

173–76. See *Vitae Patrum* IV.12 (PL 73:823).

176–77. See Dan. 3.

177–82. See *Vitae Patrum* v.xiv.4 (PL 73:948).

199–200. Anselm, *Cur Deus homo* II.5 (2:100).

202–3. Ambrose, *De paradiso* VIII. 39 (CSEL 32.1:296).

218–19. Gregory, *Moralia* XXXV. xiv.30 (PL 76:766). This passage in Gregory is the basis for the scholastic discussion of whether perfect obedience may contain any exercise of the obedient person's own will. A similar solution is given by Alanus, *De arte praedicatoria* 16 (PL 210:144), and Auxerre, f. 165c–d.

219–20. Quoted earlier, at ll. 63–65.

226–29. Gregory, *Moralia* XXXV. xiv.30 (PL 76:766).

231–32. Isa. 6:8.

232–33. See Jer. 1:6.

236–37. Phil. 3:8.

241–42. Matt. 26–38.

245–66. This question is also raised by Auxerre, f. 166a, and is given there the same solution as in *Postquam*.

246. Matt. 23:3.

247. 1 Pet. 2:18.

256. See *Decretum*, causa XXIII, qu. iv, cc. 1–15 (1:899–903).

258–60. *Decretum*, distinctio XCIII, cc. 8–9 (1:322).

260–61. Almost verbally, not in Gregory but Augustine, *De opere monachorum* XXXI.39 (PL 40:578).

NOTES TO CHAPTER VI

3–4. Cf. *MDP*, p. 30, l. 1.

4–5. *MDP*, p. 7, l. 20, from Cicero, *De inventione* II.liv.163.

7–8. Cf. Augustine, *De libero arbitrio* I.27 (CC 29:229).

8. Perhaps a reference to Prov. 31: 19.

11–12. Isa. 35:3.

13–14. Isa. 40:31.

14–15. Gregory, *Moralia* XIX. xxvii.50 (PL 76:131).

16–17. The five species of fortitude and their definitions are taken from *MDP*, p. 30, but notice that *MDP* lists a sixth species, patience, which in *Postquam* is the subject of Chapter IV.

17–18. *MDP*, p. 30, l. 4.

21–22. See 2 Mach. 8.

24–25. Wisd. 9:15.

25–26. 2 Esdras 4:10.

29. Prov. 28:1.

30–31. See Statius, *Achilleis* I.1 and II.143–50.

32–33. Deut. 33:19.

33. Cf. Gregory, *Moralia* VII.xv.18 (PL 75:775).

34–35. Job 6:6.

38–39. Gregory, *Moralia* VII.xxv. 30 (PL 75:782). This passage also contains the image of the *torrens* of ll. 35–37.

40. Job. 6:15.

45. See *MDP*, p. 30, l. 5.

46–47. Heb. 4:16.

49–50. Phil. 2:13.

51. Rom. 7:18.

53–54. Prov. 3:5.

56–58. Cf. Bernard, *In Psalmum Qui habitat*, sermo XVII.4 (4:489).

57–58. *Cum ipso . . .* : see Ps. 90: 15.

59. Cf. Ps. 9:35, "Laborem et dolorem consideras."

59–60. Job 35:13.

61. See Acts 7:55.

64–65. Jer. 17:5.

69. Job 5:1.

71–72. Acts 12:5.

73–74. See Ps. 24:22.

75–76. See *MDP*, p. 30, ll. 6–7.

77. Prov. 15:15.

79. 2 Par. 17:6.

83. Isa. 14:30.

84–85. Perhaps Gregory, *Moralia* XXII.xvi.35 (PL 76:233). The quotation appears verbatim in Peraldus, *Virtutes* III.iv.5 (p. 262).

89. See *MDP*, p. 30, ll. 7–8.

91. Ecclus. 43:32.

94–95. Not from Isidore but Jerome, *Epistula 71* ii.1 (CSEL 55:2).

96–97. See John 6:67.

97–98. See Luke 9:62.

98–103. Apparently not in *Vitae Patrum*; but the story appears in the thirteenth-century *Tractatus de viciis* in London, British Library, MS Royal 5.A.viii, f. 124.

105. See Matt. 27:5ff.; 2 Kings 17: 23.

109–10. Soph. 3:7.

110–11. See Luke 14:30.

115–16. Deut. 33:25.

117–20. *Vitae Patrum* v.x.8 (PL 73:913).

121–22. See *MDP*, p. 30, ll. 8–9.

122–24. James 1:8.

124–25. See 2 Cor. 1:17.

125–26. Ecclus. 37:20.

128. Isa. 42:4.

128–30. *Glossa* on Isa. 42:4, marginal.

130–31. Luke 19:41; John 11:35.

132–33. See John 2:15ff.

134. Ecclus. 8:1.

137. Bar. 6:31. "Those who are brought to a mourning" are hired mourners.

139–40. Gal. 2:18.

141. See Josue 6:26.

143. See Matt. 11:7.

143–44. Eph. 4:14.

146–47. Job 24:18.

150–51. John 5:17.

153–54. Ecclus. 38:32.

156–57. Isa. 6:3.

157–59. Apoc. 4:8.

162. Gen. 1:14.

165–67. Wisd. 19:17.

168–69. Perhaps Aristotle, *De generatione et corruptione* II.ix.10 (336a).

172–73. Anselm, *Meditatio I*, 13–14 (3:76).

174. 2 Thess. 3:10.

175. Gen. 3:19.

176. Prov. 31:27.

177–78. See Seneca, *De clementia* I.xix.4.

178–79. Prov. 6:6.

182–83. Ecclus. 11:3.

184. Mark 6:31.

184–85. Cf. *Glossa* on Mark 6:31, interlinear.

186–87. Isa. 32:18.

188. 1 Tim. 4:7.

190. Rom. 12:11.

192–93. Matt. 6:34.

196. Luke 22:43.

196–97. Luke 6:12.

197–98. See 1 Kings 31:4–6 and 1 Par. 10:4–6.

202. Wisd. 8:9.

204–5. Not from Gregory but Ps.-Augustine, *Sermo 302* 2 (PL 39:2324) and Isidore, *Sententiae* III.viii.2 (PL 83:679).

208–10. Ecclus. 6:35.

212–13. 1 Thess. 5:11.

2–12. Notice that Latin *pietas* means both "piety" and "pity," as at IV.407.

4–6. *MDP*, p. 27, ll. 17–18.

6–7. Augustine, *De civitate Dei* X.1 (CC 47:273).

8–9. 2 Tim. 4:7.

10–12. *MDP*, p. 25, ll. 3–4, from Cicero, *De inventione* II.liii.161.

13–14. Matt. 5:7.

14–15. Bernard, *De gradibus humilitatis et superbiae* III.6 (3:21).

15–16. Cf. Ecclus. 31:18.

18–19. Gal. 1:4.

20–21. 2 Cor. 12:15.

24–25. The quotation is not from Augustine but is based on Dionysius Areopagita, *De divinis nominibus* IV.1 (PG 3:694) or *De caelesti hierarchia* IV.1 (PG 3:178). The wording is scholastic and can be found, for example, in Bonaventure, *In Sententias* I, dist. xix, pars i, art. unicus, qu. 2 (1:344; also 9:378).

28–30. Boethius, *De consolatione Philosophiae* III, m. ix, 4–6 (CC 94:52).

31. See Aristotle, *Metaphysica* I.4 (984b).

33–34. Titus 3:5.

34–35. Cf. Ps.-Augustine, *Ad fratres in eremo*, sermo VI (PL 40:1246–47).

37–38. Jer. 31:3.

39–40. Jer. 2:2.

44–45. Wisd. 10:13.

47–48. Zach. 11:12.

50–51. Lam. 3:22.

52. Ps. 36:6.

53–54. Not from Anselm but Augustine; see *Enarrationes in Psalmos*, Ps. 32, en. ii, sermo ii.4 (CC 38:259).

55–56. Cf. Lev. 25:4.

58–59. Cf. Augustine, *Sermo 9* XIII.21 (PL 38:91).

61. Isa. 52:1.

64–65. Augustine, *Contra Felicianum* 7 (PL 42:1162), and John Damascene, *De fide orthodoxa* II.27 (PG 94: 960).

68. James 2:13.

70–72. Ecclus. 16:15.

86–87. Isa. 52:10.

87–88. See Isa. 53:5.

89–90. See 2 Cor. 12:26.

91–92. 2 Cor. 2:29.

95–96. Luke 14:13.

98. Matt. 6:20.

102. Prov. 19:17.

104. Luke 6:37.

105–6. See Matt. 18:23–35.

109. Luke 6:37.

110–11. Lam. 3:22.

112. Wisd. 12:22.

113. Heb. 7:25.

114–15. See Luke 23:34.

116. Ecclus. 35:26.

117–18. Prov. 1:24.

119–20. Isa. 30:18.

120–21. Wisd. 11:24.

122–23. Luke 1:78.

125–26. Jer. 3:1.

127–28. Gregory, *Homiliae in Evangelia* I.xii.6 (PL 76:1122).

131. Ps. 144:9.

132–33. Matt. 5:45.

134–35. Ecclus. 18:12.

135–40. Ps.-Chrysostom, *Opus imperfectum in Matthaeum* hom. IX (PG 56:682).

139–40. Matt. 5:44.

140. James 1:5.

141–42. See Ecclus. 20:15.

147–48. Isa. 54:10.

148–49. Osee 6:4.

152–54. On Saint Martin, see *Legenda aurea*, p. 742; on Saint Lawrence, ibid., pp. 488–93.

155–59. "Saint Anselm" must be a mistake in the archetype. The story is usually told of Saint John the Almoner: *Vitae Patrum* I, Vita sancti Joannis Eleemosynarii 8 (PL 73: 346).

159–64. See Gregory, *Dialogi* III.1 (PL 77:216–20).

164–67. For a saintly person who steals in order to give to the poor, see Caesarius of Heisterbach, *Dialogus miraculorum* VI.5, ed. J. Strange (Cologne: Heberle, 1851), 1:345–52. But the parallels are not close.

168–69. Jerome, *In Ionam* i.7 (CC 76:387).

169–75. See *Vitae Patrum* I, Vita sancti Joannis Eleemosynarii 22 (PL 73:359).

172. Matt. 19:21.

180–81. Acts 19:19.

185. See 1 Cor. 12:12.

186–87. Gregory, *Homiliae in Evangelia* I.xxxix.9 (PL 76:1300).

197. Isa. 1:24.

199–201. See 2 Kings 9:1ff.

210–11. Osee 10:12.

214. Matt. 25:34.

215–16. Publilius Syrus, *Sententiae* 206, ed. W. Meyer (Leipzig: Teubner, 1880), p. 33. The quotation also occurs in *MDP*, p. 27, ll. 20–21.

217. Luke 6:36.

218–19. Tob. 4:8.

220. Exod. 23:3.

222. Exod. 23:2.

224. Ecclus. 12:5.

225–26. Cf. *MDP*, p. 17, ll. 10–11; from Cicero, *De officiis* II.xviii. 61–62.

228. Matt. 6:20.

229–31. The quotation appears verbatim in Peraldus, *Virtutes* III.v.14 (p. 374). Cf. also Augustine, *Sermo 302* IX.8 (PL 38:1388–89), and Petrus Chrysologus, *Sermo 135* (PL 52: 566).

233. Job 5:24.

234–35. Ps. 80:3.

238–39. Ecclus. 35:12.

240–41. 1 Par. 29:14.

242–43. James 2:13.

244–45. Prov. 19:17.

246–47. Prov. 22:9.

248–50. Given by Vincent, *Speculum doctrinale* IV.67 (col. 338), and attributed to "Auctor."

250–51. The first definition of *pietas* is probably a rephrasing of definitions given in Vincent, *Speculum doctrinale* IV.41 (col. 323).

251–52. The second definition of *pietas* appears in Vincent, *Speculum doctrinale* IV.41 (col. 323), where it is attributed to "Auctor."

252–53. See Vincent, *Speculum doctrinale* IV.68 (col. 338), attributed to "Auctor."

253–55. The definition of *compassio* also appears in Vincent, *Speculum doctrinale* IV.67 (col. 338), attributed to "Auctor."

260. See Gen. 2:6.

262–63. For the legend of the wellspring of oil appearing at Christ's birth, see Orosius, *Historiae* VI.xviii (PL 31:1017) and xx (1053–54).

263. See Gen. 28:12ff.

268. The identification of mercy with "oil" and the following reason, ll. 268–70, also occur in Peraldus, *Virtutes* III.v.14 (p. 372).

273. See Ps. 144:9.

274–75. Cf. Peraldus, *Virtutes* III.v. 14 (p. 373).

278. Apoc. 14:13. The reference is to the Epistle as read in the Mass for the Departed; *Sarum Missal*, p. 431.

282–83. See Matt. 25:4.

285–86. Cf. *Glossa* on Lev. 25:21, interlinear.

288–89. 2 Mach. 1:20ff.

290. See Aristotle, *Meteorologica* IV.9 (385b).

293–94. Ecclus. 17:20.

296. 1 Cor. 3:17.

300–303. Cf. Ezech. 8:8–10.

305–6. Ecclus. 29:13.

306. Cf. *Glossa* on Ecclus. 29:13, interlinear.

307–8. Cf. Ecclus. 3:33.

310. 3 Kings 18:38.

312–13. Ecclus. 12:10.

313–14. See Baldricus Dolensis,

Historia Hierosolymitana III, in *Gesta Dei per Francos*, ed. Jacques Bongars (Hanover: Ex typis Wechelianis, 1611), 1:125, ll. 22–24.

315–16. Isa. 43:2.

318. Matt. 6:17.

321. Augustine, *De sermone Domini in monte* II.xii.42 (CC 35:135).

324. Ecclus. 7:33.

328. Prov. 15:27.

331. See Cant. 1:4.

332–33. See Luke 10:38ff.

334–35. See Lev. 2:4ff.

340. Luke 6:38.

341–42. Luke 6:35.

342–43. Luke 6:37.

344. See Luke 19:41; and John 11: 35.

345–46. See Gregory, *Moralia* XX. xxxvi.70 (PL 76:180).

347–48. Matt. 18:15.

348–49. See *Glossa* on Matt. 18:15, interlinear.

350–52. Prov. 28:23.

NOTES TO CHAPTER VIII

4–6. Cf. Ps.-Galen, *De dinamidis*; in *Galeni ascripti libri* (Venice: n.p., 1541), f. 18v.

7–8. Ecclus. 3:32.

10–11. *MDP*, p. 51, l. 6.

17–18. Isa. 58:5.

20–21. See above, at IV.693–94.

27. Ps. 73:14.

31. Ecclus. 31:19.

32. Ecclus. 31:20.

33. Boethius, *De consolatione Philosophiae* II, pr. v, 16 (CC 94:27).

38. Hab. 1:16.

40–41. Eccles. 10:17.

42. Ecclus. 37:32.

43–44. Eccles. 10:17.

49–50. Deut. 26:10–11.

50–51. Job 3:24.

55–56. See *Primo,* f. 67v–68.

59. 1 Thess. 5:7.

60–61. See Num. 11:34.

64. Ovid, *Metamorphoses* V.549.

65–66. Prov. 14:13.

67–69. The "companions" of abstinence are taken from *MDP*, p. 41, ll. 22–23.

70–71. See *MDP*, p. 42, ll. 1–2.

74–75. Cf. Aristotle, *Ethica Nicomachea* II.5 and 8 (1106b and 1109a).

75. Gal. 5:23.

77–78. The definition of *verecundia* is based on Augustine, *Enarrationes in Psalmos*, Ps. 68, ii.4 (CC 40:919).

82–83. Isa. 56:11.

85–86. Cf. John Damascene, *De fide orthodoxa* II.15 (PG 94:931).

87–88. See *MDP*, p. 51, l. 11.

92–93. Luke 16: 19, 22.

93–94. See *MDP*, p. 51, ll. 17–18.

96–97. Gregory, *Moralia* XXX. xviii.61 (PL 76:557).

97–98. See *MDP*, p. 51, l. 19.

98–99. Ecclus. 14:10.

100. See *MDP*, p. 51, l. 20.

102–3. Ecclus. 31:37.

103–4. See *MDP*, p. 52, l. 1.

104–5. See *MDP*, p. 52, ll. 2–3; from Sallust, *De Catilinae coniuratione* LI.3.

105–6. See *Primo*, f. 70.

107–8. See Matt. 4:2.

109. Matt. 5:6.

113–14. Matt. 5:6.

114. Isa. 49:10.

116. John 6:35.

117–18. *Glossa ordinaria* on Luke 9:17 (PL 114:278).

120. Ecclus. 24:29.

121–22. Ecclus. 42:26.

123. Ps. 104:4.

124. Augustine, *Enarrationes in Psalmos*, Ps. 104:3 (CC 40:1537).

131–32. Cf. Gregory, *Moralia* XVIII. lvi.91 (PL 76:94).

136. Aristotle, *De anima* II.3 (414b).

137–38. Cf. Ambrose, *Expositio*

Evangelii secundum Lucam VII.215 (CC 14:289).

138–39. Eccles. 5:9.

140. Matt. 5:6.

143–44. Augustine, *Regula ad servos Dei* ("*Regula tertia*") 4 (PL 32:1379).

145. Cf. Gregory, *Regula pastoralis* II.3 (PL 77:29–30).

146–47. Isa. 30:32.

150–51. Isa. 58:7.

151–53. See *Glossa* on Isa. 58:7, marginal.

154. Ecclus. 37:34.

155–56. Ecclus. 31:37.

156–57. Cf. above, ll. 4–6.

158–59. Tob. 12:8.

160–61. Cf. Acts 2: 1–4 and 15 ("*cum sit hora diei tertia*").

166–70. Ps.-Ambrose, *Commentarius in Epistulam primam ad Timotheum* V.23 (PL 17:507).

171–72. Luke 18:11.

172–73. Cf. *Glossa* on Luke 18:11, interlinear.

174. Jth. 6:15.

176. Jer. 2:33.

177–78. Matt. 6:16. The Vulgate text supports E's unique reading.

180–81. Cf. Gregory, *Moralia* XXX. xviii.63 (PL 76:558–59) and *Homiliae in Hiezechihelem prophetam* II.vii.19 (CC 142:332).

182. Isa. 61:8.

187–88. Cf. Jerome, *Epistula 130* II (CSEL 56:191).

189–90. Isa. 9:20.

190–91. See Luke 16:24.

191. See Matt. 8:12.

191–92. *Glossa* on Matt. 8:12, marginal.

193. Isa. 24:9.

193–94. Jerome, *In Esaiam* VIII. xxiv.7/13 (CC 73:318).

NOTES TO CHAPTER IX

3–4. Cicero, *De inventione* II.liv. 164.

14. 1 Cor. 7:28.

17–19. For this and the following scholastic definitions of matrimony, see Josef G. Ziegler, *Die Ehelehre der Poenitentialsummen von 1200–1350* (Regensburg: Friedrich Pustet, 1956), pp. 34–37.

21–22. *Decretum,* causa XXVII, qu. ii, introd. (1:1062).

23–25. *Digest* XXIII.ii.1, in *Corpus iuris civilis*, ed. Paul Krueger et al., 16th ed. (Berlin: Weidmann, 1954), 1:330. Notice that the letters "ff." are commonly used in medieval manuscripts as a reference to the *Digest.*

30–31. A popular mnemonic verse; also in Richard of Wethringsette, *Summa brevis*, Oxford, MS Bodley 64, f. 135.

33–35. See Eph. 5:26.

36. Cf. Augustine, *De bono coniugii* VI.6 (PL 40:377).

38. Gen. 9:7.

41–42. Not from Gregory but Lombard, *Sententiae* IV.xxvi.2 (2:913).

43. Gen. 2:24.

50–51. Tob. 6:17. For Asmodeus, see Tob. 3:8.

52–53. See Jerome, *Adversus Jovinianum* I.49 (PL 23:281).

54–55. See Matt. 14:3ff.

56–57. The remark on "*formatum puerum . . .*" comes from Augustine, *Quaestiones in Exodum* 80 (CC 33:111), which is repeated by Lombard, *Sententiae* IV.xxxi.4 (2:938), and *Decretum*, causa XXXII, qu. ii, c. 8 (1:1122). Notice that Augustine's text reads *puerperium.*

60. Gen. 4:11.

61–62. Eccles. 8:6.

67–68. Job 12:7.

71. Eph. 2:3.

74–75. See *Primo*, ff. 80v–82. This section of the chapter on lechery anticipates some of the discussion of

matrimony which appears in *Postquam.*

76. Cf. Augustine, *De bono coniugii* XVII.20 (PL 40:387).

78–79. Eph. 5:32.

79. 1 Cor. 11:3.

82–83. Matt. 6:24.

85–87. See John Damascene, *De fide orthodoxa* I.5 (PL 94:801/02).

95. See H. Walther, *Proverbia*, no. 8231.

97. Eph. 5: 25 and 28.

98. Eph. 5:25.

98–99. The gloss seems to come from Lombard on Eph. 5:25 (PL 192:214).

101–2. Job 39:16.

103–4. See Isidore, *Etymologiae* VIII. xi.102.

106–9. Cf. 1 Pet. 3:1ff.

109. 1 Cor. 7:34.

111. Isa. 42:22.

112. 2 Pet. 2:14.

114. Ibid.

115. See the section "*Quibus modis alliciunt mulieres,*" in *Primo*, ff. 75v–77.

116–63. A similar treatment of this question appears in Bonaventure, *In Sententias* IV.xxxi, art. 2 (4:721–28).

117–18. Gregory, *Responsum 10* (PL 77:1196).

121–22. 1 Cor. 7:6.

123–24. See Lombard, *Sententiae* IV.xxxii.3 (2:947), and *Decretum*, causa XXXII, qu. ii, c. 4 (1:1120). Based on Origen, *In Numeros*, hom. VI.3 (PG 12:610).

124–25. Wisd. 1:5. The Vulgate text supports E's unique reading.

126. 1 Cor. 6:16.

126–27. Cf. Augustine, *Sermo 162* 2 (PL 38:887).

127–28. Cf. Aristotle, *Topica* V.1 (129a).

131. Cf. Augustine, *De civitate Dei* XIV.15 (CC 48:438) or XXII.22 (842).

132–33. Cf. Augustine, *De bono coniugii*, passim (PL 40:373–96).

133–35. Bede, *Homiliae* XIII (PL 94: 68).

167. 1 Cor. 7:39.

168. Augustine, *Confessiones* VIII.5.

170–71. See John 19:26.

172–73. Jth. 8: 1 and 6.

174–75. Jude 23.

175–76. Gen. 37:31.

177–78. Ecclus. 35:18–19.

179. Luke 2:36–37.

180–81. *Glossa* on Luke 2:36, marginal.

182. See 3 Kings 17:7ff.

184–85. 1 Tim. 5:10.

186–87. See 1 Kings 21:1–6.

189–90. Heb. 13:10.

191–92. Num. 10:21.

197–98. See Matt. 26:7.

201–2. Antiphon for Vespers, for the first Sunday following October 28; see F. Procter and Ch. Wordsworth, eds., *Breviarium ad usum insignis ecclesiae Sarum* (Cambridge: Cambridge University Press, 1879–86), vol. 1, col. mccclxxv.

208. Job 28:13.

208–9. Prov. 31:10.

215. See Matt. 3:4.

215–16. See 4 Kings 1:8.

220–21. See Jer. 13:1ff.

224. Job 40:2.

226–27. Bernard, *Sermo ad clericos de conversione* XXI.37 (4:113).

229. 1 Cor. 7:34.

230. See Dan. 10:5.

231. See Rev. 15:6.

232–33. Luke 12:35.

233–35. Gregory, *Homiliae in Evangelia* I.xiii.1 (PL 76:1123).

236–37. Job 40:11.

239. Job 31:12.

240. Lam. 4:11.

242–43. Cf. Gregory, *Moralia* V. xxii.43 (PL 75:702–3).

244. Matt. 5:8.

246–47. See *Postquam* I.171.

251–52. Prov. 20:9.

254. Matt. 5:8.

258. Rom. 1:20.

260–61. The quotation is strongly reminiscent of certain "followers of Aristotle" (Avicenna?) discussed by William of Auvergne. The latter frequently speaks of *irradiationes* that come from (a separate) *intelligentia agens* and are given to the pure of heart. See, for instance, *De universo* II.i and iii.20, in Guilelmus Alvernus, *Opera omnia* (Orleans and Paris: Deluyne, 1674), 1: 816 and 1053–54; and *De anima* II (2:210).

264–65. Matt. 5.8.

266–68. Cf. Gregory, *Moralia* v.xxxiv.61–62 (PL 75:712–13).

269. Augustine, *De immortalitate animae* I.1 (PL 32:1021).

272–73. Isa. 51:6.

274–76. First responsory at Matins on Tuesday after Pentecost; Procter and Wordsworth, *Breviarium . . . Sarum,* vol. 1, col. mxvi.

277–78. Prov. 22:11.

281–82. Ps. 23.3.

284. Ps. 50:12.

288–89. Prov. 10:20.

290–91. Prov. 4:23.

292–93. *Vitae Patrum* v, "Verba seniorum," x.11 (PL 73:913–14).

295–96. Ps. 72:21.

297. See Gregory, *Moralia* XXI.ii.5 (PL 76:191).

300–301. Ecclus. 7:26.

302. Jer. 9:21.

303–4. Cf. Gregorius, *Moralia* XXI.ii.4 (PL 76:189–90).

306–7. From the hymn "Jam lucis orto sidere," said at Prime, in spring; Procter and Wordsworth, *Breviarium . . . Sarum*, 2:37.

309–10. Lev. 3:4.

310–11. *Glossa* on Lev. 3:4, interlinear.

316–17. Prov. 6:27–29.

318–19. Jerome, *Epistula 52, Ad Nepotianum presbyterum* 5 (CSEL 54: 423).

320–21. *Decretum*, causa XVIII, qu. ii, c. 21 (1:835).

321–22. See *Decretum*, distinctio XXXII, c. 17 (1:121).

323–24. Gal. 5:24.

325–26. Heb. 12:3–4.

326–28. For the commonplace, in prose and verse, and usually attributed to Gregory, see Siegfried Wenzel, *Verses in Sermons* (Cambridge, Mass.: Mediaeval Academy of America, 1978), p. 148.

329–30. *Glossa* on Exod. 6:6, interlinear.

332–34. Wisd. 3:13–14.

336. 2 Mach. 14:35.

337. See 1 Cor. 3:16f.

341–42. Gen. 15:6.

343–44. Ecclus. 49:12.

347. Matt. 19:27.

348. Heb. 11:37.

350. Cf. Cant. 5:8.

351. Wisd. 3:13.

353–404. For the rite of dedicating a church, see Walter H. Frere, *Pontifical Services*, vol. 1, Alcuin Club Collections no. 3 (London: Longmans, Green and Co., 1901), 1–43; and H. A. Wilson, ed., *The Pontifical of Magdalen College*, Henry Bradshaw Society, vol. 39 (London: Harrison, 1910), pp. 98–124.

355–57. 1 Mach. 4:36.

359–60. Rom. 6:19.

362–64. Eph. 4:22.

365–66. 1 Esdras 3:13.

370–71. 1 Cor. 11:28.

373–74. Jer. 6:16.

375–76. 1 John 2:27.

380–81. Luke 10:20.

382–83. Perhaps based on Ambrose, *Exameron* III.iii.12–16 (CSEL 32.1:67–69).

386–87. Ps. 68:29.

392–93. Apoc. 21:3.

393–94. Dan. 3:1.
396. 1 Mach. 1:40.
402. Eph. 5:12.
403–4. Ezech. 8: 8, 6.
409–10. Augustine, *De sancta virginitate* XIII.12 (PL 40:401).
411. 2 Cor. 11:2.
414. Lev. 21:13.
415–16. Isa. 7:14.
416. Isa. 66:7.
417. Cant. 2:16.
418–19. Gregory, *Moralia* XXIV.viii. 17 (PL 76:296).
421. Wisd. 6:20.
422. See John 13:25.
425. Deut. 28:4.
426–27. Wisd. 3:13.
429–30. The quotation, often attributed to Jerome in medieval works, comes from Paschasius Radbertus, *Epistula ad Paulam et Eustochium* 5 (PL 30:126).
432–34. Anselm, *Oratio* 7 (3:21).
435. See Gen. 40:1–19; and Dan. 1:17.
437. Jth. 15:11.
438–39. Apoc. 16:15.
440–41. Apoc. 14:4.
443. See Dan. 3.
444. For the reference to Saint Agatha, see *Legenda aurea*, p. 171, where Agatha speaks of wild beasts and fire.
446–47. Jerome, *Adversus Jovinianum* I.40 (PL 23:282).
447–48. Ibid., I.16 (PL 23:246).
449. Apoc. 14:4.
454–55. Apoc. 3:5.
456–57. Lam. 4:7.
458–60. Ambrose, *De virginibus* I. iii.10 (PL 16:202).
460–61. Cant. 4:8.
461–62. See Exod. 26:14.
467–90. The question whether virginity is a virtue is similarly treated by Auxerre, f. 160a–b, and Bonaventure, *In Sententias* IV. d. xxxiii, art. 2, qu. 1 (4:753–54).
468–69. Quoted earlier, *Postquam* II.II.
474. 1 Cor. 7:28.
476–77. Cf. Aristotle, *De generatione et corruptione* I.3 (318).
493–94. Cf. Augustine, *De mendacio* VII.10 (PL 40:495).
496–97. Jerome, *Epistula 22 Ad Eustochium* 5 (CSEL 54:150).
501–2. The quotation here attributed to Jerome is based on Ps.-Augustine, *Hypognosticon* III.ix.17 (PL 45: 1631).
502–4. Gregory, *Regula pastoralis* III.28 (PL 77:107).
504–5. Amos 5:1.
505–6. Cf. Hugh of St. Cher on Amos 5 (7:186b), quoting Jerome, *In Amos* II.v.1–3 (CC 76:272–75).
516–17. Isidore, *Sententiae* II.xl.7 (PL 83:644). For the following sentence (517–18), see Isidore, ibid., 8.
518–21. Cf. Augustine, *De nuptiis* I.xii.13 (PL 44:422).
525–27. Gregory, *Moralia* VIII.xlv. 74 (PL 75:847).
527. Ps. 44:14.
528–29. Gregory, *Moralia* XXXV. xviii.45 (PL 76:777).
530. See Gen. 34:1–2.
531–32. See Judges 11:34–39.
537–38. Ecclus. 26:13.
539–40. Ezech. 3:24–26.
542. Luke 1:28.
546–47. 2 Cor. 4:7.
552–53. See Gen. 3:5.
557. Luke 1:38.
558. Ibid.
560. Luke 1:45.
562. Luke 1:34.
564. Cf. the antiphon at Lauds on feasts of the Blessed Virgin Mary, from the first week after the Octave of Easter until the vigil of the Ascension: Procter and Wordsworth, *Breviarium . . . Sarum*, vol. 1, col. dccclxx.
567–68. Probably a reminiscence

of Bernard, *In Vigilia Nativitatis Domini, Sermo IV* 3 (4:222).

570–71. Ecclus. 25:33.

572. From the hymn "Ave mundi spes Maria," *Sarum Missal*, p. 480.

573–74. Ps. 86:3.

574. Apoc. 21:16.

582. Apoc. 12:1.

582–84. 3 Kings 10:18.

586–87. Cf. Bernard, *In laudibus Virginis Matris* I.8 (4:18).

594. Ecclus. 24:20.

597–744. This series of plant images applied to the Blessed Virgin Mary follows a very similar list in Ecclus. 24:17–23.

598–99. Bernard, *In laudibus Virginis Matris* II.1 (4:21).

600–601. Luke 1:48.

605. Bernard, *In Adventu Domini, Sermo II* 4 (4:173).

607. See Cant. 1:3.

610. From a popular prayer contained in the *Admonitio morienti* attributed to Saint Anselm (PL 158:687). See Siegfried Wenzel, *Verses in Sermons* (Cambridge, Mass.: Mediaeval Academy of America, 1978), pp. 144–45.

612–13. Bernard, *Sermo in Dominicam infra Octavam Assumptionis Beatae Virginis Mariae* 2 (5:263).

615. The phrase "uirgo ante partum, uirgo post partum" occurs in *Legenda aurea*, p. 41 (feast of the Nativity).

617. Cant. 1:16.

620–21. Augustine, *De natura et gratia* XXXVI.42 (PL 44:267).

622–23. Prov. 31:29.

624. Gen. 3:15.

625–26. Cant. 6:3.

630. Cant. 7:7.

633–34. Cant. 3:6.

637. See Ezech. 47:12.

638–39. See Cant. 7:13.

641–42. Luke 1:42.

643–44. 2 Kings 23:6.

645. Cant. 4:3.

648. Cant. 4:7.

649–50. Cant. 7:8.

652–53. Cant. 4:13.

658–59. Cant. 5:1.

660–61. Cant. 8:8.

663. Cant. 6:12.

664. Cant. 6:8.

665. Eph. 2:14.

666. Mich. 5:5.

668. Job 29:6.

670. Cant. 2:4.

673–74. Cant. 1:4.

679–80. Cant. 1:3.

682. Mal. 4:2.

684. Jth. 13:23.

688–89. Cant. 7:1.

691–92. Luke 2:35.

692. Cant. 1:12.

696–97. See 2 Par. 6:13.

699–700. Cant. 2:2.

701–2. Cant. 5:13.

707. Ps. 64:11.

709. Cant. 4:11.

711–12. Cant. 8:10.

716–17. Isa. 64:7.

717. See Gen. 6:6; and Gen. 19:13, etc.

721. Cant. 3:6.

724. Cant. 4:11.

726. Cant. 1:2.

729–30. Luke 1:42.

730–31. Bernard, *In laudibus Virginis Matris* III.6 (4:39).

732. Luke 1:38.

733–34. Cant. 7:7.

735–36. Bernard, *In laudibus Virginis Matris* II.1 (4:21).

736–38. See Exod. 15:20.

742. Cant. 5:1.

742–43. Cf. Augustine, *De musica* VI.52 (PL 32:1190).

745–871. A series of images similar to those in this section appears in Bernard, *De laudibus Virginis Matris* (4:13–58).

745. See Exod. 3:2.

746. Cf. Bernard, *In laudibus Virginis Matris* II.5 (4:24).

747. See Num. 17.

748. Bernard, *In laudibus Virginis Matris* II.5 (4:24).

748–49. See Isa. 11:1.

750. Luke 1:38.

751. Ibid.

755–56. See above, ll. 628–29.

757. Luke 1:29.

760. See Job 40:10ff.

763. See Judges 6:37ff.

765–67. Bernard, *In laudibus Virginis Matris* II.7 (4:25).

768. Cf. above, l. 610.

770. Ps. 71:6.

772–73. 3 Kings 22:30.

775. Phil. 2:7.

779–80. 3 Kings 18:44.

781. Gen. 1:2.

786–87. Jer. 31:22.

787–88. Bernard, *In laudibus Virginis Matris* II.9 (4:27).

789–91. Cf. [Albumasar], *Introductorium in astronomiam Albumasaris Abalachi octo continens libros partiales* (Venice: Erhardus Ratdolt, 1489). The passage and its author are also quoted by Jean de Meun, *Roman de la rose*, ll. 19, 147–50, ed. Félix Lecoy (Paris: Honoré Champion, 1970), 3:75; see also Lecoy's note, p. 179.

793–94. See *Postquam* III.629.

794–96. For the theory that the body of the sun was formed from a cloud that had illuminated the world for the preceding three "days," see Petrus Comestor, *Historia scholastica*, on Genesis, chaps. 3 and 6 (PL 183: 1057 and 1060).

796–97. Mal. 4:2.

799. John 1:18.

800–801. Exod. 33:20.

804–5. Wisd. 7:26.

812–13. Isa. 4:5–6.

814. Cant. 6:9.

819. Luke 2:10.

822–23. Cant. 6:3.

826–27. Wisd. 17:17.

832. Num. 24:17.

834–35. Bernard, *In laudibus Virginis Matris* II.17 (4:35).

837–38. Luke 1:49.

839–40. See above, l. 676.

840–42. See above, ll. 677–78.

848. See *Altercatio Hadriani et Epicteti*, ed. Walther Suchier, Illinois Studies in Language and Literature 24 (Urbana: University of Illinois Press, 1939), 106 (no. 41), 131 (no. 31), 139 (no. 51), and 156 (no. 6).

850–51. Ecclus. 43:6.

854. Ecclus. 43:7.

854–55. Cf. Ambrose, *Exameron* IV. vii.29 (CSEL 32.1:134).

858. Introit to the Mass of the Blessed Virgin during Advent, in the *Sarum Missal*, p. 387. Based on Isa. 45:8.

860. Cf. Apoc. 17:15.

863. Ecclus. 43:24.

866–67. This very popular exhortation, from Arnaud de Bonneval, *De laudibus Beatae Mariae Virginis* (PL 189:1726), is commonly attributed to Saint Bernard, in medieval texts.

869–70. John 2:3.

871. The *Oracio beati Anselmi* added in MS W occurs in Anselm, *Oratio* 7 (3:20), except for the name Johannes.

INDEX

INDEX TO THE TRANSLATION